Handbook of Evidence-Based Prevention of Behavioral Disorders in Integrated Care

William O'Donohue • Martha Zimmermann
Editors

Handbook of Evidence-Based Prevention of Behavioral Disorders in Integrated Care

A Stepped Care Approach

Springer

Editors
William O'Donohue
Psychology Department
University of Nevada
Reno, NV, USA

Martha Zimmermann
Psychology Department
University of Nevada
Reno, NV, USA

ISBN 978-3-030-83468-5 ISBN 978-3-030-83469-2 (eBook)
https://doi.org/10.1007/978-3-030-83469-2

This Springer imprint is published by the registered company Springer Nature Switzerland AG
The registered company address is: Gewerbestrasse 11, 6330 Cham, Switzerland

Acknowledgments

The editors would like to thank the authors for their collaboration and thoughtful contributions to this volume.

WO would like to thank all the support and kindness extended to him by his family: Jane, Katie, and Anna.

MZ would like to express gratitude to the staff and community at the Community Health Alliance for the opportunity to begin her training in integrated care. Thank you to Kenny, friends, and family for your love and support.

Contents

About the Editors

William O'Donohue Ph.D., is a Professor of clinical psychology at the University of Nevada, Reno. He has directed the Victims of Crime Treatment Center there for the past 25 years. This clinic provides free psychotherapy to child and adult victims of sexual assault and is supported by a grant from the National Institute of Justice. He received a doctorate from the State University of New York at Stony Brook in 1986. He has published over 80 books and 300 journal articles and book chapters.

Martha Zimmermann M.A., is a doctoral candidate in clinical psychology at the University of Nevada, Reno, and psychology intern in behavioral medicine at the VA Palo Alto Health Care System. She earned her B.A. in psychology and sociology from the University of Southern California in 2013 and her master's degree from the University of Nevada, Reno, in 2017.

Chapter 1
Integrated Care and Prevention

William O'Donohue and Martha Zimmermann

1.1 Integrated Care and Prevention

Many who envisioned the development of integrating behavioral health into primary care medicine gave at least some mention of the potential for integrated care to prevent both behavioral and physical problems (e.g., James & O'Donohue, 2009). For example, early screening and intervention for health behaviors (e.g., physical activity, diet) in childhood could theoretically prevent obesity; obesity-related problems such as diabetes, heart disease, and cancers; and behavioral health problems like depression, eating disorders, or social anxiety. Of course, this approach is dependent on having effective interventions for these problems particularly in a format that fits the ecology of primary care, as well as actually delivering these services. It is also fair to say that in the actual implementation of integrated care prevention, efforts in real-world settings have been less than ideal in attention and emphasis. Treatment may take priority over prevention as there are so many serious presenting behavioral health problems to address; unless the integrated care system is properly staffed, the urgency of these problem presentations could overwhelm clinical resources, and the "quieter" problems of prevention could be shunted to the side. Those evaluating the new delivery system may be more impressed with the quicker and more salient results of treating current problems, rather than the slower developing prevention results—which after all are most impressive when eventually nothing occurs. In addition, institutional and social norms and lack of funding may be barriers to delivering the preventive care, despite the existence of evidence-based programs and approaches (Leslie et al., 2016).

W. O'Donohue (✉) · M. Zimmermann
Psychology Department, University of Nevada, Reno, NV, USA
e-mail: wto@unr.edu; mzimmermann@nevada.unr.edu

W. O'Donohue, M. Zimmermann (eds.), *Handbook of Evidence-Based Prevention of Behavioral Disorders in Integrated Care*,
https://doi.org/10.1007/978-3-030-83469-2_1

1.2 Background: The Prevention Context

Mental, emotional, and behavioral disorders are common across the life span. Approximately one in two adolescents 13–18 meets diagnostic criteria for an emotional or behavioral disorder (Merikangas et al., 2010). As many as one in five adults in the United States will experience a mental, emotional, or behavioral disorder in a single year (SAMHSA, 2017). Mental illnesses affect one quarter of older adults (age 65 and above) with prevalence rates projected to increase (Bartels, 2003). Among the most prevalent include emotional disorders (anxiety and depression) and behavioral health problems such as obesity resulting from multifactorial health risk behaviors such as physical activity levels and diet (Lobstein et al., 2004; Merikangas et al., 2010). The majority of affected youth and adults do not receive appropriate or high-quality behavioral healthcare (Filter, 2003; Robinson et al., 2005; Wang et al., 2005; Wolitzky-Taylor et al., 2015; Young et al., 2001), and members of minority groups are even less likely to receive appropriate care (Cabassa et al., 2006; McGuire & Miranda, 2008; Young et al., 2001). More concerning still is that even with a rise in treatment rates, the prevalence of common mental disorders appears to be increasing (Jorm et al., 2017).

The high prevalence of emotional and behavioral disorders is of utmost relevance to medical providers, as individuals with these concerns are more likely to see a primary care provider (PCP) than a mental health specialist (Young et al., 2001). Moreover, these problems pose significant burden on the healthcare system (Lobstein et al., 2004) as they are associated with increased morbidity, mortality, financial costs, and medical service utilization (Ford et al., 2004). Approximately 70% of medical visits have a behavioral health component (O'Donohue & Cucciare, 2005).

Integrated care is a model of service delivery that may address behavioral health service delivery problems. In integrated care, behavioral health is delivered at the same location and in the same mode ("high volume, low touch") as primary care medicine. Integrated care has been widely adopted in the past two decades. As many as 44% of primary care providers are now collocated with a behavioral health provider (Richman et al., 2020). The promise of integrate care includes increased patient and PCP satisfaction, better detection of behavioral health problems, broader access to behavioral health services, and reduced medical cost (Kwan & Nease, 2013). This approach has also been effective in reducing behavioral health disparities in minoritized groups by improving access and quality of care (Bridges et al., 2014).

A key component of faithfully mirroring the ecology of primary care medicine, however, is to have an appropriate focus on prevention (A. Jorm & Yap, 2019). In primary care medicine, screens, assessments, and interventions (e.g., inoculations) are given in order to prevent physical disease. Unfortunately, in rolling out integrated care, the prevention of behavioral health disorders has been relatively neglected. Initiatives for integrating behavioral health services into primary care have often focused on *treating* rather than *preventing* behavioral health problems.

This disparity is known as the "prevention gap," in that mental health delivery systems allocate resources to treatment at the cost of expanding preventive efforts (Jorm & Yap, 2019). A growing body of research suggests that efforts to prevent behavioral health problems in youth, adults, and older adults can be effective (Barrera et al., 2007; Muñoz et al., 2010; Stockings et al., 2016) and cost-effective (Knapp et al., 2011; Mihalopoulos & Chatterton, 2015; van't Veer-Tazelaar et al., 2010) in a variety of settings including primary care (Brown et al., 2018; Leslie et al., 2016; Van Voorhees et al., 2005), yet little research, clinical, or operational infrastructure currently exists to prevent behavioral disorders within the integrated care framework. Given the magnitude of the burden of behavioral health concerns and the need for prevention of these problems at a large scale, it is essential to develop effective preventive care that can be seamlessly integrated into the infrastructure of existing integrated care programs.

1.2.1 Prevention and the Recent COVID-19 Crisis

The lack of appropriate preventive care infrastructure becomes still more salient when considering the recent spread of the novel coronavirus (SARS-CoV-2), the prevention of which depends on a variety of key health behaviors. Despite scientific consensus suggesting the importance of mask-wearing, handwashing, and being socially distant in preventing the spread (Cheng et al., 2020), cases of COVID-19 transmission continued to rise in the United States (Dong et al., 2020). The uncontrolled spread of COVID-19 was devastating with respect to loss of life and health but also mental health (Godfred-Cato et al., 2020; Xiong et al., 2020).

The ability to quickly and effectively implement behavioral health prevention programming in primary care settings could be essential in the face of a public health crisis such as COVID-19. Preventive interventions have been shown to impact both health behaviors and mental health. For instance, behavioral interventions can effectively target health-promoting behaviors such as handwashing. A face-to-face intervention conducted in Australian childcare centers including handwashing led to reduction in respiratory illness (Roberts et al., 2000). In a large trial conducted in the United Kingdom, an online intervention providing information about respiratory infection and handwashing, reinforcing positive social norms pertaining to handwashing, and providing feedback reduced the incidence of respiratory infection by an estimated 14% (Little et al., 2015). A review of studies examining interventions to prevent and lessen mental health consequences of COVID-19 found that digital and mHealth interventions are feasible and effective (Rauschenberg et al., 2021). As such, preventive interventions are available and effective both in person and online, yet they are not routinely delivered in the US primary healthcare system. This need is even greater in the context of the uncontrolled COVID-19 pandemic.

1.3 Key Considerations in Integrating Prevention into Primary Care Settings

The Institute of Medicine (IOM) stratifies levels of prevention interventions by individual risk. These levels include universal (all individuals at varying levels of risk), selective (higher-than-average risk), and indicated (higher risk levels; Muñoz et al., 1996). Value-based care, in which health promotion is seen as better than illness, is increasingly a focus in the healthcare system. Traditionally, annual physicals or wellness visits have been tools for delivering universal, selective, and indicated preventive services for asymptomatic patients and patients exhibiting risk of morbidity. Equivalent infrastructure to provide behavioral health-focused preventive care is limited. Chapters 2 and 3 describe how prevention could be integrated into primary care workflows in more detail.

Currently, there is too little information about many questions regarding integrated care and, particularly, prevention efforts in integrated care. For example, too little is known about the psychometrics of common screening devices that attempt to either identify behavioral health problems or risks for developing problems; too little is known about the clinical outcomes of the briefer often truncated interventions given in integrated care or about the short- or long-term outcomes of prevention efforts; too little is known on how integrated care should vary across differing populations or medical care practices; too little is known about the cost-effectiveness of integrated care, particularly prevention efforts that have been implemented; too little is known about proper training of professionals in an integratated care setting, especially in prevention skills; and too little is known about key operational details such as proper staffing, effective management, ideal contracting, or financial sustainability. It seems that it is unfortunate that integrated care has been adopted so widely without a proper emphasis on its being data based and data generating. Quality improvement initiatives are admittedly costly but to date seem to be given short shrift (O'Donohue & Maragakis, 2016). It is unfortunately the case that integrated care has not been practiced in the best tradition of evidence-based practice but rather seems to be all too often practiced beyond the margins of clinical science.

These diverse data gaps lead to difficulties for designing optimal prevention efforts in integrated care. Certainly, as the present volume will show, there are many choice points that need to be considered, ideally (sooner or later) with high-quality and relevant data to guide these decisions:

- How shall resources be divided between the twin tasks of the treatment of current problems and prevention of future problems? (And how should this be decided?)
- What should be the set of prevention targets? Smoking? Obesity? Suicide? Depression? Substance abuse? Social rejection? And so on.
- What should be the mix between preventing mental health problems such as depression and preventing medical health problems such as diabetes and perhaps mixed problems such as obesity?

- When should be the prevention efforts be universal (i.e., everyone receives), and when ought it to be targeted only toward high-risk individuals—and how does one validly measure such risk and determine appropriate cutoffs for prevention treatment?
- When ought prevention efforts be siloed—e.g., a single focus on for example depression—and when ought there be a prevention system that organizes multiple prevention targets and determines timing, dose, etc.? Relatedly, are there transdiagnostic processes such as tolerance of uncertainty, coping skills, relaxation skills, experiential avoidance, or anxiety sensitivity that ought to be targeted as these can prevent multiple clinical diagnoses?
- When ought these prevention efforts be delivered—e.g., should a smoking prevention be delivered at a certain age, say 10 or 12, or when some sort of sentinel event occurs—the child admits to curiosity about tobacco products or only after some initial experimentation?
- Who receives the prevention efforts—the child, the guardian, or both?
- Who delivers the prevention efforts—the behavioral health provider, the primary care provider, paraprofessionals, or some combination of these?
- How effective are such prevention efforts—is there some sort of demarcation where there is too little bang for the buck?
- How ought such prevention efforts be paid for? This is key because the costs and benefits of prevention efforts can be borne by different payers (i.e., current insurers can pay the costs of the prevention efforts), while the benefits may accrue to a payer at some distant point even decades into the future (e.g., smoking prevention decreases cancer rates many decades later).
- What sort of training does the staff (everyone from front desk staff, providers, employees in the billing department, and management) of the system need to effectively implement such as prevention orientation?
- What sort of quality control system needs to be embedded so that one has data on the outcome and processes of the preventative system? This is a key question given the short shrift data generation has been given in contemporary integrated care practice.
- Are these prevention efforts culturally sensitive, or do they require cultural adaptations (e.g., language translation or otherwise)?
- How are these services coordinated with usual medical prevention and treatment efforts in the medical setting?

These are just some of the key questions that need to be answered while designing prevention efforts.

1.4 Public Health and Prevention

Public health measures have had some of the largest impacts on physical health. Improved sanitation, particularly clean water, has probably had the largest impact on the health of developed nations. But there is a range of other public health measures such as fluoridation, food safety measures, vaccinations (as recently seen so clearly in the COVID-19 pandemic), seat belt laws, gun laws, and what is generally considered as the development of the social safety net; also, there has had clear positive impacts on the prevention of a myriad of serious physical health problems.

Candidates for similar public health measures that are targeted toward behavioral health problems are less clear. Certainly, the public health measures mentioned above have ancillary behavior health benefits. For example, successfully preventing childhood polio by universal vaccinations results in the prevention of grief, stress, and other psychological disorders associated with families who do not have to deal with a child suffering or dying from polio.

However, it is difficult to identify public health measures that have directly targeted the prevention of behavioral health problems. For instance, while interventions to prevent anxiety and depression exist across levels of prevention (e.g., Stockings et al., 2016), these do not appear to be routinely implemented or scaled to a national level. Resources have been placed on early education such as Headstart, and although these are directly aimed at educational success, these again ought to have desirable behavioral health consequences. But this effort was aimed at preventing educational problems, not preventing mental health problems. General societal trends, such as vast increases in material wealth both in the high-income countries and in lower- and middle-income OECD countries such as China, India, and Brazil, have brought numerous benefits and certainly have prevented some behavioral health problems (e.g., decreased grief due to high rates of child mortality). Various political campaigns that have resulted in societal changes such as the feminist movement and gay rights movements have in all likelihood also resulted in the prevention of a wide range of psychological problems due to adverse consequences of sexism or homophobia as well as the mental health problems that can arise due to the stress and aversiveness of being discriminated against, but these were not developed as public health campaigns to prevent mental health disorders but rather civil rights campaigns to remediate civil rights problems. The current emphasis on identifying and eliminating racism might result in similar positive effects, but again these current efforts are generally not regarded as a public health matter but again as a civil and human rights matter.

It is probably worthwhile for a clinician to understand a client's resource problems as these can be used to prevent obvious problems such as financial stress or the wide range of problems associated with homelessness. We have developed a quick screen for the integrated behavioral health provider to use. However, it is also fair to say that identifying a resource gap is only a first step—often ways to remediate these gaps are simply not available in many communities. Filling these needs could have dramatic implications for the prevention of behavioral health problems (Fig. 1.1).

1.5 The Structure of This Book

This book attempts to provide up-to-date, comprehensive, and authoritative information on prevention technologies that can be used in integrated care settings. It covers general issues related to prevention (e.g., how to finance these efforts, how to staff these efforts, and a general introduction to the advantages of including prevention efforts). It then contains 15 chapters covering specific behavioral health disorders that can be addressed. The approach will hopefully be very helpful to the practitioner as well as management in integrated care: it covers basic definitions, screens, the specific roles of both the primary care provider and the behavioral care provider, and specific resources presented in a stepped care model. Stepped care is used in physical medicine in primary care. It allows the clinician and the patient to choose treatments that vary in their level of intensity.

Each chapter is designed to include:

1. Definition/diagnostic criteria
2. Prevalence and age of onset
3. Risk factors
4. Effective screening
5. Review of evidence: What is evidence-based prevention?
6. Universal, indicated, and selective prevention
7. Stepped care prevention model: Role of PCP and BCP
    (a) Watchful waiting
    (b) Psychoeducation
    (c) Biblio-prevention
    (d) eHealth prevention tools
    (e) Groups
    (f) Individual
8. Lessons learned/implementation.

Finally, it is hoped this book will spur a research agenda to address the gaps in knowledge related to effective prevention efforts in integrated care.

Resource Plan

Please check the box for any services needed now or in the near future (within the next 12 months). If you are unsure check, "unsure." The goal of this is to make sure **all** services that are needed are being provided. Gaps in services can result in problems in health and functioning. Some services may not be available for various reasons (for example, financial); however, please still check the box as it is important to identify service gaps.

Service	Present Need	Future Need	Unsure
Housing and Shelter Childcare	☐	☐	☐
Food	☐	☐	☐
Clothing	☐	☐	☐
Employment	☐	☐	☐
Financial Aid Resources	☐	☐	☐
Transportation	☐	☐	☐
Healthcare Medical	☐	☐	☐
Dental	☐	☐	☐
Vision	☐	☐	☐
Hearing	☐	☐	☐
Disability Services	☐	☐	☐
Children and Youth Services	☐	☐	☐
Legal Services	☐	☐	☐
Mental Health Services	☐	☐	☐
Police Services	☐	☐	☐
Protective/Victims' Services	☐	☐	☐
Elderly Services	☐	☐	☐
Caregiver Support Services	☐	☐	☐
Substance Abuse Treatment	☐	☐	☐
Childcare	☐	☐	☐

Other: Please describe:

Fig. 1.1 Resource plan

References

Barrera, A. Z., Torres, L. D., & Muñoz, R. F. (2007). Prevention of depression: The state of the science at the beginning of the 21st century. *International Review of Psychiatry, 19*(6), 655–670.

Bartels, S. J. (2003). Improving the United States' system of care for older adults with mental illness: Findings and recommendations for the President's New Freedom Commission on Mental Health. *The American Journal of Geriatric Psychiatry, 11*(5), 486–497.

Bridges, A. J., Andrews, A. R., III, Villalobos, B. T., Pastrana, F. A., Cavell, T. A., & Gomez, D. (2014). Does integrated behavioral health care reduce mental health disparities for Latinos? Initial findings. *Journal of Latina/o Psychology, 2*(1), 37.

Brown, C. M., Bignall, J. R., & Ammerman, R. T. (2018). Preventive behavioral health programs in primary care: A systematic review. *Pediatrics, 141*(5). https://doi.org/10.1542/peds.2017-0611

Cabassa, L. J., Zayas, L. H., & Hansen, M. C. (2006). Latino adults' access to mental health care: A review of epidemiological studies. *Administration and Policy in Mental Health and Mental Health Services Research, 33*(3), 316–330.

Cheng, V. C.-C., Wong, S.-C., Chuang, V. W.-M., So, S. Y.-C., Chen, J. H.-K., Sridhar, S., To, K. K.-W., Chan, J. F.-W., Hung, I. F.-N., Ho, P.-L., & Yuen, K.-Y. (2020). The role of community-wide wearing of face mask for control of coronavirus disease 2019 (COVID-19) epidemic due to SARS-CoV-2. *Journal of Infection, 81*, 107–114.

Dong, E., Du, H., & Gardner, L. (2020). An interactive web-based dashboard to track COVID-19 in real time. *The Lancet Infectious Diseases.*

Filter, B. (2003). *The cause of wars & agression: Book 1.* Global Justice Publishing. Retrieved from https://unr.idm.oclc.org/login?url=https://search.ebscohost.com/login.aspx?direct=true&db=psyh&AN=2004-12435-000&site=ehost-live&scope=site

Ford, J. D., Trestman, R. L., Steinberg, K., Tennen, H., & Allen, S. (2004). Prospective association of anxiety, depressive, and addictive disorders with high utilization of primary, specialty and emergency medical care. *Social Science & Medicine, 58*(11), 2145–2148.

Godfred-Cato, S., Bryant, B., & Leung, J. (2020). COVID-19–Associated multisystem inflammatory syndrome in children—United States, March–July 2020. *MMWR. Morbidity and Mortality Weekly Report, 69.*

James, L. C., & O'Donohue, W. T. (2009). *The primary care toolkit: Practical resources for the integrated behavioral care provider*. Springer.

Jorm, A. F., Patten, S. B., Brugha, T. S., & Mojtabai, R. (2017). Has increased provision of treatment reduced the prevalence of common mental disorders? Review of the evidence from four countries. *World Psychiatry, 16*(1), 90–99.

Jorm, A., & Yap, M. (2019). The future of mental health & prevention. *Mental Health & Prevention.* https://doi.org/10.1016/j.mhp.2019.200168

Knapp, M., McDaid, D., & Parsonage, M. (2011). *Mental health promotion and mental illness prevention: The economic case.*

Kwan, B. M., & Nease, D. E. (2013). The state of the evidence for integrated behavioral health in primary care. In *Integrated behavioral health in primary care* (pp. 65–98). Springer.

Leslie, L. K., Mehus, C. J., Hawkins, J. D., Boat, T., McCabe, M. A., Barkin, S., Perrin, E. C., Metzler, C. W., Prado, G., Tait, V. F., Brown, R., & Beardslee, W. (2016). Primary health care: Potential home for family-focused preventive interventions. *American Journal of Preventive Medicine, 51*(4), S106–S118.

Little, P., Stuart, B., Hobbs, F. D., Moore, M., Barnett, J., Popoola, D., Middleton, K., Kelly, J., Mullee, M., & Raftery, J. (2015). An internet-delivered handwashing intervention to modify influenza-like illness and respiratory infection transmission (PRIMIT): A primary care randomised trial. *The Lancet, 386*(10004), 1631–1639.

Lobstein, T., Baur, L., & Uauy, R. (2004). Obesity in children and young people: A crisis in public health. *Obesity Reviews, 5*, 4–85.

McGuire, T. G., & Miranda, J. (2008). New evidence regarding racial and ethnic disparities in mental health: Policy implications. *Health Affairs, 27*(2), 393–403.

Merikangas, K. R., He, J.-P., Burstein, M., Swanson, S. A., Avenevoli, S., Cui, L., Benjet, C., Georgiades, K., & Swendsen, J. (2010). Lifetime prevalence of mental disorders in U.S. adolescents: Results from the National Comorbidity Survey Replication–Adolescent Supplement (NCS-A). *Journal of the American Academy of Child & Adolescent Psychiatry*. Elsevier Inc. *49*(10): 980–989. https://doi.org/10.1016/j.jaac.2010.05.017

Mihalopoulos, C., & Chatterton, M. Lou. (2015). Economic evaluations of interventions designed to prevent mental disorders: A systematic review. *Early Intervention in Psychiatry*. Wiley Subscription Services. https://doi.org/10.1111/eip.12156.

Muñoz, R. F., Cuijpers, P., Smit, F., Barrera, A. Z., & Leykin, Y. (2010). Prevention of major depression. *Annual Review of Clinical Psychology, 6*, 181–212. https://doi.org/10.1146/annurev-clinpsy-033109-132040

Muñoz, R. F., Mrazek, P. J., & Haggerty, R. J. (1996). Institute of Medicine report on prevention of mental disorders: Summary and commentary. *American Psychologist, 51*(11), 1116. https://doi.org/10.1037//0003-066X.51.11.1116

O'Donohue, W., & Maragakis, A. (2016). *Quality improvement in behavioral health*. Springer.

O'Donohue, W. T., & Cucciare, M. A. (2005). The role of psychological factors in medical presentations. *Journal of Clinical Psychology in Medical Settings, 12*(1), 13–24. https://doi.org/10.1007/s10880-005-0908-x

Rauschenberg, C., Schick, A., Hirjak, D., Seidler, A., Paetzold, I., Apfelbacher, C., Riedel-Heller, S. G., & Reininghaus, U. (2021). Evidence synthesis of digital interventions to mitigate the negative impact of the COVID-19 pandemic on public mental health: Rapid meta-review. *Journal of Medical Internet Research, 23*(3), e23365.

Richman, E. L., Lombardi, B. M., & Zerden, L. D. (2020). Mapping colocation: Using national provider identified data to assess primary care and behavioral health colocation. *Families, Systems, & Health, 38*(1), 16.

Roberts, L., Smith, W., Jorm, L., Patel, M., Douglas, R. M., & McGilchrist, C. (2000). Effect of infection control measures on the frequency of upper respiratory infection in child care: A randomized, controlled trial. *Pediatrics, 105*(4), 738–742.

Robinson, W. D., Geske, J. A., Prest, L. A., & Barnacle, R. (2005). Depression treatment in primary care. *The Journal of the American Board of Family Practice, 18*(2), 79–86. https://doi.org/10.3122/jabfm.18.2.79

SAMHSA. (2017). *2017 National Survey on Drug Use and Health (NSDUH)*. Retrieved from https://www.samhsa.gov/data/sites/default/files/cbhsq-reports/NSDUHDetailedTabs2017/NSDUHDetailedTabs2017.htm#tab8-33A

Stockings, E. A., Degenhardt, L., Dobbins, T., Lee, Y. Y., Erskine, H. E., Whiteford, H. A., & Patton, G. (2016). Preventing depression and anxiety in young people: A review of the joint efficacy of universal, selective and indicated prevention. *Psychological Medicine*. Cambridge University Press. https://doi.org/10.1017/S0033291715001725

van't Veer-Tazelaar, P., Smit, F., van Hout, H., van Oppen, P., van der Horst, H., Beekman, A., & van Marwijk, H. (2010). Cost-effectiveness of a stepped care intervention to prevent depression and anxiety in late life: Randomised trial. *The British Journal of Psychiatry, 196*(4), 319–325.

Van Voorhees, B. W., Ellis, J., Stuart, S., Fogel, J., & Ford, D. E. (2005). Pilot study of a primary care internet-based depression prevention intervention for late adolescents. *The Canadian Child and Adolescent Psychiatry Review, 14*(2), 40.

Wang, P. S., Lane, M., Olfson, M., Pincus, H. A., Wells, K. B., & Kessler, R. C. (2005). Twelve-month use of mental health services in the United States: Results from the National Comorbidity Survey Replication. *Archives of General Psychiatry, 62*(6), 629–640. https://doi.org/10.1001/archpsyc.62.6.629

Wolitzky-Taylor, K., Zimmermann, M., Arch, J. J., De Guzman, E., & Lagomasino, I. (2015). Has evidence-based psychosocial treatment for anxiety disorders permeated usual care in community mental health settings? *Behaviour Research and Therapy, 72*. https://doi.org/10.1016/j.brat.2015.06.010

Xiong, J., Lipsitz, O., Nasri, F., Lui, L. M. W., Gill, H., Phan, L., Chen-Li, D., Iacobucci, M., Ho, R., Majeed, A., & McIntyre, R. S. (2020). Impact of COVID-19 pandemic on mental health in the general population: A systematic review. *Journal of Affective Disorders, 277*, 55–64.

Young, A. S., Klap, R., Sherbourne, C. D., & Wells, K. B. (2001). The quality of care for depressive and anxiety disorders in the United States. *Archives of General Psychiatry, 58*(1), 55–61.

Chapter 2
The Behavioral Health Wellness Visit

Martha Zimmermann and William O'Donohue

2.1 Annual Wellness Visits and the Prevention of Physical Disease

The annual wellness visit (AWV), also referred to as the annual physical or periodic health exam, is a routine medical visit conducted for asymptomatic children and adults. This visit has traditionally been the primary format through which services to prevent physical disease are delivered in primary care settings (Gorbenko et al., 2017). Endorsed as far back as the 1920s by the American Medical Association (Emerson, 1923), a version of the AWV was a mainstay of primary care for years (Gorbenko et al., 2017; Oboler et al., 2002). The conceptual underpinnings of the AWV were grounded in an "all-encompassing" approach to detect early-stage disease and alter their course (Han, 1997). The AWV typically includes an assessment of health and risk factors for disease (e.g., substance use, family medical history) in addition to provision of preventive care services tailored to these risk factors. Services also aim to consider relevant sociodemographic risk factors, such as patient age and sex (Boulware et al., 2007). The goals of the AWV include health promotion, early disease detection, and disease prevention. The visit also serves to educate patients about risks and health services, to facilitate a relationship with the provider and organization, and to identify opportunities to intervene and improve population-level health (Boulware et al., 2007; Zaman, 2018).

The concept of a yearly physical is not without controversy. First, constraints on provider time and resources have led some to question the value of the visit relative to the costs of its delivery in both expense and optimal resource utilization (Birtwhistle et al., 2017; Mehrotra & Prochazka, 2015; Shein & Stone, 2017).

M. Zimmermann (✉) · W. O'Donohue
Psychology Department, University of Nevada, Reno, NV, USA
e-mail: mzimmermann@nevada.unr.edu; wto@unr.edu

W. O'Donohue, M. Zimmermann (eds.), *Handbook of Evidence-Based Prevention of Behavioral Disorders in Integrated Care*,
https://doi.org/10.1007/978-3-030-83469-2_2

Second, evidence has suggested that a general "prevention" approach does not demonstrate clear benefit in the prevention of physical disease (e.g., Cutler et al., 1973). A growing body of evidence suggests that general health checks do not appear to impact purported outcomes of morbidity or mortality (Krogsbøll et al., 2012). In addition, concerns related to excessive diagnosis and testing have been raised, as potential patient harm could arise from false positives and unnecessary intervention (Birtwhistle et al., 2017). It has been suggested that factors other than efficacy (e.g., insurance, patient expectations) have contributed to the continued use of the AWV (Han, 1997). Approximately two-thirds of primary care patients and providers, for example, believe an annual physical is a necessary component of healthcare (Oboler et al., 2002; Prochazka et al., 2005).

In response to these concerns, a second generation of the wellness visit approach involved more targeted and selected services aimed at prevention services for asymptomatic populations. In the 1970s, the Canadian Task Force on the Periodic Health Examination suggested replacing the general health check with a "selective plan of health protection packages appropriate to the various health needs at the different stages of human life" (Hill et al., 1979, p. 1199). According to the report, preventive care should be based on relevant demographic characteristics (e.g., age and sex) and be a "lifetime plan intended to improve or protect health at all ages" (Hill et al., 1979, p. 1199).

In 1984, the US Department of Health and Human Services created the US Preventive Services Task Force (USPSTF). The USPSTF Guide to Clinical Preventive Services provided recommendations for timing and provision of preventive care. These guidelines were published in 1989 and are continually updated with the accrual of new evidence (USPSTF, 1989, 1996, 2014). These guidelines consider the costs and benefits of delivering a particular service, alongside the strength of the evidence supporting the recommendation. Recommendations consider the net benefit or the "benefit minus harm of the preventive service as implemented in a general primary care population" (USPSTF, 1996, p. 231). Evidence is assessed on the strength and certainty of a given recommendation or the "the likelihood that the USPSTF assessment of the net benefit of a preventive service is correct (USPSTF, 1996, p. 231). Guidelines receive designations based on the degree of certainty (either "A," "B," "C," "D," or "I"). An "A" rating indicates that the service is recommended with high certainty of a benefit of that service, "B" indicates moderate to substantial benefit, and so on. An "I" rating indicates that the evidence is not conclusive.

In 1994, the American Academy of Pediatrics developed Bright Futures, a set of recommendations aimed at the AWV for children ages 0–21, or the "Well-Child Visit." Guidelines are developed for each developmental stage (i.e., infancy 0–9 months, early childhood 1–4 years, middle childhood 5–10 years, and adolescence 11–21 years) and include both the prevention of physical disease (immunizations, screening for HIV, sexually transmitted infection, etc.) and developmental and behavioral health concerns. Several limitations of these guidelines have been noted, including time constraints associated with the delivery of all suggested services (Belamarich et al., 2006) and concern for the degree to which recommendations are evidence-based (Dinkevich et al., 2001).

2.1.1 *Lessons Learned from the AWV for the Prevention of Physical Disease*

The lack of benefit associated with a general prevention approach has led to the development of new models for delivering preventive care. In contrast to a more general approach, targeted preventive care has a positive impact on health outcomes and the prevention of physical disease (Birtwhistle et al., 2017; Ploeg et al., 2005; Stuck et al., 2015). As a result, Birtwhistle (2017) and colleagues propose the periodic preventive health visit rather than a yearly physical. This format could retain benefits of maintaining a patient-provider relationship and strike a more effective balance between harms and benefits of screening and intervention. For instance, cervical cancer screening might be a worthwhile preventive care service for individuals aged 25–65 with a cervix at average risk every 5 years (Fontham et al., 2020), whereas potential harms associated with false-positive findings from mammography screening for breast cancer may not (Jørgensen & Gøtzsche, 2009; Moynihan et al., 2012). Any broad recommendation could be tempered with shared decision-making to meet the needs of an individual patient.

Shared decision-making can be defined as "a process whereby clinicians collaboratively help patients to reach evidence-informed and values-congruent medical decisions" (Grad et al., 2017, p. 682). Shared decision-making may be of particular relevance to preventive care, given the costs and benefits associated with a given service. Conversations about the value of preventive care could include providing information about risk and patient values. Grad and colleagues (2017) also suggest using decision aids such as an infographics that visually demonstrate the proportion of individuals receiving a given screening who are diagnosed with a disease, receive a false-positive diagnosis, or experience other adverse events as a result of testing.

Example of a Novel Prevention Approach: The BETTER Model An example of emerging models of the AWV includes the Building on Existing Tools to Improve Chronic Disease Prevention and Screening in Primary Care (BETTER) model (Grunfeld et al., 2013). In order to address the gap in preventive care, the BETTER model aims to deliver individually tailored, evidence-based care in a primary care setting to prevent chronic disease. Intervention targets lifestyle factors, such as alcohol and tobacco use, diet, and exercise, relevant to heart disease, diabetes, and cancer. The key to this framework is the designation of an allied health professional as a dedicated "prevention practitioner." The prevention practitioner conducts a 1-hour primary care visit specifically designed for the delivery of preventive care.

The BETTER model includes a patient health survey prior to visits and validated instruments not typically collected to assess the patient's electronic medical record, such as the General Practice Physical Activity Questionnaire [(GPPAQ; Heron et al., 2014)] (Grunfeld et al., 2013; Manca et al., 2015). This tool has been revised in response to feedback and is designed to be completed in approximately 30 minutes and prior to the visit (Manca et al., 2015). This screening serves both as an assessment tool to determine patient risk-level and intervention targets and as a means to assess progress and response to intervention over time. Prevention visits include reviewing results of this screening and connecting patients to community resources within the practice (e.g., referral to dietician), external resources (e.g., specialists, more specialized screenings, community programs), or Internet resources (Grunfeld et al., 2013). The visit includes shared decision-making and goal setting related to relevant health behaviors or lifestyle changes.

The BETTER program makes use of digital resources, including "toolkits," for providers and low-intensity patient resources. The website includes resources listed by problem or health behavior (e.g., alcohol, lifestyle, obesity, mental health, etc.). Patients can find evidence-based self-help resources, such as physical activity tracking sheets, affordable nutrition information, or computer-based self-help for depression or anxiety (e.g., MoodGYM; Twomey & O'Reilly, 2017). Receipt of prevention practitioner services is associated with an increase in overall prevention and screening actions (e.g., blood pressure screening, BMI screening, physical activity program referrals, etc.; Grunfeld et al., 2013). Clinician, stakeholder, and patient interviews suggest the value of the comprehensive nature of the BETTER approach; the personalized, patient-centered approach; integration within the primary care system; and adaptability across settings (Manca et al., 2014; Sopcak et al., 2017).

Finally, an economic evaluation of the program examined the intervention's incremental cost-effectiveness ratio, or the difference in cost between usual care and the intervention. Analyses suggested the incremental cost-effectiveness ratio was $26.42 (CAD, or $21.89 USD) for each chronic disease prevention and screening action completed. The authors suggest that this cost is relatively low compared with the likely long-term cost associated with chronic health conditions (Grunfeld et al., 2013). Qualitative interviews from patients and stakeholders were also solicited to determine other costs or barriers associated with the program (i.e., concerns regarding lack of follow-up; Sopcak et al., 2017).

Taken together, an evolving understanding of the AWV and its function has suggested the following features increase the effectiveness and value of preventive care in primary care settings: (1) selective timing; (2) targeted intervention; (3) dedicated practitioners; (4) use of digital modalities to provide low-intensity, low-resource intervention; and (5) careful cost-benefit analyses and solicitation of stakeholder input to ensure valuable services and avoid harms associated with false positives.

2.2 Need for a Behavioral Health-Focused Wellness Visit

Behavioral disorders (including mental and emotional disorders) are prevalent, impairing, and costly. One in every three to four children and nearly half of adolescents are estimated to experience a behavioral health disorder of some kind (Merikangas et al., 2010). Approximately one in five adults has experienced a mental disorder in the past year (SAMHSA, 2017). Depression, for instance, is among the most common mental disorders (Kessler et al., 2005). Individuals affected by depression experience disruptions in social relationships, education, or employment and are at greater risk for onset and more severe course of physical disease (Kessler, 2012a, b). In the year 2020, the economic burden of major depressive disorder was estimated to be $326.2 billion USD (Greenberg et al., 2021). This figure includes workplace costs, direct costs, and suicide-related costs (Greenberg et al., 2021). Particularly concerning is that depression appears to be increasing in prevalence even as treatment rates increase (Jorm et al., 2017). As such, turning attention to the prevention of such disorders is essential to the reduction of this growing burden.

Behavioral health disorders play an important role in the presentation of physical disease and health service utilization (O'Donohue & Cucciare, 2005). Accordingly, the integration of behavioral health into the medical settings has resulted in improvements in behavioral health and physical health outcomes across the lifespan and conditions (Asarnow et al., 2015; Kwan & Nease, 2013; Vogel et al., 2017; Woltmann et al., 2012). Perhaps due to the reimbursement structures and lack of community mental health access, however, integrated primary care has primarily focused on the treatment rather than the prevention of behavioral disorders (Williams, 2019). Workflows that are conducive to preventive care delivery are essential to the delivery of a given service (Litaker et al., 2005). Just as the periodic health exam provides infrastructure within primary care to deliver preventive care, wellness visits could be conducted by a dedicated behavioral health practitioner to transform the integrated care model from treatment-focused to one that emphasizes prevention.

2.2.1 Existing Behavioral Health Guidelines

USPSTF guidelines recognize the importance of behavioral health and behavior change in preventive care delivery. Existing guidelines encompass a great deal of recommendations pertinent to the prevention of behavioral health concerns. The USPSTF considers screening youth ages 12–18 and adults (including pregnant and postpartum women) for major depressive disorder (MDD) as a recommendation "B" for moderate certainty of moderate benefit (Forman-Hoffman et al., 2016; O'Connor et al., 2016). In addition to screening, the USPSTF increasingly recommends the delivery of interventions to prevent behavioral disorders. For instance, counseling to prevent perinatal depression (O'Connor et al., 2019) and to prevent tobacco use among youth (Owens et al., 2020) are services with a "B" rating. In practice, providers report assessing for behavioral health risks within AWVs (Boulware et al., 2007). Substance use, including alcohol, tobacco use, and dietary risks are the most reported risk assessments in the adult AWV, although practices vary (Boulware et al., 2007).

The American Academy of Pediatrics Bright Futures provides specific guidelines for children in the Well-Child Visit. These guidelines typically include screening for autism spectrum disorder, tobacco use, drug and alcohol use, and child and maternal depression (Hagan et al., 2007). Well-child visits have traditionally included preventive care or counseling known as *anticipatory guidance*, defined as the "provision of information to parents or children with the expected outcome being a change in parent attitude, knowledge, or behavior," and information about typical development (Telzrow, 1978, p. 14). Anticipatory guidance can be seen as covering behavioral health concerns. For instance, anticipatory guidance could include the recommendation to avoid sugar-sweetened beverages prior to 1 year of age and limit sugar-sweetened beverage consumption among older children (Turner, 2018).

2.2.2 Limitations of Existing Guidelines

Although professional organizations increasingly recommend screening and intervention either related to behavioral health or to prevent behavioral disorders, these services are often neglected. The majority of well-child visits, for instance, do not address all domains of behavioral health concerns (Irwin et al., 2009). Consultation time in the AWV in the United States appears to be on average approximately 20 minutes (Irving et al., 2017) but can include less than 10 minutes spent on anticipatory guidance (Burt et al., 2014). An observational study of well-child visits found that an average of 42% of topics recommended by the Bright Futures guidelines were covered (Norlin et al., 2011). In particular, social and family factors, behavior and discipline, physical activity, risk reduction, and substance use were less commonly recommended by primary care physicians (Norlin et al., 2011). Relying on the traditional AWV to deliver screening and prevention services with a focus on behavior change has the following limitations:

1. *Time*. An analysis conducted by Yarnall et al. (2003) suggested that if primary care providers were to provide all recommended USPSTF services, this would create 7.4 hours per day of additional time engaged in service provision. This analysis was conducted prior to the introduction of many of the USPSTF guidelines described above. Accordingly, providers report that time constraint is one important impediment to the implementation of behavioral health-focused intervention (Midboe et al., 2011).
2. *Training*. Providers may have heterogeneous training with respect to behavioral health, with general medical training including 4–8 weeks of interview training and 4–8 weeks in psychiatry in year 3 (Smith, 2011; Smith et al., 2014). Further, while behavioral change techniques, such as motivational interviewing (MI), can be implemented by medical professionals (Lundahl et al., 2013), they do require time and training to deliver with fidelity (Schumacher et al., 2018; Schwalbe et al., 2014). One study found that among advanced doctoral students and fellows, an average of nine supervised sessions were required to achieve MI competency benchmarks, ranging from 4 to 20 (Schumacher et al., 2018). Further, these techniques may be best sustained with 12–16 hours of initial training and extended follow-up (i.e., 6 months) with an expert trainer (Schwalbe et al., 2014). Accordingly, medical providers report less training in behavior change

interventions and lower self-efficacy in delivering such interventions than do their counterparts in mental health fields (Midboe et al., 2011).

3. *Scope*. While behavioral health has been to some extent incorporated into preventive care with respect to the prevention of physical disease (i.e., the BETTER model; Grunfeld et al., 2013), the prevention of behavioral health disorders themselves has been relatively unaddressed. The addition of behavioral health providers and interventions targeting behavioral health disorders themselves is key to reducing the burden of prevalent and costly disorders (e.g., depression and anxiety) in addition to health behaviors that contribute to the onset and chronicity of physical disease.

The limitations of provider capability to provide preventive care for behavioral disorders do not suggest that primary care providers are not striving to provide quality care. Provider consultation time has increased from 15 to 20 minutes in the United States in recent years, yet the proportion of primary care providers per capita is relatively low and has remained stable over time (Irving et al., 2017). As such, primary care providers experience an increasing time burden and also report high rates of burnout relative to other medical specialties (Shanafelt et al., 2019). Leveraging the unique skillsets of behavioral health professionals to deliver preventive care has the potential to both improve patient care and increase physician satisfaction.

2.3 Existing Research on Behavioral Health-Focused AWV

The structure and needs of primary care make this setting well-suited for the implementation of prevention programs (Leslie et al., 2016; Williams, 2019; Zimmermann et al., 2020). While little is known about the efficacy of the behavioral health-focused wellness visit to prevent behavioral disorders, a significant body of work suggests prevention programs are efficacious across developmental stages and settings (Leslie et al., 2016). Prevention programs developed for other settings could be adapted for use in a behavioral health-focused AWV.

An example of one program developed in a school setting and adapted for primary care is the Family Check-Up (FCU). Originally developed as a school-based prevention approach, the FCU is a risk-informed approach to increase parental motivation to monitor their child's substance use to prevent substance use initiation (Dishion et al., 2003). Several studies have demonstrated the effectiveness of the FCU in school setting in preventing behavioral health problems (Smith et al., 2018). Smith et al. (2018) describe a process for using implementation science to "scale out" existing evidence-based practices for new contexts. Specifically, scaling can include adapting an evidence-based practice or program to a different setting (e.g., from school to primary care) with the same population (Aarons et al., 2017; Smith et al., 2018).

Ridenour et al. (2021) examined the use of the FCU in a primary care setting, employing a behavioral specialist who spent 8 minutes while patients waited in a waiting room to administer the computerized *Youth Risk Index* (Ridenour et al., 2015). The majority (93.5%) of families referred to the program participated in it. At a 12-month follow-up, the FCU reduced the risk of initiating a substance by 37%. The FCU also led to a reduction in risk factors for substance use, including anxiety and deviancy tolerance (Ridenour et al., 2015). The FCU has also been adapted for obesity prevention, leading to the development of the Family Check-Up for Health (FCU4Health), which included an emphasis on goal setting, problem-solving, social support, information about health risks, restructuring environment, and gathering information (Smith et al., 2018). Taken together, evidence-based prevention programs across developmental periods exist, and the wellness visit could be a format through which to implement such services.

While research is limited in regard to the efficacy of the behavioral health wellness visit in the prevention of behavioral disorders, preliminary evidence suggests that these visits are feasible and acceptable to stakeholders. Burt et al. (2014) examined the integration of behavioral health into the well-child visit in underserved and rural primary care clinics. In this study, 94 parents and/or caregivers of children receiving a well-child visit were randomly assigned to receive usual care (i.e., standard well-child visit) or usual care with additional anticipatory guidance and behavioral health-oriented guidance delivered by a behavioral health provider, following the visit with the primary care provider. Behavioral health providers asked parents and caregivers about their child's activities and development and provided responsive recommendations if any concerns were raised. Parents and caregivers in the behavioral health-integrated group reported nearly twice the number of topics covered and an increase of 9 minutes in time compared with the usual care group (Burt et al., 2014). This preliminary investigation suggests that the addition of behavioral health into the annual wellness visit can increase the scope of topics covered as well as time spent with the provider.

The majority of adults (>90%) report that diet, physical activity, and drug and alcohol use should be discussed in an annual physical with their providers (Oboler et al., 2002). Parents and caregivers also report interest in their children's behavioral health, reporting interest in behavioral health resources and in discussing behavioral health with their pediatricians (Byrd et al., 2015; Mehus et al., 2019; Riley et al., 2019). Attitudes toward a behavioral health wellness visit specifically also appear positive. In a study of parents and caregivers of children ages 0–18, the majority of participants (>80%) agreed that prevention was important, were interested in learning their child's risk for a behavioral disorder, and were interested in learning screening results (Zimmermann et al., 2020). Parents and caregivers ranked anxiety disorders as the most important to prevent, followed by depression, alcohol use disorders, impulse control disorders, and other substance use disorder. Thus, existing research suggests that integrating behavioral health into the wellness visits and well-child visit both could increase the scope of topics covered and also would be received positively by patients, parents, and caregivers.

2.4 Behavioral Health Wellness Visit Content: Screening, Intervention, and Stepped Care Approach

The behavioral health wellness visit conducted by a dedicated behavioral health professional has high stakeholder interest, has demonstrated feasibility, and has the potential to substantially improve the quality of behavioral health-focused preventive care. What follows is an outline of an approach to a behavioral health-integrated wellness visit (Fig. 2.1).

2.4.1 Identify Tailored Prevention Target

Prevention targets could be determined based on static risk factors (e.g., age) and dynamic or variable risk factors (e.g., symptom elevations). In particular, age of onset could determine the age at which some disorders are screened (Zimmermann et al., 2020).

2.4.2 Screening

The wellness visit could include a general screen (i.e., range of behavioral health concerns) commonly reported in primary care in addition to a risk-specific screen if indicated. Screening could be provided via patient portals (e.g., Gadomski et al., 2015) so that providers could view results of the screen prior to the visit. Examples

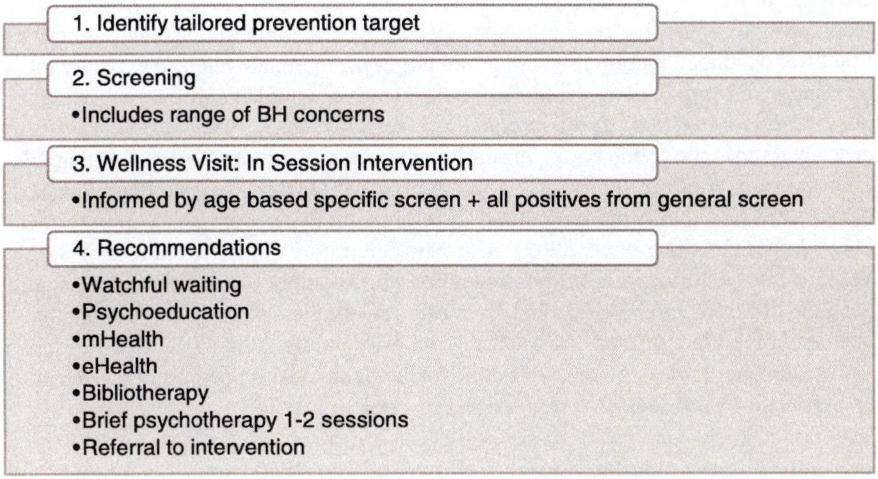

Fig. 2.1 Assessment and intervention in the behavioral health-integrated wellness visit

of general screens include the Pediatric Screening Inventory (PSI; Byrd et al., 2015), Adolescent Symptom Inventory-4 (ASI-4; Gadow et al., 1997), and the Adult Screening Inventory (ASI; Maragakis & O'Donohue, 2015). Screening could also include a more specific, risk-responsive tool (e.g., administering the Screen for Child Anxiety-Related Emotional Disorders [SCARED; Birmaher et al., 1997] close to age of onset for anxiety disorders [median age of 11; Kessler et al., 2005]). Screening tools relevant to specific behavioral disorders and how they can be interpreted are described in each chapter of this book.

2.4.3 Wellness Visit

The visit itself could be individually tailored and include a 20–30-minute visit led by a behavioral health professional to serve the following functions:

Describe the Role of Behavioral Health Provider in Patient Health One of the advantages of integrated care is the facilitation of access to quality behavioral healthcare for individuals who might not otherwise obtain access. Describing the role of behavioral health in physical health and well-being could reduce future barriers to accessing behavioral health.

Provide Screening Feedback Behavioral Health Providers (BHPs) could determine the level of risk based on positive findings from the general screen and elevations on any additional screening. For instance, SCARED scores ≥30 indicate probable anxiety disorder diagnosis. Scores below this threshold but exhibiting an elevation (e.g., SCARED score between 10 and 29) could indicate greater risk.

Deliver Brief Psychoeducation or Intervention The session could include responding to a positive screen as appropriate. Below-threshold scores might warrant brief psychoeducation relevant to the target problem, elevated scores may indicate indicated prevention, while screening positive would result in usual care for positive screening (e.g., brief intervention, referral, etc.). Brief interventions are described throughout this book pertaining to specific disorders. Prevention can take the form of a "toolbox approach," with the provider teaching brief skills relevant to the concern raised or something that is developmentally appropriate (Cuijpers et al., 2009; James & O'Donohue, 2009). A growing literature supports the role of Single Session Interventions in both the prevention and treatment of youth mental health problems (Schleider & Weisz, 2017). While few single session interventions have been examined in a primary care setting, the brief nature is ideally suited for delivery within the context of the well-child or wellness visit. Specific approaches to preventive interventions are provided in this book.

Introduce Recommendations for Follow-Up The visit would be followed by stepped care approaches to prevention.

Stepped care recommendations. Stepped care approaches are self-correcting, least restrictive approaches to maximizing healthcare resources (Bower & Gilbody, 2005; Maragakis & O'Donohue, 2018; O'Donohue & Draper, 2010). Self-correcting refers to the ability to monitor the level of care for appropriateness, whereas least restrictive refers to the progression of care from lower to higher intensity (Bower & Gilbody, 2005). Stepped care approaches to prevention have been effectively used in the primary care setting (van't Veer-Tazelaar et al., 2009) and have demonstrated cost-effectiveness (van't Veer-Tazelaar et al., 2010) and sustained effects over time (van't Veer-Tazelaar et al., 2011). Routine or built-in assessment of the target problem would allow for the decision for a more intensive step (Hermens et al., 2014). Decision-making can be informed by standardized cutoffs (e.g., van't Veer-Tazelaar et al., 2009). Steps could include eHealth and mHealth, groups, brief individual therapy, or a referral to specialty mental health.

Digital health. With respect to prevention, low intensity is particularly relevant, as asymptomatic individuals may be unlikely to perceive a significant need or be prepared to commit significant time or resources to a prevention approach. As such, digital health technologies could play an important role in the behavioral health wellness visit. First, the use of digital screening has the capacity to expand the scope of assessments, given the limitations of time face to face with a provider (Gadomski et al., 2015). One example is the *DartScreen*, a digital tool to implement validated instruments via tablet prior to a wellness visit (Gadomski et al., 2015). The tool is responsive, meaning that a brief screen (e.g., GAD-2; Kroenke et al., 2007) is followed by additional screening (e.g., GAD-7; Spitzer et al., 2006) if positive. The use of the *DartScreen* is associated with greater coverage of psychosocial topics within a wellness visit (Gadomski et al., 2015). Digital health interventions have also demonstrated effectiveness in the prevention of several behavioral health disorders (Deady et al., 2017) and health behavior change to prevent physical disease (Joiner et al., 2017).

2.4.4 Theoretical Approach

The transtheoretical model (TTM) or stages of change model (Prochaska et al., 2015) could be applied to increase motivation to engage with BHP recommendations. The TTM conceptualizes behavior change as a process and operates by identifying patient readiness to change, harnessing processes of change (e.g., stimulus control, helping relationships, reinforcement), and addressing decisional balance (i.e., costs and benefits of change) and self-efficacy to change. This model has been delivered briefly to promote health behaviors among racial/ethnic minority youth in primary care (Issner et al., 2017) and is the basis for effective multiple health behavior change (MHBC) interventions with high-risk populations (Prochaska et al., 2015). This model is designed to cohere with a range of specific, targeted interventions such as cognitive-behavioral techniques (Prochaska et al., 2015) and is described in this book.

2.5 Strengths of Behavioral Health Wellness Visit Approach

1. *Provide structure for delivery of preventive care services*. Healthcare is moving toward a value-based system, in which "maintaining good health is inherently less costly than dealing with poor health" (Porter, 2009, p. 109). There is a need for systems and technologies that can transform standard clinical practice by facilitating behavioral health-focused prevention and quickly measuring service quality and value.
2. *Reduce barriers to accessing behavioral healthcare*. Medical settings may remove barriers to behavioral health services such as stigma and privacy concerns raised in school settings (Burt et al., 2014; Gillham et al., 2006). The behavioral health-integrated wellness visit has the potential to reduce stigma by suggesting that all patients can benefit from behavioral health services (Williams, 2019). The integration of behavioral health into medical settings is associated with better follow-up into behavioral health services (Auxier et al., 2012; Kessler, 2012a, b).
3. *Reduce primary care provider burden*. The potential impact of the behavioral health annual wellness visit on primary care providers is twofold. First, behavior health providers can take on preventive care traditionally expected to be delivered by primary care providers. Second, the effective prevention of behavioral disorders could result in reduced medical service utilization and physical health problems.

2.6 Challenges and Considerations

1. *Patient factors*. Some patient factors may be associated with finding the wellness visit less acceptable. For instance, sociodemographic characteristics, including younger caregiver age, and identifying as non-Hispanic or Latino White have been associated with less favorable attitudes toward behavioral health-focused preventive care (Zimmermann et al., 2020). It may also be important to identify and address perceived risks of this service for parents/caregivers. One study found privacy to be a main concern expressed by parents declining to participate in a prevention program in a school setting (Heinrichs et al., 2005). In addition, decisional balance, or perceiving risks to outweigh benefits, is associated with less favorable attitudes toward a behavioral health-focused visit in primary care (Zimmermann et al., 2020).
2. *Provider and setting factors*. While provider attitudes and perspectives should be incorporated for program development (Proctor et al., 2007), provider attitudes are not consistently related to patient health outcomes (Litaker et al., 2005; Litaker et al., 2007). For instance, the Direct Observation of Primary Care Study examined physician attitudes and whether patients were up to date on preventive care as determined by the USPSTF guidelines. The study found generally low

rates on behavioral health-focused preventive care, with 10% of primary care patients receiving diet advice and 36% receiving smoking cessation advise. Rather than provider attitudes predicting provision of these services, however, having an office visit scheduled was the most important factor associated with service provision (Litaker et al., 2005). As such, developing a feasible and effective workflow is essential to effective implementation of a behavioral health wellness visit. Any change to workflow in integrated care can be challenging and should be coupled with adequate training and preparation (Kwan & Nease, 2013).

3. *Reimbursement.* The integration of behavioral health providers into the well-child visit or annual wellness visit would require costs of training, staff, direct costs, and time that are not currently embedded within the healthcare system. The Canadian Task Force on the Periodic Health Examination called for incentives for developing approaches for preventive care (Hill et al., 1979).

2.7 Conclusions and Future Directions

While most medical visits are focused on treatment, the AWV has long been the vehicle through which health promotion and disease prevention occur for primary care patients. The historical changes in the AWV suggest the importance of considering the value of care and delivering targeted and evidence-based screening and intervention. The integration of behavioral health into this visit presents an opportunity to expand the scope of preventive care and increase its effectiveness. More research is needed to determine the effectiveness and cost-effectiveness of a behavioral health wellness visit, as well as timing and duration of preventive interventions delivered in this format.

References

Aarons, G. A., Sklar, M., Mustanski, B., Benbow, N., & Brown, C. H. (2017). "Scaling-out" evidence-based interventions to new populations or new health care delivery systems. *Implementation Science, 12*(1), 111.

Asarnow, J. R., Rozenman, M., Wiblin, J., & Zeltzer, L. (2015). Integrated medical-behavioral care compared with usual primary care for child and adolescent behavioral health: A meta-analysis. *JAMA Pediatrics, 169*(10), 929–937.

Auxier, A., Runyan, C., Mullin, D., Mendenhall, T., Young, J., & Kessler, R. (2012). Behavioral health referrals and treatment initiation rates in integrated primary care: A collaborative care research network study. *Translational Behavioral Medicine, 2*(3), 337–344. https://doi.org/10.1007/s13142-012-0141-8

Belamarich, P. F., Gandica, R., Stein, R. E. K., & Racine, A. D. (2006). Drowning in a sea of advice: Pediatricians and American Academy of Pediatrics policy statements. *Pediatrics, 118*(4), e964–e978.

Birmaher, B., Khetarpal, S., Brent, D., Cully, M., Balach, L., Kaufman, J., & Neer, S. M. (1997). The screen for child anxiety related emotional disorders (SCARED): Scale construction and psychometric characteristics. *Journal of the American Academy of Child & Adolescent Psychiatry, 36*(4), 545–553.

Birtwhistle, R., Bell, N. R., Thombs, B. D., Grad, R., & Dickinson, J. A. (2017). *Periodic preventive medical visits: Better delivery of prevention services by the Canadian task force on preventive health care.*

Boulware, L. E., Marinopoulos, S., Phillips, K. A., Hwang, C. W., Maynor, K., Merenstein, D., … Powe, N. R. (2007). Systematic review: The value of the periodic health evaluation. *Annals of Internal Medicine, 146*(4), 289–300.

Bower, P., & Gilbody, S. (2005). Stepped care in psychological therapies: Access, effectiveness and efficiency: Narrative literature review. *The British Journal of Psychiatry, 186*(1), 11–17.

Burt, J. D., Garbacz, S. A., Kupzyk, K. A., Frerichs, L., & Gathje, R. (2014). Examining the utility of behavioral health integration in well-child visits: Implications for rural settings. In *Families systems & health.* Educational Publishing Foundation-American Psychological Assoc. https://doi.org/10.1037/a0035121

Byrd, M. R., O'Donohue, W. T., & Maragakis, A. (2015). Pilot testing of the pediatric screening inventory in the primary care setting. *Acta Psychopathologica, 01*(01). https://doi.org/10.4172/2469-6676.100008

Cuijpers, P., Muñoz, R. F., Clarke, G. N., & Lewinsohn, P. M. (2009). Psychoeducational treatment and prevention of depression: The "coping with depression" course thirty years later. *Clinical Psychology Review, 29*(5), 449–458.

Cutler, J. L., Ramcharan, S., Feldman, R., Siegelaub, A. B., Campbell, B., Friedman, G. D., … Collen, M. F. (1973). 1. Methods and population. *Preventive Medicine, 2*(2), 197–206.

Deady, M., Choi, I., Calvo, R. A., Glozier, N., Christensen, H., & Harvey, S. B. (2017). eHealth interventions for the prevention of depression and anxiety in the general population: A systematic review and meta-analysis. *BMC Psychiatry, 17*(1), 310. https://doi.org/10.1186/s12888-017-1473-1

Dinkevich, E., Hupert, J., & Moyer, V. A. (2001). Evidence based well child care. *BMJ, 323*(7317), 846–849.

Dishion, T. J., Nelson, S. E., & Kavanagh, K. (2003). The family check-up with high-risk young adolescents: Preventing early-onset substance use by parent monitoring. *Behavior Therapy, 34*(4), 553–571.

Emerson, H. (1923). Periodic medical examinations of apparently healthy persons. *Journal of the American Medical Association, 80*(19), 1376–1381.

Fontham, E. T. H., Wolf, A. M. D., Church, T. R., Etzioni, R., Flowers, C. R., Herzig, A., … Walter, L. C. (2020). Cervical cancer screening for individuals at average risk: 2020 guideline update from the American Cancer Society. *CA: a Cancer Journal for Clinicians, 70*(5), 321–346.

Forman-Hoffman, V., McClure, E., McKeeman, J., Wood, C. T., Middleton, J. C., Skinner, A. C., … Viswanathan, M. (2016). Screening for major depressive disorder in children and adolescents: A systematic review for the US Preventive Services Task Force. *Annals of Internal Medicine, 164*(5), 342–349.

Gadomski, A. M., Fothergill, K. E., Larson, S., Wissow, L. S., Winegrad, H., Nagykaldi, Z. J., … Roter, D. L. (2015). Integrating mental health into adolescent annual visits: Impact of previsit comprehensive screening on within-visit processes. *Journal of Adolescent Health.* Elsevier. https://doi.org/10.1016/j.jadohealth.2014.11.011

Gadow, K. D., Sprafkin, J., Attack, P., Phobia, S., Tics, D. M., & Anorexia, D. (1997). *Adolescent symptom inventory-4 (ASI-4).* Checkmate Plus.

Gillham, J. E., Hamilton, J., Freres, D. R., Patton, K., & Gallop, R. (2006). Preventing depression among early adolescents in the primary care setting: A randomized controlled study of the Penn Resiliency Program. *Journal of Abnormal Child Psychology, 34*(2), 203–219. https://doi.org/10.1007/s10802-005-9014-7

Gorbenko, K., Metcalf, S. A., Mazumdar, M., & Crump, C. (2017). Annual physical examinations and wellness visits: Translating guidelines into practice. *American Journal of Preventive Medicine, 52*(6), 813–816.

Grad, R., Légaré, F., Bell, N. R., Dickinson, J. A., Singh, H., Moore, A. E., ... Kretschmer, K. L. (2017). Shared decision making in preventive health care: What it is; what it is not. *Canadian Family Physician, 63*(9), 682–684.

Greenberg, P. E., Fournier, A.-A., Sisitsky, T., Simes, M., Berman, R., Koenigsberg, S. H., & Kessler, R. C. (2021). The economic burden of adults with major depressive disorder in the United States (2010 and 2018). *Pharmacoeconomics*, 1–13.

Grunfeld, E., Manca, D., Moineddin, R., Thorpe, K. E., Hoch, J. S., Campbell-Scherer, D., ... Mamdani, M. (2013). Improving chronic disease prevention and screening in primary care: Results of the better pragmatic cluster randomized controlled trial. *BMC Family Practice*. https://doi.org/10.1186/1471-2296-14-175

Hagan, J. F., Shaw, J. S., & Duncan, P. M. (2007). Bright futures: Guidelines for health supervision of infants, children, and adolescents. *American Academy of Pediatrics*.

Han, P. K. J. (1997). Historical changes in the objectives of the periodic health examination. *Annals of Internal Medicine, 127*(10), 910–917.

Heinrichs, N., Bertram, H., Kuschel, A., & Hahlweg, K. (2005). Parent recruitment and retention in a universal prevention program for child behavior and emotional problems: Barriers to research and program participation. *Prevention Science, 6*(4), 275–286.

Hermens, M. L. M., Muntingh, A., Franx, G., van Splunteren, P. T., & Nuyen, J. (2014). Stepped care for depression is easy to recommend, but harder to implement: Results of an explorative study within primary care in the Netherlands. *BMC Family Practice, 15*(1), 5.

Heron, N., Tully, M. A., McKinley, M. C., & Cupples, M. E. (2014). Physical activity assessment in practice: A mixed methods study of GPPAQ use in primary care. *BMC Family Practice, 15*(1), 1–9.

Hill, N., Frappier-Davignon, L., & Morrison, B. (1979). The periodic health examination. *Canadian Medical Association Journal, 121*, 1193–1254.

Irving, G., Neves, A. L., Dambha-Miller, H., Oishi, A., Tagashira, H., Verho, A., & Holden, J. (2017). International variations in primary care physician consultation time: A systematic review of 67 countries. *BMJ Open, 7*(10), e017902.

Irwin, C. E., Adams, S. H., Park, M. J., & Newacheck, P. W. (2009). Preventive care for adolescents: Few get visits and fewer get services. *Pediatrics, 123*(4), e565–e572.

Issner, J. H., Mucka, L. E., & Barnett, D. (2017). Increasing positive health behaviors in adolescents with nutritional goals and exercise. *Journal of Child and Family Studies, 26*(2), 548–558.

James, L. C., & O'Donohue, W. T. (2009). *The primary care toolkit: Practical resources for the integrated behavioral care provider*. Springer.

Joiner, K. L., Nam, S., & Whittemore, R. (2017). Lifestyle interventions based on the diabetes prevention program delivered via eHealth: A systematic review and meta-analysis. *Preventive Medicine, 100*, 194–207.

Jørgensen, K. J., & Gøtzsche, P. C. (2009). Overdiagnosis in publicly organised mammography screening programmes: systematic review of incidence trends. *BMJ*, 339.

Jorm, A. F., Patten, S. B., Brugha, T. S., & Mojtabai, R. (2017). Has increased provision of treatment reduced the prevalence of common mental disorders? Review of the evidence from four countries. *World Psychiatry, 16*(1), 90–99.

Kessler, R. (2012a). Mental health care treatment initiation when mental health services are incorporated into primary care practice. *The Journal of the American Board of Family Medicine, 25*(2), 255–259. https://doi.org/10.3122/jabfm.2012.02.100125

Kessler, R. C. (2012b). The costs of depression. *Psychiatric Clinics, 35*(1), 1–14.

Kessler, R. C., Berglund, P., Demler, O., Jin, R., Merikangas, K. R., & Walters, E. E. (2005). Lifetime prevalence and age-of-onset distributions of DSM-IV disorders in the National Comorbidity Survey Replication. *Archives of General Psychiatry, 62*(6), 593. https://doi.org/10.1001/archpsyc.62.6.593

Kessler, R. C., Chiu, W. T., Demler, O., & Walters, E. E. (2005). Prevalence, severity, and comorbidity of 12-month DSM-IV disorders in the National Comorbidity Survey Replication. *Archives of General Psychiatry, 62*(6), 617–627.

Kroenke, K., Spitzer, R. L., Williams, J. B. W., Monahan, P. O., & Löwe, B. (2007). Anxiety disorders in primary care: Prevalence, impairment, comorbidity, and detection. *Annals of Internal Medicine, 146*(5), 317–325.

Krogsbøll, L. T., Jørgensen, K. J., Larsen, C. G., & Gøtzsche, P. C. (2012). General health checks in adults for reducing morbidity and mortality from disease: Cochrane systematic review and meta-analysis. *BMJ, 345.*

Kwan, B. M., & Nease, D. E. (2013). The state of the evidence for integrated behavioral health in primary care. In *Integrated behavioral health in primary care* (pp. 65–98). Springer.

Leslie, L. K., Mehus, C. J., Hawkins, J. D., Boat, T., McCabe, M. A., Barkin, S., … Tait, V. F. (2016). Primary health care: Potential home for family-focused preventive interventions. *American Journal of Preventive Medicine, 51*(4), S106–S118.

Litaker, D., Flocke, S. A., Frolkis, J. P., & Stange, K. C. (2005). Physicians attitudes and preventive care delivery insights from the DOPC study. *Preventive Medicine.* https://doi.org/10.1016/j.ypmed.2004.07.015

Litaker, D., Watts, B., Samaan, R., Ober, S., & Lawrence, R. H. (2007). Are provider self-efficacy and attitudes related to cardiovascular prevention associated with better treatment outcomes? *Translational Research, 149*(4), 165–172.

Lundahl, B., Moleni, T., Burke, B. L., Butters, R., Tollefson, D., Butler, C., & Rollnick, S. (2013). Motivational interviewing in medical care settings: A systematic review and meta-analysis of randomized controlled trials. *Patient Education and Counseling, 93*(2), 157–168.

Manca, D. P., Campbell-Scherer, D., Aubrey-Bassler, K., Kandola, K., Aguilar, C., Baxter, J., … Faria, V. (2015). Developing clinical decision tools to implement chronic disease prevention and screening in primary care: The BETTER 2 program (building on existing tools to improve chronic disease prevention and screening in primary care). *Implementation Science, 10*(1), 1–10.

Manca, D. P., Greiver, M., Carroll, J. C., Salvalaggio, G., Cave, A., Rogers, J., … Bible, S. (2014). Finding a BETTER way: A qualitative study exploring the prevention practitioner intervention to improve chronic disease prevention and screening in family practice. *BMC Family Practice, 15*(1), 1–10.

Maragakis, A., & O'Donohue, W. T. (2015). *Pilot testing of multiple behavioral health screening devices in the primary care setting.*

Maragakis, A., & O'Donohue, W. T. (2018). *Principle-based stepped care and brief psychotherapy for integrated care settings.* Springer.

Mehrotra, A., & Prochazka, A. (2015). Improving value in health care – Against the annual physical. *New England Journal of Medicine, 373*(16), 1485–1487.

Mehus, C. J., Kazlauskaite, V., Colianni, S., & Borowsky, I. W. (2019). Parents' interest in resources to address their child's behavioral health through primary care. *Families, Systems & Health.* https://doi.org/10.1037/fsh0000429

Merikangas, K. R., He, J., Burstein, M., Swanson, S. A., Avenevoli, S., Cui, L., … Swendsen, J. (2010). Lifetime prevalence of mental disorders in US adolescents: Results from the National Comorbidity Survey Replication–Adolescent Supplement (NCS-A). *Journal of the American Academy of Child & Adolescent Psychiatry, 49*(10), 980–989. https://doi.org/10.1016/j.jaac.2010.05.017

Midboe, A. M., Cucciare, M. A., Trafton, J. A., Ketroser, N., & Chardos, J. F. (2011). Implementing motivational interviewing in primary care: The role of provider characteristics. *Translational Behavioral Medicine.* Springer. https://doi.org/10.1007/s13142-011-0080-9

Moynihan, R., Doust, J., & Henry, D. (2012). Preventing overdiagnosis: How to stop harming the healthy. *BMJ, 344.*

O'Connor, E., Rossom, R. C., Henninger, M., Groom, H. C., Burda, B. U., Henderson, J. T., … Whitlock, E. P. (2016). *Screening for depression in adults: An updated systematic evidence review for the US Preventive Services Task Force.*

O'Connor, E., Senger, C. A., Henninger, M., Gaynes, B. N., & Coppola, E. (2019). *Interventions to prevent perinatal depression: a systematic evidence review for the US Preventive Services Task Force.*

O'Donohue, W., & Draper, C. (2010). *Stepped care and e-health*. Springer.

O'Donohue, W. T., & Cucciare, M. A. (2005). The role of psychological factors in medical presentations. *Journal of Clinical Psychology in Medical Settings, 12*(1), 13–24. https://doi.org/10.1007/s10880-005-0908-x

Oboler, S. K., Prochazka, A. V., Gonzales, R., Xu, S., & Anderson, R. J. (2002). Public expectations and attitudes for annual physical examinations and testing. *Annals of Internal Medicine, 136*(9), 652–659.

Owens, D. K., Davidson, K. W., Krist, A. H., Barry, M. J., Cabana, M., Caughey, A. B., … Epling, J. W. (2020). Primary care interventions for prevention and cessation of tobacco use in children and adolescents: US preventive services task force recommendation statement. *JAMA, 323*(16), 1590–1598.

Ploeg, J., Feightner, J., Hutchison, B., Patterson, C., Sigouin, C., & Gauld, M. (2005). Effectiveness of preventive primary care outreach interventions aimed at older people: Meta-analysis of randomized controlled trials. *Canadian Family Physician, 51*(9), 1244–1245.

Porter, M. E. (2009). A strategy for health care reform – Toward a value-based system. *The New England Journal of Medicine, 361*(2), 109–112.

Prochaska, J. O., Redding, C. A., & Evers, K. E. (2015). The transtheoretical model and stages of change. *Health Behavior: Theory, Research, and Practice, 97*.

Prochazka, A. V., Lundahl, K., Pearson, W., Oboler, S. K., & Anderson, R. J. (2005). Support of evidence-based guidelines for the annual physical examination: A survey of primary care providers. *Archives of Internal Medicine, 165*(12), 1347–1352.

Proctor, E. K., Knudsen, K. J., Fedoravicius, N., Hovmand, P., Rosen, A., & Perron, B. (2007). Implementation of evidence-based practice in community behavioral health: Agency director perspectives. *Administration and Policy in Mental Health and Mental Health Services Research, 34*(5), 479–488.

Ridenour, T. A., Galan, C., & Shaw, D. S. (2021). *Well-child screening and referral to prevent adolescent substance use and conduct problems: 12-month outcomes*. In Society of behavioral medicine 42nd annual meeting and scientific sessions.

Ridenour, T. A., Willis, D., Bogen, D. L., Novak, S., Scherer, J., Reynolds, M. D., & Tarter, R. E. (2015). Detecting initiation or risk for initiation of substance use before high school during pediatric well-child check-ups. *Drug and Alcohol Dependence, 150*, 54–62.

Riley, A. R., Walker, B. L., Wilson, A. C., Hall, T. A., Stormshak, E. A., & Cohen, D. J. (2019). Parents' consumer preferences for early childhood behavioral intervention in primary care. *Journal of Developmental & Behavioral Pediatrics, 40*(9), 669–678. https://doi.org/10.1097/DBP.0000000000000736

SAMHSA. (2017). *2017 National Survey on Drug Use and Health (NSDUH)*. Retrieved from https://www.samhsa.gov/data/sites/default/files/cbhsq-reports/NSDUHDetailedTabs2017/NSDUHDetailedTabs2017.htm#tab8-33A

Schleider, J. L., & Weisz, J. R. (2017). Little treatments, promising effects? Meta-analysis of single-session interventions for youth psychiatric problems. *Journal of the American Academy of Child & Adolescent Psychiatry, 56*(2), 107–115.

Schumacher, J. A., Williams, D. C., Burke, R. S., Epler, A. J., Simon, P., & Coffey, S. F. (2018). Competency-based supervision in motivational interviewing for advanced psychology trainees: Targeting an a priori benchmark. *Training and Education in Professional Psychology, 12*(3), 149.

Schwalbe, C. S., Oh, H. Y., & Zweben, A. (2014). Sustaining motivational interviewing: A meta-analysis of training studies. *Addiction, 109*(8), 1287–1294.

Shanafelt, T. D., West, C. P., Sinsky, C., Trockel, M., Tutty, M., Satele, D. V., … Dyrbye, L. N. (2019). Changes in burnout and satisfaction with work-life integration in physicians and the general US working population between 2011 and 2017. In *Mayo Clinic proceedings* (Vol. 94, pp. 1681–1694). Elsevier.

Shein, D. M., & Stone, V. E. (2017). The annual physical: Delivering value. *American Journal of Medicine*. Elsevier. https://doi.org/10.1016/j.amjmed.2016.12.036

Smith, J. D., Berkel, C., Rudo-Stern, J., Montaño, Z., St George, S. M., Prado, G., … Dishion, T. J. (2018). The Family Check-Up 4 Health (FCU4Health): Applying implementation science frameworks to the process of adapting an evidence-based parenting program for prevention of pediatric obesity and excess weight gain in primary care. *Frontiers in Public Health, 6*, 293.

Smith, R. C. (2011). Educating trainees about common mental health problems in primary care: A (not so) modest proposal. *Academic Medicine: Journal of the Association of American Medical Colleges*. https://doi.org/10.1097/ACM.0b013e3182308dc8

Smith, R. C., Laird-Fick, H., D'Mello, D., Dwamena, F. C., Romain, A., Olson, J., … Frankel, R. (2014). Addressing mental health issues in primary care: An initial curriculum for medical residents. In *Patient education and counselling*. Elsevier Ireland Ltd.. https://doi.org/10.1016/j.pec.2013.09.010

Sopcak, N., Aguilar, C., Nykiforuk, C. I. J., O'Brien, M. A., Aubrey-Bassler, K., Cullen, R. M., … Manca, D. P. (2017). Patients' perspectives on BETTER 2 prevention and screening: Qualitative findings from Newfoundland & Labrador. *BJGP Open, 1*(3).

Spitzer, R. L., Kroenke, K., Williams, J. B. W., & Löwe, B. (2006). A brief measure for assessing generalized anxiety disorder: The GAD-7. *Archives of Internal Medicine, 166*(10), 1092–1097. https://doi.org/10.1001/archinte.166.10.1092

Stuck, A. E., Moser, A., Morf, U., Wirz, U., Wyser, J., Gillmann, G., … Harari, D. (2015). Effect of health risk assessment and counselling on health behaviour and survival in older people: A pragmatic randomised trial. *PLoS Medicine, 12*(10), e1001889.

Telzrow, R. W. (1978). Anticipatory guidance in pediatric practice. *Journal of Continuing Education in Pediatrics, 20*, 14–27.

The BETTER Program. (2021). Retrieved from http://better.utoronto.ca/

Turner, K. (2018). Well-child visits for infants and young children. *American Family Physician, 98*(6), 347–353.

Twomey, C., & O'Reilly, G. (2017). Effectiveness of a freely available computerised cognitive behavioural therapy programme (MoodGYM) for depression: Meta-analysis. *Australian & New Zealand Journal of Psychiatry, 51*(3), 260–269.

USPSTF. (1989). Guide to clinical preventive services. *An assessment of the effectiveness of 169 interventions*.

USPSTF. (1996). *The guide to clinical preventive services*. Williams & Wilkins.

USPSTF. (2014). *Guide to clinical preventive services, 2014: Recommendations of the U.S. Preventive Services Task Force*. Rockville, MD. Retrieved from http://www.ahrq.gov/professionals/clinicians-providers/guidelines-recommendations/guide/index.html

van't Veer-Tazelaar, P., Smit, F., van Hout, H., van Oppen, P., van der Horst, H., Beekman, A., & van Marwijk, H. (2010). Cost-effectiveness of a stepped care intervention to prevent depression and anxiety in late life: Randomised trial. *The British Journal of Psychiatry, 196*(4), 319–325.

van't Veer-Tazelaar, P. J., van Marwijk, H. W. J., van Oppen, P., van der Horst, H. E., Smit, F., Cuijpers, P., & Beekman, A. T. F. (2011). Prevention of late-life anxiety and depression has sustained effects over 24 months: A pragmatic randomized trial. *The American Journal of Geriatric Psychiatry, 19*(3), 230–239.

van't Veer-Tazelaar, P. J., van Marwijk, H. W. J., van Oppen, P., van Hout, H. P. J., van der Horst, H. E., Cuijpers, P., … Beekman, A. T. F. (2009). Stepped-care prevention of anxiety and depression in late life: A randomized controlled trial. *Archives of General Psychiatry, 66*(3), 297–304.

Vogel, M. E., Kanzler, K. E., Aikens, J. E., & Goodie, J. L. (2017). Integration of behavioral health and primary care: Current knowledge and future directions. *Journal of Behavioral Medicine, 40*(1), 69–84.

Williams, A. A. (2019). The next step in integrated care: Universal primary mental health providers. *Journal of Clinical Psychology in Medical Settings, 27*, 115–126. https://doi.org/10.1007/s10880-019-09626-2

Wiltsey Stirman, S., Gamarra, J. M., Bartlett, B. A., Calloway, A., & Gutner, C. A. (2017). Empirical examinations of modifications and adaptations to evidence-based psychotherapies:

Methodologies, impact, and future directions. *Clinical Psychology: Science and Practice, 24*(4), 396–420.

Woltmann, E., Grogan-Kaylor, A., Perron, B., Georges, H., Kilbourne, A. M., & Bauer, M. S. (2012). Comparative effectiveness of collaborative chronic care models for mental health conditions across primary, specialty, and behavioral health care settings: Systematic review and meta-analysis. *American Journal of Psychiatry, 169*(8), 790–804.

Yarnall, K. S. H., Pollak, K. I., Østbye, T., Krause, K. M., & Michener, J. L. (2003). Primary care: Is there enough time for prevention? *American Journal of Public Health, 93*(4), 635–641.

Zaman, J. A. B. (2018). The enduring value of the physical examination. *Medical Clinics, 102*(3), 417–423.

Zimmermann, M., O'Donohue, W., & Vechiu, C. (2020). A primary care prevention system for behavioral health: The behavioral health annual wellness checkup. *Journal of Clinical Psychology in Medical Settings, 27*(2). https://doi.org/10.1007/s10880-019-09658-8

Zimmermann, M., O'Donohue, W., Zepeda, M., & Woodley, A. (2020). Examining Caretaker Attitudes Towards Primary Prevention of Pediatric Behavioral Health Problems in Integrated Care. *The Journal of Behavioral Health Services & Research*, 1–13.

Chapter 3
Integrating Mental Health Prevention into the Primary Care Workflow

Laura Blanke, Lisa Herron, Stephanie Kirchner, and Benjamin F. Miller

3.1 Introduction

Primary care is first, foremost, and fundamental (Starfield, 1998; Starfield & Shi, 2004, 2007; Starfield et al., 2005). It is the bedrock, the core function of a healthy delivery system. For decades, science has recognized that without mental health as a part of this function, primary care offers inferior and insufficient care. In the seminal 1996 National Academies of Science, Engineering, and Medicine (formerly Institute of Medicine) report on Primary Care, authors described the critical necessity of investing in primary care to help achieve population health goals (deGruy, 1996; Institute of Medicine, 1996). Since then, the healthcare sector continues to work at valuing and investing in primary care, and the integration of mental health has taken a much more visible position in the primary care community, at least conceptually (Brown Levey et al., 2012; Butler et al., 2008; B.F. Miller & Hubley, 2017; Zivin et al., 2017).

The integration of primary care and mental health, as defined by the Agency for Healthcare Research and Quality (Peek, 2013) is the: *Care that results from a practice team of primary care and behavioral health clinicians, working together with*

L. Blanke · L. Herron
Well Being Trust, Oakland, CA, USA
e-mail: laura@wellbeingtrust.org; lisa@wellbeingtrust.org

S. Kirchner
University of Colorado School of Medicine, Aurora, CO, USA
e-mail: stephanie.kirchner@cuanschutz.edu

B. F. Miller (✉)
Well Being Trust, Oakland, CA, USA

Stanford School of Medicine, Stanford, CA, USA
e-mail: ben@wellbeingtrust.org

W. O'Donohue, M. Zimmermann (eds.), *Handbook of Evidence-Based Prevention of Behavioral Disorders in Integrated Care*,
https://doi.org/10.1007/978-3-030-83469-2_3

patients and families, using a systematic and cost-effective approach to provide patient-centered care for a defined population. This care may address mental health and substance use conditions, health behaviors (including their contribution to chronic medical illnesses), life stressors and crises, stress-related physical symptoms, and ineffective patterns of health care utilization.

Bringing mental health clinicians into primary care settings and onto the primary care team has significant benefit for the patient (Balasubramanian et al., 2017). From early detection of mental health problems to crisis intervention and treatment, there are a multitude of gains when mental health expertise is on site in a primary care practice. While the literature has covered the science behind integration in great detail elsewhere (Butler et al., 2008; Funk et al., 2008; Patel et al., 2013), there are two key aspects of the work that we will consistently refer to in this chapter. The first is the importance of workflow and assuring that pathways for the patient and all the clinicians involved in care are clear and consistently defined so that patients do not get lost in the system or fall through the cracks (Davis et al., 2013). The second is the range of interventions that mental health clinicians provide on the primary care team (Maragakis & O'Donohue, 2018; B. F. Miller et al., 2014). We posit that prevention and early intervention should be a core foundation of how primary care conceptualizes and implements its integrated model. This chapter will explore the need and growing effort to better integrate mental health in the primary care setting, which includes identifying ways that core prevention services can be distributed in the clinical workflow to improve care and efficiency as well as provide specific recommendations for mechanisms that can be employed to improve integration efforts among practice personnel, and system and policy changes needed to facilitate changes in the clinical setting.

3.2 Defining Prevention

Across the globe, health prevention and healthcare delivery are typically divided into three tiers: primary, secondary, and tertiary. Each tier has a unique and overlapping clinical workflow, with bidirectional flows of patient information, provider tasks, and levels of communication. Here we will briefly describe the various types of prevention.

Prevention in the primary care setting was first defined in the 1940s by Hugh Leavell and E. Guerney Clark of Harvard and Columbia Schools of Public Health as "measures applicable to a particular disease or group of diseases in order to intercept the causes of disease before they involve man…" (Cohen et al., 2010, p. 5). Primary caregivers include primary care physicians (PCPs), nurse practitioners (NPs), and physician's assistants (PAs). The primary care setting is the first point of contact for people who need healthcare and healthcare services for routine services such as vaccinations and occurs before the development of illness or disease.

The literature has robust examples of primary prevention – and many of the solutions for advancing health and preventing disease are grounded in social or community factors. If the goal of primary prevention is to avoid the onset of the disease to begin with, this means that most of the priority factors for intervention are social factors like where a person lives, their education, and their employment, also referred to as the social determinants of health (SDoH).

Mental health clinicians working in primary care will have appointees, which may range from patient navigators to social workers, to address the above issues through a network of care model. Prevention in secondary care requires a screening element and involves more clinicians and treatment than primary and is typically hospital-based. It can be routine and planned, like mammography or colonoscopy, or it can be urgent, like treatment of a fracture or severe stomach flu. Prevention in tertiary care is the highest specialization of care and occurs after diagnosis of a disease or illness, for example, neurosurgery for a brain tumor or chemotherapy for cancer patients (Centers for Disease Control, 2019).

3.3 Public Health Prevention

Public health prevention focuses on prevention of disease and health promotion, and provision of a limited set of safety net services – often outside of the primary care setting and not providing the full set of services that would be classified as a medical home, let alone robust integrated care that includes mental health services. Access to more comprehensive health and mental health services usually require referral, though there are some local and regional public health clinics that provide a wider array of services and might be considered integrated in some ways. Those clinics are sometimes affiliated with a Federally Qualified Health Center or co-located with state-level services (such as Women, Infant & Children programs).

3.4 Prevention in Primary Care

The literature is clear that having a regular source of care is the single most important factor associated with the receipt of preventive services (Bindman et al., 1996). Primary care at its core is about continuity (Schwarz et al., 2019) and comprehensiveness (O'Malley & Rich, 2015). In fact, Barbara Starfield in her seminal work on primary care (Starfield, 1998) described how comprehensiveness in primary care must include prevention and wellness, as well as acute and chronic health condition management, which includes mental health. As others have written, bringing mental health into primary care only complements these core functions of continuity and comprehensiveness (Dickinson & Miller, 2010).

Despite the hurdles, prevention matters, as it is fundamental to improving both personal and population health outcomes. Prevention means avoiding more intensive and costly services, improving quality of life, increasing productivity, and reducing morbidity/mortality outcomes (Hogg et al., 2008; HUNG et al., 2007).

Subsequent to the passage of the Patient Protection and Affordable Care Act (ACA), most health plans are required to cover preventive services, though plans vary greatly in which of those services they cover (Fox & Shaw, 2015). For the most part, preventive services include items like blood pressure, diabetes, and cholesterol tests as well as certain screenings for cancer. Specific to mental health, depression screening is the *only* item considered covered under prevention ("Preventive care benefits for adults," 2021). One of the ongoing critiques of prevention practices in primary care has been on the amount of time it takes to deliver those services. In an often-cited paper, Yarnall et al. (2003) indicated that, in the hustle and bustle of delivering primary care, to "fully satisfy the USPSTF recommendations on prevention, 1773 hours of a physician's annual time, or 7.4 hours per working day, is needed for the provision of preventive services" (p. 635). Since 2003, though some improvements have been made in delivery, there remains an increasing number of duties being assigned to primary care clinicians – all important, and all time-consuming. In fact, Bucher et al. (2016) found that the annual time required for primary care to adequately perform all the required preventive care was 20% of their total patient time or about 250 h. And perhaps most interesting, almost three quarters of the patients in this study had a prevention to care time ratio exceeding 15%. The challenge for primary care is made worse through primary care payment structures – particularly with respect to fee-for-service (FFS) contracts that incentivize volume, which artificially creates an inferior care model because primary care providers are beholden to seeing an increased number of patients due to insurance billing structure. FFS contracts translate to shorter office visits to allow the clinician to see more patients, without covering the depth and complexity that some patients require, especially with respect to mental health. As we will discuss in our policy recommendations, FFS models in primary care are an impediment to pursuing both integration and prevention and a factor that must change.

While primary care practices are being asked to do a lot in the prevention space, all health plans offered through the ACA's marketplace are required to cover preventive services without charging patient copays or coinsurance. For example, alcohol misuse screening and counseling as well as depression screening are both covered. Despite the availability and reimbursement of standard screening tools and coverage (meaning payment), for administering screening, most primary care practices still do not screen for depression – less than 5% nationally (Ayse Akincigil & Elizabeth B. Matthews, 2017). It is already hard to treat what you don't see, and without a significant uptake of screening, the progression of mental health conditions will continue to worsen individually and at a population level.

3.5 Mental Health and Primary Care Prevention

Mental health prevention ensures that all individuals have access to the full continuum of whole-person care, no matter how they come into contact with a health system – whether primary, secondary, or tertiary (Well Being Trust, 2020a).

Increasingly, mental healthcare and support is found in primary care settings, as the first line of clinical care for people across the United States (Institute of Medicine (US) Committee on the Future of Primary Care, 1996). As a result, in the last decades, research and investments have increasingly targeted primary care settings as opportunity zones to bring in mental clinicians. It is at this intersection that the opportunities to leverage mental health clinicians comes into focus. First, there are the opportunities for mental health clinicians integrated into primary care to free up more time for the primary care physician. In one study, Polaha et al. found that when a mental health clinician was on site in primary care, primary care physicians spent two fewer minutes on average for every patient seen, allowing them to see 42% more patients, and bring in $1142 more revenue per day. Of course, this was compared to the days the mental health clinician was not on site (Gouge et al., 2016). And when patients have mental health as a primary reason for coming into the practice, they spend an average of 7 min longer when compared to patients in the clinic for non-mental health reasons (Cooper et al., 2006).

Prevention for mental health conditions is often predicated on actually detecting risk factors and symptoms early. Early detection of mental health conditions is critical for young people, ages 13–18, as by age 14 half of mental health concerns and illness first emerge (Dougherty et al., 2020). Healthcare utilization patterns for adolescents underscore the benefit of a mental health vital sign. Many adolescents don't engage in well-care visits as frequently as they do at younger ages, outside of physicals for sports or school requirements –making screening at every opportunity, whether for sexual health or urgent care service, crucial. As we will discuss in our recommendations, keeping this population as a focus in the workflow is an essential way to prevent and treat serious mental illness before it worsens.

Beyond screening for specific mental health conditions, emerging mental health practice suggests that primary care settings are primed for screening for Adverse Childhood Experiences (ACEs) and long-term toxic stress. ACEs was first coined in a 1998 Centers for Disease Control and Kaiser Permanente study (Felitti et al., 1998), in which over 9000 respondents identified if they had experienced one or more of seven categories of adversities (including abuse, traumatic experiences, neglect) by age 18. ACEs have now been expanded into ten categories across three domains, as outlined below:

Abuse: Physical, emotional, and sexual abuse
Neglect: Physical and emotional neglect
Household challenges: Growing up in a household with incarceration, mental illness substance dependence, absence due to parental separation or divorce, or intimate partner violence

With respect to mental health, increased exposure to ACEs activates youths' biological stress response, can damage brain development, and disrupt healthy stress and hormonal regulation patterns. All of these are part of a toxic stress response that has both direct and indirect relationships with outcome such as depression, anxiety, PTSD, and, worse, risk for suicide. As discussed later in the chapter, ACEs can and should be addressed in integrated care settings and through changes in the clinical workflow.

3.6 Evidence

Evidence suggests that prevention is most successful when delivered consistently and with appropriate follow-up (Doyle et al., 2013). In the context of integrated care, this means assuring there is sufficient coordination among providers from screening to treatment. Similar to many of the conditions screened for in the primary care setting to identify physical health concerns, prevention continues to play a role even after screening or test results signal a concern or a diagnosis. For example, screening for cholesterol levels that indicate increased risk is often managed through changes to diet or medication in an effort to prevent more serious outcomes, such as stroke or heart attack. Similarly, primary and secondary prevention are also essential in the management of mental health conditions, such as anxiety, depression, and substance use disorders. Treatment for these mental health conditions can improve a variety of factors, with the ultimate goal of preventing Deaths of Despair (DoD) – as all continue to rise at unsustainable rates (Pain in the Nation, 2020). Primary care clinicians should be able to identify common mental health issues such as anxiety or depression. With identification, they can either collaborate with an embedded mental health clinician for treatment or, if needed, refer patients to specialty care.

Prevention and integration of mental health in primary and secondary care settings have multiple benefits for clinicians and patients:

- Operationalizing the identification and treatment of mental health issues across the spectrum thereby preventing disorders from escalating into more serious mental health issues. For example, a recent investment and evaluation from the Well Being Trust, in which six primary care clinics in Orange County, California, integrated mental healthcare, demonstrated that patients with severe to moderate depression enrolled in systematic screening had between 24 and 28% clinically significant improvement in their symptoms (Well Being Trust, 2020b).
- Physicians report feeling more comfortable talking to patients about their mental health concerns and connecting them with embedded mental health clinicians.

3.7 Importance of Workflows and Evidence on How They Best Work in Integrated Settings

According to the Agency for Healthcare Research and Quality (AHRQ), a clinical workflow is "the sequence of physical and mental tasks performed by various people within and between work environments. It can occur at several levels (one person, between people, across organizations) and can occur sequentially or simultaneously (AHRQ)." Good clinical workflows can provide better quality of care, deliver improved outcomes for patients, and control or reduce costs of care (Ross KM, et al. 2018; Davenport, et al. 2017). The overarching goals of clinical workflows are to deliver seamless, integrated mental healthcare, and build a system of trust between patient, clinician, and BHC. Examining workflow to address prevention in primary care includes considering how integrated mental health supports these goals to avoid disorganized and under-resourced clinical teams or, worse, failing to identify and provide treatment across the spectrum of mental health services, from prevention to serious mental illness.

Best practices for clinical workflows in primary care clinics have been identified, whether the clinic is at the beginning stages of integration or in a more advanced stage. These best practices are outlined in one of the most comprehensive studies to date, "Clinical Workflows and the Associated Tasks and Behaviors to Support Delivery of Integrated Behavioral Health and Primary Care." This comprehensive analysis, in conjunction with prior research from Davis, drew from two different studies focused on integration of mental health and primary care, *Advancing Care Together* and the *Integration Workforce Study*, and identified four key phases critical to prevention in clinical workflows in integrated care settings across a range of characteristics in practices (Davis et al., 2019). See Table 3.1.

Within each of these phases of clinical workflow design, it is essential to determine who is accountable for each step and have a clear understanding of how each of the phases is interconnected. For example, to systematically screen for mental health concerns, teams must identify which patients will be screened, how often patients will be screened, where and how patients will be screened, who will evaluate or score the screening tool, where will this information be stored in the electronic health record, and who on the team is responsible for follow-up and referral tracking. From this example, it is evident that the actual treatment or clinical intervention provided to the patient though clearly important is only one step in the treatment pathway. A team of individuals on staff with clearly identified roles and responsibilities sets the clinician up with the data and process required to put the patient in the right place to receive the right intervention from the right person.

Team-based care is at the heart of all of the phases of a sustainable workflow (Bodenheimer et al., 2014). Systems for communication between mental health clinicians, PCPs, and staff are essential to providing whole person care and creating the opportunity for multidisciplinary care in a shared setting. Onboarding and training new staff in an integrated setting assures that staff understand not only their unique role in patient care but the value of mental health integration and prevention. Communicating expectations and anticipating challenges in daily team huddles allow high functioning teams to be proactive versus reactive during busy clinic sessions (Stewart & Johnson, 2007). This routine communication also creates space for teams to reinforce protocols or adjust them when exceptions with individual patients arise. The ideal is working toward each individual on the care team, including front desk staff, medical assistants, clinicians, and ancillary providers, who are being utilized and functioning at the highest level of their licensure. Every individual

Table 3.1 The four phases of clinical workflows

Phase	Components
Identifying patients needing integrated care	Systematic mental health screening with clinician discretion for follow-up Use mental health as a vital sign and systematic screening of depression/anxiety, substance misuse, and unmet social needs/basic needs Develop and implement timing protocols for screening intervals and who performs screening (e.g., bi-annually through entry paperwork or by medical assistants) Schedule morning meetings in teams/"huddles" to develop integrated patient care strategy, including deciding on follow-up for rescreening
Engaging patients and integrated care team	Communicate with patient about integrated care and working with mental health clinicians using scripts: describing transition of care clearly and what next steps include, explaining commitment to "whole person care" and trust in mental health clinician as a counselor and colleague Train new and auxiliary staff early on (1) how to explain transition and how to answer questions that may arise and (2) briefing mental health clinicians outside of the clinical room with respect to patient needs
Providing integrated care treatment	Mental health clinicians conducting rapid and focused assessment based on team huddles or EHR information Mental health clinicians create a shared care plan, so that all clinicians understand goals, timeline, and respective responsibility for patient Mental health clinicians are responsible for facilitating correct tier of care, if primary care setting was not enough – establishing a continuum of care for the practice Mental health clinicians must have access to all EHR systems with patient records Mental health clinician practice and integration is reflective of the patterns of primary clinic
Monitoring immediate treatment outcomes and adjusting treatment	Mental health clinician and PCP agreed upon scheduling and follow-up with specialty care More comprehensive EHR records, with complete team access to include patient-level clinical and process outcomes

Adapted from "Clinical Workflows and Structural Workflows that Facilitate or Impede Deliver of Integrated Care"

contributes to patient care and patient experience and has a unique set of skills to contribute to improved patient outcomes.

3.8 Recommendations to Support Prevention in Integrated Health Settings

To ensure widespread adoption of integration and prevention into the clinical workflow, innovation is necessary at multiple levels. Recommendations for supporting prevention in integrated settings are broken down into three categories: clinical, system, and policy, to operationalize and incentivize individual practice change and a broader redesign of mental health service delivery.

3.8.1 Clinical Recommendations

1. **Redesign Workflow:** The benefits of team-based care are well documented and include improving outcomes while decreasing costs and increasing revenue (Coleman & Reid, 2010). A 2006 evidence review of diabetes interventions found that providing team-based care was the single most effective intervention in improving intermediate diabetes outcomes (Shojania, et al., 2006). Most physicians only deliver 55% of recommended care, and 42% report not having enough time with their patients (Bodenheimer, 2008). Providers spend 13% of their day on care coordination activities and only half of their time on activities using their medical knowledge (Loudin, et al., 2011). Many care and care coordination activities can be better provided by non-physician members of a care team (Coleman & Reid, 2010), and the following steps can help clinics move toward better integrated care that promotes prevention and maximizes personnel time and skill.

    - Engage all staff in integration efforts to promote consistency and standards across clinical personnel and reduce single points of failure.
    - Organize a multidisciplinary team with representation from each unique function within the clinic to develop redesign of workflow – front desk staff, clinical provider, mental health clinician, care manager, clinic administrators, and other roles that may contribute to care and operations.
    - Examine *current* workflow of how a patient experiences integrated mental health, including prevention, through a process mapping exercise. This process map should include every step from the point a patient enters the clinic setting to the time when they leave, including but not limited to screening, entry of screening results into the EHR, warm handoff from rooming staff to medical provider, clinical services provided, warm handoff from medical provider to mental health clinician, external referrals, and closing the communications loop on external referrals. Clearly identify (1) what are the steps in the process, (2) who is accountable for each of those steps along the way, and (3) where are results of each of these steps documented so that other members of the care team can access them for patient care. This exercise provides an opportunity to clarify assumptions that exist as well as identify possible redundancies and gaps in the *current process.*
    - Clinical workflow to support prevention efforts should include considerations related to coding and billing. Staff should be trained on appropriate codes and have a systematic approach to using appropriate billing codes. Including this element in process mapping and workflow design will assure that practices bill and receive claims to cover the services that are being provided. Z codes

are a subset of ICD-10-CM codes that can be used to help identify non-medical factors that may influence a patient's health status. Often characterized as codes that classify "social determinants of health," Z codes may hold great value in identifying factors key to prevention efforts. Though not widely used by clinics and hospitals, most likely because there is limited payment for reporting Z codes, the American Hospital Association (2019) has promoted their utility in the clinical setting – indicating that collecting this information can help providers easily identify social factors impacting prevention goals at the individual level and can be aggregated at the practice level to help inform staffing needs or identification of community resources outside of the clinical setting which might contribute to preventive efforts.

- Working from the current state, map out the *ideal* workflow for the existing clinical staff structure and/or identify where additional personnel might be necessary to better optimize integration and address prevention.
- Provide training to all staff on new processes. Ensure that each staff person can recognize the importance and benefits of prevention and their role in helping patients receive optimal care that include preventive strategies. All staff should have perspective on the workflow from beginning to end and understand responsibilities within their distinct role to ensure success of integrated care delivery that includes prevention.
- Implement changes and revisit with staff on a periodic basis to assess what is working, what additional changes might be needed, where there are gaps in knowledge and skills that require additional training or support, and if the workflow is contributing to intended outcomes.
- Implement daily care team huddles to revisit workflow, look at the day's schedule, anticipate potential needs for mental health clinicians, anticipate potential challenges that could slow the workflow or result in longer appointments, etc.

2. **Maximize Electronic Health Records (EHR):** Facilitating access to relevant patient information across all providers via EHR within the clinical setting to help to reduce redundancy in collecting and documenting patient history and background on the presenting need. This efficiency within the workflow helps to maximize the encounter and save effort in updating patient charts but also helps ensure that all providers have common access to screening, diagnosis, and treatment details.

- Implement systematic mental health screening that populates in the EHR as a vital sign. Easy access to this information at every encounter helps to assess any changes in mental health status that may be crucial for early identification and intervention purposes.
- Establish a dashboard that includes metrics to track intended outcomes, including process measures (number of patients screened, number of patients referred to BHC), outcome measures (clinical quality measures), and patient satisfaction. Prevention is often difficult to quantify and measure, but improving or stabilizing screening results, medication adherence, and comparing practice rates to state or national metrics on timely follow-up can support tracking prevention efforts.

3. **Structure Staff to Promote Integrated Care and Mental Health Prevention:** Hire staff with mental health expertise to ensure that patients have access to meet whole-person health needs. This supports improved health outcomes and frees up primary care providers to focus on their area of expertise. Of note, if access to mental healthcare staff is limited in the clinical setting, e.g., only having mental health clinicians available certain days of the week, scheduling is an important factor to consider as relates to access. Scheduling patients with expressed mental health concerns, those with more complex mental health needs (like medication management), or those with a previous concerning vital sign level on days during which the mental health provider staff is on site, may require the attention of schedulers in cooperation with the clinical team to coordinate accordingly.
4. **Leverage Telehealth:** Use technology, as appropriate, to improve access to care. The success of integration and collaborative care is predicated on having a sufficient workforce to meet the need. This is a challenge in some rural areas where mental health providers are not physically located and urban centers where demand for services may exceed supply of available providers. Increasingly, models of providing telemental health are expanding to improve access and incorporate mental health prevention in rural or medically underserved areas, and staffing needs to facilitate this functionality should be considered when designing the processes to reach patients with limited access to in person services (Waugh et al., 2019).

3.8.2 System Recommendations

1. **Diversify Payment Structures:** The most important system change recommendation to address mental health prevention is to shift the way we pay for care. Research has shown that there are alternative payment models that can support mental health integration, including prevention (Ross et al., 2018). Instead of fee-for-service (FFS), as discussed earlier, payment models that support a team-based approach allow aspects of care to be distributed across the team to appropriately leverage staff time and skill sets, maximize level of training and expertise, and increase efficiency. Distributing aspects of care across the team streamlines service provision and allows primary care and mental health providers to focus on clinical responsibilities during encounters, promoting comprehensive care while increasing their bandwidth to see more patients. New payment models can further support uptake of mental health preventive services. Medicare Advantage, an option for Medicare beneficiaries to choose to receive their benefits through a private health plan instead of the federally administrated program, is one example of a program that allows for more flexibility in what services are rendered and how care is delivered specifically because of the payment mechanism. Medicare Advantage plans are given a specific dollar amount for services, which

allows these plans to be more creative with their providers and more inclusive of services that may not always be covered, like mental health prevention.

2. **Reimburse Networks of Care:** As discussed previously, there are opportunities for mental health clinicians to work on primary and public health prevention. Traditionally, primary care physicians and mental health clinicians are not trained or paid for helping a person connect to social services including applications for vouchers for affordable housing, childcare supports, or SNAP/EBT programs. Primary care clinics are essential but not sufficient to address the complexity of all mental health needs – they need to establish ties with broader networks of care in which BHCs work closely with an interdisciplinary group of providers and supports. Studies show that health outcomes improved for patient populations who were receiving whole-person care, in which referrals and follow-up with social services were integrated into workflows (Hewner et al., 2017). This is particularly important for underserved and under resourced populations, who need a community-based network of care to address interconnected basic and mental health needs. The clearest way to do this is through incentivizing network of care models. Our payment system should move toward a place where clinics can employ mental health clinicians and support staff who can address, navigate, and bill for these types of critical interventions.

3.8.3 Policy Recommendations

1. **Promote Policy Focused on Outcomes:** Though there are opportunities to improve prevention through innovation in the clinical setting, clinical practice and workflow is, in part, structured in response to payment mechanisms. As a result, "prevention" has traditionally fallen outside of the scope of clinical service delivery, as there is often no payment that directly correlates to that aspect of care – despite evidence that investment in prevention improves both morbidity and mortality and can yield savings to the healthcare system. The relationship between care and payment methodology is particularly complex with mental health – as certain codes are not paid unless there is a mental health diagnosis. Due to demands within a primary care visit (Harris, 2015), focusing on screening and prevention for mental health when there is no payment is often not feasible. To advance prevention efforts within the clinical setting, we must acknowledge the role of payment in the organization of care delivery and design policy that allows for payment of care coordination, integration, and implementation of payment models that incentivize screening, prevention, and early identification/treatment. Policy related to healthcare financing at the federal and state level can establish the parameters necessary to restructure payment methodologies and ultimately allow clinical practice to move toward a more integrated approach that prioritizes prevention. Examples of policy action include:

- CPT codes used in Collaborative Care Models (CoCM) should be covered by all insurers at a rate that incentivizes adoption of mental health integration (BHI) models in the primary care setting. Investment at the federal or state level for the technical assistance necessary to better position practices and health systems to fully implement integrative models is also necessary to establish the structure and personnel necessary to successfully adapt workflows.
- The federal government should ensure that hospital payment models and quality programs incentivize assessing mental health at every interaction as a vital sign and not only during well visits. This should include integrating screening and treatment into episode-based payment models for health conditions for which there are frequent mental health comorbidities, such as cardiovascular diseases, cancers, and pulmonary diseases (Well Being Trust, 2020a).

2. **Establish Quality and Measurement Standards:** In addition to advancing financing mechanisms which value prevention, policy can play a role in establishing standards and practices that help promote integrated care that can help prevent crisis and improve patients' mental health outcomes.

- **Access**. Federal law increasingly supports effective preventive care in mental health, with policies such as Early and Periodic Screening, Diagnosis, and Treatment (EPSDT) in Medicaid or the requirement that most insurers cover certain services recommended by the US Preventive Services Task Force. Unfortunately, these policies mostly support screening for early detection of mental health conditions and have not translated well for young children. Although the American Academy of Pediatrics recommends screening for depression in young children and developing psychosocial needs, coverage for interventions to address these identified needs is inconsistent and often unclear – often failing to ensure that children get access to clinically indicated care. (Well Being Trust, 2020a).
- **Training**. Every year, thousands of new primary care providers enter the field – the vast majority of whom receive little to no training on integrated care (Blount & Miller, 2009; Martin et al., 2019). For those already in practice, few receive any support in learning new skills and practice models for integrated care. Mental healthcare is not so different than the countless other health conditions that primary care providers deal with, but without training, effectively addressing it becomes an unreasonable expectation. Structured training opportunities for those both pre-service and in-service is critical for making mental health a standard part of primary care.

– The federal government should provide incentives, through Graduate Medical Education (GME), Graduate Nursing Education (GNE), and other programs, for healthcare practitioner education institutions to offer training in integrated mental healthcare.
– Providers should be incentivized to take additional Continuing Medical Education (CME) classes on current best practices.

– The federal government should focus existing federally funded quality improvement organizations on mental health integration across diverse primary care practices and for serving diverse populations and financing additional learning collaboratives as necessary (Well Being Trust, 2020a).

3.9 Conclusion

Prevention is key to improving health outcomes and maximizing healthcare spending in the United States. Focusing on prevention and early intervention efforts is as critical for mental health as other physical health conditions. Creating mechanisms in the clinical workflow to capitalize on primary, secondary, and tertiary prevention opportunities benefits both patients and providers. Practice structure and payment models to support screening/identification, proper training for providers, integration to maximize clinical skills, and innovation to reach underserved populations must be considered and appropriately financed to promote prevention and realize improvement in mental health outcomes.

3.10 Resources

The following resources and tools may be helpful to practitioners and healthcare administrators in the implementation of best practices related to mental health integration and ensuring that prevention is a key consideration in structuring the clinical workflow.

- CMS Medicare Learning Network Behavioral Health Integration Services Booklet: https://www.cms.gov/Outreach-and-Education/Medicare-Learning-Network-MLN/MLNProducts/Downloads/BehavioralHealthIntegration.pdf
- AHRQ Workflow Tool Examples: https://digital.ahrq.gov/health-it-tools-and-resources/evaluation-resources/workflow-assessment-health-it-toolkit/examples
- AHRQ Workflow Tools: https://digital.ahrq.gov/health-it-tools-and-resources/evaluation-resources/workflow-assessment-health-it-toolkit/all-workflow-tools

References

American Hospital Association. (2019). *ICD-10-CM Coding for Social Determinants of Health.* Retrieved from https://www.aha.org/system/files/2018-04/value-initiative-icd-10-code-social-determinants-of-health.pdf

Akincigil, A., & Matthews, E. B. (2017). National Rates and patterns of depression screening in primary care: Results from 2012 and 2013. *Psychiatric Services, 68*(7), 660–666. https://doi.org/10.1176/appi.ps.201600096

Balasubramanian, B. A., Jetelina, K. K., Cohen, D. J., Davis, M., Gunn, R., Gowen, K., Dickinson, L. M., DeGruy, F. V., Miller, B. F., & Green, L. A. (2017). Outcomes of integrated behavioral health with primary care. *The Journal of the American Board of Family Medicine, 30*(2), 130–139. https://doi.org/10.3122/jabfm.2017.02.160234

Bindman, A. B., Grumbach, K., Osmond, D., Vranizan, K., & Stewart, A. L. (1996). Primary care and receipt of preventive services. *Journal of General Internal Medicine, 11*(5), 269–276. Retrieved from http://www.ncbi.nlm.nih.gov/entrez/query.fcgi?cmd=Retrieve&db=PubMed&dopt=Citation&list_uids=8725975

Blount, A., & Miller, B. F. (2009). Addressing the workforce crisis in integrated primary care. *Journal of Clinical Psychology in Medical Settings, 16*, 113–119.

Bodenheimer, T., Ghorob, A., Willard-Grace, R., & Grumbach, K. (2014). The 10 building blocks of high-performing primary care. *The Annals of Family Medicine, 12*(2), 166–171. https://doi.org/10.1370/afm.1616

Brown Levey, S., Miller, B. F., & deGruy, F. V. (2012). Behavioral health integration: an essential element of population-based healthcare redesign. *Translational Behavioral Medicine*, 1–8. https://doi.org/10.1007/s13142-012-0152-5

Bucher, S., Maury, A., Rosso, J., de Chanaud, N., Bloy, G., Pendola-Luchel, I., Delpech, R., Paquet, S., Falcoff, H., Ringa, V., & Rigal, L. (2016). Time and feasibility of prevention in primary care. *Family Practice, 34*(1), 49–56. https://doi.org/10.1093/fampra/cmw108

Butler, M., Kane, R. L., McAlpin, D., Kathol, R. G., Fu, S. S., Hagedorn, H., & Wilt, T. J. (2008). *Integration of Mental Health/Substance Abuse and Primary Care No. 173 (Prepared by the Minnesota Evidence-based Practice Center under Contract No. 290-02-0009.) AHRQ Publication No. 09-E003*. Retrieved from Rockville, MD:

Centers for Disease Control and Prevention. (2019). Picture of America: Prevention. Retrieved from: https://www.cdc.gov/pictureofamerica/pdfs/Picture_of_America_Prevention.pdf

Cohen, L., Chavez, V., & Chehimi, S. (Eds.). (2010). *Prevention is primary: strategies for community well being* (2nd ed.). Wiley.

Cooper, S., Valleley, R. J., Polaha, J., Begeny, J., & Evans, J. H. (2006). Running out of time: Physician management of behavioral health concerns in rural pediatric primary care. *Pediatrics, 118*(1), e132–e138. https://doi.org/10.1542/peds.2005-2612

Davis, M., Balasubramanian, B. A., Waller, E., Miller, B. F., Green, L. A., & Cohen, D. J. (2013). Integrating behavioral and physical health care in the real world: Early lessons from advancing care together. *The Journal of the American Board of Family Medicine, 26*(5), 588–602. https://doi.org/10.3122/jabfm.2013.05.130028

Davis, M. M., Gunn, R., Cifuentes, M., Khatri, P., Hall, J., Gilchrist, E., Peek, C. J., Klowden, M., Lazarus, J. A., Miller, B. F., & Cohen, D. J. (2019). Clinical Workflows and the Associated Tasks and Behaviors to Support Delivery of Integrated Behavioral Health and Primary Care. *The Journal of ambulatory care management, 42*(1), 51–65. https://doi.org/10.1097/JAC.0000000000000257

deGruy, F. (1996). Mental health care in the primary care setting. In M. S. Donaldson, K. D. Yordy, K. N. Lohr, & N. A. Vanselow (Eds.), *Primary care: America's health in a new era*. Institute of Medicine.

Dickinson, W. P., & Miller, B. F. (2010). Comprehensiveness and continuity of care and the inseparability of mental and behavioral health from the patient-centered medical home. *Families, Systems & Health, 28*(4), 348–355.

Dougherty, D., LeBlanc, N., Armstrong, P., Shah Kahani, N., Wttenberg, R., & Cope, E. (2020). *Advancing teen flourishing: Moving policy upstream*. Retrieved from https://wellbeingtrust.org/wp-content/uploads/2020/06/AdvancingTeenFlourishingFinalReport.pdf: https://wellbeingtrust.org/wp-content/uploads/2020/06/AdvancingTeenFlourishingFinalReport.pdf

Doyle, C., Lennox, L., & Bell, D. (2013). A systematic review of evidence on the links between patient experience and clinical safety and effectiveness. *BMJ Open, 3*(1), e001570. https://doi.org/10.1136/bmjopen-2012-001570

Felitti, V. J., Anda, R. F., Nordenberg, D., Williamson, D. F., Spitz, A. M., Edwards, V., Koss, M. P., & Marks, J. S. (1998). Relationship of childhood abuse and household dysfunction to many of the leading causes of death in adults: The adverse childhood experiences (ACE) study. *American Journal of Preventive Medicine, 14*(4), 245–258. https://doi.org/10.1016/S0749-3797(98)00017-8

Fox, J. B., & Shaw, F. E. (2015). Clinical preventive services coverage and the affordable care act. *American Journal of Public Health, 105*(1), e7–e10. https://doi.org/10.2105/AJPH.2014.302289

Funk, M., Saraceno, B., Drew, N., & Faydi, E. (2008). Integrating mental health into primary healthcare. *Mental Health in Family Medicine, 5*(1), 5–8. Retrieved from https://pubmed.ncbi.nlm.nih.gov/22477840; https://www.ncbi.nlm.nih.gov/pmc/articles/PMC2777555/

Gouge, N., Polaha, J., Rogers, R., & Harden, A. (2016). Integrating behavioral health into pediatric primary care: Implications for provider time and cost. *Southern Medical Journal, 109*(12), 774–778. https://doi.org/10.14423/smj.0000000000000564

Harris, S. K. (2015). Making time for mental health: Computerized previsit screening in primary care. *Journal of Adolescent Health, 56*(3), 257–258. https://doi.org/10.1016/j.jadohealth.2014.12.012

Hewner, S., Casucci, S., Sullivan, S., Mistretta, F., Xue, Y., Johnson, B., Pratt, R., Lin, L., & Fox, C. (2017). Integrating social determinants of health into primary care clinical and informational workflow during care transitions. *EGEMS (Washington, DC), 5*(2), 2–2. https://doi.org/10.13063/2327-9214.1282

Hogg, W., Lemelin, J., Moroz, I., Soto, E., & Russell, G. (2008). Improving prevention in primary care: Evaluating the sustainability of outreach facilitation. *Canadian Family Physician Medecin de famille canadien, 54*(5), 712–720. Retrieved from https://pubmed.ncbi.nlm.nih.gov/18474705; https://www.ncbi.nlm.nih.gov/pmc/articles/PMC2377224/

Hung, D. Y., Rundall, T. G., Tallia, A. F., Cohen, D. J., Halpin, H. A., & Crabtree, B. F. (2007). Rethinking prevention in primary care: Applying the chronic care model to address health risk behaviors. *The Milbank Quarterly, 85*(1), 69–91. https://doi.org/10.1111/j.1468-0009.2007.00477.x

Institute of Medicine. (1996). *Primary care: America's health in a new era*. Institute of Medicine: National Academis Press.

Maragakis, A., & O'Donohue, W. T. (Eds.). (2018). *Principle-based stepped care and brief psychotherapy for integrated care settings*. Springer.

Martin, M., Bauman, D., Allison, L., & Myerholtz, L. (2019). *Integration as both standard of care and standard of training*. Retrieved from http://journals.stfm.org/familymedicine/2019/september/lte-sept19-martin

Miller, B. F., Brown Levey, S., Payne-Murphy, J. C., & Kwan, B. (2014). Outlining the scope of behavioral health practice in integrated primary care: Dispelling the myth of the one-trick mental health pony. *Families, Systems & Health, 32*, 338–343.

Miller, B. F., & Hubley, S. H. (2017). The history of fragmentation and the promise of integration. In M. Maruish (Ed.), *Handbook of psychological assessment in primary care settings* (pp. 55–73). Routledge.

O'Malley, A. S., & Rich, E. C. (2015). Measuring comprehensiveness of primary care: Challenges and opportunities. *Journal of General Internal Medicine, 30*(Suppl 3), S568–S575. https://doi.org/10.1007/s11606-015-3300-z

Patel, V., Belkin, G. S., Chockalingam, A., Cooper, J., Saxena, S., & Unützer, J. (2013). Grand challenges: Integrating mental health services into priority health care platforms. *PLoS Medicine, 10*(5), e1001448. https://doi.org/10.1371/journal.pmed.1001448

Peek, C. J., National Integration Academy Council. (2013). *Lexicon for behavioral health and primary care integration: Concepts and definitions developed by expert consensus*. Retrieved from http://integrationacademy.ahrq.gov/sites/default/files/Lexicon.pdf

Preventive care benefits for adults. (2021). Retrieved from https://www.healthcare.gov/preventive-care-adults/

Ross, K. M., Gilchrist, E. C., Melek, S. P., Gordon, P. D., Ruland, S. L., & Miller, B. F. (2018). Cost savings associated with an alternative payment model for integrating behavioral health in primary care. *Translational Behavioral Medicine*, iby054–iby054. https://doi.org/10.1093/tbm/iby054

Schwarz, D., Hirschhorn, L. R., Kim, J.-H., Ratcliffe, H. L., & Bitton, A. (2019). Continuity in primary care: A critical but neglected component for achieving high-quality universal health coverage. *BMJ Global Health, 4*(3), e001435–e001435. https://doi.org/10.1136/bmjgh-2019-001435

Starfield, B. (1998). *Primary care: Balancing health needs, services, and technology*. Oxford University Press.

Starfield, B., & Shi, L. (2004). The medical home, access to care, and insurance: A review of the evidence. *Pediatrics, 113*, 1493–1498.

Starfield, B., & Shi, L. (2007). The impact of primary care and what States can do. *North Carolina Medical Journal, 68*(3), 204–207. Retrieved from http://www.ncbi.nlm.nih.gov/pubmed/17674698

Starfield, B., Shi, L., & Mackino, J. (2005). Contributions of primary care to health systems and health. *The Milbank Quarterly, 83*, 457–502.

Stewart, E. E., & Johnson, B. C. (2007). Improve office efficiency in mere minutes. *Family Practice Management, 14*(6), 27–29.

Trust for America's Health and Well Being Trust. [2020]. Pain in the Nation Update. Retrieved from: https://www.tfah.org/wp-content/uploads/2020/05/PiNUdpate_2020.pdf

Well Being Trust. (2020a). Healing the Nation: Advancing Mental Health and Addiction Policy. Retrieved from: https://healingthenation.wellbeingtrust.org/assets/pdfs/Healing-the-Nation-Report.pdf

Well Being Trust. (2020b). Sharing and Scaling Promising Approached to Advance Mental Health. Retrieved from: https://wellbeingtrust.org/wp-content/uploads/2021/05/WBT-Sharing-and-Scaling-Promising-Practices.pdf

Waugh, M., Calderone, J., Brown Levey, S., Lyon, C., Thomas, M., DeGruy, F., & Shore, J. H. (2019). Using Telepsychiatry to enrich existing integrated primary care. *Telemedicine Journal and E-Health, 25*(8), 762–768. https://doi.org/10.1089/tmj.2018.0132

Yarnall, K. S. H., Pollak, K. I., Østbye, T., Krause, K. M., & Michener, J. L. (2003). Primary care: Is there enough time for prevention? *American Journal of Public Health, 93*(4), 635–641. https://doi.org/10.2105/ajph.93.4.635

Zivin, K., Miller, B. F., Finke, B., Bitton, A., Payne, P., Stowe, E. C., Reddy, A., Day, T. J., Lapin, P., Jin, J. L., & Sessums, L. L. (2017). Behavioral health and the Comprehensive Primary Care (CPC) initiative: Findings from the 2014 CPC behavioral health survey. *BMC Health Services Research, 17*(1), 612. https://doi.org/10.1186/s12913-017-2562-z

Chapter 4
Cultural Factors in Prevention

Felipe González Castro and Roger Kessler

4.1 Purpose and Approach

This chapter describes the construct of *cultural factors*. Cultural factors are constructs that capture significant life experiences of people and families from major racial/ethnic minority groups, i. e., from *ethnocultural groups* (Bernal & Adames, 2017). In the United States, these major ethnocultural groups are Hispanics/Latinxs, Blacks/African Americans, Asian Americans and Pacific Islanders, and American Indians/Native Americans. We also recognize that beyond these ethnocultural groups, other important identity groups exist that are defined by gender are LGBTQ people.

We examine select studies that conducted research involving cultural factors, some of which are *culturally common* across ethnocultural groups, meaning that they occur and have recognized meaning across two or more groups, for example, *discrimination stress*. By contrast, some cultural factors are *culturally specific*, meaning that they are primarily recognized and understood within a single ethnocultural group, such as efforts to avoid *loss of face* as discussed by Asians. Accordingly, a more complete understanding of ethnocultural individuals, families, and communities within the context of their own culture is facilitated by understanding the roles and meanings conveyed by various cultural factors.

F. G. Castro (✉)
College of Nursing and Health Innovation, Arizona State University, Phoenix, AZ, USA
e-mail: Felipe.Castro@asu.edu

R. Kessler
University of Colorado School of Medicine, Aurora, CO, USA

W. O'Donohue, M. Zimmermann (eds.), *Handbook of Evidence-Based Prevention of Behavioral Disorders in Integrated Care*,
https://doi.org/10.1007/978-3-030-83469-2_4

4.2 Concepts of Culture

Culture has been a core element of human societies since the beginning of human civilization. Culture is a complex construct that has many dimensions. "Culture consists of ideals, values, and assumptions of about life," such as beliefs and expectations, "that guide specific behaviors" (Brislin, 1993)(p. 23). From a psychological perspective, the construct of *subjective culture* (Triandis et al., 1973) focuses on culture as a *human schema*, an organized "world view" or "explanatory model," that consists of symbols, attitudes, behaviors, values, and norms transmitted from one generation to the next. This "cultural world view" is constructed by members of an ethnocultural group to interpret their world. These human schemas capture the ethnocultural group's collective wisdom for living and include familial and community norms, practices, and traditions, which facilitate the group's survival and well-being (Lehman et al., 2004; Shiraev & Lewy, 2010).

Worldwide, large variations exist in expressions of culture, as manifested by the diversity of languages, religious systems of belief, sociocultural attitudes, family values, and sociocultural norms. Across societies worldwide, a dynamic tension exists between community efforts toward *modernization*, making changes to improve social structures, and efforts toward *traditionalism*, a resistance to change that favors preserving ancestral traditions (Ramirez, 1999; Shiraev & Lewy, 2010). Factors that promote *modernization*, such as international globalization, emphasize growth and standardization in monetary currencies and in consumer products, thus creating a homogenization of cultural practices. By contrast, factors that promote *traditionalism* (Ramirez, 1999) consist of distinct "local subcultures" that create *diverse communities* that have their own distinct culture, identity, traditions, and lifeways. Migrating individuals who relocate to a new cultural environment, whether between nations or within a nation, often face the challenges of *acculturation*, the process of adapting to a new community environment, and *assimilation*, the process of fully integrating into that new community, which often includes adopting the human schema of the new cultural group or society (Berry, 1980, 2005).

4.3 Cultural Factors: Operationalizing "Culture" for Prevention Research

4.3.1 Origins of Cultural Factors

Cultural factors originate as *cultural constructs*, abstract ideas drawn from everyday observations about social and family processes (Cuellar et al., 1995; Triandis et al., 1973). Established hierarchical structures based on racial and ethnic background, religious orientation, and socioeconomic status establish *expectations* and *sociocultural norms* that constitute rules of acceptable behaviors in a given situation (McGoldrick et al., 2005). Within a cultural group, widely accepted and frequently practiced norms can also become longstanding *cultural traditions*. For example, within traditional Latinx cultures, parents expect their children to respect elders, i.e., the Latinx cultural value of *respeto* (respect) (Castro & Hernandez Alarcon, 2002). In traditional families and community settings, the concept of *respeto* has become a sociocultural norm or rule that children are expected to follow. Thus, within traditional Latinx families, the norm of *respeto* prescribes familial and social expectations that a youth should show proper respect to an elder. Some Latinx families no longer adhere to this traditional sociocultural norm.

4.3.2 What Are Cultural Factors?

In summary, *culture* is a broad and rich construct that captures "real-life" aspects of an ethnocultural group's history, beliefs, practices, and traditions. A *cultural factor* operates as a specific experiential element or component of that complex culture (Castro & Nieri, 2010). Thus, cultural factors have been described as "personal, interpersonal, or environmental factors that are particularly influential or meaningful for members of a certain cultural group or population" (Castro et al., 2013)(p. 766). Another Latinx cultural factor, *cultural pride*, consists of a person's strong identification and bonding with their native ethnocultural group as expressed by asserting "I am very proud" to be a Latino or a Latina. As with other cultural factors, cultural pride captures an ethnocultural person's positive feelings toward their culture, ethnicity, and ancestry.

Among African American/Black groups, a major cultural factor is *Africentric values*. *Africentric values* emerged in popularity in the 1970s by emphasizing the longstanding sense of "peoplehood" and cultural pride that existed for years within this ethnocultural group. In the past, that pride has been expressed by the affirmation that "Black is beautiful," when endorsing an African-centered world view (Parham et al., 2011). Various cultural factors, such as *folk beliefs*, involve cultural factors about health and well-being that can influence health-related behaviors. Some cultural factors can also operate as risk or protective factors that can impede or facilitate health and wellness (Castro et al., 1984; Whaley, 2003).

As noted, some cultural factors exist within several racial/ethnic groups in the United States, such as the *individualism-collectivism* dichotomy, *traditionalism*, and *acculturation* (see Table 4.1). The cultural factor of *acculturation* is broadly applicable to Latinx and Asian ethnocultural groups, since these populations contain large sectors of immigrants or children of immigrants, who have experienced the challenges of adapting to a new and different cultural society. Conversely, and as noted, other cultural factors tend to be *culturally specific*, capturing a salient and perhaps unique feature of an ethnocultural group's ethnic beliefs and life experiences. For example, among traditional Asian Americans, loss of face refers to a concern over embarrassing oneself and family, followed by shame from engaging in some improper conduct. The consciousness and moral values directed at avoiding this embarrassment has been referred to as loss of face (Lau et al., 2009; Zane & Yeh, 2002)

Table 4.1 Major cultural factors in racial/ethnic communities

Cultural factor	Description
Multiethnic	
• **Acculturation**	Beliefs and behaviors that conform to the cultural mainstream of a host society, e.g., "the American way of life." Refers also to the process of culture change toward the mainstream culture of a new host culture, e.g., "the American lifestyle"
• **Assimilation**	A change in cultural identity and lifestyle involving a conversion from one's original native culture to a new culture, identity, and lifestyle. This can involve a total integration into the new host society
• **Ethnic pride**	A positive attitude and sense of belonging to one's ethnic cultural heritage or native culture group, e.g., stating that "I am proud to be a Mexican"
• **Folk beliefs** • **Folk remedies**	Beliefs in the therapeutic effects of herbal and other natural remedies. This can include beliefs in the healing power of spiritual healers, e.g. *curanderos* in Latinx cultures or *santeros* among Caribbean Latinx cultures
• **Collectivism-individualism**	Contrasting cultural "world views," involving preferences for an individualistic self-oriented relational style versus a group-oriented collectivistic relational style
• **Spirituality**	Beliefs in the influences of God or a higher power. This can include a strong appreciation and bonding with nature
• **Traditionalism**	Conservative beliefs and behaviors favoring an adherence to long-established cultural beliefs and norms about a correct way of life
Latinx, Hispanic	
• **Acculturation stress**	Involves chronic stress from the challenges and conflicts encountered during the process of cultural changes from one's native culture to a new host culture. Latinos and Latinas often face some culturally specific stressors involving prejudice and discrimination directed at them for being a person of Latinx heritage
• **Bicultural identity** • **Bicultural skills**	The development of a combined identity developed from living in two cultures. This includes the skills and capabilities for engaging in the languages, activities, and social relations existing within these two distinct cultures
• **Cultural flex**	The skills and capabilities for shifting back and forth in the language, activities, and social relations that exist between two distinct cultures
• ***Familismo*** **(familism)**	A strong familial orientation, bonding, and devotion to one's family
• ***Machismo*** • ***Caballerismo***	A traditional Latinx male gender role orientation that emphasizes male dominance as proper or acceptable form of male identity and conduct. *Positive machismo* emphasizes *caballerismo*, a male gender role that involves serving as a responsible family provider. By contrast, *negative machismo* emphasizes masculine power and dominance over women and members of the family, often also involving antisocial conduct, including the abuse of alcohol and drugs
• ***Marianismo***	A traditional Latinx female (Latina) gender role orientation that emphasizes a motherly, nurturant role as well as a demure posture toward males within the household. This gender role also embodies a feminine orientation that emphasizes religious and traditional Latinx beliefs and practices

(continued)

Table 4.1 (continued)

Cultural factor	Description
• ***Personalismo***	The value and preference afforded to personalized attention and courtesy expressed in interpersonal relations
• ***Respeto***	The value of expressing respect and recognition toward persons of higher social position. This includes reverence and respect for elders
• ***Simpatia***	A deferential posture toward family members directed at maintaining harmony in family relations. Includes a posture of agreeableness, respect, and politeness toward others
African American/ BLACK	
• **Africentric values**	A cultural orientation that emphasizes pride in one's identity as a person of Black and/or African American heritage
• **Intergenerational connections**	The importance of sound child development for establishing and maintaining strong social ties with caring adults who can offer guidance, support, and mentorship
• **Racial socialization**	Parental guidance provided to children and youth regarding racial discrimination and oppressive forces in society and how best to respond to these
• **Religious social support**	Social support from the church as a trusted institution and network of people who can provide aid and affective support during difficult times
• **Religious beliefs** • **Spiritual coping**	Beliefs in the power of spirituality for providing hope and comfort during stressful times
Asian American	
• **Acculturation stress**	Stress produced by challenges and conflicts during the process of adaptation from one's native culture to a new host culture. Asian Americans often face some culturally specific stressors involving prejudice and discrimination directed at them for being a person of Asian heritage
• ***Chi***	Energy, a potent life force
• **Model minority**	The stereotype that Asians constitute a "model minority," because of their pro-social behaviors that emphasize educational achievement, good citizenship, and avoiding confrontational situations
• **Shame and stigma** • **Loss of face**	Refers among traditional Asians, to "loss of face," involving anxiety and shame for improper behavior or a failure to live up to one's social obligations. This failure can reflect not only on the individual but also on the individual's entire family. A goal is to avoid a "loss of face" by taking actions directed at "saving face," which refers to acting in proper ways, to avoid "a loss of face"
Native American	
• **Family connections** • **Reflective process**	The process of thinking about the negative consequences of alcohol use. An emphasis on maintaining good relationships with family and avoiding life choices that would bring negative consequences to self and family

(continued)

Table 4.1 (continued)

Cultural factor	Description
• **Life appreciation** • **Reasons for life**	Beliefs and expectancies that make life enjoyable and worthwhile. Also, appreciations for nature and its creator, along with reflecting on reasons for following a right path toward the good life

Note. Adapted from Castro & Hernandez Alarcon (2002), and from Castro and Nieri (2010)

4.3.3 Cultural Factors and Cultural Variables for Testing Theory and Models

Given that a cultural factor consists of a specific cultural concept, it can operate as a component of a *theory* or *conceptual framework*. That cultural factor can be converted into a measurable *cultural variable* generated from a reliable and valid scale and used as a variable in statistical model analyses (Triandis et al., 1973; Zane & Yeh, 2002). For example, a multiple regression model or a structural equation model can incorporate the measured cultural variable of *ethnic pride* as a predictor or moderator variable. This model can then test the influence of ethnic pride in preventing the use of alcohol and tobacco among Latinx adolescents (Castro et al., 2009).

4.3.4 Modeling the Effects of Cultural Factors

Informed by *minority stress theory* (Carter, 2007), in a sample of Mexican heritage college students, Cheng and colleagues tested the potential moderator effect of the cultural factor, *familismo*, on the effects of another cultural factor, *acculturation stress*, as an antecedent (predictor) of the development of *depressive symptoms* (Cheng et al., 2016). These investigators reasoned that students of Mexican ancestry, who have high levels of *familismo*, relative to those having lower levels, would benefit from family-related support that can buffer exposures to acculturation stress, thus attenuating the development of depressive symptoms.

Figure 4.1 presents a simple model of this dynamic process. In this model, *acculturative stress* (Factor 1) is hypothesized as a cultural factor that can produce *depressive symptoms* (Factor 3). The cultural factor of *familismo* (familism, strong family bonds) is also hypothesized as a *moderator* (an effect modifier) that can buffer (attenuate) the effects of *acculturative stress* on the occurrence of depressive symptoms. Among other effects that Chen and collaborators tested in their hierarchical multiple regression analyses, they showed that greater acculturative stress was associated with higher levels of depressive symptoms ($\beta = 0.21$, $p < 0.01$). Then they reported the *acculturative stress-familismo* interaction, which was also significant ($\beta = 0.22$, $p < 0.01$), indicating that the interaction of *acculturative stress* and *familismo* also exerted a significant effect on depressive symptoms, ideally in the manner hypothesized. Finally, when examining the effect of *low* versus *high* levels of *familismo*, as indicated by two simple slopes, the slope for *high* level of *familismo*

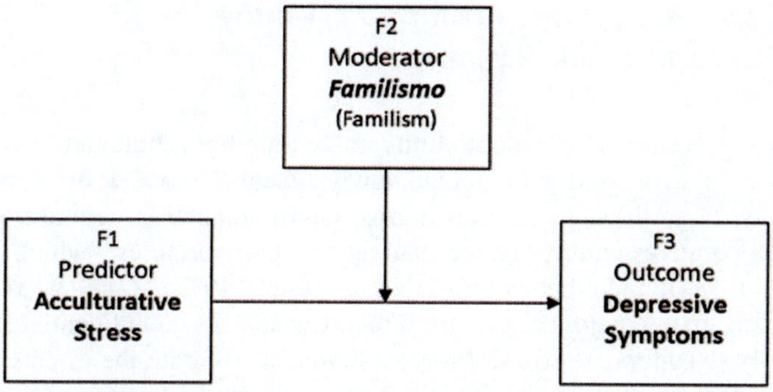

Fig. 4.1 A simple moderation model with two cultural factors

was greater (β = 0.24, $p < 0.001$) when compared with the slope at the *low* level of *familismo* (β = 0.11, $p < 0.05$). This analysis revealed that relative to *low* levels of *familismo*, *high* levels exerted a stronger moderating (attenuating or buffering) effect, which reduced the effects of acculturative stress on depressive symptoms (Cheng et al., 2016). This result suggests that for these young adults of Mexican heritage, the cultural factor of *familismo* can operate as a *protective factor* against acculturative stress in reducing the development of depressive symptoms.

4.4 Cultural Factors Toward Reducing Health Disparities

4.4.1 Pervasiveness of Health Disparities Among Communities of Color

Ethnocultural populations and their communities are affected by many types of social inequities and related health disparities. This includes limited access to healthcare services, which can also produce low rates of health service utilization, which can also perpetuate existing health disparities and inequities. A health disparity consists of a significant difference in the rates of a health problem, e.g., rates of HIV/AIDS, within a socially *disadvantaged* population as compared with a socially *advantaged* population (Braveman, 2006).

As examined across a series of health-related problems, e.g., rates of obesity, heart disease, and cancers, the profile of health disparities often reveals a greater extent of impaired health within the disadvantaged group. Unfortunately, this health disparity profile constitutes a recurring pattern among the major ethnocultural groups in the United States (Braveman et al., 2010). Within many of these ethnocultural communities, health status is influenced by the presence of several comorbidities. For example, co-existing depression can aggravate an existing somatic health problem, such as type 2 diabetes (T2D).

4.4.2 Cultural Factors to Inform Preventive Intervention Development

Beginning in the early 1970s, community and cultural psychologists observed that culture also is expressed by "human environments" created by communities. Accordingly, in addition to cultural norms, environmental structural components could also operate as cultural factors and as "cultural variables," which operate as determinants of human behavior (Triandis et al., 1973; Zane & Yeh, 2002). Unfortunately, many major sociocultural theories, such as the influential *social cognitive theory* (Bandura, 1986), did not explicitly incorporate the effects of culture and cultural factors as determinants of behaviors among ethnocultural groups in the United States.

In 1999, the National Institute on Drug Abuse (NIDA) published a research-based guide that identified 13 principles of effective drug abuse treatment (NIDA, 1999). These principles included the principles that (a) effective treatment attends to the client's multiple needs and not just to drug abuse and (b) remaining in treatment is crucial to treatment effectiveness. Ironically among these principles, a striking omission was that none of these principles referred to *cultural factors* and their possible roles as risk or protective factors in recovery from drug abuse. This omission highlighted the importance of recognizing cultural factors among ethnocultural people as additional factors that can affect recovery from drug abuse. This limitation had been mentioned a few years earlier as important for a more efficacious drug abuse treatment provided to African Americans/Blacks, Hispanics/Latinos, and Native Americans (Terrell, 1993).

Shortly after the year 2000, cultural factors gained greater recognition as important culture-related influences on drug use treatment outcomes among ethnocultural groups (Zane & Yeh, 2002). Other research studies began incorporating cultural factors into regression model analyses to model their effects as etiological, moderator, mediator, or outcome variables to better understand the determinants of drug abuse etiology and treatment (Castro & Hernandez Alarcon, 2002; Castro et al., 2007).

4.4.3 Developing and Implementing Preventive Interventions in Various Settings

4.4.3.1 Urban Contexts

A study of factors in the process of building capacity to address health disparities in urban African American neighborhoods identified five capacity building factors. These factors are (a) leadership, (b) institutional commitment, (c) trust, (d) credibility, and (e) interorganizational networks (Gilbert et al., 2010). This approach endorsed the development of community partnerships to generate resources under an ecological systems approach for reducing health disparities. These investigators conducted a case study in creating partnerships to build community capacity. They interviewed 18 participants from nonprofit, government, academic, and civic organizations. As coordinated by a Center for Minority Health, this study identified *emerging themes* for building these partnerships in an urban environment. These themes also highlighted the importance of (a) sustained funding to address health disparities, (b) creating changes in existing organizational cultures, and (c) leadership for modifying a participating organization's mission and vision statements.

Further, trust and credibility emerged as important factors for establishing and sustaining interorganizational partnerships and in creating interorganizational networks for addressing health disparities within urban environments. This effort coordinated the participating organizations' role in providing instrumental, financial, and functional support to other participating organizations.

In total, this effort included (a) building each individual organization's readiness to respond to important community needs, (b) establishing organizational leadership structures to galvanize institutional commitments for engaging in transformative change, (c) reestablishing trusting relationships with local African American communities and organizations, (d) convening a diverse network of stakeholders, (e) understanding local community infrastructures to design culturally relevant interventions, (f) promoting the adoption of a culturally relevant model that includes one or more cultural factors that influence health promotion and disease prevention, and (g) organizing and conducting data collection, analysis, monitoring, and evaluation activities (Gilbert et al., 2010). In summary, this study provides a basic framework of approaches for developing and organizing an interorganizational system of resources and support that can be mobilized to address targeted health disparities within a local urban context.

4.4.3.2 Rural Contexts

A study of rural community conditions examined the cultural beliefs, practices, and lifestyle choices of rural community residents to identify the factors that impede the utilization of healthcare services toward reducing the occurrence of chronic diseases (Murimi & Harpel, 2010). Targeting a reduction of obesity and related chronic diseases among low-income residents living within a rural setting, a group of local community members created a multidisciplinary project charged with developing a consortium of local organizations, schools, and churches. The related study investigated personal, cultural, and external barriers among community residents from participating in community-based preventive outreach program for reducing obesity, diabetes, heart disease, and hypertension. Investigators conducted six focus groups to identify specific barriers to healthcare utilization by comparing community resident who *did not* utilize healthcare services with those who did.

These focus groups identified four themes associated with barriers to participation in preventive care services: (a) *time* involving daily routines, such as family and work responsibilities, that prevented participation in health outreach program activities; (b) *low priority* given to seeking preventive care; (c) *fear of the unknown*, exemplified by fears that a screening test may reveal a disease, such as having cancer; and (d) *lack of companionship support* for accompanying individuals in seeking healthcare services.

These investigators concluded that low-income status and low education were associated with a low motivation for seeking preventive healthcare services. To improve healthcare services seeking among these vulnerable sectors of their local rural communities, these investigators endorsed *proactive disease prevention* efforts and *self-care education* that could be provided by a coalition of policy-makers, funding agents, healthcare providers, community leaders, and community residents (Murimi & Harpel, 2010).

4.4.3.3 Structural Interventions for Macrolevel Effects

Structural interventions target changing existing inequities that originate in social, physical, economic, or political environments (Brown et al., 2019). For a more comprehensive approach to health promotion and disease prevention, an *ecodevelopmental systems framework* is important for informing a multi-domain (macro-, meso-, and microlevel) analysis and design for creating multilevel structural interventions (Richard et al., 2011). From this multi-domain approach, inequities operate as drivers of health disparities, in part by shaping and constraining health behaviors and outcomes. Clearly, these inequities are detrimental to ethnocultural persons, families, and communities. To address these oppressive contexts, preventive interventions are needed, which focus on interventions delivered at one or more ecodevelopmental domains, e.g., families, organizations, and communities, as focal points for reducing and eliminating these drivers of inequity. This approach consists of increasing *protective factors* and reducing or eliminating *risk factors* to support healthful behaviors and environmental changes to reduce or eliminate these inequities (Brown et al., 2019).

A systematic review of ecodevelopmental factors was used to identify protective factors to reduce the existing "school-to-prison pipeline." This is a structural condition that leads many Latinx youth into contact with the juvenile justice system (Hoskins et al., 2020). Investigators argue that strength-based interventions that address cultural, familial, and community factors are needed to counter the effects of longstanding structural inequities and the factors that produce and perpetuate this pipeline. Investigators emphasized incorporating the Latinx familial cultural factors of *collectivism* and *familism* (*familismo*) for engaging Latinx youth to initiate and remain in treatment (Hoskins et al., 2020). These investigators endorse the design of preventive interventions that incorporate the cultural factors of *collectivism* and *familismo* as core components for greater intervention *efficacy* and *acceptability* with Latinx youth and families.

4.4.3.4 Structural Factors in Healthcare Settings

Integrating Psychological Services Into Integrated Healthcare (IHC) As noted, *health disparities* are pervasive adversities imposed on vulnerable ethnocultural communities by structural inequities in healthcare availability. One systemic action for increasing health equity is to improve the availability of *integrated healthcare* to provide preventive and treatment interventions in a culturally relevant manner. This can be directed toward reducing major chronic degenerative diseases, including cardiovascular disease, cancer, type 2 diabetes, HIV, and AIDS (Thobaben, 2004).

Integrated healthcare systems offer services provided by physicians, psychologists, and other culturally competent healthcare providers. For more effective health services to patients from ethnocultural groups, these providers can also develop cultural competence that consists of knowledge of the cultures of local ethnocultural groups. Culturally competent health professionals have an in-depth understanding of core aspects of healthcare delivery as relevant to the needs and preferences of ethnocultural individuals and families from local disadvantaged communities (Petersen et al., 2011).

In summary, given that physical illness is often accompanied and exacerbated by emotional, social, and cultural factors, implementing medical treatment without addressing illness-related psychological, social, and culture factors often compromises the effectiveness of the medical treatment that is provided. Accordingly, integrating psychological and sociocultural services into healthcare settings, especially those treating vulnerable ethnocultural populations, can increase the efficacy of the medical care provided (Petersen et al., 2011).

Integrated Care Outcome Studies with Ethnic Minority Participants Based on a *chronic disease conceptual model*, integrated care programs have been defined as those having one or more of the following components: (a) a healthcare system as a venue for the delivery of integrative services, (b) community resources that support the delivery of integrative services, (c) support for client self-management, (d) delivery systems design to deliver effective care, (e) decision-support that includes empirically based guidelines and technical support from experts, and (f) a clinical information system for information sharing and sending client reminders (Lemmens et al., 2015). The need for integrated care services is especially acute for patient populations affected by somatic disease and co-occurring psychological disorders, such as depression. Such *comorbidities* are associated with a poorer quality of life, greater disability, poor disease outcomes, and higher mortality (Lemmens et al., 2015).

The IMPACT (Improving Mood—Promoting Access to Collaborative Treatment) is an intervention that focused on reducing depression among patients from 18 primary care clinics in 5 states (Gilmer et al., 2008). Ethnocultural patients constituted 23% of the total sample of N = 1087 patients. Depression care managers and consulting psychiatrists were added to a clinic's staff to provide "collaborative stepped care," which included depression treatment that combined antidepressant medication and problem-solving psychotherapy. Compared to usual care, this integrated care intervention produced a greater reduction in depression at a 12-month assessment.

Another study focusing on depression treatment among patients in medical care (Miranda et al., 2003) utilized *co-located integrated care* that was provided to outpatients at San Francisco General Hospital and affiliated clinics. Participants were 199 primary care patients, including 77 Spanish-speaking Latinos, 46 African Americans, and 18 Asians and American Indians, who were randomly assigned to receive (a) a cognitive-behavioral therapy (CBT), (b) a group therapy intervention, or (c) the CBT intervention combined with clinical case management designed to increase engagement and reduce dropout. These investigators *adapted* the CBT intervention for low-income/low-education patients and for Latino patients as guided by Spanish and English-language manuals written at appropriate reading levels. *Cultural factors* incorporated into this study to provide cultural relevance for Latinx patients included the cultural values of *respeto*, *personalismo*, and *simpatia* (see Table 4.1).

Patients receiving the group CBT plus case management attended more CBT sessions and were less likely to drop out of therapy, when compared with those receiving the group CBT alone. The effects of treatment condition on depression outcomes were moderated by patients' language use. That is, Spanish-speaking participants, who received this group CBT plus case management, reported less depression at the 6-month follow-up, when compared with patients receiving group CBT alone. For English-speaking participants, there were no differences between treatment conditions on depression at the 6-month follow-up.

In summary, within the emerging context of *integrated care*, the need exists for policy-makers, treatment providers, and other professionals to ensure high quality in service delivery to maximize the attainment of successful treatment outcomes (Rutkowski et al., 2012). In the past, the delivery of behavioral health services has been bifurcated into treatment settings that offered substance use treatment, separate from those that offered mental health treatment. A more effective approach in integrated care is to provide both substance use and mental health treatment services as complements to medical care, with all three components provided within a single location, and as delivered by a collaborative team of health professionals. In this effort, a systems approach is necessary for a more complete and effective conceptualization of these complex processes for better service planning and delivery within a primary care setting, as this coordination can significantly improve the health and well-being of ethnocultural clients and patients, especially among those affected by co-occurring health problems (Collins, 2018).

4.4.4 *Cultural Factors Among Major US Ethnocultural Groups*

4.4.4.1 Overview

The US Census Bureau for the year 2010 reports that the total population of the United States consisted of over 308 million (U.S. Census Bureau, 2012). By contrast, in July of 2019, that total US population consisted of over 267 million persons classified as persons who are "not of Hispanic origin," along with over 60 million persons classified as being "of Hispanic origin." In total, these two sub-populations (Hispanics and non-Hispanics) comprised a total US population of over 328 million (U.S. Census Bureau, 2021). Among these, the major ethnocultural populations in the United States, when ranked in order of population size, are Hispanics or Latinxs, Blacks or African Americans, Asian Americans and Pacific Islanders, and American Indians or Native Americans. Each of these populations is also composed of several within-population populations or community sectors defined by nationality of origin, tribal subgroup, and other characteristics.

4.4.4.2 Cultural Factors in Hispanic/Latinx Communities

The US Census Bureau in 2010 reported that the population identified as being of Hispanic or Latinx heritage and who also reported being of "one or more races in combination" numbered over 50 million. This population grew to over 60 million in 2019, constituting 18.45% of the total US population of over 328 million (U.S. Census Bureau, 2021). Latinx, the largest ethnocultural population in the United States, is composed of several Hispanic/Latinx subgroups that have a family heritage from Mexico, Puerto Rico, Cuba, and other Latin American countries. Many Hispanics/Latinxs express pride in their national heritage, such as being from Mexico, although variations exist in the extent to which individuals identify with the generic term of Hispanic or Latino/a (Latinx) or in how much they identify with their national heritage, such as being Mexican, Cuban, Costa Rican, etc.

Hispanics/Latinxs have a history greatly influenced by the Spanish conquest that occurred during the 1500s. That conquest in time created racial admixtures of Europeans and indigenous heritages. From the conquest, Hispanic/Latinos inherited the Spanish language and Catholicism, although today several variation exist in the religious affiliations and linguistic practices of Latinos and Latinas, that is, there exist three acculturation-related population sectors: (a) whether they are bilingual/bicultural, (b) primarily Spanish-speaking and of low acculturation into the American society, or (c) primarily English-speaking and of high acculturation. Immigration issues constitute an important feature in the life experiences of many Latinos (Falicov, 2005).

The process of *acculturation* (cultural change) has created variations in the extent to which Latinxs identify and adopt the lifeways of the mainstream American culture and society. For some Latinxs, this process of acculturation creates *acculturation stress*. Acculturation stress often involves sociocultural and identify conflicts, an addition to other stressors that do not involve cultural issues. Becoming bilingual and bicultural constitutes a core identity for many Latinos and Latinas, although some are very traditional and prefer to retain completely their native cultural identity and to adhere to their native cultural traditions. Others prefer to integrate almost entirely into the American culture and society, integrating completely, thus *assimilating* into American society. The value of *collectivism*, which involves strong family bonds (*familismo*), respect for authority, and the observance of religious and secular traditional practices, constitutes a core cultural family value that exists among many of the more traditional Latinx families (Falicov, 2005).

The Latinx/Hispanic and Asian American and Pacific Islander ethnocultural groups contain large population sectors that have a significant immigration history. Accordingly, these immigration experiences prompt the occurrence of *acculturation* and *assimilation*, thus inducing the creation of the cultural factors of *acculturation* and *assimilation*. For Asian and Latinx immigrant individuals and their families, these two cultural factors have strong meaning and significance (Lopez-Class et al., 2011; Schwartz et al., 2010). *Acculturation* refers to a "sociocultural process in which members of one cultural group adopt the beliefs and behaviors of another group," (Lopez-Class et al., 2011)(p. 1556). *Assimilation* refers to an individual's or a group's complete integration into a new host society (Portes & Zhou, 1993). The process of developing a *bicultural identity* constitutes another cultural factor that develops as a consequence of the process acculturation change as manifested among many Latinos and Latinas.

Cultural Factors and Health-Related Outcomes Beginning about the year 2000, studies of racial/ethnic group differences in military veterans exposed to major stressors reported on ethnocultural differences in which Hispanic/Latinx veterans exhibited a higher probability of developing *post-traumatic stress disorder* (PTSD), although without higher levels of dysfunction (Ortega & Rosenstock, 2002). In a study of trauma survivors, relative to non-Hispanic white Americans and the African Americans, Hispanics reported greater overall PTSD symptom severity (Marshall et al., 2009). These investigators identified discrimination, economic hardships, and the loss of strong familial, religious, and social networks as factors in the development of PTSD among these Hispanics.

Based on the *theory of gender and power*, Wingood and colleagues identified certain Latinx cultural norms and traditional practices as influences on male-female power differentials that may operate as risk factors for increasing HIV risk behaviors (Wingood & DiClemente, 2000). Two prominent cultural factors within Latinx population are the traditional cultural factors involving gender role norms and expectations. These cultural factors are *machismo* (male dominance) and *marianismo* (female modesty and submissiveness to males). Daniel-Ulloa and collaborators conducted an analysis of studies examining the influence of Latinx cultural factors on gender-related beliefs and behaviors related to HIV/AIDS risks (Daniel-Ulloa et al., 2016). These investigators advocated for further research to develop culturally relevant theoretical models that explicitly include and test the influences of various cultural factors to better understand their effects on HIV-related risk behaviors among Latinx women and men.

In a study directed primarily at Spanish-speaking Latino patients, the IMPACT depression intervention was combined with a culturally relevant diabetes intervention (Project *Dulce*) to treat depression in Latinx persons receiving diabetes care in three southern California community clinics (Gilmer et al., 2008). By combining these two interventions, the overall project was described as a "co-located, co-managed" form of integrated care. Project *Dulce* consisted of a peer-led *diabetes self-management intervention*. IMPACT was delivered by bilingual staff and was culturally adapted by making it "more flexible for responding to cultural norms and beliefs, low literacy, socioeconomic barriers, and social stigma" (Gilmer et al., 2008) (p. 1324). In that study, a pre-post intervention evaluation revealed that depressed diabetes patients were able to significantly lower depression scores at the 6-month assessment by an average of 7.5 points as measured by the PHQ-9 while also significantly improving their nutrition.

4.4.4.3 Cultural Factors in Black/African American Communities

For the year 2010, the US Census Bureau reported that the *Black or African American* population in the United States numbered over 40 million (U.S. Census Bureau, 2012). And, the US Census Bureau reported that the Black or African American population in the United States for the year 2019 grew to over 44 million, which consisted of 13.53% of the total US population of over 328 million (U.S. Census Bureau, 2021). One of the landmark historical events among African Americans in the United States is the history and legacy of slavery and its influences on African American familial and social relations (Black & Jackson, 2005). Another prominent historical feature, a cultural resource, has been Black churches that provide *spirituality* and intergenerational connections, which serve as sources of strength, coping, and resilience in the face of chronic social stressors (Moore Hines & Boyd-Franklyn, 2005). A related historical context is segregation and the disproportionate distribution of African Americans into lower socioeconomic communities and poverty.

Institutionalized racism and discriminatory structural conditions have become significant social determinants of health, contributing to longstanding *inequities* and *health disparities*. These historical and sociocultural conditions have created social barriers and a potent "ripple effect" that produced waves of social oppression, which are still prominent among sectors of the African American population of the United States (Black & Jackson, 2005). By contrast, the emergence of *Africentric values* and traditions (Parham et al., 2011) among African Americans has rekindled a "sense of peoplehood" and collective struggle, instrumental for coping with racism and discrimination with collective strength in the face of many adversities (Moore Hines & Boyd-Franklyn, 2005).

HIV/AIDS Prevention In the area of HIV and AIDS, beyond evidence-based efforts to change individual behaviors, an ecosystemic approach has been encouraged, which gives attention to *contextual factors* in prevention and treatment. This approach is a more comprehensive and a likely efficacious approach for reducing health disparities among African American youth and adults (Lightfoot & Milburn, 2009). Toward preventing early sexual behaviors and HIV risks among African America youth, relevant *contextual factors* include low socioeconomic status, neighborhood structures and dynamics, and disproportionate sources of adversity, which adversely affect African American communities. For African Americans, these factors have produced high rates of incarceration and involvement in the criminal justice system.

Lightfoot and Milburn argue that HIV prevention should attend to African American *cultural factors* that are associated with the disproportionately high representation of African American youth as HIV/AIDS cases. Countering these adverse influences involves the incorporation of *protective cultural factors* into the design of HIV preventive interventions for African American youth. These cultural factors include *supportive family relationships*, *Africentric values*, and *racial socialization* that includes enhancing *racial/ethnic pride*. These preventive interventions should also be designed to modify some of the surrounding *contextual factors*, such as local community economic and geographic conditions. Within this approach, two guiding questions are "How can *culture* be incorporated into HIV interventions to reduce HIV-related risk behaviors among African American youth" and "What makes an HIV intervention for African American youth *culturally sensitive* and *culturally appropriate*?" (Lightfoot & Milburn, 2009).

A qualitative study of *storytelling* as shared by HIV-positive African American women has been used to provide advice to at-risk African American women (Robillard et al., 2017). This storytelling narrative approach was used to capture the richness of cultural factors for teaching about cognitive and emotional intervention contents and activities that facilitate healthful behavior change. These narratives identified five emergent themes that linked social determinants of health to HIV/AIDS prevention. These themes were (a) providing advice for prevention, (b) mobilizing support systems to aid in prevention, (c) the need for education, (d) developing empowerment and self-care capabilities, and (e) identifying barriers to prevention. Emerging issues included barriers imposed by the stigma of having HIV. These issues revealed the need to provide participants with (a) strategies for coping with an HIV-positive diagnosis, (b) understanding the challenges of interacting with sexual partners, (c) understanding gender-related power politics, (d) understanding the challenges of access to healthcare, and (d) obtaining social support. Also emphasized was the beneficial role of having HIV-positive African American women as *lay-health workers* serving as agents of change, when incorporated into community-focused HIV preventive interventions designed for young African American women.

Preventing Cigarette Use In a study of *protective cultural factors* that may "buffer" the effects of stress on cigarette smoking initiation among African American adolescents, Belgrave and collaborators examined the potential buffering effects of two cultural factors: *religious support* and *intergenerational connections*, as moderators of the effects of stressors on cigarette smoking behaviors (Belgrave et al., 2010) (see Fig. 4.1). In prior research with African American families, *religious beliefs*, *religious practices*, and *traditional family practices* emerged as potential moderators of youth substance use. Also, *spiritual ways of coping* have been found beneficial for reducing the stressors experienced from a difficult life event. Similarly, *intergenerational connections* were important in providing youth with social supports received from parents and other supportive adults from the local neighborhood. It appeared that positive family influences and youth engagement in school activities could also operate as protective factors against cigarette smoking.

Using hierarchical multiple regression model analyses, Belgrave and collaborators found that the cultural factor of *intergenerational connections* moderated the effect of stressors on the past 30-day tobacco use. Similarly, *religious support* moderated the effect of stressors on 30-day tobacco use. These results suggest that *religious beliefs* and *social support* from caring adults from the local community operated as intervention cultural factors, core components, and "active ingredients," which can be incorporated into a preventive intervention designed to prevent early cigarette use among Black/African American adolescents.

Obesity Prevention Important obesity-related issues emerge from ethnocultural group comparisons of age-adjusted obesity prevalence values based on data from the National Health and Nutrition Examination Surveys (NHANES). In those studies, obesity was assessed with body mass index (BMI) values of 30 kg/m^2 and greater. Data for *men* from the years 2017–2018 that compared non-Hispanic white, non-Hispanic black, and Hispanic groups revealed prevalence values of 44.7, 41.1, and 45.7 for these ethnocultural groups, respectively (Fryar et al., 2020). In these comparisons, Hispanic men exhibited the highest prevalence of obesity. In similar comparisons for this same time period of 2017–2018, among *women*, these prevalence values were 39.8, 56.9, and 43.7, respectively, for non-Hispanic white, non-Hispanic black, and Hispanic women (Fryar et al., 2020). These data for women reveal a remarkably higher prevalence of obesity among non-Hispanic black women. In summary, recent data from the NHANES indicates comparatively higher prevalence values of obesity among *Hispanic men* and among *Black women*.

Ickes and collaborators conducted a literature review of childhood obesity preventive interventions among African American youth for the years 2005–2010 (Ickes & Sharma, 2011). These investigators targeted empirical studies having samples of African American youths of 35% or higher. This review revealed that most studies screened *did not* contain a meaningful number of African American participants, suggesting that many studies consisted of samples of African American youths that essentially constituted unplanned samples of convenience. This review revealed that most of these studies were not designed to focus on African American youths, also suggesting that these studies lacked a focus on the cultural factors that are important to African American families and communities. Further, most studies also focused on individual behavior change, rather than examining broader systemic changes that can reduce obesity. The few studies that focused on changing social and environmental factors, such as access to resources and policy-related changes, focused on interventions deliverable in community-based, home-based, or school-based settings. This review also revealed that most of the interventions for obesity reduction focused on promoting nutrition and physical activity, including weight reduction as assessed by decreases in body mass index. Intervention activities included skill building, goal setting, and increasing self-efficacy while also making the intervention enjoyable to children and adolescents.

Regarding *cultural factors* in the design of interventions for African American youth, the culturally relevant components, such as *role modeling* and *mentorship*, can be provided by caring African American adults. One distinct weakness needing attention in future study designs was that among the identified 18 interventions, only 3 included parents in these obesity reduction interventions. Clearly, *parental inclusion* emerged as an important factor for maintaining healthful behavior changes in obesity reduction among these African American children and adolescents.

4.4.4.4 Cultural Factors in Asian American Communities

For the year 2010, the US Census Bureau reported that the population of *Asians* in the United States numbered over 16 million (U.S. Census Bureau, 2012). Further, the US Census Bureau also reported that there are over 1 million persons who identify as *Native Hawaiian and Other Pacific Islanders,* for a combined total of over 17 million Asians in the year 2010 (U.S. Census Bureau, 2012). Then for the year 2019, this combined population of *Asians and Native Hawaiian and Pacific Islanders* grew to almost 23 million, constituting 7% of the total US population of over 328 million (U.S. Census Bureau, 2021). Individuals sharing common characteristics as Asians consist of over 30 ethnocultural subgroups, with Pacific Islanders consisting of another 21 subgroups (Lee & Mock, 2005a). Among Asian Americans, the largest ethnocultural groups by population size are Chinese, Filipino, Asian Indian, Japanese, and Korean.

Among Asians, immigration and the process of *acculturation* and *assimilation* constitute core cultural themes that reflect many of their life experiences. Regarding within-group cultural variations that exist among Asians, these variations include their use of a non-English language, as well as diversity in their social, religious, and other backgrounds. Despite this extensive diversity, Asian Americans share many common cultural threads. Among these are the centrality of the family unit and the value of *collectivism* (versus American *individualism*), the pervasiveness of immigration issues in their lives, and the presence of effective cultural coping strategies despite exposures to trauma, racism, and discrimination (Lee & Mock, 2005a).

Centuries-old Confucian teachings have been a source of common Asian American characteristics. These teachings emphasize the importance of harmonious interpersonal relationships, interdependence, hierarchical family roles, and obligations and duties to the family (Lee & Mock, 2005b). With strong adherence to these longstanding traditional Chinese values, many Asian Americans exhibit strong family bonds, value educational achievement, practice self-discipline and hard work, and exhibit social modesty, which are often expressed as an unassuming and nonconfrontational interpersonal style. These cultural features have led to the Asian American stereotype of being a "model minority." Also, many traditional Asian Americans refrain from seeking mental health services to avoid the shame of exposing personal and family difficulties to outsiders. In summary, traditional Asian Americans exhibit a strong adherence to their cultural values and traditions, as this includes family loyalty, reverence for elders, maintaining their native language, and observing familial traditions, rituals, and customs (Lee & Mock, 2005b).

A study by Anyon and collaborators examined assets and barriers to help seeking among Asian American high school students in 15 public high schools. This study was conducted as part of a school-based mental health (SBMH) prevention program conducted in an urban community having a significant Asian population (Anyon et al., 2014). Study investigators recognized the influence of several systemic and cultural factors, such as Asian students' *internalization of distress*, their focus on somatic rather than psychological symptoms, their conformity to group norms, and the *stigma* and *shame* felt over publicly disclosing embarrassing topics, each of which could discourage their use of mental health services (Sue & Sue, 1999).

Investigators conducted multilevel regression model analyses to examine risk and protective factors in four domains: structural conditions, organizational settings, cultural factors, and social relationships, as predictors of mental health service utilization. After controlling for several covariates, including the school-based contextual variable of school racial composition, investigators found that the Asian students, when compared with Black, Latino, and multiracial students, exhibited significantly *lower* odds of using these school-based mental health services. Among the Asian students, self-reports of various risk factors (alcohol, tobacco, and drug use, externalizing behaviors, and truancy), based on teacher or self-referrals, increased the odds of using this program's mental health services. Nonetheless, among Asian students, self-reports of depressive symptoms were *not* associated with the use of these mental health services, suggesting still that cultural factors of *stigma* and *shame* (loss of face) associated with disclosing feelings of depression and suicidal ideation still operate as barriers to the use of mental health services among many Asian students.

4.4.4.5 Cultural Factors in Native American Communities

For the year 2010, the US Census Bureau reported that persons identifying as *American Indians and Alaska Natives* numbered over 4 million (U.S. Census Bureau, 2012). Further, for the year 2019, that population grew as a population of *American Indians and Alaska Natives*, numbering over 4 million, which constitutes 1.34% of the US population of over 328 million (U.S. Census Bureau, 2021).

Native Americans/American Indians are people represented by over 500 native tribes in the United States. Despite that diversity, a central feature of their cultures is the importance of kinship and family bonds. This includes respect and reverence for elders and their family ancestry. Another core feature of Native American lifeways is the importance of *spirituality* in their relationship with nature and kin (Sutton & Broken Nose, 2005). This reverence for nature and connections with kin constitute expressions of *collectivism*, whereby one's identity is based not on the individualized self but instead on the family and extended family as the unit of lifeways.

Based on a history of oppression and being relocated from their original ancestral lands into desolate frontier settings, many Native American tribes were relegated to lives of poverty and discrimination. Yet many Native American communities preserved their traditional tribal values, language, and folkways as sources of collective strengths. Despite efforts to survive, the risk of suicide has emerged as a significant problem affecting Native American youth. Suicidal ideation and intents have been associated with early alcohol use that in short time transcends to heavy alcohol use. This progression appears associated with youth conflicts in reconciling indigenous and Westernized lifeways. By contrast, preventive interventions in support of healthful beliefs and actions among Native American youth have emphasized the importance of establishing indigenous connections that promote *spirituality* and *cultural traditions* (Kulis et al., 2017). These connections seek to help Native American youth survive within Westernized environments, aided by various skills for "surviving in these two worlds."

As noted, early alcohol use among Alaska native youth constitutes a risk factor for subsequent alcohol abuse and suicidal ideation. Using indigenous theory applicable to prevention, Allen and collaborators examined two cultural factors meaningful to Native American communities (Allen et al., 2018). In a multilevel cultural intervention focusing on individual, familial, and community levels of analysis, two youth skill development outcomes were *reasons for life* and *reflective processes. Reasons for life* refers to beliefs and expectancies that make life enjoyable and worthwhile. Illustrative items assessed by this study's measurement scales are "My elders teach me that life is valuable" and "People see that I live my life in a native way." Similarly, *reflective processes* refers to thinking about the negative consequences of drinking alcohol. Illustrative items are "I would feel embarrassed to have drinking in my family" and "I do not want to lose control over myself."

These measures reflect indigenous cultural factors regarded as protective against youth alcohol use and suicide. In the Alaskan Yup'ik community, Philip and collaborators examined the protective effects of *social network components* (Philip et al., 2016). Social network characteristics examined included network size, network density, connections to adults, and connections to elders, each as a protective factor operating at community, familial, and individual levels. Using the identified cultural factors of *reasons for life* and *reflective processes*, this Qungasvik multilevel intervention examined *social network characteristics* to assess the effects of these cultural factors as protective against alcohol use disorders and suicide.

4.4.5 Mixed Methods for Designing Culturally Focused Preventive Interventions

4.4.5.1 Emergence of Mixed Methods Research

Within the past two decades, the mixed methods field has emerged as a "third paradigm" beyond the conventional *qualitative* and the *quantitative* research paradigms (Johnson et al., 2007; Tashakkori & Teddle, 2010). The mixed methods field offers novel methodologies for conducting *deep-structure* analyses that contribute rich and contextual information (Resnicow et al., 2000). Accordingly, mixed methods research designs can generate a greater "yield" when compared with the sole use of a qualitative or quantitative research methodology, thus providing "the best of both" (QUAL and QUAN) methodologies. A hallmark of mixed methods research is the aim of integrating qualitative and quantitative evidence to attain this grater *yield* (Curry & Nunez-Smith, 2015). This dual methods approach is well suited for the analysis of cultural factors as potential core components of culturally relevant preventive intervention.

4.4.5.2 Mixed Methods Research Designs

Mixed methods research designs have been used extensively in implementation research to identify factors and conditions to inform the processes of dissemination, adoption, implementation, and sustainability of *evidence-based preventive interventions* (EBPIs), as well as to apply this knowledge for informing for empirically validated treatments (EBTs) (Nastasi & Hitchckci, 2016). In principle, this information will aid in eliminating implementation barriers to improve the implementation of preventive and treatment interventions delivered within integrated care settings (Palinkas et al., 2011).

In their analysis of mixed methods studies, Palinkas et al. (2011) identified three major elements of mixed methods research when designing implementation studies. These major elements are (a) *structure*, the study's mixed methods research design which consists either of a *concurrent/convergent* or *sequential* approach and the relative importance of the study's qualitative and quantitative components (e.g., "QUAL ➔ quan" or "QUAL + QUAN"); (b) *function*, the utilization of one of four major approaches (purposes) for conducting a mixed methods study (i.e., convergence, complementarity, expansion, development); and (c) *process*, the manner in which the qualitative and quantitative data are integrated (i.e., merged, connected, embedded).

Methods guiding the conduct of mixed methods research are now available in several texts (Creamer, 2018; Curry & Nunez-Smith, 2015; Nastasi & Hitchckci, 2016), some in their second edition or beyond (Creswell & Creswell, 2018; Tashakkori & Teddle, 2010). This includes books that focus on qualitative techniques, research methods, and data analysis (Bernard et al., 2017). Both rigor and cultural sensitivity in intervention assessment as conducted within a healthcare setting can be attained by using well-specified research designs, coupled with a well-planned implementation of a mixed methods research (Castro et al., 2014).

4.4.5.3 Mixed Methods for "Unpacking" and In-Depth Analysis of Cultural Factors

"Unpacking" and In-Depth Analysis of a Cultural Factor Mixed methods analyses can generate explanatory "thick description" narratives that constitute the essence of a deep-structure analysis. This approach can be used to explore the analysis of an intervention's *core components* and their effects on targeted intervention outcomes. This approach is useful for understanding complex cultural issues that affect the health and well-being of diverse ethnocultural groups.

The identification of core themes and their structure can be linked to existing theoretical models (Ryan & Bernard, 2003). This approach aids in exploring an intervention's likely *mechanisms of change*. Textual data for conducting a thematic analysis can be gathered from participants using in-depth interviews. These interviews can generate culturally rich and informative *emergent themes* for "unpacking" meanings and nuances and the structure of complex cultural factors, such as *acculturation*, *ethnic identity*, and *traditionalism* (Castro & Coe, 2007; Castro et al., 2010).

In their mixed methods study, Castro and Coe conducted deep-structure *focus question* interviews with Latinas from two rural communities in Arizona. One study aim was to "unpack" the meaning of the complex cultural factor of *family traditionalism* as conceptualized by adult rural Latinx women (Castro & Coe, 2007). The quantitative (QUAN) assessment of the construct of *traditionalism* involved administering three cultural variable scales: *family traditionalism*, *rural lifestyles*, and *folk beliefs* (folk remedies). Furthermore, the open-ended *focus questions* were administered via one-to-one interviews conducted by *promotoras* (lay-health workers) to identify *emerging themes* that reflect traditional Latinx family beliefs and practices. For eliciting these deep-structure themes, some of these focus questions were as follows: "How 'should' husbands, wives, and children act?; What is the right way to act? What are certain family members supposed to do?"

A thematic analysis of qualitative textual responses for each of these focus question responses generated six themes: (a) male (macho) privilege, (b) family trust and respect, (c) family unity (*familismo*), (d) valuing traditions, (e) adherence to customs, and (f) resistance to change. A representative response about the theme of *family trust and respect* (*respeto*) was "[The family] always shares everything equally and there should be respect among everyone; between couples and children." An illustrative response about the theme of *resistance to change* was "[A traditional woman] does not believe in changing her ways. Everything that her parents believe, so does she." In summary, these thematic analyses "unpacked" the construct of *family traditionalism* by identifying *emergent themes*. This analysis yielded nuanced, deep-structure text narrative responses that described core features of Latinx *family traditionalism*, as manifested within rural Latinx communities (Castro & Coe, 2007).

4.4.5.4 Mixed Methods Analyses for Cultural Enhancement of EBIs for Integrated Care

Studies can be conducted within integrated care settings by utilizing mixed methods research designs that utilize *purposeful sampling* of strategically selected groups of participants to analyze the effects of a preventive or treatment intervention (Castro et al., 2014; Creswell & Creswell, 2018). For example, a mixed methods research study that interviews therapists and clients who participated in a treatment intervention can elicit responses that answer specific and well-developed focus questions about the participant's reactions to treatment. For example, (a) "What intervention activities appeared to operate as "active ingredients" for attaining the targeted outcomes?" (b) "In what ways did the intervention contribute toward attaining its targeted outcomes?" and (c) "What were some weaknesses or limitations of this intervention, and what modifications of this intervention are needed to improve it?" In a "systematic mapping review" of empirical studies that utilized a qualitative component incorporated into controlled clinical trials, O'Cathain and colleagues describe how qualitative data provided *contextual information* regarding the manner in which the intervention study was implemented and how that intervention may have produced the targeted outcomes (O'Cathain et al., 2013).

4.4.6 Developing EBPIs for Implementation in Community Settings

4.4.6.1 Challenges of Taking an Evidence-Based Intervention to Scale

In 2008, Green observed that the outcomes of most behavioral research are not implemented in practice (Green, 2008), noting that only about 17% of these findings are incorporated into practice. Further, for these findings, it takes approximately 17 years for that to occur (Balas & Boren, 2000). There are many reasons for this. The most commonly cited reason is that many clinicians do not regard these research findings to be relevant; they do not apply to their patient populations or their settings (Correa et al., 2020). We are challenged by the following mainstream conundrum: there is a massive literature considered to be elegantly designed and that supports the efficacy of psychological and behavioral interventions for the treatment of medical and psychological problems typically seen in primary care (Maragakis & O'Donohue, 2018) Nonetheless, this body of research is made irrelevant by the inherent limitations of these research designs (Holtrop et al., in press). Conventional research relies on designs that maximize *internal validity* to attribute research results with high certainty to the intervention. These pristine research designs maximize the homogeneity of participant samples by minimizing variations in patients' presenting problems. These designs also minimize variations in organizational functioning and implementation fidelity, whereby the intervention is often delivered by highly experienced research staff.

By contrast, issues of *external validity* have been greatly minimized or neglected, thus limiting the generalizability and capacity for "real-world" implementation of these research results within diverse community settings. This limited external validity has lacked attention toward external environmental contexts, including cultural variations in the participants from a local community who could be the beneficiaries of that intervention. This inattention also involves a lack of implementation planning to "real-world" variations in the types of organization or settings in which the intervention would be implemented, such as medical centers, clinics, community-based agencies, as well as attention to broader community environments and contexts (urban, suburban, rural, frontier). Given this design inattention to external validity, is it any surprise that most research-based interventions have not been taken to scale?

To make research meaningful and implementable, Kessler and Glasgow proposed that from the beginning, research should (a) be practical and have feasible interventions, (b) address key contextual factors, (c) have transparent reporting, and (d) use a design that fits the question of interest (Kessler & Glasgow, 2011). They further suggest that all these be applied to core research elements: the design selection, intervention characteristics, choice of evaluation measures, and data analyses (Kessler & Glasgow, 2011).

4.4.6.2 Strategies for Facilitating EBPI Dissemination and Implementation

Over the last 15 years, these issues involving the gap between formal research studies and their transferability to community-based services have coalesced into new frameworks and theories identified as dissemination and implementation (D&I) research. This field focuses on efforts to effectively transfer *evidence-based preventive interventions* (EBPIs) and *empirically validated treatments* (EVTs) into local community and healthcare settings. For reducing one or more health disparities among one or more ethnocultural groups, the goal is to design from the beginning an evidence-based preventive or treatment intervention that is "scale-up ready" (Fagan et al., 2019) and transferable with high *adaptability* (fit and function) (Alvidrez et al., 2019) into one of several community settings and implemented expeditiously to confer targeted benefits to clients from one or more ethnocultural groups. The following sections provide four select strategies, among many, that are important in this process of developing an intervention that is designed as readily "scale-up ready" and transferrable from the efficacy testing phase, for implementation within one of several community settings for the benefit of improving health and wellness in diverse ethnocultural groups.

Coordinating with Agency Administration and Staff

Once adopted, organization administrators need to exercise leadership in setting certain priorities for the implementation and sustainability of the intervention, as supported by their own organization. This may include administration-approved guidelines and expectations for intervention staffing, roles and responsibilities, and plans for implementation sustainability. It is important to ensure that the individuals mandating the change have the authority to do so, given that the implementers often lack such authority.

Assess Intervention "Scale-Up Readiness" and Identify Implementation Facilitators and Barriers

This assessment is typically guided by a conceptual framework or model that identifies factors that may impede implementation within various community settings. For example, an intervention's "scale-up" readiness (Fagan et al., 2019) will be impeded if the new setting lacks leadership support. Thus, effectively implementing the innovation would require a focus on leadership engagement and education to promote effective intervention delivery. That assessment may also determine whether staff from that site have prior experience in using that intervention, thus inviting them to serve as an implementation champion.

Adapting the Intervention for the Local Contexts

Identify ways that the intervention can be *adapted* to meet local needs (Barrera et al., 2017). It is useful to identify components of successful implementation. When adapting an intervention, it is critical to identify and ensure that the intervention's presumed core components are delivered with fidelity to the theory or the intervention's *logic model*, which serves as the scientific foundation believed to produce intervention's treatment outcomes (to produce intervention efficacy), i.e. ,the mechanisms by which the intervention "works." This includes identifying needed adaptations for the intervention's fit and function within the local clinical setting and meeting the needs of local community residents. In this regard, these adaptations may consist of tailoring discrete implementation strategies (intervention contents and activities) to eliminate barriers and leverage facilitators for an efficacious implementation process and capacity to attain targeted outcomes.

Engaging Consumers Under a Social Participatory Approach

Community clients are also key individuals in this implementation process – under a partnership that includes their views as consumers of this intervention. It is also important to orient these consumers to the intervention's guiding theory or logic model, in ways that consumers can understand. This orientation will allow consumers to ask questions, also clarifying their role as active participants for enhancing their own health and wellness. This includes their role as active participants in intervention-related decision-making and monitoring their own progress in attaining intervention-related goals.

4.4.7 Final Comments About Cultural Factors

This chapter provided an overview of *cultural factors* as important constructs and measurable *cultural variables* that can be used to conduct more probing deep-structure analyses about the cultural experiences of persons from the major ethnocultural groups in the United States.Cultural factors can operate as core elements of culture and can reveal rich nuances from those cultural experiences. When converted into quantitative cultural variables, these elements can be incorporated into multivariate data analyses to expand existing models or develop new models and aid in a rigorous analysis of complex relationships and associations among variables in a given model. The use of mixed methods analyses that include cultural factors introduces the combined analytic power and yield from the integration of qualitative and quantitative data, thus adding further depth of analysis that can yield more complete conclusions from this mixed methods approach. Finally, cultural factors can add depth of analysis in the design, dissemination, and implementation of evidence-based preventive and treatment interventions, at the intersection of prevention science and implementation science. This approach can improve the transfer of tested and effective interventions into community settings to promote the health and well-being of multiple constituencies, including vulnerable members of ethnocultural groups, and contribute to reducing inequities and health disparities for a more comprehensive approach for improving the nation's health.

References

Allen, J., Rasmus, S. M., Fok, C. C. T., Charles, B., Henry, D., & Team, Q. (2018). Multi-level cultural intervention for the prevention of suicide and alcohol use risk with Alaska native youth: A nonrandomized comparison of treatment study. *Prevention Science, 19*, 174–185. https://doi.org/10.1007/s11121-017-0798-9

Alvidrez, J., Napoles, A. M., Bernal, G., Lloyd, J., Cartill, V., Godette, D., Cooper, L. A., Brave Heart, M. Y. H., Das, R., & Farhat, T. (2019). Building the evidence base to inform planned intervention adaptations by practitioners serving health disparity populations. *American Journal of Public Health, 109*(S1), S94–S101. https://doi.org/10.2105/AJPH.2018.304915

Anyon, Y., Ong, S. L., & Whitaker, K. (2014). School-based mental health prevention for Asian American adolescents: Risk behaviors, protective factors, and service use. *Asian American Journal of Psychology, 5*(2), 134–144. https://doi.org/10.1037/a0035300

Balas, E. A., & Boren, S. A. (2000). Managing clinical knowledge for health care improvement. In J. Bemmel & A. T. McCray (Eds.), *Yearbook of medical informatics patient-centered systems*.

Bandura, A. (1986). *Social foundations of thought and action: A social cognitive theory*. Prentice Hall.

Barrera, M., Berkel, C., & Castro, F. G. (2017). Directions for the advancement of culturally adapted preventive interventions: Local adaptations, engagement, and sustainability. *Prevention Science, 18*, 640–648. https://doi.org/10.1007/s11121-016-0705-9

Belgrave, F. Z., Johnson, J., Nguyen, A., Hood, K., & Tademy, A. (2010). Stress and tobacco use among African-American adolescents: The buffering effect of cultural factors. *Journal of Drug Education, 40*(2), 173–188.

Bernal, G., & Adames, C. (2017). Cultural adaptations: Conceptual, ethical, contextual, and methodological issues for working with ethnocultural and majority-world populations. *Prevention Science, 18*, 681–688. https://doi.org/10.1007/s11121-017-08-06-0

Bernard, H. R., Wutich, A., & Ryan, G. W. (2017). *Analyzing qualitative data: Systematic approaches* (2nd ed.). Sage.

Berry, J. W. (1980). Acculturation as varieties of adaptation. In A. M. Padilla (Ed.), *Acculturation: Theory, models and some findings* (pp. 9–25). Westview Press.

Berry, J. W. (2005). Acculturation: Living successfully into cultures. *International Journal of Intercultural Relations, 29*, 697–712.

Black, L., & Jackson, V. (2005). Families of African origin. In M. McGoldrick, J. Giordano, & N. Garcia-Prieto (Eds.), *Ethnicity & family therapy* (3rd ed.). Guilford.

Braveman, P. A. (2006). Health disparities and health equity: Concepts and measurement. *Annual Review of Public Health, 27*, 167–194. https://doi.org/10.1146/annurev.publhealth.27.021405.102103

Braveman, P. A., Cubbin, C., Egerter, S., Williams, D. R., & Pamuk, E. (2010). Socioeconomic disparities in health in the United States: What the patterns tell us. *American Journal of Public Health, 100*(S1), S186–S196. https://doi.org/10.2105/AJPH.2009.166082)

Brislin, R. (1993). *Understanding culture's influence on behavior*. Harcourt Brace Jovanovich.

Brown, A. P., Ma, G. X., Miaranda, J., Eng, E., Casstille, D., Brockie, T., Jones, P., Airhilenbuwa, C. O., Farhat, T., Zhu, L., & Trinh-Shevrin, C. (2019). Structural interventions to reduce and eliminate health disparities. *American Journal of Public Health, 109*(51), 572–578. https://doi.org/10.2105/AJPH.2018.304844

Carter, R. T. (2007). Racism and psychological and emotional injury: Recognizing and assessing race-based traumatic stress. *The Counseling Psychologist, 35*, 13–105. https://doi.org/10.1177/0011000006292033

Castro, F. G., & Coe, K. (2007). Traditions and alcohol use: A mixed methods study. *Cultural Diversity and Ethnic Minority Psychology, 13*(4), 260–284. https://doi.org/10.1037/1099-9809.13.4.269

Castro, F. G., & Hernandez Alarcon, E. (2002). Integrating cultural variables into drug abuse prevention and treatment with racial/ethnic minorities. *Journal of Drug Issues Issues*, 783–810.

Castro, F. G., & Nieri, T. (2010). Cultural factors in drug use etiology: Concepts, methods, and recent findings. In L. M. Scheier (Ed.), *Handbook of drug use etiology: Theory, methods, and empirical findings* (pp. 305–324). American Psychological Association.

Castro, F. G., Furth, P., & Karlow, H. (1984). The health beliefs or Mexican, Mexican American and Anglo American women. *Hispanic Journal of Behavioral Sciences, 6*(4), 365–383.

Castro, F. G., Nichols, E., & Kater, K. (2007). Relapse prevention with Hispanic and other racial/ethnic populations: Can cultural resilience promote relapse prevention? In K. Witkiewitz & G. A. Marlatt (Eds.), *A therapist's guide to evidence-based relapse prevention* (pp. 259–292). Academic Press.

Castro, F. G., Stein, J. A., & Bentler, P. M. (2009). Ethnic pride, traditional family values, and acculturation in early cigarette and alcohol use among Latino adolescents. *Journal of Primary Prevention, 30*, 265–292. https://doi.org/10.1007/s10935-009-0174-z

Castro, F. G., Kellison, J. G., Boyd, S., & Kopak, S. (2010). A methodology for conducting integrative mixed methods research and data analyses. *Journal of Mixed Methods Research, 4*, 342–360.

Castro, F. G., Garvey, M., Kellison, J. G., & Marsiglia, F. F. (2013). Ethnic and cultural minority populations. In B. S. McCrady & E. E. Epstein (Eds.), *Addictions: A comprehensive guidebook* (pp. 758–787). Oxford.

Castro, F. G., Morera, O. F., Kellison, J. G., & Aguirre, K. M. (2014). Mixed methods research design for prevention science: Methods, critiques, and recommendations. In Z. Sloboda & H. Petras (Eds.), *Advances in prevention science* (pp. 453–490). Springer.

Cheng, H., Hitter, T. L., Adams, E. M., & Williams, C. (2016). Minority stress and depressive symptoms: Familism, ethnic identity, and gender as moderators. *The Counseling Psychologist, 44*(6), 841–870. https://doi.org/10.1177/0011000016660377

Collins, L. M. (2018). *Optimization of behavioral, biobehavioral, and biomedical interventions: The multiphase optimization strategy (MOST)*. Springer International Publishing.

Correa, V. C., Lugo-Agudelo, L. H., Aguirre-Acevedo, D. C., Contreras, J. A. P., Borrero, A. M. P., Patino-Lugo, D. F., & Valencia, D. A. C. (2020). Individual, health system, and contextual barriers and facilitators for the implementation of clinical practice guidelines: A systematic metareview. *Health Research Policy and Systems, 18*(1), 1–11. https://doi.org/10.1186/s12961-020-00588-8

Creamer, E. G. (2018). *An introduction to fully integrated mixed methods research*. Sage.

Creswell, J. W., & Creswell, J. D. (2018). *Research design: Qualitative, quantitative and mixed methods approaches* (5th ed.). Sage.

Cuellar, I., Arnold, B., & Gonzalez, G. (1995). Cognitive referents of acculturation: Assessment of cultural constructs in Mexican Americans. *Journal of Community Psychology, 23*, 339–356.

Curry, L., & Nunez-Smith, M. (2015). *Mixed methods in health science research: A practical primer*. Sage.

Daniel-Ulloa, J., Ulibarri, M., Baquero, B., Sleeth, C., Haring, H., & Rhodes, S. D. (2016). Behavioral HIV prevention intervention among Latinas in the US: A systematic review of the evidence. *Journal of Immigrant and Minority Health, 18*, 1498–1521. https://doi.org/10.1007/s10903-015-0283-0

Fagan, A. A., Bumbarger, B. K., Barth, R. P., Bradshaw, C. P., Cooper, B. R., Supplee, L. H., & Walker, D. K. (2019). Scaling up evidence-based interventions in US public systems to prevent behavior health problems: Challenges and opportunities. *Prevention Science, 20*, 1147–1168. https://doi.org/10.1007/s11121-019-01048-8

Falicov, C. (2005). Mexican families. In M. McGoldrick, J. Giordano, & N. Garcia-Preto (Eds.), *Ethnicity & family therapy* (3rd ed.). Guilford.

Fryar, C. D., Carroll, M. D., & Afful, J. (2020). *Prevalence of overweight, obesity, and severe obesity among adults aged 20 and over: United States, 1960–1962 through 2017–2018*. National Center for Health Statistics.

Gilbert, K. L., Quinn, S. C., Ford, A. F., & Thomas, S. B. (2010). The urban context: A place to eliminate health disparities and build organizational capacity. *Journal of Prevention & Intervention in the Community, 39*(1), 77–92. https://doi.org/10.1080/10852352.2011.530168

Gilmer, T. P., Walker, C., Johnson, E. D., Philis-Tsimikas, A., & Unutzer, J. (2008). Improving treatment of depression among Latinos with diabetes using project Dulce and IMPACT. *Diabetes Care, 31*(7), 1324–1326.

Green, L. W. (2008). Making research relevant: If it is an evidence-based practice, where's the practice-based evidence. *Family Practice, 25*, 120–124.

Holtrop, J. S., Estabrooks, P. A., Gaglio, B., Harden, S. M., Kessler, R. S., King, D. K., Kwan, G. M., Ory, M. G., Rabin, B. A., Shelton, R. C., & Glasgow, R. E. (in press). Understanding and applying the RE-AIM framework: Clarifications and resources. *Journal of Clinical and Translational Science*.

Hoskins, D., Tahir, P., del Cid, M., Perez-Gualdron, L., & Tolou-Shams, M. (2020). Ecological systems in relation to Latinx youth in the juvenile justice system: A narrative literature review. *Children and Youth Services Review, 117*, 1–13. https://doi.org/10.1016/j.childyouth.2019.104669

Ickes, M. J., & Sharma, M. (2011). A review of childhood obesity prevention interventions targeting African-American children. *Vulnerable Children and Youth Studies, 6*(2), 103–123. https://doi.org/10.1080/174501128.2011.564227

Johnson, R. B., Onwuegbuzie, A. J., & Turner, L. A. (2007). Toward a definition of mixed methods research. *Journal of Mixed Methods Research, 1*, 112–133.

Kessler, R. S., & Glasgow, R. E. (2011). A proposal to speed translation of healthcare research into practice: Dramatic change is needed. *American Journal of Preventive Medicine, 40*(6), 637–644.

Kulis, S. S., Ayers, S. L., & Harthun, M. L. (2017). Substance use prevention for urban American Indian youth: A efficacy trial of the culturally adapted living in 2 worlds program. *Journal of Primary Prevention, 38*(1–2), 137–158. https://doi.org/10.1007/s10935-016-0461-4

Lau, A. S., Fung, J., Wang, S., & Kung, S. (2009). Explaining elevated social anxiety among Asian Americans: Emotional attunement and cultural double bind. *Cultural Diversity and Ethnic Minority Psychology, 15*(1), 77–85. https://doi.org/10.1037/a0012819

Lee, E., & Mock, M. R. (2005a). Asian families. In M. McGoldrick, J. Giordano, & N. Garcia-Preto (Eds.), *Ethnicity & family therapy* (3rd ed.). Guilford.

Lee, E., & Mock, M. R. (2005b). Chinese families. In M. McGoldrick, J. Giordano, & N. Garcia-Preto (Eds.), *Ethnicity & family therapy* (3rd ed.). Guilford.

Lehman, D. R., Chiu, C., & Schaller, M. (2004). Psychology and culture. *Annual Review of Psychology, 55*, 699–714.

Lemmens, L. C., Molema, C. C. M., Versnel, N., Baan, C. A., & de Bruin, S. R. (2015). Integrated care programs for patients with psychological comorbidity: A systematic review and meta-analysis. *Journal of Psychosomatic Research, 79*, 580–594.

Lightfoot, M. A., & Milburn, N. G. (2009). HIV prevention and African American youth: Examination of individual-level behaviour is not the only answer. *Culture, Health & Sexuality, 11*(7), 731–742. https://doi.org/10.1080/13691050903078824

Lopez-Class, M., Castro, F. G., & Ramirez, A. (2011). Conceptions of acculturation: A review and statement of critical issues. *Social Science and Medicine, 72*, 1555–1562.

Maragakis, A., & O'Donohue, W. T. (2018). *Principle-based stepped care and brief psychotherapy for integrated care settings*. Springer.

Marshall, G. N., Schell, T. L., & Miles, J. N. V. (2009). Ethnic differences in posttraumatic distress: Hispanics' symptoms differ in kind and degree. *Journal of Consulting and Clinical Psychology, 77*(6), 1169–1178.

McGoldrick, M., Giordano, J., & Garcia-Preto, N. (2005). Overview: Ethnicity and family therapy. In M. McGoldrick, J. Giordano, & N. Garcia-Preto (Eds.), *Ethnicity & family therapy*. Guilford.

Miranda, J., Azocar, F., Organizta, K. C., Dwyer, E., & Areane, P. (2003). Treatment of depression among impoverished primary care patients from ethnic minority groups. *Psychiatric Services, 54*, 219–225.

Moore Hines, P., & Boyd-Franklyn, N. (2005). African American families. In M. McGoldrick, J. Giordano, & N. Garcia-Preto (Eds.), *Ethnicity & family therapy* (3rd ed.). Guilford.

Murimi, M. W., & Harpel, T. (2010). Practicing preventive health: The underlying culture among low-income rural populations. *Journal of Rural Health, 26*, 273–282. https://doi.org/10.1111/j.1748-0361.2010.00289.x

Nastasi, B. K., & Hitchckci, J. H. (2016). *Mixed methods research and culture-specific interventions: Program design and evaluation*. Sage.

NIDA. (1999). *Principles of drug addition treatment: A research-based guide*. National Institutes of Health.

O'Cathain, A., Thomas, K. J., Drabble, S. J., Rudolph, A., & Hewison, J. (2013). What can qualitative research do for randomized controlled trials? A systematic mapping review. *BMJ Open, 3*. https://doi.org/10.1136/bmiopen-2013-002889

Ortega, A. N., & Rosenstock, R. (2002). Posttraumatic stress disorder among Hispanic Vietnam veterans. *American Journal of Psychiatry, 157*, 615–619.

Palinkas, L. A., Aarons, G. A., Horwitz, S., Chamberlain, P., Hurlburt, M., & Landsverk, J. (2011). Mixed methods designs in implementation research. *Administration, Policy, and Mental Health, 38*, 44–53. https://doi.org/10.1007/s10488-010-0314-z

Parham, T. A., Ajamu, A., & White, J. L. (2011). *The psychology of Blacks: Centering our perspectives in the African consciousness* (4th ed.). Prentice Hall.

Petersen, S., Hutchings, P., Shrader, G., & Brake, K. (2011). Integrating health care: The clear advantage for underserved diverse populations. *Psychological Services, 8*(2), 69–81. https://doi.org/10.1037/a0023521

Philip, J., Ford, T., Henry, D., Rasmus, S., & Allen, J. (2016). Relationship of social network to protective factors in suicide and alcohol use disorder intervention for rural Yup'ik Alaska native youth. *Psychosocial Intervention, 28*, 45–54. https://doi.org/10.1016/j.psi.2015.08.002

Portes, A., & Zhou, M. (1993). The new second generation: Segmented assimilation and its variants. *Annuals of the American Academe of Political and Social Science, 530*(1), 74–96.

Ramirez, M. (1999). *Multicultural psychotherapy: On approach to individual and cultural differences* (2nd ed.). Allyn & Bacon.

Resnicow, K., Soler, R., & Braithwaite, R. L. (2000). Cultural sensitivity in substance use prevention. *Journal of Community Psychology, 28*, 271–290.

Richard, L., Gauvin, L., & Raine, K. (2011). Ecological models revisited: Their uses and evolution in health promotion over two decades. *Annual Review of Public Health, 32*, 307–326. https://doi.org/10.1146/annualrev-publhealth-031210-101141

Robillard, A., Padi, A., Lewis, K., Julious, C., & Troutman, J. (2017). Advice for prevention from HIV-positive African American women: My story is not just a story. *Culture, Health & Sexuality, 19*(5), 630–642. https://doi.org/10.1080/13691058.2016.1243732

Rutkowski, B. A., Rawson, R. A., & Freeze, T. E. (2012). Editors' introduction: The evidence for integrated care: Substance use disorders, mental health, and primary care: California substance research consortium (SARC) meetings, 2011. *Journal of Psychoactive Drugs, 44*, 281–284.

Ryan, G. W., & Bernard, H. R. (2003). Techniques to identify themes. *Field Methods, 15*(1), 85–109. https://doi.org/10.1177/1525822X02239569

Schwartz, S. J., Weisskirch, R. S., Zamboznga, B. L., Castrillo, L. G., Ham, L. S., Huyuh, Q., & Cano, M. A. (2010). Dimensions of acculturation: Associations with high risk behaviors among college students from immigrant families. *Journal of Counseling Psychology Adolescent Health, 20*, 1–15.

Shiraev, E. B., & Lewy, D. A. (2010). *Cross-cultural psychology: Critical thinking and contemporary applications*. Allyn & Bacon.

Sue, D. W., & Sue, D. (1999). *Counseling the culturally different: Theory and practice* (3rd ed.). Wiley.

Sutton, C. E. T., & Broken Nose, M. A. (2005). American Indian families. In M. McGoldrick, J. Giordano, & N. Garcia-Preto (Eds.), *Ethnicity & family therapy* (3rd ed.). Guilford.

Tashakkori, A., & Teddle, C. (2010). *Sage handbook of mixed methods in social and behavioral research* (2nd ed.). Sage.

Terrell, M. D. (1993). Ethnocultural factors and substance abuse towards culturally sensitive treatment models. *Psychology of Adductive Behaviors, 7*, 162–167.

Thobaben, M. (2004). Strategies home health care providers can use to help decrease minority health disparities. *Home Health Care Management & Practice, 17*(1), 56–57. https://doi.org/10.1177/1084822304268166

Triandis, H. C., Malpass, R. Y., & Davidson, A. R. (1973). Psychology and culture. *Annual Review of Psychology, 24*(1), 355–378. https://doi.org/10.1146/annurev.ps.020173.002035

U.S. Census Bureau. (2012). Table 1. Summary of Modified Race and Census 2010 Race Distributions for the United States (US-MR2010-01).

U.S. Census Bureau. (2021). Annual Estimates of the Resident Population by Sex, Race, and Hispanic Origin for the United States: April 1, 2010 to July 1, 2019. Retrieved from https://www.census.gov/data/datasets/time-series/demo/popest/2010s-national-detail.html

Whaley, A. L. (2003). Ethnicity/race, ethics, and epidemiology. *Journal of the National Medical Association, 95*(8), 736–742.

Wingood, G. M., & DiClemente, R. J. (2000). Application of the theory of gender and power to examine HIV-related exposures, risk factors, and effective interventions for women. *Health Education & Behavior, 27*, 539–565.

Zane, N., & Yeh, M. (2002). The use of culturally-based variables in assessment: Studies of loss of face. In K. S. Kurasaki & S. Sue (Eds.), *Asian American mental health: Assessment, methods and theories* (pp. 123–138). Kluwer.

Chapter 5
Multiple Behavior Change as Prevention

James O. Prochaska and Janice M. Prochaska

5.1 Risk Factors

Health risk behaviors like smoking, inactivity, unhealthy diets, alcohol misuse, and ineffectively managed stress significantly contribute to a population's morbidity, disability, mortality, reduced functioning and productivity, and escalating health-care costs. In contrast, accumulating evidence suggests that a healthy lifestyle, including abstinence from smoking, eating five servings of fruits and vegetables each day, adequate physical activity (e.g., moving 10,000 steps a day or doing 150 minutes of moderate exercise a week), 20 minutes of daily stress management, and striving to maintain a body mass index (BMI) of less than 25, increases life expectancy by up to 14 years (Khaw et al., 2008; Pronk et al., 2010; van den Brandt, 2011). However, having a healthy lifestyle of 0 (smoking), 1 (drink per day for women, 2 for men under 65), 5 (fruits and vegetables), 10 (10,000 steps), 20 (at least 20 minutes of mindful breathing, meditation, or other methods for reducing distress, and 25 (<25 BMI) has been an elusive goal for 97% of the population (Reeves & Rafferty, 2005). Why is it so important to do 0, 1, 2, 5, 10, 20, and 25 for one's health?

Those behaviors are fundamental functions of life: breathing, drinking, eating, moving, and feeling. If we breathe toxins, we poison our bodies. If we drink alcohol to toxic levels, we do damage to both our minds and bodies. If we eat toxins, we seriously compromise our general well-being. If we don't move it, move it, move it enough, we don't push enough toxins out of our bodies. And, if we feel distressed, we are likely to smoke more cigarettes, drink more alcohol, eat more unhealthy "comfort foods," and flop on the couch. Distress is also the number one reason why people relapse when they try to change unhealthy behaviors to healthy ones.

J. O. Prochaska (✉) · J. M. Prochaska
Prochaska Change Consultants, Mill Valley, CA, USA

W. O'Donohue, M. Zimmermann (eds.), *Handbook of Evidence-Based Prevention of Behavioral Disorders in Integrated Care*,
https://doi.org/10.1007/978-3-030-83469-2_5

Those fundamental functions of life are so important because they happen day, after day, after day for our whole lives. If the dysfunctional behaviors happen year after year, they build up the risk of producing diseases, disabilities, poor function, and premature death.

To have a significant and sustainable impact on attaining the healthy behaviors of 0, 1, 2, 5, 10, 20, and 25, a model of behavior change is needed to address the needs of the entire populations, not just the minority who are motivated to take immediate action for better health. The transtheoretical model of behavior change (TTM) reframes change from equaling progress through a series of stages. The TTM is integrated around the stages of change which can identify segments of populations in different stages of change (Prochaska & Prochaska, 2016). Then, principles and processes are applied to initiate progress through the stages of change: precontemplation (not ready to take action), contemplation (getting ready), preparation (ready), action (meeting the healthy criteria behavior change), and maintenance (keeping up the healthy criteria behavior change).

5.2 Effective Screening

In order to use the stage approach, a necessary first step is identifying which stage of readiness best classifies your patient for each relevant health behavior. A critical component is clearly operationalizing the target behavior and action criteria. This can be thought of as what one would be doing if they were in action. For example, the action criterion for smoking cessation is no smoking.

In such areas as weight management, there may be multiple behaviors that are important to assess and treat – readiness to do healthy eating and regular exercise. In working with multiple risks, it is often beneficial to prioritize the at-risk behavior that the patient is most ready to change. If someone is in the preparation stage, you can set goals and offer treatment options that will likely help them fairly quickly reach action. Upon making that successful behavior change, they will have a success under their belt and likely will have increased confidence and skills to make additional behavior changes.

There are several options by which stage of change can be assessed in clinical settings. For many health areas, reliable and valid assessment tools have been developed and can be found in published articles or online and available in the public domain. Other times, measures can be licensed through the companies that developed them and then incorporated within your patient portal or electronic medical software. A list of companies with health risk assessments certified by the National Committee for Quality Assurance (NCQA) can be found at http://www.ncqa.org. Using certified assessment tools offers the most reliable and consistent way to monitor and report patient health behaviors and risks longitudinally. For those without the resources to implement standardized protocols, providers can administer staging questions during their patient interview. In doing so, it is important to identify a specific and well-defined behavior and to ask their intention to do the behavior according to this sample:

Do you intend to {insert action criteria}?
No. I don't intend to do so in the next 6 months (precontemplation).
Yes. I intend to do so in the next 6 months (contemplation).
Yes. I intend to do so in the next 30 days (preparation).
Yes. I have been doing so for less than 6 months (action).
Yes. I have been doing so for more than 6 months (maintenance).

5.3 Using the Transtheoretical Model to Help Patients

The transtheoretical model of behavior change (TTM), also known as the stages of change model, is a comprehensive model that integrates constructs from several different theories and approaches to change (hence the name "transtheoretical") to explain and predict how and when individuals stop high-risk behaviors or adopt healthy ones (Prochaska & Norcross, 2018). The TTM construes the change process into distinct stages of intention and provides approaches to help people move forward through the stages (Prochaska & DiClemente, 1983). Decades of research on a wide variety of health behaviors have found that certain principles and processes of change work best at each stage to reduce resistance, facilitate engagement and progress, and prevent relapse (Prochaska, 1994). These include decisional balance, self-efficacy, and processes of change.

Stage of change is the TTM's central organizing construct. Longitudinal studies of change have found that people move through a series of stages when modifying behavior on their own or with the help of formal interventions (DiClemente & Prochaska, 1982; Prochaska & DiClemente, 1983). Understanding the stages of change allows one to appreciate change as a dynamic process and helps one to learn the variability in patients' responses to the uptake of health behavior interventions. The stage construct implies progress occurring over time. Traditionally, behavior change was often construed as an event, such as quitting smoking, drinking, or overeating, but the TTM recognizes change as a process that unfolds over time and involves progress through the series of stages (see Fig. 5.1).

5.3.1 Precontemplation

Patients in the precontemplation stage are not intending to take action in the foreseeable future, usually measured as the next 6 months. Being uninformed or underinformed about the consequences of one's behavior may cause a person to be in precontemplation. Multiple, unsuccessful attempts at change can lead to demoralization about one's ability to change. Both the uninformed and underinformed tend

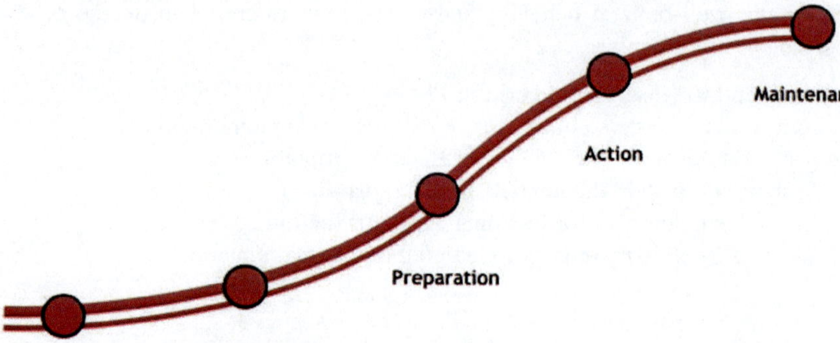

Fig. 5.1 The stages of change. © Pro-Change Behavior Systems, Inc. Reprinted with permission

to avoid reading, talking, or thinking about their high-risk behaviors. They are often characterized in other theories as resistant, unmotivated, or not ready for interventions. The fact is action-oriented programs are not ready for such individuals and are not developed to meet their needs. Messages like "Wherever you are at, we can work with that"™ need to be delivered, and interventions meeting that need to be implemented.

Contemplation Contemplation is the stage in which patients are intending to change in the next 6 months. They are more aware of the pros of changing but are also acutely aware of the cons. In a meta-analysis across 48 health risk behaviors (Hall & Rossi, 2008), the pros and cons of changing were equal for people in contemplation. This weighting between the costs and benefits of changing can produce profound ambivalence that can cause people to remain in this stage for long periods of time. This phenomenon is often characterized as chronic contemplation or behavioral procrastination. Individuals in contemplation also are not ready for traditional action-oriented programs that expect participants to act immediately.

5.3.2 *Preparation*

Preparation is the stage in which patients are intending to take action in the immediate future, usually measured as the next month. Typically, they have already taken some significant steps toward the healthier behavior in the past year. These individuals have a plan of action, such as joining an exercise class, consulting a counselor, talking to their physician, buying a self-help book, or relying on a self-change approach. These are the people who can be recruited for action-oriented programs, such as nicotine replacement therapies or Weight Watchers.

5.3.3 Action

Action is the stage in which patients have made specific overt modifications in their lifestyles within the past 6 months. Since action is observable, the overall process of behavior change often has been equated with action. But in the TTM, action is only one of the stages. Not all modifications of behavior count as action in this model. In most applications, people have to attain a criterion that scientists and professionals agree is sufficient to reduce the risk of disease. For example, reduction in the number of cigarettes and switching to low-tar and low-nicotine cigarettes were formerly considered acceptable actions for smoking. Now, the consensus is clear – only total abstinence counts, as those other changes do not necessarily lead to quitting and do not remove the risks associated with smoking to zero.

5.3.4 Maintenance

Maintenance is the stage in which people have made specific, overt modifications in their lifestyles for at least 6 months. They are working to prevent relapse, but they do not apply change processes as frequently as do people in action. They are less tempted to relapse and grow increasingly more confident (have greater self-efficacy) that they can continue their changes. Based on self-efficacy and temptation data, researchers have estimated that maintenance lasts from 6 months to about 5 years. Fitbit is a good example of a tool to help someone stay in maintenance.

5.3.5 Termination

Termination is the stage in which people are not tempted; they have 100% self-efficacy. Whether depressed, anxious, bored, lonely, angry, or stressed, individuals in this stage are sure they will not return to unhealthy habits as a way of coping. It is as if the habit was never acquired in the first place or their new behavior has become an automatic healthy habit. Examples include people who have developed automatic seatbelt use or who automatically take their medications at the same time and place each day. In a study of former smokers and alcoholics, researchers found that less than 20% of each group had reached the criteria of zero temptation and total self-efficacy (Snow et al., 1992). The criterion of 100% self-efficacy may be too strict, or it may be that this stage is an ideal goal for population health efforts. In other areas, like exercise, consistent condom use, and weight control, the realistic goal for many people may be a lifetime of maintenance.

5.4 Decisional Balance

The process of reflection and weighing of the pros and cons of changing is decisional balance. Sound decision-making requires the consideration of the potential gains (pros) and losses (cons) associated with a behavior's consequences. For example, there are more than 65 scientifically established benefits of regular physical activity. One could be encouraged to make a list to see how many can be identified. They can then take a list of 65+ pros, like from our book, *Changing to Thrive*, and see how many of the pros of changing are important to them. One can also list the cons. The more the list of pros outweighs the cons, the better prepared one will be to take effective action.

5.5 Self-Efficacy

With TTM-based interventions, self-efficacy is operationalized as confidence to make and sustain changes. Confidence is low in the precontemplation stage and increases across the stages (DiClemente et al., 1991). Given the importance of self-efficacy, it needs to be raised early by assisting patients in setting and achieving small goals that will build their confidence for taking on increasingly difficult challenges. If, for example, someone is not exercising at all but is intending to do so in the next 6 months, it would be helpful to have them set a reasonable and achievable goal to begin exercising slowly (e.g., 10 minutes, three times a week) and increase the frequency and intensity once that goal has been mastered.

5.6 Temptation

Temptation reflects the intensity of urges to engage in a specific unhealthy habit while in the midst of difficult situations. Typically, three factors reflect the most common types of tempting situations: emotional distress, positive social situations, and craving. People could ask themselves how they will cope with emotional distress (without relying on a cigarette or comfort foods) to help them cope more effectively and thereby build their confidence or self-efficacy.

5.7 Processes of Change

Table 5.1 illustrates the principles and processes of change by stage. Processes of change are the experiential and behavioral activities that people use to progress through the stages. They provide important guides for intervention programs,

Table 5.1 Integration of the stages, principles, and processes of change

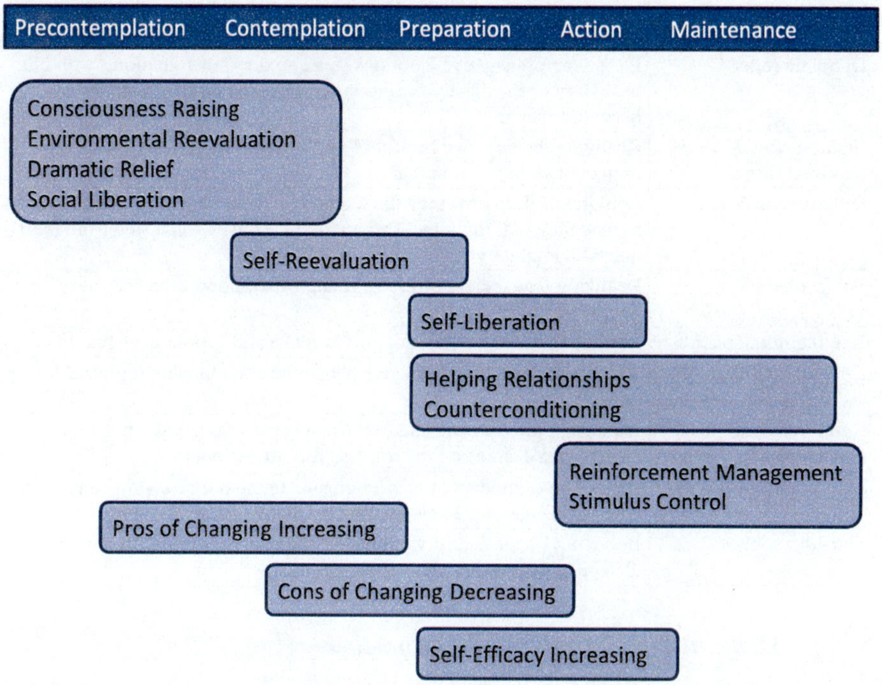

serving as activities that are applied to move from stage to stage. Ten processes have received the most scientific support to date. They are described in Table 5.2 and below.

5.7.1 Consciousness Raising (Get the Facts)

Consciousness raising involves increased awareness about the causes, consequences, and cures for a particular problem behavior. Interventions that can increase awareness include feedback, interpretations, bibliotherapy (i.e., using self-help books or manuals), and media campaigns. Sedentary people, for example, may not be aware that their inactivity can have the same risk as smoking a pack of cigarettes a day.

Table 5.2 Processes of change

Consciousness-raising	Learning new facts, ideas, and tips that support the healthy behavior change
Dramatic relief	Experiencing negative emotions (fear, anxiety) that go along with old behaviors or the positive emotions (inspirations) that go along with behavior change
Environmental reevaluation	Realizing the negative impact of one's behavior – and the positive impact of change – on others
Self-reevaluation	Looking back to how they think and feel about themselves and forward to how they will think and feel about themselves when free from their unhealthy habit
Social liberation	Realizing that social norms are changing to support the healthy behavior
Helping relationships	Seeking and using social support to make and sustain changes
Counterconditioning	Substituting healthy alternative behaviors and thoughts for unhealthy ones
Reinforcement management	Increasing the intrinsic and extrinsic rewards for healthy behavior change and decreasing the rewards for old behaviors
Stimulus control	Removing reminders or cues to engage in the old behaviors, and using cues to engage in the new healthy behavior
Self-liberation	Believing in one's ability to change and making a commitment to change based on that belief

5.7.2 *Dramatic Relief (Pay Attention to Feelings)*

Dramatic relief initially produces increased emotional experiences followed by reduced affect or anticipated relief, if appropriate action is taken. Personal testimonies, social networks, and health risk feedback delivered by text messages are examples of techniques that can move people emotionally.

5.7.3 *Self-Reevaluation (Create a New Self-Image)*

Self-reevaluation combines both cognitive and affective assessments of one's self-image with and without a particular unhealthy habit, such as one's image as a couch potato versus an active person. Values clarification, identifying healthy role models, and imagery are techniques that can help people apply self-reevaluation. One might ask "Imagine if you were free from smoking – How would you feel about yourself?"

5.7.4 Environmental Reevaluation (Notice Your Effect on Others)

Environmental reevaluation combines both affective and cognitive assessments of how the presence or absence of a personal habit affects one's social environment, such as the effect of smoking on others. It can also include the awareness that one can serve as a positive or negative role model for others. Empathy training and documentaries can lead to such assessments.

5.7.5 Social Liberation (Notice Social Trends)

Social liberation involves realizing that social norms are changing to support the healthy behavior. Examples include recognizing how few places they can smoke, salad bars at restaurants, and walking paths.

5.7.6 Self-Liberation (Make a Commitment)

Self-liberation is both the belief that one can change and the commitment as well as re-commitment to act on that belief. New Year's resolutions, public testimonies, and a contract are ways of enhancing what the public calls willpower. The intervention could state "Telling others about my commitment to take action can strengthen my willpower. Who am I going to tell?" Today with social networks, individuals can make commitments to many of their digital friends.

5.7.7 Counterconditioning (Use Substitutes)

Counterconditioning requires learning healthy behaviors as substitutes for problem behaviors. Examples of counterconditioning include mindful breathing as a health substitution for breathing smoke or walking as a healthier alternative than "comfort foods" as a way to cope with distress.

5.7.8 Stimulus Control (Manage Your Environment)

Stimulus control removes cues for unhealthy habits and adds prompts for healthier alternatives. Examples are removing all the ashtrays from the house and car or removing high-fat foods that are tempting cues for unhealthy eating.

5.7.9 Reinforcement Management (Use Rewards)

Reinforcement management provides positive consequences for taking steps in a positive direction. While contingency management can include the use of punishment, it was found that self-changers rely on reward much more than punishment. Reinforcements are emphasized since a philosophy of the stage model is to work in harmony with how people change naturally. People expect to be reinforced by others more frequently than is actually the case, so they should be encouraged to reinforce themselves through self-statements like "Nice going – you handled that temptation." They also can treat themselves at milestones as a reinforcement to increase the probability that healthy responses will be repeated.

5.7.10 Helping Relationships (Get Support)

Helping relationships combine caring, trust, openness, and acceptance, as well as support for healthy behavior change. Guiding people on how to get social support through support groups, social media, and buddy systems can be sources of social support.

5.8 Using Stage-Matched Communications

Once action criteria are identified and one understands the patient's intention to do the action criteria, the next step is to use that knowledge to target the intervention strategy. Below are guidelines for considering the patient's stage and interventions by stage of change.

Precontemplation	
Patient	Interventions
• Not ready to change/not intending to take action	• Engage them in a TTM change process, like the pros of changing
• May experience change as coerced	• Use motivational interviewing techniques (e.g., open-ended questions, reflection, evoking change talk, rolling with resistance)
• Might feel demoralized from multiple relapses	• Increase awareness of how to progress, e.g., reduces defenses
• May respond with denial, reactance, or resistance	• Move them emotionally based on current and future consequences of the unhealthy behavior
• Under or unaware of problem	• Facilitate movement to contemplation
• Identifies many cons to changing	• Suggest less intense treatment options

(continued)

Precontemplation	
Patient	Interventions
• Under-recognizes benefits of changing	• Discuss benefits of changing
Contemplation	
Patient	Interventions
• Aware that problem exists	• Resolve ambivalence so pros outweigh the cons
• Expresses some interest in changing eventually	• Help problem solve around significant cons of changing perceived by patient
• Recognizes benefits of changing	• Increase benefits to changing (the longer the list the better)
• Marked by ambivalence	• Encourage reflection of how self-image would improve if behavior changed
• Lacks commitment to change	• Encourage progress rather than action
• Lacks confidence to change	• Encourage small steps
• Might feel stuck – not sure how to make progress	
• Acutely aware of the cons or barriers to changing	
Preparation	
Patient	**Interventions**
• Intending to make a change in the next month	• Goal is to encourage, excite, and empower patient
• Preparing to act	• Provide support
• Has taken some small steps	• Create an action plan that includes start date and steps to action
• Recognizes more benefits than cons to changing	• Ensure patient has necessary support systems
• Expresses commitment to change	• Encourage reflection on how self-image will change
• Has increased confidence in ability to change	• Problem-solving barriers to change
• Developing a plan toward meeting action criteria	• Provide examples and inspiration of successful changers
	• Refer to more intense action-oriented treatment options
Action	
Patient	**Interventions**
• Recently made the behavior change	• Support action
• Still actively working (giving time and energy) to sustain the change	• Provide praise and recognition
• May experience strong urge to revert back to old behavior	• Communicate that sustaining action takes effort and commitment
• Identifying difficult times to stay adherent	• Encourage coping skills to handle urges to slip

(continued)

Precontemplation	
Patient	Interventions
• Slips and recycling to earlier stage common	• Ensure their environment and routine support lasting action
	• Assist with strategies to prevent relapse
	• Intense treatment options still appropriate
	• Encourage coping skills to handle urges to slip
Maintenance	
Patient	**Interventions**
• Maintaining the behavior change for at least 6 months	• Understand that change is dynamic and slips are the rule, not the exception
• High confidence	• Consult on challenge of ongoing doing the healthy behavior
• High commitment	• Focus on relapse prevention
• Slips still can happen, but they don't have to be a fall	• Ensure good coping skills for times of distress and ongoing stress management
• Experience fewer temptations to slip back	• Assist with keeping confidence high
• Risk for relapse highest during times of distress	• Create plan for dealing with distress
	• Encourage patients to learn from slips and plan accordingly

5.9 Evidence-Based Prevention

TTM-based approaches result in increased participation and engagement because they appeal to the whole population rather than the minority ready to take action. TTM research across many behaviors and populations have demonstrated repeatedly that only a minority of any at risk group are in preparation (typically 20%) with the majority in precontemplation and contemplation (typically 80%) (Velicer et al., 1995; Wewers et al., 2003). Yet, most behavior change messaging and treatments are action-oriented and assume readiness to participate in action-oriented programs. Such methods engage mostly the 20% or so of people who are ready to take action and misserve the majority of at-risk people who are not prepared to take action. With this information at hand, it isn't surprising that the average participation of health promotion programs is quite modest, with one worksite health promotion review of 59 studies finding a median retention rate of 57% (Soler et al., 2010), while TTM-based programs often achieve greater than 80% participation (Prochaska et al., 2001). TTM approaches engage whole populations because they are perceived as more respectful, relevant, engaging, and appealing, thereby reducing resistance and reactance among early-stage individuals.

TTM-based approaches can accelerate rates of behavior change. While action-oriented programs may do well to help those ready to change, their impact is limited to the small percentage of people who are ready to change. By using a stage approach, one not only increases participation but also the likelihood that individuals will eventually take action. Research demonstrates that helping participants move forward at least one stage of change (such as moving from precontemplation to contemplation) can as much as double the likelihood that they will move to the action stage in the next 6 months. Helping them to move two stages can triple their chances of taking action (Prochaska et al., 2001).

TTM-based approaches are often more efficacious. A large body of literature supports the increased efficacy of stage-matched programs over action-oriented and one-size-fits-all interventions. Meta-analyses conclude that tailoring on TTM constructs produces greater impacts than tailoring on most constructs of other behavior change theories (Krebs et al., 2010; Noar et al., 2007). TTM-based treatments have been found effective across dozens of behaviors and populations (Evers et al., 2006; Johnson et al., 2008; Johnson, Driskel, et al., 2006a; Johnson, Driskell, et al., 2006b; Levesque et al., 2012; Mauriello et al., 2010) and have been found to surpass the average outcomes of other behavior change programs identified as benchmarks by a national task force (Johnson et al., 2013). Recent research demonstrates the additional impact of TTM-based treatment can have overall and specific domains of well-being (Prochaska et al., 2012).

TTM-based approaches impact multiple risks. Several randomized clinical trials of TTM-based interventions have demonstrated the ability to impact multiple risks, even risks that were not specifically treated (Johnson et al., 2014; Johnson & Evers, 2015). This research includes areas such as adherence to anti-hypertension and lipid-lowering medication, weight management, obesity prevention, and prenatal care (Johnson et al., 2008; Johnson, Driskel, et al., 2006a; Johnson, Driskell, et al., 2006b; Mauriello et al., 2010; Mauriello et al., 2016; Velicer et al., 2013). Through this research, the phenomena of coaction have been described as the increased probability that individuals who adopt one health behavior will adopt another health behavior. For example, in a randomized clinical trial of a TTM-tailored weight management intervention for overweight adults, the treatment group demonstrated a 2.5–5.2 increased likelihood of success on a second behavior. The control group demonstrated a 1.2–2.6 increase likelihood of success on a second behavior (Johnson et al., 2014). Given the vast differences in probability of additional behavior change between successful changers in the treatment group compared to control, it can be concluded that this is not a naturally occurring phenomenon. Similar findings from other multiple behavior trials cumulate evidence that coaction occurs more in groups receiving TTM-tailored behavior change treatments. It can be hypothesized that by teaching individuals strategies that support the change process, they then apply those strategies successfully to other areas.

5.10 The Role of Primary Care Physicians and Behavioral Care Provider

Within a practice setting, an important first step is to have the patient assessed for all relevant health behaviors via a health risk assessment (HRA). This can be incorporated within electronic medical software or done in a patient interview with the behavioral care provider (BCP). Depending on the results, the BCP can then intervene with stage-matched communications or prescribe TTM-computerized, tailored interventions online. With multiple behavior change, a combination of personal and online interventions could be beneficial. There is a comprehensive suite of programs available at Pro-Change Behavior Systems, Inc. With the online programs, patients are assessed on their pros and cons, confidence, and processes of change. They then receive feedback on strategies for increasing the pros and decreasing the cons, ideas for coping with temptations, what processes of change to use more, and strategies for taking small steps for progressing to the next stage. Patients are then able to assess a printed report as well as an online personal activity center where they can find activities designed to reinforce their personal report.

Typically, 30 days and 60 days after the first session, patients are prompted to return to complete a follow-up session. Here they are reassessed, given feedback on their progress, and receive an updated report. In addition, patients can receive tailored text messages every 1–3 days depending on their current stage of change.

If a cluster of patients exist with a variety of risk behaviors, a group could be formed and led by the BCP to teach patients the stages of change and help patients support each other as they move through the stages. The primary care physician's role is to reinforce the use of the online and group programs and to check on progress made through the stages of change.

A helpful comparison of moving from traditional patient health to integrated prevention care is shown below:

Patient health	Integrated preventive care
Passive, wait for patient to call	Proactive, reach out to the population
Acute conditions	Prevention of chronic conditions
Action-oriented	Stage-based
Clinic-based	Clinic- or home-based
Clinician-delivered	Clinician- and technology-delivered
Standardized	Tailored
Single target behavior	Multiple target behaviors
Fragmented	Integrated
Specificity, e.g., treat just one behavior	Synergy, e.g., coaction
Reducing risks	Reducing risks and enhancing well-being

5.11 Lessons Learned/Implementation

Hopefully you are more prepared to incorporate a stage approach in your work with multiple behavior change. Recognizing the unique needs of patients in different stages and seeing progress as movement to the next stage can assist in significantly increasing the impact of your interventions.

Those who seek additional guidance can participate in an e-learning module titled "Become an Agent of Change; Applying the TTM of Behavior Change" (details at www.prochange.com\e-learning) or refer to the book *Changing To Thrive: Using The Stages Of Change to Overcome the Top Threats to Your Health and Happiness* (2016).

There are many benefits to integrating a TTM stage approach, including the following:

- Prepares you to work with entire populations of patients wherever they are in the stages of change
- Helps you reduce resistance among your patients
- Allows you to see and appreciate how your patients are making progress in stages
- Enables you to set stage-matched goals with patients
- Gets you to offer and prescribe behavior change programs that are stage-appropriate
- Teaches you the principles and processes of change that are applicable across all health behaviors
- Shows you an approach that is successful at increasing engagement, increasing healthy behaviors, reducing multiple risks, enhancing multiple domains of well-being, and productivity

Finally, how ready are you to integrate a stage approach in your work?

1. I don't intend to integrate a stage approach in my work in the next 6 months (precontemplation).
2. I intend to integrate a stage approach in my work in the next 6 months (contemplation).
3. I intend to integrate a stage approach in my work in the next month (preparation).
4. I have been integrating a stage approach in my work for less than 6 months (action).
5. I have been integrating a stage approach in my work for more than 6 months (maintenance).

Below are some ideas to guide next steps:

1. If you are in precontemplation, look for more information (e.g., *Changing to Thrive*) in using a stage approach, and consider how your work, your patient interactions, and your practice might benefit by adopting a stage approach.
2. If you are in contemplation, make a list of the pros and cons of TTM, and learn more about the pros of using a stage approach by talking with others who use it

and seeking additional training in the approach at www.prochage.com/elearning. Identify what barriers might be in your way and consider ways to overcome them. Feel inspired by how the stage approach has helped so many others to more successfully engage patients.

3. If you are in preparation, make a commitment to begin using a stage approach, and share that commitment with others. Build your confidence by role-playing or practicing the approach with patients. Ask co-workers to support and assist your efforts, and notice the benefit.

4 or 5. If you are in action or maintenance, keep this chapter and other training materials visible to make it easy to use a stage approach. Appreciate the benefits TTM offers you and your patients. Boost your confidence by using the approach even with resistant patients. And, like your patients, you may have a slip, but you don't have to fall all the way back to your old practice.

References

DiClemente, C. C., & Prochaska, J. O. (1982). Self-change and therapy change of smoking behavior: A comparison of processes of change of cessation and maintenance. *Addictive Behaviors, 7*, 133–142.

DiClemente, C. C., Prochaska, J. O., Fairhurst, S., Velicer, W. F., Velasquez, M., & Rossi, J. S. (1991). The process of smoking cessation: An analysis of precontemplation, contemplation and preparation stages of change. *Journal of Consulting and Clinical Psychology, 59*, 259–304.

Evers, K. E., Prochaska, J. O., Johnson, J. L., Mauriello, L. M., Padula, J. A., & Prochaska, J. M. (2006). A randomized clinical trial of a population- and transtheoretical model-based stress-management intervention. *Health Psychology, 25*, 521–529.

Hall, J. S., & Rossi, J. S. (2008). Meta-analytic examination of the strong and weak principles across 48 health behaviors. *Preventive Medicine, 46*, 266–274.

Johnson, S., & Evers, K. (2015). Advances in multiple behavior change. *The Art of Health Promotion-American Journal of Health Promotion, 29*(4), TAHP-6–TAHP-8.

Johnson, S., Driskel, N., Johnson, J., Prochaska, J., Zwick, W., Prochaska, J., & Bourne, L. (2006a). Transtheoretical model intervention for adherence to lipid-lowering drugs. *Disease Management, 9*, 102–114.

Johnson, S. S., Driskell, M. M., Johnson, J., Prochaska, J. M., Zwick, W., & Prochaska, J. O. (2006b). Efficacy of a transtheoretical model-based expert system for antihypertensive adherence. *Disease Management, 9*(5), 291–301.

Johnson, S. S., Paiva, A. L., Cummins, C. O., Johnson, J. L., Dyment, S. J., Wright, J. A., Prochaska, J. O., Prochaska, J. M., & Sherman, K. (2008). Transtheoretical model-based multiple behavior intervention for weight management: Effectiveness on a population basis. *Preventive Medicine, 46*(3), 238–246. https://doi.org/10.1016/j.ypmed.2007.09.010

Johnson, J. L., Prochaska, J. O., Paiva, A. L., Fernandez, A. C., DeWees, S. L., & Prochaska, J. M. (2013). Advancing bodies of evidence for population-based health promotion programs: Randomized controlled trials and case studies. *Population Health Management, 16*(6), 373–380. https://doi.org/10.1089/pop.2012.0094

Johnson, S. S., Paiva, A. L., Mauriello, L., Prochaska, J. O., Redding, C., & Velicer, W. F. (2014). Coaction in multiple behavior change interventions: Consistency across multiple studies on weight management and obesity prevention. *Health Psychology, 13*, 475–480.

Khaw, K. T., Wareham, N., Bingham, S., Welch, A., Luben, R., & Day, N. (2008). Combined impact of health behaviours and mortality in men and women: The EPIC-Norfolk prospective population study. *PLoS Medicine, 5*(1), e12.

Krebs, P., Prochaska, J. O., & Rossi, J. S. (2010). A meta-analysis of computer-tailored interventions for health behavior change. *Preventive Medicine, 51*, 214–221.

Levesque, D. A., Ciavatta, M. M., Castle, P. H., Prochaska, J. M., & Prochaska, J. O. (2012). Evaluation of a stage based computer tailored adjunct to usual care for domestic violence offenders. *Psycholoy of Violence, 2*(4), 368–384. https://doi.org/10.1037/a0027501

Mauriello, L. M., Ciavatta, M. M., Paiva, A. L., Sherman, K. J., Castle, P. H., Johnson, J. L., & Prochaska, J. M. (2010). Results of a multi-media multiple behavior obesity prevention program for adolescents. *Preventive Medicine, 51*(6), 451–456. https://doi.org/10.1016/j.ypmed.2010.08.004

Mauriello, L. M., Van Marter, D. F., Umanzor, C. D., Castle, P. H., & de Aguiar, E. L. (2016). Using mHealth to deliver behavior change interventions within prenatal Care at Community Health Centers. *American Journal of Health Promotion, 30*(7), 554–562. https://doi.org/10.4278/ajhp.140530-QUAN-248

Noar, S., Benac, C., & Harris, M. (2007). Does tailoring matter? Meta-analytic review of tailored print health behavior change interventions. *Psychological Bulletin, 133*, 673–693.

Prochaska, J. O. (1994). Strong and weak principles for progressing from precontemplation to action on the basis of twelve problem behaviors. *Health Psychology, 13*(1), 47–51. https://doi.org/10.1037/0278-6133.13.1.47

Prochaska, J. O., & DiClemente, C. C. (1983). Stages and processes of self-change of smoking: Toward an integrative model of change. *Journal of Consulting and Clinical Psychology, 51*, 390–395.

Prochaska, J. O., & Prochaska, J. M. (2016). *Changing to thrive*. Hazeldon.

Prochaska, J. O. & Norcross, J. (2018). Systems of psychotherapy: A transtheoretical analysis (9th edition). London: Oxford University Press. ISBN-13: 978-1285176024.

Prochaska, J. O., Velicer, W. F., Fava, J. L., Rossi, J. S., & Tsoh, J. Y. (2001). Evaluating a population-based recruitment approach and a stage-based expert system intervention for smoking cessation. *Addictive Behaviors, 26*, 583–602.

Prochaska, J. O., Evers, K. E., Castle, P. H., Johnson, J. L., Prochaska, J. M., Rula, E. Y., Coberley, C., & Pope, J. E. (2012). Enhancing multiple domains of Well-being by decreasing multiple health risk behaviors: A randomized clinical trial. *Population Health Management, 15*, 1–11. © Mary Ann Liebert, Inc.

Pronk, N. P., Lowry, M., Kottke, T. E., Austin, E., Gallagher, J., & Katz, A. (2010). The association between optimal lifestyle adherence and short-term incidence of chronic conditions among employees. *Population Health Management, 13*(6), 289–295. https://doi.org/10.1089/pop.2009.0075

Reeves, M. J., & Rafferty, A. P. (2005). Healthy lifestyle characteristics among adults in the United States, 2000. *Archives of Internal Medicine, 165*(8), 854–857. https://doi.org/10.1001/archinte.165.8.854

Snow, M. G., Prochaska, J. O., & Rossi, J. S. (1992). Stages of change for smoking cessation among former problem drinkers: A cross-sectional analysis. *Journal of Substance Abuse, 4*(2), 107–116. https://doi.org/10.1016/0899-3289(92)90011-l

Soler, R. E., Leeks, K. D., Razi, S., Hopkins, D. P., Griffith, M., Aten, A., Chattopadhyay, S. K., Smith, S. C., Habarta, N., Goetzel, R. Z., Pronk, N. P., Richling, D. E., Bauer, D. R., Buchanan, L. R., Florence, C. S., Koonin, L., MacLean, D., Rosenthal, A., Matson Koffman, D., … Task Force on Community Preventive Services. (2010). A systematic review of selected interventions for worksite health promotion. The assessment of health risks with feedback. *American Journal of Preventive Medicine, 38*(2 Suppl), S237–S262. https://doi.org/10.1016/j.amepre.2009.10.030

van den Brandt, P. A. (2011). The impact of a Mediterranean diet and healthy lifestyle on premature mortality in men and women. *The American Journal of Clinical Nutrition, 94*(3), 913–920. https://doi.org/10.3945/ajcn.110.008250

Velicer, W. F., Fava, J. L., Prochaska, J. O., Abrams, D. B., Emmons, K. M. & Pierce, J. P. (1995). Distribution of smokers by stage in three representative samples. *Preventive Medicine, 24*, 401–411. PMID: 7479632.

Velicer, W. F., Redding, C. A., Paiva, A. L., Mauriello, L. M., Blissmer, B., Oatley, K., Meier, K. S., Babbin, S. F., McGee, H., Prochaska, J. O., Burditt, C., & Fernandez, A. C. (2013). Multiple behavior interventions to prevent substance abuse and increase energy balance behaviors in middle school students. *Translational Behavioral Medicine: Practice, Policy and Research, 3*(1), 82–93. https://doi.org/10.1007/S13142-013-0197-0

Wewers, M. E., Stillman, F. A., Hartman, A. M., & Shopland, D. R. (2003). Distribution of daily smokers by stage of change: Current population survey results. *Preventive Medicine, 36*(6), 710–720. https://doi.org/10.1016/s0091-7435(03)00044-6

Chapter 6
Depression

L. Sophia Rintell, Katherine R. Buchholz, and Tracy R. G. Gladstone

6.1 Definition/Diagnostic Criteria

Depression is a common and serious mental health disorder that affects mood, thoughts, and behaviors. Depressive disorders are characterized by sadness, loss of interest or pleasure, disruptions to appetite or sleep, low energy, poor concentration, and low self-worth. Symptoms of depression can impact an individual's functioning in daily life, relationships, and work. The two most common forms of depressive disorders are major depressive disorder (MDD) and persistent depressive disorder (dysthymia). MDD is comprised of major depressive episodes that are defined by persistent depressive symptoms and functional impairment over at least 2 weeks. These episodes can be categorized as mild, moderate, or severe based on the symptom profile and level of functional impairment. Persistent depressive disorder is a chronic form of mild depression, involving ongoing depressive symptoms over at least 2 years, which may include episodes of major depression along with periods of less-severe symptoms (American Psychiatric Association, 2013). The criteria for diagnosis of MDD, as defined by the *Diagnostic and Statistical Manual of Mental Disorders, 5th Edition (DSM-5)*, include the presence of five or more of nine specific symptoms (listed below), one of which is either depressed mood or loss of interest or pleasure, most of the time during a 2-week period:

1. Depressed mood most of the day, nearly every day
2. Markedly diminished interest or pleasure in all, or almost all, activities most of the day, nearly every day

L. S. Rintell · K. R. Buchholz · T. R. G. Gladstone (✉)
The Wellesley Centers for Women, Wellesley, MA, USA
e-mail: tgladsto@wellesley.edu

W. O'Donohue, M. Zimmermann (eds.), *Handbook of Evidence-Based Prevention of Behavioral Disorders in Integrated Care*,
https://doi.org/10.1007/978-3-030-83469-2_6

3. Significant weight loss when not dieting, weight gain, or decrease or increase in appetite nearly every day
4. Insomnia or hypersomnia nearly every day
5. A slowing down of thought and a reduction of physical movement or increased restlessness, observable by others
6. Fatigue or loss of energy nearly every day
7. Feelings of worthlessness or excessive or inappropriate guilt nearly every day
8. Diminished ability to think or concentrate or indecisiveness nearly every day
9. Recurrent thoughts of death, recurrent suicidal ideation without a specific plan, or a suicide attempt or a specific plan for committing suicide

These symptoms must cause the individual clinically significant distress or impairment in social, occupational, or other important areas of functioning. The symptoms must not be a result of substance use or another medical condition (American Psychiatric Association, 2013).

The presentation of depression in children and adolescents is similar to that of adults, with differences that stem from children's developmental stages (Birmaher et al., 1996). For example, irritability, low frustration tolerance, somatic complaints, withdrawal, and vegetative symptoms (changes in appetite, weight, energy, and insomnia) are more common in adolescents with MDD than adults with MDD. Loss of interest (anhedonia), concentration problems, delusions, and suicide attempts are more common in adults with MDD (Birmaher et al., 2007; Mullen, 2018; Rice et al., 2019). Similarly, characteristic symptoms of depression can look different for women and men. Women with depression are more likely to report atypical symptoms, somatic complaints, and comorbid anxiety symptoms (Parker & Brotchie, 2010), while men with depression more often experience acts of aggression, anger, substance use, and risky behavior (Martin et al., 2013).

The etiology of depression is complex, and it is likely caused by a combination of psychological, social, behavioral, and biological factors. Depression can be triggered by adverse events, physical illness, loss, or other stressors, or it can occur without a specific antecedent. If triggered by a specific event, the symptoms of depression and their impairment are greater than would be expected from a typical stress response. MDD often occurs alongside other serious physical and mental illnesses. In fact, risk of depression is elevated for people with one or more chronic disease (Katon, 2011; Moussavi et al., 2007). Likewise, MDD increases the risk of several physical illnesses, including diabetes mellitus, heart disease, stroke, hypertension, obesity, cancer, cognitive impairment, and Alzheimer's disease morbidity (Penninx et al., 2013). Comorbid depression can cause negative health consequences, including increased mortality, disability, and poor quality of life, adding to disease burden and healthcare costs (Gold et al., 2020; Kang et al., 2015). A leading cause of disability worldwide, depression is a significant contributor to global economic and disease burden, accounting for 10% of the world's total nonfatal disease burden (Gold et al., 2020; Kessler, 2012; Mnookin, 2016; World Health Organization, 2016).

6.2 Prevalence and Age of Onset

Although its prevalence varies by region, depression is common all over the world and affects over 300 million people globally, equivalent to 4.4% of the world's population (World Health Organization, 2017). The average age of onset for MDD is 15 years old, although symptoms of mental health disorders can emerge a few years before meeting diagnostic criteria (National Research Council and Institute of Medicine, 2009). Rates of depression increase sharply as children transition to adolescence (Fergusson & Horwood, 2001; Mojtabai et al., 2016). Notably, the prevalence of MDD is twice as high in older adolescents as compared to younger adolescents, particularly for severe MDD (Avenevoli et al., 2015). Approximately 18.1% of US adolescents ages 12–17 have experienced major depression in their lifetime (Lu, 2019). The 12-month prevalence of major depressive episodes in adolescents increased from 8.7% in 2005 to 11.3% in 2014 (Mojtabai et al., 2016).

Among adults in the United States, the lifetime prevalence of MDD is 10.6%, and the 12-month prevalence is 10.4% (Hasin et al., 2018). In 2017 alone, 17.3 million adults in the United States were estimated to have had at least one major depressive episode, which represents 7.1% of the country's adult population. The prevalence of adults who had a major depressive episode was highest among those ages 18–25 (13.1%) (World Health Organization, 2017). Individuals tend to experience multiple episodes of depression during their lifetime. Among adults in the United States, the average number of lifetime episodes is 3.86 (Hasin et al., 2018). Over half of people who recover from a first major depressive episode will have another episode in their lifetime, and over three quarters of those who have had two episodes will experience a recurrence (Burcusa & Iacono, 2007).

Rates of depression in older patients are thought to be similar to the general adult population, though higher among those living in long-term care institutions. Depression was identified in as many as 50% of nursing home residents in their first year of stay, indicating a possible causal role for institutional stays in the onset of depression (Hoover et al., 2010).

There are no gender differences in the prevalence of depression among children (Girgus & Yang, 2015), although boys report a greater number of depressive symptoms than girls (Twenge & Nolen-Hoeksema, 2002). Beginning in adolescence, the burden of depression falls disproportionately on girls and women; girls have been found to experience a two- to threefold risk of MDD compared to adolescent boys (Avenevoli et al., 2015). Gender differences in prevalence appear after the pubertal stage and may be attributed to a number of social, biological, and psychological factors (Van de Velde et al., 2010; Yoon & Kim, 2018). These differences continue into adulthood when MDD is nearly twice as prevalent in women as it is in men (Seedat et al., 2009; Van de Velde et al., 2010).

Low-income adults have higher rates of 12-month MDD (Hasin et al., 2018). By race, 12-month MDD prevalence is lower in African American, Asian/Pacific Islander, and Hispanic adults than in White adults. Despite greater exposure to social stressors, Black adults in the United States have lower rates of MDD than non-Hispanic Whites (Barnes et al., 2013), although when Black adults do develop depression, it is generally more chronic and more severe (Williams et al., 2007). This pattern, whereby Black adults report equal or lower rates of many mental health disorders, including depression, relative to White adults, has been termed a "black-white mental health paradox." Erving et al. (2019) found that the black-white mental health paradox is consistent across gender and is still present after adjusting for socioeconomic factors (Erving et al., 2019).

6.3 Risk Factors

A risk factor, as defined by Kazdin et al. (1997), is an antecedent condition associated with an increase in the likelihood of an outcome, in this case, diagnosis of depression. Risk factors for depression can be considered specific or nonspecific. Specific risk factors are those that are related to the onset of depression. Nonspecific risk factors increase rates of depression as well as other psychiatric disorders, especially when they co-occur (Muñoz et al., 2012). Prevention efforts must address both specific and nonspecific risk factors. It is important to note that there is an overlap between these categories, which are meant only as conceptual tools. Key risk factors for depression are briefly outlined in this section.

6.3.1 Parental Depression

Having a parent with depression is one of the strongest and best studied risk factors for the development of depression (DiFonte & Gladstone, 2017; England & Sim, 2009; Evans et al., 2005; Goodman et al., 2011). Relative to offspring of nondepressed parents, offspring of parents who are depressed are at three times the risk for developing depressive disorders (Weissman et al., 2006). Children whose parents have depressive symptoms or a depressive disorder have more internalizing disorders (Pettit et al., 2008), show poorer academic performance (Shen et al., 2016), report more negative life events, use fewer positive emotion regulation strategies (Loechner et al., 2020), and report more friendship instability (Evans et al., 2005). Goodman and Gotlib's (2002) integrative model of the transmission of risk from depressed mother to offspring incorporates biological and environmental mechanisms and markers associated with risk. This model proposes that mechanisms of risk transmission overlap and interact with one another.

Familial transmission of depression can be explained in part by genetic effects and heritability. In a longitudinal study of a high-risk sample (i.e., a sample of biological relatives of individuals with MDD), the heritability of MDD was found to be 67%, adjusting for age and gender (Guffanti et al., 2016). These heritability rates contrast with the heritability of depression in community samples, which range from 31% to 42% in studies of twins and adopted children (Sullivan et al., 2000).

Predisposition to depression may be influenced by the interaction of environment and genome, a process known as phenotypic plasticity (Bagot & Meaney, 2010; Hochberg et al., 2011). In other words, an individual inherits genetic makeup from a depressed parent, but depression emerges only with the combination of genetics and certain environmental effects (Beardslee et al., 2011). For example, in a meta-analysis of the relation between the 5-HTT gene variation and stress, Bleys et al. (2018) found that people with one or two copies of the short allele in the 5-HTTLPR are more susceptible to depression when faced with stress. In addition, there is a research base for the effects of hippocampal volume (Rao et al., 2010) and cortical thickness (Bansal et al., 2016) on vulnerability to depression in children of depressed parents. Future research on genetic and biological factors involved in the intergenerational transmission of depression hold much potential (Beardslee et al., 2011).

Parental behaviors also play a significant role in the transmission of parental depression. Deficits in parenting skills may increase risk for children of depressed parents (Foster et al., 2008; Lovejoy et al., 2000; Middleton et al., 2009), particularly when combined with other external stressors, such as low socioeconomic status (Vreeland et al., 2019). Forehand et al. (2012) found that parents with depressive symptoms were more likely to engage in negative parenting practices, and Taraban et al. (2019) reported a positive correlation between overreactive parenting (i.e., anger and irritability when confronted with challenges from their children) and depressive symptoms in both mothers and fathers. Efforts to address the parenting practices of parents with depression through preventive interventions have yielded encouraging results (e.g., Beardslee et al., 2007; Forehand et al., 2012).

6.3.2 Cognitive Risk Factors

Cognitive models of depression are based on the notion that depression is caused not just by events but by the interpretation of those events. Beck's (1967, 1979) original theory on depressive self-schemas, maladaptive assumptions, and negative thoughts has driven research, suggesting that distorted thinking is associated with depressive symptoms and depressive disorders (Dozois & Beck, 2008), from early childhood (Leppert et al., 2019) through adolescence (Pössel & Pittard, 2019), young adulthood (Pearson et al., 2015), and into old age (Meyer et al., 2010). Cognitive risk factors (see Alloy et al., 2017 for a review) include learned helplessness (Abramson et al., 1978), pessimism (Schueller & Seligman, 2008), and ruminative response style (Kuyken et al., 2006; Spasojević & Alloy, 2001; Wisco & Nolen-Hoeksema, 2008).

6.3.3 Gender

Female gender is a known risk factor for depression. As noted earlier in this chapter, adolescent and adult women are at a twofold increase in risk for depression as compared to men (Avenevoli et al., 2015; Seedat et al., 2009; Van de Velde et al., 2010). In a meta-analysis examining gender differences in depression in national samples, Salk et al. (2017) reported that gender differences exist for both depressive symptoms and depressive diagnoses, the magnitude of the gender difference peaks in adolescence but exists across the lifespan, and gender differences in depression are most pronounced in countries with greater gender equity. Gender differences in depression may be attributable to psychosocial factors (i.e., increased likelihood of sexual abuse, higher rate of victimization, role overload, and financial disadvantage), neurochemical factors (i.e., activation of the hypothalamic-pituitary-adrenal axis and elevated cortisol levels), hormonal factors (i.e., gonadal steroid hormones and estrogen fluctuation during premenstrual and postpartum periods), and cognitive styles (i.e., ruminative coping styles) (Grigoriadis & Erlick Robinson, 2007).

6.3.4 Sociodemographic and Environmental Risk Factors

Social factors that are documented to increase rates of depression include income inequality (Patel et al., 2018); abuse and maltreatment (Widom et al., 2007); experienced discrimination of marginalized racial, ethnic, and gender groups (Patil et al., 2018); and stressful life events, such as interpersonal conflict, separation, loss, marital conflict or divorce, exposure to violence, and interpersonal functioning (National Research Council and Institute of Medicine, 2009). Reducing the burdens of environmental factors like poverty, exposure to violence, and maltreatment may help to reduce depressive disorders, particularly in children (National Research Council and Institute of Medicine, 2009). Many of these social and environmental risk factors are not specific to depression and present risk for a variety of other disorders and conditions as well.

There are also protective factors: environmental conditions, characteristics, or events that decrease the likelihood of depression and increase the likelihood of healthy outcomes (National Research Council and Institute of Medicine, 2009). Examples of modifiable protective factors for depression include healthy eating and sleep patterns (Cairns et al., 2014) and social support (Gariepy et al., 2016). Scott, Wallander, and Cameron (2015) review a range of individual (e.g., ethnic identity, self-esteem), family (e.g., parental support, familism), and social community (e.g., extracurricular activities, employment) protective mechanisms that are associated with lower risk for depression in racial/ethnic minority youth. Many depression prevention efforts aim to reduce or mitigate risk factors while building protective factors (National Research Council and Institute of Medicine, 2009).

It is a challenge to researchers who study risk factors to understand whether study findings represent risk factors or symptoms of MDD (Jeon et al., 2017). Though there is ample evidence to show that several risk factors are associated with depression, there is limited evidence proving a causal relationship for some risk factors. More longitudinal research is needed to better address this issue (Hammen, 2018).

The study of risk factors is complex, as many factors interact and contribute a small proportion of risk and patterns of risk vary between individuals. Risk factors must be understood within a developmental framework. Different types of risk factors interact over the course of development, and their occurrence may change over time across the lifespan (Schaakxs et al., 2017). As the onset of depression is most common during adolescence and early adulthood, identifying risk in early life is important to the prevention of depression (National Research Council and Institute of Medicine, 2009). Prevention efforts should be designed to address the multiple risk and protective factors associated with depression (Hoare et al., 2020). Risk profiles give guidance on which groups to target and the type of intervention that needs to be offered or designed for the intended target group. After all, some risk factors can be addressed using psychological interventions, while some require environmental intervention, and yet others cannot be changed, but their adverse effects can be mitigated by improving coping styles. Lastly, there are some risk factors that cannot be manipulated but can help to identify target groups or people in need of intervention (Muñoz et al., 2010).

6.4 Effective Screening

Screening for depression is important in the effort to prevent and treat depression. Evidence supports the benefits of screening for depression in conjunction with providing resources for prevention, treatment, and management of identified cases. The US Preventive Services Task Force (USPSTF) recommends screening for MDD among adolescents (ages 12–18 years), adults (age 18 and older), pregnant and postpartum women, and older adults, in clinical settings with "adequate systems in place to ensure diagnosis, effective treatment, and appropriate follow-up" (Siu, 2016; Siu et al., 2016, p. 381). Additionally, the American Academy of Pediatrics recommends annual universal screening of adolescents and monitoring of adolescents with depression risk factors (Zuckerbrot et al., 2018). The USPSTF suggests screening all adults who have not previously been screened, as well as considering risk factors, life events, and comorbidities to determine if high-risk patients should have additional screenings (Siu et al., 2016). There is little to no evidence of harm or adverse effects of screening for depressive disorders in adolescents, adults, and elderly patients (O'Connor et al., 2009; Siu, 2016).

6.4.1 Adolescents

Adolescent screening can take place in a variety of settings, including primary care and schools (Allison et al., 2014). Researchers have explored the use of paper screens, internet-based screens, and electronic screens that are accessed through a mobile device. There is little research comparing these screening methods to each other, but adolescents rarely refuse screening, although there are obstacles to using each method (Zuckerbrot et al., 2018). Several instruments have been tested in adolescent populations. The Patient Health Questionnaire (PHQ)-2 and PHQ-9 (Richardson, McCauley, et al., 2010; Richardson, Rockhill, et al., 2010) are self-report measures derived from the PRIME-MD interview (Spitzer et al., 1999) that assess for mental disorders. The items address severity of current symptoms over the past 2 weeks. The measures have demonstrated adequate psychometric properties. Evidence suggests the optimal cutoff scores for adolescents fall between 8 and 11 for the PHQ-9 (Allgaier et al., 2012; Richardson, McCauley, et al., 2010) and 2–3 for the PHQ-2 (Allgaier et al., 2012; Richardson, Rockhill, et al., 2010). The PHQ-9 contains one item (item 9) that assesses for suicidal thoughts and behaviors; evidence suggests that an affirmative response to item 9 indicates increased risk of suicide attempt and death (Rossom et al., 2017; Simon et al., 2013). Additionally, the Patient Health Questionnaire for Adolescents (PHQ-A) is an instrument that closely resembles the PHQ-9 and was designed to assess disorders that are likely to be present among adolescents (Johnson et al., 2002). In addition to the PHQ-2 and PHQ-9, the Center for Epidemiologic Studies Depression (CES-D) scale is a short self-report scale designed to measure current depressive symptomatology. It contains 20 items about symptoms that occurred in the past week (Radloff, 1977). The recommended cutoff score for the CES-D is 16, but there is evidence that a cutoff score of 20 yields a more accurate trade-off between sensitivity and specificity (Vilagut et al., 2016). A shortened, 10-item version of the CES-D has also been validated in several populations, including adolescents and older adults (Andresen et al., 1994; Bradley et al., 2010). The Beck Depression Inventory II (BDI-II) is another widely used self-report measure of the severity of depressive symptoms in adolescents and adults. It is designed for individuals 13 years and older, contains 21 items, uses a recall period of 2 weeks, and has strong psychometric properties (Beck et al., 1996; Jackson-Koku, 2016). The BDI-II has been tested and validated for use in adolescent samples (Lee, Lee, et al., 2017; Osman et al., 2008). If using measures with suicide screening questions, clinical teams must be prepared to further assess and provide sustained follow-up care and safety planning.

6.4.2 Adults

The screening measures described for adolescents are also used in adult populations. The Patient Health Questionnaire (PHQ)-2 and PHQ-9 are the most widely used measures for screening adults in primary care (Maurer et al., 2018; Mitchell et al., 2016). For adults, the optimal cutoffs for the PHQ-2 and the PHQ-9 are 2 and 10, respectively (Arroll et al., 2010; Mitchell et al., 2016). The CES-D and BDI-II are also used regularly with adults.

6.4.3 Pregnant and Postpartum Individuals

Screening is important among women who are pregnant and those who have just given birth. Perinatal depression includes major and minor depressive episodes that occur during pregnancy (prenatal depression) and in the first 12 months after pregnancy (postpartum depression). It is one of the most common medical conditions during pregnancy and the postpartum period (American College of Obstetricians and Gynecologists, 2018). The prevalence of postpartum depression has been estimated at 17%, though it often goes undetected and untreated, negatively affecting the well-being of mothers, infants, and family members (Letourneau et al., 2012; Shorey et al., 2018; Soe et al., 2016). The USPSTF and the American College of Obstetricians and Gynecologists recommend screening all postpartum women for depression at least once during the perinatal period, which may be done during postpartum visits (American College of Obstetricians and Gynecologists, 2018; Siu et al., 2016). In addition, the American Academy of Pediatrics recommends that physicians screen mothers for depression during the infant's 1-, 2-, 4-, and 6-month well-child visits (Earls et al., 2019). Women with current depression or anxiety or a history of mood disorders, risk factors, or suicidal thoughts should be screened and closely monitored. Screening pregnant and postpartum women for depression may reduce depressive symptoms for women with depression and may reduce the prevalence of depression within the population (O'Connor, Rossom, Henninger, Groom, & Burda, 2016). The most used screening tools are the Edinburgh Postnatal Depression Scale (Cox et al., 1996), the Postpartum Depression Screening Scale (Beck & Gable, 2000), and the PHQ-9.

6.4.4 Older Adults

Depression screening is important in older adults, as the prevalence of depression is high among elderly and institutionalized adults (Hoover et al., 2010). Identifying depression in older adults can be challenging because depression may manifest in somatic complaints that are common symptoms in older patients and because depression is more likely to be comorbid with other physical diseases (Rodda et al., 2011). Multiple measures exist for use specifically with elderly populations. The Geriatric Depression Scale (GDS), created originally by Yesavage et al. (1982), is the instrument most widely used for depression screening in older adults (O'Connor, Rossom, Henninger, Groom, Burda, Henderson, et al., 2016). Unlike general screening tools, the measure does not assess for somatic symptoms, as they may be attributed to common comorbid physical conditions and the process of aging. The original GDS consists of 30 items, though several briefer versions have been used, most often the GDS-15, which has been shown to be as or more effective than the GDS-30 in identifying cases of depression (Mitchell et al., 2010). The standard cutoff scores for the GDS-30 and GDS-15 are ≥10 and ≥ 5, respectively (Tsoi et al., 2017). The Even Briefer Assessment Scale for Depression (EBAS-DEP) (Allen et al., 1994) contains eight items and has a standard cutoff score of ≥7. Finally, the Cornell Scale for Depression in Dementia (CSDD) (Alexopoulos et al., 1988) is a 19-item measure designed specifically for assessing depression in patients with dementia (Alexopoulos et al., 1988; Tsoi et al., 2017).

6.4.5 Considerations for Screening

Screening measures in primary care are typically used to identify individuals who are currently experiencing MDD but may also be used to identify individuals who are experiencing depressive symptoms. If screening tools are used purposely to identify subsyndromal individuals or to measure depressive symptoms, different sensitivities, specificities, and cutoff points should be considered. The USPSTF recommendations for screening are not focused on this distinction. Several depression prevention intervention trials (Asarnow et al., 2009; Gladstone et al., 2015; Lewandowski et al., 2016) utilize screening measures to purposely screen for depressive symptoms and disorders in order to test preventive interventions or understand patterns in adolescent screening. For example, Van Voorhees et al. (2020) used the PHQ-9 to screen for depressive symptoms as inclusion criteria for participation in a randomized controlled trial of Competent Adulthood Transition with Cognitive-behavioral Humanistic and Interpersonal Training (CATCH-IT), a preventive intervention designed to prevent the onset of major depressive episodes in adolescents with subthreshold depressive symptoms or prior depressive episodes. Similarly, a randomized controlled trial of a group cognitive-behavioral preventive intervention used a score of 20 or more on the CES-D to determine eligibility based on subthreshold depressive symptoms (Beardslee et al., 2013; Garber et al., 2009).

6.5 Review of Evidence: What Is Evidence-Based Prevention?

The Institute of Medicine (IOM) of the United States has published two reports advocating for the development, evaluation, and implementation of preventive interventions for mental, emotional, and behavioral disorders, highlighting major depression as an area with great potential for prevention efforts (Mrazek & Haggerty, 1994; National Research Council and Institute of Medicine, 2009). The earlier, 1994 Institute of Medicine report made an effort to clearly define the word "prevention," noting that progress in the field of prevention had been hampered by an unclear definition and moving away from the practice of using the term "prevention" to describe research and practice in the realm of treatment, because treatment of depression can prevent subsequent episodes and symptoms of the disorder. The 1994 report, in contrast, proposed a clear distinction between treatment and prevention: interventions that take place before the onset of a clinical episode are preventive, and interventions that take place after onset are treatment (Mrazek & Haggerty, 1994, p. 23). This definition was maintained in the 2009 IOM report (National Research Council and Institute of Medicine, 2009).

Ideally, preventive interventions, once administered, would be effective over the life course; current prevention methods, however, have not shown lifetime effects. Just like vaccines, preventive interventions for depression may need to be administered or boosted during multiple developmental stages of life. Muñoz et al. (2012) conceptualize the prevention of depression as delaying onset during key developmental periods when individuals may be more vulnerable to depressive episodes. From a developmental perspective, different preventive approaches may be required for different stages and common life events or transitions.

The best way to test prevention efficacy is through a randomized controlled trial (RCT). Most RCTs test whether incidence of MDD (onset of new clinical episodes) and/or depressive symptoms is reduced in the experimental condition compared to the control. Reduction in symptoms or maintenance of subthreshold symptom level would indicate prevention of major depressive episodes and therefore the prevention of depression. In order to conduct prevention RCTs, it is important to identify the target population, the incidence of depression in that population, and the sample size required to yield significant results. Typically, depression prevention trials require participants to be evaluated with a validated diagnostic measure to ensure they do not meet the criteria for clinical depression at baseline and at later timepoints to determine if participants have onset of MDD during the trial. Significantly lower incidence in the experimental group indicates a preventive effect (Muñoz et al., 2012). Many analyses of the effectiveness of preventive interventions look at the number needed to treat (NNT), which is the number of individuals who must receive the intervention in order to prevent one case of depression, and the incidence rate ratio (IRR), which is the incidence rate of developing depression in experimental participants compared to the incidence rate in control participants (Muñoz et al., 2010).

In the past two decades, hundreds of RCTs aimed at preventing the onset of depressive episodes have been published, along with several systematic reviews of the topic. Bellón et al. (2015) conducted a systematic review of systematic reviews and meta-analyses, accounting for 12 reviews of 156 trials and over 56,000 participants, in which they found a small to medium preventive effect of depression prevention interventions. They conclude that depression is preventable. There are, however, a series of challenges to implementing preventive interventions for depression. Prevention has not been implemented widely, and adherence to prevention programs has been a problem. Populations at highest risk may be the least motivated to participate in prevention programs (Cuijpers et al., 2010). In addition, much of the extant prevention research only presents short-term outcomes for preventive interventions.

6.5.1 Children and Adolescents

Research on the onset of depression suggests that the ideal window for prevention efforts occurs during childhood and adolescence, 2–4 years before the age of highest risk for depression onset (National Research Council and Institute of Medicine, 2009). The presence of depressive symptoms in adolescence is a strong predictor of the development of MDD later in life (Kovacs & Lopez-Duran, 2010). Numerous RCTs have been conducted to test preventive interventions for depression in adolescents. Meta-analytic evidence suggests small positive effects from child and adolescent depression prevention interventions for depressive symptoms post-intervention and depression diagnosis up to 12 months (Hetrick et al., 2016), though there is a need for continuing research in this area. There have been several systematic reviews and meta-analyses that have studied the efficacy (both short and long term) of these programs, moderators of intervention effects, and other important considerations, such as cost-effectiveness, ability to be used widely, and ability to be easily taught. Such reviews have contributed to the growing wealth of knowledge in the field of prevention and have identified factors that influence outcomes of preventive interventions in order to optimize intervention effectiveness.

6.5.1.1 Prevention Type/Target Population

Adolescent depression prevention interventions that target subgroups at higher risk for depression have been found to be more effective than interventions provided to an entire population or community (Hetrick et al., 2016; Horowitz & Garber, 2006).

6.5.1.2 Therapeutic Approach

Preventive interventions for depression in children and adolescents are most often based on cognitive-behavioral and interpersonal approaches (Hetrick et al., 2015), in part due to the success of these types of interventions in the treatment of depression (Kaslow & Thompson, 1998). There is evidence that the content of the intervention, or therapeutic approach, modifies the effect size. Cognitive-behavioral therapy (CBT) can reduce the risk of developing depression, especially when used in targeted populations (Hetrick et al., 2015), and may be more effective than other therapeutic approaches for reducing depressive symptoms in children and adolescents (Dray et al., 2017). Interpersonal psychotherapy (IPT) has also shown promise in preventing depression (Hetrick et al., 2015).

6.5.1.3 Depressive Symptoms

Conejo-Cerón et al. (2020) reported mixed results for the effect of baseline depressive symptoms on intervention outcome for adolescents. Several intervention trials have found that elevated baseline symptoms of depression led to better outcomes (Brière et al., 2014; Gladstone et al., 2018; Horowitz et al., 2007; Müller et al., 2015). A handful of studies documented no moderating effects of baseline depressive symptomatology (Brent et al., 2015; Duong et al., 2016; Garber et al., 2009; Gau et al., 2012).

6.5.1.4 Personnel Delivering the Intervention

There is some data showing that intervention trials using professional interventionists or mental health professionals have favorable effects, relative to interventions delivered by other kinds of providers or teachers (Stice et al., 2009; Wahl et al., 2014).

6.5.1.5 Intervention Setting

The setting in which the intervention is delivered is important to consider, though there has been little comparison between settings for delivery of preventive interventions for children and adolescents. There is, however, meta-analytic evidence supporting prevention effects in school-based interventions (Calear & Christensen, 2010b; Feiss et al., 2019; Werner-Seidler et al., 2017) as well as trials reporting preventive effects in primary care settings (Gillham et al., 2006; Saulsberry et al., 2013).

6.5.1.6 Age

Several meta-analyses of child and adolescent depression prevention interventions report that age moderates the effect size of adolescent prevention programs. Specifically, samples with older adolescents saw greater effect sizes (Feiss et al., 2019; Horowitz & Garber, 2006; Stice et al., 2009). Notably, a systematic review by Conejo-Cerón et al. (2020) found inconsistent evidence for age as a moderator of intervention effects.

6.5.1.7 Gender

Evidence indicates that gender can moderate outcomes of depression prevention trials. Stice et al. (2009) found that samples with more females produced larger effect sizes in depressive symptoms and risk reduction. Horowitz and Garber (2006) also found in a meta-analysis including college students that studies with more female participants had greater effect sizes.

6.5.1.8 Race

Race has also been found to moderate depression prevention programs (Conejo-Cerón et al., 2020; Feiss et al., 2019; Stice et al., 2009). Understanding how factors related to social demographics moderate program effectiveness is important to ensuring equity and inclusion in the future of prevention research. For example, culturally sensitive practices like groups made up of same-race participants or same-race therapists are beneficial to the experience and outcomes of participants who belong to minority groups (Chang & Yoon, 2011; Griner & Smith, 2006; Planey et al., 2019).

Other noteworthy moderators that may increase efficacy of youth preventive interventions include lower dose or shorter duration, use of homework assignments (Stice et al., 2009), lower use of substances, and lack of parental depressive symptoms (Conejo-Cerón et al., 2020).

6.5.2 Adults

Although several meta-analyses focus specifically on preventive interventions for children and adolescents, there has been less research on the prevention of adult depression. The focus on child and adolescent depression may be due to the fact that onset of depression and depressive symptoms typically occurs during adolescence (National Research Council and Institute of Medicine, 2009). There is evidence, however, that psychological and psychoeducational depression prevention interventions can have small to moderate effect sizes in preventing adult depression as well (Conejo-Cerón et al., 2017; Cuijpers et al., 2008; van Zoonen et al., 2014).

6.5.2.1 Prevention Type/Target Population

In a meta-analytic review of depression prevention interventions for adults, Cuijpers et al. (2008) found no differences between target populations or intervention type, and van Zoonen et al. (2014) reported no difference between prevention types (selective, indicated, or universal), although their analysis included only two universal prevention trials.

6.5.2.2 Therapeutic Approach

In a meta-analytic review of depression prevention trials, van Zoonen et al. (2014) found that data on the number needed to treat (NNT) did show differences between CBT (NNT = 71), IPT (NNT = 7), and other intervention approaches (NNT = 12). Cuijpers et al. (2008) also found subgroup differences indicating that interventions using IPT were more effective than those using CBT but reported these findings cautiously, given the small number of IPT interventions examined.

6.5.2.3 Depressive Symptoms

A systematic review conducted by Conejo-Cerón et al. (2020) found some evidence for moderating the effects of baseline depressive symptomatology on intervention effects in adults. Specifically, Allart and colleagues (2007) reported that lower levels of depressive symptoms at baseline were associated with fewer symptoms post-intervention, and other trials (Barrera et al., 2015; Lara et al., 2010; Seligman et al., 1999) revealed that elevated baseline depressive symptoms were associated with a greater reduction of symptoms post-intervention. Several studies reported no moderating effects of baseline depressive symptoms.

6.5.2.4 Intervention Setting

There is evidence to support effective prevention interventions for adults in primary care settings (Conejo-Cerón et al., 2017; Willemse et al., 2004). There has been some research suggesting small positive effects of universal depression prevention interventions in workplace settings, but additional research in this area is necessary (Bellón et al., 2019; Tan et al., 2014).

6.5.2.5 Age

The evidence for age effects of adult prevention trials is inconsistent. While age was not found to moderate intervention effects in a meta-analysis by van Zoonen et al. (2014), Conejo-Cerón et al. (2020) reported that lower age was found to be associated with greater intervention effect.

6.5.2.6 Gender and Race

There is little to no evidence to support gender and race differences in the effectiveness of depression prevention interventions for adults (Conejo-Cerón et al., 2020).

6.6 Universal, Indicated, and Selective Prevention

The 1994 IOM report (Mrazek & Haggerty) outlines the three types of prevention for mental health disorders. Universal prevention targets the general public, community, or population regardless of risk level (e.g., a health education curriculum offered to all high school freshmen in a community). Indicated prevention is aimed at individuals who display symptoms of a mental health disorder but do not meet clinical diagnostic criteria. An example of an indicated preventive intervention is one that teaches depression prevention strategies to individuals who have screened positive for subthreshold clinical symptoms. Selective prevention is aimed at members of a subgroup who are at higher risk for a mental health disorder, such as children of depressed parents.

Meta-analytic data indicate that selective and indicated prevention programs for children, adolescents, and adults are more effective than universal programs, though they typically show only small to moderate effects. This trend has been observed several months post-intervention in multiple analyses (Hetrick et al., 2016; Horowitz & Garber, 2006; Mendelson & Eaton, 2018). This may be attributable to the finding that, in universal samples, participants in the control group often do not show a high enough level of symptoms at follow-up to demonstrate a preventive effect. In selective and indicated studies, the sample, which is targeted for higher-risk status, is likely to have a higher level of symptoms at baseline and to show an increase in depressive symptoms over time (Horowitz & Garber, 2006). Adding to the challenge of conducting universal prevention studies, in order to achieve statistically significant power, studies would need extremely large numbers of participants, in the tens of thousands, which is more than typically feasible (Cuijpers, 2003). Although universal interventions do not have to take the step of screening for risk and depressive symptoms, they require service delivery to large numbers of individuals with low risk or little need. There is, however, potential for universal prevention programs to be cost-effective despite low effect sizes if they are able to prevent even a somewhat small number of cases of depression at a low cost

(Horowitz & Garber, 2006). In fact, Lee, Barendregt, et al. (2017) found that school-based universal and indicated prevention involving group-based psychological interventions can be cost-effective. There may be other benefits to universal interventions, including reduction in stigma of singling out individuals and lower drop-out rates.

Universal, indicated, and selective interventions may be conducted in a variety of settings with children, adolescents, and adults. Schools are a common setting for preventing depression in children and adolescents. School settings easily facilitate the delivery of universal interventions, but subgroups can be targeted within school settings as well. In fact, a systematic review of school-based prevention showed that indicated preventive interventions were most effective in schools (Calear & Christensen, 2010b). School-based interventions offer an accessible way to reach children and adolescents and the ability to implement population-level interventions (Werner-Seidler et al., 2017). The equivalent of a school setting for adults may be the workplace, where universal interventions may be feasible (Tan et al., 2014). The primary care setting is amenable to all kinds of prevention efforts (Conejo-Cerón et al., 2017).

6.7 Stepped Care Prevention Model

6.7.1 Role of the Primary Care Provider and the Behavioral Care Provider

The aim of a stepped care model for depression prevention is to identify patients with depressive symptoms and connect them with an intervention that will lead to symptom improvement and prevent future symptoms or development of MDD. While some stepped care models have patients move from lower-intensity steps to higher-intensity steps, other models use assessments to determine the level of intervention intensity at which a patient should start. When embedded in primary care clinics, stepped care models can reach patients who may be apprehensive about pursuing specialty mental healthcare.

In stepped care for depression, the primary care provider (PCP) collaborates closely with the behavioral care provider (BCP), who is embedded in the medical clinic. The initial role of the PCP is to identify patients who might benefit from depression prevention or treatment interventions. Many self-report, screening measures such as the Patient Health Questionnaire-9 item (PHQ-9), the Patient Health Questionnaire-2 item (PHQ-2), or the Beck Depression Inventory-II (BDI-II) provide a brief assessment of depressive symptoms to help PCPs determine which patients may need further follow-up. In addition, it is important for PCPs to conduct safety assessments to identify patients who are experiencing suicidal ideation or planning to engage in taking steps to hurt or kill themselves. Nearly half of patients who die of suicide have seen a PCP in the last month. This finding suggests that PCPs can play an important role in depression and suicide prevention.

Following these brief assessments, the PCP may coordinate with the BCP who may conduct further assessment or manage safety concerns. The BCP may conduct a more comprehensive assessment to understand the severity of symptoms and potential functional impairment related to symptoms. Furthermore, the BCP may assess for comorbid mental health concerns and work collaboratively with the patient to determine the best prevention plan or treatment intervention. In a stepped care model, the PCP and BCP collaborate across the steps in care. Some common steps included in stepped care models for depression prevention are detailed below.

6.7.2 Watchful Waiting

The first step of many stepped care models for depression is watchful waiting, sometimes called active monitoring. For a patient who reports mild symptoms on a depression screening measure, a PCP or BCP may decide the best course of action is to see if the patient's depressive symptoms remit on their own. No formal intervention is provided to the patient, but the PCP or BCP monitors the change in symptoms over time (typically ranges from every 2 weeks to 3 months; Iglesias-González et al., 2017; van Straten et al., 2010). Research on watchful waiting varies in regard to outcomes. One study found that of adolescents who screened positive for depression on the PHQ-9, 47% continued to screen positive at 6 weeks and 35% screened positive at 6 months. Higher baseline depression scores and a positive screen at 6 weeks were found to be associated with the persistence of a positive screen at 6 months (Richardson et al., 2012). Another study of adults in primary care found that only 9–13% of patients remitted from minor depression over a 1-month watchful waiting period (Hegel et al., 2006). Given this study only reported outcomes for the first month, it may be that a longer period of watchful waiting may have resulted in more patients remitting. Finally, a study of subthreshold depression and anxiety in visually impaired older adults demonstrated that just over a third of patients no longer qualified as having subthreshold depression after a 3-month watchful waiting period, while 18% met the criteria for depression or an anxiety disorder. Follow-up analyses suggested that female sex, adjustment problems due to vision loss, greater baseline symptoms, and a history of depressive disorder were associated with lower odds of recovery from subthreshold symptoms (van der Aa et al., 2015). Together, these studies suggest that watchful waiting can be an effective first step for some people who report elevated symptoms of depression on screening measures.

In conjunction with watchful waiting or as a step-up from watchful waiting, PCPs or BCPs may provide some brief psychoeducation or provide information regarding another self-guided, low-intensity intervention (Bauer & Areán, 2016; Iglesias-González et al., 2017; Van Straten et al., 2015).

6.7.3 Psychoeducation

Psychoeducation is a low-intensity brief intervention for depression. It may include passive methods of providing information through brochures and websites as well as active administration of psychoeducation, in which a professional or peer provides and discusses relevant information (Donker et al., 2009). The aim of psychoeducation is to provide patients with information on the symptoms of depression; how depression can affect peoples' thoughts, behaviors, and emotions; interventions; and how professionals will work with them to support prevention or recovery (Ratzliff et al., 2016). Many interventions start with psychoeducation prior to introducing skills work. For adolescents, psychoeducation often involves parents or caregivers, and some psychoeducation interventions are designed specifically for parents (for review, see Jones et al., 2018).

Psychoeducation has been found to be helpful in increasing knowledge of depression, symptom identification, engagement, and improving depressive symptoms (Donker et al., 2009; Jones et al., 2018). A meta-analysis that reviewed studies on passive psychoeducation (including leaflets, brochures, and websites) found patients with depression or elevated depressive symptoms reported decreased symptoms after receiving the informational materials, although the pooled effect size was small ($d = 0.20$; Donker et al., 2009). This study also reported larger between-group effect sizes for psychoeducation that included evidence-based information on depression and anxiety versus test feedback and advice. Tursi et al. (2013) reviewed a combination of active and passive psychoeducation programs for adults and families. They concluded that while more research is needed to fully understand the efficacy of psychoeducational interventions, there is evidence to suggest these interventions improved symptoms, engagement in treatment, and functioning among people experiencing depressive symptoms.

In an integrative, stepped care model, the PCP and BCP may deliver psychoeducation to patients. While the PCP may provide an initial overview of information, the BCP may have the opportunity to review psychoeducational material in depth either individually or in a group format. BCPs may engage the patient in discussion and ensure that the patient has a good understanding of the psychoeducational material.

6.7.4 Biblio-Prevention

Biblio-prevention programs are books developed to teach cognitive-behavioral techniques to the reader and provide strategies to manage stress and mood (McNaughton, 2009). Examples of these books include *Feeling Good: The New Mood Therapy* (Burns, 1980, revised in 2008) and *Control Your Depression* (Lewinsohn, 2010). While biblio-prevention is typically self-led, patient engagement can be increased through support from a BCP. The BCP may provide motivational interviews to help the patient remain engaged in the self-directed intervention, or they may discuss new skills with the patient to help build mastery and find ways for the patient to use skills in their daily life (Bilich et al., 2008; Van Straten et al., 2010).

Research suggests that biblio-prevention for depression is associated with an immediate (at posttreatment) decrease in depressive symptoms, while longer-term effects are not always found (for review see, Gualano et al., 2017; Anderson et al., 2005). Other research suggests that biblio-prevention is efficacious only in indicated samples (people who are experiencing a certain number of depressive symptoms). For example, in one study, adolescents provided with a copy of *Feeling Good* (Burns, 1980), who received two reminder calls to use and engage with the book, demonstrated a significant decrease in depressive symptoms as compared to adolescents who received an informational brochure only if the adolescents had higher baseline depressive symptoms (Müller et al., 2015).

6.7.5 E-Health Prevention Tools

E-health prevention tools are online interventions that can be accessed through mobile devices, tablets, and computers. They may take the form of an application or website. Similar to biblio-prevention, these interventions are self-led, and support from the BCP through motivational interviews or discussions on skill mastery may improve patient engagement in the intervention (Cuijpers, Quero, et al., 2019). Ease of access and privacy are benefits of e-health prevention tools. Many people have devices that they carry with them and can access programs without anyone seeing what they are doing.

"Project CATCH-IT" (Competent Adulthood Transition with Cognitive-behavioral, Humanistic and Interpersonal Training) is an example of an e-health prevention tool. Developed by Van Voorhees et al. (2009), Project CATCH-IT is an Internet-based depression prevention intervention for adolescents with elevated depressive symptomatology or a prior history of depression in primary care. CATCH-IT demonstrated preventive effects for depressive episodes compared to a health education intervention at 6 months post-intervention for those with higher symptomatology at baseline, supporting the benefits of indicated prevention efforts, but these effects were no longer significant at 12 or 24 months follow-up (Gladstone et al., 2018; Van Voorhees et al., 2020). Van Voorhees et al. (2009) also found that motivational interviewing by the PCP in conjunction with CATCH-IT increased engagement and satisfaction in the program, demonstrating that periodic provider support may encourage adolescent participation in Internet-based programs.

Another example of an e-health prevention tool is MoodGYM (Calear & Christensen, 2010a; Christensen et al., 2002), a free, online, interactive program designed to prevent and decrease symptoms of depression. MoodGYM has been used in many settings, including adult primary care. The intervention is based on CBT and contains five interactive modules aimed to change dysfunctional thoughts, improve interpersonal relationships, improve self-esteem, and teach skills like problem-solving and relaxation. A large-scale, three-arm RCT of MoodGYM, Beating the Blues (a commercial, web-based e-health program), and usual PCP care found no difference in positive screens on the PHQ-9 across arms at 4 months (Gilbody et al., 2015; Littlewood et al., 2015), although MoodGYM demonstrated fewer positive PHQ-9 screens and lower depression scores at 12 months. These group differences, however, were not maintained at 24 months (Gilbody et al., 2015). Other primary care studies of MoodGYM supported by a clinician demonstrate stronger results. For example, MoodGYM in conjunction with brief face-to-face therapist support demonstrated a significantly greater reduction in depressive symptoms compared to delayed treatment (Høifødt et al., 2013), and MoodGYM plus telephone support resulted in lower depression scores at 4 months compared to MoodGYM with minimal support (Gilbody et al., 2017).

6.7.6 Group Prevention Interventions

Within a stepped care model, a BCP may provide group interventions for patients that would benefit from a greater treatment intensity. A group format provides consistent intervention over time with built-in patient/provider interaction. While groups require more resources (e.g., space, provider time, patient travel) than watchful waiting, psychoeducation, biblio-prevention, or e-health prevention, groups require fewer resources than individual intervention. Typically, randomized clinical trials find stronger evidence for group interventions than passive psychoeducation or other self-led interventions (Müller et al., 2015; Rohde et al., 2018).

There are evidence-based depression prevention groups targeted at all age groups. One of the most well-known and researched group interventions for depression prevention is the Coping with Depression (CWD) course (Cuijpers et al., 2009). CWD is a CBT-based program that was developed by Lewinsohn and colleagues in the late 1970s and has been used by numerous other researchers and practitioners in trials with subjects of all age groups, including adolescents and adults. A meta-analysis of CWD studies found that studies aimed at the prevention of MDD onset reduced risk by 38% (Cuijpers et al., 2009). Allart-van Dam et al. (2007) evaluated the long-term preventive effects of CWD on the incidence of depressive episodes and symptoms in adults with subthreshold depressive symptoms and found that the CWD course was effective in preventing depressive symptomatology but not depressive disorder. CWD has been adapted for primary care settings (van den Berg et al., 2011).

More recently, other depression prevention and treatment groups have been implemented in the primary care setting. For example, Behavioral Activation with Mindfulness (BAM) groups conducted in a primary care setting have demonstrated decreased depressive symptoms and significantly lower incidence of MDD compared to treatment as usual at 12 months (Wong et al., 2018). Another study found that Spanish-speaking patients who participated in a modified CBT group in primary care reported decreased depressive symptoms during treatment (Aguilera et al., 2018). In addition to the groups described here, many of the individual interventions discussed below may be delivered in group format.

6.7.7 Individual Prevention Interventions

Individual intervention for depression requires the most resources (e.g., provider time, space, patient travel) and provides patients with the most provider contact. One-on-one sessions with the provider allow the intervention to be specifically tailored to the patient and can often feel more personal to the patient. Individual intervention within primary care is typically short term compared to specialty mental health, where patients may be seen regularly over a longer period of time. Multiple individual treatments have been found to be effective for the treatment of depression (or subthreshold depression) in the primary care setting. These treatments include cognitive-behavioral therapy and interpersonal therapy for adolescents (Weersing et al., 2017) and cognitive-behavioral therapy, behavioral activation, interpersonal therapy, and problem-solving therapy in adults (Ramanuj et al., 2019; for review see, Cuijpers, Quero, et al., 2019).

An example of a primary care depression intervention specifically for adolescents is a CBT protocol designed by Clarke et al. (1999). This CBT program can be delivered in group or individual formats, and it consists of two-, four-session modules. One module focuses on increasing pleasant activities, while the other module addresses cognitive distortions. In a primary care setting, adolescents who had declined treatment with antidepressants were randomized to either the CBT protocol plus treatment as usual or a treatment as usual control condition. The CBT condition was found to be superior to treatment as usual as measured by recovery from MDD. These findings were maintained over a 2-year period. Additionally, adolescents who were assigned to the CBT condition reported decreased depressive symptoms as compared to adolescents in the treatment as usual group across the first year (Clarke et al., 2016). This same CBT protocol has also been successfully used as one intervention in a collaborative care model (Richardson et al., 2014). In this study, at 1 year follow-up, adolescents who received the collaborative care model reported significant improvement in their depressive symptoms compared to adolescents assigned to the usual care group.

While cognitive-behavioral therapy is the most researched, the other evidence-based therapies appear to have similar outcomes (Cuijpers, Quero, et al., 2019). For example, a pilot study of interpersonal therapy for adolescents in primary care found a significant reduction in depressive symptoms (Mufson et al., 2015), and a small follow-up study examining interpersonal therapy in the context of a stepped care model found this model to be feasible and acceptable (Mufson et al., 2018).

6.8 Lessons Learned/Implementation

There is ample evidence that depression can be prevented (Muñoz et al., 2012; Muñoz & Bunge, 2016), yet most people with depression, or with symptoms of depression, do not receive any treatment at all. In fact, according to Thornicroft et al. (2017), in high-income countries, only approximately 1/5 people with symptoms of depression receive minimally adequate treatment, and this "treatment gap" is much more significant among people in low- or lower-middle-income countries. In addition, within the United States, the lowest percentages of adults receiving treatment are those without health insurance and also men and those from racial or ethnic minority groups (Olfson et al., 2016). There are many reasons why people struggling with depressive symptoms do not receive adequate care, including shortage of mental health clinicians, multiple barriers to access (e.g., high cost and poor insurance coverage, clinic hours that interfere with work schedules, wait times for appointments), the stigma associated with acknowledging symptoms of depression, and the fact that many people with symptoms of depression do not even recognize the need for intervention (Hodgkinson et al., 2017; Szlyk et al., 2020; Thornicroft et al., 2017).

Primary care physicians provide an important resource for attending to the high rates of depression among children, adolescents, adults, and the elderly. In fact, many primary care physicians recognize their role in identifying their patients' depressive symptoms (Heneghan et al., 2008), but they often lack the training and the time to manage depression in the primary care setting (Weissman et al., 2014). Additionally, the attitudes of healthcare staff, and the perception that physical and psychological concerns should be addressed separately, can be a significant barrier to managing depression within primary care (Wood et al., 2017). Nonetheless, depression *can* be well-managed within the primary care setting, both in youth (e.g., Asarnow et al., 2015; Richardson et al., 2014) and in adults (Archer et al., 2012). Ultimately, given the barriers to accessing mental health specialists, as well as the importance of providing routine access to preventive interventions for individuals with subthreshold depressive symptoms (Muñoz et al., 2012), primary care physicians must play a significant role in identifying signs of depression and implementing strategies to address depression in their patients (Cheung et al., 2018; Nimalasuriya et al., 2009; Zuckerbrot et al., 2018).

Below are several specific recommendations to assist with the management of depression within primary care:

1. *Primary care physicians need to add behavioral care providers to their healthcare teams* so that they are able to provide their patients with psychotherapeutic interventions that may be better suited to lower levels of depressive symptomatology rather than just prescribing antidepressant medications (Cuijpers, Quero, et al., 2019). In fact, the majority of patients presenting in primary care with depression report mild to moderate levels of symptoms (Bitsko et al., 2018; Cuijpers, Quero, et al., 2019), for which medication is not recommended as a first level of intervention. And both youth (Jaycox et al., 2006) and adults

(McHugh et al., 2013) report that they prefer psychotherapeutic interventions to medication in addressing symptoms of depression. Mufson and Rynn (2019) note that the current structure of most primary care settings does not allow for adequate care of depressed individuals without adding behavioral care providers (BCPs) to the healthcare team.

2. *Medical school and residency programs need to include behavioral care providers as part of their training teams*, so that students and residents can learn to identify and address patients' depressive symptoms prior to beginning practice. Enhancing in-school training has the potential to reduce the costs of on-the-job training and ultimately may enable primary care physicians to manage mild to moderate cases of depression independently, without relying on consultations with behavioral care providers (Mufson & Rynn, 2019).
3. *It is essential that high quality, evidence-based interventions be available to patients who present with symptoms of depression in primary care* (Asarnow et al., 2015; Thornicroft et al., 2017). For example, behavioral activation has a strong evidence base, even when administered by non-mental health specialists (Cuijpers et al., 2007; Ekers et al., 2014). Similarly, there is ample evidence for the effectiveness of cognitive-behavioral interventions in primary care (e.g., Twomey et al., 2015), both for people with diagnosed depression and for those who present with depressive symptoms, for whom such interventions are more preventive in nature (Santoft et al., 2019). Finally, there is emerging evidence for the use of interpersonal psychotherapy to address depression in primary care, both in adolescents (Mufson et al., 2018) and in adults (Weissman et al., 2014).
4. *Technology-based interventions hold promise for the prevention of depression in primary care, among both youth* (Gladstone et al., 2018) *and adults* (Buntrock et al., 2016). Such technology-based formats have the potential to reduce barriers to treatment for individuals with depression, as they are accessible, private, and affordable. Overall, telehealth or therapeutic interventions delivered remotely have been found to be as effective as face-to-face or group psychotherapy in addressing symptoms of depression (Cuijpers, Noma, et al., 2019; Santoft et al., 2019).
5. *Finally, interventions that more indirectly address symptoms of depression may be more acceptable in the primary care setting*. Muñoz & Bunge (2016) suggest a creative approach to addressing the stigma associated with mental health interventions by highlighting the work of Christensen et al. (2016), who found evidence supporting an online intervention targeting insomnia among adults with depressive symptoms (Christensen et al., 2016). Munoz and Bunge argue that interventions focusing on more indirect methods of addressing depressive symptoms, such as healthy eating or exercise, may be more acceptable to consumers and may ultimately have significant preventive effects on depression. Such interventions that target health behaviors *related to* depression have tremendous potential for dissemination in the primary care setting and ultimately may support broader depression prevention efforts.

References

Abramson, L. Y., Seligman, M. E., & Teasdale, J. D. (1978). Learned helplessness in humans: Critique and reformulation. *Journal of Abnormal Psychology, 87*(1), 49.

Aguilera, A., Bruehlman-Senecal, E., Liu, N., & Bravin, J. (2018). Implementing group CBT for depression among Latinos in a primary care clinic. *Cognitive and Behavioral Practice, 25*(1), 135–144.

Alexopoulos, G. S., Abrams, R. C., Young, R. C., & Shamoian, C. A. (1988). Cornell scale for depression in dementia. *Biological Psychiatry, 23*(3), 271–284.

Allart-van Dam, E., Hosman, C. M., Hoogduin, C. A., & Schaap, C. (2007). Prevention of depression in subclinically depressed adults: Follow-up effects on the 'coping with Depression' course. *Journal of Affective Disorders, 97*(1–3), 219–228.

Allen, N., Ames, D., Ashby, D., Bennetts, K., Tuckwell, V., & West, C. (1994). A brief sensitive screening instrument for depression in late life. *Age and Ageing, 23*(3), 213–218.

Allgaier, A. K., Pietsch, K., Frühe, B., Sigl-Glöckner, J., & Schulte-Körne, G. (2012). Screening for depression in adolescents: Validity of the patient health questionnaire in pediatric care. *Depression and Anxiety, 29*(10), 906–913.

Allison, V. L., Nativio, D. G., Mitchell, A. M., Ren, D., & Yuhasz, J. (2014). Identifying symptoms of depression and anxiety in students in the school setting. *The Journal of School Nursing, 30*(3), 165–172.

Alloy, L. B., Salk, R., Stange, J. P., & Abramson, L. Y. (2017). Cognitive vulnerability and unipolar depression. *Oxford Handbook of Mood Disorders*, 142–153.

American College of Obstetricians and Gynecologists. (2018). ACOG Committee Opinion No. 757: Screening for perinatal depression. *Obstetrics and Gynecology, 132*(5), e208–e212.

American Psychiatric Association. (2013). *Diagnostic and statistical manual of mental disorders (DSM-5®)*. American Psychiatric Pub.

Anderson, L., Lewis, G., Araya, R., Elgie, R., Harrison, G., Proudfoot, J., Schmidt, U., Sharp, D., Weightman, A., & Williams, C. (2005). Self-help books for depression: How can practitioners and patients make the right choice? *British Journal of General Practice, 55*(514), 387–392.

Andresen, E. M., Malmgren, J. A., Carter, W. B., & Patrick, D. L. (1994). Screening for depression in well older adults: Evaluation of a short form of the CES-D. *American Journal of Preventive Medicine, 10*(2), 77–84.

Archer, J., Bower, P., Gilbody, S., Lovell, K., Richards, D., Gask, L., Dickens, C., & Coventry, P. (2012). Collaborative care for depression and anxiety problems. *Cochrane Database of Systematic Reviews, 10*.

Arroll, B., Goodyear-Smith, F., Crengle, S., Gunn, J., Kerse, N., Fishman, T., Falloon, K., & Hatcher, S. (2010). Validation of PHQ-2 and PHQ-9 to screen for major depression in the primary care population. *The Annals of Family Medicine, 8*(4), 348–353.

Asarnow, J. R., Jaycox, L. H., Tang, L., Duan, N., LaBorde, A. P., Zeledon, L. R., Anderson, M., Murray, P. J., Landon, C., & Rea, M. M. (2009). Long-term benefits of short-term quality improvement interventions for depressed youths in primary care. *American Journal of Psychiatry, 166*(9), 1002–1010.

Asarnow, J. R., Rozenman, M., Wiblin, J., & Zeltzer, L. (2015). Integrated medical-behavioral care compared with usual primary care for child and adolescent behavioral health: A meta-analysis. *JAMA Pediatrics, 169*(10), 929–937.

Avenevoli, S., Swendsen, J., He, J.-P., Burstein, M., & Merikangas, K. R. (2015). Major depression in the National Comorbidity Survey–Adolescent Supplement: Prevalence, correlates, and treatment. *Journal of the American Academy of Child and Adolescent Psychiatry, 54*(1), 37–44. e32.

Bagot, R. C., & Meaney, M. J. (2010). Epigenetics and the biological basis of gene× environment interactions. *Journal of the American Academy of Child and Adolescent Psychiatry, 49*(8), 752–771.

Bansal, R., Peterson, B. S., Gingrich, J., Hao, X., Odgerel, Z., Warner, V., Wickramaratne, P. J., Talati, A., Ansorge, M., & Brown, A. S. (2016). Serotonin signaling modulates the effects

of familial risk for depression on cortical thickness. *Psychiatry Research: Neuroimaging, 248*, 83–93.
Barnes, D. M., Keyes, K. M., & Bates, L. M. (2013). Racial differences in depression in the United States: How do subgroup analyses inform a paradox? *Social Psychiatry and Psychiatric Epidemiology, 48*(12), 1941–1949.
Barrera, A. Z., Wickham, R. E., & Muñoz, R. F. (2015). Online prevention of postpartum depression for Spanish-and English-speaking pregnant women: A pilot randomized controlled trial. *Internet Interventions, 2*(3), 257–265.
Bauer, A., & Areán, P. (2016). Mood disorders-major depression. In A. Ratzliff, J. Unützer, W. Katon, & K. A. Stephens (Eds.), *Integrated care: Creating effective mental and primary health care teams* (pp. 27–54). Wiley.
Beardslee, W. R., Brent, D. A., Weersing, V. R., Clarke, G. N., Porta, G., Hollon, S. D., Gladstone, T. R., Gallop, R., Lynch, F. L., & Iyengar, S. (2013). Prevention of depression in at-risk adolescents: Longer-term effects. *JAMA Psychiatry, 70*(11), 1161–1170.
Beardslee, W. R., Gladstone, T. R., & O'Connor, E. E. (2011). Transmission and prevention of mood disorders among children of affectively ill parents: A review. *Journal of the American Academy of Child and Adolescent Psychiatry, 50*(11), 1098–1109.
Beardslee, W. R., Wright, E. J., Gladstone, T. R., & Forbes, P. (2007). Long-term effects from a randomized trial of two public health preventive interventions for parental depression. *Journal of Family Psychology, 21*(4), 703.
Beck, A. T. (1967). *Depression: Clinical, experimental, and theoretical aspects*. Hoeber Medical Division, Harper & Row.
Beck, A. T. (1979). *Cognitive therapy and the emotional disorders*. Penguin.
Beck, A. T., Steer, R. A., & Brown, G. K. (1996). *Manual for the Beck depression inventory-II*. Psychological Corporation.
Beck, C. T., & Gable, R. K. (2000). Postpartum depression screening scale: Development and psychometric testing. *Nursing Research, 49*(5), 272–282.
Bellón, J., Conejo-Cerón, S., Cortés-Abela, C., Pena-Andreu, J. M., Garcia-Rodriguez, A., & Moreno-Peral, P. (2019). Effectiveness of psychological and educational interventions for the prevention of depression in the workplace: A systematic review and meta-analysis. *Scandinavian Journal of Work, Environment and Health, 45*(4), 324–332.
Bellón, J. Á., Moreno-Peral, P., Motrico, E., Rodríguez-Morejón, A., Fernandez, A., Serrano-Blanco, A., Zabaleta-del-Olmo, E., & Conejo-Ceron, S. (2015). Effectiveness of psychological and/or educational interventions to prevent the onset of episodes of depression: A systematic review of systematic reviews and meta-analyses. *Preventive Medicine, 76*, S22–S32.
Bilich, L. L., Deane, F. P., Phipps, A. B., Barisic, M., & Gould, G. (2008). Effectiveness of bibliotherapy self-help for depression with varying levels of telephone helpline support. *Clinical Psychology & Psychotherapy: An International Journal of Theory & Practice, 15*(2), 61–74.
Birmaher, B., Brent, D., & AACAP Work Group on Quality Issues. (2007). Practice parameter for the assessment and treatment of children and adolescents with depressive disorders. *Journal of the American Academy of Child and Adolescent Psychiatry, 46*(11), 1503–1526.
Birmaher, B., Ryan, N. D., Williamson, D. E., Brent, D. A., Kaufman, J., Dahl, R. E., Perel, J., & Nelson, B. (1996). Childhood and adolescent depression: A review of the past 10 years. Part I. *Journal of the American Academy of Child and Adolescent Psychiatry, 35*(11), 1427–1439.
Bitsko, R. H., Holbrook, J. R., Ghandour, R. M., Blumberg, S. J., Visser, S. N., Perou, R., & Walkup, J. T. (2018). Epidemiology and impact of health care provider–diagnosed anxiety and depression among US children. *Journal of Developmental and Behavioral Pediatrics: JDBP, 39*(5), 395.
Bleys, D., Luyten, P., Soenens, B., & Claes, S. (2018). Gene-environment interactions between stress and 5-HTTLPR in depression: A meta-analytic update. *Journal of Affective Disorders, 226*, 339–345.

Bradley, K. L., Bagnell, A. L., & Brannen, C. L. (2010). Factorial validity of the Center for Epidemiological Studies Depression 10 in adolescents. *Issues in Mental Health Nursing, 31*(6), 408–412.

Brent, D. A., Brunwasser, S. M., Hollon, S. D., Weersing, V. R., Clarke, G. N., Dickerson, J. F., Beardslee, W. R., Gladstone, T. R., Porta, G., & Lynch, F. L. (2015). Effect of a cognitive-behavioral prevention program on depression 6 years after implementation among at-risk adolescents: A randomized clinical trial. *JAMA Psychiatry, 72*(11), 1110–1118.

Brière, F. N., Rohde, P., Shaw, H., & Stice, E. (2014). Moderators of two indicated cognitive-behavioral depression prevention approaches for adolescents in a school-based effectiveness trial. *Behaviour Research and Therapy, 53*, 55–62.

Buntrock, C., Ebert, D. D., Lehr, D., Smit, F., Riper, H., Berking, M., & Cuijpers, P. (2016). Effect of a web-based guided self-help intervention for prevention of major depression in adults with subthreshold depression: A randomized clinical trial. *JAMA, 315*(17), 1854–1863.

Burcusa, S. L., & Iacono, W. G. (2007). Risk for recurrence in depression. *Clinical Psychology Review, 27*(8), 959–985.

Burns, D. (1980). *Feeling good. The new mood therapy*. Willian Morrow and Company.

Cairns, K. E., Yap, M. B. H., Pilkington, P. D., & Jorm, A. F. (2014). Risk and protective factors for depression that adolescents can modify: A systematic review and meta-analysis of longitudinal studies. *Journal of Affective Disorders, 169*, 61–75.

Calear, A. L., & Christensen, H. (2010a). Review of internet-based prevention and treatment programs for anxiety and depression in children and adolescents. *Medical Journal of Australia, 192*, S12–S14.

Calear, A. L., & Christensen, H. (2010b). Systematic review of school-based prevention and early intervention programs for depression. *Journal of Adolescence, 33*(3), 429–438.

Chang, D. F., & Yoon, P. (2011). Ethnic minority clients' perceptions of the significance of race in cross-racial therapy relationships. *Psychotherapy Research, 21*(5), 567–582.

Cheung, A. H., Zuckerbrot, R. A., Jensen, P. S., Laraque, D., Stein, R. E., & Group, G.-P. S. (2018). Guidelines for adolescent depression in primary care (GLAD-PC): Part II. Treatment and ongoing management. *Pediatrics, 141*(3).

Christensen, H., Batterham, P. J., Gosling, J. A., Ritterband, L. M., Griffiths, K. M., Thorndike, F. P., Glozier, N., O'Dea, B., Hickie, I. B., & Mackinnon, A. J. (2016). Effectiveness of an online insomnia program (SHUTi) for prevention of depressive episodes (the GoodNight Study): A randomised controlled trial. *The Lancet Psychiatry, 3*(4), 333–341.

Christensen, H., Griffiths, K. M., & Korten, A. (2002). Web-based cognitive behavior therapy: Analysis of site usage and changes in depression and anxiety scores. *Journal of Medical Internet Research, 4*(1), e3.

Clarke, G., DeBar, L. L., Pearson, J. A., Dickerson, J. F., Lynch, F. L., Gullion, C. M., & Leo, M. C. (2016). Cognitive behavioral therapy in primary care for youth declining antidepressants: A randomized trial. *Pediatrics, 137*(5), e20151851.

Clarke, G. N., Rohde, P., Lewinsohn, P. M., Hops, H., & Seeley, J. R. (1999). Cognitive-behavioral treatment of adolescent depression: Efficacy of acute group treatment and booster sessions. *Journal of the American Academy of Child and Adolescent Psychiatry, 38*(3), 272–279.

Conejo-Cerón, S., Bellón, J. Á., Motrico, E., Campos-Paíno, H., Martín-Gómez, C., Ebert, D. D., Buntrock, C., Gili, M., & Moreno-Peral, P. (2020). Moderators of psychological and psychoeducational interventions for the prevention of depression: A systematic review. *Clinical Psychology Review, 101859*.

Conejo-Cerón, S., Moreno-Peral, P., Rodríguez-Morejón, A., Motrico, E., Navas-Campaña, D., Rigabert, A., Martín-Pérez, C., Rodríguez-Bayón, A., Ballesta-Rodríguez, M. I., & de Dios Luna, J. (2017). Effectiveness of psychological and educational interventions to prevent depression in primary care: A systematic review and meta-analysis. *The Annals of Family Medicine, 15*(3), 262–271.

Cox, J. L., Chapman, G., Murray, D., & Jones, P. (1996). Validation of the Edinburgh Postnatal Depression Scale (EPDS) in non-postnatal women. *Journal of Affective Disorders, 39*(3), 185–189.

Cuijpers, P. (2003). Examining the effects of prevention programs on the incidence of new cases of mental disorders: The lack of statistical power. *American Journal of Psychiatry, 160*(8), 1385–1391.

Cuijpers, P., Cristea, I. A., Karyotaki, E., Reijnders, M., & Hollon, S. D. (2019). Component studies of psychological treatments of adult depression: A systematic review and meta-analysis. *Psychotherapy Research, 29*(1), 15–29.

Cuijpers, P., Muñoz, R. F., Clarke, G. N., & Lewinsohn, P. M. (2009). Psychoeducational treatment and prevention of depression: The "coping with depression" course thirty years later. *Clinical Psychology Review, 29*(5), 449–458.

Cuijpers, P., Noma, H., Karyotaki, E., Cipriani, A., & Furukawa, T. A. (2019). Effectiveness and acceptability of cognitive behavior therapy delivery formats in adults with depression: A network meta-analysis. *JAMA Psychiatry, 76*(7), 700–707.

Cuijpers, P., Quero, S., Dowrick, C., & Arroll, B. (2019). Psychological treatment of depression in primary care: Recent developments. *Current Psychiatry Reports, 21*(12), 129.

Cuijpers, P., van Straten, A., Smit, F., Mihalopoulos, C., & Beekman, A. (2008). Preventing the onset of depressive disorders: A meta-analytic review of psychological interventions. *American Journal of Psychiatry, 165*(10), 1272–1280.

Cuijpers, P., Van Straten, A., & Warmerdam, L. (2007). Behavioral activation treatments of depression: A meta-analysis. *Clinical Psychology Review, 27*(3), 318–326.

Cuijpers, P., van Straten, A., Warmerdam, L., & van Rooy, M. J. (2010). Recruiting participants for interventions to prevent the onset of depressive disorders: Possibile ways to increase participation rates. *BMC Health Services Research, 10*(1), 1–6.

DiFonte, M., & Gladstone, T. R. (2017). Children of parents with depression. In T. Gullotta & G. Blau (Eds.), *Handbook of childhood behavioral issues: Evidence-based approaches to prevention and treatment* (pp. 159–176). Routledge/Taylor & Francis Group.

Donker, T., Griffiths, K. M., Cuijpers, P., & Christensen, H. (2009). Psychoeducation for depression, anxiety and psychological distress: A meta-analysis. *BMC Medicine, 7*(1), 1–9.

Dozois, D. J., & Beck, A. T. (2008). Cognitive schemas, beliefs and assumptions. In *Risk factors in depression* (pp. 119–143). Elsevier.

Dray, J., Bowman, J., Campbell, E., Freund, M., Wolfenden, L., Hodder, R. K., McElwaine, K., Tremain, D., Bartlem, K., & Bailey, J. (2017). Systematic review of universal resilience-focused interventions targeting child and adolescent mental health in the school setting. *Journal of the American Academy of Child and Adolescent Psychiatry, 56*(10), 813–824.

Duong, M. T., Kelly, B. M., Haaland, W. L., Matsumiya, B., Huey, S. J., & McCarty, C. A. (2016). Mediators and moderators of a school-based cognitive-behavioral depression prevention program. *Cognitive Therapy and Research, 40*(5), 705–716.

Earls, M. F., Yogman, M. W., Mattson, G., Rafferty, J., & Committee on Psychosocial Aspects of Child and Family Health. (2019). Incorporating recognition and management of perinatal depression into pediatric practice. *Pediatrics, 143*(1).

Ekers, D., Webster, L., Van Straten, A., Cuijpers, P., Richards, D., & Gilbody, S. (2014). Behavioural activation for depression; an update of meta-analysis of effectiveness and sub group analysis. *PLoS One, 9*(6), e100100.

England, M. J. E., & Sim, L. J. (2009). *Depression in parents, parenting, and children: Opportunities to improve identification, treatment, and prevention.* National Academies Press.

Erving, C. L., Thomas, C. S., & Frazier, C. (2019). Is the black-White mental health paradox consistent across gender and psychiatric disorders? *American Journal of Epidemiology, 188*(2), 314–322.

Evans, D. L., Foa, E. B., Gur, R. E., Hendin, H., O'Brien, C. P., Seligman, M. E., & Walsh, B. T. (2005). *Treating and preventing adolescent mental health disorders: What we know and what we don't know.* Oxford University Press.

Feiss, R., Dolinger, S. B., Merritt, M., Reiche, E., Martin, K., Yanes, J. A., Thomas, C. M., & Pangelinan, M. (2019). A systematic review and meta-analysis of school-based stress, anxiety, and depression prevention programs for adolescents. *Journal of Youth and Adolescence, 48*(9), 1668–1685.

Fergusson, D. M., & Horwood, J. L. (2001). The Christchurch Health and Development Study: Review of findings on child and adolescent mental health. *Australian and New Zealand Journal of Psychiatry, 35*(3), 287–296.

Forehand, R., Thigpen, J. C., Parent, J., Hardcastle, E. J., Bettis, A., & Compas, B. E. (2012). The role of parent depressive symptoms in positive and negative parenting in a preventive intervention. *Journal of Family Psychology, 26*(4), 532.

Foster, C. E., Webster, M. C., Weissman, M. M., Pilowsky, D. J., Wickramaratne, P. J., Rush, A. J., Hughes, C. W., Garber, J., Malloy, E., & Cerda, G. (2008). Course and severity of maternal depression: Associations with family functioning and child adjustment. *Journal of Youth and Adolescence, 37*(8), 906–916.

Garber, J., Clarke, G. N., Weersing, V. R., Beardslee, W. R., Brent, D. A., Gladstone, T. R., DeBar, L. L., Lynch, F. L., D'Angelo, E., & Hollon, S. D. (2009). Prevention of depression in at-risk adolescents: A randomized controlled trial. *JAMA, 301*(21), 2215–2224.

Gariepy, G., Honkaniemi, H., & Quesnel-Vallee, A. (2016). Social support and protection from depression: Systematic review of current findings in Western countries. *The British Journal of Psychiatry, 209*(4), 284–293.

Gau, J. M., Stice, E., Rohde, P., & Seeley, J. R. (2012). Negative life events and substance use moderate cognitive behavioral adolescent depression prevention intervention. *Cognitive Behaviour Therapy, 41*(3), 241–250.

Gilbody, S., Brabyn, S., Lovell, K., Kessler, D., Devlin, T., Smith, L., Araya, R., Barkham, M., Bower, P., & Cooper, C. (2017). Telephone-supported computerised cognitive–behavioural therapy: REEACT-2 large-scale pragmatic randomised controlled trial. *The British Journal of Psychiatry, 210*(5), 362–367.

Gilbody, S., Littlewood, E., Hewitt, C., Brierley, G., Tharmanathan, P., Araya, R., Barkham, M., Bower, P., Cooper, C., Gask, L., Kessler, D., Lester, H., Lovell, K., Parry, G., Richards, D. A., Andersen, P., Brabyn, S., Knowles, S., Shepherd, C., … White, D. (2015). Computerised cognitive behaviour therapy (cCBT) as treatment for depression in primary care (REEACT trial): Large scale pragmatic randomised controlled trial. *BMJ, 351*, h5627. https://doi.org/10.1136/bmj.h5627

Gillham, J. E., Hamilton, J., Freres, D. R., Patton, K., & Gallop, R. (2006). Preventing depression among early adolescents in the primary care setting: A randomized controlled study of the Penn Resiliency Program. *Journal of Abnormal Child Psychology, 34*(2), 195–211. https://doi.org/10.1007/s10802-005-9014-7

Girgus, J. S., & Yang, K. (2015). Gender and depression. *Current Opinion in Psychology, 4*, 53–60.

Gladstone, T., Terrizzi, D., Stinson, A., Nidetz, J., Canel, J., Ching, E., Berry, A., Cantorna, J., Fogel, J., Eder, M., Bolotin, M., Thomann, L. O., Griffith, K., Ip, P., Aaby, D. A., Brown, C. H., Beardslee, W., Bell, C., Crawford, T. J., … Van Voorhees, B. W. (2018). Effect of internet-based cognitive behavioral humanistic and interpersonal training vs. internet-based general health education on adolescent depression in primary care: A randomized clinical trial. *JAMA Network Open, 1*(7), e184278. https://doi.org/10.1001/jamanetworkopen.2018.4278

Gladstone, T. G., Marko-Holguin, M., Rothberg, P., Nidetz, J., Diehl, A., DeFrino, D. T., Harris, M., Ching, E., Eder, M., Canel, J., Bell, C., Beardslee, W. R., Brown, C. H., Griffiths, K., & Van Voorhees, B. W. (2015). An internet-based adolescent depression preventive intervention: Study protocol for a randomized control trial. *Trials, 16*, 203–203. https://doi.org/10.1186/s13063-015-0705-2

Gold, S. M., Köhler-Forsberg, O., Moss-Morris, R., Mehnert, A., Miranda, J. J., Bullinger, M., Steptoe, A., Whooley, M. A., & Otte, C. (2020). Comorbid depression in medical diseases. *Nature Reviews Disease Primers, 6*(1), 1–22.

Goodman, S. H., & Gotlib, I. H. (2002). Transmission of risk to children of depressed parents: Integration and conclusions. In S. H. Goodman & I. H. Gotlib (Eds.), *Children of depressed parents: Mechanisms of risk and implications for treatment* (pp. 307–326). American Psychological Association. https://doi.org/10.1037/10449-012

Goodman, S. H., Rouse, M. H., Connell, A. M., Broth, M. R., Hall, C. M., & Heyward, D. (2011). Maternal depression and child psychopathology: A meta-analytic review. *Clinical Child and Family Psychology Review, 14*(1), 1–27.

Grigoriadis, S., & Erlick Robinson, G. (2007). Gender issues in depression. *Annals of Clinical Psychiatry, 19*(4), 247–255.

Griner, D., & Smith, T. B. (2006). Culturally adapted mental health intervention: A meta-analytic review. *Psychotherapy: Theory, Research, Practice, Training, 43*(4), 531.

Gualano, M., Bert, F., Martorana, M., Voglino, G., Andriolo, V., Thomas, R., Gramaglia, C., Zeppegno, P., & Siliquini, R. (2017). The long-term effects of bibliotherapy in depression treatment: Systematic review of randomized clinical trials. *Clinical Psychology Review, 58*, 49–58.

Guffanti, G., Gameroff, M. J., Warner, V., Talati, A., Glatt, C. E., Wickramaratne, P., & Weissman, M. M. (2016). Heritability of major depressive and comorbid anxiety disorders in multi-generational families at high risk for depression. *American Journal of Medical Genetics Part B: Neuropsychiatric Genetics, 171*(8), 1072–1079.

Hammen, C. (2018). Risk factors for depression: An autobiographical review. *Annual Review of Clinical Psychology, 14*, 1–28.

Hasin, D. S., Sarvet, A. L., Meyers, J. L., Saha, T. D., Ruan, W. J., Stohl, M., & Grant, B. F. (2018). Epidemiology of adult DSM-5 major depressive disorder and its specifiers in the United States. *JAMA Psychiatry, 75*(4), 336–346.

Hegel, M. T., Oxman, T. E., Hull, J. G., Swain, K., & Swick, H. (2006). Watchful waiting for minor depression in primary care: Remission rates and predictors of improvement. *General Hospital Psychiatry, 28*(3), 205–212.

Heneghan, A., Garner, A. S., Storfer-Isser, A., Kortepeter, K., Stein, R. E., & Horwitz, S. M. (2008). Pediatricians' role in providing mental health care for children and adolescents: Do pediatricians and child and adolescent psychiatrists agree? *Journal of Developmental and Behavioral Pediatrics, 29*(4), 262–269.

Hetrick, S. E., Cox, G. R., & Merry, S. N. (2015). Where to go from here? An exploratory meta-analysis of the most promising approaches to depression prevention programs for children and adolescents. *International Journal of Environmental Research and Public Health, 12*(5), 4758–4795.

Hetrick, S. E., Cox, G. R., Witt, K. G., Bir, J. J., & Merry, S. N. (2016). Cognitive behavioural therapy (CBT), third-wave CBT and interpersonal therapy (IPT) based interventions for preventing depression in children and adolescents. *Cochrane Database of Systematic Reviews, 8*. https://doi.org/10.1002/14651858.CD003380.pub4

Hoare, E., Callaly, E., & Berk, M. (2020). Can depression be prevented? If so, how? *JAMA Psychiatry*. https://doi.org/10.1001/jamapsychiatry.2020.1273

Hochberg, Z. e., Feil, R., Constancia, M., Fraga, M., Junien, C., Carel, J.-C., Boileau, P., Le Bouc, Y., Deal, C., & Lillycrop, K. (2011). Child health, developmental plasticity, and epigenetic programming. *Endocrine Reviews, 32*(2), 159–224.

Hodgkinson, S., Godoy, L., Beers, L. S., & Lewin, A. (2017). Improving mental health access for low-income children and families in the primary care setting. *Pediatrics, 139*(1), e20151175.

Høifødt, R. S., Lillevoll, K. R., Griffiths, K. M., Wilsgaard, T., Eisemann, M., & Kolstrup, N. (2013). The clinical effectiveness of web-based cognitive behavioral therapy with face-to-face therapist support for depressed primary care patients: Randomized controlled trial. *Journal of Medical Internet Research, 15*(8), e153.

Hoover, D. R., Siegel, M., Lucas, J., Kalay, E., Gaboda, D., Devanand, D., & Crystal, S. (2010). Depression in the first year of stay for elderly long-term nursing home residents in the USA. *International Psychogeriatrics, 22*(7), 1161.

Horowitz, J. L., & Garber, J. (2006). The prevention of depressive symptoms in children and adolescents: A meta-analytic review. *Journal of Consulting and Clinical Psychology, 74*(3), 401.

Horowitz, J. L., Garber, J., Ciesla, J. A., Young, J. F., & Mufson, L. (2007). Prevention of depressive symptoms in adolescents: A randomized trial of cognitive-behavioral and interpersonal prevention programs. *Journal of Consulting and Clinical Psychology, 75*(5), 693.

Iglesias-González, M., Aznar-Lou, I., Gil-Girbau, M., Moreno-Peral, P., Peñarrubia-María, M. T., Rubio-Valera, M., & Serrano-Blanco, A. (2017). Comparing watchful waiting with antidepressants for the management of subclinical depression symptoms to mild–moderate depression in primary care: A systematic review. *Family Practice, 34*(6), 639–648.

Jackson-Koku, G. (2016). Beck depression inventory. *Occupational Medicine, 66*(2), 174–175.

Jaycox, L. H., Asarnow, J. R., Sherbourne, C. D., Rea, M. M., LaBorde, A. P., & Wells, K. B. (2006). Adolescent primary care patients' preferences for depression treatment. *Administration and Policy in Mental Health and Mental Health Services Research, 33*(2), 198–207.

Jeon, S. W., Amidfar, M., & Kim, Y.-K. (2017). Bio-psycho-social risk factors for depression. In *Major depressive disorder: Risk factors, characteristics and treatment options* (pp. 71–90). Nova Science Publisher.

Johnson, J. G., Harris, E. S., Spitzer, R. L., & Williams, J. B. (2002). The patient health questionnaire for adolescents: Validation of an instrument for the assessment of mental disorders among adolescent primary care patients. *Journal of Adolescent Health, 30*(3), 196–204.

Jones, R. B., Thapar, A., Stone, Z., Thapar, A., Jones, I., Smith, D., & Simpson, S. (2018). Psychoeducational interventions in adolescent depression: A systematic review. *Patient Education and Counseling, 101*(5), 804–816.

Kang, H.-J., Kim, S.-Y., Bae, K.-Y., Kim, S.-W., Shin, I.-S., Yoon, J.-S., & Kim, J.-M. (2015). Comorbidity of depression with physical disorders: Research and clinical implications. *Chonnam Medical Journal, 51*(1), 8–18.

Kaslow, N. J., & Thompson, M. P. (1998). Applying the criteria for empirically supported treatments to studies of psychosocial interventions for child and adolescent depression. *Journal of Clinical Child Psychology, 27*(2), 146–155.

Katon, W. J. (2011). Epidemiology and treatment of depression in patients with chronic medical illness. *Dialogues in Clinical Neuroscience, 13*(1), 7.

Kazdin, A. E., Kraemer, H. C., Kessler, R. C., Kupfer, D. J., & Offord, D. R. (1997). Contributions of risk-factor research to developmental psychopathology. *Clinical Psychology Review, 17*(4), 375–406.

Kessler, R. C. (2012). The costs of depression. *Psychiatric Clinics, 35*(1), 1–14.

Kovacs, M., & Lopez-Duran, N. (2010). Prodromal symptoms and atypical affectivity as predictors of major depression in juveniles: Implications for prevention. *Journal of Child Psychology and Psychiatry, 51*(4), 472–496.

Kuyken, W., Watkins, E., Holden, E., & Cook, W. (2006). Rumination in adolescents at risk for depression. *Journal of Affective Disorders, 96*(1–2), 39–47.

Landback, J., Prochaska, M., Ellis, J., Dmochowska, K., Kuwabara, S. A., Gladstone, T., Larson, J., Stuart, S., Gollan, J., & Bell, C. (2009). From prototype to product: Development of a primary care/internet based depression prevention intervention for adolescents (CATCH-IT). *Community Mental Health Journal, 45*(5), 349–354.

Lara, M. A., Navarro, C., & Navarrete, L. (2010). Outcome results of a psycho-educational intervention in pregnancy to prevent PPD: A randomized control trial. *Journal of Affective Disorders, 122*(1–2), 109–117.

Lee, E.-H., Lee, S.-J., Hwang, S.-T., Hong, S.-H., & Kim, J.-H. (2017). Reliability and validity of the Beck Depression Inventory-II among Korean adolescents. *Psychiatry Investigation, 14*(1), 30.

Lee, Y., Barendregt, J., Stockings, E., Ferrari, A., Whiteford, H., Patton, G., & Mihalopoulos, C. (2017). The population cost-effectiveness of delivering universal and indicated school-based interventions to prevent the onset of major depression among youth in Australia. *Epidemiology and Psychiatric Sciences, 26*(5), 545–564.

Leppert, K. A., Wasserbach, M.-C., & Dougherty, L. R. (2019). Cognitive styles in preschool-age children: Associations with depression risk and evidence of stability. *Journal of Psychopathology and Behavioral Assessment, 41*(4), 612–626.

Letourneau, N. L., Dennis, C.-L., Benzies, K., Duffett-Leger, L., Stewart, M., Tryphonopoulos, P. D., Este, D., & Watson, W. (2012). Postpartum depression is a family affair: Addressing the impact on mothers, fathers, and children. *Issues in Mental Health Nursing, 33*(7), 445–457.

Lewandowski, R. E., O'Connor, B., Bertagnolli, A., Beck, A., Tinoco, A., Gardner, W. P., Jelinek-Berents, C. X., Newton, D. A., Wain, K. F., & Boggs, J. M. (2016). Screening for and diagnosis of depression among adolescents in a large health maintenance organization. *Psychiatric Services, 67*(6), 636–641.

Lewinsohn, P. (2010). *Control your depression* (Rev ed.). Simon and Schuster.

Littlewood, E., Duarte, A., Hewitt, C., Knowles, S., Palmer, S., Walker, S., Andersen, P., Araya, R., Barkham, M., & Bower, P. (2015). A randomised controlled trial of computerised cognitive behaviour therapy for the treatment of depression in primary care: The Randomised Evaluation of the Effectiveness and Acceptability of Computerised Therapy (REEACT) Trial. *Health Technology Assessment (Winchester, England), 19*(101), 1.

Loechner, J., Sfärlea, A., Starman, K., Oort, F., Thomsen, L. A., Schulte-Koerne, G., & Platt, B. (2020). Risk of depression in the offspring of parents with depression: The role of emotion regulation, cognitive style, parenting and life events. *Child Psychiatry and Human Development, 51*(2), 294–309.

Lovejoy, M. C., Graczyk, P. A., O'Hare, E., & Neuman, G. (2000). Maternal depression and parenting behavior: A meta-analytic review. *Clinical Psychology Review, 20*(5), 561–592.

Lu, W. (2019). Adolescent depression: National trends, risk factors, and healthcare disparities. *American Journal of Health Behavior, 43*(1), 181–194.

Martin, L. A., Neighbors, H. W., & Griffith, D. M. (2013). The experience of symptoms of depression in men vs women: Analysis of the National Comorbidity Survey Replication. *JAMA Psychiatry, 70*(10), 1100–1106.

Maurer, D. M., Raymond, T. J., & Davis, B. N. (2018). Depression: Screening and diagnosis. *American Family Physician, 98*(8), 508–515.

McHugh, R. K., Whitton, S. W., Peckham, A. D., Welge, J. A., & Otto, M. W. (2013). Patient preference for psychological vs. pharmacological treatment of psychiatric disorders: A meta-analytic review. *The Journal of Clinical Psychiatry, 74*(6), 595.

McNaughton, J. L. (2009). Brief interventions for depression in primary care: A systematic review. *Canadian Family Physician, 55*(8), 789–796.

Mendelson, T., & Eaton, W. W. (2018). Recent advances in the prevention of mental disorders. *Social Psychiatry and Psychiatric Epidemiology, 53*(4), 325–339.

Meyer, T. D., Gudgeon, E., Thomas, A. J., & Collerton, D. (2010). Cognitive style and depressive symptoms in elderly people–extending the empirical evidence for the cognitive vulnerability–stress hypothesis. *Behaviour Research and Therapy, 48*(10), 1053–1057.

Middleton, M., Scott, S. L., & Renk, K. (2009). Parental depression, parenting behaviours, and behaviour problems in young children. *Infant and Child Development: An International Journal of Research and Practice, 18*(4), 323–336.

Mitchell, A. J., Bird, V., Rizzo, M., & Meader, N. (2010). Diagnostic validity and added value of the Geriatric Depression Scale for depression in primary care: A meta-analysis of GDS30 and GDS15. *Journal of Affective Disorders, 125*(1–3), 10–17.

Mitchell, A. J., Yadegarfar, M., Gill, J., & Stubbs, B. (2016). Case finding and screening clinical utility of the Patient Health Questionnaire (PHQ-9 and PHQ-2) for depression in primary care: A diagnostic meta-analysis of 40 studies. *BJPsych open, 2*(2), 127–138.

Mnookin, S. (2016). *Out of the shadows: Making mental health a global development priority*. T. W. Bank. http://documents.worldbank.org/curated/en/270131468187759113/Out-of-the-shadows-making-mental-health-a-global-development-priority

Mojtabai, R., Olfson, M., & Han, B. (2016). National trends in the prevalence and treatment of depression in adolescents and young adults. *Pediatrics, 138*(6), e20161878.

Moussavi, S., Chatterji, S., Verdes, E., Tandon, A., Patel, V., & Ustun, B. (2007). Depression, chronic diseases, and decrements in health: Results from the World Health Surveys. *The Lancet, 370*(9590), 851–858.

Mrazek, P. J., & Haggerty, R. J. (1994). *Reducing risks for mental disorders: Frontiers for preventive intervention research.* National Academies Press.

Mufson, L., Rynn, M., Yanes-Lukin, P., Choo, T. H., Soren, K., Stewart, E., & Wall, M. (2018). Stepped care interpersonal psychotherapy treatment for depressed adolescents: A pilot study in pediatric clinics. *Administration and Policy in Mental Health and Mental Health Services Research, 45*(3), 417–431.

Mufson, L., & Rynn, M. A. (2019). Primary care: Meeting the mental health care needs of adolescents with depression. *Journal of the American Academy of Child and Adolescent Psychiatry, 58*(4), 389–391. https://doi.org/10.1016/j.jaac.2018.10.014

Mufson, L., Yanes-Lukin, P., & Anderson, G. (2015). A pilot study of Brief IPT-A delivered in primary care. *General Hospital Psychiatry, 37*(5), 481–484.

Mullen, S. (2018). Major depressive disorder in children and adolescents. *Mental Health Clinician, 8*(6), 275–283.

Müller, S., Rohde, P., Gau, J. M., & Stice, E. (2015). Moderators of the effects of indicated group and bibliotherapy cognitive behavioral depression prevention programs on adolescents' depressive symptoms and depressive disorder onset. *Behaviour Research and Therapy, 75*, 1–10.

Muñoz, R. F., Beardslee, W. R., & Leykin, Y. (2012). Major depression can be prevented. *American Psychologist, 67*(4), 285.

Muñoz, R. F., & Bunge, E. L. (2016). Prevention of depression worldwide: A wake-up call. *The Lancet Psychiatry, 3*(4), 306.

Muñoz, R. F., Cuijpers, P., Smit, F., Barrera, A. Z., & Leykin, Y. (2010). Prevention of major depression. *Annual Review of Clinical Psychology, 6*, 181–212.

National Research Council and Institute of Medicine. (2009). *Preventing mental, emotional, and behavioral disorders among young people: Progress and possibilities* (M. E. O'Connell, T. Boat, & K. E. Warner, Eds.). National Academies Press.

Nimalasuriya, K., Compton, M. T., & Guillory, V. J. (2009). Screening adults for depression in primary care: A position statement of the American College of Preventive Medicine. *Journal of Family Practice, 58*(10), 535–539.

O'Connor, E., Rossom, R. C., Henninger, M., Groom, H. C., & Burda, B. U. (2016). Primary care screening for and treatment of depression in pregnant and postpartum women: Evidence report and systematic review for the US Preventive Services Task Force. *JAMA, 315*(4), 388–406.

O'Connor, E., Rossom, R. C., Henninger, M., Groom, H. C., Burda, B. U., Henderson, J. T., Bigler, K. D., & Whitlock, E. P. (2016). Screening for depression in adults: An updated systematic evidence review for the U.S. Preventive Services Task Force Evidence Syntheses, Issue.

O'Connor, E., Whitlock, E. P., Beil, T. L., & Gaynes, B. N. (2009). Screening for depression in adult patients in primary care settings: A systematic evidence review. *Annals of Internal Medicine, 151*(11), 793–803.

Olfson, M., Blanco, C., & Marcus, S. C. (2016). Treatment of adult depression in the United States. *JAMA Internal Medicine, 176*(10), 1482–1491.

Osman, A., Barrios, F. X., Gutierrez, P. M., Williams, J. E., & Bailey, J. (2008). Psychometric properties of the Beck Depression Inventory-II in nonclinical adolescent samples. *Journal of Clinical Psychology, 64*(1), 83–102.

Parker, G., & Brotchie, H. (2010). Gender differences in depression. *International Review of Psychiatry, 22*(5), 429–436.

Patel, V., Burns, J. K., Dhingra, M., Tarver, L., Kohrt, B. A., & Lund, C. (2018). Income inequality and depression: A systematic review and meta-analysis of the association and a scoping review of mechanisms. *World Psychiatry, 17*(1), 76–89.

Patil, P. A., Porche, M. V., Shippen, N. A., Dallenbach, N. T., & Fortuna, L. R. (2018). Which girls, which boys? The intersectional risk for depression by race and ethnicity, and gender in the US. *Clinical Psychology Review, 66*, 51–68.

Pearson, R., Heron, J., Button, K., Bentall, R., Fernyhough, C., Mahedy, L., Bowes, L., & Lewis, G. (2015). Cognitive styles and future depressed mood in early adulthood: The importance of global attributions. *Journal of Affective Disorders, 171*, 60–67.

Penninx, B. W., Milaneschi, Y., Lamers, F., & Vogelzangs, N. (2013). Understanding the somatic consequences of depression: Biological mechanisms and the role of depression symptom profile. *BMC Medicine, 11*(1), 129.

Pettit, J. W., Olino, T. M., Roberts, R. E., Seeley, J. R., & Lewinsohn, P. M. (2008). Intergenerational transmission of internalizing problems: Effects of parental and grandparental major depressive disorder on child behavior. *Journal of Clinical Child and Adolescent Psychology, 37*(3), 640–650.

Planey, A. M., Smith, S. M., Moore, S., & Walker, T. D. (2019). Barriers and facilitators to mental health help-seeking among African American youth and their families: A systematic review study. *Children and Youth Services Review, 101*, 190–200.

Pössel, P., & Pittard, C. M. (2019). Integrating the hopelessness model and the response style theory in an adolescent sample. *Journal of Abnormal Child Psychology, 47*(4), 695–706.

Radloff, L. S. (1977). The CES-D scale: A self-report depression scale for research in the general population. *Applied Psychological Measurement, 1*(3), 385–401.

Ramanuj, P., Ferenchick, E. K., & Pincus, H. A. (2019). Depression in primary care: Part 2—Management. *BMJ, 365*, l835. https://doi.org/10.1136/bmj.l835

Rao, U., Chen, L.-A., Bidesi, A. S., Shad, M. U., Thomas, M. A., & Hammen, C. L. (2010). Hippocampal changes associated with early-life adversity and vulnerability to depression. *Biological Psychiatry, 67*(4), 357–364.

Ratzliff, A., Cerimele, J., Katon, W., & Unützer, J. (2016). Working as a team to provide collaborative care. In A. Ratzliff, J. Cerimele, W. Katon, & J. Unützer (Eds.), *Integrated care: Creating effective mental health care teams* (pp. 1–24). Wiley. https://doi.org/10.1002/9781119276579.ch1

Rice, F., Riglin, L., Lomax, T., Souter, E., Potter, R., Smith, D., Thapar, A., & Thapar, A. (2019). Adolescent and adult differences in major depression symptom profiles. *Journal of Affective Disorders, 243*, 175–181.

Richardson, L. P., Ludman, E., McCauley, E., Lindenbaum, J., Larison, C., Zhou, C., Clarke, G., Brent, D., & Katon, W. (2014). Collaborative care for adolescents with depression in primary care: A randomized clinical trial. *JAMA, 312*(8), 809–816.

Richardson, L. P., McCauley, E., Grossman, D. C., McCarty, C. A., Richards, J., Russo, J. E., Rockhill, C., & Katon, W. (2010). Evaluation of the Patient Health Questionnaire-9 Item for detecting major depression among adolescents. *Pediatrics, 126*(6), 1117–1123.

Richardson, L. P., McCauley, E., McCarty, C. A., Grossman, D. C., Myaing, M., Zhou, C., Richards, J., Rockhill, C., & Katon, W. (2012). Predictors of persistence after a positive depression screen among adolescents. *Pediatrics, 130*(6), e1541–e1548.

Richardson, L. P., Rockhill, C., Russo, J. E., Grossman, D. C., Richards, J., McCarty, C., McCauley, E., & Katon, W. (2010). Evaluation of the PHQ-2 as a brief screen for detecting major depression among adolescents. *Pediatrics, 125*(5), e1097–e1103.

Rodda, J., Walker, Z., & Carter, J. (2011). Depression in older adults. *BMJ, 343*, d5219. https://doi.org/10.1136/bmj.d5219

Rohde, P., Brière, F. N., & Stice, E. (2018). Major depression prevention effects for a cognitive-behavioral adolescent indicated prevention group intervention across four trials. *Behaviour Research and Therapy, 100*, 1–6.

Rossom, R. C., Coleman, K. J., Ahmedani, B. K., Beck, A., Johnson, E., Oliver, M., & Simon, G. E. (2017). Suicidal ideation reported on the PHQ9 and risk of suicidal behavior across age groups. *Journal of Affective Disorders, 215*, 77–84.

Salk, R. H., Hyde, J. S., & Abramson, L. Y. (2017). Gender differences in depression in representative national samples: Meta-analyses of diagnoses and symptoms. *Psychological Bulletin, 143*(8), 783.

Santoft, F., Axelsson, E., Öst, L.-G., Hedman-Lagerlöf, M., Fust, J., & Hedman-Lagerlöf, E. (2019). Cognitive behaviour therapy for depression in primary care: Systematic review and meta-analysis. *Psychological Medicine, 49*(8), 1266–1274.

Saulsberry, A., Marko-Holguin, M., Blomeke, K., Hinkle, C., Fogel, J., Gladstone, T., Bell, C., Reinecke, M., Corden, M., & Van Voorhees, B. W. (2013). Randomized clinical trial of a primary care internet-based intervention to prevent adolescent depression: One-year outcomes. *Journal of the Canadian Academy of Child and Adolescent Psychiatry = Journal de l'Academie canadienne de psychiatrie de l'enfant et de l'adolescent, 22*(2), 106–117.

Schaakxs, R., Comijs, H. C., van der Mast, R. C., Schoevers, R. A., Beekman, A. T., & Penninx, B. W. (2017). Risk factors for depression: Differential across age? *The American Journal of Geriatric Psychiatry, 25*(9), 966–977.

Schueller, S. M., & Seligman, M. E. (2008). Optimism and pessimism. In *Risk factors in depression* (pp. 171–194). Elsevier.

Scott, S. M., Wallander, J. L., & Cameron, L. (2015). Protective mechanisms for depression among racial/ethnic minority youth: Empirical findings, issues, and recommendations. *Clinical Child and Family Psychology Review, 18*(4), 346–369.

Seedat, S., Scott, K. M., Angermeyer, M. C., Berglund, P., Bromet, E. J., Brugha, T. S., Demyttenaere, K., De Girolamo, G., Haro, J. M., & Jin, R. (2009). Cross-national associations between gender and mental disorders in the World Health Organization World Mental Health Surveys. *Archives of General Psychiatry, 66*(7), 785–795.

Seligman, M. E., Schulman, P., DeRubeis, R. J., & Hollon, S. D. (1999). The prevention of depression and anxiety. *Prevention & Treatment, 2*(1), 8a.

Shen, H., Magnusson, C., Rai, D., Lundberg, M., Le-Scherban, F., Dalman, C., & Lee, B. K. (2016). Associations of parental depression with child school performance at age 16 years in Sweden. *JAMA Psychiatry, 73*(3), 239–246.

Shorey, S., Chee, C. Y. I., Ng, E. D., Chan, Y. H., San Tam, W. W., & Chong, Y. S. (2018). Prevalence and incidence of postpartum depression among healthy mothers: A systematic review and meta-analysis. *Journal of Psychiatric Research, 104*, 235–248.

Simon, G. E., Rutter, C. M., Peterson, D., Oliver, M., Whiteside, U., Operskalski, B., & Ludman, E. J. (2013). Does response on the PHQ-9 Depression Questionnaire predict subsequent suicide attempt or suicide death? *Psychiatric Services, 64*(12), 1195–1202.

Siu, A. L. (2016). Screening for depression in children and adolescents: US Preventive Services Task Force recommendation statement. *Pediatrics, 137*(3), e20154467. https://doi.org/10.1542/peds.2015-4467

Siu, A. L., Bibbins-Domingo, K., Grossman, D. C., Baumann, L. C., Davidson, K. W., Ebell, M., García, F. A., Gillman, M., Herzstein, J., & Kemper, A. R. (2016). Screening for depression in adults: US Preventive Services Task Force recommendation statement. *JAMA, 315*(4), 380–387.

Soe, N. N., Wen, D. J., Poh, J. S., Li, Y., Broekman, B. F., Chen, H., Chong, Y. S., Kwek, K., Saw, S.-M., & Gluckman, P. D. (2016). Pre-and post-natal maternal depressive symptoms in relation with infant frontal function, connectivity, and behaviors. *PLoS One, 11*(4), e0152991.

Spasojević, J., & Alloy, L. B. (2001). Rumination as a common mechanism relating depressive risk factors to depression. *Emotion, 1*(1), 25.

Spitzer, R. L., Kroenke, K., Williams, J. B., & Group, P. H. Q. P. C. S. (1999). Validation and utility of a self-report version of PRIME-MD: The PHQ primary care study. *JAMA, 282*(18), 1737–1744.

Stice, E., Shaw, H., Bohon, C., & Marti, C. N. (2009). A meta-analytic review of depression prevention programs for children and adolescents: Factors that predict magnitude of intervention effects. *Journal of Consulting and Clinical Psychology, 77*(3), 486–503. https://doi.org/10.1037/a0015168

Sullivan, P. F., Neale, M. C., & Kendler, K. S. (2000). Genetic epidemiology of major depression: Review and meta-analysis. *American Journal of Psychiatry, 157*(10), 1552–1562.

Szlyk, H., Deng, J., Xu, C., Krauss, M. J., & Cavazos-Rehg, P. A. (2020). Leveraging social media to explore the barriers to treatment among individuals with depressive symptoms. *Depression and Anxiety, 37*(5), 458–465. https://doi.org/10.1002/da.22990

Tan, L., Wang, M.-J., Modini, M., Joyce, S., Mykletun, A., Christensen, H., & Harvey, S. B. (2014). Preventing the development of depression at work: A systematic review and meta-analysis of universal interventions in the workplace. *BMC Medicine, 12*(1), 74.

Taraban, L., Shaw, D. S., Leve, L. D., Natsuaki, M. N., Ganiban, J. M., Reiss, D., & Neiderhiser, J. M. (2019). Parental depression, overreactive parenting, and early childhood externalizing problems: Moderation by social support. *Child Development, 90*(4), e468–e485.

Thornicroft, G., Chatterji, S., Evans-Lacko, S., Gruber, M., Sampson, N., Aguilar-Gaxiola, S., Al-Hamzawi, A., Alonso, J., Andrade, L., & Borges, G. (2017). Undertreatment of people with major depressive disorder in 21 countries. *The British Journal of Psychiatry, 210*(2), 119–124.

Tsoi, K. K., Chan, J. Y., Hirai, H. W., & Wong, S. Y. (2017). Comparison of diagnostic performance of Two-Question Screen and 15 depression screening instruments for older adults: Systematic review and meta-analysis. *The British Journal of Psychiatry, 210*(4), 255–260.

Tursi, M. F. D. S., Baes, C. V. W., Camacho, F. R. D. B., Tofoli, S. M. D. C., & Juruena, M. F. (2013). Effectiveness of psychoeducation for depression: A systematic review. *Australian and New Zealand Journal of Psychiatry, 47*(11), 1019–1031.

Twenge, J. M., & Nolen-Hoeksema, S. (2002). Age, gender, race, socioeconomic status, and birth cohort difference on the children's depression inventory: A meta-analysis. *Journal of Abnormal Psychology, 111*(4), 578.

Twomey, C., O'Reilly, G., & Byrne, M. (2015). Effectiveness of cognitive behavioural therapy for anxiety and depression in primary care: A meta-analysis. *Family Practice, 32*(1), 3–15.

Van de Velde, S., Bracke, P., & Levecque, K. (2010). Gender differences in depression in 23 European countries. Cross-national variation in the gender gap in depression. *Social Science and Medicine, 71*(2), 305–313.

van den Berg, M., Smit, F., Vos, T., & van Baal, P. H. (2011). Cost-effectiveness of opportunistic screening and minimal contact psychotherapy to prevent depression in primary care patients. *PLoS One, 6*(8), e22884.

van der Aa, H. P., Comijs, H. C., Penninx, B. W., van Rens, G. H., & van Nispen, R. M. (2015). Major depressive and anxiety disorders in visually impaired older adults. *Investigative Ophthalmology and Visual Science, 56*(2), 849–854.

Van Straten, A., Hill, J. J., Richards, D., & Cuijpers, P. (2015). Stepped care treatment delivery for depression: A systematic review and meta-analysis. *Psychological Medicine, 45*(2), 231–246. https://doi.org/10.1017/S0033291714000701

Van Straten, A., Seekles, W., Van 't Veer-Tazelaar, N. J., Beekman, A. T., & Cuijpers, P. (2010). Stepped care for depression in primary care: What should be offered and how? *Medical Journal of Australia, 192*(11), S36–S39.

Van Voorhees, B., Gladstone, T. R., Sobowale, K., Brown, C. H., Aaby, D. A., Terrizzi, D. A., Canel, J., Ching, E., Berry, A. D., & Cantorna, J. (2020). 24-month outcomes of primary care web-based depression prevention intervention in adolescents: Randomized clinical trial. *Journal of Medical Internet Research, 22*(10), e16802.

Van Voorhees, B. W., Fogel, J., Pomper, B. E., Marko, M., Reid, N., Watson, N., Larson, J., Bradford, N., Fagan, B., & Zuckerman, S. (2009). Adolescent dose and ratings of an Internet-based depression prevention program: A randomized trial of primary care physician brief advice versus a motivational interview. *Journal of cognitive and behavioral psychotherapies: the official journal of the International Institute for the Advanced Studies of Psychotherapy and Applied Mental Health, 9*(1), 1.

van Zoonen, K., Buntrock, C., Ebert, D. D., Smit, F., Reynolds, C. F., III, Beekman, A. T., & Cuijpers, P. (2014). Preventing the onset of major depressive disorder: A meta-analytic review of psychological interventions. *International Journal of Epidemiology, 43*(2), 318–329.

Vilagut, G., Forero, C. G., Barbaglia, G., & Alonso, J. (2016). Screening for depression in the general population with the Center for Epidemiologic Studies Depression (CES-D): A systematic review with meta-analysis. *PLoS One, 11*(5), e0155431. https://doi.org/10.1371/journal.pone.0155431

Vreeland, A., Gruhn, M. A., Watson, K. H., Bettis, A. H., Compas, B. E., Forehand, R., & Sullivan, A. D. (2019). Parenting in context: Associations of parental depression and socioeconomic factors with parenting behaviors. *Journal of Child and Family Studies, 28*(4), 1124–1133.

Wahl, M. S., Adelson, J. L., Patak, M. A., Pössel, P., & Hautzinger, M. (2014). Teachers or psychologists: Who should facilitate depression prevention programs in schools? *International Journal of Environmental Research and Public Health, 11*(5), 5294–5316.

Weersing, V. R., Jeffreys, M., Do, M.-C. T., Schwartz, K. T., & Bolano, C. (2017). Evidence base update of psychosocial treatments for child and adolescent depression. *Journal of Clinical Child and Adolescent Psychology, 46*(1), 11–43.

Weissman, M. M., Hankerson, S. H., Scorza, P., Olfson, M., Verdeli, H., Shea, S., Lantigua, R., & Wainberg, M. (2014). Interpersonal counseling (IPC) for depression in primary care. *American Journal of Psychotherapy, 68*(4), 359–383.

Weissman, M. M., Wickramaratne, P., Nomura, Y., Warner, V., Pilowsky, D., & Verdeli, H. (2006). Offspring of depressed parents: 20 years later. *American Journal of Psychiatry, 163*(6), 1001–1008.

Werner-Seidler, A., Perry, Y., Calear, A. L., Newby, J. M., & Christensen, H. (2017). School-based depression and anxiety prevention programs for young people: A systematic review and meta-analysis. *Clinical Psychology Review, 51*, 30–47.

Widom, C. S., DuMont, K., & Czaja, S. J. (2007). A prospective investigation of major depressive disorder and comorbidity in abused and neglected children grown up. *Archives of General Psychiatry, 64*(1), 49–56.

Willemse, G. R., Smit, F., Cuijpers, P., & Tiemens, B. G. (2004). Minimal-contact psychotherapy for sub-threshold depression in primary care: Randomised trial. *The British Journal of Psychiatry, 185*(5), 416–421.

Williams, D. R., Gonzalez, H. M., Neighbors, H., Nesse, R., Abelson, J. M., Sweetman, J., & Jackson, J. S. (2007). Prevalence and distribution of major depressive disorder in African Americans, Caribbean blacks, and non-Hispanic whites: Results from the National Survey of American life. *Archives of General Psychiatry, 64*(3), 305–315.

Wisco, B. E., & Nolen-Hoeksema, S. (2008). Ruminative response style. In *Risk factors in depression* (pp. 221–236). Elsevier.

Wong, S. Y., Sun, Y. Y., Chan, A. T., Leung, M. K., Chao, D. V., Li, C. C., Chan, K. K., Tang, W. K., Mazzucchelli, T., & Au, A. M. (2018). Treating subthreshold depression in primary care: A randomized controlled trial of behavioral activation with mindfulness. *The Annals of Family Medicine, 16*(2), 111–119.

Wood, E., Ohlsen, S., & Ricketts, T. (2017). What are the barriers and facilitators to implementing Collaborative Care for depression? A systematic review. *Journal of Affective Disorders, 214*, 26–43.

World Health Organization. (2016). World Health Organization depression: Fact sheet.

World Health Organization. (2017). *Depression and other common mental disorders: Global health estimates* (Licence: CC BY-NC-SA 3.0 IGO.).

Yesavage, J. A., Brink, T. L., Rose, T. L., Lum, O., Huang, V., Adey, M., & Leirer, V. O. (1982). Development and validation of a geriatric depression screening scale: A preliminary report. *Journal of Psychiatric Research, 17*(1), 37–49.

Yoon, S., & Kim, Y.-K. (2018). Gender differences in depression. In *Understanding depression* (pp. 297–307). Springer.

Zuckerbrot, R. A., Cheung, A., Jensen, P. S., Stein, R. E., Laraque, D., & Group, G.-P. S. (2018). Guidelines for adolescent depression in primary care (GLAD-PC): Part I. Practice preparation, identification, assessment, and initial management. *Pediatrics, 141*(3), e20174081.

Chapter 7
Preventing Anxiety Disorders in Integrated Care

Brendan Willis and Martha Zimmermann

Anxiety disorders are the most common form of mental disorders worldwide (Bienvenu & Ginsburg, 2007). In primary care settings, an estimated 19.5%, nearly 1 in 5, patients have at least one anxiety disorder for which they currently meet criteria (Combs & Markman, 2014). It is also shocking to note that despite the high prevalence of these disorders, patients will often be delayed years if not decades before seeking help (Bienvenu & Ginsburg, 2007). This points to a need to both be able to detect anxiety issues sooner as well as intervene earlier in the hopes of preventing the development of any anxiety disorder.

The prevention literature in the field of anxiety disorders has grown significantly (Lau & Rapee, 2011). Various forms of prevention for anxiety disorders have been attempted, with universal methods (i.e., providing anxiety prevention to individuals regardless of risk), and have seen modest success as have school-based programs (Lau & Rapee, 2011). These efforts have also made progress in reducing the stigma surrounding anxiety disorders (Lau & Rapee, 2011). However, there is still a need to implement high-quality preventative interventions in the primary care setting, which serves as a vital point of access to the healthcare system for many (Finley et al., 2018; García-Campayo et al., 2015).

The primary care setting is especially ideal for preventing anxiety disorders or helping to prevent symptoms from worsening. Characteristics unique to primary care include the the availibility of providers, the possibility of enhancing continuity of care, as well as its accessibility to the majority of the general population (García-Campayo et al., 2015). The goal of this chapter, therefore, is to provide a tool kit for providers working in integrated primary care settings to help screen for, identify, and intervene effectively to help prevent anxiety symptoms, or to prevent anxiety

B. Willis (✉) · M. Zimmermann
Psychology Department, University of Nevada, Reno, NV, USA
e-mail: brendanwillis@nevada.unr.edu; mzimmermann@nevada.unr.edu

W. O'Donohue, M. Zimmermann (eds.), *Handbook of Evidence-Based Prevention of Behavioral Disorders in Integrated Care*,
https://doi.org/10.1007/978-3-030-83469-2_7

symptoms from becoming worse. In order to do so, first, this chapter will focus on reviewing the definitions, diagnostic criteria, and prevalence data for anxiety disorders. Next, this chapter will review risk factors, in an effort to prepare healthcare personnel with warning signs that can be used to increase awareness of possible anxiety symptoms. The chapter will conclude by offering recommendations for screening and a stepped-care model that can be used as a framework for building interventions to aid in the prevention of anxiety disorders.

7.1 Definition/Diagnostic Criteria

Anxiety disorders include panic disorder (PD), agoraphobia (AP) with and without panic, specific phobia (SP), social anxiety disorder (SAD), generalized anxiety disorder (GAD), and separation anxiety disorder. Previously, obsessive compulsive disorder (OCD) and posttraumatic stress disorder (PTSD) were considered under the umbrella of anxiety disorders but have since been classified in a separate diagnostic category. For the purposes of this chapter, OCD will be considered along with other anxiety disorders, whereas PTSD will be discussed elsewhere in this book (see Chap. 8). OCD shares core features with anxiety disorders and may also share risk factors (Storch et al., 2008).

In terms of specific diagnostic factors, the *Diagnostic and Statistical Manual of Mental Disorders, Fifth Edition* lists the following as criteria for the previously mentioned anxiety disorders:

1. *Panic Disorder (*American Psychiatric Association, 2013*, p. 214–217)*
   (a) Panic disorder is defined as recurrent unexpected panic attacks. A panic attack is an abrupt surge of intense fear or intense discomfort that reaches a peak within minutes. This surge can occur from a calm state or from an anxious state. During the surge, four (or more) of the following symptoms occur.
      (i) Palpitations, pounding heart, or accelerated heart rate
      (ii) Sweating
      (iii) Trembling or shaking
      (iv) Sensations of shortness of breath or smothering
      (v) Feelings of choking
      (vi) Chest pain or discomfort
      (vii) Nausea or abdominal distress
      (viii) Feeling dizzy, unsteady, light-headed, or faint
      (ix) Chills or heat sensations
      (x) Paresthesias (numbness or tingling sensations)
      (xi) Derealization (feelings of unreality) or depersonalization (being detached from oneself)
      (xii) Fear of losing control or "going crazy"
      (xiii) Fear of dying

(b) At least one of the attacks has been followed by 1 month (or more) of one or both of the following:

   (i) Persistent concern or worry about additional panic attacks or their consequences (e.g., losing control, having a heart attack, "going crazy")
   (ii) A significant maladaptive change in behavior related to the attacks (e.g., behaviors designed to avoid having panic attacks, such as avoidance of exercise or unfamiliar situations)

2. *Agoraphobia (*American Psychiatric Association, 2013*, p. 217–222)*

   (a) Agoraphobia is defined as a marked fear or anxiety about two (or more) of the following five situations:

      (i) Using public transportation (e.g., automobiles, buses, trains, ships, planes)
      (ii) Being in open spaces (e.g., parking lots, marketplaces, bridges)
      (iii) Being in enclosed places (e.g., shops, theaters, cinemas)
      (iv) Standing in line or being in a crowd
      (v) Being outside of the home alone

   (b) The individual fears or avoids these situations because of thoughts that escape might be difficult or help might not be available in the event of developing panic-like symptoms or other incapacitating or embarrassing symptoms (e.g., fear of falling in the elderly; fear of incontinence).
   (c) The agoraphobic situations almost always provoke fear or anxiety.
   (d) The agoraphobic situations are actively avoided, require the presence of a companion, or are endured with intense fear or anxiety.
   (e) The fear or anxiety is out of proportion to the actual danger posed by the agoraphobic situations and to the sociocultural context.
   (f) The fear, anxiety, or avoidance is persistent, typically lasting for 6 months or more.
   (g) The fear, anxiety, or avoidance causes clinically significant distress or impairment in social, occupational, or other important areas of functioning.
   (h) If another medical condition (e.g., inflammatory bowel disease, Parkinson's disease) is present, the fear, anxiety, or avoidance is clearly excessive.

3. *Specific Phobia (*American Psychiatric Association, 2013*, p. 197–202)*

   (a) Specific phobia is defined as a marked fear or anxiety about a specific object or situation (e.g., flying, heights, animals, receiving an injection, seeing blood).
   (b) The phobic object or situation almost always provokes immediate fear or anxiety.
   (c) The phobic object or situation is actively avoided or endured with intense fear or anxiety.
   (d) The fear or anxiety is out of proportion to the actual danger posed by the specific object or situation and to the sociocultural context.

(e) The fear, anxiety, or avoidance is persistent, typically lasting for 6 months or more.
(f) The fear, anxiety, or avoidance causes clinically significant distress or impairment in social, occupational, or other important areas of functioning.

4. *Social Anxiety Disorder* (American Psychiatric Association, 2013, *p. 202–208)*

(a) Social anxiety disorder is defined as marked fear or anxiety about one or more social situations in which the individual is exposed to possible scrutiny by others. Examples include social interactions (e.g., having a conversation, meeting unfamiliar people), being observed (e.g., eating or drinking), and performing in front of others (e.g., giving a speech).
(b) The individual fears that he or she will act in a way or show anxiety symptoms that will be negatively evaluated (i.e., will be humiliating or embarrassing, will lead to rejection or offend others).
(c) The social situations almost always provoke fear or anxiety.
(d) Note: In children, the fear or anxiety may be expressed by crying, tantrums, freezing, clinging, shrinking, or failing to speak in social situations.
(e) The social situations are avoided or endured with intense fear or anxiety.
(f) The fear or anxiety is out of proportion to the actual threat posed by the social situation and to the sociocultural context.
(g) The fear, anxiety, or avoidance is persistent, typically lasting for 6 months or more.
(h) The fear, anxiety, or avoidance causes clinically significant distress or impairment in social, occupational, or other important areas of functioning.
(i) The fear, anxiety, or avoidance is not attributable to the physiological effects of a substance (e.g., a drug of abuse, a medication) or another medical condition.
(j) The fear, anxiety, or avoidance is not better explained by the symptoms of another mental disorder, such as panic disorder, body dysmorphic disorder, or autism spectrum disorder.
(k) If another medical condition (e.g., Parkinson's disease, obesity, disfigurement from burns or injury) is present, the fear, anxiety, or avoidance is clearly unrelated or is excessive.

5. *Generalized Anxiety Disorder* (American Psychiatric Association, 2013, *p. 222–226)*

(a) Generalized anxiety disorder is defined as excessive anxiety and worry (apprehensive expectation), occurring more days than not for at least 6 months, about a number of events or activities (such as work or school performance).
(b) The individual finds it difficult to control the worry.
(c) The anxiety and worry are associated with three (or more) of the following six symptoms (with at least some symptoms having been present for more days than not for the past 6 months):

(i) Restlessness or feeling keyed up or on edge
(ii) Being easily fatigued
(iii) Difficulty concentrating or mind going blank
(iv) Irritability
(v) Muscle tension
(vi) Sleep disturbance (difficulty falling or staying asleep, or restless, unsatisfying sleep)

(d) The anxiety, worry, or physical symptoms cause clinically significant distress or impairment in social, occupational, or other important areas of functioning.
(e) The disturbance is not attributable to the physiological effects of a substance (e.g., a drug of abuse, a medication) or another medical condition (e.g., hyperthyroidism).

6. *Separation Anxiety Disorder* (American Psychiatric Association, 2013, *p. 190–202)*

(a) Defined as developmentally inappropriate and excessive fear or anxiety concerning separation from those to whom the individual is attached, as evidenced by at least three of the following:

(i) Recurrent excessive distress when anticipating or experiencing separation from home or from major attachment figures
(ii) Persistent and excessive worry about losing major attachment figures or about possible harm to them, such as illness, injury, disasters, or death
(iii) Persistent and excessive worry about experiencing an untoward event (e.g., getting lost, being kidnapped, having an accident, becoming ill) that causes separation from a major attachment figure
(iv) Persistent reluctance or refusal to go out, away from home, to school, to work, or elsewhere because of fear of separation
(v) Persistent and excessive fear of or reluctance about being alone or without major attachment figures at home or in other settings
(vi) Persistent reluctance or refusal to sleep away from home or to go to sleep without being near a major attachment figure
(vii) Repeated nightmares involving the theme of separation
(viii) Repeated complaints of physical symptoms (e.g., headaches, stomachaches, nausea, vomiting) when separation from major attachment figures occurs or is anticipated

(b) The fear, anxiety, or avoidance is persistent, lasting at least 4 weeks in children and adolescents and typically 6 months or more in adults.
(c) The disturbance causes clinically significant distress or impairment in social, academic, occupational, or other important areas of functioning.

7. *Obsessive Compulsive Disorder* (American Psychiatric Association, 2013, *p. 237–242)*

(a) Obsessive compulsive disorder is defined as the presence of obsessions, compulsions, or both.

Obsessions are defined by (1) and (2):

(i) Recurrent and persistent thoughts, urges, or images that are experienced, at some time during the disturbance, as intrusive and unwanted and that in most individuals cause marked anxiety or distress.
(ii) The individual attempts to ignore or suppress such thoughts, urges, or images, or to neutralize them with some other thought or action (i.e., by performing a compulsion).

Compulsions are defined by (1) and (2):

(i) Repetitive behaviors (e.g., hand washing, ordering, checking) or mental acts (e.g., praying, counting, repeating words silently) that the individual feels driven to perform in response to an obsession or according to rules that must be applied rigidly.
(ii) The behaviors or mental acts are aimed at preventing or reducing anxiety or distress, or preventing some dreaded event or situation; however, these behaviors or mental acts are not connected in a realistic way with what they are designed to neutralize or prevent or are clearly excessive.

(b) The obsessions or compulsions are time-consuming (e.g., take more than 1 hour per day) or cause clinically significant distress or impairment in social, occupational, or other important areas of functioning.
(c) The obsessive-compulsive symptoms are not attributable to the physiological effects of a substance (e.g., a drug of abuse, a medication) or another medical condition.

8. *Posttraumatic Disorder* (American Psychiatric Association, 2013*, p. 271–280)*

(a) Posttraumatic stress disorder occurs after exposure to actual or threatened death, serious injury, or sexual violence in one (or more) of the following ways:

(i) Directly experiencing the traumatic event(s).
(ii) Witnessing, in person, the event(s) as it occurred to others.
(iii) Learning that the traumatic event(s) occurred to a close family member or close friend. In cases of actual or threatened death of a family member or friend, the event(s) must have been violent or accidental.
(iv) Experiencing repeated or extreme exposure to aversive details of the traumatic event(s) (e.g., first responders collecting human remains; police officers repeatedly exposed to details of child abuse). Note that this does not apply to exposure through electronic media, television, movies, or pictures, unless this exposure is work related.

(b) Posttraumatic stress disorder is defined as experiencing the following symptoms. The presence of one (or more) of the following intrusion symptoms associated with the traumatic event(s), beginning after the traumatic event(s) occurred:

(i) Recurrent, involuntary, and intrusive distressing memories of the traumatic event(s).
(ii) Recurrent distressing dreams in which the content and/or affect of the dream are related to the traumatic event(s).
(iii) Dissociative reactions (e.g., flashbacks) in which the individual feels or acts as if the traumatic event(s) were recurring. (Such reactions may occur on a continuum, with the most extreme expression being a complete loss of awareness of present surroundings.)
(iv) Intense or prolonged psychological distress at exposure to internal or external cues that symbolize or resemble an aspect of the traumatic event(s).
(v) Marked physiological reactions to internal or external cues that symbolize or resemble an aspect of the traumatic event(s).

(c) Persistent avoidance of stimuli associated with the traumatic event(s), beginning after the traumatic event(s) occurred, as evidenced by one or both of the following:

(i) Avoidance of or efforts to avoid distressing memories, thoughts, or feelings about or closely associated with the traumatic event(s)
(ii) Avoidance of or efforts to avoid external reminders (people, places, conversations, activities, objects, situations) that arouse distressing memories, thoughts, or feelings about or closely associated with the traumatic event(s)

(d) Negative alterations in cognitions and mood associated with the traumatic event(s), beginning or worsening after the traumatic event(s) occurred, as evidenced by two (or more) of the following:

(i) Inability to remember an important aspect of the traumatic event(s) (typically due to dissociative amnesia and not to other factors such as head injury, alcohol, or drugs)
(ii) Persistent and exaggerated negative beliefs or expectations about oneself, others, or the world (e.g., "I am bad," "No one can be trusted," "The world is completely dangerous," "My whole nervous system is permanently ruined")
(iii) Persistent, distorted cognitions about the cause or consequences of the traumatic event(s) that lead the individual to blame himself/herself or others
(iv) Persistent negative emotional state (e.g., fear, horror, anger, guilt, or shame)
(v) Markedly diminished interest or participation in significant activities
(vi) Feelings of detachment or estrangement from others
(vii) Persistent inability to experience positive emotions (e.g., inability to experience happiness, satisfaction, or loving feelings)

(e) Marked alterations in arousal and reactivity associated with the traumatic event(s), beginning or worsening after the traumatic event(s) occurred, as evidenced by two (or more) of the following:
   (i) Irritable behavior and angry outbursts (with little or no provocation) typically expressed as verbal or physical aggression toward people or objects
   (ii) Reckless or self-destructive behavior
   (iii) Hypervigilance
   (iv) Exaggerated startle response
   (v) Problems with concentration
   (vi) Sleep disturbance (e.g., difficulty falling or staying asleep or restless sleep)

(f) Duration of the disturbance (Criteria B, C, D, and E) is more than 1 month.
(g) The disturbance causes clinically significant distress or impairment in social, occupational, or other important areas of functioning.

It is important to note that all of the preceding disorders require careful differential diagnosis to ensure that the symptoms a patient presents with are not better explained by another similar disorder. For additional information on differentiating the various anxiety disorders, we refer readers to pages 189–291 in the *Diagnostic and Statistical Manual of Mental Disorders, Fifth Edition* (American Psychiatric Association, 2013).

7.2 Prevalence and Age of Onset

7.2.1 Prevalence

The lifetime prevalence of anxiety disorders is 32.4%[1] among youth ages 13–17 and 33.7% among adults ages 18–64 in the United States (Kessler et al., 2012). The lifetime prevalence of specific anxiety disorders among adults age 18–64 from most to least common is 13.8% for SP, 13.0% for SAD, 6.6% for separation anxiety disorder, 6.2% for GAD, 5.2% for PD, 2.7% for OCD, and 2.6% for AP. Comorbidity is common across conditions (Kessler et al., 2012; van Balkom et al., 2008). Commensurate with this high prevalence among youth, parents/caregivers rank anxiety disorders as the most important behavioral disorder to prevent for their children (Zimmermann, O'Donohue, et al., 2020).

[1] PTSD is included under "any anxiety disorder," in the Comorbidity Survey Replication (NCS-R) and Adolescent Supplement (NCS-A) (Kessler et al., 2012).

7.2.2 *Age of Onset (AOO)*

According to meta-analytic work, the mean age of onset (AOO) for any anxiety disorder is an estimated 21.3 years (de Lijster et al., 2017). The AOO for separation anxiety disorder is 10.6 years, SP 11.0 years, SAD 14.3 years, AP with panic 21.1 years, OCD 24.0 years, PD 30.3 years, and GAD 34.9 years. Median age of onset is 11 for any anxiety disorder, although this age varies substantially by disorder. Reported median AOO for SP and separation anxiety is 7 years (IQR is 4–7 years), SAD is 13 years (IQR of 7 years). Other anxiety disorders have a notably wider range of AOO (age 19–31; Kessler et al., 2005). Earlier age of onset is associated with greater comorbidities and anxiety disorder recurrence (Ramsawh et al., 2011).

7.3 Risk Factors

Risk factors can be defined as characteristics that both precede an outcome and are associated with an increase in likelihood of that outcome occurring (Kraemer et al., 1997). Protective factors are variables that are associated with a reduction in likelihood of a particular outcome occurring. Importantly, the term "risk factor" does not necessitate causality, and many other pathways (e.g., third variable, shared vulnerability, mutual maintenance) can explain the relationship between a given risk factor and subsequent anxiety disorder development (Kraemer et al., 1997). Risk factors for anxiety disorders may be nonspecific and confer risk broadly across many specific anxiety disorders or even across other disorders (e.g., depression) or specific to a particular disorder (Hayward et al., 2000). Negative affect, the trait-like tendency to experience more negative emotions (e.g., anxiety, anger, guilt, sadness), for instance, may be associated with internalizing disorders more generally (Anthony et al., 2002). Other factors may confer more specific risk, such as specific physiological mechanisms that implicate cigarette smoking in the development of PD (Zvolensky et al., 2004).

Kraemer et al. (1997) also distinguish between static risk factors (e.g., birth year) and dynamic risk factors (e.g., occupation). A further distinction is that among dynamic risk factors, some may be *modifiable risk factors*, or those factors that can be reasonably modified by an individual without outside intervention (Cairns et al., 2014). If a risk factor is modifiable and causally associated with a particular outcome, it may be appropriate for intervention (Cairns et al., 2014; Jacka et al., 2013). Otherwise, risk factors may be thought of as indicators of greater likelihood of developing a disorder. A systematic review of modifiable risk factors for new-onset anxiety disorders found several studies identifying prospective associations between modifiable behaviors and incident anxiety disorders (Zimmermann, Chong, et al., 2020). Notably, just 19 studies examined prospective associations between modifiable behaviors and incident anxiety disorders, suggesting a need for more research in this area.

Finally, risk factors do not operate in isolation. Biopsychosocial diathesis-stress models of anxiety pathology suggest that multiple vulnerability factors interact with stressors to cause the onset of a given disorder (Barlow, 2004). For instance, exposure to stressful conditions (e.g., absence of medical help, financial difficulties, social stressors) appears to interact with pre-disposing cognitive factors such as anxiety sensitivity (AS), a trait-like fear of bodily sensations, to increase risk for panic attacks (Zvolensky et al., 2005). Diathesis-stress models suggest that the presence of a risk factor may not be sufficient for the development of a disorder but rather part of a causal pathway in its development. Taken together, it is important to note that the presence of any given risk factor does not necessitate the development of an anxiety disorder, nor does it describe a causal relation.

7.4 Review

The following review of risk factors describes potentially relevant variables that confer risk and could be useful factors to identify patients who may benefit from intervention to prevent incident anxiety disorders. These include sociodemographic, social/environmental, mental health and health, and cognitive behavioral and temperament domains associated with anxiety disorder risk. This list is not exhaustive and may also reflect gaps in the literature on risk and protective factors for anxiety disorders. There are more prospective studies examining cigarette smoking and PD, for instance, than most other relationships (Zimmermann, Chong, et al., 2020). Despite these limitations, the following review may provide guidance in the identification of patients at greater risk for new-onset anxiety disorders.

7.4.1 Sociodemographic Risk Factors

Several sociodemographic factors have been shown to be related to the development of anxiety disorders. Perhaps the most notable risk factor is the association between female gender and anxiety disorders. The lifetime prevalence of anxiety disorders is 40.4% among women and 26.4% among men (Kessler et al., 2012). Women appear to be at significantly greater risk for the development of PD, SP, and GAD (Grant et al., 2009) although this elevated risk has not been found in every study (Moreno-Peral et al., 2014). Individuals identifying as Non-Hispanic Black and Hispanic appear to be at lower risk than those identifying as Non-Hispanic White (Grant et al., 2009; Kessler et al., 2005). Family income between 0 and $19,999 is associated with great risk of PD, SP, and GAD (Grant et al., 2009). No association was found for education, urbanicity, or region (Grant et al., 2009). One study found that being divorced or widowed was associated with new-onset GAD (Grant et al., 2009), but this is not the case in a study of older adults (Schoevers et al., 2005).

7.4.2 Social/Environmental Risk Factors

Social Support Evidence for the relationship between social support and incident anxiety disorders is mixed. Some studies have suggested a prospective relationship between lower social support and SAD (Reinelt et al., 2014), although others have suggested no link (Vriends et al., 2011).

Parental Factors Parental factors such as overcontrol, rejection, and other parental styles have been implicated in the development of anxiety disorders (Brook & Schmidt, 2008). Several studies have suggested that the presence of parental depression, anxiety, and other psychopathology (i.e., personality disorders, bipolar disorder, and sleep disturbance) has been shown to be associated with PD and GAD onset (Moreno-Peral et al., 2014).

Occupational Factors Psychological demands of work have been shown to be associated with new-onset GAD (Melchior et al., 2007; Niedhammer et al., 2015). Other work factors such as lack of social support at work, limited autonomy in decision-making, emotional demands, role and ethical conflict, and job security may also be risk factors for GAD (Niedhammer et al., 2015).

Stressful Life Events Studies have suggested a relationship between financial difficulties and new-onset anxiety disorders (Moreno-Peral et al., 2014). Some studies have also suggested a relationship between adverse childhood experiences and later-onset GAD (Moreno-Peral et al., 2014). Independent of the actual event, appraising stressful life events as more impactful is associated with risk of any new-onset anxiety disorder (Espejo et al., 2012).

Perinatal Period While estimates vary, the prevalence of OCD and PD is higher among pregnant women than in the general population, with an estimated 3% prevalence of both PD and OCD, nearly double that of non-pregnant women (Viswasam et al., 2019). Some evidence suggests that the perinatal period may also be a risk factor for the recurrence of PD for those in remission (Viswasam et al., 2019).

7.4.3 Physical and Mental Health Risk Factors

Depression Anxiety and depression frequently co-occur and are thought to have shared vulnerability features (Barlow et al., 2004). Individuals with any type of depressive disorder are at nearly three times the risk of developing a subsequent anxiety disorder and more than six times at risk for the development of SAD specifically (Jacobson & Newman, 2017).

Substance Use Disorders According to substance-induced theories, physiological arousal, both as a direct effect of the substance and also from withdrawal symptoms, may contribute to incident anxiety disorders (Garey et al., 2020; Wolitzky-Taylor et al., 2011). Individuals with anxiety disorders are nearly three times as likely to report meeting diagnostic criteria for a drug use disorder within the past 12 months than their counterparts without an anxiety disorder.

Physical Health Anxiety disorders are more prevalent among individuals with physical health conditions, even when adjusting for depression, substance use disorders, and demographic characteristics (Sareen et al., 2005). Individuals with any neurologic, vascular, respiratory, gastrointestinal, metabolic/autoimmune, bone/joint, or other physical disorders are all more likely to report a past-year anxiety disorder (Sareen et al., 2005). A prospective relationship has been found between having a greater number of physical diseases and PD (Rudaz et al., 2010).

7.4.4 Health Behaviors

Tobacco Use Several studies have suggested a link between cigarette use and PD (Breslau & Klein, 1999; Isensee et al., 2003; Johnson, 2000; Mojtabai & Crum, 2013; Pohl et al., 1992; Zvolensky et al., 2008). Cigarette smoking has been associated with new-onset AP (Johnson, 2000) and SP (Isensee et al., 2003; Mojtabai & Crum, 2013). Cigarette smoking has mixed evidence in the development of GAD, associated with risk in two studies (Johnson, 2000; Mojtabai & Crum, 2013) but not in a third (Isensee et al., 2003). Evidence does not support a link between tobacco use and OCD (Johnson, 2000). Cigarette smoking has demonstrated a link with SAD, although this may be dependent on level of use (Isensee et al., 2003; Mojtabai & Crum, 2013).

Cannabis Use Some studies have suggested a prospective relationship between cannabis use and incident social anxiety disorder but not panic disorder or specific phobia controlling for cigarette smoking and demographic characteristics (Feingold et al., 2016; Zvolensky et al., 2008).

Alcohol Use Alcohol quantity has demonstrated a relationship between new-onset anxiety disorders, but only for women (Flensborg-Madsen et al., 2011). In this study, high levels of drinking were characterized by 4 drinks or more per week for women and 21 drinks per week for men. Women drinking at higher levels were twice as likely to develop an anxiety disorder (Flensborg-Madsen et al., 2011). Similarly, occasional binge drinking was associated with more than two times the risk of PD among women but not for men in a prospective study (Chou et al., 2011).

Caffeine Use Caffeine has acute anxiogenic effects and is associated with nervousness and jitteriness. Caffeine intake is associated with greater risk of GAD, and PD (Kendler et al., 2006), although causal evidence is limited and other studies have found no such relationship using a case-control design (Pohl et al., 1992).

Physical Activity Cross-sectional evidence and prospective studies are suggestive of a link between physical activity and anxiety disorders (Schuch et al., 2019). A meta-analysis indicated that greater self-reported engagement in physical activity is associated with a decrease in likelihood of developing an anxiety disorder and, specifically, lower likelihood of developing AP (Schuch et al., 2019). Sports participation has also been shown to be a protective factor (Hiles, Lamers et al., 2017).

7.4.5 Cognitive, Behavioral, and Temperamental Risk Factors

Several cognitive, behavioral, and temperamental or personality factors have been associated with incident anxiety disorders. Behavioral avoidance of social situations has been associated with new-onset SAD, even when controlling for social anxiety symptom severity (Trumpf et al., 2010). Similarly, behavioral inhibition can be defined as a more trait or temperament consisting of the tendency to avoid, or respond cautiously to, novel stimuli (Fox et al., 2005). Behavioral inhibition has been found to be a risk for incident anxiety disorders (Muris et al., 2011).

Anxiety sensitivity (AS) is a trait-like fear of anxiety-related physical sensations that are perceived as potentially harmful. AS has been descried as an "anxiety amplifier," in that individuals perceiving bodily sensations associated with anxiety experience greater anxiety as a result of this perception (Taylor et al., 2007, *p*. 177). AS is conceptualized as having three dimensions. These include physical concerns, such as the belief that increasing heart rate will result in a heart attack; social concerns, or the belief that others are noticing anxiety symptoms and may be evaluating these negatively; and cognitive concerns, or beliefs that bodily sensations are an indicator of losing control (Taylor et al., 2007). A large body of work has demonstrated a relationship between AS and the development of anxiety symptoms and disorders (Schmidt et al., 1999; 2006; 2010).

Finally, it is not surprising that coping skills may be a protective factor in the development of anxiety disorders. Coping skills, including problem-focused and emotion-focused coping have been shown to be a protective factor in the development of SP (Trumpf et al., 2010). Problem-focused coping includes the use of resources to solve a problem or source of stress. In contrast, emotion-focused coping includes efforts to change the internal experience of emotion rather than an external problem. For instance, emotion-focused coping could include cognitive restructuring or distraction (Trumpf et al., 2010)

7.5 Screening for Anxiety

The detection of the beginning stages of anxiety issues is crucial in the prevention of anxiety disorders. This is especially apparent when considering the sobering statistic that on average, individuals with anxiety disorders often lag between 9 and 23 *years* in seeking treatment (Bienvenu & Ginsburg, 2007). Some of this lag time may be reduced by effective screening procedures utilized in primary care settings, leading healthcare professionals to be more aware of the presence or the severity of anxious symptoms. Therefore, especially in integrated care settings where a behavioral health clinician is more available, it is crucial to develop a method of screening patients efficiently for the presence of anxiety disorders. The quicker that anxiety symptoms can be found, the faster interventions can be implemented to prevent those symptoms from worsening.

In addition, screening for existing disorders, effective screening, and detection of risk factors can be used by clinicians to know when to be more aware of when preventive care is indicated. Qualitative information (e.g., observation, patient report) should be a part of the screening process and should also be combined with more quantitative measures. Quantitative measures are useful due to the relative speed with which they can be administered as well as the ability of those measures to provide more objective data on the presence and possibly severity of anxiety symptoms (Goldberg et al., 2017).

7.5.1 Guidance when Selecting Measures

Selection of the appropriate measures is key when designing or modifying a screening program. Humeniuk et al. (2010) have indicated in their recommendations for screening instruments that cost be factored into the decision-making process. Given that a screening instrument may be administered dozens, if not hundreds, of times each day, the cost of such an assessment needs to be taken into account in order to assure a sustainable program.

In addition to cost, the validity of potential screening instruments should be considered as well. Not all measures labeled as "anxiety screens" or "anxiety inventories" perform adequately at assessing anxiety. The selection of a problematic screening instrument may result in too many false-positives or false-negatives, depending on the measure selected. For example, Muntingh et al., (2011) examined the use of the *Beck Anxiety Inventory* (Beck et al., 1988) and found the inventory could be used as an indicator of anxiety with patients in primary care settings. However, the researchers also indicated their findings suggested that the measure is not a suitable instrument to discriminate between anxiety and depression, as it is sensitive to both the severity of depressive symptoms as well as the severity of anxiety symptoms (Muntingh et al., 2011).

Finally, length of the screen is an important consideration. Shorter measures may not always perform as well as longer measures, but this must be weighed against the amount of time that it takes to complete longer measures. Especially in the context of a primary care waiting room, a patient may not have an overabundance of time to complete assessments, so care should be taken to ensure that the length of selected screens is not excessive.

7.5.2 Administration Guidelines

Once measures have been selected, there are a number of general administration suggestions to consider in order to effectively deploy the screening tools. Spear et al. (2016) conducted a feasibility and acceptability study of a computer-assisted screen for alcohol and substance use disorders which, while focusing on substance use and not anxiety, still provides valuable insight into general guidelines when implementing behavioral health screening measures. Spear et al. (2016) focused their efforts on a screen that was designed to be administered in the waiting room of a primary care clinic. Given that most primary care physicians may only have 10 min to attend to a patient before needing to move on to the next patient, being able to complete assessments ahead of the planned appointment can be an efficient time saver (Wiesche et al., 2017). While many clinics are already implementing their own screening processes, the following points may be useful when starting, or working to improve an existing, system of screening patients.

1. *Methods of Delivery*: Pen and paper screening tests are rapidly becoming more and more difficult to administer for many reasons, including issues of language and literacy (Goldberg et al., 2017). Therefore, consideration must be given to how to deliver the screening instruments. Overall, computer-assisted methods have become more common and represent a viable alternative to traditional pen and paper assessments. While computerized assessments do have their own special requirements (detailed below), they can be an effective means to bridge the gap of language or literacy barriers via translations of assessments and via audio-assisted screen, where the screen is either partially or fully read to the patient by the device administering the test (Goldberg et al., 2017; Spear et al., 2016). However, care must be taken in the selection of the actual hardware that will be utilized to deliver the assessments. The tablet or computer should be durable and easy to use. Additionally, if a system of electronic assessments is not already in place, consultation should be sought with appropriate information technology experts with training in regulations outlined under the *Health Insurance Portability and Accountability Act* (HIPAA). This is to ensure that the data transmissions from any mobile screening device (such as a laptop or tablet) or from any stationary computer are sent in a secure and encrypted manner back to the central medical database (Department of Health and Human Services, 2013).

2. *The Importance of Screening Before the Appointment*: Given the aforementioned limited time most physicians can spend with patients, having them complete measures either in the waiting room or before coming to their appointment can save valuable time. Additionally, given the advent of electronic health records systems, physicians may be able to access and view the completed screens before seeing the patient themselves (Garrett, 2010). Ideally, being able to see the results of any administered measures should allow a primary care physician to be able to identify possible warning signs and plan on what should the focus of session should be during their time with the patient. If anxiety issues are detected, then information can be provided on prevention strategies. In the case of integrated care settings, the measures can also alert the physician to involve the on-staff behavioral health specialist, should the need arise.
3. *Consider "At Home" Delivery Options*: Increasingly, clinics that have access to electronic health records systems are also gaining access to patient portals were patients can log in remotely and complete intake paperwork and respond to questionnaires (Titanium Software, 2019; Epic, 2021). Patient portals permit individuals to complete check-in paperwork, intake procedures, and, depending on the capabilities of the system in question, questionnaires related to their health and functioning. As these technologies become more widely available, it is worth considering the possibility of administering screens before a patient arrives at the clinic. By completing paperwork at home, it potentially allows for slightly longer, and thereby more detailed, screens to be administered. Additionally, scores that exceed predetermined cutoff points can be flagged before the patient is seen, allowing for more time to prepare intervention options. Furthermore, these technologies allow for the administration of behavioral health screens in rural telehealth settings, where having the patient be physically present may be infeasible.
4. *The Need for Orientation*: When considering an electronic assessment system, some concern might be raised regarding the acceptability of such measures to individuals with limited experience using computers. Spear et al. (2016) found that electronic assessments were preferred to other forms of assessment (such as clinical interviews), especially when discussing symptoms of a private or sensitive nature (in their case, alcohol use). However, to achieve this effect, the researchers indicated that an orientation was needed, where the patient would be introduced to the interface and be shown how to use the device. Additionally, such orientations can review topics such as confidentiality and ensure that patients know how the information they will be providing might be utilized by the healthcare staff. Orientations such as these have been shown to help even those with limited to no computer experience navigate the screening process successfully (Spear et al., 2016). Additionally, the orientation can be delivered either in person or can be integrated into the device used in the assessment process, such as in the form of an information slide or short introductory video.

7.5.3 *Example Screening Measure for Anxiety*

While a number of screening measures do exist for anxiety disorders, the Generalized Anxiety Disorder Screener (GAD-7) stands out as being short, efficient, and freely available (Kroenke et al., 2007). The GAD-7 is a 7-item self-report measure capable of assessing the severity of anxious symptoms that an individual is experiencing. Additionally, the GAD-7 has been demonstrated to be able to screen the presence of four different anxiety disorders: generalized anxiety disorder, posttraumatic stress disorder, social anxiety disorder, and panic disorder. While the screener cannot differentially diagnose those disorders, it can flag a clinician to ask further questions in order to hone in a specific diagnosis if symptoms have progressed that far. A cut score of 8 may be used as a point of identifying when further questioning might be employed to detect the development of an anxiety disorder. Given the brief nature of the GAD-7, it is possible to combine it with other behavioral health measures that can be quickly administered during the check-in process at an outpatient clinic visit. Thus, the scale can serve as an early warning system, helping to alert clinicians to elevations in anxiety symptom severity that might indicate the need of prompt preventative intervention.

Another freely available measure in the prevention tool box is the Anxiety Sensitivity Index, version 3 (ASI-3; Taylor et al., 2007). As mentioned previously, the construct of anxiety sensitivity is a potential risk factor in the development of anxiety disorders. Therefore, the ASI-3 can be utilized when deciding who should receive interventions to help prevent the development of anxiety disorders, even when anxiety symptoms are not present or not yet severe. The scale is an 18-item multiple choice survey and with scores between 0 and 17 indicating almost no anxiety sensitivity, 18 and 35 indicating low anxiety sensitivity, 36 and 53 indicating moderate anxiety sensitivity, and anything above 54 indicating high anxiety sensitivity. The ASI-3 can be used both as a means of assessing the overall risk of developing an anxiety disorder, with high scores indicating greater risk, as well as a means of tracking the effectiveness of any deployed interventions. However, depending on resources available, even scoring beyond 0 on the ASI-3 may indicate a brief, preventative action, such as the Anxiety Sensitivity Amelioration Training (Schmidt et al., 2007; detailed below), or the implementation of self-guided e-Health options may be useful to prevent the development of anxiety symptoms later on.

7.6 Prevention Strategies

Using the information from the screens listed above, the next question revolves around methods to prevent the development or worsening of detected anxiety symptoms. A great deal of research has been performed on various methods of responding early in order to prevent or at least lessen mood disorders in general and anxiety in specific (Griffiths, Farrer, Christensen, 2010). However, when deciding on what interventions to select and which ones to use with a particular patient, several principles as well as the model of stepped-care deserve consideration.

7.6.1 General Principles: Behavioral Health Literacy

A key ingredient for treatment programs in general lies in the construct of behavioral health literacy. Behavioral health literacy is construct that goes beyond the boundaries of traditional psychoeducation. Psychoeducation is usually defined as interventions that provide informative materials, such as lectures, leaflets, or information websites (Clarke et al., 2015). Psychoeducation is a part of many existing interventions, such as for GAD (Zinbarg, Craske, & Barlow, 2006) and PTSD (Foa et al., 2019). As defined in Willis and O'Donohue (2018), behavioral health literacy incorporates elements of psychoeducation but also includes a focus on the ability to use that information to make healthcare-related decisions. Specifically, Willis and O'Donohue (2018) defined behavioral health literacy as a series of competencies including the ability to obtain valid and relevant behavioral health information, evaluate and utilize that information in making healthcare decisions, and understand the factors that contribute to the prevention of psychological disorders. In particular, good behavioral health literacy is thought to include being able to recognize when a disorder is in its initial stages or is becoming worse as well as how to prevent behavioral health issues in the first place. This call to effective action is especially important in behavioral health literacy, as evidence is currently mixed on the ability of solely psychoeducational treatments to effect short-term or long-term improvements in anxiety disorders (Clarke et al., 2015). Behavioral health literacy focuses on informing the patient of their options and supporting them in taking the necessary action for their specific situation.

It is important to note that behavioral health literacy by itself is not a treatment or intervention. Rather, it is an important part of an overall treatment strategy. Providing information to the patient is thought to help increase their willingness to participate in treatment and help them feel that they understand what is required of them and why. Specifically applied to the domain of anxiety prevention, behavioral health literacy focuses on ensuring that patients understand the factors that may be increasing their anxiety, such as avoidance of feared stimuli, and what factors may serve to reduce their anxious responses, such as graduated exposure (Foa et al., 2019). Behavioral health literacy may be especially important in anxiety prevention, as it may be that some patients will require more information to help clarify why they may need to undergo a preventative treatment for anxiety. Finally, behavioral health literacy is vital as it allows patients to more fully participate in shared decision-making with their provider, the act of patients exercising their voice in treatment planning (Willis & O'Donohue, 2018).

7.6.2 General Principles: Shared Decision-Making

Similar to behavioral health literacy, shared decision-making is not an intervention; rather, it is a principle that is important to include in the construction of a prevention program. Willis & O'Donohue (2018) indicated that, like behavioral health literacy, shared decision-making may help to improve patient adherence with treatment recommendations. Shared decision-making itself consists of ensuring that the patient has an active voice in the treatment planning phase. Treatment options should be explained, and patients should be given the chance to make their opinions known to the provider. This process may include the exploration of alternative options that a clinic may not be able to provide (e.g., if a patient wanted to try exposure-based therapy, but the staff at their provider's office was unable to offer this service). Additionally, shared decision-making entails the various levels of care (i.e., watchful waiting, guided self-help, referral to a specialist) and making sure that the patient has a clear idea of which level of care their current presenting symptoms best correspond to. Shared decision-making is thought to increase treatment adherence by fostering a sense of investment in the treatment plan (Willis & O'Donohue, 2018). The patient, ideally, feels that it is "their" treatment plan, not a plan that has been forced on them by a medical authority.

7.6.3 Primary Prevention

Primary prevention of anxiety is a continuing goal of treatment providers due to the potential for the efficacy and cost-effectiveness of such interventions (García-Campayo et al., 2015). Effective interventions for anxiety disorders in adolescents exist, although, they may be difficult to apply in the primary care setting without some degree of modification, especially as many established interventions were initially designed to be delivered in the school setting (García-Campayo et al., 2015). One of the most effective prevention programs for anxiety in adolescents is the FRIENDS program, a universal 10-session cognitive behavioral therapy intervention that is designed to promote emotional resilience. The intervention includes modules on emotion identification, cognitive methods to challenge unhelpful thoughts, relaxation techniques, and problem-solving skills. The program is designed to be delivered in a classroom setting and include all children, regardless of emotional health statue (Stallard et al., 2005).

The FRIENDS program has since been updated and modified for other groups, such as adults and families, with training available online for interested providers at https://friendsresilience.org/ (Barrett, 2019). The current FRIENDS Resilience program, while originally intended for school use, can be adapted into a number of different forms, depending on the setting. For example, the program can be compressed into a 2–3 full day intensive workshop, a 2-hour 5-day workshop, 45-min weekly sessions spread out over several weeks, or 15-min daily sessions spread out over several weeks. This suggests that the FRIENDS program might be useful as a guide when developing a prevention program that can be delivered in an integrated care setting, taking into account available resources and constraints.

7.6.4 A Stepped Care Approach to Prevention

In general, stepped care refers to planning treatments that proceed in order of ascending intensity (Richards, 2012). The core idea in stepped care is to match the needs of the patient to the appropriate level of care (e.g., outpatient vs. intensive outpatient treatment), with the focus being on starting at the lowest appropriate level of care and then escalating upward as needed. This stepped care model can be utilized to organize differing treatments intended to prevent the continuing development of anxiety symptoms (O'Donohue & Draper, 2011). In integrated care settings, it will be vital to coordinate these treatment efforts with the behavioral health specialist. This is especially important in the event that medications are present, as some forms of anxiety treatment will require medications to be stable before starting (Foa et al., 2019).

Once a provider has identified an individual experiencing the beginning stages of anxiety, such as someone scoring between 1 and 8 on the GAD-7 (Kroenke et al., 2007), then it may be a good opportunity to have a conversation with the patient discussion option for symptoms from worsening. Furthermore, if a provider suspects that a patient may possess any of the previously mentioned risk factors for the development of anxiety disorders, then intervention should be considered to prevent the development of symptoms, even if those symptoms have yet to manifest. The provider should strive to ensure that enough information has been given to the patient that they feel that they can make an informed decision on what to do next. Then, the provider and patient can collaboratively construct a treatment plan for preventing the development of the identified anxious symptoms. Below is a model of how the stepped care approach can be brought to bear on the issue of anxiety prevention.

A note before proceeding, the following information is intended to be used as soon as anxiety symptoms begin to present themselves or when individuals may be at risk for developing anxiety symptoms (see anxiety risk factors previously mentioned in this chapter). The goal of any prevention program in primary care targeting anxiety should be to provide the needed tools to prevent anxiety symptoms from happening or to intervene early enough to prevent an anxiety disorder from forming.

7.6.4.1 Step 1: Watchful Waiting

Watchful waiting represents the lowest intensity option and therefore may be best reserved for those experiencing relatively low symptoms of anxiety or anxiety symptoms that can clearly be tied to a temporary situation or event (i.e., a major test in school or a job interview). This also may be a good step for individuals with a low likelihood of developing anxiety disorders, such as those suffering from few or none of the risk factors previously mentioned in this chapter. The watchful waiting step can be useful in cases where anxiety is starting to develop but has not yet reached a point of concern for the patient. Additionally, watchful waiting provides the opportunity to see if the anxious symptoms spontaneously remit during the period of waiting.

7.6.4.2 Step 2: Self-Directed and Health Behaviors

The next step up from watchful waiting is guided self-help and self-directed interventions delivered via books, pamphlets or reading material, and digital modalities. If an individual's anxiety symptoms do not remit spontaneously after a set period of time, then it may be time to escalate to a more direct form of intervention. Additionally, if the patient started with higher (though still subclinical) levels of anxiety, then they may start the prevention process here. Finally, this step may be seen as a starting point in the event that an individual is experiencing some of the previously mentioned risk factors (such as stressful life events, physical health conditions, etc.), even if they are not yet beginning to experience symptoms of anxiety.

This step involves more action on the part of the patient as they take part in self-directed and guided self-help interventions. Computerized Cognitive Behavioral Therapy (cCBT) packages represent on form of guided self-help, and they have become more commonplace. Importantly, current evidence suggests that they can be as effective as in person, face-to-face sessions in the treatment of anxiety disorders (Pauley et al., 2021; Krebber et al., 2012). Furthermore, evidence-based cCBT has been shown to have similar impacts on symptom improvement as face-to-face therapy for PD and for SP, indicating that a wide range of anxiety symptoms can be treated via computerized CBT systems. cCBT can take multiple forms; however, the system described by Proudfoot et al. (2003) represents a good example. Participants in their study used the *Beating the Blues* cCBT intervention developed by Gray et al. (2000). In this intervention, participants attended nine online sessions, starting with a 15-min introductory video, followed by 9 weekly therapy sessions lasting 50 min. The software generated homework for each patient and customized sessions to the unique needs of each individual. At the end of each session, a report on progress was sent to the patient's provider, including information on any risk factors such as suicidal ideation. Systems similar to *Beating the Blues* represent a potentially crucial source of guided self-help, as computer systems usually lack the long wait times that traditional one and one therapy may have before a patient can be seen by a provider. cCBT offers the chance for someone to be seen quickly and potentially slow or prevent the progress of their anxiety symptoms. Two examples of currently available self-help, CBT-informed online options are the following:

1. Get-Better: Self-Help (Health Promotion Agency, 2021)
    (a) Available at: https://depression.org.nz/get-better/self-help/

2. Anxiety Self-Help Guide (NHS Inform, 2021)
   (a) Available at: https://www.nhsinform.scot/illnesses-and-conditions/mental-health/mental-health-self-help-guides/anxiety-self-help-guide

Bibliotherapy, or the assigning of evidence-based books containing self-guided treatment information, has also become an area of focus in the treatment of anxiety (Wootton et al., 2018). Bibliotherapy can be especially useful in integrated care settings. It allows a provider to provide patients with effective information regarding anxiety while allowing patients to read the material at their own pace without needing additional guidance from the provider. Bibliotherapy may also serve as an effective intervention when risk factors for anxiety have been identified, but no symptoms have arisen yet (Bienvenu & Ginsburg, 2007). The following are self-help books that have been utilized in the reviewed literature and that have the benefit of currently being available for purchase.

1. *The Mindful Way Through Anxiety: Break Free from Chronic Worry and Reclaim Your Life* (Orsillo & Roemer, 2011)
   (a) Available both online on www.amazon.com and in print. An audiobook version is also available as of this writing on www.amazon.com.
2. *The Shyness and Social Anxiety Workbook* (Antony & Swinson, 2018)
   (a) Available both online on www.amazon.com and in print.
3. *Worry Less, Live More: The Mindful Way Through Anxiety* (Orsillo & Roemer, 2016)
   (a) Available both online on www.amazon.com and in print.

Guided self-help also can incorporate the growing field of mobile applications. Drissi et al. (2020) found in an examination of the Google Play Store and the iPhone app store 167 anxiety-related mobile apps (123 Android apps and 44 iOS apps). These apps covered a wide range of anxiety coping skills, such as providing psychoeducation, interactive breathing exercises, mindfulness practices, meditation, and day planning. These apps themselves represent another potential fruitful avenue where patients can receive help at their own pace without having to wait for a provider. However, it is recommended that providers examine apps before recommending them to patients. Drissi et al. (2020) found a small (but still non-zero) number of apps based on pseudoscientific and non-evidence-based practices. For example, at least one application that was investigated was entirely based around management of anxiety via horoscopes.

A final entry that deserves mentioning in the guided self-help stage is health behavior-based interventions. As previously noted, several health behaviors have been identified as risk factors for anxiety disorder development. While more research is needed to determine causality, it is possible that modifying these health behaviors could reduce risk for anxiety disorders. Some evidence suggests that modifying health behaviors can have an impact on anxiety symptom severity. For instance, physical activity has demonstrated strong effects in helping to reduce mild to moderate anxiety, potentially being as effective in the long-term as the use of medications such as clomipramine in panic disorder (Jorm et al., 2004). Given that exercise has reported strong effects for mild anxiety, encouraging healthy physical activity via apps or as part of a cCBT treatment protocol may also serve to increase the effects of prevention efforts. Similarly, caffeine reduction has been found to be associated with decrease levels of anxiety (Jorm et al., 2004). Individuals with GAD, PD, and SAD have reported higher levels of anxiety after consuming caffeine in a double-blind, placebo-controlled study (Jorm et al., 2004). While patients are making use of self-directed interventions, modifying these and other health behaviors (e.g., diet, tobacco, drug, and alcohol use) may prove helpful in managing or reducing their anxiety symptoms. Chapter 5 in this volume reviews multiple behavior change interventions as prevention.

7.6.4.3 Step 2: Brief Interventions

If a patient's anxiety symptoms continue to increase despite guided self-help interventions, then it is likely time to consider brief interventions that can be carried out by either the primary care provider or the behavioral health clinician in integrated care clinics. The goal of these brief interventions is to reduce or manage the anxiety symptoms without the need to resort to a full course of psychotherapy. This step is useful for when self-help methods have not been successful or when a clinician feels that a short, in person intervention may serve to prevent symptoms from getting worse without the need for additional treatment.

One potential method of prevention at this step involves Anxiety Sensitivity Amelioration Training (ASAT; Schmidt et al., 2007). ASAT is a brief, 40-min intervention designed to address how stress impacts the body as well as information regarding conditioned fear responses to bodily cues (i.e., interoceptive conditioning). Training is also provided in exercises to help reduce fear reactions to body cues that are commonly connected to fears and anxiety. In its original form, the ASAT program was delivered as a 30-min training video followed up by a 10-min session with a provider where practices were discussed and questions were answered. In this modality, ASAT may be especially helpful in the primary care setting, as the instructional video could potentially be assigned to a patient as homework, with the provider using the 10-min in person session to problem solve and provide feedback on practicing exposures at home. Additionally, there is a longer version of ASAT intended for use with adolescents that is detailed below in the next section (Knapp et al., 2020).

Reeves and Stace (2005) examined a treatment package for mild to moderate anxiety symptoms called assisted bibliotherapy. Assisted bibliotherapy involves slightly more provided input than traditional bibliotherapy and consists of an 8-week course of treatment with limited clinician contact (20-min weekly sessions). Six module booklets are presented and discussed throughout the course of treatment, with each booklet focusing on a different aspect of anxiety management, such as breathing exercises or reducing worry. Assisted bibliotherapy overall is an effective brief intervention, and in trials more than 80% of participants reported that the self-help strategies became part of their daily routines by the end of treatment. Additionally, patients who participated reported significant improvements in their anxiety symptoms. Unfortunately, the authors used proprietary self-help materials currently not available online. However, the principles illustrated in their study suggest that other bibliotherapy packages, such as *Feeling Good: The New Mood Therapy*, may be effective in an assisted bibliotherapy context (Burns, 1999; Yuan et al., 2018).

Other brief interventions include the Anxiety Sensitivity Amelioration Program for Youth (ASAP-Y; Knapp et al., 2020). This program adapted from the standardized Anxiety Sensitivity Amelioration Training program for adults (ASAT; Schmidt et al., 2007) and includes psychoeducation, exposure to fear stimuli (in this case breathing through a straw), homework assignments parent training, and parental monitoring of at home exposures targeted at patients under the age of 18. Patients who have undergone ASAP-Y on average report lower levels of anxiety sensitivity both immediately afterwards and at follow-up assessments a year later. ASAP-Y is time limited, consisting of only two pieces, psychoeducation and direct exposure in Part I and parent training and exposure monitoring in Part II, once per week for 4 weeks. This time limited nature makes the ASAP-Y more feasible to deploy in integrated care situations were behavioral health specialists and providers may not have the time to see a patient for an extended period of time. Despite the time limited nature, ASAP-Y appears to be effective at targeting anxiety sensitivity and thus effective at reducing overall anxiety (Reiss & Bootzin, 1985). Furthermore, the program from which ASAP-Y is derived, ASAT, has been shown to have similar effects on adults with a similar timeline (Schmidt et al., 2007).

7.6.4.4 Step 3: Referral for Specialized Treatment

If a patient still has not experienced significant anxiety symptoms relief after attempting a brief intervention, or if anxiety symptoms increase significantly (e.g., if a patient's GAD-7 screening score rises above 8; Kroenke et al., 2007), then it may be time to consider a referral to a behavioral health provider and a full course of anxiety treatment. It is recommended that such a referral be made to a provider capable of offering evidence-based treatments in general and exposure-based therapy, specifically based on the long-standing empirical foundation supporting exposure-based treatments for anxiety disorders (Deacon et al., 2013).

Even if a patient escalates to this level of care, however, and requires more intensive one on one psychotherapy, the time spent in previous steps is not wasted. Hopefully, the patient will have accrued new coping skills and knowledge that can aid in maintaining treatment gains in the long run once their course of treatment has been completed. For a graphical representation of the preceding steps, please see Fig. 7.1.

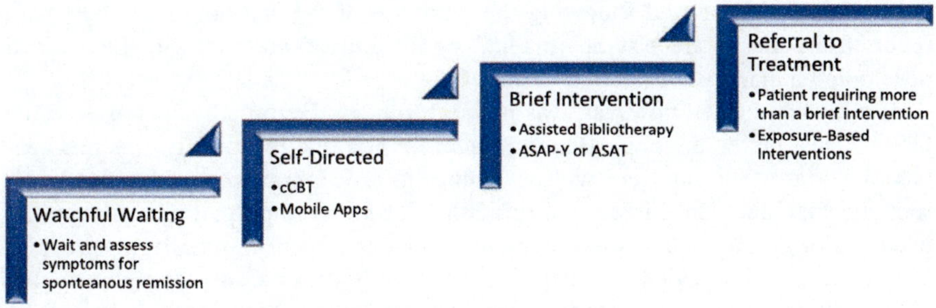

Fig. 7.1 The stepped care model applied to anxiety prevention

7.6.5 Deploying the Model

A potential model for summarizing and utilizing the information presented above is as follows. Before attempting any interventions for preventing anxiety disorders, the first issue to address is how to screen for anxiety symptoms and risk factors and then establishing clear criteria on when interventions will be delivered. Once initial screening measures are in place, they can be used as warning signs to trigger further assessment surrounding anxiety risk factors that a provider should be aware of (such as occupational stress, see above). Depending on the available resources, once anxiety risk factors have been identified, then the stepped care model depicted above can be implemented at the lowest appropriate stage. If needed, patients can escalate up the steps of care until they find the right one for their situation.

7.6.6 A Hypothetical Example

To further illustrate the stepped care approach outlined above, the following hypothetical case examples are presented. The hypothetical case involves two individuals, Kira, aged 29, and her husband Cael, aged 30. Kira has not been experiencing symptoms of anxiety, while Cael has recently begun to experience some minor anxiety, but not serious enough to be diagnosed with a specific anxiety disorder.

While at her primary care doctor's office, Kira completes a number of behavioral health screens, including the GAD-7 and ASI-3. Kira scores a 3 on the GAD-7, below the usual clinical cutoff. However, she scores an 18 on the ASI-3, indicating the presence of elevated anxiety sensitivity, a potential risk factor for the development of anxiety disorders, though it is still low. Based on the elevated ASI-3 score, Kira's provider asks some additional questions regarding Kira's risk factors and identifies that Kira is experiencing an increase in stress at work as well as has been drinking a higher amount of caffeine than usual. Kira's provider recommends that she start with some guided self-help options and recommends both an app she can utilize on her phone with anxiety coping skills, relaxation techniques. By titrating her coffee use down and following the guidance of the self-help materials, Kira reported that her anxiety symptoms had significantly decreased, and she avoided developing a diagnosable anxiety disorder.

Her husband Cael, however, was not so fortunate. He initially scored 7 on the GAD-7, just below the clinical cutoff, and reported that his anxiety was manageable, but starting to interfere with his ability to function at work. Specifically, he reported that since encountering a difficulty during an important presentation, he had been struggling with anxiety about his work performance. Initially, his provider started Cael on the guided self-help step, but after 3 weeks, Cael was reporting that his anxiety had worsened, though it was still at subclinical levels. At this point, he was close to meeting criteria for social anxiety disorder, and his provider contacted the behavioral health clinician at the integrated care clinic and set Cael up with a brief intervention. The intervention, which incorporated elements of exposure as defined in the ASAT manual, lasted approximately 5 weeks. At the end of the treatment, Cael reported that his anxiety symptoms had returned to normative levels and he was performing better at work. Better still, he reported that the skills he had acquired in the guided self-help section were helping him to maintain the positive changes in his life.

While these cases are brief and admittedly somewhat idealized, they nonetheless represent a possible course of treatment in the effort to prevent anxiety disorders. In Kira's case, she was able to succeed at a lower level of care and avoid significant increases in her anxiety. Cael required a step up but one that still represents a smaller time commitment than a full course of psychotherapy. Both represent cases where a clinician can intervene when screening measures indicate a possible risk to develop significant anxiety and then prevent that anxiety from getting worse or developing into a diagnosable disorder.

7.7 Conclusion

Overall, the goal of this chapter was to provide a tool kit healthcare personnel working in integrated care settings. This tool kit consists of information on risk factors, screening tools, and intervention options to help prevent anxiety symptoms from becoming worse. Given the access that primary care has for the general population, implementing preventative anxiety treatments in integrated settings is an important component of anxiety prevention broadly (Finley et al., 2018).

One final note on the prevention efforts was described here in this chapter. True to the spirit of integrated healthcare, proper implementation of the suggestions contained herein will require the cooperation of multiple specialists. Physicians will need to cooperate with the behavioral health professionals to ensure timely interventions when needed. Behavioral health specialists will need to partner with medical information technology experts to make screening tools more available and easier to use. Like integrated care in general, it is through the combining of these various skillsets that effective progress can be made in both screening and preventing the development of anxiety disorders.

References

American Psychiatric Association. (2013). *Diagnostic and statistical manual of mental disorders (DSM-5®)*. American Psychiatric Pub.

Anthony, J. L., Lonigan, C. J., Hooe, E. S., & Phillips, B. M. (2002). An affect-based, hierarchical model of temperament and its relations with internalizing symptomatology. *Journal of Clinical Child and Adolescent Psychology, 31*(4), 480–490.

Antony, M. M., & Swinson, R. P. (2018). The Shyness and social anxiety workbook. : New Harbinger Publications

Barlow, D. H. (2004). *Anxiety and its disorders: The nature and treatment of anxiety and panic*. Guilford Press.

Barlow, D. H., Allen, L. B., & Choate, M. L. (2004). Toward a unified treatment for emotional disorders. *Behavior Therapy, 35*(2), 205–230.

Barrett, P. (2019). *Friends resilience*. Retrieved June 21, 2021, from Friends Resilience Hub: friendsresilience.org

Beck, A. T., Epstein, N., Brown, G., & Steer, R. A. (1988). N inventory for measuring clinical anxiety: Psychometric properties. *Journal of Consulting and Clinical Psychology, 56*, 893–897.

Bienvenu, O. J., & Ginsburg, G. S. (2007). Prevention of anxiety disorders. *International Review of Psychiatry, 19*(6), 647–654.

Breslau, N., & Klein, D. F. (1999). Smoking and panic attacks. *Archives of General Psychiatry, 56*(12), 1141. https://doi.org/10.1001/archpsyc.56.12.1141

Brook, C. A., & Schmidt, L. A. (2008). Social anxiety disorder: A review of environmental risk factors. *Neuropsychiatric Disease and Treatment*.

Burns, D. D., & Beck, A. T. (1999). *Feeling good: The new mood therapy*. HarperCollins Publishers.

Cairns, K. E., Yap, M. B. H., Pilkington, P. D., & Jorm, A. F. (2014). Risk and protective factors for depression that adolescents can modify: A systematic review and meta-analysis of longitudinal studies. *Journal of Affective Disorders, 169*, 61–75. https://doi.org/10.1016/j.jad.2014.08.006

Chou, K.-L., Liang, K., & Mackenzie, C. S. (2011). Binge drinking and Axis I psychiatric disorders in community-dwelling middle-aged and older adults: Results from the National Epidemiologic Survey on Alcohol and Related Conditions (NESARC). *The Journal of Clinical Psychiatry, 72*(5), 640–647.

Clarke, A. M., Kuosmanen, T., & Barry, M. M. (2015). A systematic review of online youth mental health promotion and prevention interventions. *Journal of Youth and Adolescence, 44*(1), 90–113.

Combs, H., & Markman, J. (2014). Anxiety disorders in primary care. *Medical Clinics, 98*(5), 1007–1023.

Deacon, B. J., Farrell, N. R., Kemp, J. J., Dixon, L. J., Sy, J. T., Zhang, A. R., & McGrath, P. B. (2013). Assessing therapist reservations about exposure therapy for anxiety disorders: The therapist beliefs about exposure scale. *Journal of Anxiety Disorders, 27*(8), 772–780.

de Lijster, J. M., Dierckx, B., Utens, E. M. W. J., Verhulst, F. C., Zieldorff, C., Dieleman, G. C., & Legerstee, J. S. (2017). The age of onset of anxiety disorders: A meta-analysis. *Canadian Journal of Psychiatry. Revue Canadienne de Psychiatrie, 62*(4), 237.

Department of Health and Human Services. (2013). *HIPAA Administrative Simplification*. Retrieved July 21, 2020, from U.S. Department of Health and Human Services: https://www.hhs.gov/sites/default/files/hipaa-simplification-201303.pdf

Drissi, N., Ouhbi, S., Idrissi, M. A. J., & Ghogho, M. (2020). An analysis on self-management and treatment-related functionality and characteristics of highly rated anxiety apps. *International Journal of Medical Informatics*, 104243.

Espejo, E. P., Hammen, C., & Brennan, P. A. (2012). Elevated appraisals of the negative impact of naturally occurring life events: A risk factor for depressive and anxiety disorders. *Journal of Abnormal Child Psychology*. https://doi.org/10.1007/s10802-011-9552-0

Epic. (2021). *MyChart Features*. Retrieved June 10, 2021, from MyChart: https://www.mychart.com/Features

Feingold, D., Weiser, M., Rehm, J., & Lev-Ran, S. (2016). The association between cannabis use and anxiety disorders: Results from a population-based representative sample. *European Neuropsychopharmacology*. https://doi.org/10.1016/j.euroneuro.2015.12.037

Finley, C. R., Chan, D. S., Garrison, S., Korownyk, C., Kolber, M. R., Campbell, S., Eurich, D. T., Lindblad, A. J., Vandermeer, B., & Allan, G. M. (2018). What are the most common conditions in primary care?: Systematic review. *Canadian Family Physician, 64*(11), 832–840.

Flensborg-Madsen, T., Becker, U., Grønbæk, M., Knop, J., Sher, L., & Mortensen, E. L. (2011). Alcohol consumption and later risk of hospitalization with psychiatric disorders: Prospective cohort study. *Psychiatry Research*. https://doi.org/10.1016/j.psychres.2010.11.016

Foa, E. B., Hembree, E. A., Rothbaum, B. O., & Rauch, S. A. (2019). *Proloned exposure therapy for PTSD: Emotional processing of traumatic experiences*. Oxford University Press.

Fox, N. A., Henderson, H. A., Marshall, P. J., Nichols, K. E., & Ghera, M. M. (2005). Behavioral inhibition: Linking biology and behavior within a developmental framework. *Annual Review of Psychology, 56*, 235–262.

García-Campayo, J., del Hoyo, Y. L., Valero, M. S., Yus, M. C. P., Esteban, E. A., Guedea, M. P., & Botaya, R. M. (2015). Primary prevention of anxiety disorders in primary care: A systematic review. *Preventive Medicine, 76*, S12–S15.

Garrett, D. (2010). Tapping into the value of health data through secondary use: As electronic health records (EHRs) proliferate across the nation, an important new opportunity awaits healthcare organizations that can find meaningful commercial uses for the data contained in their EHR systems. *Healthcare Financial Management, 64*(2), 76–84.

Garey, L., Olofsson, H., Garza, T., Rogers, A. H., Kauffman, B. Y., & Zvolensky, M. J. (2020). Directional effects of anxiety and depressive disorders with substance use: A review of recent prospective research. *Current Addiction Reports*, 1–12.

Goldberg, D. P., Reed, G. M., Robles, R., Minhas, F., Razzaque, B., Fortes, S., … Saxena, S. (2017). Screening for anxiety, depression, and anxious depression in primary care: A field study for ICD-11 PHC. *Journal of Affective Disorders, 213*, 199–206.

Grant, B. F., Goldstein, R. B., Chou, S. P., Huang, B., Stinson, F. S., Dawson, D. A., … Pickering, R. P. (2009). Sociodemographic and psychopathologic predictors of first incidence of DSM-IV substance use, mood and anxiety disorders: Results from the wave 2 National Epidemiologic Survey on alcohol and related conditions. *Molecular Psychiatry, 14*(11), 1051–1066.

Gray, J. A., Proudfoot, J., & Swain, S. (2000). 'Beating the blues': Computerised cognitive-behavioural therapy. *Journal of Primary Care Mental Health, 4*, 17–18.

Griffiths, K. M., Farrer, L., & Christensen, H. (2010). The efficacy of internet interventions for depression and anxiety disorders: a review of randomised controlled trials. *Medical Journal of Australia, 192*, S4–S11. Chicago.

Hayward, C., Killen, J. D., Kraemer, H. C., & Taylor, C. B. (2000). Predictors of panic attacks in adolescents. *Journal of the American Academy of Child & Adolescent Psychiatry, 39*(2), 207–214.

Health Promotion Agency. (2021). *Self-Help*. Retrieved June 21, 2021, from Depression and Anxiety: https://depression.org.nz/get-better/self-help

Hiles, S. A., Lamers, F., Milaneschi, Y., & Penninx, B. W. J. H. (2017). Sit, step, sweat: Longitudinal associations between physical activity patterns, anxiety and depression. *Psychological Medicine*. https://doi.org/10.1017/S0033291716003548

Humeniuk, R. E., Henry-Edwards, S., Ali, R. L., Poznyak, V., & Monteiro, M. (2010). *The alcohol, smoking and substance involvement screening test (ASSIST): manual for use in primary care*. World Health Organization.

Isensee, B., Wittchen, H.-U., Stein, M. B., Höfler, M., & Lieb, R. (2003). Smoking increases the risk of panic findings. *Archives of General Psychiatry, 60*(315), 692–700. https://doi.org/10.1001/archpsyc.60.7.692

Jacka, F. N., Reavley, N. J., Jorm, A. F., Toumbourou, J. W., Lewis, A. J., & Berk, M. (2013). Prevention of common mental disorders: What can we learn from those who have gone before and where do we go next? *Australian & New Zealand Journal of Psychiatry, 47*(10), 920–929. https://doi.org/10.1016/j.jad.2015.05.019

Jacobson, N. C., & Newman, M. G. (2017). Anxiety and depression as bidirectional risk factors for one another: A meta-analysis of longitudinal studies. *Psychological Bulletin, 143*(11), 1155.

Johnson, J. G. (2000). Association between cigarette smoking and anxiety disorders during adolescence and early adulthood. *Journal of the American Medical Association*. https://doi.org/10.1001/jama.284.18.2348

Jorm, A. F., Christensen, H., Griffiths, K. M., Parslow, R. A., Rodgers, B., & Blewitt, K. A. (2004). Effectiveness of complementary and self-help treatments for anxiety disorders. *Medical Journal of Australia, 181*, S29–S46.

Kendler, K. S., Myers, J., & Gardner, C. O. (2006). Caffeine intake, toxicity and dependence and lifetime risk for psychiatric and substance use disorders: An epidemiologic and co-twin control analysis. *Psychological Medicine, 36*(12), 1717.

Kessler, R. C., Berglund, P., Demler, O., Jin, R., Merikangas, K. R., & Walters, E. E. (2005). Lifetime prevalence and age-of-onset distributions of DSM-IV disorders in the National Comorbidity Survey Replication. *Archives of General Psychiatry, 62*(6), 593. https://doi.org/10.1001/archpsyc.62.6.593

Kessler, R. C., Petukhova, M., Sampson, N. A., Zaslavsky, A. M., & Wittchen, H. (2012). Twelve-month and lifetime prevalence and lifetime morbid risk of anxiety and mood disorders in the United States. *International Journal of Methods in Psychiatric Research, 21*(3), 169–184. https://doi.org/10.1002/mpr.1359

Knapp, A. A., Feldner, M., Allan, N. P., Schmidt, N. B., Keough, M. E., & Leen-Feldner, E. W. (2020). Test of an Anxiety sensitivity amelioration program for at-risk youth (ASAP-Y). *Behaviour Research and Therapy, 126*, 103544.

Kraemer, H. C., Kazdin, A. E., Offord, D. R., Kessler, R. C., Jensen, P. S., & Kupfer, D. J. (1997). Coming to terms with the terms of risk. *Archives of General Psychiatry, 54*(4), 337–343. https://doi.org/10.1001/archpsyc.1997.01830160065009

Krebber, A. M. H., Leemans, C. R., de Bree, R., van Straten, A., Smit, F., Smit, E. F., … Verdonck-de Leeuw, I. M. (2012). Stepped care targeting psychological distress in head and neck and lung cancer patients: A randomized clinical trial. *BMC Cancer, 12*(1), 1–8.

Kroenke, K., Spitzer, R. L., Williams, J. B., Monahan, P. O., & Löwe, B. (2007). Anxiety disorders in primary care: Prevalence, impairment, comorbidity, and detection. *Annals of Internal Medicine, 146*(5), 317–325.

Lau, E. X., & Rapee, R. M. (2011). Prevention of anxiety disorders. *Current Psychiatry Reports, 13*(4), 258–266.

Melchior, M., Caspi, A., Milne, B. J., Danese, A., Poulton, R., & Moffitt, T. E. (2007). Work stress precipitates depression and anxiety in young, working women and men. *Psychological Medicine*. https://doi.org/10.1017/S0033291707000414

Mojtabai, R., & Crum, R. M. (2013). Cigarette smoking and onset of mood and anxiety disorders. *American Journal of Public Health*. https://doi.org/10.2105/AJPH.2012.300911

Moreno-Peral, P., Conejo-Cerón, S., Motrico, E., Rodríguez-Morejón, A., Fernández, A., García-Campayo, J., … Bellón, J. Á. (2014). Risk factors for the onset of panic and generalised anxiety disorders in the general adult population: A systematic review of cohort studies. *Journal of Affective Disorders, 168*, 337–348.

Muntingh, A. D., van der Feltz-Cornelis, C. M., van Marwijk, H. W., Spinhoven, P., Penninx, B. W., & van Balkom, A. J. (2011). Is the beck anxiety inventory a good tool to assess the severity of anxiety? A primary care study in The Netherlands study of depression and anxiety (NESDA). *BMC Family Practice, 12*(1), 1–6.

Muris, P., van Brakel, A. M. L., Arntz, A., & Schouten, E. (2011). Behavioral inhibition as a risk factor for the development of childhood anxiety disorders: A longitudinal study. *Journal of Child and Family Studies, 20*(2), 157–170.

NHS Inform. (2021). *Anxiety self-help guide*. Retrieved June 21, 2021, from Illnesses and Conditions: nhsinform.scot/illnesses-and-conditions/mental-health/mental-health-self-help-guides/anxiety-self-help-guide.

Niedhammer, I., Malard, L., & Chastang, J.-F. (2015). Occupational factors and subsequent major depressive and generalized anxiety disorders in the prospective French national SIP study. *BMC Public Health*. https://doi.org/10.1186/s12889-015-1559-y

O'Donohue, W. T., & Draper, C. (Eds.). (2011). *Stepped care and e-health: Practical applications to behavioral disorders*. Springer. https://doi.org/10.1007/978-1-4419-6510-3

Orsillo, S. M., & Roemer, L. (2011). *The mindful way through Anxiety: Break free from chronic worry and reclaim your life*. Guilford Press.

Orsillo, S. M., & Roemer, L. (2016). *Worry less, live more: The mindful way through anxiety workbook*. Guilford Press.

Pauley, D., Cuijpers, P., Papola, D., Miguel, C., & Karyotaki, E. (2021). Two decades of digital interventions for anxiety disorders: A systematic review and meta-analysis of treatment effectiveness. *Psychological Medicine*, 1–13.

Pohl, R., Yeragani, V. K., Balon, R., Lycaki, H., & McBride, R. (1992). Smoking in patients with panic disorder. *Psychiatry Research*. https://doi.org/10.1016/0165-1781(92)90058-B

Proudfoot, J., Goldberg, D., Mann, A., Everitt, B., Marks, I., & Gray, J. A. (2003). Computerized, interactive, multimedia cognitive-behavioural program for anxiety and depression in general practice. *Psychological Medicine, 33*(2), 217.

Ramsawh, H. J., Weisberg, R. B., Dyck, I., Stout, R., & Keller, M. B. (2011). Age of onset, clinical characteristics, and 15-year course of anxiety disorders in a prospective, longitudinal, observational study. *Journal of Affective Disorders, 132*(1–2), 260–264.

Reeves, T., & Stace, J. M. (2005). Improving patient access and choice: Assisted bibliotherapy for mild to moderate stress/anxiety in primary care. *Journal of Psychiatric and Mental Health Nursing, 12*(3), 341–346.

Reinelt, E., Aldinger, M., Stopsack, M., Schwahn, C., John, U., Baumeister, S. E., … Barnow, S. (2014). High social support buffers the effects of 5-HTTLPR genotypes within social anxiety disorder. *European Archives of Psychiatry and Clinical Neuroscience*. https://doi.org/10.1007/s00406-013-0481-5

Reiss, S., & Bootzin, R. (1985). *Theoretical issues in behavior therapy*. Academic.

Richards, D. A. (2012). Stepped care: A method to deliver increased access to psychological therapies. *The Canadian Journal of Psychiatry, 57*(4), 210–215.

Rudaz, M., Craske, M. G., Becker, E. S., Ledermann, T., & Margraf, J. (2010). Health anxiety and fear of fear in panic disorder and agoraphobia vs. social phobia: A prospective longitudinal study. *Depression and Anxiety, 27*(4), 404–411.

Sareen, J., Cox, B. J., Clara, I., & Asmundson, G. J. G. (2005). The relationship between anxiety disorders and physical disorders in the US National Comorbidity Survey. *Depression and Anxiety, 21*(4), 193–202.

Schmidt, N. B., Eggleston, A. M., Woolaway-Bickel, K., Fitzpatrick, K. K., Vasey, M. W., & Richey, J. A. (2007). Anxiety Sensitivity Amelioration Training (ASAT): A longitudinal primary prevention program targeting cognitive vulnerability. *Journal of Anxiety Disorders, 21*(3), 302–319.

Schmidt, N. B., Keough, M. E., Mitchell, M. A., Reynolds, E. K., MacPherson, L., Zvolensky, M. J., & Lejuez, C. W. (2010). Anxiety sensitivity: Prospective prediction of anxiety among early adolescents. *Journal of Anxiety Disorders, 24*(5), 503–508.

Schmidt, N. B., Lerew, D. R., & Jackson, R. J. (1999). Prospective evaluation of anxiety sensitivity in the pathogenesis of panic: Replication and extension. *Journal of Abnormal Psychology, 108*(3), 532.

Schmidt, N. B., Zvolensky, M. J., & Maner, J. K. (2006). Anxiety sensitivity: Prospective prediction of panic attacks and Axis I pathology. *Journal of Psychiatric Research, 40*(8), 691–699.

Schoevers, R. A., Deeg, D. J. H., Van Tilburg, W., & Beekman, A. T. F. (2005). Depression and generalized anxiety disorder: Co-occurrence and longitudinal patterns in elderly patients. *The American Journal of Geriatric Psychiatry, 13*(1), 31–39.

Schuch, F. B., Stubbs, B., Meyer, J., Heissel, A., Zech, P., Vancampfort, D., … Ward, P. B. (2019). Physical activity protects from incident anxiety: A meta-analysis of prospective cohort studies. *Depression and Anxiety, 36*(9), 846–858.

Spear, S. E., Shedlin, M., Gilberti, B., Fiellin, M., & McNeely, J. (2016). Feasibility and acceptability of an audio computer-assisted self-interview version of the Alcohol, Smoking and Substance Involvement Screening Test (ASSIST) in primary care patients. *Substance Abuse, 37*(2), 299–305.

Stallard, P., Simpson, N., Anderson, S., Carter, T., Osborn, C., & Bush, S. (2005). An evaluation of the FRIENDS programme: A cognitive behaviour therapy intervention to promote emotional resilience. *Archives of Disease in Childhood, 90*(10), 1016–1019.

Storch, E. A., Abramowitz, J., & Goodman, W. K. (2008). Where does obsessive–compulsive disorder belong in DSM-V? *Depression and Anxiety, 25*(4), 336–347.

Taylor, S., Zvolensky, M. J., Cox, B. J., Deacon, B., Heimberg, R. G., Ledley, D. R., … Stewart, S. H. (2007). Robust dimensions of anxiety sensitivity: Development and initial validation of the Anxiety sensitivity Index-3. *Psychological Assessment, 19*(2), 176.

Titanium Software. (2019). *Titanium schedule*. Retrieved March 13, 2019, from titaniumschedule.com: http://www.titaniumschedule.com/Main/Default.aspx

Trumpf, J., Margraf, J., Vriends, N., Meyer, A. H., & Becker, E. S. (2010). Predictors of specific phobia in young women: A prospective community study. *Journal of Anxiety Disorders*. https://doi.org/10.1016/j.janxdis.2009.09.002

van Balkom, A. J. L. M., van Boeijen, C. A., Boeke, A. J. P., van Oppen, P., Kempe, P. T., & van Dyck, R. (2008). Comorbid depression, but not comorbid anxiety disorders, predicts poor outcome in anxiety disorders. *Depression and Anxiety, 25*(5), 408–415. https://doi.org/10.1002/da.20386

Viswasam, K., Eslick, G. D., & Starcevic, V. (2019). Prevalence, onset and course of anxiety disorders during pregnancy: A systematic review and meta analysis. *Journal of Affective Disorders, 255*, 27–40.

Vriends, N., Becker, E. S., Meyer, A. H., & Margraf, J. (2011). Incidence of DSM-IV social phobia in a community sample of young German women. *German Journal of Psychiatry, 14*(2).

Wiesche, L., Schacht, M., & Werners, B. (2017). Strategies for interday appointment scheduling. in primary care. *Health Care Management Science, 20*(3), 403–418.

Willis, B. M., & O'Donohue, W. T. (2018). The neglected constructs of health literacy, shared decision making, and patient centered care in behavioral health: An integrated model. In M. Duckworth (Ed.), *Behavioral medicine and integrated care: Efficient delivery of effective treatments*. Springer.

Wolitzky-Taylor, K., Operskalski, J. T., Ries, R., Craske, M. G., & Roy-Byrne, P. (2011). Understanding and treating comorbid anxiety disorders in substance users: Review and future directions. *Journal of Addiction Medicine, 5*(4), 233–247.

Wootton, B. M., Steinman, S. A., Czerniawski, A., Norris, K., Baptie, C., Diefenbach, G., & Tolin, D. F. (2018). An evaluation of the effectiveness of a transdiagnostic bibliotherapy program for anxiety and related disorders: results from two studies using a benchmarking approach. *Cognitive Therapy and Research, 42*(5), 565–580.

Yuan, S., Zhou, X., Zhang, Y., Zhang, H., Pu, J., Yang, L., … Xie, P. (2018). Comparative efficacy and acceptability of bibliotherapy for depression and anxiety disorders in children and adolescents: A meta-analysis of randomized clinical trials. *Neuropsychiatric Disease and Treatment.*

Zimmermann, M., Chong, A. K., Vechiu, C., & Papa, A. (2020). Modifiable risk and protective factors for anxiety disorders among adults: A systematic review. *Psychiatry Research, 285*, 112705. https://doi.org/10.1016/j.psychres.2019.112705

Zimmermann, M., O'Donohue, W., Zepeda, M., & Woodley, A. (2020). Examining caretaker attitudes towards primary prevention of pediatric behavioral Health problems in integrated care. *The Journal of Behavioral Health Services & Research*, 1–13.

Zinbarg, R. E., Craske, M. G., & Barlow, D. H. (2006). *Mastery of your anxiety and worry*. Oxford University Press.

Zvolensky, M. J., Kotov, R., Antipova, A. V., & Schmidt, N. B. (2005). Diathesis stress model for panic-related distress: A test in a Russian epidemiological sample. *Behaviour Research and Therapy, 43*(4), 521–532.

Zvolensky, M. J., Leen-Feldner, E. W., Feldner, M. T., Bonn-Miller, M. O., Lejuez, C. W., Kahler, C. W., & Stuart, G. (2004). Emotional responding to biological challenge as a function of panic disorder and smoking. *Journal of Anxiety Disorders, 18*(1), 19–32.

Zvolensky, M. J., Lewinsohn, P., Bernstein, A., Schmidt, N. B., Buckner, J. D., Seeley, J., & Bonn-Miller, M. O. (2008). Prospective associations between cannabis use, abuse, and dependence and panic attacks and disorder. *Journal of Psychiatric Research*. https://doi.org/10.1016/j.jpsychires.2007.10.012

Chapter 8
Evidence-Based Interventions for Posttraumatic Disorder in Primary Healthcare Settings

Funlola Are, Hannah Espeleta, Carla Newman, Leigh E. Ridings, Elizabeth Wallis, and Rochelle F. Hanson

8.1 Introduction

This chapter provides information related to diagnosis, prevalence, and risk factors for posttraumatic stress disorder (PTSD), followed by an overview of a stepped care, multi-component approach to prevent and/or mitigate the risk of PTSD among patients seen in primary care settings. In the first section, we define diagnostic criteria and delineate risk factors for PTSD. We then describe current evidence-based interventions for PTSD prevention. The final section outlines the use of a stepped, collaborative care approach to address trauma-related mental health problems in primary care that includes screening to identify individuals who are at risk or have experienced a potentially traumatic event, brief prevention interventions, and the role of behavioral health and primary care providers (PCPs). The chapter concludes with lessons learned and suggestions for implementing PTSD prevention models in primary care settings.

In Handbook of Evidence-Based Prevention of Behavioral Disorders in Integrated Care: A Stepped Care Approach (original submission12/21/2020; revised submission 2/8/2021).

F. Are · C. Newman · R. F. Hanson (✉)
National Crime Victims Research and Treatment Center, Department of Psychiatry and Behavioral Sciences, Medical University of South Carolina, Charleston, SC, USA
University of Texas Health Science Center at Houston, Houston, TX, USA
e-mail: hansonrf@musc.edu

H. Espeleta · L. E. Ridings
College of Nursing, Medical University of South Carolina, Charleston, SC, USA

E. Wallis
Department of Pediatrics, Medical University of South Carolina, Charleston, SC, USA

W. O'Donohue, M. Zimmermann (eds.), *Handbook of Evidence-Based Prevention of Behavioral Disorders in Integrated Care*,
https://doi.org/10.1007/978-3-030-83469-2_8

8.2 Overview of Posttraumatic Stress Disorder (PTSD)

8.2.1 Definition/Diagnostic Criteria

The Diagnostic and Statistical Manual (DSM-5) defines a traumatic event *as* "a distressing or dangerous experience, occurring outside of ordinary human experiences that evokes intense and overwhelming emotional, physical, and behavioral responses" (American Psychiatric Association, 2013; Weathers & Keane, 2007). Traumatic events may include (1) serious injury or witnessing the serious injury or death of another person, (2) imminent threats of serious injury or death to oneself or others, and/or (3) a repeated or extreme indirect exposure to aversive details of the traumatic event(s) that occurs in the course of one's professional obligations (e.g., first responders: law enforcement, fire fighters, health professionals). Traumatic events may be acute in nature (i.e., short-lived, one-time events), such as mass shootings, natural disasters, motor vehicle accidents, physical/sexual assaults, and violent loss of a loved one, or chronic (e.g., ongoing physical and sexual abuse, interpersonal violence, and war). Additionally, race-related traumatic events are increasingly recognized as a Criterion A stressor (Bryant-Davis & Ocampo, 2005; Carter, 2007; Williams et al., 2018).

In the immediate aftermath of a traumatic event, nearly all individuals will experience acute symptoms of distress, such as increased reactivity to trauma reminders, difficulty concentrating, hypervigilance, and sleep problems, meeting criteria for a diagnosis of acute stress disorder (ASD). However, most will evidence a reduction in these symptoms over time (Pineles et al., 2011). During this "natural recovery process," most individuals are able to process the memories associated with their traumatic experience, manage trauma-related negative emotions, and gradually experience a reduction in fears associated with trauma reminders (Foa & Rothbaum, 2001), enabling them to return to their previous levels of functioning (Bonanno, 2004; Bonanno & Mancini, 2008). This process, however, can be disrupted for any number of reasons (e.g., avoidant coping styles, personality characteristics), resulting in development of PTSD (Pineles et al., 2011). To be diagnosed with PTSD, symptoms must cause clinically significant distress or impairment in social, occupational, or other important areas of functioning for more than 1 month and must not be attributable to the physiological effects of a substance (e.g., medication, alcohol) or another medical condition (APA, 2013) (see Table 8.1).

Posttraumatic stress and PTSD can manifest differently across the lifespan. Both adults and youth may experience intense distress and difficulties coping, including anger, irritability, repeated and intrusive thoughts, and/or extreme distress when faced with trauma reminders (APA, 2013; Dyregrov & Yule, 2006). However, with children, these symptoms may result in behavioral difficulties, aggression, destructiveness, repetitive play, increased attention seeking, and concentration difficulties, which can cause school-related problems (Anda et al., 2006; Hanson et al., 2008). For children younger than 6 years of age, the DSM-5 includes a preschool subtype of PTSD. See Tedeschi and Billick (2017) for a review of diagnostic criteria.

Table 8.1 DSM-5 diagnostic criteria for PTSD (APA, 2013)

Criterion A	Trauma exposure	Exposure to death, threatened death, actual or threatened serious injury, or actual or threatened sexual violence via direct exposure, witnessing the trauma, learning that a relative or close friend was exposed to a trauma, or indirect exposure to aversive details of the trauma, usually in the course of professional duties
Criterion B	Intrusion symptoms	***Two or more of the following:*** Unwanted upsetting memories; Nightmares; Flashbacks; Emotional distress after exposure to traumatic reminders; Physical reactivity after exposure to traumatic reminders
Criterion C	Avoidance symptoms	***One or more of the following:*** Avoidance of trauma-related thoughts or feelings; Avoidance of trauma-related external reminders
Criterion D	Negative alterations in cognitions and mood	***Two or more of the following:*** Inability to recall key features of the trauma; Overly negative thoughts and assumptions about oneself or the world; Exaggerated blame of self or others for causing the trauma; Negative affect; Decreased interest in activities; Feeling isolated; Difficulty experiencing positive affect
Criterion E	Alterations in arousal and reactivity	***Two or more of the following:*** Irritability or aggression; Risky or destructive behavior; Hypervigilance; Heightened startle reaction; Difficulty concentrating; Difficulty sleeping

8.2.2 Prevalence

An estimated 50–60% of adults experience a traumatic event at least once in their lifetimes (Mitchell et al., 2012). Prevalence estimates of ASD are difficult to ascertain given that ASD must be diagnosed within 1 month of a traumatic experience. Furthermore, most studies of ASD focus on a specific population of individuals, such as car accident victims or victims of violent injury; thus, prevalence rates across traumatic events are difficult to identify (Ophuis et al., 2018). Nevertheless, studies have estimated ASD prevalence rates to fall between 11.7% and 41%, depending on the population sampled (Liebschutz et al., 2007). Notably, prevalence rates for PTSD are much lower. While trauma exposure is fairly common, studies indicate that only 7–8% of individuals will meet full criteria for PTSD (Brewin et al., 2000; Kessler et al., 2005; Weathers & Keane, 2007). Prevalence rates vary across genders, with ~10% of women developing PTSD versus 4% of men. While median age of onset is approximately 23 years of age (Kessler et al., 2005), data indicate that an estimated 40–80% of youth will experience some type of traumatic event before age 18 (Finkelhor et al., 2013; Kilpatrick et al., 2003). Estimated PTSD prevalence rates among adolescents is between 6 and 10% (Kessler et al., 1995; Kilpatrick et al., 2003), with higher rates among girls (7%) versus boys (2%) (McLaughlin et al., 2013).

8.2.3 *Risk Factors*

A large body of empirical work indicates that certain factors increase risk for PTSD (Howlett & Stein, 2016). These include female gender (Breslau et al., 1999), preexisting psychiatric disorders, family history of psychiatric disorders (Banerjee et al., 2017), lower IQ (Breslau et al., 2013), earlier age of traumatic event (Dunn et al., 2017), personality traits such as neuroticism (Ogle et al., 2017), and low social support (Breslau, 2012). Development of PTSD also is influenced by the severity and chronicity (Kira et al., 2008; Neuner et al., 2004; Ogle et al., 2014) of the traumatic stressor and the type of trauma. For example, assaultive trauma, which is more likely to be experienced by women than men, is related to increased PTSD risk (McCutcheon et al., 2009). Individuals from low socioeconomic backgrounds are also at heightened risk for developing PTSD (Bonanno et al., 2010; Hobfoll et al., 2009). Advances in neurobiological understanding of genetic markers, such as the serotonin transporter gene (5-HTTLPR) and genes associated with the hypothalamic-pituitary-adrenal (HPA) axis, are also being studied as additional risk factors for PTSD (McCutcheon et al., 2009; Zhao et al., 2017).

Early life adversities also may create a neurobiological vulnerability that predisposes individuals to anxiety and traumatic stress-related disorders, such as PTSD. In a national survey of adolescents, 61.8% of youth had experienced a potentially traumatic event (e.g., interpersonal violence, accidents, injuries) during their lifetime; the prevalence of PTSD was 4.7%, with girls having higher prevalence rates (7.3%) than boys (2.2%) (McLaughlin et al., 2013). The probability of having a PTSD diagnosis was higher for victims of interpersonal violence and for teens with preexisting fear and distress disorders (McLaughlin et al., 2013). Furthermore, youth who have been exposed to multiple traumatic events, have a history of family adversity, and who have a past history of anxiety or other psychological problems are at greater risk of developing PTSD (Bonanno & Mancini, 2008).

8.2.3.1 Disparities in Prevalence Rates

Researchers have documented differences in PTSD prevalence rates across racial and ethnic minority groups, as well as among individuals who identify as sexual and gender minorities. Disparities in PTSD prevalence rates are complex, and researchers are continuing to study what accounts for these disparities. Possible reasons include rates of trauma exposure, trauma type, and number of traumatic events experienced (Liu et al., 2017). For example, several studies have observed racial and ethnic differences related to exposure to traumatic events and subsequent development of PTSD (Roberts et al., 2011, Andrews et al., 2015, Crouch et al., 2000). Roberts and colleagues (2011) found that PTSD rates were the highest among Blacks (8.7%), followed by Whites (7.0%) and Hispanics (7.4%) and lowest among Asians (4.0%).

Similar patterns for prevalence of trauma and PTSD have been observed for racial/ethnic minority children, as well. For instance, African American and Latinx adolescents report substantially higher rates of sexual assault, physical assault, physical abuse, and witnessing violence compared to Caucasians, as well as a higher risk for development of PTSD, in nationally representative surveys (Andrews et al., 2015; Crouch et al., 2000). However, the nature of the relations between race and ethnicity and posttraumatic stress reactions remains unclear (Kilpatrick & Acierno, 2003; Meiser-Stedman, 2002) and may stem from complex risk factors that influence the development of PTSD (Perilla et al., 2002). For example, some studies have suggested that after accounting for factors, such as gender, severity, or nature of the traumatic event, racial/ethnic disparities in rates of PTSD or number of posttraumatic stress symptoms are no longer present (Meiser-Stedman, 2002).

Lesbian, gay, bisexual, transgender, and queer (LGBTQ+) adults and youth are also at high risk for trauma exposure and victimization by peers, including verbal and physical assault, bullying, and hate crimes (D'Augelli et al., 2002; Stoddard et al., 2009), as well as social isolation, rejection, and homelessness (Tyler & Cauce, 2002). LGBTQ+ youth are also particularly vulnerable to trauma-related consequences, such as alcohol abuse (Talley et al., 2014), suicidality (Almazan et al., 2014), and other self-harm behaviors (Batejan et al., 2015). Given the increased risk for experiencing interpersonal traumatic events, LGBTQ youth are also at increased risk for developing PTSD (Stenersen et al., 2019).

8.2.4 Screening in Primary Care

The high prevalence rates of trauma exposure and related mental health consequences discussed above make screening and early identification critical priorities for healthcare settings. Early detection of trauma can help mitigate potential lifelong health consequences (Pardee et al., 2017), and there has been increasing support for integration of trauma assessment in primary care (Carey et al., 2010; Institute of Medicine Committee on Preventive Services for Women, 2011; Machtinger et al., 2015), including routine screening for physical, sexual, and psychological abuse (American Medical Assocation, 2017).

There are several key reasons why primary care providers (PCPs) should assess for the potential impact of trauma exposure as part of standard practice. First, many patients seen in primary care settings have a history of trauma exposure and PTSD. A nationally representative study, conducted by Kessler et al. (2005), found that over 50% of men and women reported trauma exposure at the time of their primary care visit, with a lifetime PTSD prevalence rate of 6.8% across primary care settings (Kartha et al., 2008; Kessler et al., 1995; Liebschutz et al., 2007). This rate can be even higher in certain settings. For example, a study by Breslau et al. (1998) reported a 90% prevalence rate for trauma exposure in their urban primary care sample. Studies also indicate that individuals with PTSD utilize medical health services at a higher rate than those without PTSD (Kartha et al., 2008; Stein et al., 2000). Second, research suggests that many patients, particularly those that are traditionally underserved, prefer to seek mental health services in primary care settings, compared to specialty mental health clinics (Goldstein et al., 2017; Guevara et al., 2001; Howard et al., 1996). Finally, without trauma screening, the related symptoms often go undetected, leading providers to misdiagnose and direct services toward symptoms that only partially explain individuals' treatment needs (SAMHSA, 2014b). Thus, primary care settings have a unique opportunity to bridge behavioral and physical health care, and routine screening for trauma history and related symptoms increases the likelihood that individuals are identified and referred for further evaluation and treatment, when warranted (Cohen et al., 2008; Dubowitz et al., 2011; Hanson et al., 2018; Sonis, 2013).

Similar to screening for other medical conditions, screening for trauma history and trauma-related symptoms should be feasible (i.e., time efficient, easy to use) and inform whether further evaluation or intervention is warranted (Brooks et al., 2020; Hanson et al., 2018). A more thorough assessment may include the use of evidence-based standardized assessment instruments to determine if the patient is experiencing diagnostic level symptoms, including PTSD (Hanson et al., 2018; Schneider et al., 2013). It is also important to assess for other high-risk behaviors that commonly co-occur with trauma, such as substance use, self-harm/suicidality, and risky sexual behaviors (SAMHSA, 2014b; Ullman et al., 2013).

8.2.5 Selecting Screening Tools

A key component to integrate trauma screening as part of standard practice is through the use of effective screening tools. When selecting instruments, it is critical to assess not only for exposure to trauma but also to identify the presence and severity of trauma-related symptoms. Previous attempts to screen for trauma in primary care have relied heavily on tools, such as the Adverse Childhood Experiences (ACEs) survey, which focuses solely on *exposure* to trauma. The limitations of these screening instruments are that they fail to identify specific trauma-related symptoms and/or provide sufficient information to facilitate appropriate referrals (Brooks et al., 2020). Therefore, it is recommended that PCPs adopt screening tools that promote resiliency (SAMHSA, 2014a), inform treatment planning, and are appropriate for the patient population, including age/developmental level, gender, cultural background, and language (Hanson et al., 2018; SAMHSA, 2014a). PCPs also should select screening tools that fit within the clinical work flow (Schulman & Maul, 2019). Specifically, PCPs should select measures that are brief, publicly accessible, have strong psychometric properties, and are easy to administer and interpret. Examples of several cost-effective, accessible, brief and psychometrically sound measures, for children and adults, are provided in the table below (*See* Table 8.2).

Table 8.2 Screening measures

Name of instrument	Author	Domains assessed	Age	Format	Where to obtain
Child measures					
Child PTSD Symptom Scale for DSM-V (CPSS-VSR)	(Foa et al., 2001)	PTSD symptoms	Ages 8–18	Child/caregiver report 24 items	http://www.episcenter.psu.edu
Child and Adolescent Trauma Screen (CATS)	(Sachser et al., 2017)	Trauma exposure and PTSD symptoms	Ages 3-6 and ages 7–17	Child/caregiver report 15 items – exposure 25 items – symptoms	Depts.washington.edu
Child Trauma Screen (CTS)	(Lang & Connell, 2017)	Trauma exposure and PTSD symptoms	Ages 6–17	Child/caregiver report 4 items – exposure 6 items – symptoms	Chdi.org
Pediatric Symptom Checklist-17 (PSC-17)	(Gardner et al., 1999)	Attention, mood, and conduct-related problems	Ages 4–16	Child report 17 items	Massgeneral.org
Adult measures					
Primary Care PTSD Screen for DSM-5 (PC-PTSD-5)	(Prins et al., 2016)	Trauma exposure and PTSD symptoms	Adult	5 items	Ptsd.va.gov
PTSD Checklist for DSM-5 (PCL-5)	(Weathers et al., 2013)	Trauma-related symptoms	Adult	20 items	Ptsd.va.gov
Brief Trauma Questionnaire (BFQ)	(Schnurr et al., 1999)	Trauma exposure	Adult	10 items	Ptsd.va.gov
Trauma Screening Questionnaire (TSQ)	(Brewin et al., 2002)	Trauma-related symptoms	Adult	10 items	Ptsd.va.gov

8.2.6 Challenges to Screening in Primary Care Settings

Despite the growing evidence supporting trauma screening in primary care and the availability of brief screening tools, it is important to acknowledge the inherent challenges faced by PCPs to engage in these activities as part of their standard practice. These include lack of training and knowledge in behavioral health, uncertainty about how to respond to abuse disclosure, concerns about alienating patients, limited access to and knowledge of appropriate referrals or follow-up procedures, and limited availability of screening tools to assess for traumatic stress (Dueweke et al.,

2019; Kerker et al., 2016), as well as system level barriers (e.g., insufficient time to conduct screening and coordinate referrals, lack of reimbursement for screening) (Diamond et al., 2012; Dueweke et al., 2019).

8.3 Trauma-Informed Care (TIC) Approach

In the past several years, there has been increased attention to a trauma-informed care (TIC) approach as a way to increase awareness of trauma and related sequelae and implement procedures and protocols that can improve services to better meet the needs of patients, families, and staff across different service settings, including primary care (Brooks et al., 2020; Dueweke et al., 2019; Oral et al., 2016; Pardee et al., 2017). The TIC approach highlights the importance of trauma screening and can offer a useful framework to address the noted barriers described above. Several key TIC principles have been identified that are applicable to the primary care setting, including (1) increased provider awareness about the prevalence and impact of trauma (SAMHSA, 2014b); (2) use of effective screening procedures that outline steps to follow after a positive or negative trauma screen (Raja et al., 2015), including knowledge of available on-site or community-based resources (Brooks et al., 2020); (3) methods to identify and respond to ongoing safety risks (Brooks et al., 2020); (4) efficient care coordination with the preferred provider (U.S. Department of Veterans Affairs, 2019); and (5) the use of patient-centered communication (e.g., active listening, empathy, understanding the patient's perspective) when discussing the purpose of assessment, as well as the results and possible referrals (U.S. Department of Veterans Affairs, 2019).

8.4 What Is Evidence-Based Prevention?

An important purpose of trauma screening is to determine whether any prevention or intervention efforts may be warranted. *Evidence-based* prevention strategies are programs, policies, or techniques that have demonstrated effectiveness at preventing health problems through rigorous, empirical research (Health Policy Institute of Ohio, 2013). PTSD *prevention models*, which may include one or a collection of evidence-based strategies, occur at two main time points: (1) prior to trauma exposure, targeting individuals at high risk for trauma, based on community, familial, or individual risk factors, or (2) immediately following trauma exposure, targeting individuals during the acute phases of trauma recovery (e.g., within first 3 months following traumatic event) to reduce the likelihood of developing severe, long-lasting trauma-related mental health problems.

PTSD prevention among individuals *at risk* for trauma exposure aim to (1) decrease the likelihood that a traumatic event will occur and (2) bolster resiliency among individuals, families, and communities at risk for these events (Howlett &

Stein, 2016). Prevention strategies within these models can include public health and policy changes (e.g., laws requiring seat belt use, sexual assault prevention and awareness campaigns, and laws restricting carrying guns in public places), screening to identify risk factors for trauma exposure (e.g., trauma and mental health history, substance abuse, negative parenting practices), as well as psychosocial support (e.g., building coping skills, increasing social support, increasing access to case management and therapeutic resources). However, few of these trauma prevention initiatives occur within the context of primary care and are instead typically offered in community settings, such as child welfare agencies (Chaffin et al., 2012; Edwards & Lutzker, 2008), schools, and specialty mental health clinics (Mendelson et al., 2015; Skeffington et al., 2013). As noted throughout the chapter, primary care offers ideal opportunities to conduct trauma screening and to reinforce several of these prevention strategies. For example, PCPs can discuss healthy sexual practices to reduce risk for victimization, assess for gun safety in the home, inquire about available social supports, and facilitate access to additional therapeutic resources when indicated.

Models of prevention that occur immediately *after exposure* to a potentially traumatic event are situated within the initial phase of recovery and are often implemented in trauma centers or emergency departments. During this acute phase of recovery, individuals may be experiencing natural posttraumatic stress symptoms, but they do not yet qualify for a PTSD diagnosis (APA, 2013) (e.g., symptoms must persist for at least 30 days) that would warrant a more intensive intervention. Thus, prevention strategies during this initial recovery phase aim to provide education on normative trauma reactions and support the implementation of positive, evidence-based coping strategies to manage acute posttraumatic stress responses, making them ideally suited for delivery in primary care.

8.5 Examples of Prevention Interventions

One example of a brief, acute prevention intervention is psychological debriefing (PD). PD involves a single session to target all individuals exposed to a potentially traumatic event in the early aftermath, regardless of trauma-related symptoms (e.g., Mitchell, 1983). PD was one of the earliest and most widely used PTSD prevention strategies. However, despite its widespread implementation, several reviews have since deemed it not only *ineffective* at preventing PTSD (Bastos et al., 2015; Van Emmerik et al., 2002) but also associated with an increased risk for PTSD (Rose et al., 2002). Thus, PD programs are no longer recommended as an appropriate prevention intervention.

In response to the lack of evidence and increased risks associated with PD, multiple-session psychosocial prevention models subsequently have been developed and tested for efficacy in the immediate aftermath of a trauma (Kearns et al., 2012; Qi et al., 2016; Roberts et al., 2019). Of these models, *Psychological First Aid (PFA)*, a brief modular approach designed to provide comfort, psychoeducation, and support for physical and mental health needs, has been recommended as a front-line prevention model, offered within the first 2 weeks of a traumatic event (Litz & Gray, 2002; National Child Traumatic Stress Network and National Center for PTSD, 2006). Since PFA can be delivered by an array of trained first responders (i.e., does not require a licensed mental health professional), it may be particularly viable in primary care.

Skills for Psychological Recovery (SPR; Berkowitz et al., 2010) is another multimodal brief intervention that can be delivered by trained first responders and thus may be viable in primary care settings. SPR includes problem-solving, positive activities scheduling, managing reactions, helpful thinking, and building healthy social connections, all of which can reduce risk for PTSD.

Although psychosocial models of PTSD prevention remain understudied, emerging literature (Guay et al., 2019; Kassam-Adams, 2014) has highlighted key intervention targets (e.g., avoidance, parent-child interaction, trauma-related appraisals, enhancing support) to inform prevention programs. Continued research is necessary to demonstrate their effectiveness in preventing the onset of PTSD and their delivery in primary care settings (Kearns et al., 2012). Importantly, there are several trauma-focused mental health treatment interventions, such as prolonged exposure (Foa et al., 2019; Powers et al., 2010), cognitive processing therapy (Resick et al., 2016), and trauma-focused cognitive behavioral therapy (Cohen et al., 2016), that have been demonstrated to be effective at ameliorating PTSD. These interventions are designed to target individuals who have developed PTSD and, as such, are mental health treatments, rather than prevention interventions. However, an advantage of an integrated healthcare setting is the availability of a behavioral healthcare provider with the knowledge and skills to deliver these more complex interventions for those suffering from PTSD.

8.6 Pharmacological Interventions

Pharmacotherapy also has been investigated as a preventative strategy for PTSD, with preliminary findings suggesting that early use of medication may help prevent the onset of PTSD symptoms. While current evidence remains limited, due to few randomized clinical trials and small sample sizes, the pharmacological intervention with moderate quality evidence is the administration of hydrocortisone (Schelling et al., 2001; Schelling et al., 2004). Across several small studies, patients administered hydrocortisone were less likely to meet criteria for PTSD at follow-up than a placebo group at a median of 4.5 months (Howlett & Stein, 2016; Sijbrandij et al., 2015). Other pharmacologic interventions that have been tested for PTSD prevention include propranolol (Hoge et al., 2012; Pitman et al., 2002; Stein et al., 2007; Vaiva et al., 2003), escitalopram (a selective serotonin reuptake inhibitor) (Jonas et al., 2013; Shalev et al., 2012; Stoddard et al., 2011; Suliman et al., 2015; Zohar et al., 2017), temazepam, and gabapentin. Whether due to study design or medication efficacy is unclear, none of these medications separated from placebo and did not show benefit in reducing the development of PTSD in adults (Amos et al., 2014). Further work is needed to determine the efficacy of pharmacotherapy in preventing PTSD in adults and to identify potential moderators of treatment effect. This could be a promising area of primary care intervention if a medication is identified that would reduce the likelihood of developing PTSD following a traumatic event.

8.7 Universal, Indicated, and Selective Prevention

High rates of exposure to potentially traumatic events highlight the need for multifaceted prevention approaches to reduce the likelihood that individuals will develop PTSD. Prevention models historically have been classified as primary (i.e., to reduce onset of an illness or traumatic event), secondary (i.e., to detect illness/disease at an early stage), and tertiary (i.e., to mitigate severity among already affected individuals) (Caplan, 1964; Commission on Chronic Illness, 1957). An alternative framework (Gordon 1983) classifies prevention models according to the group being targeted. Universal prevention approaches target an entire population, whereas selective prevention approaches target a specific subgroup of the population at higher risk for the disorder. Indicated prevention approaches target those individuals who are at the highest risk for disease and/or may already be experiencing subthreshold disease symptoms. Additional details about these three classifications, as applied to PTSD prevention, are provided below.

8.7.1 Universal Prevention of PTSD

Universal prevention models or strategies address an entire population to prevent exposure to potentially traumatic events and/or to reduce the likelihood of developing PTSD (Howlett & Stein, 2016). These primarily focus on broad, public health-based interventions to address PTSD prevention at the population level rather than the subgroup or individual level. However, there are relevant examples for use in primary care, including universal PTSD screening and injury prevention educational programs.

8.7.2 Selective Prevention of PTSD

Selective prevention strategies target groups of people at risk for developing PTSD. These subgroups can be based on factors, such as age, gender, race/ethnicity, occupation, family history, socioeconomic status, or other characteristics. For instance, women are more likely to be victims of interpersonal violence, such as sexual assault, and, as a result, are often targeted for PTSD prevention initiatives.

Thus, identification and referral for psychosocial interventions (e.g., sexual assault survivor support groups) may be helpful in preventing PTSD and can be easily implemented in primary care settings.

8.7.3 Indicated Prevention of PTSD

Indicated prevention refers to strategies designed to prevent the onset of PTSD in those individuals who have not yet met full criteria for a PTSD diagnosis or are experiencing subclinical symptoms of PTSD. Many of these individuals may meet diagnostic criteria for acute stress disorder (*see criteria above*). In this instance, *indicated* prevention can ward off a future diagnosis of PTSD or reduce the severity of PTSD symptoms, which may result in shorter treatment and/or necessitate treatment of a lesser intensity. For example, one study found that five sessions of prolonged exposure therapy or brief exposure therapy and anxiety management treatment resulted in fewer people meeting criteria for PTSD when compared to those who received supportive counseling following a traumatic event (Bryant et al., 1998).

8.8 Stepped Care Prevention Model: Collaborative Care

This chapter has emphasized the role of PCPs in early identification of patients who have experienced or are at risk for PTSD as a way to offer prevention interventions. We now discuss a stepped care model, which can be implemented within primary care settings, as an optimal way to meet the needs of these patients. Stepped care models of treatment begin with the lowest dosage of an intervention and increase dosage as necessary. Thus, they have the potential to provide efficient, evidence-based mental health services to individuals (Ahmedani & Vannoy, 2014; Bower & Gilbody, 2005). Further, given the high prevalence of exposure to traumatic events and relatively low prevalence of PTSD (Pineles et al., 2011), stepped care prevention models can be especially useful in preventing PTSD. *Collaborative care* is a stepped care model of treatment intervention that engages clinic case managers, PCPs, and behavioral health providers to perform specific functions or tasks as part of a collaborative team. The focus is on an initial screening of the patient's symptoms, matching them to an intervention intensity consistent with their symptom presentation, facilitating transfer and coordination among service providers, and conducting regular review of their progress to move them through the stepped care treatment stages as necessary. Consequently, collaborative care models have emerged as an evidence-based approach to addressing mental health concerns (Ratzliff et al., 2014), including prevention and treatment of PTSD (Zatzick et al., 2011) in primary care settings.

8.9 Role of Primary Care Provider (PCP)

Within the collaborative care model, a PCP's main roles include completion of initial screening and assessment measures with the patient, discussion of any identified symptoms including posttraumatic stress symptoms, and psychoeducation about PTSD symptoms. While some PCPs have the knowledge to address mental health concerns in primary care, many lack the skills and training to identify PTSD symptoms outside of specialized mental health settings (Green et al., 2011; Weinreb et al., 2010). This further underscores the advantages of utilizing a collaborative care model to address concerns related to PTSD. Using this model, the PCP continues to oversee many aspects of the patient's care (i.e., initial identification of behavioral health problems, completing initial screening) and then facilitates a "warm hand-off" to a behavioral healthcare provider. The PCP transfers the patient to the behavioral healthcare provider during the medical appointment, to increase the likelihood that the patient will effectively engage in further behavioral health interventions (Roy-Byrne et al., 2010) to address PTSD symptoms.

8.10 Role of Behavioral Healthcare Provider (BHCP)

BHCPs fulfill a unique role on the collaborative care team. Depending on the severity of the patient symptoms, this may take different forms; however, the primary role of the BHCP is to help the patient manage their behavioral health symptoms. The BHCP may provide psychoeducation about PTSD and/or conduct additional assessments to gather information on patient's symptoms. They are in charge of monitoring for signs of symptom progression and can focus on developing strengths and coping mechanisms as an additional means to build patient resilience (Maragakis & Hatzigeorgiou, 2018). As members of the collaborative care team, BHCPs are often able to play a unique role in that they can share knowledge about warning signs and risk factors for PTSD with other members of the collaborative team who may be less able to recognize PTSD symptoms. Finally, they may provide psychosocial interventions, such as those discussed previously, to prevent symptom progression and are aptly skilled to identify the most appropriate referral source should the patient's needs require a higher level of care.

8.11 Lessons Learned/Implementation

In conclusion, aims of this chapter were to (1) provide an overview of PTSD prevalence and its impact, (2) discuss key risk factors, (3) highlight effective screening practices, (4) review evidence-based models of prevention, and (5) introduce a stepped care approach – collaborative care – for primary care settings. Lessons learned and key points about implementing prevention models for PTSD in primary care settings are discussed below.

In general, there is growing empirical support for preventive interventions for PTSD (Howlett & Stein, 2016). Furthermore, this work addresses multiple critical junctions at which prevention initiatives are to be implemented, including universal prevention interventions, which seek to reduce exposure to potentially traumatic events. However, given that a majority of individuals will experience a traumatic event at least once in their lifetime, additional prevention approaches, such as selective prevention strategies that target groups at high risk for developing acute stress disorder or PTSD, are also warranted. Complex challenges remain around screening and assessing posttraumatic stress symptoms and implementing integrated care interventions. Additionally, our knowledge of how these interventions translate to primary care settings is limited. While some interventions, such as multiple-session CBT-based interventions and pharmacological agents (e.g., hydrocortisone), are gaining increasing support in primary care settings, they require further empirical evidence to demonstrate their effectiveness at preventing PTSD (Howlett & Stein, 2016). Perhaps the most promising intervention for preventing PTSD is not a true intervention at all but rather a framework for addressing patients' symptoms in a cost- and resource-effective manner that engages multiple members of a collaborative care team. This collaborative care model, described above, is a stepped care model that screens patients for symptoms and problems, such as PTSD, and then matches them with a prevention intervention appropriate for their level of symptom severity. Patients are subsequently monitored by their PCPs and/or other members of their collaborative care team (i.e., case managers, BHCPs) and moved to different steps of the model as needed. However, collaborative care approaches are not without challenges, and in order for this model to be implemented successfully, members of the care team must have clearly defined areas of expertise but also be open to the flexibility that is required when tailoring a treatment plan specific to an individual patient's needs (Ratzliff et al., 2014). While stepped care models for other mental health disorders have shown promise (Gilbody et al., 2006; Thota et al., 2012; Zatzick et al., 2011), PTSD may pose unique challenges, which warrant further empirical work. Unlike other mental health disorders, implementing PTSD prevention models in primary care settings requires an understanding of risk factors for PTSD, as well as specialized training to adequately screen and triage patients to the appropriate step in the model.

Additional research efforts, including randomized clinical trials evaluating PTSD prevention and intervention during the peri- and post-trauma phases; mixed-methods studies designed to facilitate interprofessional, collaborative care in PTSD treatment assessment and delivery; and identification of novel, cost-effective, scalable solutions to address traumatic stress, are critical to identify the most effective treatments and implementation strategies in healthcare settings for trauma survivors. Advances can only be made with rigorous studies led by collaborative disciplines across practice settings through a dissemination and implementation lens from the design onset. Trauma-informed prevention and intervention research in primary care settings has advanced over the last few decades. However, additional research is warranted to establish clearer roadmaps for PCPs facing ongoing challenges to address the mental health needs of their patients. This is particularly salient for patients who may have experienced or be at risk for trauma and related mental health problems, which require further intervention to maximize positive health outcomes.

References

Ahmedani, B. K., & Vannoy, S. (2014). National pathways for suicide prevention and health services research. *American Journal of Preventive Medicine, 47*(3), S222–S228.

Almazan, E. P., Roettger, M. E., & Acosta, P. S. (2014). Measures of sexual minority status and suicide risk among young adults in the United States. *Archives of Suicide Research, 18*(3), 274–281.

American Medical Assocation. (2017). Code of Medical Ethics Opinion 8.10: preventing, identifying, and treating violence and abuse. *AMA Code of Medical Ethics*. Retrieved November 1, 2020, from https://www.ama-assn.org/delivering-care/preventing-identifying-treating-violence-abuse

American Psychiatric Association. (2013). *Diagnostic and statistical manual of mental disorders (DSM-5®)*. American Psychiatric Association.

Amos, T., Stein, D. J., & Ipser, J. C. (2014). Pharmacological interventions for preventing posttraumatic stress disorder (PTSD). *Cochrane Database of Systematic Reviews, 7*.

Anda, R. F., Felitti, V. J., Bremner, J. D., Walker, J. D., Whitfield, C., Perry, B. D., Dube, S. R., & Giles, W. H. (2006). The enduring effects of abuse and related adverse experiences in childhood. *European Archives of Psychiatry and Clinical Neuroscience, 256*(3), 174–186.

Andrews, A. R., Jobe-Shields, L., López, C. M., Metzger, I. W., De Arellano, M. A., Saunders, B., & Kilpatrick, D. G. (2015). Polyvictimization, income, and ethnic differences in trauma-related mental health during adolescence. *Social Psychiatry and Psychiatric Epidemiology, 50*(8), 1223–1234.

Banerjee, S. B., Morrison, F. G., & Ressler, K. J. (2017). Genetic approaches for the study of PTSD: Advances and challenges. *Neuroscience Letters, 649*, 139–146.

Bastos, M. H., Furuta, M., Small, R., McKenzie-McHarg, K., & Bick, D. (2015). Debriefing interventions for the prevention of psychological trauma in women following childbirth. *Cochrane Database of Systematic Reviews, 4*.

Batejan, K. L., Jarvi, S. M., & Swenson, L. P. (2015). Sexual orientation and non-suicidal self-injury: A meta-analytic review. *Archives of Suicide Research, 19*(2), 131–150.

Berkowitz, S., Bryant, R., Brymer, M., Hamblen, J., Jacobs, A., Layne, C., & Watson, P. (2010). *The National Center for PTSD & the National Child Traumatic Stress Network, skills for psychological recovery: Field operations guide*. American Psychiatric Pub.

Bonanno, G. A. (2004). Loss, trauma, and human resilience: Have we underestimated the human capacity to thrive after extremely aversive events? *American Psychologist, 59*(1), 20.

Bonanno, G. A., & Mancini, A. D. (2008). The human capacity to thrive in the face of potential trauma. *Pediatrics, 121*(2), 369–375.

Bonanno, G. A., Brewin, C. R., Kaniasty, K., & Greca, A. M. L. (2010). Weighing the costs of disaster: Consequences, risks, and resilience in individuals, families, and communities. *Psychological Science in the Public Interest, 11*(1), 1–49.

Bower, P., & Gilbody, S. (2005). Stepped care in psychological therapies: Access, effectiveness and efficiency: Narrative literature review. *The British Journal of Psychiatry, 186*(1), 11–17.

Breslau, N. (2012). Epidemiology of posttraumatic stress disorder in adults. In *The Oxford handbook of traumatic stress disorders* (pp. 84–97). Oxford University Press.

Breslau, N., Kessler, R. C., Chilcoat, H. D., Schultz, L. R., Davis, G. C., & Andreski, P. (1998). Trauma and posttraumatic stress disorder in the community: The 1996 Detroit Area Survey of Trauma. *Archives of General Psychiatry, 55*(7), 626–632.

Breslau, N., Chilcoat, H. D., Kessler, R. C., Peterson, E. L., & Lucia, V. C. (1999). Vulnerability to assaultive violence: Further specification of the sex difference in post-traumatic stress disorder. *Psychological Medicine, 29*(4), 813–821.

Breslau, N., Chen, Q., & Luo, Z. (2013). The role of intelligence in posttraumatic stress disorder: Does it vary by trauma severity? *PLoS One, 8*(6), e65391.

Brewin, C. R., Andrews, B., & Valentine, J. D. (2000). Meta-analysis of risk factors for posttraumatic stress disorder in trauma-exposed adults. *Journal of Consulting and Clinical Psychology, 68*(5), 748.

Brewin, C. R., Rose, S., Andrews, B., Green, J., Tata, P., McEVEDY, C., Turner, S., & Foa, E. B. (2002). Brief screening instrument for post-traumatic stress disorder. *The British Journal of Psychiatry, 181*(2), 158–162.

Brooks, K., Byrne, K., Thorn, B., & Shepard, L. (2020). Screening for trauma in Pediatric primary care. *Current Psychiatry Reports, 22*(11).

Bryant, R. A., Harvey, A. G., Dang, S. T., Sackville, T., & Basten, C. (1998). Treatment of acute stress disorder: A comparison of cognitive-behavioral therapy and supportive counseling. *Journal of Consulting and Clinical Psychology, 66*(5), 862.

Bryant-Davis, T., & Ocampo, C. (2005). Racist incident–based trauma. *The Counseling Psychologist, 33*(4), 479–500.

Caplan, G. (1964). *Principles of preventive psychiatry*. Basic Books.

Carey, T., Crotty, K., Morrissey, J., Jonas, D., Viswanathan, M., Thaker, S., Ellis, A., Woodell, C., & Wines, C. (2010). Future research needs for the integration of mental health/substance abuse and primary care: Identification of future research needs from evidence report/technology assessment No. 173. *Agency for Healthcare Research and Quality.*

Carter, R. T. (2007). Racism and psychological and emotional injury: Recognizing and assessing race-based traumatic stress. *The Counseling Psychologist, 35*(1), 13–105.

Chaffin, M., Hecht, D., Bard, D., Silovsky, J. F., & Beasley, W. H. (2012). A statewide trial of the SafeCare home-based services model with parents in child protective services. *Pediatrics, 129*(3), 509–515.

Cohen, J. A., Kelleher, K. J., & Mannarino, A. P. (2008). Identifying, treating, and referring traumatized children: The role of pediatric providers. *Archives of Pediatrics & Adolescent Medicine, 162*(5), 447–452.

Cohen, J. A., Mannarino, A. P., & Deblinger, E. (2016). *Treating trauma and traumatic grief in children and adolescents*. Guilford Publications.

Commission on Chronic Illness. (1957). *Chronic illness in the United States: The Baltimore study. Chronic Illness in a Large City. IV.* Harvard University Press.

Crouch, J. L., Hanson, R. F., Saunders, B. E., Kilpatrick, D. G., & Resnick, H. S. (2000). Income, race/ethnicity, and exposure to violence in youth: Results from the national survey of adolescents. *Journal of Community Psychology, 28*(6), 625–641.

D'Augelli, A. R., Pilkington, N. W., & Hershberger, S. L. (2002). Incidence and mental health impact of sexual orientation victimization of lesbian, gay, and bisexual youths in high school. *School Psychology Quarterly, 17*(2), 148.

Diamond, G. S., O'Malley, A., Wintersteen, M. B., Peters, S., Yunghans, S., Biddle, V., O'Brien, C., & Schrand, S. (2012). Attitudes, practices, and barriers to adolescent suicide and mental health screening: A survey of Pennsylvania primary care providers. *Journal of Primary Care & Community Health, 3*(1), 29–35.

Dubowitz, H., Lane, W. G., Semiatin, J. N., Magder, L. S., Venepally, M., & Jans, M. (2011). The safe environment for every kid model: Impact on pediatric primary care professionals. *Pediatrics, 127*(4), e962–e970.

Dueweke, A. R., Hanson, R. F., Wallis, E., Fanguy, E., & Newman, C. (2019). Training Pediatric primary care residents in trauma-informed care: A feasibility trial. *Clinical Pediatrics, 58*(11–12), 1239–1249.

Dunn, E. C., Nishimi, K., Powers, A., & Bradley, B. (2017). Is developmental timing of trauma exposure associated with depressive and post-traumatic stress disorder symptoms in adulthood? *Journal of Psychiatric Research, 84*, 119–127.

Dyregrov, A., & Yule, W. (2006). A review of PTSD in children. *Child and Adolescent Mental Health, 11*(4), 176–184.

Edwards, A., & Lutzker, J. R. (2008). Iterations of the SafeCare model: An evidence-based child maltreatment prevention program. *Behavior Modification, 32*(5), 736–756.

Finkelhor, D., Turner, H. A., Shattuck, A., & Hamby, S. L. (2013). Violence, crime, and abuse exposure in a national sample of children and youth: An update. *JAMA Pediatrics, 167*(7), 614–621.

Foa, E. B., & Rothbaum, B. O. (2001). *Treating the trauma of rape: Cognitive-behavioral therapy for PTSD*. Guilford Press.

Foa, E. B., Johnson, K. M., Feeny, N. C., & Treadwell, K. R. (2001). The child PTSD symptom scale: A preliminary examination of its psychometric properties. *Journal of Clinical Child Psychology, 30*(3), 376–384.

Foa, E. B., Hembree, E., Rothbaum, B. O., & Rauch, S. (2019). *Prolonged exposure for PTSD: Emotional processing of traumatic experiences* (2nd ed.). Oxford University Press.

Gardner, W., Murphy, M., Childs, G., Kelleher, K., Pagano, M., Jellinek, M., McInerny, T., Wasserman, R. C., Nutting, P., & Chiappetta, L. (1999). The PSC-17: A brief pediatric symptom checklist with psychosocial problem subscales. A report from PROS and ASPN. *Ambulatory Child Health, 5*, 225–225.

Gilbody, S., Bower, P., Fletcher, J., Richards, D., & Sutton, A. J. (2006). Collaborative care for depression: A cumulative meta-analysis and review of longer-term outcomes. *Archives of Internal Medicine, 166*(21), 2314–2321.

Goldstein, E., Athale, N., Sciolla, A. F., & Catz, S. L. (2017). Patient preferences for discussing childhood trauma in primary care. *The Permanente Journal, 21*.

Gordon, R. S., Jr. (1983). An operational classification of disease prevention. *Public Health Reports, 98*(2), 107.

Green, B. L., Kaltman, S., Frank, L., Glennie, M., Subramanian, A., Fritts-Wilson, M., Neptune, D., & Chung, J. (2011). Primary care providers' experiences with trauma patients: A qualitative study. *Psychological Trauma: Theory, Research, Practice, and Policy, 3*(1), 37.

Guay, S., Beaulieu-Prévost, D., Sader, J., & Marchand, A. (2019). A systematic literature review of early posttraumatic interventions for victims of violent crime. *Aggression and Violent Behavior, 46*, 15–24.

Guevara, J., Lozano, P., Wickizer, T., Mell, L., & Gephart, H. (2001). Utilization and cost of health care services for children with attention-deficit/hyperactivity disorder. *Pediatrics, 108*(1), 71–78.

Hanson, R. F., Self-Brown, S., Borntrager, C., Kilpatrick, D. G., Saunders, B. E., Resnick, H. S., & Amstadter, A. (2008). Relations among gender, violence exposure, and mental health: The national survey of adolescents. *American Journal of Orthopsychiatry, 78*(3), 313–321.

Hanson, R. F., Moreland, A. D., & Orengo-Aguayo, R. E. (2018). Treatment of trauma in children and adolescents. In *APA handbook of psychopathology: Child and adolescent psychopathology, Vol.2* (pp. 511–534). American Psychological Association.

Health Policy Institute of Ohio. (2013). *Online guide: Guide to evidence-based prevention*. https://nnphi.org/wp-content/uploads/2015/08/GuideToEvidence-BasedPrevention.pdf

Hobfoll, S. E., Watson, P., Bell, C. C., Bryant, R. A., Brymer, M. J., Friedman, M. J., Friedman, M., Gersons, B. P., & Jong, J. T. d., & Layne, C. M. (2009). Five essential elements of immediate and mid-term mass trauma intervention: Empirical evidence. *Focus, 7*(2), 221–242.

Hoge, E. A., Worthington, J. J., Nagurney, J. T., Chang, Y., Kay, E. B., Feterowski, C. M., Katzman, A. R., Goetz, J. M., Rosasco, M. L., & Lasko, N. B. (2012). Effect of acute posttrauma pro-

pranolol on PTSD outcome and physiological responses during script-driven imagery. *CNS Neuroscience & Therapeutics, 18*(1), 21–27.
Howard, K. I., Cornille, T. A., Lyons, J. S., Vessey, J. T., Lueger, R. J., & Saunders, S. M. (1996). Patterns of mental health service utilization. *Archives of General Psychiatry, 53*(8), 696–703.
Howlett, J. R., & Stein, M. B. (2016). Prevention of trauma and stressor-related disorders: A review. *Neuropsychopharmacology, 41*(1), 357–369.
Institute of Medicine Committee on Preventive Services for Women. (2011). *Clinical preventive services for women: Closing the gaps*. National Academies Press.
Jonas, D. E., Cusack, K., Forneris, C. A., Wilkins, T. M., Sonis, J., Middleton, J. C., Feltner, C., Meredith, D., Cavanaugh, J., & Brownley, K. A. (2013). *Psychological and pharmacological treatments for adults with posttraumatic stress disorder (PTSD)*. Agency for Healthcare Research and Quality.
Kartha, A., Brower, V., Saitz, R., Samet, J. H., Keane, T. M., & Liebschutz, J. (2008). The impact of trauma exposure and post-traumatic stress disorder on healthcare utilization among primary care patients. *Medical Care, 46*(4), 388.
Kassam-Adams, N. (2014). Design, delivery, and evaluation of early interventions for children exposed to acute trauma. *European Journal of Psychotraumatology, 5*(1), 22757.
Kearns, M. C., Ressler, K. J., Zatzick, D., & Rothbaum, B. O. (2012). Early interventions for PTSD: A review. *Depression and Anxiety, 29*(10), 833–842.
Kerker, B. D., Storfer-Isser, A., Szilagyi, M., Stein, R. E., Garner, A. S., O'Connor, K. G., Hoagwood, K. E., & Horwitz, S. M. (2016). Do pediatricians ask about adverse childhood experiences in pediatric primary care? *Academic Pediatrics, 16*(2), 154–160.
Kessler, R. C., Sonnega, A., Bromet, E., Hughes, M., & Nelson, C. B. (1995). Posttraumatic stress disorder in the National Comorbidity Survey. *Archives of General Psychiatry, 52*(12), 1048–1060.
Kessler, R. C., Berglund, P., Demler, O., Jin, R., Merikangas, K. R., & Walters, E. E. (2005). Lifetime prevalence and age-of-onset distributions of DSM-IV disorders in the National Comorbidity Survey Replication. *Archives of General Psychiatry, 62*(6), 593–602.
Kilpatrick, D. G., & Acierno, R. (2003). Mental health needs of crime victims: Epidemiology and outcomes. *Journal of Traumatic Stress: Official Publication of The International Society for Traumatic Stress Studies, 16*(2), 119–132.
Kilpatrick, D. G., Saunders, B. E., & Smith, D. W. (2003). *Youth victimization: Prevalence and implications. Research in brief*. US Department of Justice, Office of Justice Programs.
Kira, I. A., Lewandowski, L., Templin, T., Ramaswamy, V., Ozkan, B., & Mohanesh, J. (2008). Measuring cumulative trauma dose, types, and profiles using a development-based taxonomy of traumas. *Traumatology, 14*(2), 62–87.
Lang, J. M., & Connell, C. M. (2017). Development and validation of a brief trauma screening measure for children: The child trauma screen. *Psychological Trauma: Theory, Research, Practice, and Policy, 9*(3), 390.
Liebschutz, J., Saitz, R., Brower, V., Keane, T. M., Lloyd-Travaglini, C., Averbuch, T., & Samet, J. H. (2007). PTSD in urban primary care: High prevalence and low physician recognition. *Journal of General Internal Medicine, 22*(6), 719–726.
Litz, B. T., & Gray, M. J. (2002). Early intervention for mass violence: What is the evidence? What should be done? *Cognitive and Behavioral Practice, 9*(4), 266–272.
Liu, H., Petukhova, M. V., Sampson, N. A., Aguilar-Gaxiola, S., Alonso, J., Andrade, L. H., Bromet, E. J., De Girolamo, G., Haro, J. M., & Hinkov, H. (2017). Association of DSM-IV posttraumatic stress disorder with traumatic experience type and history in the World Health Organization world mental health surveys. *JAMA Psychiatry, 74*(3), 270–281.
Machtinger, E. L., Cuca, Y. P., Khanna, N., Rose, C. D., & Kimberg, L. S. (2015). From treatment to healing: The promise of trauma-informed primary care. *Women's Health Issues, 25*(3), 193–197.
Maragakis, A., & Hatzigeorgiou, M. N. (2018). The transformation of the healthcare system: Integrated primary care and the role of stepped care interventions for behavioral health pro-

viders. In *Principle-based stepped care and brief psychotherapy for integrated care settings* (pp. 9–15). Springer.
McCutcheon, V. V., Heath, A. C., Nelson, E., Bucholz, K. K., Madden, P. A., & Martin, N. (2009). Accumulation of trauma over time and risk for depression in a twin sample. *Psychological Medicine, 39*(3), 431.
McLaughlin, K. A., Koenen, K. C., Hill, E. D., Petukhova, M., Sampson, N. A., Zaslavsky, A. M., & Kessler, R. C. (2013). Trauma exposure and posttraumatic stress disorder in a national sample of adolescents. *Journal of the American Academy of Child & Adolescent Psychiatry, 52*(8), 815–830. e814.
Meiser-Stedman, R. (2002). Towards a cognitive–behavioral model of PTSD in children and adolescents. *Clinical Child and Family Psychology Review, 5*(4), 217–232.
Mendelson, T., Tandon, S. D., O'Brennan, L., Leaf, P. J., & Ialongo, N. S. (2015). Brief report: Moving prevention into schools: The impact of a trauma-informed school-based intervention. *Journal of Adolescence, 43*, 142–147.
Mitchell, J. T. (1983). When disaster strikes: The critical incident stress debriefing process. *Journal of Emergency Medical Services*, 36–39.
Mitchell, K. S., Mazzeo, S. E., Schlesinger, M. R., Brewerton, T. D., & Smith, B. N. (2012). Comorbidity of partial and subthreshold PTSD among men and women with eating disorders in the national comorbidity survey-replication study. *International Journal of Eating Disorders, 45*(3), 307–315.
National Child Traumatic Stress Network and National Center for PTSD. (2006). *Psychological first aid: field operations guide* (2nd ed.). resources/pfa field operations guide.pdf.
Neuner, F., Schauer, M., Karunakara, U., Klaschik, C., Robert, C., & Elbert, T. (2004). Psychological trauma and evidence for enhanced vulnerability for posttraumatic stress disorder through previous trauma among West Nile refugees. *BMC Psychiatry, 4*(1), 1–7.
Ogle, C. M., Rubin, D. C., & Siegler, I. C. (2014). Cumulative exposure to traumatic events in older adults. *Aging & Mental Health, 18*(3), 316–325.
Ogle, C. M., Siegler, I. C., Beckham, J. C., & Rubin, D. C. (2017). Neuroticism increases PTSD symptom severity by amplifying the emotionality, rehearsal, and centrality of trauma memories. *Journal of Personality, 85*(5), 702–715.
Ophuis, R. H., Olij, B. F., Polinder, S., & Haagsma, J. A. (2018). Prevalence of post-traumatic stress disorder, acute stress disorder and depression following violence related injury treated at the emergency department: A systematic review. *BMC Psychiatry, 18*(1), 1–9.
Oral, R., Ramirez, M., Coohey, C., Nakada, S., Walz, A., Kuntz, A., Benoit, J., & Peek-Asa, C. (2016). Adverse childhood experiences and trauma informed care: The future of health care. *Pediatric Research, 79*(1), 227–233.
Pardee, M., Kuzma, E., Dahlem, C. H. Y., Boucher, N., & Darling-Fisher, C. S. (2017). Current state of screening high-ACE youth and emerging adults in primary care. *Journal of the American Association of Nurse Practitioners, 29*(12), 716–724.
Perilla, J. L., Norris, F. H., & Lavizzo, E. A. (2002). Ethnicity, culture, and disaster response: Identifying and explaining ethnic differences in PTSD six months after Hurricane Andrew. *Journal of Social and Clinical Psychology, 21*(1), 20–45.
Pineles, S. L., Mostoufi, S. M., Ready, C. B., Street, A. E., Griffin, M. G., & Resick, P. A. (2011). Trauma reactivity, avoidant coping, and PTSD symptoms: A moderating relationship? *Journal of Abnormal Psychology, 120*(1), 240.
Pitman, R. K., Sanders, K. M., Zusman, R. M., Healy, A. R., Cheema, F., Lasko, N. B., Cahill, L., & Orr, S. P. (2002). Pilot study of secondary prevention of posttraumatic stress disorder with propranolol. *Biological Psychiatry, 51*(2), 189–192.
Powers, M. B., Halpern, J. M., Ferenschak, M. P., Gillihan, S. J., & Foa, E. B. (2010). A meta-analytic review of prolonged exposure for posttraumatic stress disorder. *Clinical Psychology Review, 30*(6), 635–641.
Prins, A., Bovin, M. J., Smolenski, D. J., Marx, B. P., Kimerling, R., Jenkins-Guarnieri, M. A., Kaloupek, D. G., Schnurr, P. P., Kaiser, A. P., & Leyva, Y. E. (2016). The primary care PTSD

screen for DSM-5 (PC-PTSD-5): Development and evaluation within a veteran primary care sample. *Journal of General Internal Medicine, 31*(10), 1206–1211.

Qi, W., Gevonden, M., & Shalev, A. (2016). Prevention of post-traumatic stress disorder after trauma: Current evidence and future directions. *Current Psychiatry Reports, 18*(2), 20.

Raja, S., Hasnain, M., Hoersch, M., Gove-Yin, S., & Rajagopalan, C. (2015). Trauma informed care in medicine. *Family & Community Health, 38*(3), 216–226.

Ratzliff, A. D., Christensen, C. L., & Unützer, J. (2014). Building value-added teams to care for behavioral health needs in primary care. In *Integrated Care in Psychiatry* (pp. 103–126). Springer.

Resick, P. A., Monson, C. M., & Chard, K. M. (2016). *Cognitive processing therapy for PTSD: A comprehensive manual.* Guilford Publications.

Roberts, N. P., Kitchiner, N. J., Kenardy, J., Robertson, L., Lewis, C., & Bisson, J. I. (2019). Multiple session early psychological interventions for the prevention of post-traumatic stress disorder. *Cochrane Database of Systematic Reviews, 8.*

Rose, S. C., Bisson, J., Churchill, R., & Wessely, S. (2002). Psychological debriefing for preventing post traumatic stress disorder (PTSD). *Cochrane Database of Systematic Reviews, 2.*

Roy-Byrne, P., Craske, M. G., Sullivan, G., Rose, R. D., Edlund, M. J., Lang, A. J., Bystritsky, A., Welch, S. S., Chavira, D. A., & Golinelli, D. (2010). Delivery of evidence-based treatment for multiple anxiety disorders in primary care: A randomized controlled trial. *JAMA, 303*(19), 1921–1928.

Sachser, C., Berliner, L., Holt, T., Jensen, T. K., Jungbluth, N., Risch, E., Rosner, R., & Goldbeck, L. (2017). International development and psychometric properties of the Child and Adolescent Trauma Screen (CATS). *Journal of Affective Disorders, 210*, 189–195.

Schelling, G., Briegel, J., Roozendaal, B., Stoll, C., Rothenhäusler, H.-B., & Kapfhammer, H.-P. (2001). The effect of stress doses of hydrocortisone during septic shock on posttraumatic stress disorder in survivors. *Biological Psychiatry, 50*(12), 978–985.

Schelling, G., Kilger, E., Roozendaal, B., Dominique, J.-F., Briegel, J., Dagge, A., Rothenhäusler, H.-B., Krauseneck, T., Nollert, G., & Kapfhammer, H.-P. (2004). Stress doses of hydrocortisone, traumatic memories, and symptoms of posttraumatic stress disorder in patients after cardiac surgery: A randomized study. *Biological Psychiatry, 55*(6), 627–633.

Schneider, S. J., Grilli, S. F., & Schneider, J. R. (2013). Evidence-based treatments for traumatized children and adolescents. *Current Psychiatry Reports, 15*(1), 332.

Schnurr, P., Vielhauer, M., Weathers, F., & Findler, M. (1999). Brief trauma questionnaire [database record]. *APA PsycTests.*

Schulman, M., & Maul, A. (2019). *Screening for adverse childhood experiences and trauma.* Trauma-Informed Care Implementation Resource Center. Retrieved December 1, 2020, from TraumaInformedCare.chcs.org

Shalev, A. Y., Ankri, Y., Israeli-Shalev, Y., Peleg, T., Adessky, R., & Freedman, S. (2012). Prevention of posttraumatic stress disorder by early treatment: Results from the Jerusalem trauma outreach and prevention study. *Archives of General Psychiatry, 69*(2), 166–176.

Sijbrandij, M., Kleiboer, A., Bisson, J. I., Barbui, C., & Cuijpers, P. (2015). Pharmacological prevention of post-traumatic stress disorder and acute stress disorder: A systematic review and meta-analysis. *The Lancet Psychiatry, 2*(5), 413–421.

Skeffington, P. M., Rees, C. S., & Kane, R. (2013). The primary prevention of PTSD: A systematic review. *Journal of Trauma & Dissociation, 14*(4), 404–422.

Sonis, J. (2013). PTSD in primary care—An update on evidence-based management. *Current Psychiatry Reports, 15*(7), 373.

Stein, M. B., McQuaid, J. R., Pedrelli, P., Lenox, R., & McCahill, M. E. (2000). Posttraumatic stress disorder in the primary care medical setting. *General Hospital Psychiatry, 22*(4), 261–269.

Stein, M. B., Kerridge, C., Dimsdale, J. E., & Hoyt, D. B. (2007). Pharmacotherapy to prevent PTSD: Results from a randomized controlled proof-of-concept trial in physically injured patients. *Journal of Traumatic Stress: Official Publication of The International Society for Traumatic Stress Studies, 20*(6), 923–932.

Stenersen, M., Ovrebo, E., Emery, H., Brown, E., New, C., Brasfield, C., & Turner, L. (2019). Interpersonal trauma, and PTSD symptomology among lesbian, gay, and bisexual individuals: A closer look at gender, minority stress, and help-seeking behaviors. *Journal of LGBT Issues in Counseling, 13*(3), 216–231.

Stoddard, F. J., Jr., Luthra, R., Sorrentino, E. A., Saxe, G. N., Drake, J., Chang, Y., Levine, J. B., Chedekel, D. S., & Sheridan, R. L. (2011). A randomized controlled trial of sertraline to prevent posttraumatic stress disorder in burned children. *Journal of Child and Adolescent Psychopharmacology, 21*(5), 469–477.

Stoddard, J. P., Dibble, S. L., & Fineman, N. (2009). Sexual and physical abuse: A comparison between lesbians and their heterosexual sisters. *Journal of Homosexuality, 56*(4), 407–420.

Substance Abuse and Mental Health Services Administration. (2014a). *SAMHSA's concept of trauma and guidance for a trauma-informed approach.*

Substance Abuse and Mental Health Services Administration. (2014b). *Trauma-informed Care in Behavioral Health Services* (Substance Abuse and Mental Health Services Administration, Ed.). HHS Publication No. (SMA) 13-4801.

Suliman, S., Seedat, S., Pingo, J., Sutherland, T., Zohar, J., & Stein, D. J. (2015). Escitalopram in the prevention of posttraumatic stress disorder: A pilot randomized controlled trial. *BMC Psychiatry, 15*(1), 24.

Talley, A. E., Hughes, T. L., Aranda, F., Birkett, M., & Marshal, M. P. (2014). Exploring alcohol-use behaviors among heterosexual and sexual minority adolescents: Intersections with sex, age, and race/ethnicity. *American Journal of Public Health, 104*(2), 295–303.

Tedeschi, F. K., & Billick, S. B. (2017). Pediatric PTSD in the DSM-5 and the forensic interview of traumatized youth. *The Journal of the American Academy of Psychiatry and the Law, 45*(2), 175–183.

Thota, A. B., Sipe, T. A., Byard, G. J., Zometa, C. S., Hahn, R. A., McKnight-Eily, L. R., Chapman, D. P., Abraido-Lanza, A. F., Pearson, J. L., & Anderson, C. W. (2012). Collaborative care to improve the management of depressive disorders: A community guide systematic review and meta-analysis. *American Journal of Preventive Medicine, 42*(5), 525–538.

Tyler, K. A., & Cauce, A. M. (2002). Perpetrators of early physical and sexual abuse among homeless and runaway adolescents. *Child Abuse & Neglect, 26*(12), 1261–1274.

U.S. Department of Veterans Affairs. (2019). *PTSD screening and referral: For health care providers*. PTSD: National Center for PTSD. https://www.ptsd.va.gov/professional/treat/care/screening_referral.asp

Ullman, S. E., Relyea, M., Peter-Hagene, L., & Vasquez, A. L. (2013). Trauma histories, substance use coping, PTSD, and problem substance use among sexual assault victims. *Addictive Behaviors, 38*(6), 2219–2223.

Vaiva, G., Ducrocq, F., Jezequel, K., Averland, B., Lestavel, P., Brunet, A., & Marmar, C. R. (2003). Immediate treatment with propranolol decreases posttraumatic stress disorder two months after trauma. *Biological Psychiatry, 54*(9), 947–949.

Van Emmerik, A. A., Kamphuis, J. H., Hulsbosch, A. M., & Emmelkamp, P. M. (2002). Single session debriefing after psychological trauma: A meta-analysis. *The Lancet, 360*(9335), 766–771.

Weathers, F. W., & Keane, T. M. (2007). The criterion a problem revisited: Controversies and challenges in defining and measuring psychological trauma. *Journal of Traumatic Stress, 20*(2), 107–121.

Weathers, F. W., Litz, B. T., Keane, T. M., Palmieri, P. A., Marx, B. P., & Schnurr, P. P. (2013). The ptsd checklist for dsm-5 (pcl-5). Scale available from the National Center for PTSD at www. ptsd. va. gov, 10.

Weinreb, L., Savageau, J. A., Candib, L. M., Reed, G. W., Fletcher, K. E., & Hargraves, J. L. (2010). Screening for childhood trauma in adult primary care patients: A cross-sectional survey. *Primary Care Companion to the Journal of Clinical Psychiatry, 12*(6).

Williams, M. T., Metzger, I. W., Leins, C., & DeLapp, C. (2018). Assessing racial trauma within a DSM–5 framework: The UConn racial/ethnic stress & trauma survey. *Practice Innovations, 3*(4), 242.

Zatzick, D., Rivara, F., Jurkovich, G., Russo, J., Trusz, S. G., Wang, J., Wagner, A., Stephens, K., Dunn, C., & Uehara, E. (2011). Enhancing the population impact of collaborative care interventions: Mixed method development and implementation of stepped care targeting posttraumatic stress disorder and related comorbidities after acute trauma. *General Hospital Psychiatry, 33*(2), 123–134.

Zhao, M., Yang, J., Wang, W., Ma, J., Zhang, J., Zhao, X., Qiu, X., Yang, X., Qiao, Z., & Song, X. (2017). Meta-analysis of the interaction between serotonin transporter promoter variant, stress, and posttraumatic stress disorder. *Scientific Reports, 7*(1), 1–10.

Zohar, J., Fostick, L., Juven-Wetzler, A., Kaplan, Z., Shalev, H., Schreiber, G., Miroshnik, N., Shalev, A. Y., Stein, D. J., & Seedat, S. (2017). Secondary prevention of chronic PTSD by early and short-term administration of escitalopram: A prospective randomized, placebo-controlled, double-blind trial. *The Journal of Clinical Psychiatry, 79*(2), 0–0.

Chapter 9
Prevention of Conduct Problems in Integrated Pediatric Primary Care

Deborah Y. Pickford, Trenesha L. Hill, Prerna G. Arora, and Courtney N. Baker

Conduct problems include disruptive, oppositional, and argumentative behavior; physical, relational, and verbal aggression; and delinquency. Conduct problems are also known as externalizing behavior problems because they involve acting in unwanted ways toward others, such as caregivers or peers (CDC, 2020). The period prevalence of clinically significant externalizing behavior problems in children and youth in the United States is estimated to range from 7% to 19% (Ghandour et al., 2019; Merikangas et al., 2010a, b), with about one in ten children experiencing severe impairment or distress (Ghandour et al., 2019; Merikangas et al., 2010a). Lifetime prevalence estimates suggest that conduct problems are common: one in four individuals in the United States will experience a conduct problem within their lifetimes (Kessler et al., 2005).

Recent data suggest that conduct problems are most common in middle childhood (i.e., elementary school- and early middle school-age children), as opposed to early childhood and adolescence (Ghandour et al., 2019). Research conducted a decade earlier suggests a slightly later median onset of conduct problems and a trend in which older children experience more problems (Kessler et al., 2005; Merikangas et al., 2010a). The band within which onset occurs is relatively narrow, however, with the onset of most conduct problems occurring between the ages of 7

D. Y. Pickford · C. N. Baker (✉)
Department of Psychology, Tulane University, New Orleans, LA, USA
e-mail: dpickford@tulane.edu; cnbaker@tulane.edu

T. L. Hill
Department of Psychology, University of Texas Health Science Center at Tyler, Tyler, TX, USA
e-mail: trenesha.hill@uthct.edu

P. G. Arora
Departments of Health and Behavioral Sciences, Columbia University, New York, NY, USA
e-mail: pa2542@tc.columbia.edu

W. O'Donohue, M. Zimmermann (eds.), *Handbook of Evidence-Based Prevention of Behavioral Disorders in Integrated Care*,
https://doi.org/10.1007/978-3-030-83469-2_9

and 15 (Kessler et al., 2005). This differs from many chronic physical health issues, like diabetes and cardiovascular issues, in which risk for developing the condition increases with age (Kessler et al., 2005).

Of course, for many externalizing behavior problems, both risk factors and subthreshold symptoms appear earlier in life, providing a window for prevention and early intervention. For example, the first manifestation of oppositional defiant disorder (ODD) and conduct disorder (CD) was estimated by one study to occur at ages 2.5 and 5.5, respectively, which is significantly earlier than the median onset typically documented by epidemiological studies (Rowe et al., 2010). Thus, prodromal conduct problems are almost certainly more common than these estimates suggest. Intervening early has the potential to course-correct developmental trajectories associated with harmful and sometimes lifelong consequences. Unsurprisingly, having conduct problems puts individuals at risk for developing a host of psychiatric issues as adults. Individuals with childhood-onset CD are at particular risk of being diagnosed with antisocial personality disorder, which is the adult version of the CD diagnosis (Goldstein et al., 2006). Children with disruptive behavior problems are also at increased risk of developing other personality disorders, substance use disorders, mood disorders, and anxiety disorders (Goldstein et al., 2006; Lahey et al., 2005; Morcillo et al., 2011).

If left untreated, conduct problems can lead to significant short- and long-term problems for the individual and also for society in general. For example, conduct problems in childhood and adolescence are predictive of delinquency, criminal behavior, arrests, and adult antisocial behavior (McMahon et al., 2010; Olino et al., 2010). Individuals who experienced conduct problems as children or teens are more likely to become teen parents, drop out of school, get divorced, be incarcerated, and experience lower life satisfaction, with the driver of many of these problems being continued adult antisocial behavior (Colman et al., 2009; Olino et al., 2010). Youth with conduct problems also experience more academic failure and social rejection than their peers (Glenn, 2019). The accumulation of these experiences is one hypothesized driver of the finding that young children with externalizing behavior problems are at increased risk of later developing comorbid internalizing problems such as anxiety and depression (Colman et al., 2009; Willner et al., 2016). Unsurprisingly, conduct problems put individuals at risk for developing a host of psychiatric issues as adults, including antisocial personality disorder and other personality disorders, substance use disorders, mood disorders, and anxiety disorders (Goldstein et al., 2006; Lahey et al., 2005; Morcillo et al., 2011). The impacts of conduct problems are also felt by society. Estimates have calculated a savings of between \$2.6 million and \$4.4 million per child when initiating prevention with high-risk children from birth and a savings of between \$2.6 million and \$5.3 million when intervening with high-risk youth at the age of 14 (Cohen & Piquero, 2008).

9.1 Conduct Problems

9.1.1 Oppositional Defiant Disorder and Conduct Disorder

ODD is characterized by a profile of argumentative, oppositional, and defiant behavior that is developmentally inappropriate and causes significant problems at home, school, and/or with peers (APA, 2013). The hallmarks of ODD are anger or irritable mood, argumentative or defiant behavior, and vindictiveness. These symptoms and behaviors are more common in interactions with adults whom the child knows well, such as caregivers or teachers. The demonstration of these symptoms across multiple settings is the primary indicator of ODD severity.

Children with CD demonstrate a persistent pattern of behavior that includes aggressive behaviors toward people and animals, destroying property, lying and stealing, and seriously violating rules and norms (APA, 2013). Severity is determined by a combination of the frequency of the conduct problems and the amount of harm they cause to others. The childhood-onset type of CD is present before age 10 and is more common in boys, those who had ODD in early childhood, and those with comorbid attention deficit hyperactivity disorder (ADHD) (Frick & Nigg, 2012; Mohan, 2020). The developmental trajectory for childhood-onset CD is characterized as a process of cascading risk, in which a temperamentally vulnerable child experiences inadequate home and school environments, leading to enduring vulnerabilities including poor interpersonal relationships and psychosocial maladjustment (Frick & Nigg, 2012; Moffitt, 2006). In contrast, the developmental trajectory for adolescent-onset CD, in which symptoms become present after age 10, is conceptualized as an exaggeration of typical adolescent rebellion and independence-seeking behaviors. Thus, the teen's behaviors are more likely to resolve by adulthood, although the consequences of those behaviors may persist (Frick & Nigg, 2012; Mohan, 2020; Moffitt, 2006). The presentation of adolescent-onset CD is also more balanced between boys and girls than childhood-onset CD (APA, 2013).

Children who lack empathy and guilt, which are called "callous-unemotional traits" or "limited prosocial emotions," are particularly at risk for severe, stable, and aggressive behavior (Frick & Nigg, 2012). Ongoing research suggests that the developmental psychopathology of this callous-unemotional subgroup of children may differ in meaningful ways from other children diagnosed with CD and also that treatment may need to be tailored to this group (Frick & Nigg, 2012). For these reasons, boys in middle childhood with CD, callous-unemotional traits, comorbid ADHD, and a history of disruptive behavior or ODD since early childhood require immediate intervention.

ODD and CD differ in that ODD is typically less severe than CD; is characterized by emotional dysregulation such as irritable mood, whereas CD is not; and does not include the aggression toward people and animals, destruction of property, and pattern of deceit or theft that characterizes CD (APA, 2013). The onset of ODD typically occurs during the preschool years, while CD tends to onset in middle childhood or later. Some children with ODD may go on to develop CD (Burke et al.,

2005; Rowe et al., 2010). This is especially the case for children who are male with preschool-onset ODD, severe ODD symptoms, and comorbid ADHD and who present primarily with the ODD symptom cluster of defiance, argumentativeness, and vindictiveness (Burke et al., 2005; Rowe et al., 2010). For children whose primary ODD symptoms are angry and irritable mood, ODD is more predictive of anxiety and depression later in life than of CD (Copeland et al., 2009; Rowe et al., 2010).

9.1.2 Attention Deficit Hyperactivity Disorder

Because disruptive behavior is a common feature of ADHD, ADHD is frequently bundled with ODD and CD in studies of childhood behavior problems. ADHD is a neurodevelopmental disorder characterized by inattention, hyperactivity, and impulsivity (APA, 2013). Symptoms must be present before adolescence and are typically identified in middle childhood when children begin to struggle in school. ADHD is typically stable across the life span, though hyperactive behaviors, in particular, may shift from excessive motor movement during early childhood to an internal experience of restlessness or impatience during adolescence and adulthood (Resnick, 2005). ADHD has three subtypes: predominantly inattentive presentation, predominantly hyperactive/impulsive presentation, and combined presentation (APA, 2013). Of note, ADHD symptoms must be present in more than one setting, such as at home and at school, and are often not present in novel, rewarding, and highly interactive situations such as when playing video games or when being interviewed in the clinician's office. Thus, in order to meet the diagnostic criteria requiring symptoms to be present in two or more settings, accurate screening and diagnosis must incorporate the perspective of collateral reporters, typically through the use of a standardized questionnaire (APA, 2013; Weitzman & Wegner, 2015).

Conduct problems are more likely to occur in either the hyperactive/impulsive or combined presentations, because children's externalizing behavior is more closely linked to the social disinhibition and emotion dysregulation features of the diagnosis than the executive functioning challenges (Frick & Nigg, 2012). For example, children's high activity levels and impulsive behaviors, such as grabbing a toy away from another child or interrupting conversations, may cause interpersonal problems with both adults and peers, which compound over time and can lead to social problems and psychological maladjustment. ADHD is also highly comorbid with ODD, the combination of which is a risk factor for later CD (Frick & Nigg, 2012).

ADHD can be treated behaviorally, pharmacologically, or by using a combination approach. Behavioral interventions focus on creating structure to support executive functioning, providing more frequent rewards for prosocial and adaptive behaviors, training lagging social and academic skills, and improving home-school communication (Jensen et al., 2001). Pharmacological interventions rely on stimulant medications such as methylphenidate (Jensen et al., 2001). The combination, when behavioral interventions are implemented with sufficient fidelity and stimulant medication is titrated both initially and over time, as children grow, can be highly effective at managing symptoms, and it is the recommended approach for treating ADHD in children with comorbid disruptive behavior disorders (Jensen et al., 2001). This finding drives the recommendation that children with comorbid ADHD and ODD or CD be treated for ADHD first to try to alleviate psychological distress and remediate symptoms (Lillig, 2018).

9.1.3 Autism Spectrum Disorder, Anxiety Disorders, and Depressive Disorders

Finally, autism spectrum disorder (ASD), anxiety disorders, and depressive disorders may present with features of externalizing behavior problems. In all three cases, children's externalizing problems should remediate at least in part when their primary diagnoses are treated, which emphasizes the importance of screening, appropriate referrals, and accurate diagnosis. Children with ASD, which is a neurodevelopmental disorder like ADHD, tend to be inflexible in their thinking, feel safe in the context of routine, and lack verbal skills (APA, 2013). Taken together, some children with ASD may "get stuck" when their expectations or schedules change unexpectedly or when they feel overwhelmed, appearing defiant and sometimes lashing out aggressively either against themselves (i.e., head banging) or against others. This may be particularly common when children lack the verbal ability to get their needs met through more adaptive channels. Though the treatment plan for ASD should be comprehensive, some strategies and interventions can reduce these other-directed aggressive or oppositional behaviors, including providing advance notice of changes, sticking to routines, training the child's coping skills, and providing the child with alternative means of communication such as a Picture Exchange Communication System (PECS; Bondy & Frost, 2011).

Children with anxiety disorders are distressed by external or internal (i.e., thoughts, physiological experiences) stimuli and lack the coping skills to regulate their emotional responses to the stressors. For example, children worried about separating from their caregivers or taking tests may appear oppositional, defiant, or argumentative in contexts specific to their anxiety. These externalizing features are behavioral expressions of the child's attempts to avoid or, in extreme situations, escape the anxiety-provoking stimuli. Cognitive-behavioral treatment of anxiety disorders is effective (Barrett et al., 2001). It helps decouple previously conditioned responses to anxiety-provoking stimuli and trains children in generic skills for coping with stress. Sometimes true skill deficits underlie anxiety, such as when a child is asked to read in front of the class but does not know how to read. Without understanding and remediating those skill deficits, anxiety and the disruptive and oppositional behaviors that sometimes accompany it will remain. Chapter 7 in this text describes the prevention of anxiety in integrated pediatric primary care in more detail.

Finally, children with depressive disorders often present with irritable mood, in addition to or instead of sad mood, as well as a loss of pleasure, which is known clinically as anhedonia (APA, 2013). Though irritability may appear across depressive disorders in children, disruptive mood dysregulation disorder (DMDD), in particular, features chronic irritable mood peppered with temper outbursts that include verbal rages or physical aggression, are disproportionate to the situation, and are developmentally inappropriate (APA, 2013). Cognitive-behavioral therapy and interpersonal therapy are both effective psychosocial treatments for depression (Ryan, 2005). The former helps children revise problematic thinking patterns, increase experiences of mastery and pleasure, become more behaviorally activated, and gain coping and other lagging skills such as problem-solving. The latter focuses more heavily on maladaptive interpersonal behavior patterns and is more typically used for teens than for children. Depression is also frequently treated with antidepressant medication, though there continue to be concerns about the increase in suicidal ideation and attempts in children who are prescribed selective serotonin reuptake inhibitors (Ryan, 2005). The prevention of depressive disorders in pediatric primary care is discussed in more detail in Chap. 6 in this text.

9.2 Risk Factors for Developing Conduct Problems

The theory of developmental psychopathology posits that genetic, individual, family, and social/environmental influences interact over time to promote either typical or atypical developmental outcomes (Achenbach, 2015; Cicchetti, 1984). These interactive influences are sometimes referred to as the biopsychosocial model (George & Engel, 1980), and it can be helpful to remember that key influences exist both within the child and in the child's context, allowing for numerous avenues of intervention (Bronfenbrenner, 1992). Influences that boost developmental trajectories over time are called protective factors or resiliencies and may include, for example, reading to young children at home, responsive parenting with adequate supervision, access to high-quality schools, and learning coping skills to manage stress and regulate emotions. Influences that dampen developmental trajectories over time are called risk factors. Psychological disorders manifest when risk factors outweigh protective factors (Achenbach, 2015; Cicchetti, 1984). The goal of prevention efforts is to reduce or eliminate risk while boosting resilience. In the case of conduct problems, risk and resilience should be evaluated early in life, before any or early indicators of future psychological disorders manifest. When children have risk factors for conduct problems, prevention or early intervention efforts to reduce risk and boost resilience are indicated to reduce the likelihood of developing the full-blown syndrome.

9.2.1 Biological

Biological risk factors include genetic and teratogenic exposures before birth or early in life (Dodge & Pettit, 2003). Genetic factors include being male and having genetic predispositions for characteristics common in conduct problems such as aggression; impulsivity, problems with emotion regulation, and other temperamental vulnerabilities; executive functioning deficits; and low intelligence (Dodge & Pettit, 2003; Frick & Viding, 2009; Ghandour et al., 2019; Kessler et al., 2005; Merikangas et al., 2010a, b; Moffitt, 2006). Temperamental vulnerabilities present early in development and begin the hallmark pattern of cascading developmental risk that underpins conduct problems. For example, babies as young as 6 months old who present with a pattern of being fussy and hard to soothe, overly resistant to control, and difficult are at risk for developing conduct problems later in childhood (Goodnight et al., 2008). Prenatal and early exposures to teratogens through parental smoking, parental use of other substances, and lead introduce similar vulnerabilities (Carter et al., 2008; Dodge & Pettit, 2003). It is thought that together, these biological precursors negatively impact the ways that children sustain attention, process punishment and reward, and regulate mood and behavior, all of which are key drivers of conduct problems (Dodge & Pettit, 2003; Frick & Viding, 2009; Moffitt, 2006; Rogers et al., 2019; van Goozen et al., 2007).

9.2.2 Psychological

Research has focused on callous-unemotional personality traits, which include a lack of guilt, remorse, and empathy, as a highly predictive psychological risk factor for severe and persistent conduct problems (Frick & Morris, 2004; Frick & Nigg, 2012). Many of the other psychological risk factors that have been identified are part of the sequence of cascading developmental risk experienced by children with conduct problems. These psychological vulnerabilities interact with biological risk factors and unsupportive, invalidating, and antisocial environments over time, a process which shapes them to be even more antisocial, harmful, and atypical from a developmental perspective (Dodge & Pettit, 2003; Frick & Viding, 2009; Patterson et al., 1989). Examples include executive functioning challenges, such as fearlessness, lack of behavioral inhibition, impulsivity, poor attention, and lack of persistence (Moffitt, 2006; Nigg, 2000); cognitive or verbal deficits (Moffitt, 2006); problems with emotion regulation and deficits in coping skills; and poor social skills (Daly et al., 2018; Frick & Morris, 2004). Finally, though it is intrapersonal rather than strictly psychological, child physical health is also a risk factor for behavior problems; one in three children with fair or poor physical health also experiences a clinically significant conduct problem (Ghandour et al., 2019).

9.2.3 Social/Environmental

The final element in the model of cascading developmental risk that characterizes children with conduct problems is the social or environmental context. The first risk context, which comes into play during early childhood, is the home. Dysfunctional family environments are risk factors for the development of conduct problems, which include harsh parenting, lack of structure, poor monitoring, extinction of prosocial behaviors (i.e., ignoring regulated or helpful behaviors), reinforcement of antisocial behaviors (i.e., granting requests or providing attention only after explosive or dysregulated behavior), and other ineffective parenting strategies (Dodge & Pettit, 2003; Frick & Viding, 2009). Dysfunctional households predictive of conduct problems also include conflict or interpersonal violence, neglect, abuse, instability, parental psychopathology, and inconsistent caregiving (Bares et al., 2020; Frick & Viding, 2009; Ghandour et al., 2019; Kopp et al., 2007; Rey et al., 2000).

Once children become school-age, school becomes a second risk context. Poorly managed classrooms not only decrease children's opportunities for learning but also increase the likelihood that children with have negative interactions with their teachers, demonstrate behavior problems, and experience punitive or exclusionary discipline, which is the first step in the school-to-prison pipeline (Dodge & Pettit, 2003; Gregory et al., 2016; Reinke et al., 2008; Webster-Stratton et al., 2004). Academic failure and peer rejection in school lead children to associate with deviant peers, which is the third risk context (Dodge & Pettit, 2003; Patterson et al., 1989). These deviant peers increase the child's exposure to and positive reinforcement of antisocial and other risky behaviors, such as delinquency, truancy, early initiation of sex, and substance abuse (Patterson et al., 1989).

The child's developmental trajectory is embedded in the larger societal context (Bronfenbrenner, 1992). Poverty is a key risk factor for conduct problems (Ghandour et al., 2019). Researchers are beginning to tease apart the mechanisms of this effect. For example, children who live in poverty tend to live in neighborhoods with high poverty rates, high rates of violence, low social mobility, and low-quality public education (Eron et al., 1997). These neighborhood stressors interact with biological, psychological, and social factors to increase risk for conduct problems (Bares et al., 2020). Taken together, this transactional model describes a pattern that worsens over time, both because children's negative experiences with family, school, and peers continue to add up and because the consequences of aggression and property damage become more severe as children age (Dodge & Pettit, 2003; Patterson et al., 1989). Thus, even though most conduct problems onset by the mid-teens, individuals with these challenges experience their consequences across the life span via pervasive skill deficits; entrenchment in unsupportive, invalidating, and antisocial environments; and the long-term sequelae of antisocial behavior such as having a criminal record.

9.3 Screening and Prevention of Conduct Problems in Integrated Care

Currently, only about half of those with conduct problems receive treatment from a mental health professional (Ghandour et al., 2019; Merikangas et al., 2010b), with younger children less likely to receive services (Lavigne et al., 2009). Even fewer receive evidence-based interventions (Kazdin, 1997). Older children with severe conduct problems or with comorbid psychiatric conditions such as depression are more likely to receive treatment (Ghandour et al., 2019), a pattern that explicates the US perspective that problems should be treated rather than prevented. Both the risk of developing conduct problems and the challenges inherent in accessing high-quality interventions to treat them are greater in low-income, marginalized communities, which directly contributes to disparities in health and other outcomes (Arnold & Doctoroff, 2003; Smedley et al., 2003). Unsurprisingly, the prevalence and impact of conduct problems, combined with the inadequacy of the status quo with regard to addressing them, has elicited calls for prevention and early intervention (Merikangas et al., 2010b). A key component of evidence-based prevention is effective screening.

9.3.1 Effective Screening

Research has shown that screening for conduct problems during early childhood (in this case, at age 6) can effectively predict externalizing and delinquent behavior at age 10, school difficulties across middle childhood and adolescence, ADHD diagnoses at 14, cigarette use at 17, and criminal convictions at 25 for children who already had social risk factors such as living in poverty (Hill et al., 2004; Kassing et al., 2019; Racz et al., 2013). The true costs of screening, which could include stigma, psychological distress, and false positives, have not yet been carefully evaluated. However, the bulk of the evidence suggests that the importance of the benefits – preventing and intervening early upon conduct problems – outweighs these costs (Hill et al., 2004). For this reason, screening in pediatric primary care is recommended. The best practice screening is family-centered, which includes careful attention to families' cultures and contexts (AAP, 2012).

Screening can happen universally, in which all children in the practice complete an annual or more frequent screening. One consideration when planning for universal screening is the ethical obligation that the provider will have to follow up with all children who screen into at-risk or clinical levels of problems. It is helpful to have a tiered plan for follow-up assessments and interventions in place before completing the first wave of screenings. Screening can also happen when the provider is concerned either because of the presence of risk factors or of disruptive behaviors. Either way, the goal is to catch disruptive behavior early to prevent children from moving too far down the pathway of cascading developmental risk.

Screening should also be initiated at the request of families. Research suggests that about half of the time, parents of young children who are concerned about behavior problems ask their pediatricians for help (Fanton et al., 2008). In those instances, half of the children eventually saw a mental health provider, suggesting that those parents' concerns were valid. However, the most common response from pediatricians was that the behavior was "not a problem." Equally concerning, of the half of parents who did *not* consult with their pediatricians, one third later met criteria for ODD, CD, or ADHD. These cases reflect missed opportunities for prevention. Taken together, it is recommended that integrated pediatric primary care take a proactive approach to screening, which intentionally includes a thorough and thoughtful examination of parents' concerns.

Screening for conduct problems in pediatric primary care is typically completed by asking the parent or primary caregiver to complete a psychometrically validated questionnaire. Children may also complete the questionnaires as long as they are old enough to understand and respond to the items, which is typically during middle childhood. Of note, however, children are typically viewed as underreporters of their own externalizing behavior problems (i.e., Handwerk et al., 1999). For this reason, child-report data should never be used in isolation. Each validated survey will specify the appropriate population, which should be attended to carefully both for caregiver proxy and child reports, since the items are keyed to development, and the scoring typically relies on age- and sometimes gender-referenced norms.

It is almost always useful and sometimes also necessary to obtain a collateral report from a teacher or other caregivers. Evidence that the child demonstrates conduct problems in settings outside the home is an indicator of severity. In addition, for ADHD, it is a requirement of the diagnostic process (APA, 2013). Teachers tend to be more adept than other reporters at identifying nonnormative externalizing behavior (Hinshaw et al., 1992), presumably because they know the child well and they have a large mental set of typically developing children to which they can compare him or her. Finally, the sensitivity of predictions typically improves when data from multiple informants can be triangulated (Hill et al., 2004).

Several screeners with robust psychometric properties are available either for free or for purchase at an affordable price. They tend to be fairly quick and easy to administer, often taking 3–5 min, and straightforward to score either by hand or using accompanying software. With the exception of the SDQ, the measures are typically administered by an individual with at least a master's degree in psychology, counseling, social work, special education, or a related field, though other professionals can also pursue professional development to become certified in this type of psychological assessment. The screeners are often available in English and Spanish, and sometimes they also include additional translations with accompanying norms.

For thorough reviews of available measures, see McMahon and Frick (2005), Severson et al. (2007), and the Mental Health section of the American Academy of Pediatrics website (e.g., AAP, 2012). We will discuss commonly used instruments in the following paragraphs, including the Strengths and Difficulties Questionnaire (SDQ; Goodman et al., 2000); the Swanson, Nolan, and Pelham-IV (SNAP-IV;

Bussing et al., 2008); the NICHQ Vanderbilt Assessment Scale (Wolraich et al., 2003), the Conners-3 (Conners, 2008); the Child Behavior Checklist (CBCL) and related instruments (Achenbach, 1999); and the Behavior Assessment System for Children Third Edition (BASC-3; Reynolds & Kamphaus, 2015).

The SDQ is a 25-item screening questionnaire for children aged 2 and up (Goodman et al., 2000). Child-report versions exist for children 11–17 years old, and parent and teacher versions exist for children aged 2 and up. It is freely available online at www.sdqinfo.org, it can be administered by non-clinicians, it takes 3–5 min to complete, and it can be scored using a key or online. The instrument has five subscales, including emotional symptoms (i.e., anxiety and mood), conduct problems, hyperactivity/inattention, peer relationship problems, and prosocial behavior. The SDQ can be administered by non-clinicians. The test has been translated into over 75 languages and thus can be used with a multilingual population.

The SNAP-IV is a 26-item screener for children aged 6–18 (Bussing et al., 2008). The SNAP-IV focuses on ADHD and ODD. Some SNAP-IV versions also include additional items relevant to these disorders and other disorders. In line with the recommendation that child-report data are less reliable for externalizing disorders, the SNAP-IV only includes parent and teacher versions. It is freely available online, though more support around scoring is available with an annual subscription at www.myADHD.com.

The Vanderbilt (Wolraich et al., 2003) and the Conners-3 (Conners, 2008) are commonly used in screeners for ADHD. The Vanderbilt, in particular, is favored in pediatric primary care settings (Wolraich et al., 2003). It is an 18-item screener for children aged 6–18 that focuses on ADHD. Similar to the SNAP-IV, the Vanderbilt only includes parent and teacher versions, and some versions include additional items relevant to other disorders. It is available for purchase from the American Academy of Pediatrics' online store at shop.aap.org, where older versions can be downloaded for free. The Conners-3 is a 10-item screener for children aged 6–18 that focuses on ADHD, called the "ADHD Index" (Conners, 2008). Longer versions of the Conners also include items relevant to common comorbid conditions. The Conners includes parent and teacher report versions as well as a self-report version for children aged 8 and up. The flexibility of the Conners and the software package that accompanies it offer advantages for those who are interested in different levels of screening (i.e., ADHD only vs. related issues), prefer easy online scoring, and would benefit from support around creating intervention plans. The Conners is available for purchase at www.wpspublish.com.

Finally, two common "broadband" screeners contain information relevant to a host of problems, including externalizing behavior problems. Each takes 10–20 min for adults to complete and slightly longer for children to complete. They are most commonly used by specialists, such as the behavioral care provider in the integrated care practice. The CBCL and related instruments are a suite of measures that are used to detect behavioral and emotional problems in children and teens beginning at age 18 months (Achenbach, 1999). The CBCL is the parent-report measure, the Teacher-Report Form (TRF) is for teachers, and the Youth Self-Report (YSR) is for children aged 11–18. Additional instruments in the suite can support providers with progress monitoring, behavioral observation, and clinical interviewing, and all of the tools are available for purchase at www.aseba.org. The BASC-3 suite similarly is designed to assess a range of behavioral and emotional issues. The parent and teacher forms are appropriate for children aged 2 and up, and the self-report forms are appropriate for children aged 6 and up (Reynolds & Kamphaus, 2015). The BASC-3 suite includes a screener called the Behavioral and Emotional Screening System (BESS), which includes parent and teacher forms for children aged 3 and up and child-report forms for children aged 8 and up. Additional instruments in the suite can support progress monitoring, child observations, collection of a developmental history, and intervention development, and the suite is available for purchase at www.pearsonassessments.com. The instruments in these two "broadband" screening suites are, for the most part, comparable to one another (e.g., McClendon et al., 2011), and decisions to opt for one suite over the other are likely based mostly on the training background of the purchaser.

9.4 Evidence-Based Prevention

Evidence-based prevention of conduct problems has been shown to be effective both for the general population and for high-risk groups (David-Ferdon et al., 2016). Evidence-based prevention can target everyone, which is called universal or primary prevention. This type of approach is intended to provide support and education and/or reduce risk before problems arise. In the context of pediatric primary care, providers can provide information about the harms of, for example, lead and prenatal smoking to families. Related to psychological risk, children may have lagging skills in executive functioning, emotion regulation, and other areas that introduce risk. Providers can offer skills training programs to the full population of children or, more commonly, help families find schools that incorporate this sort of education into their curriculum. These child-focused curricula are often referred to as social-emotional learning. Social-emotional learning programs, which typically teach children about emotions, coping, peer relations, and problem-solving, have been shown to prevent behavior problems and emotional distress and promote prosocial behavior and academic achievement (Durlak et al., 2011).

Finally, universal prevention may also target the social/environmental risk associated with unsupportive, invalidating, and antisocial environments. The home environment plays a key role in promoting developmental risk (Dodge & Pettit, 2003; Patterson et al., 1989) and is also the environment most malleable from the perspective of the primary care provider. Pediatricians play an important role in educating families about positive and effective approaches to parenting and discipline. The most common method to teach the full suite of positive parenting strategies is through behavioral parent management training, which is a curriculum designed to teach parents these skills. Later in development, both school and peer environments become more important (Dodge & Pettit, 2003; Patterson et al., 1989). Providers in pediatric primary care may consult with families about finding high-quality schools and reinforcing youth's involvement with prosocial peers. For example, schools that train their teachers to use evidence-based classroom behavior management strategies will have fewer punitive and coercive interactions in the classroom and more opportunities for child prosocial behavior to be rewarded and reinforced (Kellam et al., 2011; Reinke et al., 2008; Webster-Stratton et al., 2008).

Behavioral parent management training and effective teacher classroom behavior management have a lot in common. The training typically teaches parents or teachers how to foster positive relationships with their children/students, proactive parenting skills such as routines and effective commands, and positive discipline strategies such as behavior-specific praise, ignoring, and natural and logical consequences. Behavioral parent management training and effective classroom behavior management can reduce disruptive behavior and increase emotion regulation, social skills, and academic achievement (Dretzke et al., 2009; MacSuga-Gage & Simonsen, 2015; Webster-Stratton et al., 2008).

Selective or secondary prevention is defined as early intervention following screening for either early manifestations of the problems or their risk factors. The goal is to catch disruptive behavior early to prevent children from moving too far down the pathway of cascading developmental risk. We discussed screening extensively in the section above. For this type of prevention, only a subset of the population is targeted based on the presence of risk factors. Thus, this group may be those children who have already started displaying antisocial behaviors such as aggression. Alternatively, it may be those children who have not yet started showing externalizing behavior but have one or several risk factors for developing it, such as early temperamental indicators, physical health problems, or living in poverty. Finally, indicated or tertiary prevention is focused on managing the problem once it has already onset to either reduce its negative impacts or remediate it. Selective prevention is most appropriate for those children who already demonstrate conduct problems. Thus, the subset of the population eligible for indicated prevention is even smaller than that of selective prevention.

The intervention classes described above are also appropriate for both selective and indicated prevention, though the sense of urgency about implementing the interventions, the number and intensity of the interventions, and the level of care used to deliver those interventions are typically greater. For example, although training lagging emotion regulation skills will be universally helpful to children, for children who already experience symptoms relevant to emotional dysregulation (i.e., frequent and intense temper tantrums), a course of outpatient cognitive-behavioral therapy may also be indicated. As the problem becomes more severe, the child may also receive these interventions across home, school, and community settings. Unsurprisingly, researchers often see larger positive effects of intervention for those children in the selective and, even more so, the indicated prevention groups (i.e., Dawson-McClure et al., 2015; Webster-Stratton et al., 2001).

When aggression and other symptoms of conduct problems become severe, the child also becomes more likely to be involved with mental health specialists in addition to pediatric primary care providers. Urgent and more intensive action is specifically recommended when children display more persistent, pervasive patterns of antisocial behavior with functional impairment (see Subsection "Watchful Waiting" for more information) and/or when they have multiple concerning risk factors, such as callous-unemotional traits, comorbid ADHD, and a history of disruptive behavior or ODD since early childhood, and/or are living in poverty. Children with high levels of clinical need may require intensive interventions such as multisystemic therapy (MST; Curtis et al., 2004) and are sometimes prescribed risperidone (Barterian et al., 2017), an atypical antipsychotic often associated with significant side effects including weight gain, in addition to a well-titrated stimulant. These interventions should be managed by specialists.

9.5 Stepped Care Prevention Model for Conduct Problems

In the stepped care prevention model, pediatricians and integrated behavioral health providers collaborate with families to provide preventative interventions along a continuum, from least (i.e., watchful waiting) to most invasive and intensive (i.e., individual treatment) or even inpatient admission. Where to start along the continuum is influenced by whether the child is already displaying antisocial behaviors, which may be learned in the context of screening, and/or whether the child has risk factors for conduct problems.

9.5.1 Watchful Waiting

Not all children with behavior or impulse-control difficulties will go on to develop externalizing behavior problems. In fact, a pattern of behavior that causes functional impairment must be present to diagnose a conduct problem (APA, 2013). On the other hand, it is important from a prevention perspective to catch developmental psychopathology early in its course (Burke et al., 2002). Taken together, in cases where the intensity, frequency, and duration of the child's behavior problems are unclear, and especially if the child is in early childhood, caregivers and providers may opt to undergo a period of watchful waiting. Key constructs to be aware of during watchful waiting include the persistence, quality, and pervasiveness of the problematic behaviors. These constructs can be evaluated in the context of the patient's history. In some cases, asking the caregivers to track and document the child's behaviors may also be helpful.

Persistent behaviors repeat and may escalate over time. The *quality* of the behaviors will also be indicative of a clinical profile (Wakschlag et al., 2007). For example, for noncompliance, whereas low-level defiance followed by compliance after a prompt is normative for young children, active defiance, requiring multiple prompts to meet the expectation, or never meeting the expectation is not. Similarly, with regard to emotion regulation, mild difficulty recovering from being upset or needing a little adult support is normative. Moderate or substantial difficulty recovering even with the help of an adult is not. Finally, for aggression, low-intensity aggression that seems impulsive is normative, while multiple incidents of mild aggression, moderate aggression, or serious and intense aggression are not. In all cases, more concerning behaviors are those that are more *pervasive*, meaning that they are present across multiple settings such as home, school, and community settings like church or the grocery store (Wakschlag et al., 2007). Of course, this guidance is nested within the child's risk context. Providers may wish to intervene earlier if the child and family present with a lot of risk, even if the persistence, quality, and pervasiveness of the conduct problems are less significant.

During the watchful waiting period, caregivers should be educated on generic strategies that have been shown to boost mood and physical well-being and, through that pathway, decrease conduct problems (Aarons et al., 2008; Penedo & Dahn, 2005). Specific recommendations include engaging in regular physical activity, maintaining a healthy diet, practicing good sleep hygiene, and developing and maintaining strong relationships with family members and other positive social supports (CDC, 2020). Sleep habits are a particularly common sticking point, with many children getting far less sleep at nighttime than is suggested by the American Academy of Pediatrics (AAP, 2016) due to media use, inconsistent bedtime routines, and caregivers' need to work split shifts or shifts in the gig economy. Occasionally, simply increasing sleep to the recommended hours per night can resolve behavior problems characterized by noncompliance and irritability, especially in early childhood.

9.5.2 Psychoeducation

The goal of psychoeducation is to provide education about the problem, including its prevalence, impact, course, risk and protective factors, and associated prevention and intervention options. This effort can also empower caregivers to make the best choices for their children, ease worries, build rapport, engage families in care, and destigmatize the problem. Almost universally, interventions further along the continuum of the stepped care model begin with psychoeducation. Providers interested in finding resources related to psychoeducation can begin with general information such as that provided by the CDC (2020) or the family-friendly guides created by the Child Mind Institute accessible at https://childmind.org/audience/for-families (Child Mind Institute, 2021a).

Alternatively, especially if providers have the appropriate training in behavioral health, they can pull psychoeducation information from the beginning of any of the more intensive interventions described later in this chapter. Psychoeducation can be shared with families verbally during their consultation or sent home in the form of materials to review. Providers should ensure that the material they communicate, either verbally or in written form, is evidence-based, accessible, family-centered, and culturally competent. In some cases, simply providing this guidance to families can help them make changes to the home or school environment that will resolve the challenging behavior.

9.5.3 Biblio-prevention

Children's books have been demonstrated to help children manage uncomfortable emotions and learn problem-solving and social skills (Hébert & Furner, 1997; Forgan, 2002; McCarty & Chalmers, 1997). They tap into humankind's deep connection with narratives and storytelling and can serve as instruction manuals for children with lagging skills in certain areas, such as emotion regulation or social skills. In addition, when caregivers and children read them together, they provide opportunities to build positive relationships and create a common language. Providers can recommend specific books for caregivers to purchase or can keep some on hand to give away or lend to families with lower incomes. Individual books are rarely evaluated in research as stand-alone interventions; instead, providers learn through experience which books appeal to families, are culturally competent, and align well with theories of psychopathology and evidence-based intervention. We describe several books we personally use below. Early in the continuum of stepped care, providing a book recommendation may be enough to help a child and family. Children's books are also incorporated as one part of larger protocols into the interventions that are situated further down the continuum.

Numerous children's books aim to promote emotional development by teaching children how to identify and cope with uncomfortable emotions. *Today I Feel Silly & Other Moods That Make My Day* by Jamie Lee Curtis uses playful rhymes to help children identify different feelings that they may experience on a given day. Books focused on anger can be particularly helpful in the prevention of conduct problems. In *When Sophie Gets Angry – Really, Really Angry* by Molly Bang (2007), readers observe the intensity of Sophie's feelings, how she behaves when she's angry, and, ultimately, how she is able to calm herself down. Coping with anger is also the focus of *Tamir and Naya Take on Anger* by Prosser Project, (2020) and coauthored by one of the authors of this chapter. *Tamir and Naya Take on Anger* is a beautifully illustrated story featuring Black children that was written by three mental health professionals who identify as women of color. Notably, *Tamir and Naya Take on Anger* includes dialogic questions at the end of the book to increase children's engagement with the story as well as three activities (e.g., deep breathing) to help further promote coping skills, prosocial behavior, and positive feelings about Blackness. *Tamir and Naya Take on Anger*, which was written to address the lack of diversity in traditional publishing, serves as a powerful resource for Black and Brown families who don't often see themselves and their culture positively portrayed in media.

In addition to books that foster emotional development, reading books that focus on building children's problem-solving and social skills can be effective in preventing conduct problems. *Talk and Work It Out* by Cheri Meiners (2005), for example, uses simple language to help children learn conflict resolution. *Join In and Play*, also by Cheri Meiners (2003), teaches appropriate social skills such as how to join in and play with peers, and it emphasizes the importance of cooperation, getting along, and being kind. These books and the others in the Learning to Get Along series include discussion questions, games, and activities that caregivers and providers can use to reinforce what children have learned. Many of the titles are also available in English-Spanish bilingual editions. Finally, *How Do Dinosaurs Play with Their Friends* by Jane Yolen (2006), is another children's book that teaches appropriate social skills. *How Do Dinosaurs Play with Their Friends* is a vibrant, fun story that uses dinosaurs to teach children about friendship and the importance of playing nicely with others. As an added bonus, the names of the dinosaurs are discreetly included in the illustrations.

9.5.4 eHealth Prevention Tools

Online prevention services allow families to access information and support, often at their convenience and from the comfort of their homes, or, in the case of mobile devices and mHealth, from anywhere. The year 2020 brought about a surge in the online and mobile tool space for telehealth and prevention because of the COVID-19 pandemic. Research on many of these tools is ongoing, with most efforts focusing on the development of the applications and the evaluation of their feasibility and acceptability, which has been favorable (Badawy & Kuhns, 2017). First, the Child Mind Institute's website includes a symptom checker (https://childmind.org/symptomchecker/; Child Mind Institute, 2021b). Although it is not a substitute for a clinical diagnosis, the checker can provide a list of disorders or learning problems associated with the symptoms, link families to psychoeducation, and facilitate a focused conversation with a provider. Second, the Fussy Baby Network at the Erikson Institute (2020) helps families with difficult-to-soothe infants and offers free phone consultations via their "warmline," video home visits, parent web groups, and referral information. Online resources that offer suites of preventative interventions via an eHealth or mHealth platform will likely become more common. Finally, it will become increasingly possible to use mobile phones to provide support to parents or older teens either through texting or applications, though scientists have truly just begun to apply mHealth to the prevention of conduct problems and mHealth in and of itself is a new area (i.e., Chu et al., 2019). For example, applications such as CopeSmart, Calm, Headspace, and iMoodJournal offer ways to easily learn and practice coping skills and monitor mood.

9.5.5 Group Programs

Generally, group treatments are highly efficacious while also being cost-effective (Burlingame et al., 2003). Group programs are also flexible enough that they can be used in the context of prevention. Group programs typically span either teach children lagging skills or teach caregivers or teachers how to create more supportive, validating, and prosocial environments.

The programs that target children's lagging skills, such as emotion regulation, are called social-emotional learning curricula. These group-based interventions for the prevention of conduct problems are often available in schools and are rarely delivered in integrated pediatric primary care settings. Therefore, school-based prevention programs will be the focus of this section. School-based prevention programs are delivered at multiple tiers based on students' needs. Universal school-based prevention programs are delivered to all students regardless of their risk, whereas secondary prevention programs provide targeted support to at-risk students.

The most widely used evidence-based universal prevention programs for conduct problems include the Incredible Years Child Training Program (Dinosaur School), Promoting Alternative Thinking Strategies (PATHS), I Can Problem Solve, and Second Step. Each of these prevention programs is designed to reduce conduct problems by promoting social-emotional development (Durlak et al., 2011). There is a strong evidence base for the effectiveness of Dinosaur School (Pidano & Allen, 2015; Webster-Stratton et al., 2008; Webster-Stratton & Reid, 2011), PATHS (Crean & Johnson, 2013; Kam et al., 2004), I Can Problem Solve (Boyle & Hassett-Walker, 2008; Shure & Spivack, 1982), and Second Step (Espelage et al., 2013; Frey et al., 2005; Low et al., 2015) on the prevention of conduct problems in children.

The Coping Power Program (Lochman et al., 2008) and the Friend to Friend (F2F) Program (Leff et al., 2015, 2016) are two evidence-based selective prevention programs for at-risk youth. Coping Power is designed to address deficits in social cognition (e.g., hostile attribution bias), self-regulation, and peer relations and improve positive parental involvement, and it includes child and parent components (Lochman & Wells, 2004). The effectiveness of Coping Power on reducing conduct problems has been demonstrated in several studies (Lochman & Wells, 2004; Muratori et al., 2015). The F2F Program, which is partially based on the Coping Power Program, aims to reduce relational aggression among girls by improving their social problem-solving abilities. Participation in the F2F Program has been shown to reduce aggression, particularly relational aggression (Leff et al., 2015), and increase prosocial behavior (Leff et al., 2016) among girls.

Although group treatments may be a convenient and cost-effective approach for youth with conduct problems, providers should be aware of potential iatrogenic effects of group treatments. In group settings, deviancy training (i.e., the process in which peers reinforce each other's antisocial behaviors) can occur, leading to an increase in antisocial and other problematic behavior rather than a decrease (Dishion et al., 1999). To counteract this problem, the group facilitator should be well trained, closely monitor group interactions, and recruit prosocial peers to join the group.

Trainings for caregivers and teachers related to creating more supportive, validating, and prosocial environments also typically occur in groups. Behavioral parent management training is one of the most substantiated interventions in child mental health, especially for children with significant externalizing behavior problems (Hutchings et al., 2020; Kazdin, 1997; Obsuth et al., 2006). It can be offered in the integrated pediatric primary care setting, typically in partnership with internal or external behavioral health providers. Involving caregivers and family members into the training process is important for decreasing negative behaviors over time, especially when compared with child or parent training alone (Webster-Stratton & Hammond, 1997). For this reason, it is extremely atypical to provide treatment in a clinical setting for externalizing behavior problems without involving the caregivers significantly.

Over the course of about 8–16 sessions, parents learn skills to proactively manage and monitor their children's behavior. The programs focus on improving the child-caregiver relationship, creating structure in the home, reinforcing prosocial behavior, extinguishing antisocial behavior, providing consistent discipline, and generally reshaping the child and caregivers' maladaptive patterns of behavior. Strong evidence exists for the effectiveness of the Incredible Years Parent Program (Leijten et al., 2017; Webster-Stratton & Reid, 2003), including the prevention (as opposed to treatment) version of the protocol. Some efficacious programs more commonly delivered in the individual setting, which we describe in the next section, can also be used in groups.

Finally, teachers can also be trained to create supportive environments that offer rewards for prosocial and regulated behavior and therefore improve children's access to instructional time. One example is classroom contingency management, which involves establishing clear behavior goals and a system to reinforce desired behaviors. For example, in the Good Behavior Game (Flower et al., 2014; Kellam et al., 2011), students are divided into two teams, and a point is given to a team if a team member engages in inappropriate behavior. At the end of the game, the team with the fewest points wins a group reward. If both teams keep their points below a predetermined level, the teams share the reward. Other approaches share many similarities with behavioral parent management training, including the Incredible Years Incredible Beginnings (for early childhood) and Teacher Classroom Management programs (Webster-Stratton et al., 2008). Either type of teacher training program may also be supported by a wraparound coaching model to help translate teachers' didactic learnings into the classroom (i.e., Becker et al., 2013; Reinke et al., 2008). Though these interventions are highly unlikely to occur in integrated pediatric primary care, providers can counsel families around identifying high-quality schools.

9.5.6 Individual Treatment

Individual treatments for conduct problems are easily integrated into pediatric primary care settings, especially when they can be provided by the behavioral care provider. As described above, behavioral parent management training is considered the gold standard treatment for young children with conduct problems (Kazdin, 1997). The goals and course of individual treatment for caregivers mirror that of the group versions of this treatment. In some cases, children and teens may exhibit such extreme antisocial behavior that regular outpatient treatment is not sufficient. In these cases, referrals to higher levels of care such as multisystemic therapy (which is the best practice intervention for youth with this presentation), intensive day treatment, partial hospitalization, or inpatient hospitalization are options (Henggeler & Schaeffer, 2019).

Well-established interventions and caregiver-focused interventions include the Triple P Positive Parenting Program (De Graaf et al., 2008), Defiant Children/ Defiant Teens (Costin & Chambers, 2007), and Parent-Child Interaction Therapy (PCIT; Thomas et al., 2017). PCIT includes many of the elements common in behavioral parent management training but also includes "bug-in-the-ear" coaching, during which providers can help shape caregiver-child interactions in real time. Moreover, although parent management training programs were originally developed as treatments for children with conduct problems, these programs are also effective prevention programs for at-risk children (Gershenson et al., 2010).

Individual, child-focused approaches to the treatment and prevention of conduct problems involve skills training. Children with conduct problems, particularly aggression, have distorted and maladaptive social-cognitive processes (Crick & Dodge, 1996). For example, aggressive children have difficulty generating alternative solutions to problems (Lochman & Curry, 1986). As such, children with conduct problems often benefit from individual skills-based training such as problem-solving skills training. Other skills that are commonly targeted in individual, child-focused interventions include emotion regulation, social skills, and perspective-taking. Either type of individual treatment – behavioral parent management training or child-focused skills training – can be supported by a wraparound assessment and coaching model called the Family Checkup (Dishion & Stormshak, 2007). The Family Checkup works with the full family, uses motivational interviewing to enhance caregiver engagement, and has been demonstrated to effectively prevent early conduct problems (Shaw et al., 2006).

9.6 Lessons Learned

Preventing conduct problems in integrated pediatric primary care is feasible, family-centered, and cost-effective and improves the likelihood that children who need care will be able to access it (Arora et al., 2017; Gleason et al., 2016; Martini et al.,

2012). However, several barriers exist to the successful implementation of both integrated pediatric primary care and prevention efforts relevant to conduct problems in these settings. For example, behavioral care needs to be fully integrated into the pediatric primary care practice. One mechanism to improve this integration is to provide opportunities for interprofessional training in primary care, such as that modeled by the Leadership Education in Neurodevelopmental and Related Disabilities (LEND) and Leadership Education in Adolescent Health (LEAH) programs, both funded by the Maternal Child Health Bureau, and other best practice team training and learning community models. Such training may eventually address some of the other common barriers to the successful integration of behavioral care into primary care, including challenges with financing, colocation, staffing, collaboration, and communication (Brady et al., 2020; King et al., 2018; Weitzman & Wegner, 2015).

Preventing and treating conduct problems in integrated pediatric primary care also introduces diagnosis-specific challenges. Providers must be trained in evidence-based practices for disruptive behavior disorders and the most common comorbid disorders. As is clear from this chapter, many of the best practice behavioral interventions target caregivers and teachers. Parent engagement, which includes, among other things, attendance and treatment adherence, is central to the effectiveness of parent management training programs. However, engagement in parent management training programs is an ongoing issue, with studies reporting high attrition rates among families receiving parent management training (Fernandez & Eyberg, 2009; Thomas & Zimmer-Gembeck, 2007), perhaps especially in prevention contexts (Baker et al., 2011). The same dysfunctional family environments that increase risk for conduct problems in the first place can also get in the way of treatment, including parental psychopathology and distrust of systems that failed the caregivers when they, themselves, were children. Similarly, providers must also coordinate effectively with teachers or school-based mental health providers. Because these collateral contacts are critical but are rarely billable, the reimbursement plan for the practice must take this into account.

References

AAP supports childhood sleep guidelines. (2016). HealthyChildren.Org. https://www.healthychildren.org/English/news/Pages/AAP-Supports-Childhood-Sleep-Guidelines.aspx

Aarons, G. A., Monn, A. R., Leslie, L. K., Garland, A. F., Lugo, L., Hough, R. L., & Brown, S. A. (2008). Association between mental and physical health problems in high-risk adolescents: A longitudinal study. *Journal of Adolescent Health, 43*(3), 260–267.

Achenbach, T. M. (1999). The child behavior checklist and related instruments. In M. E. Maruish (Ed.), *The use of psychological testing for treatment planning and outcomes assessment* (pp. 429–466). Lawrence Erlbaum Associates Publishers.

Achenbach, T. M. (2015). *Developmental psychopathology*. Oxford University Press.

American Academy of Pediatrics Committee on Hospital Care and Institute for Patient- and Family-Centered Care. (2012). Patient- and family-centered care and the pediatrician's role. *Pediatrics, 129*, 394–404.

American Psychiatric Association. (2013). *Diagnostic and statistical manual of mental disorders (DSM-5®)*. American Psychiatric Publishing.

Arnold, D. H., & Doctoroff, G. L. (2003). The early education of socioeconomically disadvantaged children. *Annual Review of Psychology, 54*(1), 517–545.

Arora, P. G., Godoy, L., & Hodgkinson, S. (2017). Serving the underserved: Cultural considerations in behavioral health integration in pediatric primary care. *Professional Psychology: Research and Practice, 48*(3), 139–148. https://doi.org/10.1037/pro0000131

Badawy, S. M., & Kuhns, L. M. (2017). Texting and mobile phone app interventions for improving adherence to preventive behavior in adolescents: A systematic review. *JMIR mHealth and uHealth, 5*(4), e50.

Baker, C. N., Arnold, D. H., & Meagher, S. (2011). Enrollment and attendance in a parent training prevention program for conduct problems. *Prevention Science, 12*(2), 126–138.

Bang, M. (2007). *When Sophie gets angry—Really, really angry*. Scholastic.

Bares, C. B., Chartier, K. G., Karriker-Jaffe, K., Aliev, F., Mustanski, B., & Dick, D. (2020). Exploring how family and neighborhood stressors influence genetic risk for adolescent conduct problems and alcohol use. *Journal of Youth and Adolescence, 49*(7), 1365–1378.

Barrett, P. M., Duffy, A. L., Dadds, M. R., & Rapee, R. M. (2001). Cognitive–behavioral treatment of anxiety disorders in children: Long-term (6-year) follow-up. *Journal of Consulting and Clinical Psychology, 69*(1), 135.

Barterian, J. A., Arnold, L. E., Brown, N. V., Farmer, C. A., Williams, C., Findling, R. L., … Aman, M. G. (2017). Clinical implications from the Treatment of Severe Childhood Aggression (TOSCA) study: A re-analysis and integration of findings. *Journal of the American Academy of Child & Adolescent Psychiatry, 56*(12), 1026–1033.

Becker, K. D., Bradshaw, C. P., Domitrovich, C., & Ialongo, N. S. (2013). Coaching teachers to improve implementation of the good behavior game. *Administration and Policy in Mental Health and Mental Health Services Research, 40*(6), 482–493.

Bondy, A., & Frost, L. (2011). *A picture's worth: PECS and other visual communication strategies in autism*. Woodbine House.

Boyle, D., & Hassett-Walker, C. (2008). Reducing overt and relational aggression among young children: The results from a two-year outcome evaluation. *Journal of School Violence, 7*(1), 27–42.

Brady, K. J. S., Durham, M. P., Francoeur, A., Henneberg, C., Adhia, A., Morley, D., Tamene, M., Singerman, A., Morris, A., Fortuna, L. R., Feinberg, E., & Bair-Merritt, M. (2020). Barriers and facilitators to integrating behavioral health services and pediatric primary care. *Clinical Practice in Pediatric Psychology*. Advance online publication. https://doi.org/10.1037/cpp0000356

Bronfenbrenner, U. (1992). *Ecological systems theory*. Jessica Kingsley Publishers.

Burke, J. D., Loeber, R., & Birmaher, B. (2002). Oppositional defiant disorder and conduct disorder: A review of the past 10 years, part II. *Journal of the American Academy of Child & Adolescent Psychiatry, 41*(11), 1275–1293.

Burke, J. D., Loeber, R., Lahey, B. B., & Rathouz, P. J. (2005). Developmental transitions among affective and behavioral disorders in adolescent boys. *Journal of Child Psychology and Psychiatry, 46*, 1200–1210. https://doi.org/10.1111/j.1469-7610.2005.00422.x

Burlingame, G. M., Fuhriman, A., & Mosier, J. (2003). The differential effectiveness of group psychotherapy: A meta-analytic perspective. *Group Dynamics: Theory, Research, and Practice, 7*(1), 3.

Bussing, R., Fernandez, M., Harwood, M., Hou, W., Garvan, C. W., Eyberg, S. M., & Swanson, J. M. (2008). Parent and teacher SNAP-IV ratings of attention deficit hyperactivity disorder symptoms: Psychometric properties and normative ratings from a school district sample. *Assessment, 15*(3), 317–328. https://doi.org/10.1177/107319110731388

Carter, S., Paterson, J., Gao, W., & Iusitini, L. (2008). Maternal smoking during pregnancy and behaviour problems in a birth cohort of 2-year-old pacific children in New Zealand. *Early Human Development, 84*(1), 59–66.

Centers for Disease Control and Prevention. (2020). Behavior or conduct problems in children. https://www.cdc.gov/childrensmentalhealth/behavior.html

Child Mind Institute. (2021a). *Resources for families.* https://childmind.org/audience/for-families/

Child Mind Institute. (2021b). *Symptom checker.* https://childmind.org/symptomchecker/.

Chu, J. T. W., Wadham, A., Jiang, Y., Whittaker, R., Stasiak, K., Shepherd, M., & Bullen, C. (2019). Effect of MyTeen SMS-based mobile intervention for parents of adolescents: A randomized clinical trial. *JAMA Network Open, 2*(9), e1911120.

Cicchetti, D. (1984). The emergence of developmental psychopathology. *Child Development, 55*(1), 1–7.

Cohen, M. A., & Piquero, A. R. (2008). New evidence on the monetary value of saving a high risk youth. *Journal of Quantitative Criminology, 25*(1), 25–49.

Colman, I., Murray, J., Abbott, R. A., Maughan, B., Kuh, D., Croudace, T. J., & Jones, P. B. (2009). Outcomes of conduct problems in adolescence: 40 year follow-up of national cohort. *BMJ, 338*, a2981.

Conners, C. K. (2008). *Conners 3*. MHS.

Copeland, W. E., Shanahan, L., Costello, E. J., & Angold, A. (2009). Childhood and adolescent psychiatric disorders as predictors of young adult disorders. *Archives of General Psychiatry, 66*, 764–772. https://doi.org/10.1001/archgenpsychiatry.2009.8

Costin, J., & Chambers, S. M. (2007). Parent management training as a treatment for children with oppositional defiant disorder referred to a mental health clinic. *Clinical Child Psychology and Psychiatry, 12*(4), 511–524. https://doi.org/10.1177/135910450708097

Crean, H. F., & Johnson, D. B. (2013). Promoting alternative thinking strategies (PATHS) and elementary school aged children's aggression: Results from a cluster randomized trial. *American Journal of Community Psychology, 52*(1–2), 56–72.

Crick, N. R., & Dodge, K. A. (1996). Social information-processing mechanisms in reactive and proactive aggression. *Child Development, 67*(3), 993–1002.

Curtis, N. M., Ronan, K. R., & Borduin, C. M. (2004). Multisystemic treatment: A meta-analysis of outcome studies. *Journal of Family Psychology, 18*(3), 411–419. https://doi.org/10.1037/0893-3200.18.3.411

Daly, B. P., DeMatteo, D., Hildenbrand, A., Baker, C. N., & Fisher, J. H. (2018). Psychosocial treatment and prevention in the adolescent years for ODD and CD. In *The Wiley handbook of disruptive and impulse-control disorders* (p. 467). Wiley Blackwell.

David-Ferdon, C., Vivolo-Kantor, A. M., Dahlberg, L. L., Marshall, K. J., Rainford, N., & Hall, J. E. (2016). *A comprehensive technical package for the prevention of youth violence and associated risk behaviors*. Centers for Disease Control and Prevention.

Dawson-McClure, S., Calzada, E., Huang, K. Y., Kamboukos, D., Rhule, D., Kolawole, B., Petkova, E., & Brotman, L. M. (2015). A population-level approach to promoting healthy child development and school success in low-income, urban neighborhoods: Impact on parenting and child conduct problems. *Prevention Science, 16*(2), 279–290. https://doi.org/10.1007/s11121-014-0473-3

De Graaf, I., Speetjens, P., Smit, F., De Wolff, M., & Tavecchio, L. (2008). Effectiveness of the triple P positive parenting program on parenting: A meta-analysis. *Family Relations, 57*(5), 553–566.

Dishion, T. J., & Stormshak, E. A. (2007). *Intervening in children's lives: An ecological, family-centered approach to mental health care*. American Psychological Association. https://doi.org/10.1037/11485-000

Dishion, T. J., McCord, J., & Poulin, F. (1999). When interventions harm. Peer groups and problem behavior. *The American Psychologist, 54*(9), 755–764. https://doi.org/10.1037//0003-066x.54.9.755

Dodge, K. A., & Pettit, G. S. (2003). A biopsychosocial model of the development of chronic conduct problems in adolescence. *Developmental Psychology, 39*(2), 349.

Dretzke, J., Davenport, C., Frew, E., Barlow, J., Stewart-Brown, S., Bayliss, S., et al. (2009). The clinical effectiveness of different parenting programmes for children with conduct problems: A systematic review of randomised controlled trials. *Child and Adolescent Psychiatry and Mental Health, 3*, 7–16.

Durlak, J. A., Weissberg, R. P., Dymnicki, A. B., Taylor, R. D., & Schellinger, K. B. (2011). The impact of enhancing students' social and emotional learning: A meta-analysis of school-based universal interventions. *Child Development, 82*(1), 405–432.

Eron, L. D., Guerra, N., & Huesmann, L. R. (1997). Poverty and violence. In *Aggression* (pp. 139–154). Springer.

Espelage, D. L., Low, S., Polanin, J. R., & Brown, E. C. (2013). The impact of a middle school program to reduce aggression, victimization, and sexual violence. *Journal of Adolescent Health, 53*(2), 180–186.

Fanton, J., MacDonald, B., & Harvey, E. (2008). Preschool parent-pediatrician consultations and predictive referral patterns for problematic behaviors. *Journal of Developmental and Behavioral Pediatrics, 29*(6), 475.

Fernandez, M. A., & Eyberg, S. M. (2009). Predicting treatment and follow-up attrition in parent–child interaction therapy. *Journal of Abnormal Child Psychology, 37*(3), 431–441.

Flower, A., McKenna, J. W., Bunuan, R. L., Muething, C. S., & Vega, R., Jr. (2014). Effects of the good behavior game on challenging behaviors in school settings. *Review of Educational Research, 84*(4), 546–571.

Forgan, J. W. (2002). Using bibliotherapy to teach problem solving. *Intervention in School and Clinic, 38*(2), 75–82.

Frey, K. S., Nolen, S. B., Edstrom, L. V. S., & Hirschstein, M. K. (2005). Effects of a school-based social–emotional competence program: Linking children's goals, attributions, and behavior. *Journal of Applied Developmental Psychology, 26*(2), 171–200.

Frick, P. J., & Morris, A. S. (2004). Temperament and developmental pathways to conduct problems. *Journal of Clinical Child and Adolescent Psychology, 33*(1), 54–68.

Frick, P. J., & Nigg, J. T. (2012). Current issues in the diagnosis of attention deficit hyperactivity disorder, oppositional defiant disorder, and conduct disorder. *Annual Review of Clinical Psychology, 8*, 77–107.

Frick, P. J., & Viding, E. (2009). Antisocial behavior from a developmental psychopathology perspective. *Development and Psychopathology, 21*(4), 1111–1131. https://doi.org/10.1017/S0954579409990071

Fussy Baby Network – National network of family support. (2020, March 31). Erikson Institute. https://www.erikson.edu/fussy-baby-network/

George, E., & Engel, L. (1980). The clinical application of the biopsychosocial model. *American Journal of Psychiatry, 137*(5), 535–544.

Gershenson, R. A., Lyon, A. R., & Budd, K. S. (2010). Promoting positive interactions in the classroom: Adapting parent-child interaction therapy as a universal prevention program. *Education and Treatment of Children, 33*(2), 261–287.

Ghandour, R. M., Sherman, L. J., Vladutiu, C. J., Ali, M. M., Lynch, S. E., Bitsko, R. H., & Blumberg, S. J. (2019). Prevalence and treatment of depression, anxiety, and conduct problems in US children. *The Journal of Pediatrics, 206*, 256–267.

Gleason, M. M., Goldson, E., Yogman, M. W., & Committee on Psychosocial Aspects of Child and Family Health. (2016). Addressing early childhood emotional and behavioral problems. *Pediatrics, 138*(6), e20163025.

Glenn, A. L. (2019). Using biological factors to individualize interventions for youth with conduct problems: Current state and ethical issues. *International Journal of Law and Psychiatry, 65*, 101348.

Goldstein, R. B., Grant, B. F., Ruan, W. J., Smith, S. M., & Saha, T. D. (2006). Antisocial personality disorder with childhood- vs. adolescence-onset conduct disorder: Results from the National Epidemiologic Survey on Alcohol and Related Conditions. *The Journal of Nervous and Mental Disease, 194*(9), 667–675.

Goodman, R., Ford, T., Simmons, H., Gatward, R., & Meltzer, H. (2000). Using the Strengths and Difficulties Questionnaire (SDQ) to screen for child psychiatric disorders in a community sample. *British Journal of Psychiatry, 177*(6), 534–539. https://doi.org/10.1192/bjp.177.6.534

Goodnight, J. A., Bates, J. E., Pettit, G. S., & Dodge, K. A. (2008). Parents' campaigns to reduce their children's conduct problems: Interactions with temperamental resistance to control. *International Journal of Developmental Science, 2*(1–2), 100–119.

Gregory, A., Hafen, C. A., Ruzek, E., Mikami, A. Y., Allen, J. P., & Pianta, R. C. (2016). Closing the racial discipline gap in classrooms by changing teacher practice. *School Psychology Review, 45*(2), 171–191.

Handwerk, M. L., Larzelere, R. E., Soper, S. H., & Friman, P. C. (1999). Parent and child discrepancies in reporting severity of problem behaviors in three out-of-home settings. *Psychological Assessment, 11*(1), 14–23. https://doi.org/10.1037/1040-3590.11.1.14

Hébert, T. P., & Furner, J. M. (1997). Helping high ability students overcome math anxiety through bibliotherapy. *Journal of Secondary Gifted Education, 8*(4), 164–178.

Henggeler, S. W., & Schaeffer, C. M. (2019). Multisystemic therapy: Clinical procedures, outcomes, and implementation research. *Family Process, 55*(3), 514–528.

Hill, L. G., Coie, J. D., Lochman, J. E., & Greenberg, M. T. (2004). Effectiveness of early screening for externalizing problems: Issues of screening accuracy and utility. *Journal of Consulting and Clinical Psychology, 72*(5), 809.

Hinshaw, S. P., Han, S. S., Erhardt, D., & Huber, A. (1992). Internalizing and externalizing behavior problems in preschool children: Correspondence among parent and teacher ratings and behavior observations. *Journal of Clinical Child Psychology, 21*(2), 143–150.

Hutchings, J., Pye, K. L., Bywater, T., & Williams, M. E. (2020). A feasibility evaluation of the Incredible Years® school readiness parenting programme. *Intervención Psicosocial, 29*(2), 83–91.

Jensen, P. S., Hinshaw, S. P., Swanson, J. M., Greenhill, L. L., Conners, C. K., Arnold, L. E., … Wigal, T. (2001). Findings from the NIMH Multimodal Treatment Study of ADHD (MTA): Implications and applications for primary care providers. *Journal of Developmental & Behavioral Pediatrics, 22*(1), 60–73.

Kam, C. M., Greenberg, M. T., & Kusché, C. A. (2004). Sustained effects of the PATHS curriculum on the social and psychological adjustment of children in special education. *Journal of Emotional and Behavioral Disorders, 12*(2), 66–78.

Kassing, F., Godwin, J., Lochman, J. E., Coie, J. D., & Conduct Problems Prevention Research Group. (2019). Using early childhood behavior problems to predict adult convictions. *Journal of Abnormal Child Psychology, 47*(5), 765–778.

Kazdin, A. E. (1997). Parent management training: Evidence, outcomes, and issues. *Journal of the American Academy of Child & Adolescent Psychiatry, 36*(10), 1349–1356.

Kellam, S. G., Mackenzie, A. C., Brown, C. H., Poduska, J. M., Wang, W., Petras, H., & Wilcox, H. C. (2011). The good behavior game and the future of prevention and treatment. *Addiction Science & Clinical Practice, 6*(1), 73.

Kessler, R. C., Chiu, W. T., Demler, O., & Walters, E. E. (2005). Prevalence, severity, and comorbidity of 12-month DSM-IV disorders in the National Comorbidity Survey Replication. *Archives of General Psychiatry, 62*(6), 617–627.

King, M. A., Wissow, L. S., & Baum, R. A. (2018). The role of organizational context in the implementation of a statewide initiative to integrate mental health services into pediatric primary care. *Health Care Management Review, 43*(3), 206–217.

Kopp, L., Kopp, L., Beauchaine, T., & Beauchaine, T. (2007). Patterns of psychopathology in the families of children with conduct problems, depression, and both psychiatric conditions. *Journal of Abnormal Child Psychology, 35*(2), 301–312.

Lahey, B. B., Loeber, R., Burke, J. D., & Applegate, B. (2005). Predicting future antisocial personality disorder in males from a clinical assessment in childhood. *Journal of Consulting and Clinical Psychology, 73*(3), 389–399.

Lavigne, J. V., LeBailly, S. A., Hopkins, J., Gouze, K. R., & Binns, H. J. (2009). The prevalence of ADHD, ODD, depression, and anxiety in a community sample of 4-year-olds. *Journal of Clinical Child & Adolescent Psychology, 38*(3), 315–328.

Leff, S. S., Paskewich, B. S., Waasdorp, T. E., Waanders, C., Bevans, K. B., & Jawad, A. F. (2015). Friend to friend: A randomized trial for urban African American relationally aggressive girls. *Psychology of Violence, 5*(4), 433.

Leff, S. S., Waasdorp, T. E., & Paskewich, B. S. (2016). The broader impact of friend to friend (F2F) effects on teacher–student relationships, prosocial behaviors, and relationally and physically aggressive behaviors. *Behavior Modification, 40*(4), 589–610.

Leijten, P., Raaijmakers, M. A., Orobio de Castro, B., van den Ban, E., & Matthys, W. (2017). Effectiveness of the incredible years parenting program for families with socioeconomically disadvantaged and ethnic minority backgrounds. *Journal of Clinical Child & Adolescent Psychology, 46*(1), 59–73.

Lillig, M. (2018). Conduct disorder: Recognition and management. *American Family Physician, 98*(10), 584–592.

Lochman, J. E., & Curry, J. F. (1986). Effects of social problem-solving training and self-instruction training with aggressive boys. *Journal of Clinical Child Psychology, 15*(2), 159–164.

Lochman, J. E., & Wells, K. C. (2004). The coping power program for preadolescent aggressive boys and their parents: Outcome effects at the 1-year follow-up. *Journal of Consulting and Clinical Psychology, 72*(4), 571.

Lochman, J. E., Wells, K. C., & Lenhart, L. A. (2008). *Coping power child group program: Facilitator guide*. New York.

Low, S., Cook, C. R., Smolkowski, K., & Buntain-Ricklefs, J. (2015). Promoting social–emotional competence: An evaluation of the elementary version of Second Step®. *Journal of School Psychology, 53*(6), 463–477.

MacSuga-Gage, A. S., & Simonsen, B. (2015). Examining the effects of teacher-directed opportunities to respond on student outcomes: A systematic review of the literature. *Education and Treatment of Children, 38*(2), 211–239.

Martini, R., Hilt, R., Marx, L., Chenven, M., Naylor, M., Sarvet, B., & Ptakowski, K. K. (2012). *Best principles for integration of child psychiatry into the pediatric health home*. American Academy of Child & Adolescent Psychiatry.

McCarty, H., & Chalmers, L. (1997). Bibliotherapy intervention and prevention. *Teaching Exceptional Children, 29*(6), 12–17.

McClendon, D. T., Warren, J. S., Green, M. K., Burlingame, G. M., Eggett, D. L., & McClendon, R. J. (2011). Sensitivity to change of youth treatment outcome measures: A comparison of the CBCL, BASC-2, and Y-OQ. *Journal of Clinical Psychology, 67*(1), 111–125.

McMahon, R. J., & Frick, P. J. (2005). Evidence-based assessment of conduct problems in children and adolescents. *Journal of Clinical Child and Adolescent Psychology, 34*(3), 477–505.

McMahon, R. J., Witkiewitz, K., & Kotler, J. S. (2010). Predictive validity of callous–unemotional traits measured in early adolescence with respect to multiple antisocial outcomes. *Journal of Abnormal Psychology, 119*(4), 752.

Meiners, C. J. (2003). *Join in and play*. Free Spirit Publishing.

Meiners, C. J. (2005). *Talk and work it out*. Free Spirit Publishing, Incorporated.

Merikangas, K. R., He, J. P., Burstein, M., Swanson, S. A., Avenevoli, S., Cui, L., … Swendsen, J. (2010a). Lifetime prevalence of mental disorders in US adolescents: Results from the National Comorbidity Survey Replication–Adolescent Supplement (NCS-A). *Journal of the American Academy of Child & Adolescent Psychiatry, 49*(10), 980–989.

Merikangas, K. R., He, J. P., Brody, D., Fisher, P. W., Bourdon, K., & Koretz, D. S. (2010b). Prevalence and treatment of mental disorders among US children in the 2001–2004 NHANES. *Pediatrics, 125*(1), 75–81.

Moffitt, T. E. (2006). Life-course-persistent versus adolescence-limited antisocial behavior. In D. Cicchetti & D. J. Cohen (Eds.), *Developmental psychopathology: Risk, disorder, and adaptation* (pp. 570–598). Wiley.

Mohan, L. (2020, November 19). *Conduct disorder*. Retrieved December 30, 2020, from https://www.ncbi.nlm.nih.gov/books/NBK470238/

Morcillo, C., Duarte, C. S., Sala, R., Wang, S., Lejuez, C. W., Kerridge, B. T., et al. (2011). Conduct disorder and adult psychiatric diagnoses: Associations and gender differences in the U.S. adult population. *Journal of Psychiatric Research, 46*(3), 323–330.

Muratori, P., Bertacchi, I., Giuli, C., Lombardi, L., Bonetti, S., Nocentini, A., ... Lochman, J. E. (2015). First adaptation of coping power program as a classroom-based prevention intervention on aggressive behaviors among elementary school children. *Prevention Science, 16*(3), 432–439.

Nigg, J. T. (2000). On inhibition/disinhibition in developmental psychopathology: Views from cognitive and personality psychology and a working inhibition taxonomy. *Psychological Bulletin, 126*(2), 220.

Obsuth, I., Moretti, M. M., Holland, R., Braber, K., & Cross, S. (2006). Conduct disorder: New directions in promoting effective parenting and strengthening parent-adolescent relationships. *Journal of the Canadian Academy of Child and Adolescent Psychiatry, 15*(1), 6.

Olino, T., Seeley, J., & Lewinsohn, P. (2010). Conduct disorder and psychosocial outcomes at age 30: Early adult psychopathology as a potential mediator. *Journal of Abnormal Child Psychology, 38*(8), 1139–1149.

Patterson, G. R., DeBaryshe, B. D., & Ramsey, E. (1989). A developmental perspective on antisocial behavior. *American Psychologist, 44*(2), 329–335. https://doi.org/10.1037/0003-066X.44.2.329

Penedo, F. J., & Dahn, J. R. (2005). Exercise and well-being: A review of mental and physical health benefits associated with physical activity. *Current Opinion in Psychiatry, 18*(2), 189–193.

Pidano, A. E., & Allen, A. R. (2015). The incredible years series: A review of the independent research base. *Journal of Child and Family Studies, 24*(7), 1898–1916.

Prosser Project. (2020). *Tamir and Naya Take on Anger*. Prosser Project.

Racz, S. J., King, K. M., Wu, J., Witkiewitz, K., & McMahon, R. J. (2013). The predictive utility of a brief kindergarten screening measure of child behavior problems. *Journal of Consulting and Clinical Psychology, 81*(4), 588.

Reinke, W. M., Lewis-Palmer, T., & Merrell, J. (2008). The classroom check-up: A classwide teacher consultation model for increasing praise and decreasing disruptive behavior. *School Psychology Review, 37*, 315–332.

Resnick, R. J. (2005). Attention deficit hyperactivity disorder in teens and adults: They don't all outgrow it. *Journal of Clinical Psychology, 61*, 529–533. https://doi.org/10.1002/jclp.20117

Rey, J. M., Walter, G., Plapp, J. M., & Denshire, E. (2000). Family environment in attention deficit hyperactivity, oppositional defiant and conduct disorders. *Australian and New Zealand Journal of Psychiatry, 34*(3), 453–457.

Reynolds, C. R., & Kamphaus, R. W. (2015). *BASC-3: Behavior assessment system for children* (3rd ed.). Pearson.

Rogers, J. C., Gonzalez-Madruga, K., Kohls, G., Baker, R. H., Clanton, R. L., Pauli, R., et al. (2019). White matter microstructure in youths with conduct disorder: Effects of sex and variation in callous traits. *Journal of the American Academy of Child and Adolescent Psychiatry, 58*(12), 1184–1196.

Rowe, R., Costello, E. J., Angold, A., Copeland, W. E., & Maughan, B. (2010). Developmental pathways in oppositional defiant disorder and conduct disorder. *Journal of Abnormal Psychology, 119*(4), 726.

Ryan, N. D. (2005). Treatment of depression in children and adolescents. *The Lancet, 366*(9489), 933–940.

Severson, H. H., Walker, H. M., Hope-Doolittle, J., Kratochwill, T. R., & Gresham, F. M. (2007). Proactive, early screening to detect behaviorally at-risk students: Issues, approaches, emerging innovations, and professional practices. *Journal of School Psychology, 45*(2), 193–223.

Shaw, D. S., Dishion, T. J., Supplee, L., Gardner, F., & Arnds, K. (2006). Randomized trial of a family-centered approach to the prevention of early conduct problems: 2-year effects of the family check-up in early childhood. *Journal of Consulting and Clinical Psychology, 74*(1), 1.

Shure, M. B., & Spivack, G. (1982). Interpersonal problem-solving in young children: A cognitive approach to prevention. *American Journal of Community Psychology, 10*(3), 341–356.

Smedley, B. D., Stith, A. Y., & Nelson, A. R. (2003). Racial and ethnic disparities in diagnosis and treatment: A review of the evidence and a consideration of causes. In *Unequal treatment: Confronting racial and ethnic disparities in health care*. National Academy of Sciences.

The ASEBA approach—Homepage. https://aseba.org/

Thomas, R., & Zimmer-Gembeck, M. J. (2007). Behavioral outcomes of parent-child interaction therapy and triple P—Positive parenting program: A review and meta-analysis. *Journal of Abnormal Child Psychology, 35*(3), 475–495.

Thomas, R., Abell, B., Webb, H. J., Avdagic, E., & Zimmer-Gembeck, M. J. (2017). Parent-child interaction therapy: A meta-analysis. *Pediatrics, 140*(3), e20170352.

van Goozen, S. H. M., Fairchild, G., Snoek, H., & Harold, G. T. (2007). The evidence for a neurobiological model of childhood antisocial behavior. *Psychological Bulletin, 133*(1), 149–182.

Wakschlag, L. S., Briggs-Gowan, M. J., Carter, A. S., Hill, C., Danis, B., Keenan, K., … Leventhal, B. L. (2007). A developmental framework for distinguishing disruptive behavior from normative misbehavior in preschool children. *Journal of Child Psychology and Psychiatry, 48*(10), 976–987.

Webster-Stratton, C., & Hammond, M. (1997). Treating children with early-onset conduct problems. *Journal of Consulting and Clinical Psychology, 65*(1), 93–109.

Webster-Stratton, C., & Reid, M. J. (2003). The IY parents, teachers, and children training series. In A. Kazdin & J. Weisz (Eds.), *Evidence-based psychotherapies for children and adolescents* (pp. 224–240). The Guilford Press.

Webster-Stratton, C. H., & Reid, M. J. (2011). The incredible years program for children from infancy to pre-adolescence: Prevention and treatment of behavior problems. In *Clinical handbook of assessing and treating conduct problems in youth* (pp. 117–138). Springer.

Webster-Stratton, C., Reid, M. J., & Hammond, M. (2001). Preventing conduct problems, promoting social competence: A parent and teacher training partnership in Head Start. *Journal of Clinical Child & Adolescent Psychology, 30*(3), 283–302. https://doi.org/10.1207/S15374424JCCP3003_2

Webster-Stratton, C., Reid, M. J., & Hammond, M. (2004). Treating children with early-onset conduct problems: Intervention outcomes for parent, child, and teacher training. *Journal of Clinical Child and Adolescent Psychology, 33*(1), 105–124.

Webster-Stratton, C., Reid, J. M., & Stoolmiller, M. (2008). Preventing conduct problems and improving school readiness: Evaluation of the Incredible Years teacher and child training programs in high-risk schools. *Journal of Child Psychology and Psychiatry, 49*(5), 471–488.

Weitzman, C., & Wegner, L. (2015). Promoting optimal development: Screening for behavioral and emotional problems. *Pediatrics, 135*(2), 384–395.

Willner, C. J., Gatzke-Kopp, L. M., & Bray, B. C. (2016). The dynamics of internalizing and externalizing comorbidity across the early school years. *Development and Psychopathology, 28*(4pt1), 1033–1052. https://doi.org/10.1017/S0954579416000687

Wolraich, M. L., Lambert, W., Doffing, M. A., Bickman, L., Simmons, T., & Worley, K. (2003). Psychometric properties of the Vanderbilt ADHD diagnostic parent rating scale in a referred population. *Journal of Pediatric Psychology, 28*(8), 559–568.

Yolen, J. (2006). *How do dinosaurs play with their friends?* Blue Sky Press.

Chapter 10
Nicotine Dependence and Prevention in Integrated Care Settings

Ellen Galstyan and Steve Sussman

10.1 Introduction: Tobacco Use Prevalence and Nicotine Dependence

Tobacco use is the leading global cause of preventable death and kills more than 8 million people each year, of whom more than 7 million are from direct tobacco use and around 1.2 million are nonusers exposed to secondhand smoke (Tobacco Fact Sheet: World Health Organization (WHO), 2019). More than 16 million Americans live with a smoking-related disease (CDC, 2021). It is estimated that there were 1.1 billion current smokers worldwide in 2018, 82% of whom were males. Among children between the ages of 13 and 15, 24 million were smokers. Although global tobacco use has fallen over the past two decades, this progress is still far from achieving the World Health Organization's (WHO) target of cutting tobacco use by 30% between 2010 and 2025, as part of global efforts to reduce mortality from the four main noncommunicable diseases (cardiovascular disease, cancers, chronic lung diseases, and diabetes) (Tobacco Fact Sheet: WHO, 2019).

This research was supported by a National Cancer Institute Grant #: 5P30CA014089-45 (PI: Caryn Lerman) Supplement (Project Leads: Matt Kirkpatrick/Adam Leventhal) Expansion of the C3I Program to develop tobacco cessation treatment capacity and infrastructure for cancer patients.
Citation: Galstyan, E., Sussman, S. Y. (2021) Nicotine dependence and prevention in integrated care settings. *Handbook of evidence-based prevention of behavioral disorders in integrated care: A stepped care approach.* Springer. (pp. 221–249).

E. Galstyan (✉) · S. Sussman
Department of Preventive Medicine, Keck School of Medicine, Institute for Health Promotion and Disease Prevention Research, University of Southern California, Los Angeles, CA, USA
e-mail: egalstya@usc.edu; ssussma@usc.edu

W. O'Donohue, M. Zimmermann (eds.), *Handbook of Evidence-Based Prevention of Behavioral Disorders in Integrated Care*,
https://doi.org/10.1007/978-3-030-83469-2_10

In 2019, an estimated 14.0% (34.1 million) of US adults were current cigarette smokers. Current cigarette smokers were defined as persons who had smoked ≥100 cigarettes during their lifetime and now smoked cigarettes either every day or some days (CDC: Burden of Tobacco Use, 2021). Men are more likely to be cigarette smokers, with about 15 of every 100 adult men (15.3%) and nearly 13 of every 100 adult women (12.7%) reporting being current smokers. Current cigarette smoking in the United States is highest among people aged 25–44 years and 45–64 years, among non-Hispanic American Indians/Alaska Natives and people of non-Hispanic "other" races (includes individuals in "other" group or "other single and multiple race"), and among those who have received a general education development (GED) certificate. Current cigarette smoking was lowest among people aged 18–24 years, among non-Hispanic Asians, and among those with a graduate degree.

There are now more former cigarette smokers than current smokers in the United States, and this has been noted for at least 8 years (e.g., US Department of Health and Human Services [National Center for Chronic Disease Prevention and Health Promotion], 2014). For more than a decade, national surveillance data on smoking cessation have revealed a similar pattern, with modest improvement—two-thirds of adult cigarette smokers indicate a desire to quit, and just over half try to quit each year; however, less than 10% of smokers who try to quit succeed in quitting for 6 months or longer (Babb et al., 2017). Clinician intervention with smokers and those dependent on nicotine is recommended (Fiore et al., 2008). In addition, while the number of current cigarette smokers has decreased, there are other types of tobacco products that have increased a great deal in popularity, primarily e-cigarettes; the percentage of persons using tobacco products overall has not noticeably decreased.

10.1.1 New and Emerging Tobacco Products

Although cigarette smoking remains the leading cause of preventable disease and death in the United States, a variety of new combustible, noncombustible, and electronic tobacco products are now being sold and marketed. The tobacco product landscape is rapidly changing, and the use of emerging tobacco products is increasing, particularly among youth and young adults (Mermelstein, 2014).

Several types of noncombustible, electronic cigarettes are now available with varying levels of nicotine, some that may contain up to 50 mg. These devices have been used for a variety of behaviors and may be considered a novelty or hobby (i.e., smoke tricks, creating "clouds" of smoke, vaping contests). Since 2011, electronic cigarettes have become the most commonly used tobacco product among US middle and high school students, surpassing combustible cigarettes (USDHHS, 2020). In 2020, 19.6% of high school students (3.02 million) and 4.7% of middle school students (550,000) reported current e-cigarette use. Among current e-cigarette users, 38.9% of high school students and 20.0% of middle school students reported using e-cigarettes on 20 or more of the past 30 days; 22.5% of high school users and 9.4% of middle school users reported daily use. Among all current e-cigarette users, 82.9% used flavored e-cigarettes, including 84.7% of high school users (2.53 million) and 73.9% of middle school users (400,000) (CDC: Office on Smoking and Health at a Glance, 2021). Evidence suggests an association between e-cigarette use in nonsmoking adolescents and subsequent cigarette smoking in young adults (Barrington-Trimis, 2018). Evidence also is accumulating that e-cigarette use, while less harmful than combustible cigarettes, is not harmless and may contribute to heart disease, cancers, and lung conditions (Qasim et al., 2017).

"Heat-not-burn" tobacco products (HnB) are electronic devices that heat processed tobacco instead of combusting it to deliver an aerosol with fewer toxicants than in cigarette smoke. Commercially available HnB systems like glo (produced by British American Tobacco (BAT)), Ploom (Japan Tobacco Inc. (JT)), or IQOS (Philip Morris International (PMI)) include a charger, a holder and tobacco sticks, plugs, or capsules. Inserted into the holder, tobacco sticks are heated with an electronically controlled heating element (Simonavicius et al., 2019). As it is a relatively newer tobacco product in the United States, there is limited research on the prevalence and use of HnB systems. A study of HnB and e-cigarette use in Japan, the largest HnB market in the world, reported that 6.6% had ever used the product(s) and 1.3% had used in the previous 30 days. Among electronic smoking device ever users, e-cigarettes accounted for the majority; Ploom and IQOS only accounted for 7.8% and 8.4%, respectively, in 2015 (Tabuchi et al., 2016). These findings warrant additional research on the health risks of HnB products and devices. While apparently much less harmful than combustible tobacco, HnB products are not harmless (Simonavicius et al., 2019). Potential carcinogenic and cardiovascular qualities of HnB products will need to be explored much more.

As they are marketed as a "harm reduction device," an aid to smoking cessation, research on the health risks of HnB products is still limited. In one study analyzing the content and nicotine delivery to the aerosol of a HnB product (IQOS) in comparison with e-cigarettes and a combustible cigarette, Farsalinos et al. found that HnB tobacco sticks contained similar nicotine concentrations as combustible cigarettes and the levels of nicotine delivered to the aerosol of the HnB products were lower than combustible cigarettes and higher than electronic cigarettes at low puff duration but lower than e-cigarettes at longer puff durations (Farsalinos et al., 2018). These findings warrant additional research on the health risks of HnB products and devices.

The use of hookah or water pipe smoking is prevalent worldwide, especially among young adults (Centers for Disease Control and Prevention, 2014; Maziak et al., 2015). Although most users in Western countries smoke water pipe intermittently, they often use other tobacco products concurrently. The spread of water pipe tobacco smoking is promoted by the use of sweetened and flavored tobacco (shisha), social acceptance, and misperceptions about the addictive potential and adverse health effects of water pipe smoking and the presumption that there is no potential for addiction (Salloum et al., 2016).

Despite the rise in hookah use and its known risks, there is limited research on the correlates of hookah use in the general adult population, as most research comes from convenience samples (Daniels & Roman, 2013; Linde et al., 2015). In a 2016 study using a nationally representative sample examining the correlates of hookah use among adults aged 18–40 years old in the United States, Grinberg and Goodwin found that hookah use was twice as common among cigarette smokers compared with nonsmokers; in particular, non-daily cigarette smokers had the highest levels of hookah use. Hookah use was also significantly more common among various demographic subgroups of the general adult population and was significantly more common among cigarette smokers compared with nonsmokers. The prevalence of hookah use among current, non-daily cigarette smokers was 10.7%, more than double that of the general adult population at 3.9% (Grinberg & Goodwin, 2016).

Hookah smoking is linked to many of the same adverse health effects as cigarette smoking, such as lung, bladder, and oral cancers, as well as heart disease (El-Zaatari et al., 2015). Users believe mistakenly that hookah smoking is less harmful than cigarette smoking and that the probability of addiction is low. The risk of secondhand smoke is considerable given that hookah is traditionally smoked in tight and enclosed spaces, such as hookah cafés and private homes. In addition, the risk of initiation of combustible cigarette smoking is higher among water pipe smokers than among never smokers, and the level of nicotine to which water pipe tobacco smokers are exposed can produce dependence with repeated exposure (Bhatnagar et al., 2019).

There are three main types of cigars sold in the United States, cigars (95% of the market), little cigars, and cigarillos (LCC), which are rolls of tobacco wrapped in leaf tobacco and cause many of the same health conditions as cigarette smoking. Regular cigar smoking is associated with an increased risk for cancers of the lung, esophagus, larynx (voice box), and oral cavity (lip, tongue, mouth, throat) (American Cancer Society, 2019). Those who smoke cigars heavily or inhale deeply also increase their risk of developing chronic obstructive pulmonary disease (COPD), which includes chronic bronchitis and emphysema (Centers for Disease Control and Prevention: *Cigars*, 2021). Cigars are generally used by older men; however, little cigar and cigarillo products have become popular among young adults (18–24) (Johnson et al., 2018). Results from the 2017 National Survey on Drug Use and Health show that 4.9% of all adults (18 and over; 8.0% of adult males) were current cigar smokers. In 2018, an estimated 12.2 million people in the United States aged 12 years or older (or 4.5%) were current cigar smokers (SAMHSA, 2018).

Increased use and appeal of LCCs can be attributed to the variety of LCC flavors, their affordability compared to cigarettes, and the perception that they are less harmful than combustible cigarettes. Racial disparities in cigar and LCC use exist; 8.0% of African American adults use cigars (SAMHSA, 2018; Smiley et al., 2019). In a study by Dunn et al., Black/African American ever users were more likely to report using LCCs due to their affordability and appealing advertising. Furthermore, Black/African American LCC users were more likely to report using LCCs because of the perception that they are less harmful than cigarettes (Smiley et al., 2019).

These findings are in accord with past research demonstrating that LCCs are advertised more heavily in predominantly Black communities (Dunn et al., 2021).

Smokeless tobacco, such as snuff or chewing tobacco, is used by individuals of all ages but particularly by white males. In the United States, smokeless tobacco companies have evolved their products, such as manufacturing spitless smokeless tobacco (i.e., placing a pouch with moist snuff in the mouth) and marketing tobacco lozenges (Piano et al., 2010). More than 2 in every 100 (2.4%) adults aged 18 or older reported current use of smokeless tobacco products. This represents 5.9 million adults. Most adult smokeless tobacco users reported daily use, and nearly 5 in every 100 (4.7%) men were current users of smokeless tobacco. Among racial/ethnic groups, non-Hispanic whites had the highest prevalence of smokeless tobacco use. Around 3 of every 100 (3.4%) non-Hispanic whites were current users of smokeless tobacco (*Smokeless Tobacco Use in the United States*, 2020). Smokeless tobacco users may be at risk for gum disease, tooth decay, cancers of the mouth, esophagus, and pancreas (Piano et al., 2010; National Center for Chronic Disease Prevention and Health Promotion, 2014). Smokeless tobacco contains more nicotine than cigarettes and has more potential for nicotine dependence.

10.2 Nicotine Addiction

Long-term tobacco use is maintained by addiction to nicotine; the addictive nature of nicotine makes tobacco use cessation quite difficult. Nicotine dependence is recognized as a medical condition in the Diagnostic and Statistical Manual (DSM-V) of the American Psychiatric Association (APA, 2013), and tobacco dependence is recognized in the International Classification of Diseases (WHO, 2019). According to the Diagnostic and Statistical Manual of Mental Disorders Fifth Edition (see Table 10.1; 2013), the criteria for tobacco use disorder include experiencing any 2 of 11 criteria within a 1-year time span. These criteria are shown in Table 10.1.

Nicotine withdrawal is classified as a nicotine-induced disorder that includes symptoms such as difficulty concentrating, nervousness, headaches, weight gain, stomach aches, decreased heart rate, restlessness, irritability, depressed mood, and insomnia (APA, 2013; Sussman, 2017). A majority of serious health hazards related to nicotine use result from smoking tobacco (i.e., "combustible tobacco use").

10.3 Considering the Risk Factors

The risk of tobacco (nicotine) dependence increases if tobacco use begins early. Tobacco use typically begins in childhood or adolescence; about 80% of smokers begin smoking by the age of 18. Although two-thirds of young people try cigarette smoking, only 20–25% of them become dependent daily smokers, usually as adults. Risk factors for escalating levels of smoking in childhood or adolescence, leading

Table 10.1 DSM-V criteria for tobacco use disorder

A problematic pattern of tobacco use leading to clinically significant impairment or distress, as manifested by at least two of the following, occurring within a 12-month period:
1. Tobacco is often taken in larger amounts or over a longer period than was intended
2. There is a persistent desire or unsuccessful efforts to cut down or control tobacco use
3. A great deal of time is spent in activities necessary to obtain or use tobacco
4. Craving, or a strong desire or urge to use tobacco
5. Recurrent tobacco use resulting in a failure to fulfill major role obligations at work, school, or home
6. Continued tobacco use despite having persistent or recurrent social or interpersonal problems caused or exacerbated by the effects of tobacco (e.g., arguments with others about tobacco use)
7. Important social, occupational, or recreational activities are given up or reduced because of tobacco use
8. Recurrent tobacco use in situations in which it is physically hazardous (e.g., smoking in bed)
9. Tobacco use is continued despite knowledge of having a persistent or recurrent physical or psychological problem that is likely to have been caused or exacerbated by tobacco
10. Tolerance, as defined by either of the following:
(a) A need for markedly increased amounts of tobacco to achieve the desired effect
(b) A markedly diminished effect with continued use of the same amount of tobacco
11. Withdrawal, as manifested by either of the following:
(a) The characteristic withdrawal syndrome for tobacco (refer to criteria A and B of the criteria set for tobacco withdrawal)
(b) Tobacco (or a closely related substance, such as nicotine) is taken to relieve or avoid withdrawal symptoms

American Psychiatric Association (2013)

to nicotine dependence, include peer and parental influences (indirect modeling and direct offers), behavioral problems (e.g., poor school performance, other substance use), personality characteristics (e.g., delinquency, conduct disorder, rebelliousness, and risk taking), psychiatric difficulties (e.g., depression, anxiety), and genetic influences (Lynch & Bonnie, 1994; Bozzini et al., 2021; Harrison et al., 2020).

In turn, heavy smoking and nicotine dependence may facilitate of worsen psychiatric disorders, particularly mood and anxiety disorders (Fluharty et al., 2016), as well as other substance use disorders. Alcohol and tobacco use are highly comorbid, and the consequences of concurrent use are multiplicative. Epidemiological data suggest that daily smokers are more likely to meet criteria for hazardous drinking and other alcohol-related diagnoses by threefold, and this risk increases by fivefold and 16-fold in non-daily smoking adults and non-daily smoking young adults (Husky et al., 2007; Verplaetse & McKee, 2017).

Significant discoveries in the behavioral and social sciences have broadened and deepened understanding of psychosocial influences on the nature and treatment of nicotine dependence. As acute nicotine withdrawal dissipates as the length of the quit attempt increases, several factors—including intermittent negative emotional states, repeated urges to smoke, diminished motivation, and decreased self-efficacy about quitting—can persist throughout the cessation process and undermine quitting (Liu et al., 2013).

10.4 Integrated Care for Tobacco Use Prevention and Cessation

Integrated healthcare is characterized by collaborative interactions among health professionals from different disciplines to address comprehensively the needs of a patient (APA: *Integrated Health Care*, 2021). The term *integrated care* is also used to refer broadly to behavioral healthcare resources that are referred to patients through collaborative primary care providers (PCPs) (Butler et al., 2008). Integrated care includes an umbrella of diverse models aimed at unifying behavioral health and primary care, including integrating behavioral health expertise into primary care settings using consultation, web-based, telephone-based, pamphlets, and other resources. Integrated care (IC) has been proposed as a solution to increase multidisciplinary collaboration, reduce medical errors, and improve patient access to quality care, including tobacco use cessation planning and programs in a clinical setting. When different specialties operate separately and do not coordinate care for a patient, there is often poor communication between providers, who have a variety of core competencies, all of which can be critical for establishing the correct diagnosis, treatment planning, and treatment implementation. Poor communication can result in inadequate diagnoses and treatment. Second, behavioral health correlates of physical disease are often not addressed due to the fact that primary care providers (PCPs) do not have comprehensive training in detection or treatment of co-occurring problems (e.g., tobacco dependence and cancer). Furthermore, when behavioral health concerns are addressed, patients often do not follow through with external referrals to specialty care due to factors such as perceived stigma and geographical and financial constraints (Snipes et al., 2015). Integrated care can assist in reducing such constraints.

There is strong evidence that supports the effectiveness of integrated primary medical and behavioral healthcare for adults, particularly for collaborative care models that emphasize behavioral healthcare practitioners (BCPs), such as addiction counselors, and PCPs working together to improve physical health, behavioral health, and mental health outcomes for a patient (Archer et al., 2012). Nicotine dependence usually starts at a young age, and because most US youth have access to primary care and visit primary care practitioners annually, integrated primary medical-behavioral healthcare models have a strong potential for improving access to and rates of care for behavioral health problems such as developing or developed tobacco use dependence (Asarnow et al., 2015).

The research literature on integrated care among youth tobacco use prevention is nonexistent to our knowledge. Most evidence-based tobacco use prevention programming has been conducted in a school-based setting, though other community units such as the family and policy measures have enhanced prevention efforts (Sussman et al., 2013). Of necessity, the present chapter focuses on cessation. However, we will briefly review evidence-based tobacco use prevention and suggest how the primary care setting might be utilized as a means to assist prevention efforts.

Informing patients about the dangers of smoking tobacco in any form, as well as using smokeless tobacco, can be accomplished in a variety of ways. The professional may have conversations about the potential harm of these products and provide educational print materials, videos, and guides outlining the health consequences of use. Materials can be tailored to the age and the tobacco use and health history of the user. Although the evidence for new and emerging tobacco products' potential for attributable disease is not as robust as cigarette smoking, primary care providers should ask patients, especially youth and young adults, about all tobacco use and provide additional information about the potential harms of using these tobacco products.

A particularly important challenge for primary care physicians working in an integrated care setting is strengthening the connection between science and practice to increase the probability that the most effective interventions reach the targeted audience it is intended for. It is important for tobacco use prevention and cessation programming to accumulate an evidence-based research through controlled trials. Evidence-based treatment of nicotine dependence increased the chances of achieving long-term abstinence (Fiore et al., 2008), but utilization of evidence-based approaches remains very low (National Center for Chronic Disease Prevention and Health Promotion, 2014).

One of the main reasons that it takes time for an evidence-based program to reach general use by clinicians, especially in integrated care settings, may be the time it takes from research findings to become an intervention ready for dissemination and then have clinicians and healthcare providers integrate them into practice ("bench to bedside"). Another issue with evidence-based practice implementation could be lack of consensus and clarity on what "evidence-based" actually means and what qualifies as such among providers (Gray et al., 2013). For example, simply a high prevalence of acceptability and willingness to be involved in a particular program may make that program appear to be evidence-based to some clinicians, but that does not mean it will exert a behavioral change impact (which is the essence of what is intended by researchers). Research-based evidence can indicate whether a prevention strategy has been shown to be highly effective, moderately effective, or ineffective in achieving its desired outcomes. This is referred to as level of effectiveness. Presentations by the research community may assist in educating practitioners on what is and is not evidence-based. Group discussion and problem-solving across primary care providers and other professionals involved in care also may help to develop a shared understanding of evidence-based practices that may be useful in combating nicotine dependence and target individuals with the most effective prevention or cessation methods that fit their specific needs and lifestyle.

10.5 Review of Evidence-Based Prevention

Evidence-based prevention refers to prevention programs, strategies, and policies that have been rigorously tested under research conditions (e.g., controlled trials, statistical controls for confounders) and found to be effective to inhibit the initiation or escalation of unhealthy or risky behavior (Pentz, 2003), such as tobacco initiation and use. Preventing tobacco use can have long-term benefits for individuals and for public health in general. State and federal government agencies, healthcare organizations, and other groups that promote public health have developed and implemented tobacco control programs to help to prevent or reduce tobacco use. These programs use taxation (making products notably more expensive to use), access restrictions, mass media campaigns (to reach wide audiences), and school-based and family-based programming. Preventive services may be provided to varied target audiences, including young people (in particular), people with comorbid health problems, those of diverse ethnicities and socioeconomic status, and women (Sussman et al., 2013; Committee on Smoking Cessation in Military and Veteran Populations; Institute of Medicine (IOM), 2009).

10.5.1 Universal, Indicated, and Selective Prevention

Tobacco interventions would not be effective if they did not reach their intended audiences: tobacco users and those at risk of initiating tobacco use. The Institute of Medicine (IOM) model (IOM, 1994), often referred to as a "continuum of services, care, or prevention," classifies prevention interventions according to their target population. Classification by population provides clarity to differing objectives of various interventions and matches the objectives to the needs of the target population. The IOM identifies the following three categories based on level of risk: universal, selective, and indicated. Universal interventions target the general population and thus are not directed at a specific risk group. Universal prevention strategies involve addressing an entire population (national, local, community, school, or neighborhood) with tobacco prevention messages and programs aimed at preventing or delaying the use of tobacco. The mission of universal prevention is to deter the initiation of use by providing all individuals with the information and skills necessary to prevent the problem behavior. The entire population is considered at risk and able to benefit from prevention programming. For example, this group can include the general population and subgroups such as junior high school-aged children and include strategies such as lessons about tobacco use in schools, training parents on what to do if they suspect their child may be using nicotine-containing substances, and mass media campaigns targeted at tobacco use (e.g., TRUTH campaigns). Such anti-tobacco programming can be delivered to large groups, regardless of any prior history of nicotine use or dependence (Sussman et al., 2013).

Selective interventions target those at higher-than-average risk for tobacco use. These individuals are identified by the magnitude and nature of risk factors for tobacco use to which they are exposed. These can include children of smokers or high school dropouts. Risk groups may be identified on the basis of biological, psychological, social, or environmental risk factors known to be associated with tobacco or other substance use (Institute of Medicine, 1994). Selective prevention targets the entire subgroup, regardless of the degree of risk of any individual within the group. Examples of selective prevention of tobacco use may include motivation-skills-decision-making programming delivered in alternative high schools, support groups for children of smokers at junior high schools, and targeted mass media campaigns (Sussman & Ames, 2008).

Indicated prevention strategies are designed to prevent addiction to tobacco use in individuals who do not meet the DSM criteria for addiction but who are showing early danger signs of becoming addicted (e.g., failing grades, using other substances, continual tobacco use experimentation). The mission of indicated prevention is to identify individuals who are exhibiting problem behaviors associated with substance use and to divert them into special substance use prevention programs. Many youths in alternative high school settings may be candidates for indicated prevention, assisted through a motivation-skills-decision-making-type program (Sussman & Ames, 2008). However, many older teens may already be addicted to nicotine. At the community level, the training of primary care providers and other providers in an integrated care setting can provide tools to screen for nicotine dependence and offer resources to provide to young patients looking for cessation methods.

10.6 Tobacco Cessation Programming for Youth in Primary Care Settings

Primary care treatment may include involvement of any number of health professionals, often in a medical office setting. In fact, one meta-analysis revealed a significant impact on youth smoking cessation when delivered in medical settings (9 studies, 4.62 treatment minus control group absolute cessation difference; error = 1.88, $t = 2.46$, $p < 0.05$, two-tailed; Sussman & Sun, 2009, p. 6). The program contents tended to rely on motivation enhancement communications to tobacco-using youth. Pharmacologic adjuncts are not effective with youth. Unfortunately, perhaps, such care generally involves one setting and is not well integrated across different health professional settings.

10.7 Tobacco Cessation Among Adults

There is a literature on integrated care and smoking cessation among adult populations (e.g., Champassak et al., 2014; Rittenmeyer et al., 2016; Knudsen, 2017). Each year, 70% of all adult smokers make at least one visit to a physician. According to a 2015 survey, about 70% of current adult smokers in the United States wanted to quit, and although about 55% had attempted to do so in the past year, only 7% were successful in quitting for 6–12 months (CDC, 2017). Limited access to tobacco cessation treatment is a barrier to quitting smoking in many healthcare settings. Smokers are infrequently referred to specialized tobacco cessation clinics, and those referred often fail to attend or dropout prematurely, due to fluctuation in motivation to quit, conflicting life demands, need to travel, or cost. Nicotine dependence is a chronic, relapsing addiction that responds best to intensive treatment extended over time (USDHHS, 2020).

Back in 1997, only 25% of managed healthcare plans covered any tobacco dependence treatment; this figure approached 90% by 2003 although coverage often included requirements that serve as barriers to its use (e.g., large co-pays). Numerous states have now added Medicaid and Medicare to the treatment of tobacco dependence (Fiore et al., 2008). In 2002, the Joint Commission (formerly, JCAHO), which accredits some 15,000 hospitals and healthcare programs, instituted an accreditation requirement for the delivery of evidence-based tobacco dependence interventions for patients with diagnoses of acute myocardial infarction, congestive heart failure, or pneumonia. Currently, Medicare, the Veteran's Health Administration, and the US military now provide coverage for tobacco dependence and cessation treatment (Clinical Practice Guideline Treating Tobacco Dependence (2008); Committee on Smoking Cessation in Military and Veteran Populations (2009)). Comprehensive Cancer Centers in the United States also have been attempting to integrate tobacco use cessation services with provision of treatments for cancer (National Comprehensive Cancer Network, 2021). These changes in policies and systems have proved worthwhile in terms of increased rates of clinical assessment, treatment care, and maintenance of tobacco use cessation.

10.8 Barriers to Tobacco Use Cessation Treatment in Primary Care Settings

Effective tobacco use cessation interventions are readily available, but underutilized, in part due to lack of clinician training and organizational support. Barriers that can prevent clinicians from consistently conducting even brief cessation interventions include time constraints; a lack of knowledge, training, and confidence; inadequate clinical and/or institutional support; a lack of adequate reimbursement for delivering tobacco treatment; and inadequate or confusing insurance cessation coverage (Fiore et al., 2008; Sheffer et al., 2018). Concerns about the lack of adequate training to effectively deliver cessation interventions are also reported by other healthcare providers, such as nurses, psychologists, and social workers (Caplan et al., 2011; Sheffer et al., 2018).

Clinicians historically did not inquire about tobacco use or use available interventions, felt that it was less of a priority given time constraints, and may still not believe the effort of tobacco cessation intervention is worth the benefit to the patient (e.g., Anczak & Nogler, 2003). The US medical schools often do not put emphasis on teaching tobacco intervention skills. Many programs do request that physicians in training assess patient tobacco use and advise tobacco-using patients to quit, and while available, physicians in training often are not taught how to counsel patients to quit (Spangler et al., 2002). For those trained, there is also a lack of training that encompasses the breadth of various tobacco products, tobacco intervention training that addresses cultural issues, and long-term studies showing implementation and maintenance of the outcomes of such training (Sheffer et al., 2021). Physician use of clinical practice guidelines is low in the United States. The Public Health Service has issued updated smoking cessation guidelines for patients and physicians, healthcare administrators, insurers, and purchasers. Successful guideline implementation is highly dependent on administrative supports from healthcare organizations and insurers. There also are some initiatives to encourage assessment of tobacco use and cessation counseling in cancer centers (Croyle et al., 2019; Wiseman et al., 2020).

10.9 The Mechanics of Tobacco Use Cessation

The goal of a tobacco use cessation intervention must be abstinence. Reducing the number of cigarettes smoked does not provide any direct health benefits to the individual smoker. The only known way to reduce cancer risk in smokers is complete cessation, which results in a 35% lower risk of death due to tobacco-related illness and a 64% reduced risk of tobacco-related cancer (Shields, 2002).

Healthcare systems in the United States have unmatched access to smokers and can provide unparalleled care for those looking to quit. The National Comprehensive Cancer Network (NCCN) Guidelines for Smoking Cessation advocate for smoking status to be updated in the patient's health record at regular checkups to indicate any status changes or quit attempts (National Comprehensive Cancer Network, 2021). The panel recommends the healthcare providers determine (1) whether the patient has ever smoked and, if so, regularly assess (2) whether the patient is a current smoker and (3) whether the patient has smoked in the last 30 days. All information should be recorded in their medical record. As a follow-up to the initial evaluation, these guidelines may direct primary care providers to a tailored patient assessment based on smoking status and history.

It is important to note that the guidelines provide specific recommendations for managing patients not yet ready to quit smoking and acknowledge the importance of an inclusive, patient-centered approach to treating tobacco dependence. The guidelines further acknowledge that tobacco dependence is a chronic, relapsing disorder, and therefore providers should discuss smoking relapse and encourage reevaluation of cessation treatment with their patients.

For many smokers, the benefits of smoking cessation can be appreciated immediately through reduced blood carbon monoxide levels, decreased irritative respiratory symptoms (e.g., cough, shortness of breath), and improved lung function. In the long term, cessation is associated with reduced risk of smoking-related disease and mortality.

10.9.1 The Five A's: A Hallmark Model of Providing Adult Smoking Cessation Treatment in Primary Care Settings

The five A's (ask, advise, assess, assist, arrange) is a stepwise approach for primary care physicians to efficiently and effectively assess and provide smoking cessation counseling to their patients. Effective smoking prevention interventions based on the National Cancer Institute's "five A's" model (Epps & Manley, 1990; Fiore et al., 2008), the Agency for Healthcare Research and Quality guidelines (Agency for Healthcare Research and Quality, 2012), and the transtheoretical model (TTM) of behavioral change (Prochaska & DiClemente, 1983) have been demonstrated to be effective in identifying and treating tobacco users. The essential features of individual smoking cessation advice which integrate these models are as follows: (1) ask (about smoking during visits), (2) advise (all smokers to quit), (3) assess (measure extent of tobacco use dependence, use triggers, assess readiness to quit), (4) assist (provide the smoker with the tools to quit), and (5) arrange (follow-up visits) (Chase et al., 2007; Park et al., 2015; Searight, 2018; Agency for Healthcare Research and Quality, 2012). The five A's model has been used within the Moonshot Initiative at several cancer centers (Croyle et al., 2019; Wiseman et al., 2020).

First, the provider should systematically identify all tobacco users by *asking* at every visit. Second, one should give clear, strong, and personalized *advice* about the importance of total cessation. Patients not willing to quit despite clinical advice may be uninformed, concerned about the effects of quitting, or discouraged by previous relapses. If they are not interested in quitting, the health professional may provide materials that the patient can use to calculate the costs and benefits of tobacco use. When the costs reliably rise above the benefits, the patient may want to take action to quit (CDC, 2021). Once identified, a smoking *assessment* form should be used for all patients and the information updated by placing a smoker identifier sticker on their chart by their primary care provider. Means of assessing nicotine dependence often includes the use of measures of nicotine dependence such as the Fagerstrom Test of Nicotine Dependence (FTND) (Heatherton et al., 1991) and the use of the Diagnostic and Statistical Manual (DSM-V) criteria as applied in a structured interview (APA, 2013). A key item that identifies nicotine dependence is whether or not the tobacco users begin use within 30 minutes of awakening in the morning. Motivational interventions for patients unwilling to quit at the present time are characterized by the "five R's": relevance, risks, rewards, roadblocks, repetition (Epps & Manley, 1990; Fiore et al., 2008; Stead et al., 2013; CDC, 2021; see table below).

Tobacco Cessation Brief Clinical Intervention: The Five As

(Derived from Centers for Disease Control and Prevention [CDC])

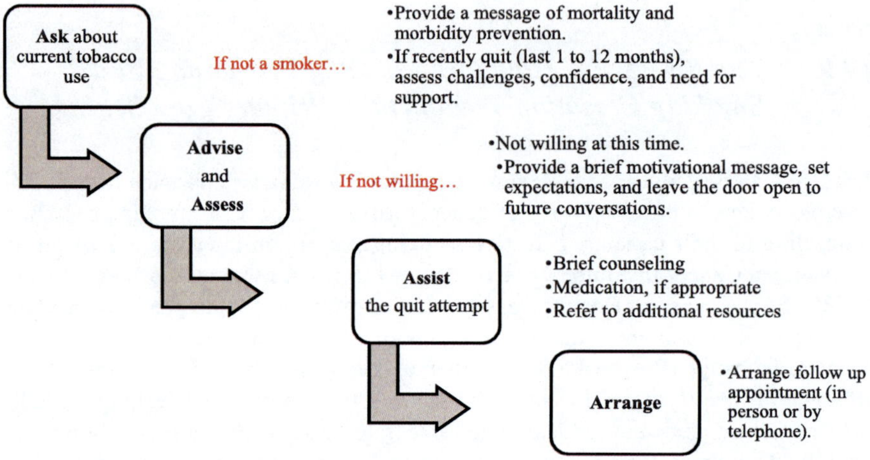

Tobacco cessation brief clinical intervention: the five A's (Derived from Centers for Disease Control and Prevention [CDC])

Since so many smokers are hesitant about quitting or lack the motivation to sustain a quit attempt, a fourth hypothetical version of the five A's might build on such approaches as the five R's (relevance, risks, rewards, roadblocks, and repetition) (Agency for Healthcare Research and Quality, 2012), which may help motivate initiation of quit attempts, even those who are initially assessed as not ready to quit. This approach is appealing because of the lack of clear evidence demonstrating that a very brief assessment of readiness to quit is sufficient to motivate quit efforts. One potential downside of this approach could be that providing support to smokers who are not ready to quit could turn out to be time-consuming and inefficient in an already time-sensitive environment.

10.9.2 The Five R's (from the Clinical Practice Guideline: Treating Tobacco Use and Dependence, *2008)*

Relevance: Encourage the patient to indicate why quitting is personally relevant, being as specific as possible. Motivational information has the greatest impact if it is relevant to a patient's disease status or risk; family or social situation (e.g., having children in the home); health concerns (morning cough, better sense of taste and smell, better breath); and age, sex, and other important patient characteristics (e.g., prior quitting experience, personal barriers to cessation).

Risks: The clinician should ask the patient to identify potential negative consequences of tobacco use. The clinician may suggest and highlight those consequences that seem most relevant to the patient. The clinician should emphasize that smoking low-tar/low-nicotine cigarettes or the use of other forms of tobacco (e.g., smokeless tobacco, cigars, and pipes) will not eliminate these risks. Examples of risks are:

- Acute risks: shortness of breath, exacerbation of asthma, harm to pregnancy, impotence, infertility, and increased serum carbon monoxide levels
- Long-term risks: myocardial infarction and strokes, lung and other cancers (larynx, oral cavity, pharynx, esophagus, pancreas, bladder, cervix), chronic obstructive pulmonary diseases (chronic bronchitis and emphysema), long-term disability, and need for extended care
- Environmental risks: increased risk of lung cancer and heart disease in spouses, higher rates of smoking by children of tobacco users, increased risk for low birth weight, sudden infant death syndrome, asthma, middle ear disease, and respiratory infections in children of smokers

Rewards: The clinician should ask the patient to identify potential benefits of improved health by quitting: food will taste better; improved sense of smell; save money; feel better about oneself; home, car, clothing, and breath will smell better; can stop worrying about quitting; set a good example for children; have healthier babies and children; not worry about exposing others to smoke; feel better physically; perform better in physical activities; and reduced wrinkling/aging of skin.

Roadblocks: The clinician should ask the patient to identify barriers or impediments to quitting and note elements of treatment (problem-solving, pharmacotherapy) that could address barriers. Typical barriers might include withdrawal symptoms, fear of failure, weight gain, lack of support, depression, and enjoyment of tobacco.

Repetition: The motivational intervention should be repeated every time an unmotivated patient visits the clinical setting. Tobacco users who have failed in previous quit attempts should be told that most people make repeated quit attempts before they are successful.

Fourth, one should assist patients willing to quit by setting a quit date and preparing the patient for the quit date. Besides setting a quit date, the health professional may provide self-help materials, quitting advice, and nicotine replacement therapy (NRT). A smoking contract can be useful to establish a quit date. The professional could make patients aware of nicotine withdrawal symptoms, so they know what to expect. If the clinician and patient feel a more intensive treatment is warranted, the patient can be referred to an intensive treatment program. Finally, the health professional should *arrange* follow-up contact for all patients attempting to quit. Following up patients can notably increase maintenance of cessation efforts (Anczak & Nogler, 2003).

10.9.3 Use of Pharmacologic Adjuncts for Nicotine Replacement

NRT may aid in abstinence from tobacco use by reducing general withdrawal symptoms and lessen craving, a bad mood, and inattention states. Nicotine replacement approaches are based on the concept that the administration of a maintenance level in a less or nontoxic format will alleviate the withdrawal symptoms associated with smoking cessation and reduce the risk associated with the inhalation format.

Numerous effective medications are available for tobacco dependence, and clinicians should encourage their use by all patients attempting to quit smoking—except when medically contraindicated or with specific populations for which there is insufficient evidence of effectiveness (i.e., pregnant women, smokeless tobacco users, light smokers, and adolescents) (Fiore et al., 2008). The general standard of replacement therapies is to present the patient with a safer and more manageable form of the drug that directly alleviates the signs and symptoms of withdrawal and craving. Seven first-line medications (five nicotine and two non-nicotine) reliably increase long-term smoking abstinence rates (Fiore et al., 2008). These include bupropion SR, nicotine gums, nicotine inhalers, nicotine lozenges, nicotine nasal spray, nicotine patches, and varenicline (a nicotinergic partial agonist and antagonist) (Fiore et al., 2008). Factors a primary care provider should consider when recommending NRTs include clinician familiarity with the medications, contraindications for selected patients, patient preference, previous patient experience with a specific pharmacotherapy (positive or negative), and patient characteristics (e.g., history of depression, concerns about weight gain) (Clinical Guidelines for Prescribing Pharmacotherapy for Smoking Cessation, 2012). Some discussion has been raised over the last 5 years regarding the use of e-cigarettes as a means of harm reduction for older, chronic combustible cigarette smokers. However, there is a lack of consensus on whether it is really a relatively safe alternative or whether it even helps the tobacco user stay away from combustible products as opposed to engaging in dual use (Cahn & Siegel, 2010; Lee et al., 2014).

10.10 Utilization of the Five A's Model in Primary Care Settings

In nationally representative data from 2000 to 2015, Babb et al. (2017) found that 57% of smokers who had seen a health professional in the past year reported receiving advice to quit. In an earlier study, King et al. (2013) found that patient reports of their physicians providing each of the five A's typically decreased as the steps progressed, with "asking" about tobacco use (87.9%) being more prevalent than "advising," "assessing," or "assisting" with a quit attempt (78.2% of those who wanted to quit) and the prevalence of "advising/assessing/assisting" being far more prevalent than "arranging for follow-up" (17.5% overall). Thus, in practice, clinicians are rarely performing all five actions in the five A's approach. One way to address this problem is by delegating some of the steps of the five A's (e.g., ask, assist, arrange) in whole or in part to other members of the healthcare team (e.g., nurses, physician assistants, receptionists) (Fiore et al., 2008). This approach lessens the burden on physicians, others on the team are considered as credible by patients, and it emphasizes the importance of quitting to patients in contact with multiple professionals. While it is doubtful that many clinicians use the five R's, it is a useful approach to help motivate tobacco users to enter contemplation and action stages of cessation (Agency for Healthcare Research and Quality, 2012).

As tobacco cessation interventions are increasingly integrated into inpatient and outpatient care, and care in other settings such as pharmacies and behavioral health treatment facilities, updates to the five A's model (as integrated with the stages of change and five R's conceptualizations) may emerge that more explicitly coordinate and distribute cessation interventions across an integrated care team and across different clinical environments (USDHHS, 2020).

10.11 Considering the Stages of Change Model When Contemplating Using the Five A's Approach

Tobacco users dependent on nicotine may transition through the five stages of behavioral change before, during, and after the smoking cessation process: precontemplation, contemplation, preparation, action, and maintenance. The stages of change model was originally developed from studying successful smoking cessation techniques. This approach was derived from an appreciation that many patients lack the motivation or are indecisive about choosing whether or not to change their habits (Prochaska & DiClemente, 1983). This model provides a framework for assessing the patient's degree of commitment to change and can guide physicians in choosing counseling strategies and methods, such as the five A's. By asking questions about the patient's motivation and determining which stage they may experience, physicians can assist and support the patient to achieve behavior change.

Precontemplation Stage
In this stage of change, the smoker is not seriously considering quitting in the next 6 months. Motivational interventions to increase awareness of adverse effects of smoking are beneficial. Smokers in this stage overestimate the benefits of smoking, underestimate the risks, and avoid information to help them change. In this stage, the clinician's role is primarily to advise and inform the patient and request the patient consider the costs and benefits of their tobacco use. As noted earlier in this chapter, when the costs reliably rise above the benefits, the patient may want to take action to quit (DiClemente et al., 1991). The five R's are most useful in this stage.

Contemplation Stage
The smoker is seriously planning to quit smoking in the next 6 months, however, not immediately, and no quit date is set. At this stage, smokers recognize that the risks of smoking outweigh the benefits. Smokers are the most ambivalent to change and are often stuck in "chronic contemplation." They tend to substitute thinking for acting. Motivational interventions to increase awareness of the patient's equivocation regarding quitting and of the adverse effects of smoking are beneficial. Clinicians should emphasize the negative effects of smoking (Anczak & Nogler, 2003).

Preparation Stage
The smoker is planning to quit in the near future, and a stop date has been set in the next month. Clinical assessment using the Fagerström measure is useful at this point (Heatherton et al., 1991). Assistance in initiating steps toward cessation is pursued, e.g., delaying the first cigarette of the morning, cutting down ("tapering") for a couple weeks, prior quit attempts with a duration of 24 h, informing family and friends and obtaining their support, and initial trials of NRT therapies. The smoker identifies that the risks outweigh the benefits. Interventions to assist patients in this stage to quit smoking include focus on NRT and developing cognitive-behavior modification skills (e.g., self-management, waiting out urges, keeping busy, learning relaxation skills).

Action Stage
Individuals have taken steps to stop smoking. Smokers may quit by using medication and NRT, cognitive-behavior modification, an informal quitting strategy (e.g., quitting and being involved with an exercise group), or a combination of some or all of these methods (USDHHS, 2020). This stage lasts from onset of the efforts to 6 months after cessation. This is also when relapse needs consideration, which varies with therapy, coffee and alcohol consumption, history of depression, and gender. High initial relapse occurs during the first 2–3 weeks (almost 50%). Difficulties with concentration and irritability, the two most common withdrawal symptoms, need to be accepted as something to adapt to by the quitter as well as significant others. Certainly, though, severity of this withdrawal varies across new quitters and may be quite mild for some. This action stage and need to surmount craving through the use of cognitive and behavioral coping strategies then tapers off during the next 2–3 months. Thus, initial support is most important. Support after 3–4 months has much smaller effects on relapse. Frequent contact with the clinician or other support persons is important for continuation of this stage, redirecting efforts, and celebrating successes.

Maintenance Stage
At this stage, the patients have not smoked for 6 months. Successful patients are now avoiding relapse. The majority of individuals that use tobacco-containing substances want to quit but attempt to quit multiple times before actually succeeding (Fiore et al., 2008; Babb et al., 2017; USDHHS, 2020). The most successful quitters relapse and cycle through the stages of change an average of three to four times before becoming free from cigarettes. It is crucial that misconceptions about

nicotine cessation are dispelled by the provider. Activities that may include weight control, engaging in exercise, and regular use of relaxation techniques may need to be included in the patients' daily schedule.

10.12 Additional Considerations in Tobacco Use Cessation Treatment in Primary Care Settings

Advice to quit from primary care providers is fundamental and often necessary for patients thinking about quitting tobacco use. Many tobacco users cannot stop without the help of a healthcare professional, or team of healthcare providers, to assist them in their quit attempts, particularly if they are heavier tobacco users or more heavily dependent on nicotine. These persons should be referred to a specialist treatment service with monitoring from their primary care provider. A cessation specialist would have at least two functions: helping tobacco users who cannot stop on their own or with only brief interventions and training and supporting other health professionals to deliver tobacco use cessation interventions. For nicotine-dependent chronic adult tobacco users, a combination of behavior support from mental-behavioral health specialists and pharmacologic therapy from a primary care provider can produce higher quit rates than either service provided alone.

Some individuals may find more success when they are treated in groups. This is partly for reasons of efficiency (cost and time savings) and because group members can motivate each other to maintain an attempt to stop. Those who do not want to be part of a group or are unable to join a group (e.g., difficulties with transportation or time of group meetings) should be offered individual treatment. In a prototypical primary care group smoking cessation program, five weekly evening sessions, of about 1 h each, are offered over 4 weeks after the quit date. The first meeting is introductory, with participants expected to stop smoking after it and by the second session. NRT is distributed and discussed at the first session. From the second session on, the meetings focus primarily on input from group members. They discuss their experiences of the past week, including difficulties encountered, and offer mutual encouragement and support. Sessions are client (not therapist) oriented, meaning they emphasize mutual support rather than didactic input from the therapist. The therapist facilitates client interaction and mutual support outside formal sessions. When the course of meetings is completed, follow-up meetings can be offered at various times up to 12 months from the beginning of the course, depending on resources. Some form of self-help materials may be provided and have been shown to be affective when no other form of intervention is offered (Livingstone-Banks et al., 2019). Evidence-based treatment—including counseling and cessation medications approved by the US Food and Drug Administration (FDA)—significantly increases success in quitting tobacco.

10.13 More on Integrated Care and Tobacco Use Cessation: A Stepped-Care Approach

Integrated care is theorized to improve quality of care in multiple ways, including access to behavioral health experts that may specialize in tobacco cessation, which is important because individuals in the primary care setting often exhibit comorbid behavioral and physical issues that may complicate their medical treatment (Cummings and O'Donohue, 2011). Behavioral health issues associated with nicotine dependence may include depression, anxiety, stress, parenting difficulties, chronic disease management, and severe mental illness. Multidisciplinary teams can promote collaborative treatment plans, decrease redundancies, provide more comprehensive diagnosis and treatment, and provide a clinical pathway for addressing cessation-associated behavioral health problems, which are often missed by PCPs (Sheldrick et al., 2011).

Coordination of a care team is crucial when providing a healthcare plan to those experiencing nicotine dependence and looking for assistance in initiating cessation. Integrated care can offer major changes in healthcare delivery systems and is thought to be "low touch, high volume," like primary care medicine, and is a model that allows providers to disseminate care to a large number of patients in an efficient and low-cost manner (Snipes et al., 2015). The creation of standardized clinical models and pathways for patients to access these low-cost interventions would provide an avenue for healthcare systems to address drivers of healthcare costs (i.e., preventable disease) in a cost-efficient manner. Further examination of other modalities of delivering behavioral healthcare in integrated care settings (e.g., eHealth, telehealth, and bibliotherapy) and how these interventions fit within a larger stepped-care model of integrated care may prove useful.

Screening of individuals dependent on nicotine should capture a wide variety of behavioral health issues (e.g., depression, anxiety, and substance abuse), physical health issues (e.g., weight management), and general problems in the patient's life (e.g., financial issues). Effective screening aids in problem identification and subsequently supports assessment of patient severity. It is imperative that stepped-care screening be comprehensive to thoroughly characterize patient dysfunction (Snipes et al., 2015). This process serves to inform which members of the team should have contact with the patient and is team-based because the PCP is responsible for directing the patient to necessary services with other health providers. This process may result in a referral to a behavioral care expert or another appropriate team member. After patient contact, the additional provider should then follow up with the PCP to obtain care plan approval before proceeding with care.

For integrated care to be most effective and efficient, care should be implemented in a stepped fashion. Stepped care suggests that providers offer care that achieves the following: minimal disruption in the patient's life; least extensive treatment required for a reasonable probability of producing positive results; least intensive for positive results, especially with respect to the side effect profile; least expensive for positive results; least expensive with respect to staff training and involvement required to provide effective service; and most efficient with respect to team-based integrated care (IC) (i.e., uses all the professionals necessary and none which are unnecessary) (O'Donohue and Draper, 2011).

These attributes of stepped care contribute to increased patient choice, an opportunity for increased coordination between interdisciplinary team members, and achieving medical cost offset. A brief outline of stepped care for nicotine dependence follows.

Watchful waiting can often be considered an appropriate method of treatment for very-low-level cases—where the individual is not using tobacco. Healthcare providers should be mindful and recognize not all patients are "at peace" with the decision of choosing watchful waiting, which may induce feelings of anxiety and uncertainty (Rittenmeyer et al., 2016).

Psychoeducation: Brochures or materials on the long-term effects of nicotine use and dependence, encouragement of seeking social support with similar individuals.

eHealth tools and quit smoking lines (the patient is referred to evidence-based eHealth sites and telehealth programs): A helpline or "quit smoking lines" are a telephone-based service that provides information, support, and advice to callers that are looking to quit using tobacco products. Quit lines can improve an individual's chance of achieving cessation. Perhaps the most widely used in the United States, 1-800-Quit-Now is available in every state. Smokefree text messaging programs are also available; Smokefree.gov offers free text messaging programs that can give encouragement, advice, and tips to smokers 24/7 (CDC, 2020). This service offers targeted messages and texts to various populations (e.g., SmokefreetTXT is designed for the general population, SmokefreeMOM is for pregnant women who want to quit smoking, SmokefreeVET is targeting for veterans with VA healthcare benefits, and SmokefreeTXT is for teens and for teenagers aged 13–17 looking to quit smoking) (Smokefree.gov).

Evidence supports the effectiveness of certain non-face-to-face delivery approaches for tobacco cessation, including telephone-based quit lines (The Community Guide, 2012) and mHealth-based interventions (The Community Guide, 2011). These approaches have characteristics that can remove or reduce time, transportation, and childcare issues that may hinder face-to-face service delivery, thereby potentially leading to more widespread use.

Staffed by trained counselors or coaches, tobacco quit lines typically deliver a variety of services, including individual counseling, practical information on how to quit, referrals to other cessation or health-related resources, mailed self-help materials, information on FDA-approved cessation medications, and, in some cases, provision of limited quantities of free or discounted cessation medications (Keller et al., 2010; Anderson, 2016). Publicly funded quit lines are available at no cost to US residents in every state, the District of Columbia, Guam, and Puerto Rico. However, specific services vary across states, largely as a result of funding constraints that vary across states and jurisdictions and over time (Centers for Disease Control and Prevention [CDC], 2014; Anderson, 2016). In addition to publicly funded state quit lines, some public and private health insurance plans and employers also offer quit line services (CDC, 2014). Quit line counseling is readily accessible because it is free, convenient, and confidential, and it removes or reduces barriers related to time, transportation, childcare, and other factors (World Health Organization [WHO], 2011). As a result, quit line counseling has the potential for broad reach. Quit line counseling has also been found to be effective with an array of subpopulations (Baezconde-Garbanati et al., 2011). Most state quit lines provide at least one counseling session to any adult tobacco user who calls, and some state lines may prioritize multi-call services for subpopulations with a higher prevalence of tobacco use or with limited access to other tobacco cessation services (Tobacco Use: Quitline Interventions, 2014).

Telemedicine services in general have become quite prevalent since the COVID-19 pandemic began in 2020. In response to the COVID-19 pandemic, the Centers for Medicare & Medicaid Services and commercial health plans largely have waived co-pays for telemedicine visits as a means to encourage utilization in this time of need and may benefit those hesitant to utilize these services because of cost (CMMS, 2020). It is possible that services delivered over such media channels as Facetime or Zoom will become a major means of delivery of tobacco use cessation programming. This may provide an opportunity for primary care providers to set up an infrastructure for providing care using telemedicine more widely. Research to establish the evidence base for this modality of delivery is ongoing.

Bibliotherapy (the patient is referred to evidence-based self-help books, etc.): A vast array of self-help materials designed to promote smoking cessation exist, from motivational pamphlets (e.g., American Cancer Society) to comprehensive manuals addressing initial cessation, through relapse prevention (e.g., American Lung Association). These manuals are often based on cognitive behavioral models (e.g., social learning, TTM of change, and relapse prevention) and are designed as translations of therapist-administered multicomponent cessation programs. Self-help programs generally produce small effects on quitting. This failure may be due at least in part to the populations used to evaluate self-help techniques, the majority of which have involved volunteer smokers who tend to be older and more addicted and have less social support than the general population of smokers (Fiore et al., 2008). Bibliotherapeutic efficacy appears to increase in some cases by tailoring the cessation materials to individual characteristics (e.g., stages of readiness to quit) relative to more general cessation materials (Johnson, 2013). The most promising effects for bibliotherapeutic interventions appear to be found in combinations of personalized supplementary materials, such as written feedback in combination with outreach telephone counseling. Bibliotherapeutic interventions' greatest efficacy may be as an important supplemental component of a more comprehensive minimal-intervention smoking cessation package.

Group psychotherapy (the patient is referred to an ongoing cognitive behavioral mood management group where multiple patients can be treated simultaneously).

Individual psychotherapy, medication intervention: Numerous effective medications are available for tobacco dependence, and clinicians should encourage their use by all patients attempting to quit smoking—except when medically contraindicated or with specific populations for which there is insufficient evidence of effectiveness (i.e., pregnant women, smokeless tobacco users, light smokers, and adolescents; see Fiore et al., 2008 for more details on a list of frontline and promising medications).

10.14 Conclusions: Lessons Learned

The prevalence of cigarette smoking in the general US population has declined steadily since the 1960s (National Center for Chronic Disease Prevention and Health Promotion, 2014) and may be assisted in part by the development and concerted implementation of evidence-based tobacco control interventions, including cessation interventions, coordinated team delivery in healthcare, and stepped-care approaches to address nicotine dependence and achieving cessation. This chapter highlighted key topics related to initiation of use and developments associated with the delivery of tobacco use prevention and cessation interventions, with a relative focus on evidence that can inform future smoking cessation efforts among healthcare providers.

Smoking prevention programming in a primary care setting may involve primarily advice from a clinician to youth to not begin tobacco use and provision of written materials. Mentioning awareness of local school-based efforts by the clinician may help facilitate a community-wide, integrated care perspective that could bolster school-based efforts (Sussman et al., 2013). Increasing smoking cessation will require several strategies, including increasing the appeal, reach, and use of existing evidence-based cessation interventions and more primary care provider intervention delivery or referrals to behavioral care providers and other members of an integrated care team in assisting with cessation.

In this chapter, we focused most attention on the five A's approach to tobacco use cessation, which is the main protocol utilized in integrated care programming. However, there are various substantive approaches to tobacco cessation assistance that were only briefly mentioned. For example, behavioral and psychological strategies that have been shown to be effective in treating tobacco use and nicotine dependence include cognitive behavioral therapy or CBT (Fiore et al., 2008), motivational interviewing (Lindson-Hawley et al., 2015), acceptance and commitment therapy (ACT), and contingency management (CM) (see Fiore et al., 2008; USDHHS, 2020). These strategies can be individual or group-based and can vary in intensity (from brief to more intensive) and in the mode of delivery (e.g., delivery by a clinician, counselor, telephone, or computer) (USDHHS, 2020). Developing additional cessation interventions for integrated care that have greater effectiveness than existing interventions, and constructing regular follow-up from healthcare providers, can be crucial in achieving cessation at the population level. Also, given the popularity of emerging tobacco products (e.g., e-cigarettes, hookah use), healthcare providers should ask users about the use of various tobacco products as well as advise users to quit, assist them in their efforts, and refer tobacco users to credible sources of information on the addictiveness and health consequences of other tobacco use (which are the same as cigarette smoking).

A difficulty in integrated care is that we currently do not have a metric that can evaluate the extent to which team-based care actually occurs or needs to occur. While providers are often colocated and work from the same electronic health records, there are no systems that ensure multiple providers are appropriately involved in the same treatment plan, which may lead to inefficiencies and reduce the overall benefit of the integrated care model. Indeed, an important related problem is identifying when team-based care is not necessary. Researchers and integrated care practitioners will need to work together to "iron out" such issues and develop multiple pathway protocols that match the needs of different patients.

In general, the success in an integrated care system depends on the type of providers that comprise the multidisciplinary team. At a minimum, a care team must include a PCP and a psychologist to treat both primary (medical, need for pharmacologic adjuncts) and behavioral health issues (cessation techniques). In an ideal case, these professionals would be joined by a care manager, psychiatrist, health behavior coach, a social worker, nurses, dietician, and dentists. Coordination of the care team is the most crucial part of providing a healthcare plan to address those individuals experiencing nicotine dependence and looking for assistance in initiating cessation. The involvement of health professionals in offering interventions for tobacco use cessation should be based on factors such as access to smokers or other tobacco users and level of training rather than professional discipline. The recommendations for health professionals are relevant for all health professionals and not only those in primary care.

Comprehensive training and certification of providers and quality assurance procedures are important to ensure high quality of delivery of care. An integrated approach to preventive healthcare is needed to truly improve quality of life for individuals dependent on nicotine. Accelerating the integration of cessation services across multiple platforms and within healthcare systems and developing new tobacco cessation medications and new indications for existing cessation medications are worth exploring in future research on tobacco cessation in integrated care settings.

References

Agency for Healthcare Research and Quality. (2012). *Patients not ready to make a quit attempt now (the "5 R's")*. Agency for Healthcare Research and Quality.

American Cancer Society. (2019). *Cigar smoking*. American Cancer Society.

American Psychiatric Association. (2013). *Diagnostic and statistical manual of mental disorders* (5th ed.). Author.

Anczak, J. D., & Nogler, R. A. (2003). Tobacco cessation in primary care: Maximizing intervention strategies. *Clinical Medicine & Research, 1*(3), 201–216. https://doi.org/10.3121/cmr.1.3.201

Anderson, C. M. (2016). *Quitline services: Current practice and evidence base*. North American Quitline Consortium. http://c.ymcdn.com/sites/www.naquitline.org/resource/resmgr/issue_papers/Quitline_Services_issue_pape.pdf. Accessed: 24 Mar 2021

Archer, J., Bower, P., Gilbody, S., Lovell, K., Richards, D., Gask, L., Dickens, C., & Coventry, P. (2012). Collaborative care for depression and anxiety problems. *The Cochrane Database of Systematic Reviews, 10*, CD006525. https://doi.org/10.1002/14651858.CD006525.pub2

Asarnow, J. R., Rozenman, M., Wiblin, J., & Zeltzer, L. (2015). Integrated medical-behavioral care compared with usual primary care for child and adolescent behavioral health: A meta-analysis. *JAMA Pediatrics, 169*(10), 929–937. https://doi.org/10.1001/jamapediatrics.2015.1141

Babb, S., Malarcher, A., Schauer, G., Asman, K., & Jamal, A. (2017). Quitting smoking among adults—United States, 2000–2015. *MMWR Morbidity and Mortality Weekly Report, 65*(52), 1457–1464. https://doi.org/10.15585/mmwr.mm6552a1

Baezconde-Garbanati, L., Guy, M., & Soto, C. (2011). *The use of quitlines among priority populations in the U.S.: Lessons from the scientific evidence*. North American Quitline Consortium. https://cdn.ymaws.com/www.naquitline.org/resource/resmgr/Issue_Papers/IssuePaperTheUseofQuitlinesA.pdf

Barrington-Trimis, J. L. (2018, December 1). *E-cigarette use and subsequent smoking frequency among adolescents*. American Academy of Pediatrics. https://pediatrics.aappublications.org/content/142/6/e20180486

Bhatnagar, A., Maziak, W., Eissenberg, T., Ward, K. D., Thurston, G., King, B. A., Sutfin, E. L., Cobb, C. O., Griffiths, M., Goldstein, L. B., & Rezk-Hanna, M. (2019). Water pipe (hookah) smoking and cardiovascular disease risk: A scientific statement from the American Heart Association. *Circulation, 139*(19), e917–e936. https://doi.org/10.1161/CIR.0000000000000671

Bozzini, A. B., Bauer, A., Maruyama, J., Simões, R., & Matijasevich, A. (2021). Factors associated with risk behaviors in adolescence: a systematic review. *Revista brasileira de psiquiatria (Sao Paulo, Brazil : 1999), 43*(2), 210–221. https://doi.org/10.1590/1516-4446-2019-0835

Burden of tobacco use in the U.S. (2021, March 7). Centers for Disease Control and Prevention. https://www.cdc.gov/tobacco/campaign/tips/resources/data/cigarette-smoking-in-united-states.html

Butler, M., Kane, R. L., McAlpine, D., Kathol, R. G., Fu, S. S., & Hagedorn, H. (2008). *Integration of mental health/substance abuse and primary care* (AHRQ Publication 09-E003). Agency for Healthcare Research and Quality.

Cahn, Z., & Siegel, M. (2010). Electronic cigarettes as a harm reduction strategy for tobacco control: A step forward or a repeat of past mistakes? *Journal of Public Health Policy, 32*(1), 16–31. https://doi.org/10.1057/jphp.2010.41

Caplan, L., Stout, C., & Blumenthal, D. S. (2011). Training physicians to do office-based smoking cessation increases adherence to PHS guidelines. *Journal of Community Health, 36*(2), 238–243. https://doi.org/10.1007/s10900-010-9303-0

Centers for Disease Control and Prevention (CDC). (2017). Quitting smoking among adults – United States, 2000–2015. *MMWR Morbidity and Mortality Weekly Report, 65*(52), 1457–1464.

Centers for Medicare & Medicaid Services. (2020). *Coverage and payment related to COVID-19 Medicare*. https://www.cms.gov/files/document/03052020-medicare-covid-19-fact-sheet.pdf

Champassak, S. L., Catley, D., Finocchario-Kessler, S., Farris, M., Ehtesham, M., Schoor, R., & Goggin, K. (2014). Physician smoking cessation counseling and adherence to a clinical practice guideline. *European Journal for Person Centered Healthcare, 2*(4), 477–484. https://doi.org/10.5750/ejpch.v2i4.833

Chase, E. C., McMenamin, S. B., & Halpin, H. A. (2007). Medicaid provider delivery of the 5A's for smoking cessation counseling. *Nicotine & Tobacco Research: Official Journal of the Society for Research on Nicotine and Tobacco, 9*(11), 1095–1101. https://doi.org/10.1080/14622200701666344

Cigars. (2021, March 31). Centers for Disease Control and Prevention. https://www.cdc.gov/tobacco/data_statistics/fact_sheets/tobacco_industry/cigars/

Clinical guidelines for prescribing pharmacotherapy for smoking cessation. (2012). Agency for Healthcare Research and Quality. https://www.ahrq.gov/prevention/guidelines/tobacco/prescrib.html

Clinical Practice Guideline Treating Tobacco Use and Dependence 2008 Update Panel, Liaisons, and Staff. (2008). A clinical practice guideline for treating tobacco use and dependence: 2008 update. A U.S. Public Health Service report. *American Journal of Preventive Medicine, 35*(2), 158–176. https://doi.org/10.1016/j.amepre.2008.04.009

Committee on Smoking Cessation in Military and Veteran Populations, Board on Population Health and Public Health Practice, & Institute of Medicine. (2009). *Combating tobacco use in military and veteran populations* (S. Bondurant & R. Wedge, Eds.). National Academies Press.

Croyle, R. T., Morgan, G. D., & Fiore, M. C. (2019). Addressing a core gap in cancer care—The NCI Moonshot Program to help oncology patients stop smoking. *New England Journal of Medicine, 380*(6), 512–515. https://doi.org/10.1056/nejmp1813913

Cummings, N. A., & O'Donohue, W. T. (Eds.). (2011). *Understanding the behavioral healthcare crisis: The promise of integrated care and diagnostic reform* (pp. 1–18). Routledge.

Daniels, K. E., & Roman, N. V. (2013). A descriptive study of the perceptions and behaviors of waterpipe use by university students in the Western Cape, South Africa. *Tobacco Induced Diseases, 11*(1), 4. https://doi.org/10.1186/1617-9625-11-4

DiClemente, C. C., Prochaska, J. O., Fairhurst, S. K., Velicer, W. F., Velasquez, M. M., & Rossi, J. S. (1991). The process of smoking cessation: An analysis of precontemplation, contemplation, and preparation stages of change. *Journal of Consulting and Clinical Psychology, 59*(2), 295–304. https://doi.org/10.1037/0022-006X.59.2.295

Dunn, D. S., Johnson, A. L., Sterling, K. L., & Cohn, A. M. (2021). Differences in reasons for little cigar/cigarillo use across white and black/African American young adult users. *Addictive Behaviors, 118*, 106884. https://doi.org/10.1016/j.addbeh.2021.106884

El-Zaatari, Z. M., Chami, H. A., & Zaatari, G. S. (2015). Health effects associated with waterpipe smoking. *Tobacco Control, 24*(Suppl 1), i31–i43. https://doi.org/10.1136/tobaccocontrol-2014-051908

Epps, R. P., & Manley, M. W. (1990). How to help your patients stop smoking. A National Cancer Institute program for physicians. *The Journal of the Florida Medical Association, 77*(4), 454–456.

Farsalinos, K. E., Yannovits, N., Sarri, T., Voudris, V., & Poulas, K. (2018). Nicotine delivery to the aerosol of a heat-not-burn tobacco product: Comparison with a tobacco cigarette and E-cigarettes. *Nicotine & Tobacco Research, 20*(8), 1004–1009. https://doi.org/10.1093/ntr/ntx138

Fiore, M. C., Jaén, C. R., Baker, T. B., Bailey, W. C., Benowitz, N. L., Curry, S. J., Dorfman, S. F., Froelicher, E. S., Goldstein, M. G., Healton, C. G., et al. (2008). *Treating Tobacco Use and Dependence: 2008 Update. U.S. Public Health Service Clinical Practice Guideline*. Rockville (MD): U.S. Department of Health and Human Services.

Fluharty, M., Taylor, A. E., Grabski, M., & Munafò, M. R. (2016). The association of cigarette smoking with depression and anxiety: A systematic review. *Nicotine & Tobacco Research, 19*(1), 3–13. https://doi.org/10.1093/ntr/ntw140

Gray, M., Joy, E., Plath, D., & Webb, S. A. (2013). Implementing evidence-based practice: A review of the empirical research literature. *Research on Social Work Practice, 23*(2), 157–166. https://doi.org/10.1177/1049731512467072

Grinberg, A., & Goodwin, R. D. (2016). Prevalence and correlates of hookah use: A nationally representative sample of US adults ages 18–40 years old. *The American Journal of Drug and Alcohol Abuse, 42*(5), 567–576. https://doi.org/10.3109/00952990.2016.1167214

Harrison, A., Ramo, D., Hall, S. M., Estrada-Gonzalez, V., & Tolou-Shams, M. (2020). Cigarette smoking, mental health, and other substance use among court-involved youth. *Substance Use & Misuse, 55*(4), 572–581. https://doi.org/10.1080/10826084.2019.1691593

Heatherton, T. F., Kozlowski, L. T., Frecker, R. C., & Fagerström, K. O. (1991). The Fagerström test for nicotine dependence: A revision of the Fagerström tolerance questionnaire. *British Journal of Addiction, 86*(9), 1119–1127. https://doi.org/10.1111/j.1360-0443.1991.tb01879.x

Husky, M. M., Paliwal, P., Mazure, C. M., & McKee, S. A. (2007). Gender differences in association with substance use diagnoses and smoking. *Journal of Addiction Medicine, 1*(3), 161–164.

Integrated health care. (2021). American Psychological Association. https://www.apa.org/health/integrated-health-care

IOM (Institute of Medicine). (1994). *Reducing risks for mental disorders: Frontiers for preventive intervention research*. National Academy Press.

Johnson, B. A. (Ed.). (2013). *Addiction medicine: Science and practice* (Vol. 1, pp. 805–806). Springer.

Johnson, A. L., Collins, L. K., Villanti, A. C., Pearson, J. L., & Niaura, R. S. (2018). Patterns of nicotine and tobacco product use in youth and young adults in the United States, 2011–2015. *Nicotine & Tobacco Research, 20*(suppl_1), S48–S54. https://doi.org/10.1093/ntr/nty018

Keller, P. A., Feltracco, A., Bailey, L. A., Li, Z., Niederdeppe, J., Baker, T. B., & Fiore, M. C. (2010). Changes in tobacco quitlines in the United States, 2005–2006. *Preventing Chronic Disease, 7*(2), A36.

King, B. A., Dube, S. R., Babb, S. D., & McAfee, T. A. (2013). Patient-reported recall of smoking cessation interventions from a health professional. *Preventive Medicine, 57*(5), 715–717. https://doi.org/10.1016/j.ypmed.2013.07.010

Knudsen, H. K. (2017). Implementation of smoking cessation treatment in substance use disorder treatment settings: A review. *The American Journal of Drug and Alcohol Abuse, 43*(2), 215–225.

Lee, Y. O., Hebert, C. J., Nonnemaker, J. M., & Kim, A. E. (2014). Multiple tobacco product use among adults in the United States: Cigarettes, cigars, electronic cigarettes, hookah, smokeless tobacco, and snus. *Preventive Medicine, 62*, 14–19. https://doi.org/10.1016/j.ypmed.2014.01.014

Linde, B. D., Ebbert, J. O., Pasker, C. K., Wayne Talcott, G., Schroeder, D. R., Hanson, A. C., & Klesges, R. C. (2015). Prevalence and predictors of hookah use in US air force military recruits. *Addictive Behaviors, 47*, 5–10. https://doi.org/10.1016/j.addbeh.2015.03.012

Lindson-Hawley, N., Thompson, T. P., & Begh, R. (2015). Motivational interviewing for smoking cessation. *The Cochrane Database of Systematic Reviews, 3*, CD006936. https://doi.org/10.1002/14651858.CD006936.pub3

Liu, X., Li, R., Lanza, S. T., Vasilenko, S. A., & Piper, M. (2013). Understanding the role of cessation fatigue in the smoking cessation process. *Drug and Alcohol Dependence, 133*(2), 548–555. https://doi.org/10.1016/j.drugalcdep.2013.07.025

Livingstone-Banks, J., Ordóñez-Mena, J. M., & Hartmann-Boyce, J. (2019). Print-based self-help interventions for smoking cessation. *Cochrane Database of Systematic Reviews, 1*, CD001118.

Lynch, B. S., & Bonnie, R. J. (1994). *Growing up tobacco free—Preventing nicotine addiction in children and youths* (The nature of nicotine addiction) (pp. 28–68). National Academy Press.

Maziak, W., Taleb, Z. B., Bahelah, R., Islam, F., Jaber, R., Auf, R., & Salloum, R. G. (2015). The global epidemiology of waterpipe smoking. *Tobacco Control, 24*(Suppl 1), i3–i12. https://doi.org/10.1136/tobaccocontrol-2014-051903

Mermelstein, R. J. (2014). Adapting to a changing tobacco landscape: Research implications for understanding and reducing youth tobacco use. *American Journal of Preventive Medicine, 47*(2 Suppl 1), S87–S89. https://doi.org/10.1016/j.amepre.2014.04.015

National Center for Chronic Disease Prevention and Health Promotion (US) Office on Smoking and Health. (2014). *The health consequences of smoking—50 years of progress: A report of the surgeon general*. Atlanta (GA): Centers for Disease Control and Prevention (US); 2014. Available from: https://www.ncbi.nlm.nih.gov/books/NBK179276/

NCCN. (2021). *Guidelines panel: NCCN clinical practice guidelines in oncology for smoking cessation (NCCN guidelines): Smoking cessation*. NCCN.

O'Donohue, W. T., & Draper, C. (2011). The case for evidence-based stepped care as part of a reformed delivery system. In *Stepped care and e-health* (pp. 1–16). Springer New York.

Office on smoking and health at a glance | CDC. (2021). Centers for Disease Control and Prevention. https://www.cdc.gov/chronicdisease/resources/publications/aag/tobacco-use.htm

Park, E. R., Gareen, I. F., Japuntich, S., Lennes, I., Hyland, K., DeMello, S., Sicks, J. D., & Rigotti, N. A. (2015). Primary care provider-delivered smoking cessation interventions and smoking cessation among participants in the national lung screening trial. *JAMA Internal Medicine, 175*(9), 1509–1516. https://doi.org/10.1001/jamainternmed.2015.2391

Pentz, M. A. (2003). Evidence-based prevention: Characteristics, impact, and future direction. *Journal of Psychoactive Drugs, 35*(Suppl 1), 143–152. https://doi.org/10.1080/02791072.2003.10400509

Piano, M. R., Benowitz, N. L., Fitzgerald, G. A., Corbridge, S., Heath, J., Hahn, E., Pechacek, T. F., Howard, G., & American Heart Association Council on Cardiovascular Nursing. (2010). Impact of smokeless tobacco products on cardiovascular disease: Implications for policy, prevention, and treatment: A policy statement from the American Heart Association. *Circulation, 122*(15), 1520–1544. https://doi.org/10.1161/CIR.0b013e3181f432c3

Prochaska, J. O., & DiClemente, C. C. (1983). Stages and processes of self-change of smoking: Toward an integrative model of change. *Journal of Consulting and Clinical Psychology, 51*(3), 390–395. https://doi.org/10.1037/0022-006X.51.3.390

Qasim, H., Karim, Z. A., Rivera, J. O., Khasawneh, F. T., & Alshbool, F. Z. (2017). Impact of electronic cigarettes on the cardiovascular system. *Journal of the American Heart Association, 6*(9), e006353. https://doi.org/10.1161/JAHA.117.006353

Rittenmeyer, L., Huffman, D., Alagna, M., & Moore, E. (2016). The experience of adults who choose watchful waiting or active surveillance as an approach to medical treatment: A qualitative systematic review. *JBI Database of Systematic Reviews and Implementation Reports, 14*(2), 174–255.

Salloum, R. G., Asfar, T., & Maziak, W. (2016). Toward a regulatory framework for the waterpipe. *American Journal of Public Health, 106*(10), 1773–1777. https://doi.org/10.2105/AJPH.2016.303322

Searight, H. R. (2018). Counseling patients in primary care: Evidence-based strategies. *American Family Physician, 98*(12), 719–728.

Sheffer, C. E., Bickel, W. K., Brandon, T. H., Franck, C. T., Deen, D., Panissidi, L., & Mantovani, A. (2018). Preventing relapse to smoking with transcranial magnetic stimulation: Feasibility and potential efficacy. *Drug and Alcohol Dependence, 182*, 8–18.

Sheffer, C. E., Al-Zalabani, A., Aubrey, A., Bader, R., Beltrez, C., Bennett, S., Carl, E., Cranos, C., Darville, A., Greyber, J., Karam-Hage, M., Hawari, F., Hutcheson, T., Hynes, V., Kotsen, C., Leone, F., McConaha, J., McCary, H., Meade, C., … Wendling, A. (2021). The emerging global tobacco treatment workforce: Characteristics of tobacco treatment specialists trained in council-accredited training programs from 2017 to 2019. *International Journal of Environmental Research and Public Health, 18*(5), 2416. https://doi.org/10.3390/ijerph18052416

Sheldrick, R. C., Merchant, S., & Perrin, E. C. (2011). Identification of developmental-behavioral problems in primary care: A systematic review. *Pediatrics, 128*(2), 356–363. https://doi.org/10.1542/peds.2010-3261

Shields, P. G. (2002). Tobacco smoking, harm reduction, and biomarkers. *Journal of the National Cancer Institute, 94*(19), 1435–1444. https://doi.org/10.1093/jnci/94.19.1435

Simonavicius, E., McNeill, A., Shahab, L., & Brose, L. S. (2019). Heat-not-burn tobacco products: A systematic literature review. *Tobacco Control, 28*(5), 582–594. https://doi.org/10.1136/tobaccocontrol-2018-054419

Smiley, S. L., Kintz, N., Rodriguez, Y. L., Barahona, R., Sussman, S., Cruz, T. B., Chou, C. P., Pentz, M. A., Samet, J. M., & Baezconde-Garbanati, L. (2019). Disparities in retail marketing for little cigars and cigarillos in Los Angeles, California. *Addictive Behaviors Reports, 9*, 100149. https://doi.org/10.1016/j.abrep.2018.100149

Smokeless tobacco use in the United States. (2020, November 16). Centers for Disease Control and Prevention. https://www.cdc.gov/tobacco/data_statistics/fact_sheets/smokeless/use_us/

Snipes, C., Maragakis, A., & O'Donohue, W. (2015). Team-based stepped care in integrated delivery settings. *Family Medicine and Community Health, 3*(1), 39–46. https://doi.org/10.15212/fmch.2015.0101

Spangler, J. G., George, G., Foley, K. L., & Crandall, S. J. (2002). Tobacco intervention training: Current efforts and gaps in US medical schools. *JAMA, 288*(9), 1102–1109. https://doi.org/10.1001/jama.288.9.1102

Stead, L. F., Buitrago, D., Preciado, N., Sanchez, G., Hartmann-Boyce, J., & Lancaster, T. (2013). Physician advice for smoking cessation. *The Cochrane Database of Systematic Reviews, 2013*(5), CD000165. https://doi.org/10.1002/14651858.CD000165.pub4

Substance Abuse and Mental Health Services Administration. (2018). *Results from the 2017 National Survey on Drug Use and Health: Detailed Tables, Table 2.32Bexternal icon*. Substance Abuse and Mental Health Services Administration, Center for Behavioral Health Statistics and Quality.

Sussman, S. (2017). *Substance and behavioral addictions: Concepts, causes, and cures* (1st ed.). Cambridge University Press.

Sussman, S., & Ames, S. L. (2008). *Drug abuse: Concepts, prevention and cessation* (1st ed.). Cambridge University Press.

Sussman, S., & Sun, P. (2009). Youth tobacco use cessation: 2008 update. *Tobacco Induced Diseases, 5*(1), 3. https://doi.org/10.1186/1617-9625-5-3

Sussman, S., Levy, D., Lich, K. H., Cené, C. W., Kim, M. M., Rohrbach, L. A., & Chaloupka, F. J. (2013). Comparing effects of tobacco use prevention modalities: Need for complex system models. *Tobacco Induced Diseases, 11*(1), 2. https://doi.org/10.1186/1617-9625-11-2

Tabuchi, T., Kiyohara, K., Hoshino, T., Bekki, K., Inaba, Y., & Kunugita, N. (2016). Awareness and use of electronic cigarettes and heat-not-burn tobacco products in Japan. *Addiction, 11*, 706–713. https://doi.org/10.1111/add.13231

The Community Guide. (2011). *Tobacco use and secondhand smoke exposure: Mobile phone-based cessation interventions*. https://www.thecommunityguide.org/findings/tobacco-use-and-secondhand-smoke-exposure-mobile-phone-based-cessation-interventions. Accessed 12 Apr 2021.

The Community Guide. (2012). *Tobacco*. 2012a; https://www.thecommunityguide.org/topic/tobacco?field_recommendation_tid=All&items_per_page=5. Accessed 12 Apr 2021.

Tobacco Fact Sheet. World Health Organization; (2019, July 26). Available at: https://www.who.int/news-room/fact-sheets/detail/tobacco

Tobacco Use: Quitline Interventions. (2014, April 17). Retrieved April 10, 2021, from Thecommunityguide.org website: https://www.thecommunityguide.org/findings/tobacco-use-quitline-interventions

U.S. Department of Health and Human Services. (2010). *What you need to know about quitting smoking: Advice from the surgeon general*. US Department of Health and Human Services, Centers for Disease Control and Prevention, National Center for Chronic Disease Prevention and Health Promotion, Office on Smoking and Health.

United States Public Health Service Office of the Surgeon General, & National Center for Chronic Disease Prevention and Health Promotion (US) Office on Smoking and Health. (2020). Smoking Cessation: A Report of the Surgeon General. US Department of Health and Human Services.

Verplaetse, T. L., & McKee, S. A. (2017). An overview of alcohol and tobacco/nicotine interactions in the human laboratory. *The American Journal of Drug and Alcohol Abuse, 43*(2), 186–196. https://doi.org/10.1080/00952990.2016.1189927

Wiseman, K. P., Hauser, L., Clark, C., Odumosu, O., Dahl, N., Peregoy, J., Sheffield, C. W., Klesges, R. C., & Anderson, R. T. (2020). An evaluation of the process and quality improvement measures of the University of Virginia Cancer Center Tobacco Treatment Program. *International Journal of Environmental Research and Public Health, 17*(13), 4707. https://doi.org/10.3390/ijerph17134707

World Health Organization. (2011). Benefits and rationale for establishing quit-line services. In: *Developing and Improving National Toll-Free Tobacco Quit Line Services: A World Health Organization Manual*. Geneva (Switzerland): World Health Organization, 7–11.

World Health Organization. (2019). *World Health Organization report on the global tobacco epidemic*. World Health Organization.

World Health Organization. *Noncommunicable diseases. Key facts; 2018*. (2021, March 25). https://www.who.int/news-room/fact-sheets/detail/noncommunicable-diseases

Chapter 11
Marijuana Use

John W. Toumbourou, Jess Heerde, Adrian Kelly, and Jen Bailey

11.1 Definition/Diagnostic Criteria

Marijuana refers to the psychoactive compound tetrahydrocannabinol [THC] derived from the cannabis plant. In what follows, we focus on THC but also provide some information on other compounds derived from the cannabis plant or through chemical synthesis, collectively known as cannabinoids.

The legal status of marijuana is rapidly changing. At the international level, it has been an illicit drug for half a century with most countries signatories to the United Nations convention that defines illicit drugs. Because it has been the most widely used illicit drug, with relatively low acute harms, and because some cannabinoids appear to have therapeutic benefits, a popular movement has been successful in legalizing marijuana use in a growing number of states and nations (Hall et al., 2019).

This section describes the consequences and harms associated with different patterns of marijuana use behaviors, to provide a basis for establishing diagnostic

J. W. Toumbourou (✉)
School of Psychology, Deakin University, Geelong, VIC, Australia
e-mail: john.toumbourou@deakin.edu.au

J. Heerde
The University of Melbourne, Melbourne, VIC, Australia
e-mail: jessica.heerde@unimelb.edu.au

A. Kelly
Queensland University of Technology, Brisbane, QLD, Australia
e-mail: a.kelly@qut.edu.au

J. Bailey
Social Development Research Group, School of Social Work, University of Washington, Washington, DC, USA
e-mail: jabailey@uw.edu

W. O'Donohue, M. Zimmermann (eds.), *Handbook of Evidence-Based Prevention of Behavioral Disorders in Integrated Care*,
https://doi.org/10.1007/978-3-030-83469-2_11

criteria to guide prevention. Although we focus on THC, the effects of other cannabinoids are also briefly discussed.

There is variation in the patterns of marijuana use that have been associated with harms. Psychiatric guidelines recognize marijuana (cannabis) use disorder as a diagnostic category (Compton et al., 2019). This is assessed using indicators such as frequency, tolerance, and time spent using or getting over effects. In what follows, we note there is increasing evidence that frequent use (monthly or more frequent use) of marijuana may increase the risk of disorders, be harmful to mental health, and have long-term adverse intergenerational effects on the offspring of users.

Longitudinal studies have identified early age marijuana use as a predictor of progression to frequent and daily adolescent use (e.g., Scholes-Balog et al., 2020). This has led to the target of preventing any use of marijuana through childhood and adolescence. In their review of available epidemiological data, Hall et al. (2019) note that adolescents who use cannabis are at greater risk than adults of developing disorders, cognitive impairment, leaving school early, progressing to other illicit drug use, and mental health problems (including schizophrenia, affective disorders, and suicidal thoughts).

A comprehensive literature review (National Academies of Sciences, Engineering, and Medicine, 2017) established that there have been relatively few studies of the longitudinal consequences of marijuana use. Longitudinal studies face the difficulty that marijuana is often used in combination with other drugs (polydrug use). For example, among young Australians, we found that approximately 8.2% reported polydrug use, including cannabis use, and that this subgroup of drug users reported higher levels of psychological distress than adolescents who typically consumed alcohol only (Kelly et al., 2015). It is often difficult in longitudinal studies to estimate the dose of marijuana being used. Chan et al. (2017) observed that very-high-potency THC products like butane hash oil have more significant associations with mental health problems and health risk behaviors, including depressed mood and polydrug use, than herbal cannabis. These issues increase the difficulty of answering questions of the consequences of marijuana use required for clinical guidelines.

In their review, Hall et al. (2019) note that epidemiological studies have tended to focus on the adverse health effects of daily marijuana use, with clear evidence of harm for this pattern of use. Silins et al. (2014) integrated data from three large longitudinal studies from Australia and New Zealand. After adjusting for other predictors, daily marijuana use before age 17 years consistently predicted a range of adult outcomes including reductions in high school completion, and adult degree attainment and increases in cannabis dependence, other illicit drug use, and suicide attempts.

There is evidence that adult frequent marijuana use (monthly or more frequent) is a risk factor for mental health problems. A large epidemiological study combined data from the US National Survey of Drug Use and Health (NSDUH) with geographically linked community surveys (Reece & Hulse, 2020a). From 2011 to 2016, state-level marijuana use in the past month (a measure of frequent use) was causally associated with higher rates of mental health problems indicated by any mental illness, major depressive illness, serious mental illness, and suicidal thinking. In explaining their effects, these authors note laboratory studies that show that cannabinoid exposure leads to adverse psychiatric outcomes by adversely impacting neural stem cell activity, which reduces neuroplasticity, resulting in premature brain aging. These authors note that these destructive neuro-cellular mechanisms not only apply to THC but also to other cannabinoids including cannabidiol and cannabichromene.

There is evidence that frequent adult marijuana use is harmful to the next generation. The offspring of frequent adult marijuana users have higher rates of congenital abnormalities (Reece & Hulse, 2020b) and adverse mental health problems including autism and ADHD symptoms (Reece & Hulse, 2020a). Geographic differences in rates of frequent adult marijuana use in Canada have been associated with higher rates of congenital abnormalities including cardiovascular defects, Down's syndrome, and gastroschisis (a birth defect of the belly wall) (Reece & Hulse, 2020b). Reece and Hulse also describe how neurobiological effects of THC and other cannabinoids explain these intergenerational harms.

11.2 Prevalence and Age of Onset

In what follows, we summarize what is known of patterns of marijuana use in different age groups and countries. In their review, Hall et al. (2019) summarize international patterns of marijuana use, noting that in 2015 around 4% of the global adult population used marijuana. Use was more common in North America and high-income countries in Europe and Oceania than in low- and middle-income countries. In the intervening years, cannabis use increased in low- and middle-income countries but remained low in Asia.

In high-income countries, population rates of marijuana use have until recent decades tended to peak in the late 20s and then declined slowly from age 30 (Compton et al., 2007). However, since 2008, cannabis use in the USA has tended to extend longer into the 30s (Hall et al., 2019). Hall et al. (2019) note that the THC content of the marijuana that is used has increased in past decades in the USA and Europe, from around 5% to more than 15%. Compton et al. (2019) analyzed data from US National Surveys on Drug Use and Health (NSDUH) collected from 2002 to 2017, noting that marijuana use increased from 10.4% to 15.3%, while daily/near daily use increased from 1.9% to 4.2%. Despite these rises, the past year prevalence of marijuana use disorders remained stable at around 1.5%.

Presently, marijuana remains by far the most used illicit drug among adolescents and young people (Kelly et al., 2018). The Monitoring the Future (MTF) survey provides annual epidemiological trend estimates of the prevalence of marijuana use among young people (early age use) in the USA (Miech et al., 2020). Surveys of the last year of secondary school (grade 12 students) reveal that lifetime use peaked in 1979 when 60.4% reported use. Since that time lifetime use declined until 1992 to

32.6% and then increased to 49.6% in 1997. In 2019, 43.7% of US grade 12 students reported lifetime use.

In Europe, similar surveys to the MTF have been n implemented. In Central Europe, past year prevalence of marijuana use among young adults (up to 34 years of age) varies from 10% in Belgium to 22% in France (EMCDDA, 2016). In Australia, around 12% of 14–17-year-olds have used cannabis in the previous year (Weier et al., 2016).

11.3 Risk Factors

In efforts to prevent harmful patterns of marijuana use, risk factors are identified based on evidence that they act as independent predictors of behavior targets in longitudinal and epidemiological research studies. Although protective factors are often defined as the reverse of risk factors, they are more clearly differentiated as characteristics that buffer, mediate, or moderate the influence of risk factors, thereby reducing the likelihood of later problems such as frequent marijuana use (Catalano et al., 1996; Toumbourou & Catalano, 2005). Resilience researchers have identified several protective factors by studying children who have avoided adversity after being exposed to difficult childhood experiences such as parental mental illness or extreme poverty (Catalano et al., 1996).

Longitudinal studies typically show a developmental behavioral sequence whereby marijuana use begins with a first experience and then progresses to more frequent use, which in turn increases the risk of marijuana use disorders (Toumbourou & Catalano, 2005). This developmental behavioral sequence has a neurobiological substrate and social relationship overlay. Neuroadaptation begins from the first exposure to marijuana use observable from higher doses being required over time to experience similar levels of intoxication. Laboratory studies show that neuroadaptation caused by both marijuana and other cannabinoid use is associated with destructive neuro-cellular changes that weaken neurological stem cell activity and therefore reduce brain plasticity (Reece & Hulse, 2020a, b). These changes in part explain the behavioral progression from marijuana use to disorder symptoms such as narrowing of life interests and aspirations. These behavioral and neurological changes also associate with social relationship overlays whereby peer, intimate, family, and community relationships are attenuated to accommodate changes such as increasing time spent in marijuana use.

Neonates are extremely vulnerable to destructive neurobiological changes following in utero exposure to maternal use of marijuana and other cannabinoids. Laboratory studies show the destructive neuro-cellular changes that arise through both marijuana and other cannabinoid use are transmitted to offspring (Reece & Hulse, 2020a, b).

Risk factors for harmful patterns of marijuana use tend to show variation across communities and are often contrasted with structural and societal determinants such as marijuana policies and laws that affect large population aggregations but show differences across states and nations (Toumbourou et al., 2014). Reviews of longitudinal and program evaluation studies identify risk factors for early age marijuana use across a range of child and adolescent development settings.

The review paper by Hawkins et al. (1992) was influential in organizing what was known to that point of developmental risk and protective factors for youth drug use, including marijuana use. Subsequent reviews have confirmed their conclusion that predictors are evident at the individual level and within the family, school, peer, and community ecological settings (Toumbourou & Catalano, 2005).

At the societal and community level, socioeconomic disadvantage is a characteristic that is consistently associated with developmental problems for neonates, children, and adolescents. In addition to socioeconomic disadvantage, several sets of community risk factors influence early age marijuana exposure (e.g., Catalano et al., 1996; Toumbourou et al., 2014) including normative expectations and acceptance of marijuana use and availability.

The International Youth Development Study (IYDS) is a cross-nationally matched longitudinal study that uses the Communities That Care Youth Survey to monitor risk factors and youth health behaviors (Rowland et al., 2019a). Longitudinal analyses of cross-nationally matched analyses of the IYDS data showed a wide range of adolescent (age 12) family, peer-group, school, and community risk factors were predictive of marijuana use (past month) 1 year later, in both US and Australian adolescents (Hemphill et al., 2011). At the family level, unique multivariate predictors included less positive family management practices (e.g., permissive parenting styles, lower relationship quality), higher levels of family conflict, a family history of substance use, and parental attitudes more favorable toward both drug use and antisocial behavior. Higher levels of attachment to both the mother and father, as well as greater opportunities and rewards for prosocial involvement within the family environment, showed protective effects.

Hemphill et al. (2011) found that similar risk and protective factors predicted both marijuana and other forms of substance use. These findings parallel research findings on the association of family and parenting factors with other types of substance use, including early use of tobacco and alcohol. For example, low emotional closeness to parents predicts tobacco use cross-sectionally and longitudinally (Kelly et al., 2011; Kelly, 2012) and alcohol use cross-sectionally and longitudinally (Kelly et al., 2011, 2012). Poor parental supervision is more associated with adolescents who show early and steep rises in alcohol use compared to those who show limited and stable growth trajectories that more strongly predicts early and strong escalation in alcohol use relative to use (Chan et al., 2013). These findings suggest that efforts to reduce social environmental risk factors for early age marijuana use are likely to also reduce other substance use problems.

A consistent observation in prevention science is that risk factors have a cumulative impact. The more risk factors that are present and the longer they persist over time, the greater the subsequent developmental impact (e.g., Toumbourou et al., 2014). There is no single risk factor that fully explains developmental problems; rather, these problems can be regarded as having complex causes involving influences and interaction of multiple risk and protective factors. For example, low emotional closeness to parents and poor supervision may serve to increase the likelihood of engagement with drug-using peer networks during the pubertal stage of development, and major school transitions may heighten this risk (Kelly et al., 2012; Li et al., 2014).

One heuristic proposed to describe the cumulative effect of risk factors is to use the analogy of a snowball (Toumbourou & Catalano, 2005). According to this view, risk factors that emerge early in life (e.g., maternal marijuana use) can lead to subsequent risk factors that tend to "adhere" and accumulate as a consequence of the experience of earlier problems (e.g., child disability, child-onset behavior problems, school failure).

Social and economic mobility patterns in competitive market economies have increased socioeconomic differentials and led to a situation whereby children experiencing snowball risk trajectories tend to be disproportionately clustered within disadvantaged geographic communities and schools (Reece & Hulse, 2020a; Toumbourou et al., 2014). Using this analogy, the solution is to invest within these targeted areas to prevent the potential for an avalanching snowball by building protective solutions and reducing early life risk factors. For example, by increasing illicit drug laws and their enforcement, it may be possible to reduce the availability and normative acceptance of marijuana and to in this way encourage adults to reduce regular marijuana use before they conceive, in this way preventing the sequence of events that can result in the cumulative escalation of risk for future generation.

In many cases, the cumulative effect of risk is more temporal and can be better described with the analogy of a snowstorm (Toumbourou & Catalano, 2005; Toumbourou et al., 2014). According to this view, a healthy child without protective clothing can be put at risk by temporal events such as exposure to extreme weather. If such unprotected exposure continues for long enough, adverse health outcomes can result. Where the adolescent has low protective factors (such as parents being unavailable to supervise activities or poor relationships with teachers) in a community with high rates of marijuana use and availability, the likelihood of the adolescent using marijuana increases. The protective advantages of positive relationships with adults suggest there is potential to protect health within risky social environments by increasing healthy adult relationships or other protective factors (analogous to providing warm clothing and shelter in stormy weather). From this perspective, solutions lie in improving social environments (by increasing protective social relationships) through the course of development (Catalano et al., 1996; Toumbourou et al., 2014).

The cumulative effect of risk across social environments for the initiation of different patterns of adolescent marijuana use has been demonstrated in an Australian longitudinal study (Scholes-Balog et al., 2020). Scholes-Balog et al. (2020) reported the cumulative effect of risk across family, peer, and community factors, accounting for early (childhood) substance use (cigarette, alcohol and illicit drug use, and drinking until drunk), predicted early adolescent-onset marijuana use. The cumulative effect of risk within the family and early adolescent substance use also predicted late adolescent-onset occasional marijuana use (relative to non-marijuana users).

Given the range of risk and protective factors, the social development model (SDM) has been proposed to organize knowledge of how risk and protective factors work together to predict marijuana use and related problems. The SDM is an explicit developmental theory of health behavior that has been well supported in empirical tests during childhood, adolescence, and young adulthood. The SDM proposes that social relationships are critical proximal influences that affect health behaviors, including marijuana use. Social relationships can conversely encourage either healthy (prosocial) or unhealthy behavior, depending on the norms and standards of the relationship influence. The development of social relationship bonds are in turn affected by more distal factors related to interaction opportunities; social, emotional, and cognitive skills; and the rewards experienced from social interactions. The SDM provides a basis for coherently evaluating health behavior influences in a range of child, adolescent, and adult social contexts.

The SDM theorizes that liberalizing marijuana laws changes key risk factors including social acceptability, perceived prevalence, risk, and availability (Kosterman et al., 2016). Fischer et al. (2020) summarize what is known of patterns of use and harms following state and national legalization of marijuana use. They observe that legalization has reduced the perceived risk and increased the normative acceptance of marijuana use among young people and adults. Legalization has been associated with a reduced price of marijuana, increased availability, and higher potency products.

Available studies show increases in use Marijuana: risk factors among adults following legalization, in line with SDM predictions. For example, a large epidemiological study combining data across geographic areas in the USA from 2011 to 2016 found state legalization changes caused increases in frequent use. These increases have in turn caused increases in mental health problems across large state populations (Reece & Hulse, 2020a).

11.4 Review of Evidence-Based Prevention

Evidence-based prevention can be defined based on programs or policies that result in reduced early age use, frequent use, or marijuana use disorders. To identify preventative interventions, we searched for literature reviews of program evaluation studies that had rigorous randomized trial and quasi-experimental or epidemiological designs. As outlined in the SDM, prevention effects operate within a social ecological setting context and may be disrupted in locations where the legalization of marijuana use results in community norms that are accepting of marijuana use for medical or recreational use.

11.5 Effective Screening

In community settings, screening includes epidemiological surveillance using instruments such as the Communities That Care Youth Survey to monitor population patterns of marijuana use and risk and protective factors, which can be targeted in prevention (Rowland et al., 2019b). Rowland et al. (2019b) reported similar risk and protective factors predicted community rates of adolescent marijuana use in both Australia and the Netherlands. These findings tend to confirm the validity and utility of the Communities That Care Youth Survey as a community surveillance instrument for monitoring population patterns of marijuana use and risk and protective factors (Hemphill et al., 2011). In Australia, the Communities That Care Youth Survey has been used successfully to guide community coalitions to reduce community rates of adolescent marijuana use and other substance use (Toumbourou et al., 2019).

Evidence from systematic literature reviews suggests that screening assessments for youth marijuana use in settings such as secondary schools (Carney et al., 2016), tertiary education institutions, or health services can be combined with brief interventions (typically one to five counseling sessions) to encourage reduction in use (Tanner-Smith et al., 2015). In their systematic review, Tanner-Smith et al. (2015) included 13 studies and demonstrated a small significant effect in reducing marijuana use. Brief counseling interventions included strategies such as motivational interviewing, goal setting, and relapse prevention. Similar effects have been demonstrated in one study implemented in the secondary school setting (Carney et al., 2016).

Screening and brief counseling strategies have also been incorporated in some online and telehealth interventions offered in tertiary education settings (Gulliver et al., 2015). However, there have been insufficient studies to assess the impacts on marijuana use.

Faced with rising rates of marijuana use following legalization, employers and injury prevention agencies have expressed concerns about potential increases in marijuana-related occupational injuries (Smith et al., 2018). Screening surveys in Colorado of occupations where workers have responsibility for their own safety or the safety of others (e.g., construction and extraction, farming, fishing, and forestry and healthcare support) reveal around 16% of workers report frequent marijuana use. Although biological screening (e.g., urine testing) is feasible in workplace injury prevention (Price, 2014), the legal status of marijuana use poses challenges to the mandatory application of such screening procedures.

11.6 Universal, Indicated, and Selective Prevention

Prevention refers here to strategies or programs that avert or delay the onset or escalation of marijuana use toward frequent use and use disorders that are implicated as causes of mental health and next-generation problems. Prevention responses can be classified as universal where they apply to an entire population, selective, or indicated where they target groups with elevated risk. This conceptualization of prevention addresses the progression from risk factor to behavior within populations (Toumbourou et al., 2014).

For the prevention of early age marijuana use, there is evidence that universal interventions are effective where they focus on improving child social-emotional competence and/or healthy social development environments at the school and/or community level. The effectiveness of interventions of this type concurs with evidence of social developmental risk factors in the early onset of marijuana use.

Policies and laws are an important community-level factor that influence population levels of marijuana use. There is evidence that the legalization of marijuana for medical and recreational use in US states has acted as a risk factor for harmful use. Reece and Hulse (2020a) present a causal analysis which implicates US state legalization as a direct cause of increasing rates of frequent marijuana use across US states, which in turn has caused increased population rates of mental health problems. The increase in population rates of frequent adult marijuana use is predicted to increase rates of congenital damage to the next generation (Reece & Hulse, 2020b).

In their international literature review, Fischer et al. (2020) note several harms that have increased in states and nations that have legalized cannabis use. These include increases in cannabis-related hospitalizations (e.g., emergency room visits, trauma incidents, calls to poison control centers), including cases involving children, as well as increases in treatment-seeking for cannabis use disorders. Fischer et al. (2020) also summarize evidence that marijuana-related road fatalities have increased in association with legalization. These trends align with evidence that frequent marijuana use increases the risk of road accidents (Asbridge et al., 2012).

In nations where marijuana remains illegal, there is early evidence that community-level interventions may be able to prevent child and adolescent marijuana use. Community-level prevention frameworks, such as Communities That Care, which address the cumulative effect of risk across multiple social contexts, have been recommended for preventing early marijuana use (Scholes-Balog et al., 2020). Communities That Care is a five-phase training process that assists the formation and strategic action of community coalitions (e.g., comprised of community workers, local health services, schools, youth agencies, and police). These coalitions are guided to use knowledge from social developmental ecological theories and prevention science. An observational study in Australia associated the implementation of Communities That Care with reductions in adolescent reports of marijuana use (Toumbourou et al., 2019). The strength of a community coalition approach is that it fortifies the skills and resources of communities to address adolescent risks in a manner that is sustainable and flexible (Rowland et al., 2013; Kelly et al., 2020).

A variety of systematic literature reviews note the potential for school-level universal interventions to prevent marijuana use in countries where marijuana is illegal. In their Cochrane review, Faggiano et al. (2014) summarize evidence for universal school-based interventions in preventing marijuana and illicit drug use. Social competence approaches were found to be effective when compared to usual curricula or no intervention in preventing school-age marijuana use. Four studies were included that had assessed effects at less than 12-month follow-up and one study after 12 months. In their systematic review, Hodder et al. (2017) also identified universal school-based resiliency interventions (teaching social-emotional competency) as an effective strategy for preventing marijuana and other illicit drug use.

Cochrane reviews note some promise for family interventions to prevent early age marijuana use, in contexts where marijuana is illegal (Gates et al., 2006). Three family interventions (Focus on Families, Iowa Strengthening Families Program, and Preparing for the Drug-Free Years) were identified in a Cochrane review as having at least one study demonstrating effects in preventing marijuana use (Gates et al., 2006).

Although the current review focuses on THC, it is possible that some cannabinoids may be associated with therapeutic effects. Hall et al. (2019) summarize evidence regarding the effectiveness of cannabinoids for medicinal use. Their evidence suggests that cannabinoids might be effective in treating anxiety symptoms. They also note there is reasonable evidence that medical quality cannabis preparations and cannabinoids modestly reduce the symptoms of chronic pain, epilepsy, and nausea and vomiting.

11.7 Stepped Care Prevention Model: Role of PCP (Primary Care Provider) and BCP (Behavioral Care Provider)

Based on the information summarized in earlier sections, there are several possibilities for stepped care prevention models. In what follows, we distinguish different models for locations where marijuana use remains illegal versus those where it is has been legalized for medical or recreational use.

In all settings, it is important to promote an accurate understanding of the patterns of marijuana use that are harmful, such that they warrant intervention. Unfortunately, there continues to be public confusion as to the effects of marijuana, with many unaware of the harms. In localities where marijuana is legally available, the SDM predicts that there is likely to be an erroneous assumption that because marijuana use is normal, it is in fact safe. Within the stepped care prevention models, there is a hierarchy of more assertive and active responses available for service agencies including (a) watchful waiting, (b) psychoeducation, (c) biblio-prevention, (d) e-health prevention tools, (e) groups, and (f) individual services. In the sections that follow, we consider the evidence base for each of these possible responses as they relate to the prevention of early age and frequent marijuana use.

(a) Watchful waiting may be applicable within the period that elapses between experimental marijuana use and the development of problems that may lead users to seek help. As early age marijuana use is typically not associated with readily observable problems such as violence or injuries, watchful waiting may fail to detect and intervene to prevent the development of frequent use and subsequent life-disrupting consequences including educational failure, marijuana use disorders, illicit drug use, and mental health problems (Silins et al., 2014).

As it applies to frequent adult marijuana use in localities where marijuana use has been legalized, watchful waiting is leading to increasing numbers approaching health services seeking assistance (Fischer et al., 2020). The problem with this strategy is that health services do not have the capacity or resources to assist the increasingly large numbers with intractable disorders (Fischer et al., 2020), mental health problems (Reece & Hulse, 2020a), and disabled children (Reece & Hulse, 2020b) that are projected to be increasingly caused by legalization.

(b) Psychoeducation is effectively used as one component in universal programs in settings such as schools to prevent early age marijuana use (e.g., Faggiano et al., 2014) and as a component in screening and brief counseling interventions to reduce frequent and disordered use (e.g., Tanner-Smith et al., 2015). While psychoeducation is a necessary component, evaluation studies suggest it is not a sufficient stand-alone component compared to critical elements such as the building of social-emotional competence skills (Hodder et al., 2017).

(c) Biblio-prevention in the form of books and brochures has shown promise as a means of conveying brief behavioral messages to prevent early and frequent marijuana use (Faggiano et al., 2014). They have also been used as a service delivery format in some screening and brief counseling strategies to prevent frequent use (Tanner-Smith et al., 2015).

(d) e-Health prevention tools have been feasible to incorporate in interventions offered in tertiary education settings (Gulliver et al., 2015). However, there have been insufficient studies to assess the impacts on marijuana use.

(e) Groups are effective service delivery formats for the implementation of school-level programs to prevent early age use. Systematic reviews identify classroom (Faggiano et al., 2014; Hodder et al., 2017) and peer-led intervention group programs (Georgie et al., 2016) as effective strategies to prevent early marijuana use.

(f) Individual services are effective service delivery formats for the implementation of brief counseling interventions, which are linked to screening assessments in contexts such as secondary schools (Carney et al., 2016) and tertiary education settings (e.g., Tanner-Smith et al., 2015). Cochrane reviews of interventions for marijuana disorders and frequent use note limited evidence for the use of pharmacotherapies (Nielsen et al., 2019) but some short-term effects for psychosocial interventions (Gates et al., 2016). Psychosocial interventions of around four sessions combining motivational enhancement and cognitive-behavioral therapy reduced frequency of use and severity of dependence posttreatment (Gates et al., 2016).

11.8 Lessons Learned/Implementation

The overview presented in this chapter reveals evidence for prevention opportunities to reduce early age and frequent adult marijuana use. International trends in prevalence show rising rates of use and increased potency of the marijuana that is used. An examination of evidence-based prevention programs and policies suggests legalization as the major policy change that is currently driving increased marijuana use and harm. The potential for stepped care prevention models is outlined. Lessons learned to date are that it is feasible to implement evidence-based prevention approaches. Perhaps the most pertinent lesson from the studies summarized in this chapter is the importance of countering the popular misconception that marijuana legalization may offer benefits for reducing harms related to marijuana use. The available evidence from the nations and states that have legalized marijuana use to date now shows a clear and causal contribution to increase in frequent use and harm.

References

Asbridge, M., Hayden, J. A., & Cartwright, J. L. (2012). Acute cannabis consumption and motor vehicle collision risk: Systematic review of observational studies and meta-analysis. *BMJ, 344*, e536. https://doi.org/10.1136/bmj.e536

Carney, T., Myers, B. J., Louw, J., & Okwundu, C. I. (2016). Brief school-based interventions and behavioural outcomes for substance-using adolescents. *Cochrane Database of Systematic Reviews, 2016*(1), Art. No.: CD008969. https://doi.org/10.1002/14651858.CD008969.pub3

Catalano, R. F., Kosterman, R., Hawkins, J. D., Newcomb, M. D., & Abbott, R. D. (1996). Modeling the etiology of adolescent substance use: A test of the social development model. *Journal of Drug Issues, 26*(2), 429–455. https://doi.org/10.1177/002204269602600207

Chan, G. C., Kelly, A. B., Toumbourou, J. W., Hemphill, S. A., Young, R. M., Haynes, M. A., & Catalano, R. F. (2013). Predicting steep escalations in alcohol use over the teenage years: Age-related variations in key social influences. *Addiction (Abingdon, England), 108*(11), 1924–1932. https://doi.org/10.1111/add.12295

Chan, G. C. K., Hall, W., Freeman, T. P., Kelly, A. B., Ferris, J., & Winstock, A. (2017). User characteristics and effect profiles of butane hash oil: Findings across 20 countries. *Drug and Alcohol Dependence, 178*, 32–38. https://doi.org/10.1016/j.drugalcdep.2017.04.014

Compton, W. M., et al. (2007). Prevalence, correlates, disability, and comorbidity of DSM-IV drug abuse and dependence in the United States…. *Archives of General Psychiatry, 64*, 566–576.

Compton, W. M., Han, B., Jones, C. M., & Blanco, C. (2019). Cannabis use disorders among adults in the United States during a time of increasing use of cannabis. *Drug and Alcohol Dependence, 204*, 107468. https://doi.org/10.1016/j.drugalcdep.2019.05.008

EMCDDA. (2016). *Prevalence maps – Prevalence of drug use in Europe*. European Drug Report European Monitoring Centre for Drugs and Drug Addiction; 2016.

Faggiano, F., Minozzi, S., Versino, E., & Buscemi, D. (2014). Universal school-based prevention for illicit drug use. *Cochrane Database of Systematic Reviews, 2014*(12), Art. No.: CD003020. https://doi.org/10.1002/14651858.CD003020.pub3. Accessed 25 November 2020.

Fischer, B., Daldegan-Bueno, D., & Boden, J. M. (2020). Facing the option for the legalisation of cannabis use and supply in New Zealand: An overview of relevant evidence, concepts and considerations. *Drug and Alcohol Review, 39*(5), 555–567. https://doi.org/10.1111/dar.13087

Gates, S., McCambridge, J., Smith, L. A., & Foxcroft, D. (2006). Interventions for prevention of drug use by young people delivered in non-school settings. *Cochrane Database of Systematic Reviews, 2006*(1), Art. No.: CD005030. https://doi.org/10.1002/14651858.CD005030.pub2. Accessed 30 November 2020.

Gates, P. J., Sabioni, P., Copeland, J., Le Foll, B., & Gowing, L. (2016). Psychosocial interventions for cannabis use disorder. *Cochrane Database of Systematic Reviews, 2016*(5), Art. No.: CD005336. https://doi.org/10.1002/14651858.CD005336.pub4

Georgie, J. M., Sean, H., Deborah, M. C., Matthew, H., & Rona, C. (2016). Peer-led interventions to prevent tobacco, alcohol and/or drug use among young people aged 11–21 years: A systematic review and meta-analysis. *Addiction, 111*(3), 391–407. https://doi.org/10.1111/add.13224

Gulliver, A., Farrer, L., Chan, J. K., Tait, R. J., Bennett, K., Calear, A. L., & Griffiths, K. M. (2015). Technology-based interventions for tobacco and other drug use in university and college students: A systematic review and meta-analysis. *Addiction Science & Clinical Practice, 10*(1), 5. https://doi.org/10.1186/s13722-015-0027-4

Hall, W., Stjepanović, D., Caulkins, J., Lynskey, M., Leung, J., Campbell, G., & Degenhardt, L. (2019). Public health implications of legalising the production and sale of cannabis for medicinal and recreational use. *Lancet, 394*(10208), 1580–1590. https://doi.org/10.1016/S0140-6736(19)31789-1

Hawkins, J. D., Catalano, R. F., & Miller, J. Y. (1992). Risk and protective factors for alcohol and other drug problems in adolescence and early adulthood: Implications for substance abuse prevention. *Psychological Bulletin, 112*, 64–105.

Hemphill, S. A., Heerde, J. A., Herrenkohl, T. I., Patton, G. C., Toumbourou, J. W., & Catalano, R. F. (2011). Risk and protective factors for adolescent substance use in Washington State, United States and Victoria, Australia: A longitudinal study. *Journal of Adolescent Health, 49*(3), 312–320. https://doi.org/10.1016/j.jadohealth.2010.12.017

Hodder, R. K., Freund, M., Wolfenden, L., Bowman, J., Nepal, S., Dray, J., Kingsland, M., Yoong, S. L., & Wiggers, J. (2017). Systematic review of universal school-based 'resilience' interventions targeting adolescent tobacco, alcohol or illicit substance use: A meta-analysis. *Preventive Medicine, 100*, 248–268. https://doi.org/10.1016/j.ypmed.2017.04.003

Kelly, A. B. (2012). Perceived father's care: Protects adolescents from transitions to tobacco use at a highly vulnerable age: A short-term longitudinal study. *Mental Health and Substance Use, 5*(2), 173–181. https://doi.org/10.1080/17523281.2011.619502

Kelly, A. B., Chan, G. C. K., Toumbourou, J. W., O'Flaherty, M., Homel, R., Patton, G. C., & Williams, J. (2012). Very young adolescents and alcohol: Evidence of a unique susceptibility to peer alcohol use. *Addictive Behaviors, 37*, 414–419. https://doi.org/10.1016/j.addbeh.2011.11.038

Kelly, A. B., O'Flaherty, M., Toumbourou, J. W., Connor, J. P., Hemphill, S., & Catalano, R. F. (2011). Gender differences in the impact of families on alcohol use: A lagged longitudinal study of pre-teens. *Addiction, 106*, 1427–1436. https://doi.org/10.1111/j.1360-0443.2011.03435.x

Kelly, A. B., Chan, G. C. K., Mason, W. A., & Williams, J. W. (2015). The relationship between psychological distress and adolescent polydrug use. *Psychology of Addictive Behaviors, 29*, 787–793. https://doi.org/10.1037/adb0000068

Kelly, A. B., Weier, M., & Hall, W. D. (2018). First use of illicit drugs: The state of current knowledge. In G. Girolamo, P. McGorry, & N. Sartorius (Eds.), *Age of onset of mental disorders: Etiopatogenetic and treatment implications*. Springer International. isbn 978-3-319-72619-9.

Kelly, A. B., Rowland, B., Kuhn, R. A., Munnings, A. W., & Toumbourou, J. W. (2020). Chapter 7: High school students at risk of exclusion: Systemic approaches to reducing risk factors and strengthening protective factors. In P. Towl & S. A. Hemphill (Eds.), *Safe, supportive, and inclusive learning environments for young people in crisis and trauma: Plaiting the rope*. Routledge. isbn: 9780367243722. www.routledge.com/Safe-Supportive-and-Inclusive-Learning-Environments-for-Young-People/Towl-Hemphill/p/book/9780367243722

Kosterman, R., Bailey, J. A., et al. (2016). Marijuana legalization and parents' attitudes, use, and parenting in Washington State. *Journal of Adolescent Health, 59*(4), 450–456.

Li, H. K., Kelly, A. B., Chan, G. C. K., Toumbourou, J. W., Patton, G. C., & Williams, J. (2014). The association of puberty and young adolescent alcohol use: Do parents have a moderating role? *Addictive Behaviors, 39*, 1389–1393. https://doi.org/10.1016/j.addbeh.2014.05.006

Miech, R. A., Johnston, L. D., O'Malley, P. M., Bachman, J. G., Schulenberg, J. E., & Patrick, M. E. (2020). *Monitoring the future national survey results on drug use, 1975–2019: Volume I, secondary school students* (590 pp). Institute for Social Research, The University of Michigan.

National Academies of Sciences, Engineering, and Medicine. (2017) The health effects of cannabis and cannabinoids: The current state of evidence and recommendations for research. www.nationalacademies.org/hmd/Reports/2017/health-effects-of-cannabis-and-cannabinoids.aspx

Nielsen, S., Gowing, L., Sabioni, P., & Le Foll, B. (2019). Pharmacotherapies for cannabis dependence. *Cochrane Database of Systematic Reviews, 2019*(1), Art. No.: CD008940. https://doi.org/10.1002/14651858.CD008940.pub3

Price, J. W. (2014). Marijuana and workplace safety: An examination of urine drug tests. *Journal of Addictive Diseases, 33*(1), 24–27. https://doi.org/10.1080/10550887.2014.882729

Reece, A. S., & Hulse, G. K. (2020a). Co-occurrence across time and space of drug- and cannabinoid- exposure and adverse mental health outcomes in the National Survey of Drug Use and Health: Combined geotemporospatial and causal inference analysis. *BMC Public Health, 20*(1), 1655. https://doi.org/10.1186/s12889-020-09748-5

Reece, A. S., & Hulse, G. K. (2020b). Canadian cannabis consumption and patterns of congenital anomalies: An ecological geospatial analysis. *Journal of Addiction Medicine, 14*(5), e195–e210. https://doi.org/10.1097/ADM.0000000000000638

Rowland, B., Toumbourou, J. W., Osborn, A., Smith, R., Hall, J., Kremer, P., Kelly, A., Williams, J., & Leslie, E. (2013). A clustered randomised trial examining the effect of social marketing and community mobilisation on the age of uptake and levels of alcohol consumption by Australian adolescents: Study protocol. *BMJ Open, 3*(1), 1–8.e002423. https://doi.org/10.1136/bmjopen-2012-002423

Rowland, B., Jonkman, H., Steketee, M., Solomon, R., Solomon, S., & Toumbourou, J. W. (2019a). A cross-national comparison of the development of adolescent problem behavior: A 1-year longitudinal study in India, the Netherlands, USA and Australia. *Prevention Science*. https://doi.org/10.1007/s11121-019-01007-3

Rowland, B., Jonkman, H., Williams, J., Kremer, P., & Toumbourou, J. W. (2019b). Community variation in adolescent cannabis use in Australia and the Netherlands. *Addictive Behaviors, 90*, 204–209. https://doi.org/10.1016/j.addbeh.2018.10.027

Scholes-Balog, K. E., Hemphill, S. A., Heerde, J. A., Toumbourou, J. W., & Patton, G. C. (2020). Childhood social environmental and behavioural predictors of early adolescent onset cannabis use. *Drug and Alcohol Review, 39*(4), 384–393. https://doi.org/10.1111/dar.13077

Silins, E., Horwood, J., Patton, G. C., Fergusson, D. H., Olsson, C. A., Hutchinson, D. M., Spry, E., Toumbourou, J. W., Degenhardt, L., Swift, W., Coffey, C., Tait, R. J., Letcher, P., Copeland, J., & Mattick, R. P. (2014). Young adult sequelae of adolescent cannabis use: An integrative analysis across three Australasian Cohorts. *Lancet Psychiatry, 1*(4), 286–293. https://doi.org/10.1016/S2215-0366(14)70307-4

Smith, R., Hall, K. E., Etkind, P., & Van Dyke, M. (2018). Current marijuana use by industry and occupation – Colorado, 2014–2015. *MMWR Morbidity and Mortality Weekly Report, 67*(14), 409–413. https://doi.org/10.15585/mmwr.mm6714a1

Tanner-Smith, E. E., Steinka-Fry, K. T., Hennessy, E. A., Lipsey, M. W., & Winters, K. C. (2015). Can brief alcohol interventions for youth also address concurrent illicit drug use? Results from

a meta-analysis. *Journal of Youth and Adolescence, 44*(5), 1011–1023. https://doi.org/10.1007/s10964-015-0252-x
Toumbourou, J. W., & Catalano, R. F. (2005). Predicting developmentally harmful substance use. In T. Stockwell, P. Gruenewald, J. W. Toumbourou, & W. Loxley (Eds.), *Preventing harmful substance use: The evidence base for policy and practice* (pp. 53–66). Wiley.
Toumbourou, J. W., Olsson, C., Rowland, B., Renati, S., & Hallam, B. (2014). Health Psychology intervention in key social environments to promote adolescent health. *Australian Psychologist, 49*, 66–74. https://doi.org/10.1111/ap.12043
Toumbourou, J. W., Rowland, B., Williams, J., Smith, R., & Patton, G. C. (2019). Community intervention to prevent adolescent health behavior problems: Evaluation of communities that care in Australia. *Health Psychology, 38*(6), 536–544. https://doi.org/10.1037/hea0000735
Weier, M., Chan, G. C. K., Quinn, C., Hides, L., & Hall, W. D. (2016). *Cannabis use in 14 to 25 year old Australians 1998–2013: Technical report*. Centre for Youth Substance Abuse Research, University of Queensland.

Chapter 12
Integrated Care Approach to the Prevention of Opioid Use Disorder

Lisa M. Schainker, Maren Wright Voss, and Ashley C. Yaugher

12.1 Definition/Diagnostic Criteria

Opioids are a class of substances that include all natural, synthetic, and semisynthetic formulations (e.g., morphine, fentanyl, etc.) and include both prescription pain medications and illicit substances such as heroin (Centers for Disease Control and Prevention [CDC], 2020b; American Society of Addiction Medicine [ASAM], 2020). In the medical setting, opioids are generally used to manage acute or chronic moderate to severe pain; however, they have a high potential for misuse due to their ability to create feelings of euphoria in some individuals. Opioid misuse includes heroin use or taking opioid medications for longer durations or in higher amounts than originally prescribed, taking them to feel intoxicated, or taking someone else's prescription (National Institute on Drug Abuse [NIDA], 2020a, b). Chronic misuse can lead to the development of a substance use disorder (SUD; American Psychiatric Association [APA], 2013). SUDs can occur from continued use of a substance even when biological (physiological), social (behavioral), and psychological (cognitive) problems result from their use (APA, 2013; Cunningham et al., 2020).

Opioid use disorder (OUD) is the sixth of ten disorders categorized in the Substance-Related and Addictive Disorders section within the DSM-5 (APA, 2013). The symptoms of an OUD are indicative of a problematic pattern of opioid use (e.g., nonmedical use or using higher doses of pain medication than prescribed) which leads to clinically significant distress or impairment. In order to meet the *diagnostic criteria for OUD*, an individual must experience two or more of the following symptoms within the previous 12 months:

L. M. Schainker (✉) · M. W. Voss · A. C. Yaugher
Utah State University, Logan, UT, USA
e-mail: lisa.schainker@usu.edu; maren.voss@usu.edu; ashley.yaugher@usu.edu

W. O'Donohue, M. Zimmermann (eds.), *Handbook of Evidence-Based Prevention of Behavioral Disorders in Integrated Care*,
https://doi.org/10.1007/978-3-030-83469-2_12

1. The individual uses larger amounts or for a longer duration than initially prescribed.
2. The individual has difficulty controlling use or reducing use of opioids, often with unsuccessful attempts.
3. The individual spends a significant amount of time in pursuit of, use of, or recovery from opioid use.
4. The individual experiences cravings or urges to use opioids.
5. The individual is unable to fulfill school, home, or work duties as a result of opioid use.
6. The individual persistently uses opioids even after interpersonal or social issues directly caused by or related to opioid use.
7. The individual cannot continue activities or must decrease them (e.g., recreational, work, or important social activities) due to opioid use.
8. The individual continues to use opioids in physically dangerous situations.
9. The individual continues to use opioids despite psychological or physical issues that may be worsened or caused by opioid use.
10. The individual develops a higher tolerance (e.g., higher dose is needed to achieve intoxication or reduced physiological response with original dose, not related to medically supervised dosing) to opioids.
11. The individual develops withdrawal symptoms (e.g., negative physical and physiological effects such as muscle aches or fever, use of other/related substances to relieve symptoms, not related to medically supervised dosing) from ceasing opioid use.

OUD severity falls into one of three categories based on the number of symptoms present—mild (two to three symptoms), moderate (four to five symptoms), and severe (six or more symptoms). Additional diagnostic features include seeking opioid prescriptions from multiple providers (i.e., "doctor shopping") and seeking illicit opioids such as heroin (APA, 2013). Once diagnosed, OUD tends to be a chronic condition that lasts for decades, with individuals often experiencing periods of recovery with subsequent return to use. It is estimated that up to approximately 30% of people with OUD are able to maintain long-term recovery (APA, 2013).

12.2 Prevalence and Age of Onset

According to the 2018 National Survey on Drug Use and Health (NSDUH; SAMHSA, 2019), it is estimated that approximately 0.4% of adolescents aged 12–17 years, 0.9% of 18- to 25-year-olds, and 0.7% of adults aged 26 years or older had a diagnosable OUD in the past year—totaling two million. Generally, OUD prevalence rates have been decreasing over time across all groups. However, OUD prevalence rates have consistently been higher among young adults and then decrease with age, with much lower rates in those 65 years and older (0.09%; APA, 2013). Rates of OUD are typically higher in men compared to women (three to one for heroin and 1.5 to one for opioid prescriptions; APA, 2013). OUD affects people of all races and ethnicities; however, rates are relatively higher among Native Americans (1.25%) compared to White, Hispanic, and Asian or Pacific Islanders (0.38%, 0.39%, and 0.35%, respectively) and are relatively lower among African Americans (0.18%; APA, 2013). Although an OUD can occur at any point in the life span, symptoms often first present or become problematic in late adolescence or early adulthood (APA, 2013).

12.2.1 *Opioid Misuse and Overdose*

Compared to the number of individuals with a diagnosable OUD, the number of people who *misuse* any type of opioid is substantially higher. It is estimated that around 3.7% of the US population over the age of 12 years have misused opioids. The majority of these cases involve the misuse of prescription opioids (9.7 million), while a smaller number (745,000) involve the use of heroin (SAMHSA, 2019). Opioid misuse has become a major public health problem in the United States, with unintentional overdose deaths on the rise since the early 2000s (CDC, 2020b; Hser et al., 2017). In fact, opioids were related to almost 70% of all substance-related overdose deaths in the United States in 2017 and 2018, with increasing rates resulting from synthetic opioids such as fentanyl (CDC, 2020b; Scholl et al., 2019).

Among the different age groups, individuals in the 18–25-year group tend to have the highest rate of prescription opioid misuse (5.2%), followed by those aged 26 years or older and those aged 12 years or older on the whole (3.4% and 3.5%), while the lowest misuse of prescription opioids was seen among those aged 12–17 years (2.3%; SAMHSA, 2019). The most commonly misused opioid pain medications were hydrocodone products (1.8%, e.g., Lortab®, Vicodin®), followed by oxycodone (1.2%, e.g., OxyContin®, Percocet®), buprenorphine, and fentanyl products in individuals 12 years and older (SAMHSA, 2019).

12.3 Risk Factors for OUD

Major categories of risk for OUD and opioid misuse include sociodemographic factors, levels of pain, opioid medication-related factors, genetics, environmental, psychosocial, family history, psychopathology, and history of other SUDs (Ballantyne, 2007; Katz et al., 2013; Kaye et al., 2017a; Liebschutz et al., 2010). Having only one risk factor from one of these categories is not likely to increase an individual's chances of developing an OUD; however, a combination of risk factors, especially if they are psychosocial, genetic, and opioid medication-related in nature, is likely to increase someone's risk (Kaye et al., 2017a). As an example, someone with a family history of SUD and a co-occurring mental health disorder who is on long-term opioid therapy (LOT) that is not well structured or monitored is at increased risk for developing an OUD (Ballantyne, 2007). The following research findings illustrate different types of risk factors that have been associated with OUD and/or opioid misuse:

- Having a higher number of adverse childhood experiences (ACEs) has been associated with both illicit substance use and prescription opioid misuse (Dube et al., 2003; Merrick et al., 2020).
- Approximately 5% of chronic pain patients on LOT develop OUD (i.e., iatrogenic addiction), and approximately 20–30% of patients misuse prescribed opioids (Higgins et al., 2018; Vowles et al., 2015). Being prescribed multiple pain medications from multiple providers is also a risk factor (Boscarino et al., 2010; Pino et al., 2019).
- Having higher levels of subjective pain, multiple pain complaints, and pain-related limitations have been associated with being at higher risk for opioid misuse (Jamison et al., 2009; Liebschutz et al., 2010; Sullivan et al., 2010).
- Past or current co-occurring mental health disorders, such as depression (e.g., major depressive disorder), anxiety (e.g., generalized anxiety disorder, panic disorder), posttraumatic stress disorder (PTSD), and any other mood disorder (e.g., bipolar disorder) as well as the use of psychotropic medications (Boscarino et al., 2010; Kaye et al., 2017a; Martins et al., 2012; Van Rijswijk et al., 2019) in associated with a higher risk for OUD.
- Prior history of a SUD or polysubstance use (i.e., use of multiple substances at the same time), particularly use of tobacco products, opioids, alcohol, and other substances (Boscarino et al., 2010; John et al., 2019; Kaye et al., 2017a; Liebschutz et al., 2010), is strongly associated with OUD and opioid misuse.

Research suggests that individuals in rural areas may have earlier and increased access to prescription opioids due to increased reports of pain. Unfortunately, due to limited treatment availability in these areas, they may also experience higher rates of opioid misuse than those who live in urban areas (García et al., 2019; Keyes et al., 2014; Monnat & Rigg, 2016). Initiation of substance use in early adolescence, including exposure to opioid prescriptions for injuries or dental procedures, may predispose an individual to develop a subsequent SUD or experience a fatal overdose (Compton et al., 2019; Dash et al., 2018; Hudgins et al., 2019; Nguyen et al., 2020; McCabe et al., 2016; Schroeder et al., 2019). Finally, of NSDUH participants who reported misusing prescription opioids in the last year, over 50% reported that they got them from family or friends (SAMHSA, 2019). This access to opioids and the increased risk associated with it is noteworthy, particularly for youth and those with a history of SUD.

12.4 Effective Screening of Opioid Use Disorder

SUDs, such as OUD, are believed to develop over time after multiple episodes of misuse, which means that it is critical to identify emerging OUDs and to use evidence-based interventions as early as possible to stop the addiction process (McLellan, 2017). Given this, the US Preventive Services Task Force and SAMHSA now recommend screening all adults aged 18 years and older for illicit substance use and prescription medication misuse, especially when more comprehensive diagnostic services, effective care, and treatment can be provided to patients (Patnode et al., 2020; SAMHSA, 2020).

Primary care providers (PCPs) are uniquely positioned to identify unhealthy substance use, including the misuse of opioids, because they serve as the frontline of the healthcare system, they have long-standing relationships with patients that allow them to see changes in health over time, and patients may perceive less stigma when substance misuse is addressed in this setting (Donroe et al., 2020). Unlike almost all other substances that fall under the SUD section of the DSM-5, opioids are prescribed by providers for the legitimate treatment of acute and chronic pain. Before PCPs decide to put a patient on LOT, they need to discuss the treatment options with the patient and weigh the risks and benefits for that individual (Dowell et al., 2016). A set of tools has been designed to aid in this process by predicting the likelihood that a patient will go on to develop an OUD if LOT is prescribed. Once patients are on LOT, providers may use yet another type of screening tool to determine if a patient is engaging in aberrant drug-related behaviors (ADRBs), which may be indicative of an OUD or put them at risk for experiencing a life-threatening overdose. In the section that follows, specific opioid misuse screening tools are discussed that PCPs can use with general patient populations and chronic pain patients being considered for LOT and to monitor for ADRB in patients on LOT.

12.4.1 General Patient Population

Brief screening for substance misuse during annual visits creates an opportunity for providers to open a dialogue with patients about their behavioral health (Gryczynski et al., 2017) and may help patients open up to their provider about their unhealthy substance use and ask for help (SAMHSA, 2020). In addition to universal screening for illicit substance use and prescription drug misuse, SAMHSA also recommends screening for alcohol misuse (i.e., binge drinking) and tobacco use because these are both related to increased risk for OUD (SAMHSA, 2020). When providers have information about a patient's substance use, they can take steps to avoid harmful interactions with medications they prescribe (Smith et al., 2010), and it opens the door to discuss the risks of mixing substances such as opioids with alcohol, which increases the risk of death from an overdose (Warner-Smith et al., 2001).

Table 12.1 Brief screening tools for use in general population patients

Author and year	Name	Description	Format
Tiet et al. (2015) and Tiet et al. (2019)	Screen of Drug Use (SoDU)	Designed to identify use of any substance in adults Designed for use in PCP setting	Two total items Number of days used and number of days used more than intended in the past 12 months
Smith et al. (2010)	Single-Item Drug Screener	Designed to identify both illicit and prescription drug misuse in adults Designed for use in PCP setting	One item Clinician administered
Gryczynski et al. (2017)	Tobacco, Alcohol, Prescription Medication, and Other Substance Use (TAPS-1)	Part 1-rapid screen of two-step tool Designed to identify unhealthy substance use in adults Designed for use in PCP setting Best used with part 2 as follow-up	Four items addressing frequency of use in past 12 months Self-administered and clinician-administered options
McNeely et al. (2015)	Substance Use Brief Screen (SUBS)	Designed to identify unhealthy use of tobacco, alcohol, and illicit and prescription drug misuse Designed for use in PCP setting	Four items with response options of 3 or more days, 1–2 days, never in the past 12 months Computer self-administered
NIDA (2012)	NIDA Quick Screen/ Modified Alcohol, Smoking, and Substance Involvement Screening Test (NM ASSIST)	Designed to identify unhealthy use of tobacco, alcohol, and illicit and prescription drug misuse Designed for use in general medical settings	One item with four parts Computer-assisted self-administered Found here: https://archives.drugabuse.gov/nmassist/

The majority of screening tools validated for use with general patient populations in primary care settings include items related to alcohol, tobacco, illicit substance use, and prescription drug misuse. Universal screening tools often do not indicate the specific illicit or prescription drug being misused; however, research suggests that general substance misuse screenings can be used to detect opioid misuse. For example, the Screen of Drug Use (SoDU) has been shown to identify OUD in a primary care setting even though the questions do not specifically ask about opioid misuse (Tiet et al., 2019). Some of the brief screening tools available for use in adult populations in the primary care setting are provided in Table 12.1.

Research is ongoing to develop new screening tools or modify administration methods of existing screening tools to make them more feasible to implement in real-world primary care settings. For example, the myTAPS (Adam et al., 2019) is a modified version of the TAPS that can be administered on a tablet while patients are waiting for their appointment. Some advantages of computer-assisted screening tools are that they can be programmed with skip patterns so patients are only asked follow-up questions about the substances they report using, scoring can be automated, and results can be integrated into a patient's electronic health record (Cheatle & Barker, 2014).

According to SAMHSA's OUD Treatment Improvement Protocol (2020), if an initial brief screening is positive for any substance misuse, a more comprehensive follow-up assessment should be conducted to determine if opioids are being misused and to what extent. The comprehensive assessment should first determine whether a patient meets the diagnostic criteria for OUD and how severe it is using the DSM-5 criteria. Other important data to collect include medical, mental health, substance use, treatment, social, and family histories as well as results from appropriate laboratory tests and a physical exam. PCPs should determine if and when to bring a behavioral healthcare provider (BHP) in to assist with the nonmedical aspects of the assessment based on their comfort, training, and capacity to provide the level of support necessary if a brief screening is positive.

12.4.2 Screening for Chronic Pain Patients Before Initiating Long-Term Opioid Therapy

The second set of screening tools are designed to help PCPs identify chronic pain patients who are at higher risk for developing an OUD if LOT were to be the treatment of choice. These tools tend to be a little longer and address many of the risk factors for OUD that were discussed in Sect. 12.3 of this chapter, including history of substance misuse, prescription adherence, mental health issues, and history of social problems. A urine drug test (UDT) or other lab test(s) as well as a check of the state's prescription drug monitoring program (PDMP) should be conducted before putting patients on LOT to confirm self-reported substance use and identify

Table 12.2 Screening tools to use before initiating LOT

Author and year	Name	Description	Format
Butler et al. (2008) and Butler et al. (2009)	Screener and Opioid Assessment for Patients with Pain-Revised (SOAPP-R)	Designed to predict ADRB among chronic pain patients prior to initiation of LOT	24 items Self-administered Five-point Likert scale
Adams et al. (2004)	Pain Medication Questionnaire (PMQ)	Designed to predict ADRB among chronic pain patients prior to initiation of LOT	26 items Self-administered Five-point Likert scale

inconsistencies (Dowell et al., 2016; Hamill-Ruth et al., 2013). Two example screening tools that patients can complete before starting on LOT are described in Table 12.2.

The results of these tools should be used to stratify patients into low-, moderate-, and high-risk groups for the purpose of determining the appropriate level of care, support, and monitoring they need while on LOT (Cheatle & Barker, 2014; Kaye et al., 2017b). The results should not be used as a means to deny LOT in higher risk patients when it could improve their quality of life and the benefits outweigh the potential risks (Kaye et al., 2017b). Cheatle and Barker (2014) and Kaye et al. (2017b) have suggested that patients in the low-risk group should receive routine follow-up (e.g., about every 3 months) and can be managed by a PCP, moderate-risk patients should be seen about once a month and be comanaged by the PCP and BHP, and patients in the high-risk group (i.e., patients currently misusing opioids or who have an untreated psychiatric disorder) should either be referred to an interdisciplinary pain center or to a behavioral health center.

12.4.3 Screening for Patients on Long-Term Opioid Therapy

A recent systematic review suggests that on average, 20–30% of chronic pain patients misuse their opioid prescriptions and between 8% and 10% develop OUD (Vowles et al., 2015). Given the high prevalence rates that some research has shown for opioid misuse and OUD among chronic pain patients on LOT, providers may elect to screen these patients periodically to assess current ADRBs and/or to assess compliance with their LOT protocol. The frequency of screening administration and other monitoring methods (e.g., UDT, medical record audits) should be tailored to each patient based on their baseline risk level and indications of ongoing adherence (Kaye et al., 2017a, b). Example screening tools for patients on LOT are described in Table 12.3.

The results of a patient's screenings and UDT can be used to help PCPs determine whether more or less restrictive opioid prescribing and monitoring practices

Table 12.3 Screening tools for patients on LOT

Butler et al. (2007)	Current Opioid Misuse Measure (COMM)	Designed to identify OUD and current opioid misuse in chronic pain patients on LOT	17 items Self-administered
McCaffrey et al. (2019)	Current Opioid Misuse Measure (COMM-9)	Designed to identify current aberrant opioid-related behavior in chronic pain patients on LOT	Nine items Self-administered Computerized
Jamison et al. (2014)	Opioid Compliance Checklist (OCC)	Monitoring opioid adherence in chronic pain patients on LOT	Eight items Self-administered

need to be implemented and whether the patient requires additional support or therapeutic services from a BHP.

12.5 Review of Evidence: What Is Evidence-Based Prevention for OUD?

Currently, there is a lack of prevention strategies for OUD in adult populations that have been evaluated rigorously enough to be considered evidence based. Compton et al. (2019) highlighted this as a current gap that needs to be addressed along with finding ways to move emerging research on preventive interventions into clinical practice. The best evidence comes from randomized controlled trials of preventive interventions implemented during early adolescence in family and school settings that enhance protective factors and reduce risk factors for substance misuse, including opioids (SAMHSA & Office of the Surgeon General, 2016; Spoth et al., 2013).

Prevention of OUD requires a combination of approaches that include system-level strategies (e.g., PDMPs, installing prescription drop-off boxes), provider-level strategies (e.g., following CDC opioid prescribing guidelines, using UDTs before and during LOT), and patient-level strategies (e.g., selecting non-opioid pain management methods when possible, skill-building programs). Compton et al. (2019) argued that while policy and practice approaches are needed to reduce exposure to both prescription and illicit opioids in adults, expanding the use of primary prevention practices with children and adolescents should also be part of a comprehensive strategy. Implementing practices that build resilience and reduce risk factors for initiating substance use during this key developmental period should reduce the number of individuals who develop an OUD and the related consequences. Finally, although it is outside the scope of the present chapter, there is substantial evidence that medication-assisted therapy (MAT) is a safe and effective treatment for OUD and that it can help individuals achieve remission and maintain recovery (SAMHSA, 2020).

12.6 Universal, Selective, and Indicated Prevention for OUD

The Institute of Medicine, now known as the National Academy of Medicine, defined three categories of preventive interventions—universal, selective, and indicated (US HHS, 2018). In the context of OUD, universal interventions would be used with the general public, selective interventions would be used with individuals who are at a higher risk for developing OUD, and indicated interventions would be used with high-risk individuals who have started to misuse opioids but have not been officially diagnosed. Table 12.4 provides examples of the populations that

Table 12.4 Example OUD prevention strategies that fall under each type of intervention

Type	Example populations targeted	Strategy
Universal	Youth who have not initiated substance use Patients with no known risks for OUD Healthcare providers	Use public awareness-building campaigns to educate the public on the risks of opioid misuse Implement programs that enhance protective factors and reduce risk factors for SUD starting in childhood (see SAMHSA & Office of Surgeon General, 2016, for list) Use brief screening for SUD annually in adults Use PDMP and CDC guidelines for prescribing opioids
Selective	Patients with past or current SUD Patients with a mental health condition Chronic pain patients on LOT Patients with any combination of risk factors discussed in Sect. 12.3	Use brief screening specifically for OUD Use more comprehensive follow-up assessment and UDT before prescribing opioids Use universal precautions approach PCPs and BHPs ensure coexisting SUD and/or mental health conditions are managed while on LOT Implement adherence monitoring strategy that matches patient's identified level of risk for OUD
Indicated	Chronic pain patients taking higher or more frequent doses of opioid medications Patients whose UTD indicates illicit opioids or nonmedical use of prescription opioids	Use of more restrictive prescribing practices (e.g., weekly refills) and more frequent office visits Use more frequent UTDs to monitor severity of misuse Conduct regular screenings/assessments to ascertain whether patient meets diagnostic criteria for OUD Naloxone prescription/training to prevent overdose

might be addressed by each type of intervention as well as some examples of strategies that would fit within each type.

12.7 Stepped Care Model for OUD Prevention

An integrated approach for prevention of OUD should involve careful collaboration between PCPs and BHPs who can provide many of the more intensive services offered through a stepped care model. OUD is complex and requires both medical and behavioral health support and monitoring once a positive screen occurs. Therefore, providers should share concerning signs and symptoms of opioid misuse with BHPs and should keep BHPs aware of any changes in chronic pain patients' opioid medication regimen. The recommended prevention activities will vary at each step depending on whether their risk for OUD is related to being a chronic pain patient or if their risk for opioid misuse is due to other factors. In the sections that follow, we discuss how watchful waiting, psychoeducation, biblio-prevention, e-health tools, group interventions, and individual interventions can be used for patients that fall into each of these groups:

Group 1: General population patients who screen positively for illicit opioid use or prescription opioid misuse
Group 2: Chronic pain patients whose screening indicates a higher risk for OUD and who are being considered for LOT
Group 3: Chronic pain patients on LOT whose screening indicates ADRB and/or indications of OUD are occurring

12.7.1 Watchful Waiting

Watchful waiting suggests understanding that a risk for opioid misuse and OUD is always imminent, but intervention is not currently warranted. Watchful waiting is indicated when there is a low level of concern for developing OUD based on screening results and other physical and psychological evaluations. This is likely the wary stance taken by many medical professionals who have become aware of opioid overdose risks. As a prevention plan decision for patients in Group 1, watchful waiting could be appropriate when opioid misuse has not been confirmed or if misuse appears to result from a misunderstanding of prescribed doses, as might happen with older adult patients who manage multiple medications.

Watchful waiting when used with patients in Groups 2 and 3 could include practicing the universal precautions approach of prescribing opioid therapy recommended by Gourlay et al. (2005). Because of the nature of physical dependence and the risks of iatrogenic addiction when on LOT, regular screenings should be part of the watchful waiting approach in a stepped care model (see Table 12.4). The nature of opioid overdose risk suggests that watchful waiting is not a safe approach unless it is included alongside other screening, self-management, and opioid safety measures.

12.7.2 Psychoeducation

There are two types of psychoeducation that can be used in primary care settings to address risk for OUD—information about opioid risks, safety, and overdose prevention and information about alternative pain management approaches. Both types of education can be offered as best practice management for all general population patients showing no indication of opioid misuse or OUD at screening as well as for Group 1, 2, and 3 patients.

12.7.2.1 Psychoeducation for Opioid Safety

Group 1 patients: Education on safe usage, storage, and disposal of opioids is a universal prevention practice that can be reinforced in primary care and behavioral health settings. NIDA (2020a, b) has recommended that patients prescribed opioids receive information on medication safety that includes the following instructions:

- Follow the directions as explained on the label or by the pharmacist.
- Be aware of potential interactions with other substances, including alcohol.
- Never stop or change a dosing regimen without first discussing it with the doctor.
- Never use another person's prescription and never give your prescription medications to others.
- Store prescription stimulants, sedatives, and opioids safely.

Psychoeducational materials to promote opioid safety are available through federal and state agencies. The information, brochures, and signage can be incorporated into patient waiting room reading materials or used as part of direct patient education. In 2015, the US government launched initiatives to reduce opioid misuse and overdose, and opioid safety education has been promoted through public health outreach campaigns (NIDA, 2020b). The Food and Drug Administration's (FDA, 2019) "Remove the Risk" campaign includes an online toolkit with accessible psychoeducational materials like fact sheets that can be included in patient education: https://www.fda.gov/drugs/ensuring-safe-use-medicine/safe-opioid-disposal-remove-risk-outreach-toolkit.

Additional educational materials are available through the federally funded State Targeted Response to the Opioid Crisis grants that included public message campaigns about opioid safety and psychoeducational materials with slogans like "Use Only as Directed," "Speak Out, Opt Out, Throw Out," and "Don't add addiction to injury." Supportive psychoeducational materials can be found at https://knowrx.org/ and https://useonlyasdirected.org/.

Group 2 and 3 patients: Additional psychoeducational materials that may be beneficial for patients in Groups 2 and 3 are overdose education for the patient and their family members. Overdose safety education includes understanding what an overdose is (i.e., repressed breathing, lack of oxygen to the brain, brain damage at 3–5-minute oxygen loss, followed by death). Overdose education then includes information on risk factors and signs of an opioid overdose (unresponsive, slow breathing, blue lips/fingertips, pinpoint pupils), information about rescue medicines (naloxone), and information on how to access and use rescue medications. NIDA has produced a video for clinicians on how to provide overdose prevention education: https://www.drugabuse.gov/videos/overdose-prevention-education-clinicians-treating-patients-opioid-use-disorder.

12.7.2.2 Psychoeducation for Pain Management

Group 1 patients: If a general population patient who is not on LOT has a positive screen, providers may want to take extra time to discuss how to generally promote a healthy lifestyle that reduces known physical and psychological risk factors for SUD. Providers using an integrated care approach will promote emotional well-being and stress reduction when screenings indicate higher risk. The integrated approach also stresses communication, referrals, and collaborative practices between both PCPs and BHPs, which support an individualized and wholistic plan for pain management.

Group 2 patients: Using an integrated health model approach with patients considering LOT for pain management should incorporate a multimodal and individualized approach to best address patient pain and reduce the risks of iatrogenic causes of OUD. Strong meta-analytic review suggests that multidisciplinary approaches to pain management are evidence-based and more effective than usual care (Kamper et al., 2015) as well as being considered an OUD prevention best practice.

The HHS Pain Management Best Practices Inter-Agency Task Force identified multimodal pain management strategies in four domains (Kamper et al., 2015). The Task Force recommendations include *restorative therapies* (e.g., physiotherapy and exercise), *interventional approaches* (e.g., trigger point injections and neuromodulation), *behavioral approaches* (e.g., psychological and cognitive therapies), *and complementary health therapies* (e.g., massage, yoga, etc.). Some of the multidisciplinary approaches are strategies that can be administered through self-care and psychoeducation, while others must be offered in clinic, or through referrals to behavioral health practitioners or specialists and are discussed below in the stepped care level for individualized care.

The Task Force-recommended pain management strategies that can be offered through psychoeducation include exercise, cold therapy, heat therapy, behavioral pain management, cognitive pain management, mindfulness, stress reduction, yoga, tai chi, and spirituality: https://www.hhs.gov/sites/default/files/pmtf-final-report-2019-05-23.pdf. These psychoeducational and self-management approaches, when incorporated with interventional and professionally supported strategies used in treatment settings, are more likely to address the full spectrum of biopsychosocial factors impacting pain and will reduce long-term risks of OUD compared to LOT alone for pain management.

For Group 2 patients who screen at a higher risk for iatrogenic addiction or in cases where the provider and patient are weighing pros and cons before going on LOT, there are decision-making resources and tools available to assist patients in deciding whether LOT is the ideal treatment option. The informational resources have been formatted as fact sheets, patient-provider agreements, or decision-making tools. These decision-making tools provide information on potential side effects, risk of OUD, tolerance over time, contraindicated medications and medical diagnoses, medication alternatives, safe storage and disposal, and how to recognize the signs of misuse. CDC and FDA resources for shared decision-making can be found here: https://www.cdc.gov/drugoverdose/pdf/AHA-Patient-Opioid-Factsheet-a.pdf and https://www.fda.gov/media/114694/download.

Group 3: Psychoeducation for patients already on LOT who screen positively for ADRB can be taken a step further to ensure patients have the information they need to be aware of the risks of SUD. Both PCPs and BHPs can provide information to patients about opioid dependence. The US Department of Health and Human Services has developed a suite of information and resources to help providers, patients, and family members identify the risks, assess needs, and access resources for opioid safety. The available information at https://www.hhs.gov/opioids/ addresses the continuum from prevention to treatment and recovery. The primary goal for patients in this group is to ensure that support is provided alongside referrals to better assess their level of risk.

For individuals already showing signs of OUD, a more targeted, shared decision-making tool for considering medication-assisted treatment options is available as well: https://mat-decisions-in-recovery.samhsa.gov/ and other tools are under development (Bart et al., 2020). The American Society of Addiction Medicine has also created fact sheets for providers and patients that summarize medications approved by the FDA to treat OUD: https://www.asam.org/docs/default-source/advocacy/mat-factsheet.pdf?sfvrsn=e0b743c2_2.

12.7.3 Biblio-prevention

Biblio-prevention can offer patients more comprehensive insights into the risks and benefits of opioid use than in handouts typically offered in psychoeducation. Readings can be used in a group setting with someone leading a book group at the clinic, or patients can be assigned readings as part of patient education. Some patients may be interested to learn more about opioids, and book readings can be included as part of a comprehensive treatment plan. Benefits of bibliotherapy include its low cost and low levels of stigma as patients complete readings on their own time. There is research indicating the general effectiveness of bibliotherapy approaches to improve outcomes in addressing psychiatric disorders in general (Evans et al., 1999; Kar, 2012), though no studies show specific effectiveness for OUD prevention.

In a review of the use of bibliotherapy for alcohol use disorders (AUD), it was found that the use of books and readings was more effective for reducing risks in problem drinkers than those who were determined to be at higher risk of AUD (Apodaca & Miller, 2003). Research also indicates that bibliotherapy for AUD is more effective when combined with brief counseling (World Health Organization, 1996) and should be used in combination with other types of prevention strategies. While there is not yet an evidence base for using bibliotherapy in OUD prevention, these studies suggest that bibliotherapy techniques might be similarly beneficial if used before OUD has fully developed. As with psychoeducation, book-based interventions can focus either on managing pain to reduce the need for LOT or they can directly focus on understanding and avoiding potential harms and reducing the risks of opioid treatment (i.e., risk of overdose).

Group 1, 2, and 3 patients: For all patients, whether or not they are currently being considered for LOT, bibliotherapy to prevent OUD provides benefits related to learning about the risks of using illicit opioids or misusing prescription opioids and how opioids can affect the brain and change response patterns. When patients are currently on or are considering LOT, bibliotherapy may be helpful in the multimodal treatment of pain conditions. The American Chronic Pain Association (ACPA) has a list of helpful reading materials, with over 100 recommended books: https://www.theacpa.org/external-resources/helpful-reading/ https://www.theacpa.org/external-resources/helpful-reading/. The recommended bibliotherapy topics range from direct readings on pain management to emotional management, journaling, mind and body awareness, diet and exercise, relationships, sexuality, and self-care. The wide-ranging ACPA-recommended reading list indicates the importance of tailoring bibliotherapy to the circumstances and needs of individual patients.

For a more targeted approach to helping patients see the risks of LOT, a number of best-selling books in the past decade have highlighted the opioid crisis in the United States. Additionally, the CDC has taken a storytelling approach to prevention in providing vignettes of individuals impacted by OUD in their "Rx Awareness" campaign (https://www.cdc.gov/rxawareness/). For patients screened at highest risk, targeted materials to understand the risks of OUD might be considered helpful, though there is not yet an evidence base to support their use.

12.7.4 E-Health Tools

Opioid risk prevention is an issue for everyone because of the high frequency of pain conditions and the potential risks of LOT. For these reasons, e-health is an excellent way to engage patients in Groups 1, 2, and 3. There are e-health interventions targeted to clinical staff to ensure safe opioid practices and to improve patient treatment. As with all prevention strategies in the stepped care model, the focus of e-health tools can be on either safe opioid use or pain education and management.

12.7.4.1 E-Health for Opioid Harm Prevention

A 2020 scoping review identified multiple technologies that can be used to address OUD, with some of these relevant to preventing opioid misuse (Nuamah et al., 2020). Of 72 apps identified that dealt with opioid use specifically, 43% were directed toward clinicians and 32% were designed for patients and/or the public, with 16 offering patient education. Mobile app functions included guidance on treatment modalities, opioid conversions, professional support, education, peer support, withdrawal support, and patient monitoring.

The *most* downloaded apps in Nuamah's review (5000+ downloads, excluding dosing calculators) include:

- CDC's Opioid Guideline Mobile App for clinicians with a free download: https://www.cdc.gov/drugoverdose/prescribing/app.html. The CDC recognizes that while treating chronic pain is complex, accessing the guidelines for best practice opioid prescribing should not be. This app includes a Morphine Milligram Equivalent (MME) calculator, prescribing guideline summaries, and an interactive motivational interviewing feature.
- FEND (Full Energy, No Drugs) by Preventum for patients and family members with a free download: https://wearefend.org/. The FEND app provides opioid education, how to respond to an opioid crisis, and connects community members to prevention initiatives.

12.7.4.2 E-Health for Pain Education and Management

Like psychoeducation and bibliotherapy, the cost of e-health is low, and the advantages include easy access to resources and little to no stigma related to their use. For these reasons, e-health can be recommended for Group 1, 2, and 3 patients. An online systematic review found 939 available apps for pain management and reviewed the 19 apps that met inclusion criteria (Devan et al., 2019). The authors identified three selected pain management apps including Curable (https://www.curablehealth.com/), PainScale-Pain Diary and Coach (https://www.painscale.com/), and SuperBetter (https://www.superbetter.com/), which included eight out of 14 of the author's best practice criteria for pain self-management.

The Veteran's Administration has provided a tool for resilience building called the Acceptance and Commitment Therapy (ACT) Coach that is particularly useful for increasing wellness in Group 1 patients as well as patients dealing with pain. It includes the basics of ACT, mindfulness practices, coping strategies, and interactive tools to track progress (https://www.ptsd.va.gov/appvid/mobile/actcoach_app_public.asp). For Group 2 and 3 patients dealing with pain and/or on LOT, Macquarie University in Sydney, Australia, has developed a free online pain education course. It includes five online research-based pain management lessons with do-it-yourself guides to understand and practice skills (https://ecentreclinic.org/?q=PainCourse). E-health is a rapidly evolving industry, and as such, the available e-health tools cannot be listed comprehensively and have not been fully evaluated for efficacy in OUD prevention. The tools identified above serve as examples of the available options that may be of benefit to patients.

12.7.5 *Group Interventions*

While many therapy and support groups exist to support individuals in recovery after a SUD has been diagnosed (i.e., NA, AA, etc.), prevention-focused groups are also available to support pain treatment and prevent opioid misuse and OUD. Prevention-focused groups address managing pain in a way that minimizes the risks of OUD and opioid harms. As Group 1 patients are not likely to need treatment for pain management, this level of stepped care may be considered more appropriate for those in Group 2 or 3.

Many of the group-format resources are offered as community classes and resources rather than as a billable treatment modality. The resource-focused pain support groups can be divided into those that provide information on coping skills, patient pain education, or social support (Keefe et al., 2018). There is also evidence to support the use of billable group therapy modalities to treat pain conditions, particularly with cognitive behavioral therapy (CBT) approaches for pain management. This approach is recommended in the best practice pain management guidelines and is a type of stepped care that can be considered opioid harm prevention (U.S. Department of Health and Human Services, 2019).

12.7.5.1 Pain Support Groups

The ACPA has established a network of pain support groups to provide support, validation, and education in basic pain management and life skills to chronic pain sufferers. As of 2021, there were 30 participating states with access to ACPA support groups (https://www.theacpa.org/about-us/support-groups/). The US Pain Foundation offers support groups in 13 states as of 2021 (https://painconnection.org/support-groups/). There is also a 12-step organization for pain support, Chronic Pain Anonymous (https://chronicpainanonymous.org/), with face-to-face meetings available in some states. Some free online support groups are available, which may increase access for patients living in more geographically isolated areas.

12.7.5.2 Pain Education Groups

The Stanford-based Chronic Disease Self-Management Program has been recommended by the CDC and HealthyPeople.gov as an evidence-based program to deliver information on self-help tools to manage chronic conditions, including pain (Brady et al., 2011). The Self-Management Resource Center has developed a manual and a version of the workshop series specifically for chronic pain management. The workshops are taught by trained facilitators as a six-week series at community centers, hospitals, or clinics and can be found in most states (https://www.selfmanagementresource.com/programs/find-a-workshop/).

12.7.5.3 Group Therapy

CBT has been shown to be an effective treatment for pain management and can be offered in group settings (Garland & Howard, 2018; Hofmann et al., 2012; National Academy of the Sciences, 2011). CBT teaches cognitive flexibility to help patients manage pain symptoms, teaches cognitive-based coping strategies, and helps individuals learn active management strategies vs. passive reactions to pain sensations.

Resources for learning more about CBT for pain management can be found at:

- Beck Institute CBT for pain resources: https://beckinstitute.org/%D1%81ondition/chronic-pain/
- Association for Behavioral and Cognitive Therapies-approved resources: http://www.abct.org/SHBooks/
- National Alliance on Mental Illness list of self-help cognitive therapy resources: https://www.nami.org/Blogs/NAMI-Blog/November-2016/Discovering-New-Options-Self-Help-Cognitive-Behav

12.7.6 *Individual Interventions*

In a stepped care model, individual-level intervention modalities are the most time-intensive approaches available and would be appropriate when other options have been tried with limited success or the severity of the patient's opioid misuse requires a more intensive approach.

Recommended individual intervention modalities for managing the pain response include restorative therapies (e.g., bracing, therapeutic exercise, massage therapies), behavioral therapies (e.g., behavior therapy, CBT, ACT, mindfulness-based stress reduction [MBSR], emotional awareness therapy, biofeedback/relaxation/hypnotherapy), and complementary therapies (e.g., acupuncture, massage therapies, yoga, tai chi), though there is some crossover in these classifications (Kamper et al., 2015). Individual interventions can be offered in the primary care setting or referred to another provider as indicated. One of the primary goals of these interventions is to lessen the need for LOT, thereby reducing the patient's exposure to opioids and the likelihood that they will develop an OUD.

12.7.6.1 Compliance Enhancement

Some specific primary care-based interventions have been developed to prevent SUDs. While evidence conclusively supports the use of brief screenings of individuals for unhealthy substance use in primary care settings (Patnode et al., 2020; US Preventative Services Task Force, 2004), the evidence for brief interventions in primary care is less clear. A brief intervention that has shown promise for alcohol-related issues that may be relevant to preventing OUD is brief behavioral compliance enhancement treatment (Johnson et al., 2003). It is delivered over 3 months in 10–20-min sessions in a primary care setting and emphasizes medication use with realistic expectations of success. However, a 10–45-min brief intervention following a screening for unsafe substance use implemented in a primary care setting was not efficacious in a randomized clinical trial (Saitz et al., 2014). More research is needed, but current evidence suggests that when the patient is showing indications of OUD, referral to a BHP for specialized assessment and counseling is a better option than trying to manage the issue in the primary care setting (Cheatle & Barker, 2014; Gourlay et al., 2005; Kaye et al., 2017b).

Medical management is another type of compliance enhancement that is more intensive but can still be offered in primary care settings. The method focuses on education, adherence to opioid medication protocols, and support to reduce iatrogenic addiction risk. The method was derived from brief interventions to address problematic alcohol use. Medical management sessions take 40–60 minutes and are delivered over a period of 4 months in nine sessions. While the method was shown to successfully prevent AUD (Anton et al., 2006), it is not clear that this would work to prevent OUD.

12.7.6.2 Mental Health Support

An important consideration in planning tailored OUD prevention plans is to address comorbidities of mental health and SUD when addressing chronic pain. Care should be taken, as there is a tendency to stigmatize patients with chronic pain as complainers and malingerers because many pain conditions are not well understood (Collier, 2018). Stigma is a challenge for patients and families and has been cited as a barrier to adequate care (Kamper et al., 2015). While there should be no assumption of co-occurring mental health conditions or SUD, chronic pain, depression, and anxiety are linked through changes in the opioid functioning of the amygdala, with approximately 50% of chronic pain patients reporting clinical depression (Wells, 2011). Additionally, there is evidence that individuals with psychiatric disorders are more likely to experience problematic opioid use when treated for chronic pain (Van Rijswijk et al., 2019). The overlap is so common it has been recommended that clinicians treating chronic pain either be proficient in treating common psychiatric disorders or be willing to refer as needed (Wells, 2011). Considering a natural overlap between psychological symptoms and chronic pain-induced symptoms, it is important to address the behavioral health needs of patients with appropriate treatment and referrals to BHPs (Kamper et al., 2015).

12.8 Lessons Learned/Implementation Primary Care Settings for OUD

Primary care settings have been suggested as ideal for identifying and managing OUD; however, there are still barriers that keep many PCPs from wanting to address the general topic of SUDs in their practice. These include discomfort with discussing the topic, lacking knowledge about diagnostic procedures, and having the time, resources, and capacity to both identify an emerging OUD and help the patient manage it. This in combination with the high proportion of patients seen in the primary care setting who seek treatment for pain has created an issue that would be solved with an integrated care approach.

PCPs and BHPs should work in partnership so that the PCP monitors physical health by conducting medical exams, UDTs, and medical treatment as indicated, while the BHP conducts diagnostic interviews and determines the best course of prevention in the stepped care model. Ideally, after a positive OUD screen has occurred, a BHP would administer a more intensive diagnostic interview and determine what kind of support the patient might need related to their opioid misuse or OUD. The BHP is also able to partner with the PCP during LOT to use CBT or other counseling approaches that may help reduce the perceived pain level of the patient, thereby potentially reducing their need for opioid medications.

The goal of a stepped care approach is to provide the minimal amount of preventive intervention necessary tailored to the needs of the patient. However, when this approach is applied to the prevention of OUD, providers need to be mindful that patients at higher risk for experiencing an OUD are not necessarily the same patients that will experience an overdose (Volkow et al., 2018). Therefore, while the stepped care approach can be effective, the potential deadly consequence of an opioid overdose means that more intensive intervention may be needed at any time and all patients, even those identified as being at lower risk for OUD, should be carefully monitored. Finally, it is very important for both PCPs and BHPs to ensure that they use non-stigmatizing approaches and language as they interact and work with patients who are experiencing indications of OUD. This is recommended as part of a “whole-person treatment” approach, and research has shown that it can improve patient outcomes (CDC, 2020a, b; Corrigan et al., 2005; da Silveira et al., 2018; Wu et al., 2011).

References

Adam, A., Schwartz, R. P., Wu, L. T., Subramaniam, G., Laska, E., Sharma, G., Mili, S., & McNeely, J. (2019). Electronic self-administered screening for substance use in adult primary care patients: Feasibility and acceptability of the tobacco, alcohol, prescription medication, and other substance use (myTAPS) screening tool. *Addiction Science & Clinical Practice, 14*(1), 39. https://doi.org/10.1186/s13722-019-0167-z

Adams, L. L., Gatchel, R. J., Robinson, R. C., Polatin, P., Gajraj, N., Deschner, M., & Noe, C. (2004). Development of a self-report screening instrument for assessing potential opioid medication misuse in chronic pain patients. *Journal of Pain and Symptom Management, 27*(5), 440–459. https://doi.org/10.1016/j.jpainsymman.2003.10.009

American Psychiatric Association. (2013). *Diagnostic and statistical manual of mental disorders (DSM-5®)*. American Psychiatric Publishing.

American Society of Addiction Medicine. (2020). The ASAM national practice guideline for the treatment of opioid use disorder: 2020 focused update. *Journal of Addiction Medicine, 14*(2S), 1–91. https://doi.org/10.1097/ADM.0000000000000633

Anton, R. F., O'Malley, S. S., Ciraulo, D. A., Cisler, R. A., Couper, D., Donovan, D. M., Gastfriend, D. R., Hosking, J. D., Johnson, B. A., LoCastro, J. S., Longabaugh, R., Mason, B. J., Mattson, M. E., Miller, W. R., Pettinati, H. M., Randall, C. L., Swift, R., Weiss, R. D., Williams, L. D., … COMBINE Study Research Group. (2006). Combined pharmacotherapies and behavioral interventions for alcohol dependence: The COMBINE study: A randomized controlled trial. *JAMA, 295*(17), 2003–2017. https://doi.org/10.1001/jama.295.17.2003

Apodaca, T. R., & Miller, W. R. (2003). A meta-analysis of the effectiveness of bibliotherapy for alcohol problems. *Journal of Clinical Psychology, 59*(3), 289–304. https://doi.org/10.1002/jclp.10130

Ballantyne, J. C. (2007). Opioid analgesia: Perspectives on right use and utility. *Pain Physician, 10*(3), 479–491.

Bart, G. B., Saxon, A., Fiellin, D. A., McNeely, J., Muench, J. P., Shanahan, C. W., Huntley, K., & Gore-Langton, R. E. (2020). Developing a clinical decision support for opioid use disorders: A NIDA center for the clinical trials network working group report. *Addiction Science & Clinical Practice, 15*(1), 4. https://doi.org/10.1186/s13722-020-0180-2

Boscarino, J. A., Rukstalis, M., Hoffman, S. N., Han, J. J., Erlich, P. M., Gerhard, G. S., & Stewart, W. F. (2010). Risk factors for drug dependence among out-patients on opioid therapy in a large US health-care system. *Addiction, 105*(10), 1776–1782. https://doi.org/10.1111/j.1360-0443.2010.03052.x

Brady, T. J., Murphy, L., Beauchesne, D., Bhalakia, A., Chervin, D., Daniels, B., Greenberg, M., House, M., & O'Colmain, B. (2011). *Sorting through the evidence for the arthritis self-management program and the chronic disease self-management program. Executive Summary of ASMP/CDSMP Meta-Analysis* (p. 24). CDC.

Butler, S. F., Budman, S. H., Fernandez, K. C., Houle, B., Benoit, C., Katz, N., & Jamison, R. N. (2007). Development and validation of the current opioid misuse measure. *Pain, 130*(1–2), 144–156. https://doi.org/10.1016/j.pain.2007.01.014

Butler, S. F., Fernandez, K., Benoit, C., Budman, S. H., & Jamison, R. N. (2008). Validation of the revised screener and opioid assessment for patients with pain (SOAPP-R). *The Journal of Pain, 9*(4), 360–372. https://doi.org/10.1016/j.jpain.2007.11.014

Butler, S. F., Budman, S. H., Fernandez, K. C., Fanciullo, G. J., & Jamison, R. N. (2009). Cross-validation of a screener to predict opioid misuse in chronic pain patients (SOAPP-R). *Journal of Addiction Medicine, 3*(2), 66–73. https://doi.org/10.1097/ADM.0b013e31818e41da

Centers for Disease Control and Prevention. (2020a). *Rx awareness*. https://www.cdc.gov/rxawareness/

Centers for Disease Control and Prevention. (2020b, March 19). *Opioid basics*. https://www.cdc.gov/drugoverdose/opioids/index.html

Cheatle, M. D., & Barker, C. (2014). Improving opioid prescription practices and reducing patient risk in the primary care setting. *Journal of Pain Research, 7*, 301–311. https://doi.org/10.2147/JPR.S37306

Collier, R. (2018). "Complainers, malingerers and drug-seekers" – The stigma of living with chronic pain. *CMAJ Canadian Medical Association Journal, 190*(7), E204–E205. https://doi.org/10.1503/cmaj.109-5553

Compton, W. M., Jones, C. M., Baldwin, G. T., Harding, F. M., Blanco, C., & Wargo, E. M. (2019). Targeting youth to prevent later substance use disorder: An underutilized response to the US opioid crisis. *American Journal of Public Health, 109*(S3), S185–S189. https://doi.org/10.2105/AJPH.2019.305020

Corrigan, P., Kerr, A., & Knudsen, L. (2005). The stigma of mental illness: Explanatory models and methods for change. *Applied and Preventive Psychology, 11*(3), 179–190. https://doi.org/10.1016/j.appsy.2005.07.001

Cunningham, C., Edlund, F. M. J., Fishman, M., Gordon, D. A. J., Jones, D. H. E., Langleben, D., & Woodworth, A. (2020) The ASAM National Practice Guideline for the Treatment of Opioid Use Disorder: Focused Update. https://www.asam.org/docs/default-source/quality-science/npg-jam-supplement.pdf?sfvrsn=a00a52c2_2

da Silveira, P. S., Casela, A. L. M., Monteiro, E. P., Ferreira, G. C. L., de Freitas, J. V. T., Machado, N. M., Noto, A. R., & Ronzani, T. M. (2018). Psychosocial understanding of self-stigma among people who seek treatment for drug addiction. *Stigma and Health, 3*(1), 42–52. https://doi.org/10.1037/sah0000069

Dash, G. F., Wilson, A. C., Morasco, B. J., & Feldstein Ewing, S. W. (2018). A model of the intersection of pain and opioid misuse in children and adolescents. *Clinical Psychological Science, 6*(5), 629–646. https://doi.org/10.1177/2167702618773323

Devan, H., Farmery, D., Peebles, L., & Grainger, R. (2019). Evaluation of self-management support functions in apps for people with persistent pain: Systematic review. *JMIR mHealth and uHealth, 7*(2), e13080. https://doi.org/10.2196/13080

Donroe, J. H., Bhatraju, E. P., Tsui, J. I., & Edelman, E. J. (2020). Identification and management of opioid use disorder in primary care: An update. *Current Psychiatry Reports, 22*(5), 23. https://doi.org/10.1007/s11920-020-01149-0

Dowell, D., Haegerich, T. M., & Chou, R. (2016). CDC guideline for prescribing opioids for chronic pain – United States, 2016. *JAMA, 315*(15), 1624–1645. https://doi.org/10.1001/jama.2016.1464

Dube, S. R., Felitti, V. J., Dong, M., Chapman, D. P., Giles, W. H., & Anda, R. F. (2003). Childhood abuse, neglect, and household dysfunction and the risk of illicit drug use: The adverse childhood experiences study. *Pediatrics, 111*(3), 564–572. https://doi.org/10.1542/peds.111.3.564

Evans, K., Tyrer, P., Catalan, J., Schmidt, U., Davidson, K., Dent, J., Tata, P., Thornton, S., Barber, J., & Thompson, S. (1999). Manual-assisted cognitive-behaviour therapy (MACT): A randomized controlled trial of a brief intervention with bibliotherapy in the treatment of recurrent deliberate self-harm. *Psychological Medicine, 29*(1), 19–25. https://doi:10.1017/S003329179800765X

Food and Drug Administration. (2019). *Press release: FDA launches public education campaign to encourage safe removal of unused opioid pain medicines from homes*. Retrieved January 3, 2021 at https://www.fda.gov/news-events/press-announcements/fda-launches-public-education-campaign-encourage-safe-removal-unused-opioid-pain-medicines-homes

García, M. C., Heilig, C. M., Lee, S. H., Faul, M., Guy, G., Iademarco, M. F., Hempstead, K., Raymond, D., & Gray, J. (2019). Opioid prescribing rates in nonmetropolitan and metropolitan counties among primary care providers using an electronic health record system – United States, 2014–2017. *MMWR Morbidity Mortality Weekly Report, 68*(2), 25–30. https://doi.org/10.15585/mmwr.mm6802a1

Garland, E. L., & Howard, M. O. (2018). Mindfulness-based treatment of addiction: Current state of the field and envisioning the next wave of research. *Addiction Science & Clinical Practice, 13*(1), 14. https://doi.org/10.1186/s13722-018-0115-3

Gourlay, D. L., Heit, H. A., & Almahrezi, A. (2005). Universal precautions in pain medicine: A rational approach to the treatment of chronic pain. *Pain Medicine, 6*(2), 107–112. https://doi.org/10.1111/j.1526-4637.2005.05031.x

Gryczynski, J., McNeely, J., Wu, L. T., Subramaniam, G. A., Svikis, D. S., Cathers, L. A., Sharma, G., King, J., Jelstrom, E., Nordeck, C. D., Sharma, A., Mitchell, S. G., O'Grady, K. E., & Schwartz, R. P. (2017). Validation of the TAPS-1: A four-item screening tool to identify unhealthy substance use in primary care. *Journal of General Internal Medicine, 32*(9), 990–996. https://doi.org/10.1007/s11606-017-4079-x

Hamill-Ruth, R. J., Larriviere, K., & McMasters, M. G. (2013). Addition of objective data to identify risk for medication misuse and abuse: The inconsistency score. *Pain Medicine (Malden, Mass.), 14*(12), 1900–1907. https://doi.org/10.1111/pme.12221

Higgins, C., Smith, B. H., & Matthews, K. (2018). Incidence of iatrogenic opioid dependence or abuse in patients with pain who were exposed to opioid analgesic therapy: A systematic review and meta-analysis. *British Journal of Anaesthesia, 120*(6), 1335–1344. https://doi.org/10.1016/j.bja.2018.03.009

Hofmann, S. G., Asnaani, A., Vonk, I. J., Sawyer, A. T., & Fang, A. (2012). The efficacy of cognitive behavioral therapy: A review of meta-analyses. *Cognitive Therapy and Research, 36*(5), 427–440. https://doi.org/10.1007/s10608-012-9476-1

Hser, Y. I., Mooney, L. J., Saxon, A. J., Miotto, K., Bell, D. S., Zhu, Y., Liang, D., & Huang, D. (2017). High mortality among patients with opioid use disorder in a large healthcare system. *Journal of Addiction Medicine, 11*(4), 315–319. https://doi.org/10.1097/ADM.0000000000000312

Hudgins, J. D., Porter, J. J., Monuteaux, M. C., & Bourgeois, F. T. (2019). Prescription opioid use and misuse among adolescents and young adults in the United States: National survey study. *PLoS Medicine, 16*(11), e1002922. https://doi.org/10.1371/journal.pmed.1002922A

Jamison, R. N., Link, C. L., & Marceau, L. D. (2009). Do pain patients at high risk for substance misuse experience more pain? A longitudinal outcomes study. *Pain medicine (Malden, Mass.), 10*(6), 1084–1094. https://doi.org/10.1111/j.1526-4637.2009.00679.x

Jamison, R. N., Martel, M. O., Edwards, R. R., Qian, J., Sheehan, K. A., & Ross, E. L. (2014). Validation of a brief opioid compliance checklist for patients with chronic pain. *The Journal of Pain, 15*(11), 1092–1101. https://doi.org/10.1016/j.jpain.2014.07.007

John, W. S., Zhu, H., Mannelli, P., Subramaniam, G. A., Schwartz, R. P., McNeely, J., & Wu, L. T. (2019). Prevalence and patterns of opioid misuse and opioid use disorder among primary care patients who use tobacco. *Drug and Alcohol Dependence, 194*, 468–475. https://doi.org/10.1016/j.drugalcdep.2018.11.011

Johnson, B. A., Ait-Daoud, N., Bowden, C. L., DiClemente, C. C., Roache, J. D., Lawson, K., & Ma, J. Z. (2003). Oral topiramate for treatment of alcohol dependence: a randomised controlled trial. *The Lancet, 361*(9370), 1677–1685. https://doi.org/10.1016/S0140-6736(03)13370-3

Kamper, S. J., Apeldoorn, A. T., Chiarotto, A., Smeets, R. J., Ostelo, R. W., Guzman, J., & van Tulder, M. W. (2015). Multidisciplinary biopsychosocial rehabilitation for chronic low back pain: Cochrane systematic review and meta-analysis. *BMJ (Clinical Research ed.), 350*, h444. https://doi.org/10.1136/bmj.h444

Kar, N. (2012). Bibliotherapy in psychiatric practice. *The Orissa Journal of Psychiatry, 19*, 25–29.

Katz, C., El-Gabalawy, R., Keyes, K. M., Martins, S. S., & Sareen, J. (2013). Risk factors for incident nonmedical prescription opioid use and abuse and dependence: Results from a longitudinal nationally representative sample. *Drug and Alcohol Dependence, 132*(1–2), 107–113. https://doi.org/10.1016/j.drugalcdep.2013.01.010

Kaye, A. D., Jones, M. R., Kaye, A. M., Ripoll, J. G., Galan, V., Beakley, B. D., Calixto, F., Bolden, J. L., Urman, R. D., & Manchikanti, L. (2017a). Prescription opioid abuse in chronic pain: An updated review of opioid abuse predictors and strategies to curb opioid abuse: Part 1. *Pain Physician, 20*(2S), S93–S109.

Kaye, A. D., Jones, M. R., Kaye, A. M., Ripoll, J. G., Jones, D. E., Galan, V., Beakley, B. D., Calixto, F., Bolden, J. L., Urman, R. D., & Manchikanti, L. (2017b). Prescription opioid abuse in chronic pain: An updated review of opioid abuse predictors and strategies to curb opioid abuse: Part 2. *Pain Physician, 20*(2S), S111–S133.

Keefe, F. J., Beaupre, P. M., Rumble, M. E., Kelleher, S. A., & Van Denburg, A. N. (2018). Group therapy for patients with chronic pain. In D. C. Turk & R. J. Gatchel (Eds.), *Psychological approaches to pain management: A practitioner's handbook* (pp. 205–229). The Guilford Press.

Keyes, K. M., Cerdá, M., Brady, J. E., Havens, J. R., & Galea, S. (2014). Understanding the rural-urban differences in nonmedical prescription opioid use and abuse in the United States. *American Journal of Public Health, 104*(2), e52–e59. https://doi.org/10.2105/AJPH.2013.301709

Liebschutz, J. M., Saitz, R., Weiss, R. D., Averbuch, T., Schwartz, S., Meltzer, E. C., Claggett-Borne, E., Cabral, H., & Samet, J. H. (2010). Clinical factors associated with prescription drug use disorder in urban primary care patients with chronic pain. *The Journal of Pain, 11*(11), 1047–1055. https://doi.org/10.1016/j.jpain.2009.10.012

Martins, S. S., Fenton, M. C., Keyes, K. M., Blanco, C., Zhu, H., & Storr, C. L. (2012). Mood and anxiety disorders and their association with non-medical prescription opioid use and prescription opioid-use disorder: Longitudinal evidence from the national epidemiologic study on alcohol and related conditions. *Psychological Medicine, 42*(6), 1261–1272.

McCabe, S. E., Veliz, P., & Schulenberg, J. E. (2016). Adolescent context of exposure to prescription opioids and substance use disorder symptoms at age 35: A national longitudinal study. *Pain, 157*(10), 2173–2178. https://doi.org/10.1097/j.pain.0000000000000624

McCaffrey, S. A., Black, R. A., Villapiano, A. J., Jamison, R. N., & Butler, S. F. (2019). Development of a brief version of the Current Opioid Misuse Measure (COMM): The COMM-9. *Pain medicine (Malden, Mass.), 20*(1), 113–118. https://doi.org/10.1093/pm/pnx311

McLellan, A. T. (2017). Substance misuse and substance use disorders: Why do they matter in healthcare? *Transactions of the American Clinical and Climatological Association, 128*, 112–130.

McNeely, J., Strauss, S. M., Saitz, R., Cleland, C. M., Palamar, J. J., Rotrosen, J., & Gourevitch, M. N. (2015). A brief patient self-administered substance use screening tool for primary care: Two-site validation study of the Substance Use Brief Screen (SUBS). *The American Journal of Medicine, 128*(7), 784.e9–784.e19. https://doi.org/10.1016/j.amjmed.2015.02.007

Merrick, M. T., Ford, D. C., Haegerich, T. M., & Simon, T. (2020). Adverse childhood experiences increase risk for prescription opioid misuse. *The Journal of Primary Prevention, 41*(2), 139–152. https://doi.org/10.1007/s10935-020-00578-0

Monnat, S. M., & Rigg, K. K. (2016). Examining rural/urban differences in prescription opioid misuse among US adolescents. *The Journal of Rural Health, 32*(2), 204–218.

National Academy of the Sciences. (2011). *Relieving pain in America: A blueprint for transforming prevention, care, education, and research* (22553896). Washington DC: National Academy of Sciences. https://doi.org/10.17226/13172

National Institute on Drug Abuse. (2012, March 1). *Resource guide: Screening for drug use in general medical settings*. Retrieved January 28, 2021 from https://archives.drugabuse.gov/publications/resource-guide-screening-drug-use-in-general-medical-settings

National Institute on Drug Abuse. (2020a, May 27). *Prescription opioids drug facts*. Retrieved January 19, 2021, from https://www.drugabuse.gov/publications/drugfacts/prescription-opioids

National Institute on Drug Abuse. (2020b, June 3). *How can prescription drug misuse be prevented?*. Retrieved January 3, 2021, from https://www.drugabuse.gov/publications/research-reports/misuse-prescription-drugs/how-can-prescription-drug-misuse-be-prevented

Nguyen, A. P., Glanz, J. M., Narwaney, K. J., & Binswanger, I. A. (2020). Association of opioids prescribed to family members with opioid overdose among adolescents and young adults. *JAMA Network Open, 3*(3), e201018.

Nuamah, J., Mehta, R., & Sasangohar, F. (2020). Technologies for opioid use disorder management: Mobile app search and scoping review. *JMIR mHealth and uHealth, 8*(6), e15752.

Patnode, C. D., Perdue, L. A., Rushkin, M., Dana, T., Blazina, I., Bougatsos, C., Grusing, S., O'Connor, E. A., Fu, R., & Chou, R. (2020). Screening for unhealthy drug use: Updated evidence report and systematic review for the US Preventive Services Task Force. *JAMA, 323*(22), 2310–2328. https://doi.org/10.1001/jama.2019.21381

Pino, C. A., Covington, M., & Wakeman, S. E. (2019). *Prescription of opioids for acute pain in opioid naïve patients*. UpToDate, Inc. https://www.uptodate.com/contents/prescription-of-opioids-for-acute-pain-in-opioid-naive-patients/print

Saitz, R., Palfai, T. P., Cheng, D. M., Alford, D. P., Bernstein, J. A., Lloyd-Travaglini, C. A., Meli, S. M., Chaisson, C. E., & Samet, J. H. (2014). Screening and brief intervention for drug use in primary care: The ASPIRE randomized clinical trial. *JAMA, 312*(5), 502–513.

Scholl, L., Seth, P., Kariisa, M., Wilson, N., & Baldwin, G. (2019). Drug and opioid-involved overdose deaths—United States, 2013–2017. *Morbidity and Mortality Weekly Report, 67*, 1419–1427. https://doi.org/10.15585/mmwr.mm675152e1

Schroeder, A. R., Dehghan, M., Newman, T. B., Bentley, J. P., & Park, K. T. (2019). Association of opioid prescriptions from dental clinicians for US adolescents and young adults with subsequent opioid use and abuse. *JAMA Internal Medicine, 179*(2), 145–152. https://doi.org/10.1001/jamainternmed.2018.5419

Smith, P. C., Schmidt, S. M., Allensworth-Davies, D., & Saitz, R. (2010). A single-question screening test for drug use in primary care. *Archives of Internal Medicine, 170*(13), 1155–1160. https://doi.org/10.1001/archinternmed.2010.140

Spoth, R., Trudeau, L., Shin, C., Ralston, E., Redmond, C., Greenberg, M., & Feinberg, M. (2013). Longitudinal effects of universal preventive intervention on prescription drug misuse: Three randomized controlled trials with late adolescents and young adults. *American Journal of Public Health, 103*(4), 665–672. https://doi.org/10.2105/AJPH.2012.301209

Substance Abuse and Mental Health Services Administration (SAMHSA). (2019). *Key substance use and mental health indicators in the United States: Results from the 2018 National Survey on Drug Use and Health* (HHS Publication No. PEP19-5068, NSDUH Series H-54). Center for Behavioral Health Statistics and Quality, Substance Abuse and Mental Health Services Administration. Retrieved from https://www.samhsa.gov/data/

Substance Abuse and Mental Health Services Administration (SAMHSA). (2020). *Medications for opioid use disorder* (Treatment Improvement Protocol (TIP) Series 63. Publication No. PEP20-02-01-006). SAMHSA. Retrieved from https://store.samhsa.gov/product/TIP-63-Medications-for-Opioid-Use-Disorder-Full-Document/PEP20-02-01-006

Substance Abuse and Mental Health Services Administration (SAMHSA) & Office of the Surgeon General. (2016). *Facing addiction in America: The surgeon general's report on alcohol, drugs, and health*. US Department of Health and Human Services. Retrieved from https://addiction.surgeongeneral.gov/sites/default/files/surgeon-generals-report.pdf

Sullivan, M. D., Von Korff, M., Banta-Green, C., Merrill, J. O., & Saunders, K. (2010). Problems and concerns of patients receiving chronic opioid therapy for chronic non-cancer pain. *Pain, 149*(2), 345–353. https://doi.org/10.1016/j.pain.2010.02.037

Tiet, Q. Q., Leyva, Y. E., Moos, R. H., Frayne, S. M., Osterberg, L., & Smith, B. (2015). Screen of drug use: Diagnostic accuracy of a new brief tool for primary care. *JAMA Internal Medicine, 175*(8), 1371–1377. https://doi.org/10.1001/jamainternmed.2015.2438

Tiet, Q. Q., Leyva, Y. E., & Moos, R. H. (2019). Screen of drug use: Diagnostic accuracy for opioid use disorder. *Drug and Alcohol Dependence, 198*, 176–179. https://doi.org/10.1016/j.drugalcdep.2019.01.044

US Department of Health and Human Services (HHS). (2019, May). *Pain management best practices inter-agency task force report: Updates, gaps, inconsistencies, and recommendations*. Retrieved from HHS website: https://www.hhs.gov/ash/advisory-committees/pain/reports/index.html

US Department of Health and Human Services (HHS), Office of the Surgeon General. (2018). *Facing addiction in America: The surgeon General's spotlight on opioids*. HHS. Retrieved from https://addiction.surgeongeneral.gov/sites/default/files/OC_SpotlightOnOpioids.pdf

US Preventive Services Task Force. (2004). Screening and behavioral counseling interventions in primary care to reduce alcohol misuse: Recommendation statement. *Annals of Internal Medicine, 140*(7), 554. https://doi.org/10.7326/0003-4819-140-7-200404060-00016

Van Rijswijk, S. M., van Beek, M. H. C. T., Schoof, G. M., Schene, A. H., Steegers, M., & Schellekens, A. F. (2019). Iatrogenic opioid use disorder, chronic pain and psychiatric comorbidity: A systematic review. *General Hospital Psychiatry, 59*, 37–50. https://doi.org/10.1016/j.genhosppsych.2019.04.008

Volkow, N., Benveniste, H., & McLellan, A. T. (2018). Use and misuse of opioids in chronic pain. *Annual Review of Medicine, 69*, 451–465. https://doi.org/10.1146/annurev-med-011817-044739

Vowles, K. E., McEntee, M. L., Julnes, P. S., Frohe, T., Ney, J. P., & van der Goes, D. N. (2015). Rates of opioid misuse, abuse, and addiction in chronic pain: A systematic review and data synthesis. *Pain, 156*(4), 569–576. https://doi.org/10.1097/01.j.pain.0000460357.01998.f1

Warner-Smith, M., Darke, S., Lynskey, M., & Hall, W. (2001). Heroin overdose: Causes and consequences. *Addiction, 96*(8), 1113–1125. https://doi.org/10.1046/j.1360-0443.2001.96811135.x

Wells, L. T. (2011). Pain and addiction. In B. A. Johnson (Ed.), *Addiction medicine: Science and practice* (p. 1139). Springer. https://doi.org/10.1007/978-1-4419-0338-9

WHO Brief Intervention Study Group. (1996). A cross-national trial of brief interventions with heavy drinkers. *American Journal of Public Health, 86*(7), 948–955. https://doi.org/10.2105/ajph.86.7.948

Wu, L. T., Blazer, D. G., Li, T. K., & Woody, G. E. (2011). Treatment use and barriers among adolescents with prescription opioid use disorders. *Addictive Behaviors, 36*(12), 1233–1239. https://doi.org/10.1016/j.addbeh.2011.07.033

Chapter 13
Prevention Strategies for Unhealthy Alcohol Use

Brandon Hunley, Brendan Willis, and Monica Zepeda

It is widely known that unhealthy alcohol use and alcohol use disorder continue to be prevalent and consequential problems for the US healthcare system. Estimates place the lifetime prevalence of Alcohol Use Disorders at 29%, although this rate can be even higher for certain at-risk groups, such as among veterans where the lifetime prevalence rate approaches 32% (Williams et al., 2018; Grant et al., 2015). The consequences of alcohol dependence and alcohol use disorders are also manifold, including increased risk for serious health problems including liver cirrhosis and cancer, fetal alcohol syndrome, and motor vehicle accidents (Friedmann, 2013; WHO, 2001). Additionally, it is estimated that around 13% of total healthcare costs in most Western countries is spent in the treatment of alcohol-related disease and injuries (Rehm et al., 2009).

However, despite the widespread nature and impact of unhealthy alcohol use, it is important to note that effective treatment for alcohol misuse or alcohol dependence is not impossible (Oryna & Karpinets, 2013). Furthermore, effective, evidence-based strategies exist not only for treating alcohol dependence but also for detection and early intervention of alcohol-related issues (Babor et al., 2017). Treatment of alcohol misuse is multifaceted, and, accordingly, there are multiple methods and approaches. These include brief single-session interventions to longer, intensive treatment modalities, such as cognitive behavioral therapies and pharmacological options (Ray et al., 2019). For the purposes of this chapter on prevention, however, we will focus on certain methods that align best within a prevention modality, concentrating mainly on early stages of misuse or even when only risk factors such as early-onset drinking (i.e., by the age of 12) or using alcohol as a coping mechanism are present.

B. Hunley · B. Willis (✉) · M. Zepeda
Psychology Department, University of Nevada, Reno, NV, USA
e-mail: bhunley@nevada.unr.edu; brendanwillis@nevada.unr.edu; monicaz@nevada.unr.edu

W. O'Donohue, M. Zimmermann (eds.), *Handbook of Evidence-Based Prevention of Behavioral Disorders in Integrated Care*,
https://doi.org/10.1007/978-3-030-83469-2_13

One model that has become more accepted in the field as a means of quickly intervening and preventing alcohol use disorders is the Screening, Brief Intervention, and Referral to Treatment (SBIRT) approach (Babor et al., 2007). A great deal of research has been devoted for more than a decade into the SBIRT model (Babor et al., 2007). This approach focuses on identifying, reducing, and preventing problematic alcohol use via the identification of individuals exhibiting risky use (i.e., use that is currently not meeting the threshold dependence) and intervening with those individuals before more specialized treatment is needed (Rahm, et al., 2015). The options for intervention that correlate with these risk assessments are brief intervention, brief treatment, and referral to more intensive treatment. Because of our focus on prevention, the brief intervention component of SBIRT fits our emphasis best. SBIRT emphasizes the importance of early detection via clinician interviews or other screening measures and the impact of brief interventions that can potentially be delivered in the primary care setting.

The SBIRT model has found acceptance as an effective model for guiding prevention and treatment efforts in the realm of alcohol use disorder and related issues (Babor et al., 2007). However, a number of factors may influence the ability to successfully implement the SBIRT model. A clinician must be aware of the risk factors such as stress levels or the use of alcohol as a coping strategy that are associated with increased alcohol use (Rahm et al., 2015; Madras et al., 2008). Additionally, a clinician should be aware of methods for assessing alcohol use such as the Alcohol Use Disorders Identification Test (AUDIT; WHO, 2001) in order to better inform treatment planning and decision-making (Johnson et al., 2013; Spear et al., 2016). Therefore, the goals of this chapter are to outline risk factors that can help alert a clinician to presentations where a patient may benefit from a brief alcohol-related intervention. Additionally, this chapter will describe methods of screening for alcohol-related issues to aid in early detection and provide more information on the SBIRT model itself to facilitate the creation of practical treatment programs that can hopefully be deployed in a preventative capacity. In integrated care settings in particular, it will be vital to incorporate the participation of behavioral health specialists in the creation of a prevention program.

13.1 Diagnostic Criteria

Accurate diagnosis is key when working with any behavioral health issue. Especially in the context of prevention, it is important to know when issues have progressed to the point where a diagnoseable disorder has developed, as this information can be key to treatment planning. The *Diagnostic and Statistical Manual of Mental Disorders, 5th Edition* states that alcohol use disorder is defined by the following criteria (American Psychiatric Association, 2013, p. 490–497):

A. A problematic pattern of alcohol use leading to clinically significant impairment or distress, as manifested by at least two of the following, occurring within a 12-month period:

1. Alcohol is often taken in larger amounts or over a longer period than was intended.
2. There is a persistent desire or unsuccessful efforts to cut down or control alcohol use.
3. A great deal of time is spent in activities necessary to obtain alcohol, use alcohol, or recover from its effects.
4. Craving or a strong desire or urge to use alcohol.
5. Recurrent alcohol use resulting in a failure to fulfill major role obligations at work, school, or home.
6. Continued alcohol use despite having persistent or recurrent social or interpersonal problems caused or exacerbated by the effects of alcohol.
7. Important social, occupational, or recreational activities are given up or reduced because of alcohol use.
8. Recurrent alcohol use in situations in which it is physically hazardous.
9. Alcohol use is continued despite knowledge of having a persistent or recurrent physical or psychological problem that is likely to have been caused or exacerbated by alcohol.
10. Tolerance, as defined by either of the following:
    (a) A need for markedly increased amounts of alcohol to achieve intoxication or desired effect.
    (b) A markedly diminished effect with continued use of the same amount of alcohol.
11. Withdrawal, as manifested by either of the following:
    (a) The characteristic withdrawal syndrome for alcohol, which can be defined as experiencing increased hand tremors, insomnia, autonomic hyperactivity, nausea or vomiting, transient hallucinations or illusions, psychomotor agitation, anxiety, and seizures, developing within several hours to a few days after the reduction or cessation of alcohol use.
    (b) Alcohol (or a closely related substance, such as a benzodiazepine) is taken to relieve or avoid withdrawal symptoms.

For additional information regarding the diagnostic criteria for alcohol use disorder, we refer readers to pages 490–503 in the *Diagnostic and Statistical Manual of Mental Disorders, 5th Edition* (American Psychiatric Association, 2013).

13.2 Common Risk Factors

When examining alcohol use disorder (see criteria above) and the role of integrated care in possible intervention, it is crucial to understand possible risk factors that may indicate which patients are prone to alcohol misuse. In this section we will present risk factors associated with the development of alcohol misuse as an understanding of these risk factors will aid in the determination of which patients may require intervention. The following risk factors are not all encompassing, but their importance is highlighted because of their recurrence in the literature and is the most relevant for consideration by primary care physicians. These include early onset of alcohol use, stressful life events or trauma, family history, and psychological factors including impulsivity, aggression, drinking motivation, stress, depression, and bipolar disorder.

13.2.1 Early Onset of Alcohol Use

The use of alcohol at an early age, defined as starting by the age of 12, has been shown to lead to greater alcohol misuse later in life (Grant et al., 2001; Trenz et al., 2012; Parker et al., 1996). Of course, not everyone who drinks alcohol early in life will misuse alcohol in the future; however, it is significant for healthcare providers to be aware and consider that those who start drinking younger have a higher likelihood of alcohol use that turns into problematic use.

In a longitudinal study on age of alcohol use onset and its relationship to alcohol misuse, researchers analyzed data from The National Longitudinal Survey of Labor Market Experience in Youth (NLSY) and found that in 1989 and 1994, for each year that the age of alcohol use was delayed, the odds of alcohol misuse decreased by 5% and 9%, respectively (Grant et al., 2001). To further highlight the consistency of these findings, in a study focused specifically on alcohol, those who used alcohol (i.e., began using alcohol in greater quantities than just a sip or a taste) the first time before the age of 14 had a lifetime dependency rate of 47%, while those who used alcohol for the first time after the age of 21 had a lifetime dependency rate of only 9% (Hingson et al., 2006).

Since early use is associated with higher rates of problematic use, early detection of use in adolescents and younger adults is critical for preventing future misuse. Morrison and Flegel (2016) recommend that providers inquire about alcohol use and provide the following recommendations to facilitate the assessment process when working with children and adolescents who might be at risk for alcohol-related issues:

1. Delay asking about alcohol use until rapport has been established with the patient, usually partway through the interview (i.e., try not to start with asking about alcohol use).

2. When possible, ask about alcohol use when parents are not present in the exam room.
3. As much as possible, focus on obtaining frequency and amount of alcohol used, the valued effect of use (i.e., to ease social anxiety, the feeling of being intoxicated, etc.), the consequences of use, and the means of financing alcohol use.

Morrison and Flegel (2016) also recommend patience when assessing for alcohol use in children and adolescents. Young patients may be resistant to questions or refuse to answer; therefore working to build a sense of trust is paramount to facilitating the conversation. Additionally, where possible, reminding young patients that what they say can, within legal guidelines, stay confidential may also assist in facilitating the assessment of alcohol use.

Understanding a patient's past alcohol use patterns, specifically the age that the patient started drinking alcohol, will help to determine the likelihood of future misuse and will inform further steps for prevention or treatment. Finding methods to educate youth on the dangers of misuse and establishing strategies to delay age of first use of alcohol may decrease the likelihood for future misuse later in life. A number of online resources exist to help with this goal, such as the following:

1. The Science of Addiction: Genetics and the Brain (Genetic Science Learning Center, 2013)
   (a) Available at: https://learn.genetics.utah.edu/content/addiction/
2. Substance Resource Center (American Academy of Child and Adolescent Psychiatry, 2019)
   (a) Available at: https://www.aacap.org/aacap/Families_and_Youth/Resource_Centers/Substance_Use_Resource_Center/Home.aspx
3. ABCT Fact Sheet (Association for Behavioral and Cognitive Therapies, 2021)[1]
   (a) Available at: https://www.abct.org/Information/?m=mInformation&fa=fs_alcohol

Early use may be a symptom of other psychiatric disorders and may not play a direct causal role in developing alcohol misuse. However, regardless of the reason for the association between early-onset and later alcohol misuse, early onset is still an important indicator for health professionals to use to assess patients. Psychological factors and their association with alcohol misuse will be discussed later in the chapter.

[1] Note the ABCT website (www.abct.org) can also be used to locate more specialized psychotherapy providers when needed.

13.2.2 Stressful Life Events/Trauma

Several studies have demonstrated the link between stressful life events (SLE) and trauma and substance use disorders which specifically include alcohol; according to the Substance Abuse and Mental Health Services Administration (2020), the link between trauma or other negative life events and substance use disorders has become increasingly accepted by researchers (Cole et al., 2019; Enoch, 2011; Lo & Cheng, 2007). While researchers use various terms to discuss the effects of negative life events, there is considerable overlap; for the scope of this chapter, we will use SLE and trauma interchangeably to indicate broadly a significant traumatic negative event or a series of traumatic events that occurred which led to long-term negative psychological effects. Looking into pathways that SLE and trauma might influence addiction and misuse, Enoch (2011) found that early life stresses can lead to hormonal and structural changes in the brain and can also influence gene expression which can cause changes in the mesolimbic pathway which is responsible for dopamine being carried from one area of the brain to another; this reward pathway has been connected with addiction.

In addition, acute trauma and sexual abuse specifically can be a significant risk factor for alcohol misuse. Research supports that experience of specific types of trauma, such as sexual or physical abuse and subsequent post-traumatic stress disorder, is linked to greater alcohol and substance use (Blumenthal et al., 2008; Blumenthal et al., 2015; Harrison et al., 1997). Additionally, Lo and Cheng (2007) found that as the severity of physical abuse increased, the individual was more likely to misuse and become addicted to alcohol and other drugs. In this study, the increased likelihood of alcohol and drug addiction was also shown to be mediated by depression. The research above highlights the possible intricate interplay between abuse, depression, and alcohol misuse. The literature suggests a link between trauma and alcohol misuse, indicating a need for physicians and behavioral health specialists in integrated care to be vigilant when examining patients with possible post-traumatic stress symptoms and indications of prior traumatic exposure or abuse.

Studies have found a comorbidity, as high as 46.6%, between PTSD and substance use disorders which explicitly includes alcohol misuse (Lisak & Miller, 2003; Pietrzak et al., 2011). Primary care physicians who are aware of this risk factor can intervene early with referrals to behavioral health specialists (especially inside of integrated care setting) when their patients display symptoms or the potential for symptoms of PTSD such as a recent traumatic experience. Additionally, the mental health professionals can provide these patients with more healthy methods for coping and reduce the likelihood that they will turn to alcohol to manage their symptoms. As we will see later in this chapter, coping as the motivation for using alcohol seems to predict negative outcomes which further highlights the need for intervention by a mental health professional. Trauma symptoms can be assessed via screening tools such as the Post-Traumatic Stress Disorder Checklist for DSM-5 (PCL-5; Weathers et al., 2013) as well as via semi-structured interview guides, such as the *Interview Guide for Evaluating DSM-5 Psychiatric Disorders and The Mental*

Status Examination (Zimmerman, 2013). The PCL-5 in particular has the advantage of being freely available (at https://www.ptsd.va.gov/professional/assessment/adult-sr/ptsd-checklist.asp) as well as being fairly quick to administer.

13.2.3 Family History: Genetics and Environment

Another important risk factor to consider in alcohol misuse is family history. For the purpose of this section, family history will encompass both genetics and the environment the family engenders. Research has demonstrated the increased risk one has of developing psychopathologies similar to parents, including alcohol misuse (Elder Jr. et al., 1986; Grant, 1998; Wilens et al., 2014). Wilens et al. (2014) found that parental substance use disorders, which included alcohol misuse, were associated with a higher likelihood of offspring substance use disorder, drug use, and alcohol use. However, determining whether this comes more from the shared environment or shared genetics is a tricky question to answer. In attempts to disentangle these findings, researchers have investigated the genetic components of alcohol misuse. Using twin studies, researchers have found variation in the role of genes from 40% to 70% for alcohol abuse (Agrawal & Lynskey, 2008; Enoch & Goldman, 2001; Goldman et al., 2005; Heath et al., 2001; Lynskey et al., 2010).

It is likely from these findings that alcohol misuse has a significant genetic component. However, genetics can impact addiction at varying levels for each substance. There seems to be a difference in the impact of genetic influence related to various types of substance use disorders. But regardless of the variability in genetic influence, there seems to be considerable overlap in how genetics influence addiction among these different substances (Agrawal et al., 2012). Twin studies suggest that the overlap in pathways to addiction for various substances may be due to dopamine neurotransmission pathways (Kendler et al., 2000; Tsuang et al., 2001). While these possible common pathways have been identified, more drug-specific pathways have also been investigated but are beyond the scope of this chapter.

Consistent with the study mentioned above, genes that have been investigated in relation to addiction have been shown to be related to metabolism (alcohol dehydrogenase) or to neurotransmission such as dopamine or serotonin. According to Lopez-Leon et al. (2021), the following genes were associated to two or more substance use disorders: OPRM1, DRD2, DRD4, BDNF, and SLC6A4. SLC6A4 was found to be significant for general substance use disorder and the ADH1B specifically for alcohol misuse (Lopez-Leon et al., 2021). Further discussion of the mechanisms and role of each gene also is beyond the scope of this chapter.

In addition to genetics, childhood environment also influences the likelihood of substance use disorders. Horigian et al. (2015) found that children are two to nine times as likely to experience difficulties with drug and alcohol later in life when their parents use alcohol and other drugs and that maladaptive family interactions are strongly associated with adolescent substance use. Moreover, consistent with other studies, we have seen that early alcohol use is linked to higher likelihood of alcohol misuse later in life. Additionally, Kendler et al. (2008) point out that when substance use disorder occurs early in life, it was more strongly influenced by social and family environment with genetic influence taking over more in terms of later substance use. While research is working to disentangle which influence plays a more crucial role, it is clear that both the environment and genetics are involved. Understanding that both play independent roles and work together in the development of alcohol misuse is the important factor for a clinician to recognize. A patient who has biological parents with alcohol misuse struggles may be at risk; a patient who has a caregiver who abuses alcohol may be at risk; and a patient who has a biological parent who is also their caregiver with alcohol misuse may be at the greatest risk for alcohol misuse in the future. Clinicians should assess family history in order to get a full picture of a patient's risk of future alcohol misuse.

13.2.4 Psychological Factors

The psychological makeup of the individual should also be considered when assessing the potential of future alcohol misuse. In addition to external factors such as age of onset and environment, researchers have also found that certain psychological factors have also been associated with an increased likelihood for alcohol misuse (Schuckit, 2006). Some of the psychological factors that have been shown to be associated with substance use disorder and alcohol misuse specifically as indicated by the National Research Council and Institute of Medicine (2009) are aggression, poor impulse control, depression, and bipolar disorder. Also, stress has been found to be associated with alcohol misuse (Schuckit, 2006; Segrin et al., 2018).

13.2.5 Impulsive/Aggressive Behaviors

Researchers have repeatedly found an association between substance use disorders, specifically including alcohol misuse, and impulsivity and aggressive behaviors (Brady et al., 1998). In three small sample size studies, researchers looked at impulsive violent offenders, impulsive arsonists, intermittent explosive disorder, and kleptomania. They found that among those offenders, lifetime substance use disorders, including alcohol misuse, had misuse rates that measured 100%, 20%, 57%, and 50%, respectively. These results indicate a strong link between impulsive offenses and alcohol misuse (Linnoila et al., 1983; McElroy et al., 1991; Salomon et al., 1994; Virkkunen et al., 1989).

Determining if impulsivity leads to alcohol misuse or if alcohol misuse leads towards increased impulsivity is also a compelling research topic. Research from Perry and Carroll (2008) observed that impulsivity led to drug and alcohol misuse and drug and alcohol misuse may also lead to higher frequencies of impulsive behavior. When examining impulsive behavior, the literature usually defines an impulsive choice as the act of choosing a small immediate reinforcer instead of a larger delayed one and defines impaired inhibition as the lack of ability to stop a behavior (Perry & Carroll, 2008). When considering these definitions used by researchers, it is easy to see how there seems to be an association between impulsivity and alcohol misuse as the alcohol provides the immediate reinforcer of positive feelings or relief from negative feelings. Those deemed more impulsive are more inclined to choose immediate reinforcers over long-term and less-immediate results. Understanding that those who may be more impulsive or exhibit more impulsive and aggressive behaviors may be at greater risk for alcohol misuse can be beneficial for primary care clinicians to understand when it may be appropriate to intervene.

13.2.6 Drinking to Cope (DTC)

Additionally, drinking to cope (DTC) with negative emotions has been found to be associated with drinking-related problems (Armeli et al., 2014; Cooper et al., 1995). Research has found that the motivation for drinking is potentially more important than other factors such as amount, frequency, or context of drinking in assessing the potential for alcohol misuse. This is especially true when the motivation to drink is to cope with negative emotions (Merrill & Read, 2010). The above referenced research discovered direct links between coping motives and unique consequences associated with drinking. It also highlights the importance of considering not only how much a person drinks but also a person's motivation for drinking. Based on these findings, practitioners should be especially attentive to patients who drink to cope with negative emotions as opposed to drinking motivated by a social setting.

13.2.7 Stress

Stress has been frequently established as a risk factor for alcohol misuse (Sinha, 2001). Lazarus and Folkman (1984) defined stress as the reaction to challenging, harmful, or difficult events based on how one perceives, interprets, and reacts to the event. Because stress is experienced differently across individuals and since there are varying levels of stress, it is easy to see how varied the response to stress can be. However, based on the research by Sinha (2001), it seems clear that one of the responses to stress is using alcohol to cope which often times leads to the problematic use. Based on other risk factors discussed in this section (genetic, environment, age of onset, etc.), some people may be more predisposed than others to react to stressful events or stress in general with alcohol misuse. Despite the variability in responses to stressful events, undoubtedly stress is a risk factor for alcohol misuse and is especially so for those who use drinking to cope with stress.

If the patient shows signs of lack of coping strategies or explicitly admits the use of alcohol as a tool to cope and they have significant stress in their lives, the combined risk factors may strongly indicate a need to intervene and provide patient assistance with using healthier ways to deal with the stress (Cooper et al., 1995; Sinha, 2001). This is a key example of how intervention prior to severe misuse may be possible when a primary care physician observes the convergence of multiple risk factors.

13.2.8 Depression/Bipolar Disorder

Schuckit (2006) illustrated the frequent use of alcohol among individuals experiencing depressive symptoms. It seems that the relationship between depressive symptoms and alcohol misuse works in two ways. Alcohol misuse sometimes exacerbates preexisting disorders, such as depression, and other times the depression, or the negative feelings that accompany depression, leads an individual to use alcohol to cope which in turn leads to abuse (Cooper et al., 1995; Hasin et al., 2002; Rabinowitz et al., 1998; Schuckit, 2006; Volkow, 2004). Additionally, Vornik and Brown (2006) found that the rate of substance use disorders, including alcohol misuse specifically, among those with bipolar disorder is significantly higher than that of the general population. These authors note that substance use disorders in general affect up to as many as 61% of people diagnosed with bipolar disorder. It can be difficult to determine which is the case in a specific patient, but for the scope of this chapter, it is just important to understand the link and to understand that decreasing the alcohol use may decrease depressive symptoms; also, decreasing depressive symptoms may also decrease the desire to use alcohol to cope. Understanding the link between depression or bipolar disorder and alcohol misuse is the critical piece. In integrated care, coordination with the behavioral health specialist will allow the patient to work out better ways to cope with depression and bipolar disorder instead of turning to alcohol.

There are significant complexities when discussing disorders that are comorbid with alcohol misuse. A specific example is post-traumatic stress disorder and depression. Since both can be risk factors for alcohol misuse, and one patient may have both diagnoses, the question of which risk factor is the true pathway for the misuse becomes unclear. Understanding this in general may be important for researchers, but for the scope of this chapter, knowing which disorders and psychological factors are associated with alcohol misuse should be sufficient for primary care physicians to determine which patients may be at greater risk.

As discussed, there are various risk factors associated with alcohol misuse that have been brought to light in relevant literature. The risk factors presented are not all encompassing, but those discussed are certainly the risk factors commonly established in relevant literature. Being aware of the risk factors for alcohol misuse can be the first step to prevention, and being able to see the signs of potential future abuse can be an important piece in stopping misuse before it even occurs. For a more in-depth understanding of how each risk factor may contribute to the development of alcohol misuse, see the cited works at the end of this chapter.

13.2.9 Ethnic and Cultural Variables

An important note about ethnic and cultural variables when discussing risk factors: the fact that an individual belongs to a certain group does not automatically mean that they require alcohol prevention services. This, of course, applies to all the factors listed here in this section, but it is of special importance to not stereotype patients being seen and evaluated. Instead, this data is presented with the intention of guiding decision-making in conjunction with the other factors here in this section. For example, this guidance is intended to help clinicians be aware that if a member of a group that is at higher risk for alcohol issues also has other risk factors described here, then that might be an opportunity to discuss the topic with the patient and explore options for the prevention of alcohol misuse before problems start, especially if alcohol use is already present.

The American Psychiatric Association (2013) illustrated significant variances of alcohol use disorder across different racial and ethnic subgroups in the US population. The 12-month prevalence rates for alcohol use among the 12–17 age range appear to be greatest among the Hispanic population (6.0%) and Native Americans and Alaskan Natives (5.7%). However, these rates shift somewhat among adults; here the 12-month prevalence rate for alcohol use disorder is highest among Native Americans and Alaskan Natives (12.1%), Whites (8.9%), Hispanics (7.9%), and African Americans (6.9%). Asian Americans and Pacific Islanders had the lowest 12-month prevalence rate at 4.5%.

Other variables such as religion can play a role in alcohol use. Ellison et al. (2008) found that religions with clear expectations regarding alcohol use, such as Protestant groups or members of the Muslim faith, bear a strong inverse relationship with alcohol use behaviors in individuals belonging to those faiths. However, the researchers also described that the individual salience of personal religious beliefs was more important in predicting alcohol use than general church teachings. This means that the personal religious commitment of an individual within a faith with regulations regarding alcohol use may serve as a buffer against other risk factors. This is due to the finding that personal commitment seems to predict which religious individuals decide to restrain or abstain from drinking (Ellison et al., 2008).

13.2.10 Anxiety

Anxiety, in particular social anxiety, has a strong association with alcohol use (Morris et al., 2005). Estimates have placed the lifetime prevalence rates of alcohol dependence among those with social anxiety disorder at 24%, meaning that nearly one in four individuals that suffer from social anxiety may also be experiencing clinically significant alcohol issues as well. However, the well-documented relationship between anxiety and alcohol use does not stop with social anxiety. In general, research has demonstrated that 50% upwards or nearly one out of every two individuals receiving treatment for problematic drinking also met the criteria for one or more anxiety disorders (Anker & Kushner, 2019). Therefore, anxiety disorders in general should be viewed as a potential warning sign and an indicator that some form of intervention may be needed as well to prevent the development of alcohol use disorder.

There are a number of different screening tools for anxiety. The Generalized Anxiety Disorder Screener (GAD-7) stands out as being short, efficient, and freely available (Kroenke et al., 2007). The GAD-7 is a seven-item self-report measure capable of assessing the severity of anxious symptoms an individual is experiencing and has been designed to be effective for individuals of ages 12 and older (Kroenke et al., 2007). Additionally, the GAD-7 has been demonstrated to be able to screen for the presence of four different anxiety disorders: generalized anxiety disorder, post-traumatic stress disorder, social anxiety disorder, and panic disorder. While the screener cannot differentially diagnose between those disorders, it can indicate to a clinician the need to ask further questions in order to hone in a specific diagnosis, if the symptoms have progressed that far. Research so far has suggested that a cut score of 8 be used as a point of identifying when further questioning might be employed to detect the development of an anxiety disorder. However, even scores under 8 may indicate an increase in anxiety symptoms that could also be associated with an increased risk of alcohol use. Clinicians should pair the GAD-7 with interview questions to be able to differentiate the exact kind of anxiety that the patient is experiencing. For more information on the prevention and screening of anxiety disorders, please see Chap. 13 of this volume.

13.2.11 Practical Suggestions on Assessment

In terms of implications for integrated care, the preceding information on risk factors, such as stress, impulsivity, or other comorbid psychiatric disorders, suggests that screening for these risk factors during appointments may be useful to alert providers as to when intervention may be required. These questions can be integrated into existing questions regarding general health behaviors, such as asking about current stress levels or asking how individuals are utilizing alcohol (i.e., asking what purpose the alcohol serves in their life, with emphasis on whether their answers indicate that they are drinking to cope).

Additionally, the above information highlights the importance of reviewing patient records, especially in integrated care settings (Willis & O'Donohue, 2020). Record reviews can allow a primary care provider to know what other clinicians have been observing, allowing their evaluations and assessments to inform the primary care provider. Record reviews enable a provider to integrate information from multiple sources that may have had the chance to observe any of the preceding risk factors. If, for example, the behavioral health specialist has noted several risk factors for alcohol use (such as impulsivity, increased stress, or the presence of comorbid bipolar disorder), then that information can inform the primary care provider to be on the lookout for additional warning signs or to start the conversation with their patient regarding alcohol use disorder prevention strategies. Further quantitative screening tools for alcohol-related issues are detailed below.

13.3 Screening and Measurement

The preceding section on risk factors for alcohol use is by no means exhaustive. Instead, it is intended to serve as an effective primer on factors to be aware of when working with patients in a clinical setting. The preceding information can act as a guide when interviewing patients, with each of the identified risk factors serving as a kind of "red flag," alerting the clinician to be more aware of possible alcohol-related issues so that prompt action can be taken if needed.

However, while awareness and the ability to qualitatively assess the preceding risk factors are important, being able to collect quantifiable information on a patient's problematic alcohol behaviors and risk factors is also vital to effective prevention. Measurement is crucial in the prevention process as it facilitates decisions regarding when and how to intervene in efforts to prevent unhealthy alcohol use from escalating into an actual alcohol use disorder. However, evidence has been shown that while brief interventions in primary care setting can be effective at reducing unhealthy drinking, many patients with alcohol issues are not identified and therefore do not receive such interventions (Nilsen et al., 2006; Vinson et al., 2007. Therefore, an important piece of any plan to help prevent alcohol use disorders should involve increasing the ability in primary care settings to effectively and efficiently screen for and detect warning signs of problematic alcohol use. It is important to note that not all of the previously elucidated risk factors have a direct quantitative method of assessing them, which is why a combination of clinical interviews and quantitative measurements is recommended whenever possible to ensure a complete picture of a patient's condition is formed. Here again, the advantages of an integrated care setup may come into play. When possible, the physician may use some of the following screening tools and discover that an individual is suffering from an elevation in their anxiety symptoms. Coordinating with the behavioral health specialist can ensure a correct diagnosis if needed as well as helping to connect that individual with the right level of intervention.

13.3.1 General Suggestions on Screening Tools

Before discussing specific screening instruments, it is important to note a few general principles that can make screening more effective. Spear et al. (2016) highlighted the need to remember the immense amount of social stigma that can accompany alcohol and other substance use issues. Therefore, they recommended the following points be considered when planning a screening strategy:

1. *Rapport Building*: Spear et al. (2016) noted in their study that individuals who trusted their clinician were much more likely to respond honestly to screening questions regarding alcohol use. Specifically, they highlighted the need for clinicians to establish rapport where the patient can feel safe in disclosing potentially unpleasant personal information. While personal warmth and positive regard can help in developing trust, confidentiality (which follows below) is also a vital starting point in helping patients build trust (Huibers & Cuijpers, 2014).
2. *Confidentiality*: While maintaining confidentiality is an ethical imperative (American Psychological Association, 2017), Spear et al. (2016) noted in their study of the acceptability of alcohol screens that patients may require extra assurances that their responses to substance-related questions will be kept confidential. Several participants in the study indicated that they were only willing to allow their primary care provider to see the results of any substance use screens. They specifically indicated they did not wish for any other healthcare personnel, including nurses and support staff, to have access to their completed screening measures (Spear et al., 2016). Therefore, care must be taken to assure patients that their responses will be kept between them and their provider to the amount feasible. The increasing proliferation of electronic health records system across the United States may make this goal of confidentiality somewhat simpler (Garrett, 2010). Electronic health records systems may provide methods of compartmentalizing data, ensuring that only designated users are able to see certain sections of a client's file (Titanium Software, 2019). Additionally, careful use of file names and a working knowledge of how different medical records systems store scale data collected from patients can enable administrators to conceal more sensitive scales from easy and accidental access, thereby offering another level of security and helping patients feel they can respond more openly on the measures.
3. *Methods of Administration*: Time is at a premium in primary care settings, where physicians may only have 10 minutes to attend to a patient before needing to move on to the next individual waiting in line (Wiesche et al., 2017). Therefore, any discussion on assessment and detection of the early warning signs of alcohol issues must also include how to deliver said assessments in an efficient manner. There are multiple methods of delivering assessments to patients, either via pen and paper measures that can be completed in a waiting room or via tablets and mobile computers that can administer the needed assessments electronically. While conducting a clinical interview with a patient will likely need to be done by a clinician, electronic means of administering scales show great promise as a means of screening for alcohol use issues. In fact, research has shown that patients frequently prefer self-guided assessments of more sensitive topics, such as alcohol use, to more formal clinical interviews (Spear et al., 2016). Several factors are important to consider when implementing an online assessment system, such as whether the assessments will be text only or if they will contain some sort of narrative guide. Additionally, care should be taken to ensure that whatever hardware is eventually selected to administer the measures, the devices themselves are easy to use and fairly durable to survive constant handling in the

clinic setting. Furthermore, consultation should be sought with appropriate information technology experts with training in regulations outlined under the *Health Insurance Portability and Accountability Act* (HIPAA) to ensure that the data transmissions from any mobile screening device (such as a laptop or tablet) are sent in a secure and encrypted manner back to the central medical database (Department of Health and Human Services, 2013). Electronic administration also aids in accessibility, as screens can be translated in various languages and those translations can be easily made available upon request by the user.

4. *Consider "At Home" Options*: Given the limited amount of time a patient might actually have to spend with their primary care doctor, it may be reasonable to consider methods of having the patient complete needed screens at home before even coming into the clinic. Increasingly, clinics that have access to electronic health records systems are also gaining access to patient portals where patients can log in remotely and complete intake paperwork and respond to questionnaires (Epic, 2021; Titanium Software, 2019). These systems allow patients to securely access screening tools and complete them before coming into the clinic. This, in turn, potentially provides an added layer of confidentiality, especially in circumstances when filling out a survey may require an audio component, such as for patients who may need an on-screen narrator for accessibility purposes. It is important to be aware that not all patients may have access to compatible devices to complete screening tools at home, but the at home option still may be an effective method for maximizing the amount of time a patient can spend talking with a provider. Furthermore, being able to administer assessments remotely and at home has benefits as clinics continue to adapt to the COVID-19 pandemic. The COVID-19 pandemic has caused massive shifts in how behavioral healthcare and primary healthcare in general operate (Fisk et al., 2020; Rawaf et al., 2020). The impact of the COVID-19 pandemic is still being investigated and understood, but the increasing use of online, at home assessments has been one method adopted by our university clinic and others to adapt to the decreased frequency of having a patient physically present in the clinic. At home administration can also benefit rural telehealth clinics, where having the patient come in to fill out measures is not feasible.
5. *The Need for Orientation*: Spear et al. (2016) noted that individuals usually preferred electronic assessments via tablet or mobile computer to in person interviews regarding alcohol use. This effect remained constant regardless of the user's skill with computers and electronic devices in general. However, to achieve this effect, the study conducted by Spear et al. (2016) recommended an orientation be added before the screening assessments begin. This orientation should include the preceding information regarding confidentiality, including specific information regarding who will and will not be able to see the patient's responses. This orientation should include a brief description of the use interface, contain information on how to navigate said interface, and clearly display where users can go to get additional help if needed. This information can be presented as a set of information slides at the beginning of the assessment package, or a facility staff member can present the information verbally. This

orientation has been demonstrated to aid in the acceptability of online electronic assessment, even by individuals who may be unfamiliar with the devices in use at the facility (Spear et al., 2016).

13.3.2 Selecting Screening Tools

The selection of measures for screening battery must be handled with care. Attention must be paid to how much time it may take a patient to complete the assessment packet, along with whatever additional sign in paperwork is customary for a primary care visit. The importance of this time requirement is somewhat reduced when options exist for patients completing assessments at home. However, even in the home setting, it will be important to not overburden patients via the administration of tests that are too long or too numerous. Additionally, it will be important to consider the length of time required to score and interpret the screening instruments under use. Therefore, in this section we will present several commonly used screening tools for alcohol use and alcohol use disorders as examples that might fit well in the primary care setting.

13.3.3 Alcohol Use Disorders Identification Test

A commonly accepted method for assessing alcohol use in patients is the Alcohol Use Disorders Identification Test (AUDIT), a ten-item measure that can be administered either as a self-report questionnaire or as an oral interview (WHO, 2001). The items focus on assessing the frequency and severity of alcohol use, as well as the impact of alcohol-related problems (i.e., accidents, injuries, feelings of guilt or remorse). As the AUDIT can be used either as a self-report measure or as a clinician-directed interview, it possesses significant flexibility. The test can be used as a self-report measure when time is a critical factor, such as in the primary care setting, or can be utilized as an interview to help patients with poor reading skills. The utilization of the measure as an interview also provides the opportunity for seamless feedback to the patient and the initiation of advice while on the topic of substance use (WHO, 2001). The AUDIT can be accessed for free from the World Health Organization website, which further enhances its utility as a screening measure, as there is no overhead cost associated with acquiring or using the instrument. The AUDIT scale itself has been the subject of a variety of studies and has been demonstrated to be effective at identifying patients who are in the "at risk" category of drinking, thereby making it more applicable to the realm of prevention. The original AUDIT interpretation guide suggested that a score of 8 for men and 7 for women indicated a pattern of unhealthy alcohol use (Babor et al., 2001). However, more recent research by Johnson et al. (2013) indicated that the cutoffs should potentially be lowered to a score of 5 for men and 3 for women. In particular, these lower cutoff scores may help to identify individuals who are at risk for more serious alcohol use issues earlier, thus facilitating the use of preventative measures. The AUDIT has been shown to be effective for individuals aged 14 and older, though it is recommended that between the ages of 14 and 18 a score of 2 should be used to indicate any alcohol problem and 3 be used for alcohol misuse or dependence (National Institute on Alcohol Abuse and Alcoholism, 2017).

13.3.4 Alcohol Use Disorders Identification Test-Concise

The AUDIT scale also has a shorter variant, the Alcohol Use Disorders Identification Test-Concise (AUDIT-C), which is a three-item scale that focuses exclusively on the amount of alcohol that is typically consumed by a patient (Bush et al., 1998). Subsequent research has suggested that the cutoffs of 4 for men and 3 for women be utilized when administering the AUDIT-C (Johnson et al., 2013). The advantage of the AUDIT-C is its brevity; the screen can be administered quickly and efficiently. However, it is important to note that with the shortening of the instrument comes a loss in performance. Johnson et al. (2013) found that while the AUDIT-C is still an effective measure of unhealthy alcohol use, the full AUDIT scale seems to perform better by increasing specificity and decreasing the number of false positives. Like its larger sibling, the AUDIT-C is also freely available online. Additionally, the AUDIT-C has been shown to be effective at assessing both adults and adolescents, from the age of 12 and up (Liskola et al., 2018).

13.3.5 The Alcohol, Smoking, and Substance Involvement Screening Test

The Alcohol, Smoking, and Substance Involvement Screening Test (ASSIST) is an eight-item questionnaire also developed by the World Health Organization. It is designed to detect problematic substance use generally (Humeniuk et al., 2010) and has been validated for the adult and adolescent population, from the ages of 18 to 60. Additionally, multiple language versions of the measure exist, including Portuguese and Spanish. While not specific to alcohol use as the previous scales, the ASSIST is still effective at detecting substance use issues and has two subscales, Alcohol Involvement and All Other Substance Involvement. This scale can be useful in detecting any comorbid substance use issues that might be present in addition to risky alcohol use. Furthermore, the scale is divided into risk zones, with a score of 0–10 indicating low risk of alcohol use problems, 11–26 indicating moderate risk, and anything above 27 indicating high risk. These divisions can be useful in identifying patients who might benefit from interventions early, before they arrive at the high-risk zone. Similar to the scales mentioned above, this scale is also freely available online, which helps to remove barriers imposed by fees for use. However, the ASSIST does differ significantly from the previous examples in that it is intended to be delivered as a clinical interview lasting between 5 and 10 minutes. However, Spear et al. (2016) demonstrated that the measure can be converted into an audio computer-assisted self-interview where the screen is read to the patient via a tablet or laptop computer and the patient responds to the questions using the device's interface.

13.4 General Principles in Prevention

Clinical interviews and the above screening tools are important in identifying who might benefit from intervention. However, once those individuals are identified, the question arises of what to do next. When creating a plan to intervene with alcohol issues, even those that are subclinical, there are a number of general factors to consider. Prevention programs tend to have three aspects incorporated into them to increase effectiveness (Larimer & Cronce, 2007):

- Knowledge
- Training skills
- Motivational/feedback

First, prevention interventions tend to provide education or awareness regarding the issue or problem. These programs often use pamphlets, posters, presentations, or classes that include risk factors or statistics to inform the public of the dangers of drinking. These are often done in schools due to them being a simple way to convey information. Their primary goal in these prevention programs is to reduce or delay the use of alcohol, and these programs are often designed to target risk factors. Meredith et al. (2020) piloted a prevention program called *Just Say Know*, an interactive intervention that focused on providing information on the brain basics and the effects of substance use. Their findings on the neuroscience-informed prevention program indicated that this type of prevention may reduce or delay the use of substances in adolescents (Meredith et al., 2020). A literature review showed that to have an effective prevention program, interventions must be theory-driven, address social norms, help students resist peer pressure, and be cultural and developmentally appropriate (Stigler et al., 2011). However, knowledge-based interventions have only a small effect in reducing or delaying alcohol use (Larimer & Cronce, 2002; Larimer & Cronce, 2007). Thus, incorporating skills training in the intervention will increase the effectiveness of the intervention. An example of an intervention program utilizing these factors is the *ready4life* mobile program, developed with the intent of helping to prevent substance use in adolescents via life skills training (Haug et al., 2017). The *ready4life* program was built using a system known as MobileCoach, which is an open-source platform and thus freely available to developers. The *ready4life* software featured automated reminder messages, monitoring questions, and other engagement activities designed to increase general life skills such as stress management and social skills. Results on the software's use have been promising, with the proportion of adolescents with at risk alcohol use declining from 20.2% in the initial sample to 15.5% at follow-up (Haug et al., 2017).

Next are the intervention programs that teach the individual the skills needed to prevent alcohol use. These are often delivered in a medical or therapeutic setting by a professional. The multi-component skills training programs often consist of environmental prevention strategies and combine them with individual- or family-level change tactics. Several studies that have used multi-component skills training to reduce alcohol use has shown a reduction in alcohol use (Barnett et al., 2007; Borsari & Carey, 2005); however, not all interventions have been as effective in reducing alcohol use (Komro et al., 2008).

Lastly, prevention interventions should include a motivational and feedback approach when dealing with alcohol use. These types of interventions use motivational interviewing (MI) which is a "goal-oriented style of communication" to help identify the individual's stage of change (Miller & Rollnick, 2013). A literature review indicated that the use of MI is effective or as effective as other treatments (DiClemente et al., 2017). In addition to the motivational interventions, feedback is an essential component to increase the effectiveness of the intervention (McNally & Palfai, 2003). The combination of these three aspects in an early intervention might have a larger impact on reducing or delaying the use of alcohol.

13.5 Brief Prevention Strategies in Primary Care

Research has suggested that brief interventions following the Screening, Brief Intervention, and Referral to Treatment (SBIRT) approach may be especially helpful in the domain of preventing the development of more serious alcohol-related issues (Babor et al., 2007). Brief interventions in general consist of efficient efforts such as one to two conversations or meetings that will provide information or advice and will focus on motivating the patient to decrease their alcohol use (Babor et al., 2007). This brief intervention can be highly structured or less so with more of a focus on motivational interviewing. It also can focus on changing behaviors that will potentially reduce alcohol use. For more information on how to implement SBIRT, it would be extremely useful to refer to the toolkit provided in "SBIRT: A Step-By-Step Guide" by the Bureau of Substance Abuse Services. This toolkit is especially helpful for use with individuals who are low to moderate risk, highlighting how this approach fits well as a prevention strategy. Benefits of the brief intervention stage of SBIRT are the time-saving and cost-effectiveness, as well as the lack of invasive approaches that may be necessary if the alcohol use progressed to a higher risk or if the patient already had a substance use disorder.

This theme of time-saving and cost-effectiveness will be evident throughout the section as early intervention and prevention strategies are typically less invasive than approaches once true intervention as opposed to prevention is necessary. This is clear in the SBIRT approach as even just the next stage of brief treatment involves two to six sessions of cognitive behavioral or motivational enhancement therapy. Babor et al. (2007) also found that brief intervention with problem drinkers seems to be as effective as more extensive treatments and found further evidence for its effectiveness, especially among those with less severe problems (Moyer et al., 2002; Bien et al., 1993). When this level of care is needed, it may be possible for the behavioral health professional in an integrated care clinic to deliver the brief intervention.

Additionally, Babor et al. (2007) as well as Seigers and Carey (2010) indicate that other healthcare personnel can deliver the brief intervention as well such as nurses, nurse practitioners, counseling staff, and trained research staff furthering its cost and time efficiency. Since brief intervention can be implemented in only one to two sessions and can be performed not only by the primary care physician, this brief intervention approach can be used any time risk factors may be present without a large time or financial impact and fits well into integrated care frameworks.

Other researchers recognize the benefit of intervention strategies if implemented but identify certain barriers that could limit its application. Screening rates for alcohol have been found to be as low as 2%–26%, and researchers have also discovered the difficulty in providing high-quality alcohol-related care because of stigma, lack, of training, lack of alcohol focus in the primary care setting, and not even seeing AUDs as something primary care facilities are equipped to handle. There is also the idea that alcohol treatment should be left to specific programs such as Alcoholics Anonymous (Bobb et al., 2017). In order to address these barriers, Sustained Patient-centered Alcohol-Related Care (SPARC) was designed.

Three main strategies were used in order to implement SPARC and address the barriers mentioned. The first involved enabling the primary care teams to offer high-quality care through training, implementation design strategy, addressing stigma, and focusing on shared decision-making. SPARC trained a "champion" provider from each site and trained them with a social worker, as part of the team. In the pilot study, other than the individual training, a consultant implemented the program on site focusing on workflow and program execution. In addition, every other week this champion would participate in learning sessions. To address stigma, patient-focused materials were provided in order to reshape attitudes about alcohol in a way more in line with treatment such as helping the providers see drinking as a health issue and to see unhealthy alcohol use on a spectrum. Additionally, staff learned recommended alcohol limits and evidence-based approaches to treat AUD. Finally, the program focused on shared decision-making in order to make the patient feel more responsible for their decisions and create a more cooperative relationship between the provider and client.

The second strategy is aimed to help medical providers stay on top of assessments and treatment by using an electronic health record (EHR) for support. The EHR would alert medical assistants when a patient hadn't had a behavioral health screening in the past year and would trigger a visual prompt for medical assistant to remind providers to give a handout and engage in a brief intervention depending on the previously mentioned AUDIT-C screening score. The EHR would also provide decision support based on DSM-5 AUD symptom checklist to advise further action such as next steps to help facilitate treatment and would provide prompts to initiate treatment. Additionally, EHR would prompt the doctor for missed assessment. The third strategy involved monitoring and providing feedback for quality improvement. Strategy one focused on program implementation, while strategies two and three are designed to keep providers accountable and make sure the process to improve care was evolving and not staying stagnant.

This EHR program, like SBIRT, involves the brief intervention strategy that fits well with our prevention focus. The results of the program's pilot study that include brief intervention as well as more in-depth treatment options saw improvements in multiple domains. In the sites involved in the study, alcohol screening increased from 8.9% before implementation to 62% after implementation. There was also an increase in new AUD diagnoses and a 54% increase in treatment within 14 days of new diagnoses. Specifically, for the purpose of prevention, the percentage of positive screens for unhealthy use increased from 2.2% to 17% affording opportunities to prevent furthered disordered drinking in these patients.

The SPARC program seems to be a promising avenue for increasing the efficiency of screening for unhealthy alcohol use. In addition, it provides training that may help providers to better support their patients. Finally, the use of the electronic health record appears to be a promising tool to help busy providers stay on top of alcohol screening and direct patients to treatment.

In terms of population, college students are an extremely important population to address in terms of prevention of unhealthy alcohol use. Approximately 30% of college students meet the diagnostic criteria for alcohol misuse (Seigers & Carey, 2010). Due to this high prevalence among the college population, focusing on college students and college campuses and even high schoolers for prevention strategies is crucial. In order to get a better understanding of prevention on college campuses, Seigers and Carey (2010) reviewed 12 studies that used brief intervention in a college- or university-based student health center or university emergency department. The reviewed studies also provided pre- and post-data to evaluate change. There were four uncontrolled studies, and all four documented alcohol consumption reduction post-intervention. Out of the eight controlled studies, six found larger alcohol consumption reduction than control conditions. One that did not find a reduction focused on behaviors other than just alcohol consumption possibly diluting the alcohol focus, and the other design that didn't find a reduction didn't control only for alcohol use specifically. These findings showed a reduction in risky behavior. In terms of best practices, Seigers and Carey (2010) stressed the importance of screening and detection of alcohol-related risk factors when deciding who will receive alcohol-related interventions. Additionally, they indicated that college health centers represent a prime venue to engage with those at risk of developing alcohol problems. Of the studies that they reviewed, they found that between 63% and 80% of students who were screened for risky drinking (see the section on assessment for specific screening tools) were willing to participate in interventions to help reduce their risk of developing alcohol-related problems. Furthermore, Seigers and Carey (2010) found that brief interventions, usually no more than 75 minutes, were effective at helping to intervene with at-risk individuals and overall utilized relatively few materials, demonstrating that brief contact can effectively reduce drinking.

The intervention strategies consisted of short single conversations or brief counseling sessions of varying length. Most studies reviewed also used motivation interviewing coupled with feedback personalized to the interview. Two studies helped bring awareness to drinking patterns by focusing on timelines and calendars, and six of the studies used Web-based components to help with screening assessment and with the intervention (Ballesteros et al., 2004; Dimeff & McNeely, 2000; Ingersoll et al., 2005; Kypri et al., 2004; Kypri et al., 2008; Kypri & McAnally, 2005; Martens et al., 2007; Werch et al., 2007). Kypri et al. (2008) also found that after a Web-based intervention with a 9.3-minute median completion time, students reported less alcohol consumption and fewer academic problems than controls, and these findings held a year after completion.

Additionally, some workplace prevention programs may offer insights on how to better prevent alcohol use disorders in primary care settings. Ames and Bennet (2011) reviewed various workplace programs and found that prevention approaches in the domains of health promotion, social health promotion, and Web-based interventions are effective for primary care prevention efforts. Ames and Bennet (2011) provide a number of suggestions when planning an alcohol prevention program. Specifically, they highlighted an approach they designated Team Awareness, which embedded alcohol-related information in the context of team building, stress management, and policy learning. While useable in the workplace, their findings nonetheless suggest that alcohol-related messages embedded within other health-related information (such as information on stress management and problem-solving skills) can be impactful in reducing the risk of developing alcohol-related issues.

A critical step recommended by Bennett et al. (2004) is the replacement of alcohol-related behaviors with behaviors that are less risky. Specifically, they recommend examining why individuals utilize alcohol. As discussed previously in this chapter, those who utilize alcohol as a means of reducing stress or coping are potentially at risk for developing unhealthy alcohol use. In the same vein, some individuals use alcohol not only for emotional regulation but also for building social support with friends or co-workers. This appears especially prevalent in individuals who have physically risky or safety-related jobs (Bennett et al., 2004). Therefore, providers should work with such patients to find alternative behaviors where they can still gain needed social support. Behavior replacement is especially important to ensure that individuals do not fall back into old, risky alcohol-related behaviors due to not having their needs sufficiently met. This behavioral replacement strategy was part of a larger intervention program dubbed Team Awareness and focuses on two 4-hour sessions spread out over 2 weeks (Bennett et al., 2004). These sessions focused on stress management skills, emotional coping skills, and psychoeducation on alcohol tolerance and other risk factors. Additionally, the sessions encouraged individuals to help and support fellow co-workers, thus working to remove the shame and stigma associated with risky alcohol use. While intended for use in an employee assistance program, the Team Awareness model nonetheless contains pieces that could be adapted to the integrated care setting, such as the focus on behavioral replacement.

Adding to this, Cook et al. (2003) found that a stress-management program/nutrition program found similar reductions in alcohol consumption compared to a program that also added substance use prevention specifically into the training. These findings show that there are substance use prevention benefits in programs that focus on healthy behavior overall regardless of inclusion of substance use discussion allowing primary care facilities to potentially accomplish multiple tasks at once, i.e., general health and substance use reduction. Therefore, prevention programs should also examine the possibility of including general health promotion (i.e., exercise, sleep hygiene, stress management, proper nutrition) to help reduce risk factors that can contribute to risky alcohol use (Ames & Bennet, 2011).

Doumas and Hannah (2008) found that those who completed a personalized feedback program on drinking reported significantly lower levels of drinking than a control group. This Web-based prevention provided feedback on drinking and also included a 15-minute motivational interviewing session. This program has been delivered in the workplace but is free to the public at www.CheckYourDrinking.net and may be a simple and easy way for primary care offices to prevent problem drinking early on with minimal time commitments on both the primary care physician and the patient.

Overall, brief intervention seems to be an efficient and well-researched form of prevention that can be easily added into an integrated care setting. Additionally, the potential for combining health promotion, social health promotion, and simple Web-based prevention adapted from the workplace prevention efforts into primary care educational prevention is promising. The results from these types of prevention strategies in the workplace appear to be effective. Combining a simple educational packet, video, or presentation that includes all of these elements that can be easily distributed to patients in the primary care setting may be simple, time-efficient, and possibly beneficial. Of course, research should be done on a specific program covering these elements adapted to the primary care setting, but the potential seems favorable.

13.6 A Guide to Implementation

Stepped care is a staged hierarchical intervention system designed to be the least restrictive possible to the patient while still making significant health gains (Bower & Gilbody, 2005). According to a stepped care guidance program from the Australian Government Department of Public Health (2019), generally, the five levels of care are as follows: self-management, low-intensity services, moderate-intensity services, high-intensity services, and acute and specialist services. For the scope of this chapter, the prevention strategies will take place in steps one and two. The third step is a referral to treatment step that, in terms of prevention, is only important to understand that it should be used when prevention has failed or treatment is needed. Steps ranging from three to five would be more applicable in a treatment as opposed to a prevention model. What follows is an example model of how the preceding information can be adapted into the stepped care model for prevention in primary care.

13.6.1 Assessment and Screening

It is important to screen patients regularly in order to be proactive enough to stay in the prevention realm and not falling into the domain of the requirement for treatment. During an appointment (or preferably before), a patient completes screening measures such as the aforementioned AUDIT or AUDIT-C. Combining the scores on these measures along with data gathered when interviewing a patient, the clinician can then decide if further intervention is warranted. If a patient has an elevated AUDIT-C measure score or has indicated that they experience a number of the previously listed risk factors (such as increased stress at work), then the provider can discuss intervention options with the patient and collaboratively decide on a course of action.

13.6.2 Stepped Care Level 1: Self-Guided Intervention

Once the level of need has been established, then stepped care can be implemented. Step one of a stepped care model would be the lowest level of care and would include a referral from a PCP for the patient to complete a preventative course of treatment on their own, offering the Web-based interventions, as they would permit the patient to complete the program at their own pace (Kypri et al., 2008). Examples of Web-based interventions for alcohol prevention are as follows:

1. General Purpose: https://www.smartrecovery.org/ (SMART Recovery, 2021)
2. For Youth: https://y4y.ed.gov/tools/drug-and-alcohol-prevention-resources/ (Department of Education, 2021)
3. Alcohol Screening: www.CheckYourDrinking.net (Evolution Health Systems, 2021)
4. Both Youth and Adults: https://drugfree.org/ (Partnership to End Addiction, 2021)

This level of care will be especially useful if a patient presents one or two risk factors but doesn't present as needing care after being assessed by one of the alcohol screening tools previously discussed. For example, if a patient doesn't necessarily score in a level that would normally cause concern on an alcohol screening test but does shows signs of impulsivity that concerns the PCP, step one can be easily administered. This is especially warranted if multiple risk factors present together. Step one can also be useful if the patient screens as low risk on an alcohol use screening test. If a PCP notices a patient presents risk factors or scores low risk on a screen, they can immediately refer the patient to one of the Web-based preventions. The benefit of this is that if a PCP is at all concerned about any of the risk factors mentioned above, or if a patient scores extremely low risk on a screen, there doesn't have to be any hesitation to implement step one as is takes so little time and effort to refer a patient to Web-based intervention. Since this approach is not at all invasive nor does it require much effort or cost, it can lower the threshold of implementation of step one to the point where true early prevention can take place. This may prevent unhealthy alcohol use habits maybe even before alcohol use is present. Additionally, another way to utilize the appearance of risk factors can be to use them as an indication for the need to administer an alcohol screening test in addition to their annual screen if any time has passed since their last screening. For example, if a patient presents extreme stress or a PCP is aware of a family history of alcohol, in addition to administering step one, the PCP can then administer an alcohol screen in order to become more aware of the patient's risk for unhealthy alcohol use.

In addition to online interventions, bibliotherapy (i.e., therapy grounded in evidence-based, self-guided books) has emerged as another effective means of preventing alcohol issues from worsening, especially among those who are not experiencing clinically significant alcohol use disorder (Connors et al., 2017). Especially in rural areas, where constant phone or Internet contact may not always be feasible, bibliotherapy provides an excellent option to help patients learn more about alcohol use issues and learn strategies for preventing alcohol use from transforming into alcohol use disorder. A few examples of books that can be utilized for this process are as follows:

1. Rational Drinking: How to Live Happily With or Without Alcohol (Edelstein & Ross, 2013)
   (a) Available online and in print from www.amazon.com
2. So You Want to Cut Down Your Drinking?: A Self-help Guide to Sensible Drinking (Robertson & Heather, 1998)
   (a) Currently available only in print, ISBN-13: 978–1,902,030,036
   (b) Utilized in Connors et al. (2017) study of the effectiveness of bibliotherapy in prevention of alcohol problems in rural areas

13.6.3 Stepped Care Level 2: Brief Intervention

If a patient screens as moderate risk for alcohol use disorder or does not respond to the self-guided options in step one, step two on the model can be used. This would include meetings conducted by a PCP, nurse practitioner, nurse, or another trained staff member. The meetings would include training in skills such as stress management and coping skills that can replace alcohol use in situations when one wants to drink to cope. Additionally, these meetings would include the brief interview that was discussed above. More detailed information on how to implement the brief interview can be found in in “SBIRT: A Step-By-Step Guide” by the Bureau of Substance Abuse Services. Throughout all of the interventions, including a shared decision-making approach as used in the SPARC program is recommended to increase implementation effectiveness. Additionally, educational programs may be beneficial to implement into a practice. Cook et al. (2003) outlined a program that involved three 45-minute sessions that included information on stress management, nutrition, and substance use prevention, and results showed reductions in alcohol consumption, and results were maintained 8 months later. This prevention strategy would require adoption of a specific program, but medical practices could potentially save time if they were able to group at-risk patients together in a classroom setting for implementation. For more information, the program is discussed in further detail in the cited article by Cook et al. (2003).

Finally, step three would be if the patient screens as high risk or if actions taken in step two were unsuccessful and the patient didn’t show signs of improvement or risk worsened. This step is implemented if prevention efforts fail or if treatment is now needed as opposed to prevention. This step is significant for this chapter, however, to understand that step three is the option after steps one and two are unsuccessful or if the patient screens as high risk. It is also worth mentioning that if a primary care facility wanted to take an all-in approach to prevention and treatment, adopting and fully implementing one of the programs listed such as SPARC or SBIRT would be particularly beneficial.

13.6.4 Stepped Care Level 3: Referral

There is always the possibility that the prevention technique described above will not be successful in preventing a patient’s symptoms from progressing into alcohol use disorder. When scores on the screening tools (such as the AUDIT) combine with clinical interview data to suggest that a patient is meeting criteria for alcohol use disorder, it may be time to consider a referral to more specialized treatment, longer-term therapy. If that is the case, the database at www.abct.org can be useful in locating a skilled provider with the needed skillsets (ABCT, 2021).

13.7 Conclusion

Screening and brief interventions for alcohol use have become important parts of the toolkit in preventing alcohol use disorder and addressing other alcohol use issues (Spear et al., 2016). The SBIRT model highlighted in this chapter provides guidance for prevention programs that can be implemented in integrated care. Screening and brief interventions as well have been augmented by up-to-date screening tools, many of which can be administered in an easier-to-use online format. This gives providers a powerful set of measures that can efficiently be used to identify those who might benefit from brief interventions and thus prevent more serious alcohol-related problems.

However, more remains to be done. In many healthcare settings, patients with alcohol use issues are not identified quickly and thus do not gain access to preventative help (Vinson et al., 2007). Therefore, a key factor in the prevention of alcohol use disorder is to increase the accessibility of information regarding screening and brief intervention methods. It is hoped that this chapter will serve in this role and will aid in the building of prevention programs in integrated care clinics.

References

Agrawal, A., & Lynskey, M. T. (2008). Are there genetic influences on addiction: Evidence from family, adoption and twin studies. *Addiction (Abingdon, England), 103*(7), 1069–1081. https://doi.org/10.1111/j.1360-0443.2008.02213.x

Agrawal, A., Verweij, K. J. H., Gillespie, N. A., Heath, A. C., Lessov-Schlaggar, C. N., Martin, N. G., Nelson, E. C., Slutske, W. S., Whitfield, J. B., & Lynskey, M. T. (2012). The genetics of addiction—A translational perspective. *Translational Psychiatry, 2*(7), 140–153. https://doi.org/10.1038/tp.2012.54

American Academy of Child & Adolescent Psychiatry. (2019, May). *Substance use resource center*. Retrieved June 21, 2021, from American academy of child & adolescent psychiatry: https://www.aacap.org/aacap/Families_and_Youth/Resource_Centers/Substance_Use_Resource_Center/Home.aspx

American Psychiatric Association. (2013). Diagnostic and statistical manual of mental disorders (DSM-5®). American Psychiatric Pub.

American Psychological Association. (2017). *Ethical principles of psychologists and code of conduct* (2002, amended effective June 1, 2010, and January 1, 2017). https://www.apa.org/ethics/code/

Ames, G. M., & Bennet, J. B. (2011). Prevention interventions of alcohol problems in the workplace: A review and guiding framework. *Alcohol Research & Health, 34*(2), 175–187.

Anker, J. J., & Kushner, M. G. (2019). Co-occurring alcohol use disorder and anxiety: Bridging psychiatric, psychological, and neurobiological perspectives. *Alcohol Research: Current Reviews, 40*(1).

Anthony, J. C., & Petron (1995). Early-onset drug use and risk of later drug problems. *Drug and Alcohol Dependence, 40*(1). https://doi.org/10.1016/0376-8716(95)01194-3

Armeli, S., Dranoff, E., Tennen, H., Austad, C. S., Fallahi, C. R., Raskin, S., Wood, R., & Pearlson, G. A. (2014). A longitudinal study of the effects of coping motives, negative affect and drinking level on drinking problems among college students. *Anxiety Stress Coping: An International Journal, 27*(5), 527–541. https://doi.org/10.1080/10615806.2014.895821

Association for Behavioral and Cognitive Therapies. (2021). *Alcohol Abuse*. Retrieved June 21, 2021, from ABCT Fact Sheets: https://www.abct.org/Information/?m=mInformation&fa=fs_alcohol

Australian Government Department of Public Health. (2019). *PHN primary mental health care flexible funding pool programme guidance stepped care.* Retrieved June 12, 2021 from Australian Government Department of Public Health: STEPPED CARE (health.gov.au)

Babor, T., Higgins-Biddle, J., Saunders, J., & Monteiro, M. (2001). *AUDIT, the alcohol use disorders identification test: Guidelines for use in primary health care* (2nd ed.). World Health Organization.

Babor, T. F., McRee, B., Kassebaum, P. A., Grimaldi, P. L., Ahmed, K., & Bray, J. W. (2007). Screening, brief intervention, and referral to treatment (SBIRT): Toward a public health

approach to the management of substance abuse. *Substance Abuse: Journal of the Association for Medical Education and Research in Substance Abuse (AMERSA), 28*(3), 7–30.
Babor, T. F., Del Boca, F., & Bray, J. W. (2017). Screening, brief intervention and referral to treatment: Implications of SAMHSA's SBIRT initiative for substance abuse policy and practice. *Addiction, 112*, 110–117.
Ballesteros, J., Duffy, J. C., Querejeta, I., Arino, J., & Gonzales-Pinot, A. (2004). Efficacy of brief interventions for hazardous drinkers in primary care: Systematic review and meta-analyses. *Alcoholism Clinical and Experimental Research Colby, 28*(4), 608–618.
Barnett, N. P., Murphy, J. G., Cobly, S. M., & Monti, P. M. (2007). Efficacy of counselor vs. computer delivered intervention with mandated college students. *Addictive Behaviors, 31*, 2629–2648.
Bennett, J. B., Patterson, C. R., Reynolds, G. S., Wiitala, W. L., & Lehman, W. E. (2004). Team awareness, problem drinking, and drinking climate: Workplace social health promotion in a policy context. *American Journal of Health Promotion, 19*(2), 103–113.
Bien, T., Miller, W. R., & Tonigan, J. S. (1993). Brief interventions for alcohol problems: A review. *Addiction, 88*, 315–336.
Blumenthal, H., Blanchard, L., Feldner, M. T., Babson, K. A., Leen-Feldner, E. W., & Dixon, L. (2008). Traumatic event exposure, posttraumatic stress, and substance use among youth: A critical review of the empirical literature. *Current Psychiatry Reviews, 4*, 228–254. https://doi.org/10.2174/157340008786576562
Blumenthal, H., Leen-Feldner, E. W., Knapp, A. A., Badour, C. L., & Boals, A. (2015). Traumatic event exposure and alcohol use expectancies among adolescents. *Journal of Child & Adolescent Substance Abuse, 24*(6), 337–343. https://doi.org/10.1080/1067828x.2013.839407
Bobb, J. F., Lee, A. K., Lapham, G. T., Oliver, M., Ludman, E., Achtmeyer, C., Parrish, R., Caldeiro, R. M., Lozano, P., Richards, J. E., & Bradley, K. A. (2017). Evaluation of a pilot implementation to integrate alcohol-related care within primary care. *International Journal of Environmental Research and Public Health, 14*(9). https://doi.org/10.3390/ijerph14091030
Borsari, B., & Carey, K. B. (2005). Two brief alcohol interventions for mandated college students. *Psychology of Addictive Behaviors, 19*, 296–302.
Bower, P., & Gilbody, S. (2005). Stepped care in psychological therapies: Access, effectiveness and efficiency. *British Journal of Psychiatry, 186*(1), 11–17. https://doi.org/10.1192/bjp.186.1.11
Brady, K. T., Myrick, H., & McElroy, S. (1998). The relationship between substance use disorders, impulse control disorders, and pathological aggression. *The American Journal on Addictions, 7*(3), 221–230. https://doi.org/10.1111/j.1521-0391.1998.tb00340.x
Bray, J. W., Del Boca, F. K., McRee, B. G., Hayashi, S. W., & Babor, T. F. (2017). Screening, brief intervention and referral to treatment (SBIRT): Rationale, program overview and cross-site evaluation. *Addiction, 112*, 3–11.
Bush, K., Kivlahan, D. R., McDonell, M. B., et al. (1998). The AUDIT alcohol consumption questions (AUDIT-C): An effective brief screening test for problem drinking. Ambulatory care quality improvement project (ACQUIP). *Archives of Internal Medicine, 158*, 1789–1795.
Cole, J., Sprang, G., & Silman, M. (2019). Interpersonal trauma exposure, trauma symptoms, and severity of substance use disorder among youth entering outpatient substance abuse treatment. *Journal of Child & Adolescent Trauma, 12*(3), 341–349. https://doi.org/10.1007/s40653-018-0239-3
Connors, G. J., Walitzer, K. S., Prince, M. A., & Kubiak, A. (2017). Secondary prevention of alcohol problems in rural areas using a bibliotherapy-based approach. *Journal of Rural Mental Health, 41*(2), 162.
Cook, R. F., Back, A. S., Trudeau, J. V., & McPherson, T. (2003). Integrating substance abuse prevention into health promotion programs in the workplace: A social cognitive intervention targeting the mainstream user. In J. B. Bennett & W. E. K. Lehman (Eds.), *Preventing workplace substance abuse: Beyond drug testing to wellness* (pp. 97–133). American Psychological Association.

Cooper, L. M., Frone, M. R., Russell, M., & Mudar, P. (1995). Drinking to regulate positive and negative emotions: A motivational model of alcohol use. *Journal of Personality and Social Psychology, 69*(5), 990–1005. https://doi.org/10.1037/0022-3514.69.5.990

Department of Education. (2021). *Drug and Alcohol Prevention Resources*. Retrieved June 22, 2021, from You for Youth: https://y4y.ed.gov/tools/drug-and-alcohol-prevention-resources/

Department of Health and Human Services. (2013). *HIPAA Administrative Simplification*. Retrieved July 21, 2020, from U.S. Department of Health and Human Services: https://www.hhs.gov/sites/default/files/hipaa-simplification-201303.pdf

Detsyk, O. Z., A & Karpinets, I. M. (2013). The ways of improvement the alcohol abuse prevention in primary health care. *The Pharma Innovation-Journal, 2*(6), 20–24.

DiClemente, C. C., Corno, C. M., Graydon, M. M., Wiprovnick, A. E., & Knoblach, D. J. (2017). Motivational interviewing, enhancement, and brief interventions over the last decade: A review of reviews of efficacy and effectiveness. *Psychology of Addictive Behaviors, 31*(8), 862.

Dimeff, L. A., & McNeely, M. (2000). Computer-enhanced primary care practitioner advice for high-risk college drinkers in a primary healthcare setting. *Cognitive and Behavioral Practice, 7*(1), 82–100.

Doumas, D. M., & Hannah, E. (2008). Preventing high-risk drinking in youth in the workplace: A web-based normative feedback program. *Journal of Substance Abuse Treatment, 34*(3), 263–271.

Edelstein, M., & Ross, W. (2013). *Rational drinking: How to live happily with or without alcohol*. Will Ross.

Elder, G. H., Jr., Caspi, A., & Downey, G. (1986). Problem behavior and family relationships: Life course and intergenerational themes. In A. Sorensen, F. Weinert, & I. Sherrod (Eds.), *Human development and the life course: Multidisciplinary perspectives* (pp. 293–340). Erlbaum.

Ellison, C. G., Bradshaw, M., Rote, S., Storch, J., & Trevino, M. (2008). Religion and alcohol use among college students: Exploring the role of domain-specific religious salience. *Journal of Drug Issues, 38*(3), 821–846.

Enoch, M.-A. (2011). The role of early life stress as a predictor for alcohol and drug dependence. *Psychopharmacology, 214*(1), 17–31. https://doi.org/10.1007/s00213-010-1916-6

Enoch, M. A., & Goldman, D. (2001). The genetics of alcoholism and alcohol abuse. *Current Psychiatry Reports, 3*(2), 144–151. https://doi.org/10.1007/s11920-001-0012-3

Epic. (2021). *MyChart features*. Retrieved June 10, 2021, from MyChart: https://www.mychart.com/Features

Evolution Health Systems. (2021). *Evolution health*. Retrieved June 8, 2021, from Evolution Health: https://screen.evolutionhealth.care/cyd

Fisk, M., Livingstone, A., & Pit, S. W. (2020). Telehealth in the context of COVID-19: Changing perspectives in Australia, the United Kingdom, and the United States. *Journal of Medical Internet Research, 22*(6), e19264.

Friedmann, P. D. (2013). Alcohol use in adults. *New England Journal of Medicine, 368*(4), 365–373.

Garrett, D. (2010). Tapping into the value of health data through secondary use: As electronic health records (EHRs) proliferate across the nation, an important new opportunity awaits healthcare organizations that can find meaningful commercial uses for the data contained in their EHR systems. *Healthcare Financial Management, 64*(2), 76–84.

Genetic Science Learning Center. (2013, August 30) *The science of addiction: Genetics and the brain*. Retrieved June 04, 2021, from https://learn.genetics.utah.edu/content/addiction/

Goldman, D., Oroszi, G., & Ducci, F. (2005). The genetics of addictions: Uncovering the genes. *Nature Review Genetics, 6*, 521–532.

Grant, B. F. (1998). The impact of a family history of alcoholism on the relationship between age at onset of alcohol use and DSM–IV alcohol dependence. *Alcohol Research & Health, 22*, 144–147.

Grant, B. F., Stinson, F., & S., & Harford T., C. (2001). Age at onset of alcohol use and DSM-IV alcohol abuse and dependence: A 12-year follow-up. *Journal of Substance Abuse, 13*(4), 493–504. https://doi.org/10.1016/s0899-3289(01)00096-7

Grant, B. F., Goldstein, R. B., Saha, T. D., Chou, S. P., Jung, J., Zhang, H., Pickering, R. P., Ruan, J., Smith, S. M., Huang, B., & Hasin, D. S. (2015). Epidemiology of DSM-5 alcohol use disorder: Results from the National Epidemiologic Survey on alcohol and related conditions III. *JAMA Psychiatry, 72*(8), 757–766.

Harrison, P. A., Fulkerson, J. A., & Beebe, T. J. (1997). Multiple substance use among adolescent physical and sexual abuse victims. *Child Abuse and Neglect, 21*(6), 529–539. https://doi.org/10.1016/s0145-2134(97)00013-6

Hasin, D., Liu, X., Nunes, E., McCloud, S., Samet, S., & Endicott, J. (2002). Effects of major depression on remission and relapse of substance dependence. *Archives of General Psychiatry, 59*(4), 375–380. https://doi.org/10.1001/archpsyc.59.4.375

Haug, S., Castro, R. P., Meyer, C., Filler, A., Kowatsch, T., & Schaub, M. P. (2017). A mobile phone-based life skills training program for substance use prevention among adolescents: Pre-post study on the acceptance and potential effectiveness of the program, Ready4life. *JMIR mHealth and uHealth, 5*(10), e143.

Heath, A. C., Whitfield, J. B., Madden, P. A., Bucholz, K. K., Dinwiddie, S. H., & Slutske, W. S. (2001). Towards a molecular epidemiology of alcohol dependence: Analyzing the interplay of genetic and environmental risk factors. *British Journal of Psychiatry, 178*(40), 33–40. https://doi.org/10.1192/bjp.178.40.s33

Hingson, R. W., Heeren, T., & Winter, M. R. (2006). Age at drinking onset and alcohol dependence: Age at onset, duration, and severity. *Archives of Pediatrics & Adolescent Medicine, 160*(7), 739–746.

Horigian, V. E., Feaster, D. J., Brincks, A., Robbins, M. S., Perez, M. A., & Szapocznik, J. (2015). The effects of brief strategic family therapy (BSFT) on parent substance use and the association between parent and adolescent substance use. *Addictive Behaviors, 42*, 44–50. https://doi.org/10.1016/j.addbeh.2014.10.024

Huibers, M. J., & Cuijpers, P. (2014). Common (nonspecific) factors in psychotherapy. *The Encyclopedia of Clinical Psychology*, 1–6.

Humeniuk, R. E., Henry-Edwards, S., Ali, R. L., Poznyak, V., & Monteiro, M. (2010). *The alcohol, smoking and substance involvement screening test (ASSIST): Manual for use in primary care*. World Health Organization.

Ingersoll, K. S., Ceperich, S. D., Nettleman, M. D., Karanda, K., Brocksen, S., & Johnson, B. A. (2005). Reducing alcohol-exposed pregnancy risk in college women: Initial outcomes of a clinical trial of a motivational intervention. *Journal of Substance Abuse Treatment, 29*(3), 173–180.

Johnson, J. A., Lee, A., Vinson, D., & Seale, J. P. (2013). Use of AUDIT-based measures to identify unhealthy alcohol use and alcohol dependence in primary care: A validation study. *Alcoholism: Clinical and Experimental Research, 37*, E253–E259.

Kendler, K. S., Prescott, C. A., & Myers, J. (2003). The structure of genetic and environmental risk factors for common psychiatric and substance use disorders in men and women. *Archives of General Psychiatry, 60*(9), 929–937.

Kendler, K. S., Karkowski, L. M., Neale, M. C., & Prescott, C. A. (2000). Illicit psychoactive substance use, heavy use, abuse, and dependence in a US population-based sample of male twins. *Archives of General Psychiatry, 57*(3), 261–269. https://doi.org/10.1001/archpsyc.57.3.261

Kendler, K. S., Schmitt, J. E., Aggen, S. H., & Prescott, C. (2008). Genetic and environmental influences on alcohol, caffeine, cannabis, and nicotine use from early adolescence to middle adulthood. *Archives of General Psychiatry, 65*(6), 674–682. https://doi.org/10.1001/archpsyc.65.6.674

Komro, K. A., Perry, C. L., Veblen-Mortenson, S., Farbakhsh, K., Toomey, T. L., Stigler, M. H., Jones-Webb, R., Kugler, K. C., Pasch, K. E., & Williams, C. L. (2008). Outcomes from a randomized controlled trial of a multi-component alcohol use preventive intervention for urban youth: Project northland Chicago. *Addiction (Abingdon, England), 103*(4), 606–618. https://doi.org/10.1111/j.1360-0443.2007.02110.x

Kroenke, K., Spitzer, R. L., Williams, J. B., Monahan, P. O., & Löwe, B. (2007). Anxiety disorders in primary care: Prevalence, impairment, comorbidity, and detection. *Annals of Internal Medicine, 146*(5), 317–325.

Kypri, K., & McAnally, H. M. (2005). Randomized controlled trial of a web-based primary care intervention for multiple health risk behaviors. *Preventative Medicine, 41*(3–4), 761–766.

Kypri, K., Saunders, J. B., Williams, S. M., Mcgee, R., Langley, J. D., Cashell-Smith, M., & Gallagher, S. J. (2004). Web-based screening and brief intervention for hazardous drinking: A double-blind randomized controlled trial. *Addiction, 99*(11), 1410–1417.

Kypri, K., Langley, J. D., Saunders, J. B., & Cashell-Smith, M. (2008). Randomized controlled trial of web-based alcohol screening and brief intervention in primary care. *Archives of Internal Medicine, 168*(5), 530–536.

Larimer, M. E., & Cronce, J. M. (2002). Identification, prevention and treatment: A review of individual-focused strategies to reduce problematic alcohol consumption by college students. *Journal of Studies on Alcohol, Supplement*(14), 148–163. https://doi.org/10.15288/jsas.2002.s14.148

Larimer, M. E., & Cronce, J. M. (2007). Identification, prevention, and treatment revisited: Individual-focused college drinking prevention strategies 1999–2006. *Addictive Behaviors, 32*(11), 2439–2468. https://doi.org/10.1016/j.addbeh.2007.05.006

Lazarus, R. S., & Folkman, S. (1984). *Stress, appraisal, and coping*. Springer.

Linnoila, M., Virkkunen, M., Scheinin, M., Nuutila, A., Rimon, R., & Goodwin, F. K. (1983). Low cerebrospinal fluid 5-hydroxindoleacetic acid concentration differentiates impulsive from non-impulsive violent behavior. *Life Science, 33*, 2609–2614. https://doi.org/10.1016/0024-3205(83)90344-2

Lisak, D., & Miller, P. M. (2003). Childhood trauma, posttraumatic stress disorder, substance abuse, and violence. In P. Ouimette & P. J. Brown (Eds.), *Trauma and substance abuse: Causes, consequences, and treatment of comorbid disorders* (pp. 73–88). American Psychological Association. https://doi.org/10.1037/10460-004

Liskola, J., Haravuori, H., Lindberg, N., Niemelä, S., Karlsson, L., Kiviruusu, O., & Marttunen, M. (2018). AUDIT and AUDIT-C as screening instruments for alcohol problem use in adolescents. *Drug and Alcohol Dependence, 188*, 266–273. https://doi.org/10.1016/j.drugalcdep.2018.04.015

Lo, C. C., & Cheng, T. C. (2007). The impact of childhood maltreatment on Young Adults' substance abuse. *The American Journal of Drug and Alcohol Abuse, 33*(1), 139–146. https://doi.org/10.1080/00952990601091119

Lopez-Leon, S., González-Giraldo, Y., Wegman-Ostrosky, T., & Forero, D. A. (2021). Molecular genetics of substance use disorders: An umbrella review. *Neuroscience and Biobehavioral Reviews., 124*, 358–369. https://doi.org/10.1016/j.neubiorev.2021.01.019

Lynskey, M. T., Agrawal, A., & Heath, A. C. (2010). Genetically informative research on adolescent substance use: Methods, findings, and challenges. *Journal of the American Academy of Child & Adolescent Psychiatry, 49*(12), 1202–1214.

Madras, B. K., Compton, W. M., Avula, D., Stegbauer, T., Stein, J. B., & Clark, H. W. (2008). Screening, brief interventions, referral to treatment (SBIRT) for illicit drug and alcohol use at multiple healthcare sites: Comparison at intake and 6 months later. *Drug and Alcohol Dependence, 99*(1), 280–295.

Martens, M. P., Cimini, M. D., Barr, A. R., Rivero, E. M., Vellis, A. P., Desemone, G. A., & Horner, K. J. (2007). Implementing a screening and brief intervention for high-risk drinking in university-based health and mental health care settings: Reductions in alcohol use and correlates of success. *Addictive Behaviors, 32*(11), 2563–2572.

McElroy, S. L., Pope, H. G., Hudson, J. I., Keck, P. E., & White, K. L. (1991). Kleptomania: A report of 20 cases. *The American Journal of Psychiatry, 148*(5), 652–657. https://doi.org/10.1176/ajp.148.5.652

McNally, A. M., & Palfai, T. P. (2003). Brief group alcohol interventions with college students: Examining motivational components. *Journal of Drug Education, 33*(2), 159–176. https://doi.org/10.2190/82CT-LRC5-AMTW-C090

Meredith, L. R., Maralit, A. M., Thomas, S. E., Rivers, S. L., Salazar, C. A., Anton, R. F., … Squeglia, L. M. (2020). Piloting of the just say know prevention program: A psychoeducational approach to translating the neuroscience of addiction to youth. *The American Journal of Drug and Alcohol Abuse*, 1–10.

Merrill, J. E., & Read, J. P. (2010). Motivational pathways to unique types of alcohol consequences. *Psychology of Addictive Behaviors, 24*(4), 705–711. https://doi.org/10.1037/a0020135

Miller, W. R., & Rollnick, S. (2013). *Motivational interviewing: Helping people to change (3rd edition)*. Guilford Press.

Morris, E. P., Stewart, S. H., & Ham, L. S. (2005). The relationship between social anxiety disorder and alcohol use disorders: A critical review. *Clinical Psychology Review, 25*(6), 734–760.

Morrison, J., & Flegel, K. (2016). *Interviewing children and adolescents* (2nd ed.). Guilford Press.

Moyer, A., Finney, J., Swearingen, C., & Vergun, P. (2002). Brief interventions for alcohol problems: A meta-analytic review of controlled investigations in treatment-seeking and non-treatment seeking populations. *Addiction, 7*, 279–292.

National Research Council and Institute of Medicine. (2009). *Preventing mental, emotional, and behavioral disorders among Young people: Progress and possibilities*. The National Academies Press. https://doi.org/10.17226/12480

National Institute on Alcohol Abuse and Alcoholism (NIAAA). (2017). Nih.gov. https://www.niaaa.nih.gov/

Nilsen, P., Aalto, M., Bendtsen, P., & Seppa, K. (2006). Effectiveness of strategies to implement brief alcohol intervention in primary healthcare. *Scandinavian Journal of Primary Health Care, 24*, 5–15.

Parker, D. A., Levin, B. M., & Harford, T. C. (1996). Effects of early drinking and an antisocial orientation on the alcohol use of young Russians. *Alcoholism: Clinical and Experimental Research, 20*(7), 1179–1183.

Partnership to End Addiction. (2021). *Prevention & early action*. Retrieved June 22, 2021, from *drugfree.org*: https://drugfree.org/prevention-and-taking-action-early/

Perry, J. L., & Carroll, M. E. (2008). The role of impulsive behavior in drug abuse. *Psychopharmacology, 200*(1), 1–26. https://doi.org/10.1007/s00213-008-1173-0

Pietrzak, R. H., Goldstein, R. B., Southwick, S. M., & Grant, B. F. (2011). Prevalence and Axis I comorbidity of full and partial posttraumatic stress disorder in the United States: Results from wave 2 of the National Epidemiologic Survey on alcohol and related conditions. *Journal of Anxiety Disorders, 25*(3), 456–465. https://doi.org/10.1016/j.janxdis.2010.11.010

Rabinowitz, J., Bromet, E. J., Lavelle, J., Carlson, G., Kovasznay, B., & Schwartz, J. E. (1998). Prevalence and severity of substance use disorders and onset of psychosis in first-admission psychotic patients. *Psychological Medicine, 28*(6), 1411–1419. https://doi.org/10.1017/s0033291798007399

Rahm, A. K., Boggs, J. M., Martin, C., Price, D. W., Beck, A., Becker, T. E., & Dearing, J. W. (2015). Facilitators and barriers to implementing screening, brief intervention, and referral to treatment (SBIRT) in primary care in integrated health care settings, *Substance Abuse, 36*(3) 281–288.

Rawaf, S., Allen, L. N., Stigler, F. L., Kringos, D., Quezada Yamamoto, H., van Weel, C., & Global Forum on Universal Health Coverage and Primary Health Care. (2020). Lessons on the COVID-19 pandemic, for and by primary care professionals worldwide. *European Journal of General Practice, 26*(1), 129–133.

Ray, L. A., Bujarski, S., Grodin, E., Hartwell, E., Green, R., Venegas, A., … Miotto, K. (2019). State-of-the-art behavioral and pharmacological treatments for alcohol use disorder. *The American Journal of Drug and Alcohol Abuse, 45*(2), 124–140.

Rehm, J., Mathers, C., Popova, S., Thavorncharoensap, M., Teerawattananon, Y., & Patra, J. (2009). Global burden of disease and injury and economic cost attributable to alcohol use and alcohol-use disorders. *The Lancet, 373*(9682), 2223–2233.

Robertson, I., & Heather, N. (1998). *So you want to cut down your drinking? A self-help manual for controlled drinking*. Scottish Health Education Group.

Salomon, R. M., Mazure, C. M., Delgado, P. L., Mendia, P., & Charney, D. S. (1994). Serotonin function in aggression: The effect of acute plasma tryptophan depletion in aggressive patients. *Biological Psychiatry, 35*(8), 570–572. https://doi.org/10.1016/0006-3223(94)90105-8

Schuckit, M. A. (2006). Comorbidity between substance use disorders and psychiatric conditions. *Addiction, 101*(Supplement s1), 76–88. https://doi.org/10.1111/j.1360-0443.2006.01592.x

Segrin, C., McNelis, M., & Pavlich, C. A. (2018). Indirect effects of loneliness on substance use through stress. *Health Communication, 33*(5), 513–518. https://doi.org/10.1080/10410236.2016.1278507

Seigers, D. K. L., & Carey, K. B. (2010). Screening and brief interventions for alcohol use in college health centers: A review. *Journal of American College Health, 59*(3), 151–158. https://doi.org/10.1080/07448481.2010.502199

Sinha, R. (2001). How does stress increase risk of drug abuse and relapse? *Psychopharmacology, 158*(4), 343–359. https://doi.org/10.1007/s002130100917

SMART Recovery. (2021). *There's life beyond addiction*. Retrieved June 10, 2021, from SMART Recovery: https://www.smartrecovery.org/

Spear, S. E., Shedlin, M., Gilberti, B., Fiellin, M., & McNeely, J. (2016). Feasibility and acceptability of an audio computer-assisted self-interview version of the alcohol, smoking and substance involvement screening test (ASSIST) in primary care patients. *Substance Abuse, 37*(2), 299–305.

Stigler, M. H., Neusel, E., & Perry, C. L. (2011). School-based programs to prevent and reduce alcohol use among youth. *Alcohol Research & Health, 34*(2), 157–162.

Titanium Software. (2019). *Titanium schedule*. Retrieved March 13, 2019, from titaniumschedule.com: http://www.titaniumschedule.com/Main/Default.aspx

Trenz, R. C., Scherer, M., Harrell, P., Zur, J., Sinha, A., & Latimer, W. (2012). Early onset of drug and polysubstance use as predictors of injection drug use among adult drug users. *Addictive Behaviors, 37*(4), 367–372. https://doi.org/10.1016/j.addbeh.2011.11.011

Tsuang, M. T., Bar, J. L., Harley, R. M., & Lyons, M. J. (2001). The Harvard twin study of substance abuse: What we have learned. *Harvard Review of Psychiatry, 9*(6), 267–279. https://doi.org/10.1080/10673220127912

Vinson, D. C., Kruse, R. L., & Seale, J. P. (2007). Simplifying alcohol assessment: Two questions to identify alcohol use disorders. *Alcoholism: Clinical and Experimental Research, 31*(8), 1392–1398.

Virkkunen, M., De Jong, J., Bartko, J., & Linnoila, M. (1989). Psychobiological concomitants of history of suicide attempts among violent offenders and impulsive fire setters. *Archives of General Psychiatry, 46*(7), 604–606. https://doi.org/10.1001/archpsyc.1989.01810070030004

Volkow, N. D. (2004). The reality of comorbidity: Depression and drug abuse. *Biological Psychiatry, 56*(10), 714–717. https://doi.org/10.1016/j.biopsych.2004.07.007

Vornik, L. A., & Brown, E. S. (2006). Management of co-morbid bipolar and substance abuse. *Journal of Clinical Psychiatry, 67*(SUPPL.7), 24–30.

Weathers, F.W., Litz, B.T., Keane, T.M., Palmieri, P.A., Marx, B.P., & Schnurr, P.P. (2013). The PTSD Checklist for DSM-5 (PCL-5). Scale available from the National Center for PTSD at www.ptsd.va.gov.

Werch, C., Bian, H., Moore, M. J., Ames, S., Diclemente, C., & Weiler, R. (2007). Brief multiple behavior interventions in a college student health care clinic. *Journal of Adolescent Health, 41*(6), 577–585.

Wiesche, L., Schacht, M., & Werners, B. (2017). Strategies for interday appointment scheduling in primary care. *Health Care Management Science, 20*(3), 403–418.

Wilens, T. E., Yule, A., Martelon, M., Zulauf, C., & Faraone, S. V. (2014). Parental history of substance use disorders (SUD) and SUD in offspring: A controlled family study of bipolar disorder. *The American Journal on Addictions, 23*(5), 440–446. https://doi.org/10.1111/j.1521-0391.2014.12125.x

Williams, E. C., Achtmeyer, C. E., Young, J. P., Berger, D., Curran, G., Bradley, K. A., Richards, J., Siegel, M., Ludman, E., Lapham, G., Forehand, M., & Harris, A. H. (2018). Barriers to and facilitators of alcohol use disorder pharmacotherapy in primary care: A qualitative study in five VA clinics. *Journal of General Internal Medicine, 33*(3), 258–267.

Willis, B., & O'Donohue, W. (2020). It's not just Murphy's law: A case study of problematic records transmission. *Clinical Case Studies*. 1534650120984238.

World Health Organization. (2001). *AUDIT: The alcohol use disorders identification test: Guidelines for use in primary health care*. Department of Mental Health and Substance Dependence.

Zimmerman, M. (2013). *Interview guide for evaluating DSM-5 psychiatric disorders and the mental status exam*. Psych Products Press.

Chapter 14
Medication Adherence in Primary Care

Andrew M. Peterson

14.1 Introduction

Medication adherence is "the extent to which patients take medications as prescribed by their health care providers" (Osterberg & Blaschke, 2005). There continues to be a high concern over patients' ability to comply with a prescribed medication regimen. It is well documented that 20–30% of prescriptions are never filled and of those that are filled, only about 50% of medications used for chronic conditions are taken as prescribed (Peterson et al., 2003; Osterberg & Blaschke, 2005; Viswanathan et al., 2012). Further, this lack of adherence spans age, gender, and ethnic demographics and constitutes a health problem in and of itself. Therefore, it is imperative that practitioners working with patients understand and support the factors which contribute to good medication adherence and strive to overcome barriers which prevent it (Choudhry et al., 2008; Osterberg & Blaschke, 2005).

14.2 Definition/Diagnostic Criteria

There are two terms used to describe the phenomenon of people not taking their medication as prescribed: medication compliance and medication adherence. Various organizations and professions have put forth different yet similar definitions of these terms. The International Society of Pharmacoeconomics and Outcomes Research (ISPOR) defines medication compliance as "the extent to which a patient

A. M. Peterson (✉)
Philadelphia College of Pharmacy/University of the Sciences in Philadelphia, Philadelphia, PA, USA
e-mail: a.peters@usciences.edu

W. O'Donohue, M. Zimmermann (eds.), *Handbook of Evidence-Based Prevention of Behavioral Disorders in Integrated Care*,
https://doi.org/10.1007/978-3-030-83469-2_14

acts in accordance with the prescribed interval and dose of and dosing regime" (Cramer et al., 2008, p. 46). The World Health Organization (WHO) defines adherence as "the extent to which a person's behavior – taking medications, following diets, or executing lifestyle changes, corresponds with agreed recommendations from a health care provider" (Sabaté, 2003, p. 17). While the two terms – medication adherence and medication compliance – are similar and often used interchangeably, currently the use of adherence is more commonly employed because it implies a mutual agreement between the healthcare practitioner and the patient versus the superior/subordinate relationship implied by the term compliance.

Several factors contribute to the phenomenon of medication nonadherence including patient-related, treatment-related, and relationship-related factors. The patient-related factors include medication and disease knowledge, the patient's socioeconomic status, demographics, and their living situation. Those factors related to treatment include the medication effects, dosage form/route of administration, and dosage frequency. Lastly, the relationship factors include the patient-provider relations, the provider's communication style, and the information exchanged between the patient and the provider (Table 14.1).

Like the multitude of factors affecting adherence, there are several types of medication adherence. Vrijens and colleagues describe three major phases of medication adherence – initiation, implementation, and discontinuation (Fig. 14.1). These phases of adherence begin when the patient takes the first dose of medication and ends when the patient stops taking the medication. Prior to initiation is another phase of adherence – initial medication adherence or primary adherence. This is related to a patient's willingness and ability to obtain the medication in the first place.

Medication adherence can be seen as a fault in one of the three processes: initiation, implementation, and discontinuation (Vrijens et al., 2012). Individuals can be nonadherent in the (1) failure to present an initial prescription for filling or taking it once retrieved (initial nonadherence), (2) failure to take first dose of medication (initiation), (3) failure to follow medication instructions (implementation), and (4) failure to refill medications used for chronic conditions (discontinuation). Patients who do not initially fill their medication do so because of various factors, including

Table 14.1 General factors affecting medication adherence

Category	Factors
Patient-related	Knowledge of the medication Knowledge of the disease state Socioeconomic status Patient abilities/patient support system Patient demographics
Treatment-related	Disease characteristics Medication effects Medication dosing frequency/medication route administration/dosage form
Relationship-related	Provider-patient communication Educational support

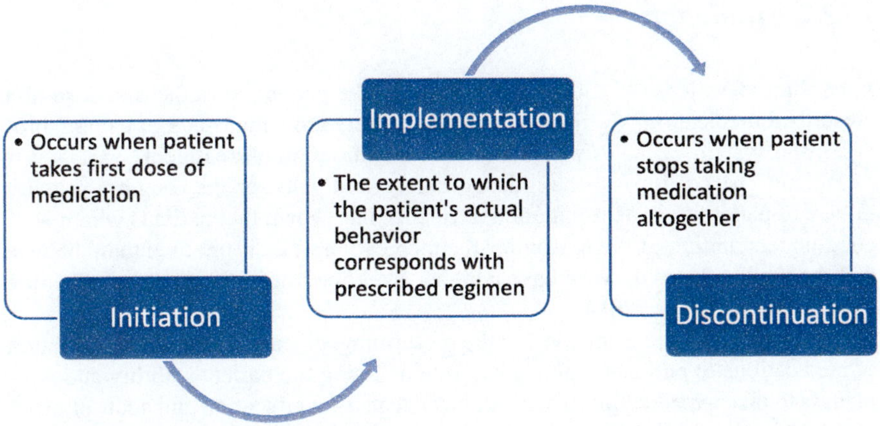

Fig. 14.1 Phases of medication adherence

due to their perception of the efficacy, safety, and cost of the medication and possibly their inability to access a pharmacy (Lehman et al., 2014; Pednekar & Peterson, 2018). For all the types of nonadherence, multiple theories exist to explain the cause and the complexity of this phenomenon.

14.2.1 Initial Medication Adherence

The first step in medication adherence is obtaining the medication in the first place. Initial adherence must occur before the three other phases of adherence occur (Hutchings et al., 2015). This includes taking the prescription to the pharmacy and retrieving the filled prescription. When patients fail to obtain a medication in an acceptable period of time, it is deemed initial nonadherence or primary medication nonadherence (PMN) (Adams & Stolpe, 2016).

Patients who fail to present the prescription for the initial fill do so either intentionally or unintentionally. The intentional failure to present may be due to health beliefs regarding the medication, fear of the side effects, or even perception of cost or lack of insurance.

Unintentional failure is usually forgetfulness or, at times, loss of the paper prescription. In either case, current technology known as electronic prescribing minimizes the failure to present as the prescription is sent directly to the patient's pharmacy electronically from the prescriber's office (Gleason et al., 2009). This leads to the second component of initial medication adherence – abandonment. Abandonment is when a prescription is filled by a pharmacist, but the patient does not pick it up, and it must be returned to stock. The primary reason for patients abandoning their prescription at the pharmacy is because it cost more than they expected and they are either unwilling or unable to pay for it. (Shrank et al., 2010)

14.2.2 Initiation

According to Vrijens, "(i)nitiation occurs when the patient takes the first dose of a prescribed medication" (Vrijens et al., 2012). There are a multitude of patient, provider, and system variables which influence the initiation of treatment.

Patients' perceptions of the efficacy, safety, and value of the drug are primary drivers of patient treatment initiation. Evidence has shown that patients who have a good understanding of the reason for the medication in their treatment and believe that the medication will work have a higher likelihood of initiating the medication therapy (Fischer et al., 2014).

The providers – those involved in the prescribing, dispensing, and administration of medications to patients – play a key role in aiding the patient's ability and willingness to take a medication. These providers can offer education and counseling on the need for the medication and how it will impact their care. Further, these providers can offer insight into what side effects to expect and how to manage them and answer questions regarding drug-drug interactions or just address patients' concerns in general. This type of communication aids in improving a patient's belief about the value of their medication in treating their disease as well as providing the level of support that making a decision to start the medication is the right one. So, good communication between the provider and the patient at the time of prescribing, along with patient counseling by the pharmacist, improves the likelihood that patients will take the medication the first time (Fischer et al., 2014).

System factors that influence the initiation, and ultimately the implementation of medication treatment, range anywhere from insurance coverage and medication cost to ease of use of the product. Patients with poor or no insurance coverage are likely not to even obtain the medication to begin with, or if there are significant hurdles to overcome (prior-authorization approvals, step therapy), the patient may feel discouraged and wonder about the value of the medication (Gleason et al., 2009).

14.2.3 Implementation

As noted earlier, with a typical PMN rate of 20–30%, that leaves 70–80% of medications in the possession of patients to be taken as prescribed. When patients have filled a prescription but do not take a medication as scheduled, Vrijens considers this a failure of implementation. This implementation failure could be due to forgetfulness, intentional dose-skipping, or delays in refilling prescriptions. The clinical consequences of implementation failure are a function of the both the disease and the drug. For example, patients taking highly active antiretroviral therapy (HAART) for HIV disease had 63% virologic failure when 80–90% compliant and only 21% failure when >95% compliant (Paterson et al., 2000). In contrast, some drugs such as aspirin are more forgiving. Due to its irreversible binding to platelet when used to prevent clotting, lack of compliance with aspirin is less troublesome because the drug activity in the body outlasts the dosing interval (Albassam & Hughes, 2021).

Patients in the implementation phase who continue to take their medication, whether as prescribed or not, are considered to be "persistent." The ISPOR defines persistence as "the accumulation of time from initiation to discontinuation of therapy. Measured by time metric" (Cramer et al., 2008).

14.2.4 Discontinuation

When patients stop taking their medication altogether, that is, they are no longer persistent, Vrijens considers them entering the discontinuation phase. Adverse effects were the most commonly cited reason for discontinuation, and others include lack of efficacy, lack of symptoms, and high cost (Gajria et al., 2014; Roborel de Climens et al., 2020).

14.3 Prevalence

Medication nonadherence knows no boundaries. Patients of any age, socioeconomic status, gender, or ethnicity are likely to be nonadherent to medications. As noted earlier, about 20–30% of prescriptions are never obtained by the patient, and in patients taking medications for chronic conditions, only about 50% adhere to long-term therapy. This lack of adherence results in about 33% to nearly 70% of all medication-related hospital admissions.

14.4 Risk Factors

A myriad of risk factors exist which can help identify patients who are at risk for not adhering to a medication regimen. This ranges from socioeconomic factors specific to a patient, the provider/patient relationship, or disease states and specific therapies which can affect a person's willingness and ability to adhere to a medication regimen.

14.4.1 Patient-Related Factors

14.4.1.1 Knowledge of the Medication and Disease State

Self-efficacy, defined as "a patient's belief in his/her ability to succeed in adhering to prescription medications" (Lee et al., 2013, p. 35), has a positive impact on medication adherence. Lee et al., (2013) used a 13-question, 3-point scale (Self-Efficacy for Appropriate Medication Use Scale – SEAMS) to measure self-efficacy as part of a broader model for predicting medication adherence. Their results showed that with each unit increase in self-efficacy score, medication adherence increased by 27% in elderly patients (Lee et al., 2013).

Rhee studied adolescents (12–20 years old) with asthma, examining medication adherence and three measures of cognitive awareness: self-efficacy, barrier perception, and outcome perception. Their results show that self-efficacy predicted better asthma medication adherence, in contrast to barrier perceptions which predicted poorer adherence and poorer asthma control. They also found that outcome expectations did not have a relationship to medication adherence or asthma outcome, but self-efficacy independently predicted fewer missed doses (Rhee et al., 2018). It is then reasoned that lack of knowledge about the disease and the reasons medication is needed are important factors but that the concept of self-efficacy is a mediator to medication adherence.

14.4.1.2 Socioeconomic Status

Patients with a good social and family support network willing and able to assist in their healthcare regimens tend to be more adherent (Barcenas et al., 2012). Patients living in an unstable living environment or with limited access to healthcare tend to have worse medication adherence. Further, these situations may be worsened if there is a lack of health insurance or complicated work schedules which prevent people from accessing medications or making time to take medications. Lastly, and not to be overlooked, is the rising cost of medications. Cost of treatment is a major factor. Co-payments decrease medication adherence in an inverse fashion – the higher the co-payment, the lower the adherence (Gast & Mathes, 2019; Gellad, 2007).

14.4.1.3 Patient Demographics

Some research shows that medication adherence decreases with increasing age (Raji et al., 2004) and others do not demonstrate the relationship (Krueger et al., 2015). Age-related nonadherence may be more directly related to factors associated with aging: impaired physical and cognitive functions or the patient's understanding of the effects of nonadherence (Barat et al., 2001). Further, males are less likely to be adherent as compared to females among elderly patients (Jin et al., 2016). Individuals belonging to different races and ethnicities can have different beliefs and attitudes toward health and medications. Studies have shown that Black and Hispanic seniors are less likely to be adherent as compared to White seniors, though this may also be a socioeconomic issue (Gellad et al., 2007).

14.4.1.4 Patient Abilities and Support Systems

While intuitive to most individuals, physical impairment by patients is one of the most overlooked reasons for medication nonadherence. Patients with conditions such as arthritis (Pasma et al., 2013) or fibromyalgia may have difficulty opening medication bottles or manipulating inhalers or syringes. Similarly, visually or cognitively impaired individuals may be unable to read or follow directions on a bottle or even a medication pamphlet. Lack of knowledge about a disease state and the reasoning for a medication also impair a person's willingness to adhere to a treatment regimen.

Physical impairments and cognitive limitations may increase the risk for nonadherence in patients. These impairments may be true limitations or barriers to a patient's adherence, and recognition of them, coupled with specific strategies for overcoming them, can improve adherence. For example, elderly patients with compromised physical dexterity such as decreased muscle strength or deformities associated with conditions such as rheumatoid arthritis can affect their ability to open medication bottles or use an inhaler. Fialová and Onder (2009) found that restrictions in mobility, fine motor skills, and upper body functioning were significant factors associated with difficulty in patients taking medications.

Further, individuals who are blind or visually impaired (due to glaucoma, loss of vision, or poor vision) may have compromised ability to read prescription labels or instructions, determine the color and markings characterizing medications, or see scales on medical devices. Such individuals may rely on their memory or caregiver to take medications or may not take medications at all. Patients with visual impairment were less likely to have good adherence compared to those with no impairment (18.42% vs 53.26%) (Shruthi et al., 2016). Similarly, patients experiencing difficulty in swallowing or dysphagia may discourage patients to take medications, and hence it may negatively impact medication adherence (Kelly et al., 2010).

14.4.2 Treatment Related

14.4.2.1 Disease State

Grenard et al. (2011) conducted a meta-analysis demonstrating that the odds of a patient with depression being nonadherent is 1.76 greater than a person without depression. This effect was seen across patients with various chronic diseases including diabetes and cardiovascular diseases and did not vary significantly across these disease states. This clearly demonstrates that practitioners need to be aware of the increased risk of nonadherence in patients who develop depression while taking other chronic medications (Grenard et al., 2011).

A meta-analysis found that for less serious diseases (e.g., hypertension, arthritis), patients with higher severity of disease are more likely to be adherent than the patients in better health. In contrast, in patients with cancer and HIV, adherence was lower in patients with a higher disease severity versus those in better health (DiMatteo et al., 2007). Similarly, Elsous et al. (2017) showed that patients suffering from the disease for longer time are more likely to be adherent than those patients with shorter duration of disease. The authors postulated that newly diagnosed patients do not understand their disease well enough and that as they learn more about it, their attitude toward the disease and treatment evolves and the interaction between their provider improves (Elsous et al., 2017).

It is often thought that patients with symptomatic diseases (e.g., hypothyroidism, pain) would be more adherent to their medication regimen than patients with asymptomatic diseases. The concept is that the absence of symptoms does not reinforce the notion that the patient has a disease; thus, there is no perceived need to take a medication. Conversely, in those diseases in which symptoms are controlled when taking a medication, adherence is more likely due to the association of symptom resolution when adherent. There are mitigating factors to this, however. Carney et al. (1998) conducted a study demonstrating that patients with symptomatic angina were *less adherent* to twice-daily aspirin than their asymptomatic counterparts. Intuitively, one could see that the patient might consider the aspirin ineffective, thus choosing not to take it.

14.4.2.2 Medication Effects

In a semi-structured interview study of community pharmacy patients, Rathbone et al. (2021) showed patients perceived that if a medication did not have a physical effect (i.e., a side effect or a therapeutic effect), the medication was considered "weak," and the patient was therefore "not motivated to take (it)." Further, the researchers noted that medication adherence had a social component. The participants voiced the notion that it was necessary to take medications as prescribed to avoid social consequences (e.g., from the healthcare providers, peers, family) of nonadherence.

14.4.2.3 Medication Route/Administration/Dosage

Patients suffering from multiple chronic disease conditions are often prescribed multiple medications which make their dosage regimen complex. Both the higher number of medications and the greater complexity of the diseases are significantly associated with lower medication adherence among older adults (Rolnick et al., 2013).

In 2013, Srivastava and colleagues published a meta-analysis demonstrating that medication adherence improves when dosing is reduced to once daily. The overall results indicated that once-daily dosing was associated with patients being three times more likely to be adherent than more than once-daily regimens. This held across all disease states studied (hypertension, diabetes, depression, HIV/AIDS). Interestingly, this also held true for once-daily vs twice-daily dosing. In general, this study confirmed that adherence rates declined as dosing frequency increased.

14.4.3 Relationship-Related

14.4.3.1 Provider-Patient Communication and Educational Support

The provider-patient relationship has tremendous impact on medication adherence. Relationships that have a higher level of trust (Schoenthaler et al., 2014) provide reinforcement and encouragement and have a more positive impact on adherence (Gu et al., 2017). Similarly, poor communication, particularly as it relates to medication purpose, side effects, and the importance of taking the medication, is associated with lower adherence. Poor or lack of communication concerning the benefits, instructions for use, and side effects of medications can also contribute to nonadherence, especially in older adults with memory problems (Gellad et al., 2011). It is evident that older patients with low levels of education are more likely to be nonadherent to the medications (Jin et al., 2016). It could be possible that more educated people may have more knowledge about the benefits of medication adherence, disease condition, and healthier habits. Further, since Velligan and colleagues' systematic review indicated that negative attitudes toward medications are directly associated with intentional nonadherence (Velligan et al., 2017), perhaps educating the patient on the importance of the medication would improve adherence.

14.5 Effective Screening

There are a number of means by which practitioners can successfully screen patients for medication nonadherence. Commonly used assessment tools include the Rapid Estimate of Adult Literacy in Medicine – Revised (REALM-R) and the Morisky Medication Adherence Scale (MMAS) (Miller, 2016). Together, these tools can be helpful to assess a patient's initial ability to adhere to a medication regimen (*initiation)* then an ongoing screening for their continued adherence (*implementation*).

The REALM-R, a tool that measures health literacy, is an eight-word recognition/pronunciation tool assessing a patient's ability to read medical words (e.g., flu, allergic, jaundice, constipation). Raehl and colleagues (2006) found a positive relationship between seniors' intention to be adherent to their regimen and better scores on the REALM-R when taking into consideration the patient's socioeconomic status, age, and over-the-counter drug use. Patients who score low on this assessment may need additional support to initiate their medication regimen.

Once the patient has initiated their regimen, there are a series of tools that can be used to assess a patient's continued adherence. Two versions of the MMAS exist – a four- and an eight-question validated assessment survey. Both the four- and eight-item scales are equally valid, and both take little time, so either may work. Either of these tools can be used to determine if nonadherence exists and are often used as screening tools in this manner. However, they are not good for identifying the reason for the nonadherence and therefore cannot provide guidance to the clinician how best to proceed (Tan et al., 2014).

14.6 Preventing Medication Nonadherence

Preventing medication nonadherence is a multifactorial process. Providers must first prevent PMN (lack of initial medication adherence) so that the patient can start medication therapy as prescribed. Aside from e-prescribing, there appears to be little that helps to improve PMN – including automated and live phone call reminders (Zeber et al., 2013; Fischer et al., 2014). The strongest association with lack of initial adherence appears to be financial, with out-of-pocket expenses (copays, coinsurances, etc.) showing a negative linear effect (Zeber et al., 2013). That is, as out-of-pocket expenses increase, initial adherence decreases.

Many of the factors affecting initial medication adherence are similar to those affecting implementation. Once the patient initiates medication, it is incumbent on the practitioner to aid in the continuation of the medication regiment. Behavioral interventions – those designed to influence or change a specific behavior – have shown promise (Peterson et al., 2003; Zeber et al., 2013). Specifically, medication pillboxes or blister packs designed to organize medications and make them more readily available have been proven to be effective (Peterson et al., 2003; Ruppar et al., 2015).

Technology has had a positive impact on medication adherence in the initial and implementation phases. For example, electronic prescribing (e-prescribing) has a positive impact on initial medication adherence. A paper by Lanham and colleagues (Lanham et al., 2016) reviewed some of the literature and found a 10% improvement in PMN using e-prescribing versus paper prescriptions. Further, using electronic reminder tools designed to record if a patient took a medication has also shown improved adherence (Checchi et al., 2014).

A study by Choudhry and colleagues (2010) demonstrated that lowering co-payments to nearly zero for patients taking statin drugs or clopidogrel had a 2.8% and 3.8% increase in monthly adherence, respectively. While the size of this effect may not appear large, from a population perspective, it may have a large impact on reducing overall healthcare costs.

Educational interventions, aimed at the patient, show promise as well, with one meta-analysis indicating nearly an 11% improvement (Peterson et al., 2003). However, team-based care, where pharmacists reconciled and tailored medication regimens in coordination with primary care providers, coupled with medication refill reminders showed a 15% higher rate of adherence compared to those not receiving these services. This is consistent with other literature suggesting that no single intervention – behavioral or educational – is more effective but that, combined, there is an overall improvement (Peterson et al., 2003).

Overall, it appears that identifying the patient-specific reason for the medication nonadherence and then tailoring an intervention aligned with that reason are the best approaches to preventing nonadherence. Practitioners must consider that the reasons for nonadherence may change over time. For example, a patient's financial situation may change, thus creating a reason for nonadherence when one did not exist before. Further, identifying populations at risk – the elderly, patients with low literacy or with a lower socioeconomic status – and tailoring interventions specific to their situation are key to improving adherence.

References

Adams, A. J., & Stolpe, S. F. (2016, May). Defining and measuring primary medication nonadherence: Development of a quality measure. *Journal of Managed Care & Specialty Pharmacy, 22*(5), 516–523.

Albassam, A., & Hughes, D. A. (2021). What should patients do if they miss a dose? A systematic review of patient information leaflets and summaries of product characteristics. *European Journal of Clinical Pharmacology, 77*, 251–260.

Barat, I., Andreasen, F., & Damsgaard, E. M. (2001, June). Drug therapy in the elderly: What doctors believe and patients actually do. *British Journal of Clinical Pharmacology, 51*(6), 615–622.

Barcenas, C. H., Zhang, N., Zhao, H., Duan, Z., Buchholz, T. A., Hortobagyi, G. N., & Giordano, S. H. (2012). Anthracycline regimen adherence in older patients with early breast cancer. *The Oncologist, 17*(3), 303–311.

Carney, R. M., Freedland, K. E., Eisen, S. A., Rich, M. W., Skala, J. A., & Jaffe, A. S. (1998). Adherence to a prophylactic medication regimen in patients with symptomatic versus asymptomatic ischemic heart disease. *Behavioral Medicine, 24*(1), 35–39.

Checchi, K. D., Huybrechts, K. F., Avorn, J., & Kesselheim, A. S. (2014, September 24). Electronic medication packaging devices and medication adherence: A systematic review. *Journal of the American Medical Association, 312*(12), 1237–1247.

Choudhry, N. K., Setoguchi, S., Levin, R., Winkelmayer, W. C., & Shrank, W. H. (2008). Trends in adherence to secondary prevention medications in elderly post-myocardial infarction patients. Pharmacoepidem. *Drug Safe, 17*,1189–1196.

Choudhry, N. K., Fischer, M. A., Avorn, J., Schneeweiss, S., Solomon, D. H., Berman, C., Jan, S., Liu, J., Lii, J., Brookhart, M. A., Mahoney, J. J., & Shrank, W. H. (2010, November). At Pitney Bowes, value-based insurance design cut copayments and increased drug adherence. *Health Affairs (Millwood), 29*(11), 1995–2001.

Cramer, J. A., Roy, A., Burrell, A., Fairchild, C. J., Fuldeore, M. J., Ollendorf, D. A., & Wong, P. K. (2008, January–February). Medication compliance and persistence: Terminology and definitions. *Value in Health, 11*(1), 44–47.

DiMatteo, M. R., Haskard, K. B., & Williams, S. L. (2007, June). Health beliefs, disease severity, and patient adherence: A meta-analysis. *Medical Care, 45*(6), 521–528.

Elsous, A., Radwan, M., Al-Sharif, H., & Abu Mustafa, A. (2017, June 9). Medications adherence and associated factors among patients with type 2 diabetes mellitus in the Gaza Strip, Palestine. *Front Endocrinol (Lausanne), 8*, 100.

Fialová, D., & Onder, G. (2009, June). Medication errors in elderly people: Contributing factors and future perspectives. *British Journal of Clinical Pharmacology, 67*(6), 641–645.

Fischer, M., Choudhry, N., Bykov, K., Brill, G., Bopp, G., Wurst, A., & Shrank, W. (2014). Pharmacy-based interventions to reduce primary medication nonadherence to cardiovascular medications. *Medical Care, 52*(12), 1050–1054.

Gajria, K., Lu, M., Sikirica, V., Greven, P., Zhong, Y., Qin, P., & Xie, J. (2014). Adherence, persistence, and medication discontinuation in patients with attention-deficit/hyperactivity disorder – A systematic literature review. *Neuropsychiatric Disease and Treatment, 10*, 1543–1569.

Gast, A., & Mathes, T. (2019, May 10). Medication adherence influencing factors-an (updated) overview of systematic reviews. *Systematic Reviews, 8*(1), 112.

Gellad, W. F., Haas, J. S., & Safran, D. G. (2007, November). Race/ethnicity and nonadherence to prescription medications among seniors: Results of a national study. *Journal of General Internal Medicine, 22*(11), 1572–1578.

Gellad, W. F., Grenard, J. L., & Marcum, Z. A. (2011, February). A systematic review of barriers to medication adherence in the elderly: Looking beyond cost and regimen complexity. *The American Journal of Geriatric Pharmacotherapy, 9*(1), 11–23.

Gleason, P. P., Starner, C. I., Gunderson, B. W., Schafer, J. A., & Sarran, H. S. (2009, October). Association of prescription abandonment with cost share for high-cost specialty pharmacy medications. *Journal of Managed Care Pharmacy, 15*(8), 648–658.

Grenard, J. L., Munjas, B. A., Adams, J. L., et al. (2011). Depression and medication adherence in the treatment of chronic diseases in the United States: A meta-analysis. *Journal of General Internal Medicine, 26*, 1175–1182.

Gu, L., Wu, S., Zhao, S., Zhou, H., Zhang, S., Gao, M., Qu, Z., Zhang, W., & Tian, D. (2017, December 6). Association of social support and medication adherence in Chinese patients with type 2 diabetes mellitus. *International Journal of Environmental Research and Public Health, 14*(12), 1522.

Hutchins, D. S., Zeber, J. E., Roberts, C. S., Williams, A. F., Manias, E., Peterson, A. M., & IPSOR Medication Adherence and Persistence Special Interest Group. (2015, July). Initial medication adherence-review and recommendations for good practices in outcomes research: An ISPOR Medication Adherence and Persistence Special Interest Group report. *Value in Health, 18*(5), 690–699.

Jin, H., Kim, Y., & Rhie, S. J. (2016, October 19). Factors affecting medication adherence in elderly people. *Patient Preference and Adherence, 10*, 2117–2125.

Kelly, J., D'Cruz, G., & Wright, D. (2010, January). Patients with dysphagia: Experiences of taking medication. *Journal of Advanced Nursing, 66*(1), 82–91.

Krueger, K., Botermann, L., Schorr, S. G., Griese-Mammen, N., Laufs, U., & Schulz, M. (2015, April 1). Age-related medication adherence in patients with chronic heart failure: A systematic literature review. *International Journal of Cardiology, 184*, 728–735.

Lee, S. K., Kang, B. Y., Kim, H. G., & Son, Y. J. (2013, March). Predictors of medication adherence in elderly patients with chronic diseases using support vector machine models. *Healthcare Information Research, 19*(1), 33–41.

Lehmann, A., Aslani, P., Ahmed, R., Celio, J., Gauchet, A., Bedouch, P., Bugnon, O., Allenet, B., & Schneider, M. P. (2014, February). Assessing medication adherence: Options to consider. *International Journal of Clinical Pharmacy, 36*(1), 55–69.

Lanham A, Cochran G, Klepser D. (2016). Electronic prescriptions: opportunities and challenges for the patient and pharmacist. *Advanced Health Care Technologies, 2*, 1–11.

Miller, T. A. (2016, July). Health literacy and adherence to medical treatment in chronic and acute illness: A meta-analysis. *Patient Education and Counseling, 99*(7), 1079–1086.

Osterberg, L., & Blaschke, T. (2005). Adherence to medication. *The New England Journal of Medicine, 353*, 487–497; 3.

Pasma, A., van't Spijker, A., Hazes, J. M. W., Busschbach, J. J. V., & Luime, J. J. (2013). Factors associated with adherence to pharmaceutical treatment for rheumatoid arthritis patients: A systematic review. *Seminars in Arthritis and Rheumatism, 43*(1), 18–28.

Paterson, D. L., Swindells, S., Mohr, J., Brester, M., Vergis, E. N., Squier, C., Wagener, M. M., & Singh, N. (2000, July 4). Adherence to protease inhibitor therapy and outcomes in patients with HIV infection. *Annals of Internal Medicine, 133*(1), 21–30.

Pednekar, P., & Peterson, A. (2018, June 4). Mapping pharmacy deserts and determining accessibility to community pharmacy services for elderly enrolled in a State Pharmaceutical Assistance Program. *PLoS One, 13*(6), e0198173.

Peterson, A. M., Takiya, L., & Finley, R. (2003, April 1). Meta-analysis of trials of interventions to improve medication adherence. *American Journal of Health-System Pharmacy, 60*(7), 657–665.

Raehl, C. L., Bond, C. A., Woods, T. J., Patry, R. A., & Sleeper, R. B. (2006, May). Screening tests for intended medication adherence among the elderly. *The Annals of Pharmacotherapy, 40*(5), 888–893.

Raji, M. A., Kuo, Y. F., Salazar, J. A., Satish, S., & Goodwin, J. S. (2004, February). Ethnic differences in antihypertensive medication use in the elderly. *The Annals of Pharmacotherapy, 38*(2), 209–214.

Rathbone, A. P., Jamie, K., Todd, A., & Husband, A. (2021). A qualitative study exploring the lived experience of medication use in different disease states: Linking experiences of disease symptoms to medication adherence. *Journal of Clinical Pharmacy and Therapeutics, 46*, 352–362.

Rhee, H., Wicks, M. N., Dolgoff, J. S., Love, T. M., & Harrington, D. (2018, May 24). Cognitive factors predict medication adherence and asthma control in urban adolescents with asthma. *Patient Preference and Adherence, 12*, 929–937.

Roborel de Climens, A., Pain, E., Boss, A., & Shaunik, A. (2020, August). Understanding reasons for treatment discontinuation, attitudes and education needs among people who discontinue type 2 diabetes treatment: Results from an online patient survey in the USA and UK. *Diabetes Therapy, 11*(8), 1873–1881.

Rolnick, S. J., Pawloski, P. A., Hedblom, B. D., Asche, S. E., & Bruzek, R. J. (2013, June). Patient characteristics associated with medication adherence. *Clinical Medicine & Research, 11*(2), 54–65.

Ruppar, T. M., Delgado, J. M., & Temple, J. (2015, October). Medication adherence interventions for heart failure patients: A meta-analysis. *European Journal of Cardiovascular Nursing, 14*(5), 395–404.

Sabaté, E. (Ed.). (2003). *Adherence to long-term therapies: Evidence for action.* World Health Organization.

Schoenthaler, A., Montague, E., Baier Manwell, L., Brown, R., Schwartz, M. D., & Linzer, M. (2014). Patient-physician racial/ethnic concordance and blood pressure control: The role of trust and medication adherence. *Ethnicity & Health, 19*(5), 565–578.

Schwartz, K. A., Schwartz, D. E., Ghosheh, K., Reeves, M. J., Barber, K., & DeFranco, A. (2005, April 15). Compliance as a critical consideration in patients who appear to be resistant to aspirin after healing of myocardial infarction. *The American Journal of Cardiology, 95*(8), 973–975.

Shrank, W. H., Choudhry, N. K., Fischer, M. A., Avorn, J., Powell, M., Schneeweiss, S., Liberman, J. N., Dollear, T., Brennan, T. A., & Brookhart, M. A. (2010, November 16). The epidemiology of prescriptions abandoned at the pharmacy. *Annals of Internal Medicine, 153*(10), 633–640.

Shruthi, R., Jyothi, R., Pundarikaksha, H. P., Nagesh, G. N., & Tushar, T. J. (2016, Descember). A study of medication compliance in geriatric patients with chronic illnesses at a tertiary care hospital. *Journal of Clinical and Diagnostic Research, 10*(12), FC40–FC43.

Srivastava, K., Arora, A., Kataria, A., Cappelleri, J. C., Sadosky, A., & Peterson, A. M. (2013, May 20). Impact of reducing dosing frequency on adherence to oral therapies: A literature review and meta-analysis. *Patient Preference and Adherence, 7*, 419–434.

Tan, X., Patel, I., Chang, J., et al. (2014). Review of the four item Morisky Medication Adherence Scale (MMAS-4) and eight item Morisky Medication Adherence Scale (MMAS-8). *Innovations of Pharmacy, 5*(3), Article 165.

Velligan, D. I., Sajatovic, M., Hatch, A., Kramata, P., & Docherty, J. P. (2017, March 3). Why do psychiatric patients stop antipsychotic medication? A systematic review of reasons for nonadherence to medication in patients with serious mental illness. *Patient Preference and Adherence, 11*, 449–468.

Viswanathan, M., Golin, C. E., Jones, C. D., Ashok, M., Blalock, S. J., Wines, R. C., Coker-Schwimmer, E. J., Rosen, D. L., Sista, P., & Lohr, K. N. (2012, December 4). Interventions to improve adherence to self-administered medications for chronic diseases in the United States: A systematic review. *Annals of Internal Medicine, 157*(11), 785–795.

Vrijens, B., De Geest, S., Hughes, D. A., Przemyslaw, K., Demonceau, J., Ruppar, T., Dobbels, F., Fargher, E., Morrison, V., Lewek, P., Matyjaszczyk, M., Mshelia, C., Clyne, W., Aronson, J. K., Urquhart, J., & ABC Project Team. (2012, May). A new taxonomy for describing and defining adherence to medications. *British Journal of Clinical Pharmacology, 73*(5), 691–705.

Zeber, J. E., Manias, E., Williams, A. F., Hutchins, D., Udezi, W. A., Roberts, C. S., Peterson, A. M., & ISPOR Medication Adherence Good Research Practices Working Group. (2013, July–August). A systematic literature review of psychosocial and behavioral factors associated with initial medication adherence: A report of the ISPOR medication adherence & persistence special interest group. *Value in Health, 16*(5), 891–900.

Chapter 15
Pain Prevention in Integrated Primary Care

Gregory P. Beehler, Paul R. King, Sarah Cercone Heavey, and Katherine M. Dollar

15.1 Definition and Diagnostic Criteria

The contemporary definition of pain was initially developed in 1975 by the International Association for the Study of Pain (IASP). Currently, IASP defines pain as "an unpleasant sensory and emotional experience associated with, or resembling that associated with, actual or potential tissue damage" (Raja et al., 2020). However, it is important to go beyond this seemingly simple definition to understand several clarifications that further develop the concept of pain. First, pain is considered subjective in nature and is influenced by biological, psychological, and social factors. Pain is a distinct phenomenon from nociception (or stimulation of pain receptors), and IASP is clear that pain cannot be assumed based on the activity of sensory neurons alone. Further, this definition acknowledges that people learn the concept of pain through their life experiences. While an individual's report of pain should be

G. P. Beehler (✉) · S. C. Heavey
VA Center for Integrated Healthcare, VA Western New York Healthcare System, Buffalo, NY, USA

Department of Community Health & Health Behavior, School of Public Health and Health Professions, University at Buffalo, Buffalo, NY, USA
e-mail: gregory.beehler@va.gov

P. R. King
VA Center for Integrated Healthcare, VA Western New York Healthcare System, Buffalo, NY, USA

Department of Counseling, School, and Educational Psychology, Graduate School of Education, University at Buffalo, Buffalo, NY, USA

K. M. Dollar
VA Center for Integrated Healthcare, Syracuse VA Medical Center, Syracuse, NY, USA

W. O'Donohue, M. Zimmermann (eds.), *Handbook of Evidence-Based Prevention of Behavioral Disorders in Integrated Care*,
https://doi.org/10.1007/978-3-030-83469-2_15

respected, verbal descriptions of pain are only one of many ways pain can be expressed.

Defining pain is fraught with challenges, and extensive scholarship is devoted to parsing the conceptualization of pain (e.g., Aydede, 2019; Cohen et al., 2018; Doleys, 2017). Throughout this scholarship, there is debate on what "counts" as pain and how to better operationalize this construct, as a way to better inform the patient and provider experience. Specifically, defining pain has a minimum of two interdependent challenges. First, the experience of pain can be ambiguous and vague (Cohen et al., 2018). Pain symptoms, or the "unpleasant sensory and emotional experience," lack the clinical specificity of other conditions that can be tested and confirmed. By comparison, a long bone fracture would be clearly viewed when imaged or the presence of biomarkers in bloodwork would indicate disease pathology. Second, appropriately translating the phenomena of pain into words is notoriously difficult (Cohen et al., 2018). Often patients describe pain using similes, such as "pain that stabs like a knife," that do not readily translate to clinically meaningful criteria. Additionally, despite the universality of pain, two individuals can describe pain in distinctly different ways.

Along with the complexities of defining pain as a phenomenon, there are inconsistencies in how acute and chronic pain are classified. Nonetheless, it is essential to distinguish between acute and chronic pain as approaches to treatment are often based on this distinction. *Acute pain* is generally linked with a specific injury or event (e.g., a surgical procedure) and lasts up to three months (King, 2007; Nugraha et al., 2019). *Sub-acute pain* has been described as pain that is present for at least 6 weeks but fewer than 3 months (King, 2007). Pain that lasts for 3 months or longer is considered *chronic pain* (IASP Task Force on Taxonomy, 1994; Treede et al., 2015). Others have defined chronic pain as pain that occurs most or all days in at least the past 6 months, while *high impact chronic pain* is chronic pain that limits routine life or work activities on most or all days in the past 6 months (Von Korff et al., 2016).

Acute pain can progress into chronic pain in a process referred to as *chronification* (Pak et al., 2018). Chronification can occur for many common medical conditions seen in primary care (e.g., musculoskeletal, neurological, cardiac, etc.) as well as postoperative pain and post-trauma pain (McGreevy et al., 2011). Most instances of acute pain do not ultimately transition to chronic pain, but a sizeable minority of patients experience chronification. In a large prognostic study of acute low back in primary care, a two-year study found that 54% of patients experienced at least one recurrence within 6 months and 47% experienced recurrence in the subsequent 18 months (Mehling et al., 2012). Similarly, in a large descriptive study of over 5000 primary care adults age 65 years and older, only 23% reported that their back pain resolved within 12 months (Rundell et al., 2015). Peripheral and central sensitization which increase sensitivity to painful stimuli (and potentially non-painful stimuli) appear to be key biological mechanisms that contribute to chronification, although the specific factors leading to chronification vary by type of pain concern (e.g., surgical, traumatic, herpetic neuralgia, etc.; McGreevy et al., 2011). The acute to chronic transition is highly complex and influenced by several risk factors described subsequently.

15.2 Prevalence and Age of Onset

National estimates for prevalence of pain conditions vary, often widely, depending on data source (e.g., national sample v. sample drawn from one health system) and definition (e.g., defining diagnoses with medical record data v. self-report). According to an analysis of the 2016 National Health Interview Survey (NHIS) by Dahlhamer et al. (2018), 50 million US adults, or about 20% of the adult population, experienced chronic pain in 2016. A further 19.6 million (an additional 8%) experienced high impact chronic pain. In general, prevalence, particularly for chronic pain, increases with age, ranging from 7% prevalence of chronic pain among 18- to 24-year-olds up to 34% prevalence among those 85 years and older. A similar relationship exists for high impact chronic pain, from 1.5% in 18- to 24-year-olds to 16% in those 85 and older. In addition to higher prevalence by age, greater pain burden may also vary by demographic factors. Women have higher prevalence rates than men (20.8% v. 17.8%, age-adjusted), and non-Hispanic White individuals have the greatest prevalence of chronic pain (21.0%, age-adjusted), compared to 17.8% for non-Hispanic Black and 16.7% for Hispanic individuals. As both education level and income increase, prevalence of chronic pain decreases.

Although a wide array of medical conditions are associated with chronic pain, it is often cited that musculoskeletal conditions are the most common specific sources of pain (Institute of Medicine of the National Academy of Science, 2011). Low back pain, in particular, is the most frequent source of concern across musculoskeletal conditions and is especially relevant for the primary care setting. In a retrospective review of national medical claims data (using ICD-9 diagnosis codes; data from 2000 through 2012), back pain was the most common diagnosis (74.5% of those with pain diagnoses), while degenerative spine disease (63.6%), neuritis/radiculitis (52.8%), and limb pain (50.0%) were also prevalent (Murphy et al., 2017). Further, only about 25% of the cohort had a single pain diagnosis, while the remaining sample had two or more. In another national survey using the 2012 NHIS, which includes self-report of pain conditions, 54.5% of US adults had a musculoskeletal pain disorder, while arthritic conditions (22.1%), lower back pain (20.3%), non-arthritic joint pain/other joint conditions (17.5%), neck pain (14.3%), and sciatica (9.8%) were also present (Clarke et al., 2016).

15.3 Pain Risk Factors

Risk factors for chronic pain are voluminous, biopsychosocial in nature, and include both modifiable and non-modifiable factors that may vary across the lifespan. Further, pain risk factors can intersect with one another in dynamic ways and fluctuate in temporal relationship to an injury event (e.g., pre- v. post-injury) or onset of a pain-causing illness. The most obvious risk for chronic pain is an underlying pain-causing condition for which the symptoms may be acute or chronic in nature. Examples of underlying illnesses include chronic musculoskeletal conditions, neurological conditions (e.g., stroke, multiple sclerosis, persistent migraine), cardiovascular or cardiopulmonary conditions (e.g., heart disease, chronic obstructive lung disease), gastrointestinal conditions (e.g., irritable bowel syndrome), metabolic conditions (e.g., diabetes), cancers, viral infections (e.g., shingles), and traumatic or polytraumatic injury, among many others. Further, the presence of at least one pain-causing condition increases the likelihood of developing a secondary pain site, and surgical correction introduces new risk for postoperative pain (Kehlet et al., 2006).

A recent review by Mills et al. (2019) described broad risk factor classifications for pain chronification, which include patient demographics, health behaviors and lifestyle, and other clinical correlates. These classifications are briefly summarized below.

15.3.1 Patient Demographics

Demographics, particularly age, racial and ethnic background, sex, socioeconomic status, and military history are typically considered to be among the most notable non-modifiable demographic correlates of all-cause chronic pain. Increased risk for chronic pain appears most consistently associated with older age, female sex, and veteran status.

15.3.1.1 Age

Most studies suggest a relative increase in risk for chronic pain beginning in middle to late middle age. This association may be intuitive given the increased risk for painful conditions and medical comorbidity with the aging process. However, some studies have also shown relatively high rates of chronic pain even among adolescents and young adults, specifically pain associated with life events (e.g., child birth) or treatment history (e.g., surgery; Kehlet et al., 2006).

15.3.1.2 Race and Ethnicity

Findings on the contribution of race and ethnicity to chronic pain risk are mixed, in part attributable to widespread differences in sampling and study methodology. Some large-scale community-based studies in the United States (Dahlhamer et al., 2018) evidence higher chronic pain risk for individuals who identify as non-Hispanic Whites, whereas a study performed in the United Kingdom showed higher risk for pain among individuals who identified as Black, Asian, or multi-racial when compared to White respondents (Macfarlane et al., 2015). In contrast, a clinical study conducted in the United States (Ndao-Brumblay & Green, 2005) showed comparable pain severity reports among Black and White women after accounting for other psychosocial covariates.

15.3.1.3 Sex and Gender

Although female sex has consistently been associated with higher pain risk (Chenot et al., 2008), it is also plausible that this finding is related to the greater likelihood that women (v. men) will evidence established pain risk factors and subsequently report and seek treatment for pain (Wijnhoven et al., 2006).

15.3.1.4 Socioeconomic and Occupational Status

In US studies, greater pain risk has consistently been found among individuals at socioeconomic disadvantage, lower educational level, and those who work in physically (e.g., repetitive movements; Palmer, 2003) and emotionally taxing positions (Leroux et al., 2005). Military veterans, in particular, have been shown to be at higher risk for chronic pain in general as well as more severe chronic pain than civilians (Nahin, 2017), likely due to the physically demanding nature of military service as well as the high burden of injury and/or combat-related trauma. Some evidence suggests women veterans report greater pain interference and intensity than male veterans (Naylor et al., 2019).

15.3.2 Health Behaviors and Lifestyle Factors

Health behaviors and lifestyle factors are considered modifiable pain risk factors. Within this domain, mixed findings exist on the linkage between chronic pain and alcohol and/or tobacco use, poor diet, time spent sitting, and physical inactivity. Importantly, these health behavior and lifestyle factors are also associated with other clinical conditions, such as diabetes (Pico-Espinosa et al., 2017), which themselves also function as pain risk factors.

15.3.2.1 Alcohol and Tobacco Use

Alcohol and tobacco use are common among patients with chronic pain (Mills et al., 2019) and often considered to be maladaptive pain coping strategies. Although data on the impact of alcohol use on pain are mixed, a recent meta-analysis (Thompson et al., 2017) supported the short-term effectiveness of alcohol as an analgesic, albeit at higher than recommended levels of alcohol intake, which in turn places individuals at risk for additional alcohol-related complications and further injury. Studies have shown a relatively consistent, positive relationship between increased tobacco use and greater pain intensity and interference (Weingarten et al., 2008).

15.3.2.2 Diet and Exercise

Insufficient evidence exists to suggest a direct link between diet and pain chronification though some work examining the role of nutritional interventions in reducing chronic pain has shown promise (Brain et al., 2019). However, poor diet is linked to other pain risk factors such as obesity and general fitness levels. While exercise is generally accepted as protective against pain, some studies have found vigorous activity (El-Metwally et al., 2007) to be a potential pain risk factor among youth.

15.3.3 Clinical Correlates

Clinical correlates, which may include mental and physical health conditions, also serve as noteworthy risk factors for the chronification of pain, and these factors may exist as pre- (non-modifiable history) or post-injury (modifiable through treatment) risks.

15.3.3.1 Fitness and Weight Control

Among young people, factors such as range of motion, flexibility, and muscle endurance have been shown to predict low back pain (Jones et al., 2005). Often considered common and modifiable risk factors (Webb et al., 2003), obesity and overweight may be especially predictive of chronic pain in older adults (Qian et al., 2020).

15.3.3.2 Mental Health Comorbidity

Generally, underlying mental health conditions are associated with greater risk for chronic pain (Viana et al., 2018). Depression, in particular, is a "yellow flag" indicator of increased risk for worse pain-related outcomes, and depression's role in developing or maintaining chronic pain is an active area of research (Glattacker et al., 2018). Studies suggest a bi-directional influence, wherein pain and mental health symptom severity have an exacerbating effect on one another (Shahidi et al., 2015).

15.3.3.3 Other Psychological Risk Factors

Other psychological risk factors, including early life stress and trauma histories (You et al., 2018), have also been associated with differential pain risks. For instance, though abuse history is associated with increased risk for chronic pain, personal resilience and adaptive coping skills (Ross et al., 2017) are protective factors. Further, an individual's personal beliefs about chronic pain (e.g., catastrophizing, treatment outcomes) and the pain experience can also serve as noteworthy risk factors (Borkum, 2010). Often included as "yellow flag" indicators (Glattacker et al., 2018), maladaptive cognitions and behaviors such as pain and activity avoidance, low pain self-efficacy, pain catastrophizing, and the expectation of long-term disability are frequently associated with increased risk of chronification and worse functional outcomes.

15.4 Effective Pain Screening

In many healthcare settings, pain is universally monitored as "the fifth vital sign" (Lorenz et al., 2009) using a standard 0–10 numeric rating scale (NRS) that gauges pain severity. Advantages of the NRS are ease of administration, brevity, and accuracy when administered using standard procedures. Critiques include that the single numeric rating does not provide information beyond pain severity, does not yield clinically actionable information, and that it is often implemented with low fidelity. Multiple derivations of this scale have been published, including verbal and visual analogues (Karcioglu et al., 2018) wherein pain intensity ratings are gathered along a linear continuum with specified anchor points (e.g., no pain to worst pain imaginable). Recent derivations include visual analogues for e-health and mobile devices (Bird et al., 2016; Escalona-Marfil et al., 2020) and item permutations that include questions related to pain interference/functional impairment. Typically, a positive endorsement of significant pain concerns or independent report of pain-related functional impairment signals a need for further clinical assessment by way of an additional clinical interview and/or standardized measure (e.g., Short-Form McGill Pain Questionnaire; Melzack, 1987). Although a comprehensive discussion of

Table 15.1 Suggested pain screening and measurement tools for the IPC setting

Name	Brief description	# Items	Exemplar reference
Measuring pain intensity and pain-related activity interference			
Brief Pain Inventory (BPI) – Short Form	Multidimensional screen for pain intensity and functional impairment	9	Cleeland & Ryan, (1994)
Defense and Veterans Pain Rating Scale (DVPRS)	11-point visual analogue rating scale coupled with questions on pain interference	5	Buckenmaier et al. (2013)
PEG	Assesses both pain severity and pain-related interference in (1) general activities and 2) enjoyment of life	3	Krebs et al. (2009)
Faces Pain Scale-Revised (FPS-R)	7-point visual display of 7 faces to assess pain levels in pediatric populations	1	Hicks et al., (2001)
Numeric rating scale (NRS)	11-point (0–10) rating of pain severity, wherein higher scores signal a higher level of pain intensity	1	Krebs et al. (2007)
Additional tools to assist with risk stratification* (i.e., *identifying those at greatest risk of developing chronic pain or significant functional impairment)			
Orebro Musculoskeletal Pain Questionnaire (OMPQ)	A self-report of musculoskeletal pain and functional impairment predictive of future employment interference	25	Linton amd Boersma (2003)
Optimal Screening for Prediction of Referral and Outcome - Yellow Flag (OSPRO-YF)	Brief multidimensional screen of "yellow flag" pain risk indicators including negative affect and fear-avoidance	10	Butera et al. (2020)
STarT Back Screening Tool (SBST)	Brief multidimensional screen of complex back pain risks	9	Storm et al. (2018)

screening and assessment instruments is beyond the scope of this chapter, several common instruments applicable to the integrated primary care (IPC) setting can be found in Table 15.1.

15.5 Review of Evidence: What Is Evidence-Based Prevention?

Evidence-based prevention of chronic pain is rooted in a biopsychosocial framework to direct intervention activities that include biomedical (e.g., algorithm-based prescribing of analgesics or other agents) and psychosocial interventions (e.g., psychological therapies). Additional non-pharmacologic modalities may include physical therapy, chiropractic, or complementary and integrative health treatments. Prevention activities will vary depending on the nature of the underlying pain concern, but the terms *primary, secondary, and tertiary prevention* as defined by the

Federal Pain Research Strategy Workgroup on the Prevention of Acute and Chronic Pain provide a useful organizing principle (Gatchel et al., 2018). According to these workgroup definitions, primary prevention of pain focuses very broadly on behaviors that will prevent acute and chronic pain by avoiding injury or accidents (e.g., use of seatbelts) or illness (e.g., immunizations), promoting healthy behaviors (e.g., weight management), or limiting pain resulting from chronic medical concerns (e.g., migraines) or procedures (e.g., post-surgical pain). Thus, the focus of primary prevention of pain is foremost on the antecedents of pain which are influenced by a host of biopsychosocial factors. All potential targets above are common prevention topics addressed by primary care teams (e.g., annual screening conducted by clinic staff to ensure patients are using seatbelts and providing education regarding the importance of this practice). Although provision of routine primary care may play an indirect role in the primary prevention of pain, no empirical studies have specifically examined the effect of IPC teams on pain prevention.

In contrast, interventions outside of the primary care clinic have shown promise in the primary prevention of low back pain in the military (George et al., 2009) and occupational settings (Sowah et al., 2018). These interventions typically include physical exercise (e.g., for strengthening, stabilizing, or increasing flexibility), education (e.g., describing causes of low back pain, reviewing strategies to avoid injury, engaging in behaviors that may reduce the impact of pain), or both. Population-based studies have also shown that educational media campaigns can be effective at changing general population beliefs and attitudes about back pain as well as reduction in disability and workers' compensation claims (Buchbinder et al., 2001). Although not specific to the primary care team, these studies provide proof of concept that primary prevention of pain is achievable using the relatively simple strategies of education and exercise promotion.

Secondary prevention of pain includes approaches that aim to limit chronification during the relatively short timeframe of three to six months following the onset of acute pain (Gatchel et al., 2018). As with the primary prevention of pain, there are no studies to date that have employed an IPC approach to address chronification. Whereas primary care clinics are likely to treat acute pain as part of standard primary care, typically these actions are designed to ameliorate acute pain rapidly rather than to purposefully prevent chronification. As chronification is a time-dependent process, prospective research can be challenging to conduct. However, some studies have shown that early psychosocial intervention in the acute phase of pain can be beneficial. For example, Linton and colleagues (2000) compared the impact of a six-session cognitive behavioral therapy (CBT) group intervention to psychoeducational materials for improving pain-related outcomes among patients with acute spinal pain receiving usual primary care. Both groups benefited over time, but those who attended the CBT group were nine times less likely to have used sick leave for their condition at one-year follow-up, compared to those who attended the psychoeducation group. Additionally, the CBT group was significantly less likely to use physician and physical therapy services relative to the education group. Although this study did not define chronification as a study endpoint, it speaks to the potential benefit of early psychosocial intervention in addressing pain.

Another challenge in preventing chronification is identifying those patients from among the many with painful conditions who are most likely to transition to chronic pain. As noted above, risk factors for chronic pain are abundant, but there are a few well-developed tools that can assist in screening patients to identify who is most likely to experience chronic pain (See Table 15.1). Finally, it should be noted that an additional challenge to this line of research is the underlying premise that there is a linear and uni-directional process underlying chronification. A simple acute-to-chronic categorization of pain is likely overly simplistic, and research has shown a variety of pain trajectories are evident (Glette et al., 2020).

Tertiary pain prevention addresses pain when it has become chronic by intervening to reduce its impact on daily functioning (Gatchel et al., 2018). Tertiary prevention has a rehabilitative focus to address the functional impairment across a variety of domains (e.g., social and occupational functioning) that often impacts those with chronic pain. Like primary and secondary pain prevention activities, IPC interventions to address chronic pain remain relatively sparse. Usual primary care treatment for chronic pain relies almost exclusively on provision of analgesics (Elder et al., 2016; Shaheed et al., 2016) despite national guidelines to incorporate non-pharmacologic approaches in light of established concerns over opioid safety (Dowell et al., 2016; US Department of Health and Human Services, 2019). These guidelines recommend evidence-based psychological therapies, such as CBT and related treatments (e.g., acceptance and commitment therapy, mindfulness-based treatments) as safer first-line treatments compared to opioid therapy.

Most psychological therapies for pain are designed for specialty care settings (e.g., a multidisciplinary chronic pain clinic), but two models of IPC have started to address tertiary prevention of chronic pain: (1) collaborative care management and 2) brief therapies delivered by co-located behavioral health providers. Generally, care management employs a nurse care manager who enacts an algorithm-based approach to care that revolves around ongoing assessment and monitoring of patient needs, as well as promoting treatment adherence, patient education, and referral management. Collaborative care approaches to pain management tend to be diverse in terms of their specific intervention approaches (e.g., guideline-adherent medication prescribing, psychosocial intervention, or both), but as a group, they appear to produce improvements in clinical outcomes. For example, one large randomized controlled trial tested tailored pain assessment by a care manager followed by routine telephone-based pain symptom assessment and self-management support provided bi-monthly for one year. Compared to primary care treatment as usual, collaborative care management for pain resulted in statistically significant albeit clinically modest improvements in pain-related disability and depression symptoms (Dobscha et al., 2009). A second, large randomized controlled trial found that automated self-management (i.e., automated symptom monitoring and nine web-based self-management modules) combined with care management to optimize non-opioid analgesic prescribing was superior to automated self-management alone for improving a combined measure of pain and mood symptoms among primary care patients (Kroenke et al., 2019). Although collaborative care management models are not often implemented in everyday IPC settings, these studies are encouraging in that they indicate the potential of this approach to address tertiary pain prevention.

Pain interventions can also be implemented under a Primary Care Behavioral Health (PCBH) model (Robinson & Reiter, 2016) of IPC that co-locates a licensed independent behavioral health provider into primary care teams to provide assessment and brief intervention. In contrast to collaborative care management, the PCBH approach tends to be more commonly implemented, but this model has limited supporting empirical evidence. For example, pain schools, or group intervention that includes pain-related psychoeducation and support, are offered in PCBH to increase patients' understanding of the nature of chronic pain and its management. However, the effectiveness of pain schools is likely modest (Straube et al., 2016) as a single approach to tertiary pain prevention. By comparison, the literature on brief psychotherapies that employ CBT and related approaches to address chronic pain is promising. For example, evidence from work conducted in Veterans Health Administration (VHA) primary care clinics suggest that both group and individual CBT-based intervention that builds pain self-management skills in six appointments or less is associated with improvements in pain-related activity interference and pain intensity (Beehler et al., 2019; Martinson et al., 2020).

15.6 Universal, Indicated, and Selective Prevention

The primary, secondary, and tertiary scheme described above delineates pain prevention based on disease stage and progression (i.e., primary prevention works to prevent the onset of acute pain from illness or injury; secondary prevention works to limit chronification; and tertiary prevention reduces functional limitations from chronic pain). Another approach to pain prevention incorporates principles of risk stratification to delineate universal, selective, and indicated prevention strategies. Risk stratification consists of subgrouping a population of patients based on established risk factors for developing chronic pain. As noted previously in this chapter, given the large number and diverse nature of risk factors for pain, risk stratification is a logical approach to identifying those from among all patients most in need of intervention. There is also a body of evidence suggesting that risk stratification can be beneficial for pain prevention. For example, a recent systematic review that included nine secondary prevention trials among patients with acute back pain identified that risk stratification procedures are advantageous (Meyer et al., 2018). More specifically, patients who screened as low risk did not benefit meaningfully from supplements to usual care, such as educational information or promotion of physical activity. Correspondingly, medium and high-risk patients who were provided with both a CBT and exercise component benefitted from this additional intervention with improved physical and emotional functioning as well as earlier return to work.

A universal prevention strategy addresses an entire population, and the primary goal is to prevent the health problem from occurring. Generally, this population has an average level of risk for developing the health problem of interest. In the present context, universal pain prevention is not a realistic or feasible goal. Many of the causes of acute pain are inadvertent (e.g., a car accident) or serve a clear adaptive function (e.g., pain when touching a hot burner on a stove). Usually, universal prevention is conducted without screening an individual for risk but can target specific sub-populations when warranted, such as wearing a seatbelt to prevent injury in a car accident. Theoretically, universal pain prevention would target all members of a population but would not account for any differences within that group (e.g., biopsychosocial factors that would alter risk for pain). Such discernment is the focus of selective prevention.

Selective prevention targets a specific group that is known to be at higher risk due to one or more biological, psychological, social, or environmental factors. Individual risk is not considered in selective prevention; the entire subgroup is targeted, even though one member of the subgroup may be at reduced personal risk while another may be at high personal risk. For example, shingles is well-known as a painful condition. The shingles vaccine is recommended specifically to those over 50 years of age because of known elevated risk in an older population. The primary goal of selective prevention is to reduce the incidence of disease and/or the related consequences, and in the context of pain, selective prevention is used to prevent chronification.

Finally, indicated prevention targets those individuals at highest risk with a focus on preventing consequences or complications of the underlying health problem. This approach includes screening or assessing an individual's specific risks, such as a military veteran who worked in a physically demanding role for many years or an athlete with a history of several acute injuries. In this context, indicated prevention focuses on reducing the morbidity associated with chronic pain including reducing the risk that chronic pain becomes high impact in nature. Indicated prevention is especially relevant for IPC practice, and as shown in Table 15.1, there are several instruments available to IPC team members to engage in individual-level risk assessment (e.g., six-item STarT screener for back pain; Storm et al., 2018).

The universal, indicated, and selective prevention approach aligns roughly with notions of primary, secondary, and tertiary prevention. Universal and primary prevention both operate with the widest lens, focusing on very similar strategies (e.g., avoiding injury and promoting healthy behaviors). Selective prevention subsumes both secondary and tertiary prevention which address subgroups with elevated risk levels. Indicated prevention also includes aspects of tertiary prevention, particularly the focus on reducing the impact of chronic pain on daily life and activities. Currently, the roles of IPC team members in each of these strategies are not well described, especially for universal and primary prevention. Given the population-based approach of most IPC models that emphasize primary prevention, it is important to consider one more perspective: the Prevention Paradox (Rose et al., 2008). This theorem states that a universal prevention program will have a greater return than a program that only targets those at high risk (i.e., indicated prevention). This phenomenon would occur because making small improvements in pain-related risk among the full population will ultimately yield larger gains in health outcomes than making large improvements in the small number of patients with the highest risk for chronic pain. While important to consider this population perspective, addressing the Prevention Paradox becomes an even greater challenge when considering the unique nature of pain. There is no way to universally prevent pain because most acute pain is adaptive. Further, Rose's theorem may be at odds with practicality – shifting the overall population's risk level prevents more cases of disease but does not necessarily consider the feasibility, costs, or intricacies of universal prevention. How (and when) do we appropriately prevent pain?

15.7 Stepped Care Prevention Model: Role of Primary Care Provider (PCP) and Behavioral Health Provider (BHP)

15.7.1 Watchful Waiting

A watchful waiting approach to chronic pain prevention is not well described in the IPC literature. In concept, watchful waiting consists of symptom monitoring to determine if the condition will resolve with no or minimal intervention to avoid treatments that are either unnecessary or those that could lead to unwanted side effects. Unfortunately, this term is a misnomer when applied to pain prevention because it reflects a biomedical framework in which psychosocial interventions are not seen as active ingredients of treatment. From a biopsychosocial perspective, there are many possible points of intervention for chronic pain and failing to provide assistance beyond symptom assessment is a missed opportunity to prevent the worsening of pain. Any member of the IPC team can provide assessment using brief measures like the NRS or the PEG (Krebs et al., 2009) in combination with simple interventions described below (e.g., psychoeducation, bibio-prevention, or e-health prevention tools) in an effort to promote patient self-management. If continued assessment shows progression of pain intensity or significant functional impairment, then more intensive intervention is warranted.

15.7.2 Psychoeducation

Psychoeducation is a typical starting point for non-pharmacologic intervention for pain, although it is most frequently offered as a tertiary prevention approach to assist those who already have chronic pain. The scope and depth of psychoeducation-based interventions varies significantly, and there is no uniform set of education that has been consistently supported by research. Psychoeducation topics can include any or all of the following: differentiating acute from chronic pain, the biopsychosocial model of pain and its relevance for preventing and treating pain, pain neuroscience, the expected course and impact of specific pain concerns, pain self-management approaches, and the importance of addressing pain-related cognitive factors, such as fear-avoidance and pain catastrophizing. In addition to variation in educational content, the modality for psychoeducation can also vary widely. Psychoeducation can be delivered informally and sporadically, as part of a routine primary care visit, or delivered in a group format to take advantage of interaction among patients with similar pain concerns. Any appropriately trained member of the IPC team can provide psychoeducation. As part of usual primary care, PCPs may provide information regarding the basic anatomy and physiology of the underlying condition, what to expect in terms of the course of acute or chronic pain, and brief essential advice regarding treatment options, including self-management. Notably, when indicated, PCPs should also strongly encourage the patient to attend more comprehensive psychoeducational sessions with BHP, nurse, or other providers who have more time allotted for counseling-based prevention strategies.

Pain psychoeducation is likely a necessary but insufficient component of addressing pain prevention effectively. The evidence suggests that, compared to no intervention, psychoeducation produces a modest effect on pain intensity and pain-related functioning, but it is difficult to draw conclusions across studies because of the above noted heterogeneity in how psychoeducation is conceptualized and delivered (Straube et al., 2016). It is also challenging to know the net effect of psychoeducation, as it is often bundled with other interventions, such as strengthening or flexibility exercises, or with psychological skill-building approaches, such as CBT.

15.7.3 Biblio-Prevention

Similar to psychoeducation, pain biblio-prevention aims to improve patients' knowledge regarding factual information about their chronic pain condition, promoting adaptive attitudes and beliefs around pain, and promotion of self-management. The prototypical biblio-therapy for management of chronic low back pain is *The Back Book*, which is focused on differentiating hurt v. harm, promoting activity engagement, and developing a positive coping-focused approach to pain management (Burton et al., 1999). Designed as a brief pamphlet, *The Back Book* has been found to be effective at improving fear-avoidance beliefs and pain-related physical functioning. This approach to education, or similar permutations of it, has become so common that *The Back Book* is often used in clinical trials as the education-control condition when compared to more comprehensive interventions like CBT (Baez et al., 2018). While biblio-prevention is useful at imparting knowledge and potentially changing patients' attitudes around pain, these approaches are likely insufficient as stand-alone strategies to substantially improve pain ratings or functional outcomes for many patients. The obvious advantage of biblio-prevention approaches is that it is convenient for the provider to offer educational materials to patients with sufficient literacy levels so that they can engage with the materials outside of clinic and at their own pace. Any member of the IPC team can initially provide these materials with follow-up appointments used to answer questions identified by the patient. As with psychoeducation, biblio-prevention can be used to build a larger, more comprehensive approach to intervention depending on the needs of the patient.

15.7.4 E-Health Prevention Tools

There has been substantial growth in the number of web-based technologies and mobile apps to assist patients with chronic pain management. These modalities have the advantage of overcoming several logistical barriers to care including removing the need for patients to travel to pre-scheduled appointments for group or individual interventions. The approach of e-health is quite broad and can include any combination of moderated discussion groups, peer support, CBT and related psychological therapies, symptom monitoring and feedback, mind-body techniques, relaxation training, or behavioral activation. Thus, e-health tools are essentially platforms in which a variety of intervention techniques and targets are embedded. Systematic reviews suggest that e-health tools can be effective approaches to chronic pain management that lead to small but significant improvement in pain intensity, physical functioning, depression symptoms, pain self-efficacy, and pain-related cognitions (Heapy et al., 2015; Moman et al., 2019). However, it is important to consider that while the e-health modality appears feasible, the impact of the intervention is based on both the quality of the delivery system (e.g., usability and design) as well as the nature of the content (e.g., degree of evidence-based information). Mobile apps for pain management have mushroomed in recent years, but despite their widespread availability, most have not been scientifically evaluated for effectiveness (Salazar et al., 2018). While most interventions are designed to be self-guided in which the patient sets the pace and goals for use of the intervention, there is growing interest in combining e-health with a level of clinician support to improve engagement. Patient adherence to e-health approaches is often modest but may be improved by offering clinician support (Mohr et al., 2011), thereby combining technology and clinician interaction. Thus, while any member of the primary care team can "prescribe" an app, BHPs or nurses may engage in orienting the patient to the technology as well as scheduling follow-up to address barriers to continued use.

15.7.5 Groups

Group interventions are flexible in format and can address a range of pain prevention targets. Primary prevention can be addressed through groups that address lifestyle and wellness topics (e.g., weight management) that are risk factors for developing chronic pain. Groups may also directly address pain psychoeducation or psychological intervention, such as CBT, as primary or secondary prevention (Linton, 2002; Linton & Andersson, 2000). The evidence supporting group psychological treatment specifically in the IPC setting exclusively addresses tertiary prevention (Lamb et al., 2010; Martinson et al., 2020). Patients may be referred to IPC group psychological interventions based on PCP recommendation or following initial consultation with the BHP who conducts additional functional assessment and symptom measurement to better understand the impact of chronic pain or contributing risk factors, such as co-occurring mental health conditions. BHPs may also assess the receptivity of the patient to group intervention or appropriateness of the patient for a group setting. Group interventions are most commonly led by the BHP (v. other members of the primary care team) or co-led with another BHP, such as a trainee. The content of group interventions can also vary, but CBT-based groups include a combination of psychoeducation, in vivo learning (e.g., engagement in relaxation exercises), review of homework, and relapse prevention. Direct interaction among group members is encouraged.

While the PCP may not play a significant role in most group formats, they are the starting point for referral to treatment and can encourage continued participation in group. Alternatively, PCPs play a larger and more well-defined role in group medical visits. Group medical visits, or shared medical appointments, can take a variety of forms but typically include the PCP in their role as medical provider and prescriber (Moitra et al., 2011). PCPs may meet with patients one-to-one as part of individualized follow-up, while the rest of the group is engaged by the BHP. A PCP may also co-lead with the BHP on topics of relevance, such as medication management or coping with chronic pain, with an effort to facilitate group interaction and learning among patients. Group medical visits may also bring in other providers, such as clinical pharmacists to assist with analgesic optimization or physical therapists to address how to safely engage in exercise or other activity-based interventions.

15.7.6 Individual

Individual intervention can address any stage of pain prevention. However, like group interventions, individual IPC interventions have been exclusively described in terms of tertiary prevention. The content of individual psychological intervention is similar to that of groups (e.g., psychoeducation, skills training with in vivo learning, review of homework, relapse prevention) but allow for more tailored assessment and treatment for the individual at the expense of group discussion and learning from peers. PCPs do not typically provide individual level psychological intervention in addition to standard components of medical care, including diagnostic assessment, brief self-management advice, prescribing analgesics and adjunctive medications, and referrals to additional services (e.g., physical therapy, chiropractic, etc.). In a collaborative care management approach, BHPs or possibly nurse care managers conduct pain symptom assessment, psychoeducation, and address barriers to self-management to improve patient engagement in care (e.g., Dobscha et al., 2009). In an approach designed for the PCBH model, the BHP uses routine measurement to guide progression through a protocolized treatment that addresses core

CBT content (i.e., psychoeducation, behavioral activation and pacing, relaxation training, cognitive skills, and relapse prevention) that have been tailored by the BHP to ensure a patient-centered approach (Beehler et al., 2019). BHPs in both collaborative care management and PCBH roles provide periodic feedback to the PCP or other members of the IPC team to indicate progress or the need for additional intervention in the form of referral or modification to the medical treatment plan.

15.8 Implementation

As noted above, there is relatively little emphasis on primary and secondary prevention of pain in the United States, and most risk factors for developing chronic pain are not routinely addressed until symptoms exacerbate beyond mild to moderate levels. A comprehensive pain prevention program in the primary care setting must include early identification of risk factors, minimize potential for chronification, and improve overall functioning. Figure 15.1 displays the goals and potential approaches to include in a pain prevention program in an IPC clinic organized by target population. Although high-quality primary care services address primary prevention targets (e.g., promoting health and wellness) for pain through routine delivery of care, many clinics may not view these services as fully meeting the goal of pain prevention. Implementation and evaluation of a stepped care approach to pain prevention that includes the IPC team is one potential strategy to begin to address this need.

15.8.1 Stepped Care Models for Pain Management

Stepped care approaches to the prevention and treatment of pain emphasize primary care-based screening and management with additional specialized resources available for more complicated presentations. Stepped care is recommended by the American Academy of Pain Medicine (Gallagher & Fraifeld, 2010) and has been implemented within the Veterans Health Administration (VHA; (Rosenberger et al., 2011), the Department of Defense, and some Federally Qualified Health Centers (Anderson et al., 2013). VHA, for example, employs a stepped care strategy to provide a continuum of effective pain care for veterans with both acute and chronic pain. This approach is highly individualized, and interventions are added or expanded with increasing patient complexity and need. The foundational step emphasizes the importance of overall wellness and self-care (e.g., weight management, social support, nutrition) and environmental safety which are reflective of primary prevention strategies. Step one focuses on multidisciplinary primary care management of the majority of pain concerns, including brief versions of CBT for chronic pain delivery by the IPC BHP, physical therapy, complementary and integrative health approaches, and a variety of other approaches. Step two brings in

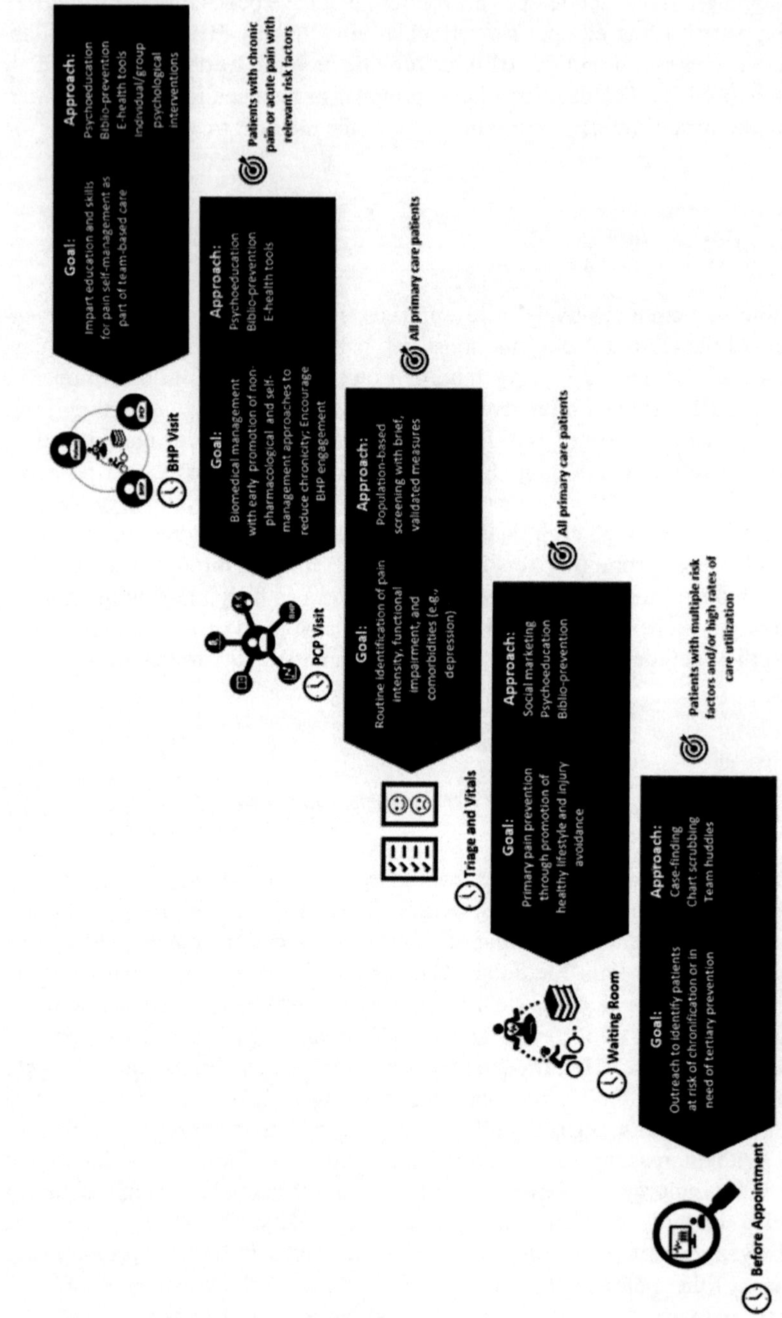

Fig. 15.1 Points of intervention for a comprehensive pain prevention program in an integrated primary care setting

specialty services such as pain medicine, physical and rehab medicine, and behavioral pain management for short-term co-management, whereas step three includes tertiary care services, such as residential pain rehabilitation programs.

The focus of the discussion that follows will address, in some detail, IPC approaches that target primary, secondary, and tertiary prevention as part of step one of a stepped care approach. Local implementation of a continuum of pain prevention services will vary based on clinic resources and contextual factors, but the approaches described below can likely be modified for many settings.

15.8.2 Addressing the Continuum of Pain Prevention in IPC

A comprehensive pain prevention program in IPC should consider four foundational intervention approaches. The first point of intervention focuses on primary pain prevention through social marketing and related approaches that publicly display persuasive educational information about pain risk factors through brochures and posters distributed through the clinic setting. Secondly, general health promotion, such as wellness groups, physical fitness groups, or stress management groups, can prevent pain by decreasing modifiable risk factors and maximizing protective factors. Thirdly, psychoeducation regarding pain management can be delivered through in-person, biblio-prevention, or e-health approaches. Fourth, the BHP, who routinely serves a broad percentage of the primary care population, is a critical component of pain prevention programming. In addition to offering biblio-prevention, e-health tools, or psychoeducation, BHPs are in the unique position to offer group or individual brief psychological interventions for pain for those needing tertiary prevention.

15.8.3 Patient Identification

Within the IPC setting, identification of patients with pain-related risk factors can begin even before the patient arrives for the medical appointment. One strategy is to engage in case finding in which an IPC team member, such as the nurse, can review the medical records of patients with upcoming appointments with the goal of identifying potential cases that have not already engaged in active wellness or biopsychosocial pain management. For example, cases might be identified based on presence of a specific pain-related condition, such as arthritis, along with other pain-related risk factors, such as depression or other mental health symptoms. The goal is to offer patients proactive outreach and engagement in interventions to reduce modifiable risk factors. As an alternative strategy, patients with pain-related conditions can be identified and prioritized for additional assessment as part of a review and discussion of upcoming appointments during routine team huddles. Routine chart scrubbing is one strategy to prepare for effective huddles and to improve overall efficiency. Chart scrubbing is a systematic and proactive review of critical information in the electronic medical record to identify gaps in care to be addressed. Typically, a nurse or a medical assistance prints the daily patient schedule and makes note of key information about each scheduled appointment, such as labs, vaccinations, recent hospitalizations or emergency department visits, review of self-management goals, and risk factors for high-priority conditions. Scrubbing also includes the identification of patient visits that may require additional time and assistance from various team members, such as the BHP. Many clinics use a standardized form when scrubbing charts to ensure consistent information for each patient is reviewed. After the scrubbing process is completed, the information is shared and discussed with the entire IPC team during huddles.

An important feature of IPC for pain prevention is assuring that the BHP is available to take warm hand-offs when at-risk patients are identified by their PCP or through the case-finding and chart scrubbing procedures noted above. Some IPC programs may make it the expectation that any patient who presents to the PCP with significant pain symptoms or functional impairment is also seen by the BHP the same day. If the patient is experiencing acute pain, for example, this collaboration across IPC team members can be a critical point of early intervention to address risk factors and maximize protective factors with the goal of preventing chronification. For those patients referred with an established history of chronic pain, the PCP's warm hand-off to the BHP provides an efficient approach to expanding the scope of services to include biopsychosocial care such as psychological therapies. For some busy clinics, this strategy may not be completely feasible due to the high volume of patients. In this scenario, a risk stratification process through additional screening is warranted.

15.8.4 Functional Assessment and Intervention

After a warm hand-off occurs, the BHP should conduct additional assessment. A functional assessment is a brief (~15–20 minutes), semi-structured approach used to identify how well a patient is functioning across life domains. Areas of functioning typically assessed include sleep, work/school, physical activity, personal relationships, mood, diet, substance use, and coping skills (Hunter et al., 2017). A functional assessment tailored for pain also explores factors that make pain better or worse, impact on daily functioning, and pain-related coping responses (positive and negative). The functional assessment should also include general descriptions of the pain as well as information about onset, frequency, and duration (Hunter et al., 2017). In addition to functional assessment, relevant symptom assessment should occur. Specifically, brief measures such as the PEG (Krebs et al., 2009) described earlier in this chapter can be incorporated into every appointment. The PEG is especially useful because of its brevity and multidimensional focus on both pain intensity and pain-related interference in general activities and enjoyment of life. Consistent use of the PEG establishes the foundation for measurement-based care.

The routine application of measurement has been found to improve the quality of care through improved early identification and assessment processes, creating a shared language for discussing symptoms, enhanced communication, as well as early identification of non-responders allowing to appropriately triage to more intensive pain management services (Dowrick et al., 2009). Additional brief, standardized assessments for mental health symptoms should be included as indicated, such as the Patient Health Questionnaire (PHQ-9; Kroenke et al., 2001).

Results of the symptom and functional assessment taken together with the patient's goals for treatment direct the approach to intervention. For example, a patient with minimal pain-specific concerns (e.g., manageable pain intensity, minimal activity interference) at the time of assessment could potentially benefit from low resource interventions such as biblio-prevention or e-health tools in an effort to provide education about the nature of chronic pain and ways to avoid chronification (e.g., staying active and managing comorbid medical and psychological conditions). Alternatively, assessment could reveal that comorbid mental health conditions are a relative priority for treatment in either the IPC or specialty setting that would ultimately reduce the risk of experiencing disabling pain subsequently. In contrast, if a patient reports significant pain intensity and reported disability and is amenable to IPC-based intervention, brief interventions can be employed to target pain management, comorbid conditions, or both. For example, enhancing problem-solving skills, providing brief interventions for depression or insomnia, and goal setting to increase self-management and general self-care are likely to improve overall functioning. Options for addressing pain management directly in the IPC setting include psychoeducation in individual or group format and brief psychological interventions for pain. Brief CBT-CP was designed specifically for use in IPC settings and has been tested in VHA clinics (Beehler et al., 2019). Brief CBT-CP can be used by any BHP with a solid foundation in basic CBT skills (e.g., relaxation training, behavioral activation, cognitive skills, etc.). Since most IPC intervention focuses on tertiary pain prevention, it is recommended that Brief CBT-CP and related interventions be made more widely available in IPC.

15.8.5 IPC Team Communication

One of the core features of IPC is communication among the interdisciplinary team members. Ideally, interprofessional communication should occur through established, routine processes across multiple modalities (e.g., written, verbal, and/or electronic). When implementing a pain prevention program, multiple points of communication should be established and maximized in order to provide the best patient care experience. Potential points of team communication include daily huddles, curbside consultations, warm hand-offs, weekly/monthly team meetings, co-signed progress notes, "view alerts" in shared electronic medical records, secure e-mails, and instant messaging.

15.8.5.1 Case Example

Consider a scenario in which a patient at risk for experiencing functional impairment from chronic pain is identified through chart scrubbing. This patient is scheduled to see the PCP regarding a flare-up in low back pain over the past several months that has resulted in several prior PCP appointments. The patient is flagged in part because of her co-occurring anxiety disorder diagnosis and tobacco use history. She is discussed among the team members during the morning huddle, and, after review, the team agrees that she might be a good candidate for meeting with the BHP. To ensure a good warm hand-off process, the PCP would discuss the concern to be addressed by the BHP with the patient using culturally appropriate language that is non-stigmatizing. The PCP would then describe the role of the BHP to the patient and ask for permission to introduce her to the BHP after the current appointment. If the patient agrees to meet with the BHP, the PCP conducts the warm hand-off through same day access scheduling slots. The PCP directly introduces the patient to the BHP and provides a brief description of the concerns based on the understanding of the patient's experience. The BHP confirms understanding the information conveyed by the PCP and engages the patient in care. After completing a pain-focused functional assessment and gathering symptom data through the PEG, the BHP provides feedback to the PCP through a quick secure instant message and briefly describes recommended team-based care interventions. The BHP offered the patient a face-to-face course of brief psychological intervention, but she declined. However, she was open to using a mobile app to track her pain to see if it changes (either worsened or improved) over the coming weeks in response to her daily activities. She also agreed to phone follow-up with the BHP to discuss barriers in using the app and to review the information she tracks.

Later that clinic day, the BHP checks-in by secure instant messaging with the PCP and suggests reinforcing the patient's use of the app as well as requests that the patient be re-referred if pain or functioning do not improve (or decline) and medication changes are being considered. This worsening of pain could indicate the need for re-assessment by the BHP at which time the CBT intervention option could be reintroduced alongside other options (e.g., referral to community resources). Next, the BHP documents key summary information for the entire IPC team through the shared electronic medical record. Finally, the next morning at the daily huddle, the BHP gives the team a brief (i.e., less than 2 minute) update on the outcomes of the functional assessment and the intervention the patient was willing to consider thereby completing the team-based care communication cycle.

15.8.6 Racial and Ethnic Disparities in Pain Care

Across a variety of medical settings, racial and ethnic disparities in pain perception, assessment, and treatment are well documented (Green et al., 2003). Physicians have been shown to be twice as likely to underestimate pain for Black patients relative to non-Black patients (Staton et al., 2007). Further, providers may hold false beliefs that Black patients are less sensitive to pain than White patients due to presumed underlying biological differences (Hoffman et al., 2016). Unfortunately, these biased and inaccurate beliefs can influence clinical practice of any member of the IPC team. Although health disparities are ultimately a product of a number of patient, provider, healthcare system factors (Anderson et al., 2009), we encourage all providers to prioritize education and training designed to address implicit bias and improve cultural competence in the screening, assessment, and management of pain among diverse patients (Tait & Chibnall, 2014). In addition to improving individual provider competencies, IPC services have been shown to improve access to mental and behavioral health care for Latinos (Bridges et al., 2014) and older Black patients (Ayalon et al., 2007) that yields outcomes comparable to those observed in non-Hispanic White patients. Thus, IPC may hold significant potential to address early treatment of pain to limit chronification while also reducing racial and ethnic inequities in care.

15.8.7 Implementation Challenges

It is challenging to implement comprehensive pain prevention programs as evidenced by the dearth of such programs on a wide scale. PCPs typically report being ill-equipped to address and prevent pain from a biopsychosocial stance. Depending on the background, training, and prior experiences of the BHP, he or she may not be knowledgeable or confident in their ability to adequately address pain prevention or management. In addition to lack of confidence and skills, there continues to be misunderstandings, stigma, and negative provider beliefs about patients who experience chronic pain. Further, there is often a misperception that pain intervention requires highly specialized expertise and should only be addressed through more intensive services than typically offered by an IPC team. Another challenge is the pace of the primary care setting: when team members feel overwhelmed by the clinic volume, there may be little time, energy, or motivation devoted to establishing comprehensive prevention programs.

In order to successfully implement pain prevention, a robust package of implementation support should be offered. This type of implementation assistance should begin with broad provider education that includes the full IPC team. Topics should include the following: identifying and reducing stigma associated with treatment of patients with chronic pain; ensuring cultural competence with diverse patient populations; embracing a prevention-oriented treatment approach; increasing provider knowledge and confidence in developing biopsychosocial case formulations and providing evidence-based treatments that include non-pharmacologic options; and employing screening and measurement practices that enhance patient care and provide a monitor for evaluating patient outcomes that can be achieved in a primary care setting. Education should also include hands-on role-playing experience in which the team practices delivering these interventions as well as direct feedback about the simulated patient interactions, thereby building providers' knowledge, skills, and confidence. If resources allow, education should be individualized and tailored for the needs of the clinic and providers.

In addition to education, more intensive forms of implementation support may be needed for many locations facing systemic implementation barriers (e.g., significant time constraints, belief that pain should be treated elsewhere, scheduling practices inconsistent with team-based care). For example, academic detailing (Davis & Taylor-Vaisey, 1997) can be used to identify the gaps between local clinic practice and current evidence-based treatment options. To conduct academic detailing, it is important to understand both current practices, and the individual beliefs, knowledge, and motivation of the providers. If gaps emerge between current practice and evidence-based guidelines, clear behavioral objectives for change should be provided. In addition to academic detailing, one of the most intensive forms of assistance is implementation facilitation. Implementation facilitation comes in many forms but typically includes multiple support strategies including routine consultation with specialists, identifying and developing champions, audit and feedback, as well as standard forms of technical assistance, which might include building policy dashboards or other resources such as note templates. Further, some IPC locations may have access to a specific form of facilitation, known as practice facilitation (Baskerville et al., 2012) in which an expert practice facilitator is hired by the organization to improve the quality of care through multiple, sequential quality improvement initiatives. Implementation of clinic-wide pain prevention is an ideal example of a target innovation for a practice facilitator.

15.9 Conclusion

Like public health measures for prevention of other chronic medical conditions, such as heart disease or diabetes, strategies to prevent chronic pain should be considered within IPC clinics. Exclusively biomedical approaches specifically targeting tertiary pain prevention have clearly been shown to be inadequate in meeting the needs of patients. Lack of attention to both primary and secondary prevention of pain results in escalation to higher-cost interventions which could have been avoidable if addressed early in the trajectory of care. A transformative approach grounded in stepped care that combines multiple supportive, educational, and evidence-based pain treatments through a multidisciplinary team approach is the key to successful pain prevention. While much research needs to be done in this area, we recommend IPC efforts to provide intervention early and often to the majority of patients who are either at risk for developing chronic pain or are experiencing the negative impact of pain already and are in need of biopsychosocial intervention.

References

Anderson, K. O., Green, C. R., & Payne, R. (2009, December). Racial and ethnic disparities in pain: Causes and consequences of unequal care. *The Journal of Pain, 10*(12), 1187–1204. https://doi.org/10.1016/j.jpain.2009.10.002

Anderson, D., Wang, S., & Zlateva, I. (2013). Comprehensive assessment of chronic pain management in primary care: A first phase of a quality improvement initiative at a multisite community health center. *Quality in Primary Care, 20*, 421–433.

Ayalon, L., Areán, P. A., Linkins, K., Lynch, M., & Estes, C. L. (2007). Integration of mental health services into primary care overcomes ethnic disparities in access to mental health services between black and white elderly. *The American Journal of Geriatric Psychiatry, 15*, 906–912.

Aydede, M. (2019, September–October). Does the IASP definition of pain need updating? *Pain Reports, 4*(5), e777. https://doi.org/10.1097/PR9.0000000000000777.

Baez, S., Hoch, M. C., & Hoch, J. M. (2018, November). Evaluation of cognitive behavioral interventions and psychoeducation implemented by rehabilitation specialists to treat fear-avoidance beliefs in patients with low back pain: A systematic review. *Archives of Physical Medicine and Rehabilitation, 99*(11), 2287–2298. https://doi.org/10.1016/j.apmr.2017.11.003

Baskerville, N. B., Liddy, C., & Hogg, W. (2012). Systematic review and meta-analysis of practice facilitation within primary care settings. *Annals of Family Medicine, 10*, 63–74.

Beehler, G. P., Murphy, J. L., King, P. R., Dollar, K. M., Kearney, L. K., Haslam, A., Wade, M., & Goldstein, W. R. (2019, October). Brief cognitive Behavioral therapy for chronic pain: Results from a clinical demonstration project in primary care Behavioral health. *The Clinical Journal of Pain, 35*(10), 809–817. https://doi.org/10.1097/AJP.0000000000000747

Bird, M.-L., Callisaya, M. L., Cannell, J., Gibbons, T., Smith, S. T., & Ahuja, K. D. (2016). Accuracy, validity, and reliability of an electronic visual Analog scale for pain on a touch screen tablet in healthy older adults: A clinical trial [original paper]. *Interactive Journal of Medical Research, 5*(1), e3. https://doi.org/10.2196/ijmr.4910

Borkum, J. M. (2010, March 1). Maladaptive cognitions and chronic pain: Epidemiology, neurobiology, and treatment. *Journal of Rational-Emotive & Cognitive-Behavior Therapy, 28*(1), 4–24. https://doi.org/10.1007/s10942-010-0109-x

Brain, K., Burrows, T. L., Rollo, M. E., Chai, L. K., Clarke, E. D., Hayes, C., Hodson, F. J., & Collins, C. E. (2019). A systematic review and meta-analysis of nutrition interventions for chronic noncancer pain. *Journal of Human Nutrition and Dietetics, 32*(2), 198–225. https://doi.org/10.1111/jhn.12601

Bridges, A. J., Andrews, A. R., III, Villalobos, B. T., Pastrana, F. A., Cavell, T. A., & Gomez, D. (2014). Does integrated behavioral health care reduce mental health disparities for Latinos? Initial findings. *Journal of Latina/o Psychology, 21*, 37–53.

Buchbinder, R., Jolley, D., & Wyatt, M. (2001). Population based intervention to change back pain beliefs and disability: Three part evaluation. *British Medical Journal, 322*, 1516–1520.

Buckenmaier, C. C., III, Galloway, K. T., Polomano, R. C., McDuffie, M., Kwon, N., & Gallagher, R. M. (2013). Preliminary validation of the defense and veterans pain rating scale (DVPRS) in a military population. *Pain Medicine, 14*(1), 110–123. https://doi.org/10.1111/j.1526-4637.2012.01516.x

Burton, A. K., Waddell, G., Tillotson, M., & Summerton, N. (1999). Information and advice to patients with back pain can have a positive effect: A randomized controlled trial of a novel educational booklet in primary care. *Spine, 24*, 2484–2491.

Butera, K. A., George, S. Z., & Lentz, T. A. (2020, May 1). Psychometric evaluation of the Optimal Screening for Prediction of Referral and Outcome Yellow Flag (OSPRO-YF) tool: Factor structure, reliability, and validity. *The Journal of Pain,* 21(5), 557–569. https://doi.org/10.1016/j.jpain.2019.09.003

Chenot, J.-F., Becker, A., Leonhardt, C., Keller, S., Donner-Banzhoff, N., Hildebrandt, J., Basler, H.-D., Baum, E., Kochen, M. M., & Pfingsten, M. (2008). Sex differences in presentation, course, and management of low back pain in primary care. *The Clinical Journal of Pain, 24*(7), 578–584. https://doi.org/10.1097/AJP.0b013e31816ed948

Clarke, T., Nahin, R., Barnes, P., & Stussman, B. (2016). *Use of complementary health approaches for musculoskeletal pain disorders among adults: United States*. N. C. f. H. Statistics.

Cleeland, C. S., & Ryan, K. M. (1994). Pain assessment: Global use of the brief pain inventory. *Annals of the Academy of Medicine Singapore, 23*, 129–138.

Cohen, M., Quintner, J., & van Rysewyk, S. (2018, March). Reconsidering the International Association for the Study of pain definition of pain. *Pain Reports, 3*(2), e634. https://doi.org/10.1097/PR9.0000000000000634

Dahlhamer, J., Lucas, J., Zelaya, C., Nahin, R., Mackey, S., DeBar, L., Kerns, R., Von Korff, M., Porter, L., & Helmick, C. (2018, September 14). Prevalence of chronic pain and high-impact chronic pain among adults – United States, 2016. *Mmwr-Morbidity and Mortality Weekly Report, 67*(36), 1001–1006. https://doi.org/10.15585/mmwr.mm6736a2.

Davis, D. A., & Taylor-Vaisey, A. (1997). Translating guidelines into practice: A systematic review of theoretic concepts, practical experience and research evidence in the adoption of clinical practice guidelines. *Canadian Medical Association Journal, 15*, 408–416.

Dobscha, S. K., Corson, K., Perrin, N. A., Hanson, G. C., Leibowitz, R. Q., Doak, M. N., Dickinson, K. C., Sullivan, M. D., & Gerrity, M. S. (2009, March 25). Collaborative care for chronic pain in primary care: A cluster randomized trial. *JAMA, 301*(12), 1242–1252.

Doleys, D. M. (2017). Chronic pain as a hypothetical construct: A practical and philosophical consideration. *Frontiers in Psychology, 8*, 664. https://doi.org/10.3389/fpsyg.2017.00664

Dowell, D., Haegerich, T. M., & Chou, R. (2016, April 19). CDC guideline for prescribing opioids for chronic pain – United States, 2016. *JAMA, 315*(15), 1624–1645. https://doi.org/10.1001/jama.2016.1464

Dowrick, C., Leydon, G. M., McBride, A., Howe, A., Burgess, H., Clarke, P., & Kendrick, T. (2009). Patients' and doctors' views on depression severity questionnaires incentivized in UK quality and outcomes framework: qualitative study. *British Medical Journal*, 338.

Elder, N., Penm, M., Pallerla, H., Vonder Meulen, M. B., Short, A. D., Diers, T., Imhoff, R. J., Wilson, B., & Boone, J. M. (2016, Jul-Aug). Provision of recommended chronic pain assessment and management in primary care: Does Patient-Centered Medical Home (PCMH) recognition make a difference? *Journal of American Board of Family Medicine, 29*(4), 474–481. https://doi.org/10.3122/jabfm.2016.04.160037

El-Metwally, A., Salminen, J. J., Auvinen, A., Macfarlane, G., & Mikkelsson, M. (2007, May 23). Risk factors for development of non-specific musculoskeletal pain in preteens and early adolescents: A prospective 1-year follow-up study. *BMC Musculoskeletal Disorders, 8*(1), 46. https://doi.org/10.1186/1471-2474-8-46

Escalona-Marfil, C., Coda, A., Ruiz-Moreno, J., Riu-Gispert, L. M., & Gironès, X. (2020). Validation of an electronic visual Analog scale mHealth tool for acute Pain assessment: Prospective cross-sectional study [original paper]. *Journal of Medical Internet Research, 22*(2), e13468. https://doi.org/10.2196/13468

Gallagher, R. M., & Fraifeld, E. M. (2010). Vision and purpose: AAPM members lead national initiative to improve pain care, education, and training. *Pain Medicine, 11*(154–157).

Gatchel, R. J., Reuben, D. B., Dagenais, S., Turk, D. C., Chou, R., Hershey, A. D., Hicks, G. E., Licciardone, J. C., & Horn, S. D. (2018, August). Research agenda for the prevention of pain and its impact: Report of the work group on the prevention of acute and chronic pain of the federal pain research strategy. *The Journal of Pain, 19*(8), 837–851. https://doi.org/10.1016/j.jpain.2018.02.015

George, S. Z., Teyhen, D. S., Wu, S. S., Wright, A. C., Dugan, J. L., Yang, G., Robinson, M. E., & Childs, J. D. (2009, July). Psychosocial education improves low back pain beliefs: Results from a cluster randomized clinical trial (NCT00373009) in a primary prevention setting. *European Spine Journal, 18*(7), 1050–1058. https://doi.org/10.1007/s00586-009-1016-7

Glattacker, M., Heyduck, K., & Jakob, T. (2018, August). Yellow flags as predictors of rehabilitation outcome in chronic low back pain. *Rehabilitation Psychology, 63*(3), 408–417. https://doi.org/10.1037/rep0000200

Glette, M., Stiles, T. C., Borchgrevink, P. C., & Landmark, T. (2020, May–June). The natural course of chronic pain in a general population: Stability and change in an eight-wave longitudinal study over four years (the HUNT Pain study). *The Journal of Pain, 21*(5–6), 689–699. https://doi.org/10.1016/j.jpain.2019.10.008

Green, C. R., Anderson, K. O., Baker, T. A., Campbell, L. C., Decker, S., Fillingim, R. B., Kalauokalani, D. A., Lasch, K. E., Myers, C., Tait, R. C., Todd, K. H., & Vallerand, A. H. (2003, September). The unequal burden of pain: Confronting racial and ethnic disparities in pain. *Pain Medicine, 4*(3), 277–294. https://doi.org/10.1046/j.1526-4637.2003.03034.x

Heapy, A. A., Higgins, D. M., Cervone, D., Wandner, L., Fenton, B. T., & Kerns, R. D. (2015). A systematic review of technology-assisted self-management interventions for chronic pain: Looking across treatment modalities. *Clinical Journal of Pain, 6*, 470–492.

Hicks, C. L., von Baeyer, C. L., Spafford, P. A., van Korlaar, I., & Goodenough, B. (2001). The faces pain scale – Revised: Toward a common metric in pediatric pain measurement. *Pain, 93*(2), 173–183. https://doi.org/10.1016/s0304-3959(01)00314-1

Hoffman, K. M., Trawalter, S., Axt, J. R., & Oliver, M. N. (2016, April 19). Racial bias in pain assessment and treatment recommendations, and false beliefs about biological differences between blacks and whites. *Proceedings of the National Academy of Sciences of the United States of America, 113*(16), 4296–4301. https://doi.org/10.1073/pnas.1516047113

Hunter, C. L., Goodie, J. L., Oordt, M. S., & Dobmeyer, A. C. (2017). *Integrated Behavioral health in primary care: Step-by-step guidance for assessment and intervention* (2nd ed.). APA.

IASP Task Force on Taxonomy. (1994). *Classification of chronic Pain*. IASP Press.

Institute of Medicine of the National Academy of Science. (2011). Relieving Pain in America: A blueprint for transforming prevention, care, education, and research. Institute of Medicine. https://www.nap.edu/catalog/13172/relieving-pain-in-america-a-blueprint-for-transforming-prevention-care

Jones, M. A., Stratton, G., Reilly, T., & Unnithan, V. B. (2005). Biological risk indicators for recurrent non-specific low back pain in adolescents. *British Journal of Sports Medicine, 39*(3), 137–140. https://doi.org/10.1136/bjsm.2003.009951

Karcioglu, O., Topacoglu, H., Dikme, O., & Dikme, O. (2018, April 1). A systematic review of the pain scales in adults: Which to use? *The American Journal of Emergency Medicine, 36*(4), 707–714. https://doi.org/10.1016/j.ajem.2018.01.008

Kehlet, H., Jensen, T. S., & Woolf, C. J. (2006, May 13). Persistent postsurgical pain: Risk factors and prevention. *The Lancet, 367*(9522), 1618–1625. https://doi.org/10.1016/S0140-6736(06)68700-X

King, W. (2007). Acute pain, subacute pain and chronic pain. In R. F. Schmidt & W. D. Willis (Eds.), *Encyclopedia of pain* (pp. 35–36). Springer. https://doi.org/10.1007/978-3-540-29805-2_75

Krebs, E. E., Carey, T. S., & Weinberger, M. (2007, October 1). Accuracy of the Pain numeric rating scale as a screening test in primary care. *Journal of General Internal Medicine, 22*(10), 1453–1458. https://doi.org/10.1007/s11606-007-0321-2

Krebs, E. E., Lorenz, K. A., Bair, M. J., Damush, T. M., Wu, J., Sutherland, J. M., Asch, S. M., & Kroenke, K. (2009, June 1). Development and initial validation of the PEG, a three-item scale assessing Pain intensity and interference. *Journal of General Internal Medicine, 24*(6), 733–738. https://doi.org/10.1007/s11606-009-0981-1

Kroenke, K., Spitzer, R. L., & Williams, J. B. (2001). The PHQ-9: Validity of a brief depression severity measure. *Journal of General Internal Medicine, 16*, 606–613.

Kroenke, K., Baye, F., Lourens, S. G., Evans, E., Weitlauf, S., McCalley, S., Porter, B., Matthias, M. S., & Bair, M. J. (2019, September). Automated self-management (ASM) vs. ASM-enhanced collaborative care for chronic pain and mood symptoms: The CAMMPS randomized clinical trial. *Journal of General Internal Medicine, 34*(9), 1806–1814. https://doi.org/10.1007/s11606-019-05121-4

Lamb, S. E., Hansen, Z., Lall, R., Castelnuovo, E., Withers, E. J., Nichols, V., Potter, R., & Underwood, M. R. (2010, March 13). Group cognitive behavioural treatment for low-back pain in primary care: A randomised controlled trial and cost-effectiveness analysis. *Lancet, 375*, 916–923. https://doi.org/10.1016/s01406736(09)62164-4

Leroux, I., Brisson, C., & Montreuil, S. (2005). Job strain and neck–shoulder symptoms: A prevalence study of women and men white-collar workers. *Occupational Medicine, 56*(2), 102–109. https://doi.org/10.1093/occmed/kqj005

Linton, S. J. (2002, May). Early identification and intervention in the prevention of musculoskeletal pain. *American Journal of Industrial Medicine, 41*(5), 433–442. https://doi.org/10.1002/ajim.10052

Linton, S. J., & Andersson, T. (2000). Can chronic disability be prevented? A randomized trial of a cognitive-behavior intervention and two forms of information for patients with spinal pain. *Spine, 25*, 2825–2831.

Linton, S. J., & Boersma, K. (2003). Early identification of patients at risk of developing a persistent back problem: The predictive validity of the Örebro musculoskeletal pain questionnaire. *The Clinical Journal of Pain, 19*(2), 80–86. https://journals.lww.com/clinicalpain/Fulltext/2003/03000/Early_Identification_of_Patients_at_Risk_of.2.aspx

Lorenz, K. A., Sherbourne, C. D., Shugarman, L. R., Rubenstein, L. V., Wen, L., Cohen, A., Goebel, J. R., Hagenmeier, E., Simon, B., Lanto, A., & Asch, S. M. (2009). How reliable is pain as the fifth vital sign? *The Journal of the American Board of Family Medicine, 22*(3), 291–298. https://doi.org/10.3122/jabfm.2009.03.080162

Macfarlane, G. J., Beasley, M., Smith, B. H., Jones, G. T., & Macfarlane, T. V. (2015). Can large surveys conducted on highly selected populations provide valid information on the epidemiology of common health conditions? An analysis of UK biobank data on musculoskeletal pain. *British Journal of Pain, 9*(4), 203–212. https://doi.org/10.1177/2049463715569806

Martinson, A., Craner, J., & Clinton-Lont, J. (2020, December 18). Outcomes of a 6-week cognitive-behavioral therapy for chronic pain group for veterans seen in primary care. *Translational Behavioral Medicine, 10*, 254–266. https://doi.org/10.1093/tbm/iby127

McGreevy, K., Bottros, M. M., & Raja, S. N. (2011). Preventing chronic pain following acute pain: Risk factors, preventive strategies, and their efficacy. *European Journal of Pain Supplements, 5*(2), 365–372. https://doi.org/10.1016/j.eujps.2011.08.013

Mehling, W. E., Gopisetty, V., Bartmess, E., Acree, M., Pressman, A., Goldberg, H., Hecht, F. M., Carey, T., & Avins, A. L. (2012). The prognosis of acute low back pain in primary care in the United States: A 2-year prospective cohort study. *Spine, 37*(8), 678–684. https://doi.org/10.1097/BRS.0b013e318230ab20

Melzack, R. (1987). The short-form McGill pain questionnaire. *Pain, 30*(2), 191–197. https://doi.org/10.1016/0304-3959(87)91074-8

Meyer, C., Denis, C. M., & Berquin, A. D. (2018, September). Secondary prevention of chronic musculoskeletal pain: A systematic review of clinical trials. *Annals of Physical and Rehabilitation Medicine, 61*(5), 323–338. https://doi.org/10.1016/j.rehab.2018.03.002

Mills, S. E. E., Nicolson, K. P., & Smith, B. H. (2019, August 1). Chronic pain: A review of its epidemiology and associated factors in population-based studies. *British Journal of Anaesthesia, 123*(2), e273–e283. https://doi.org/10.1016/j.bja.2019.03.023

Mohr, D. C., Cuijpers, P., & Lehman, K. (2011). Supportive accountability: A model for providing human support to enhance adherence to eHealth interventions [viewpoint]. *Journal of Medical Internet Research, 13*(1), e30. https://doi.org/10.2196/jmir.1602

Moitra, E., Sperry, J. A., Mongold, D., Kyle, B. N., & Selby, J. (2011). A group medical visit program for primary care patients with chronic pain. *Professional Psychology: Research and Practice, 42*(2), 153–159. https://doi.org/10.1037/a0022240

Moman, R. N., Dvorkin, J., Pollard, E. M., Wanderman, R., Murad, M. H., Warner, D. O., & Hooten, W. M. (2019, November 1). A systematic review and meta-analysis of unguided electronic and mobile health technologies for chronic pain-is it time to start prescribing electronic health applications? *Pain Medicine, 20*(11), 2238–2255. https://doi.org/10.1093/pm/pnz164

Murphy, K. R., Han, J. L., Yang, S., Hussaini, S. M., Elsamadicy, A. A., Parente, B., Xie, J., Pagadala, P., & Lad, S. P. (2017, February). Prevalence of specific types of pain diagnoses in a sample of United States adults. *Pain Physician, 20*(2), E257–E268. https://www.ncbi.nlm.nih.gov/pubmed/28158163.

Nahin, R. L. (2017, March 1). Severe pain in veterans: The effect of age and sex, and comparisons with the general population. *The Journal of Pain, 18*(3), 247–254. https://doi.org/10.1016/j.jpain.2016.10.021

Naylor, J. C., Wagner, H. R., Johnston, C., Elbogen, E. E., Brancu, M., Marx, C. E., Group, V. A. M.-A. M. W, Group, V. A. M.-A. M. W. V. W, & Strauss, J. L. (2019, June 25). Pain intensity and pain interference in male and female Iraq/Afghanistan-era veterans. *Womens Health Issues, 29*(Suppl 1), S24–S31. https://doi.org/10.1016/j.whi.2019.04.015

Ndao-Brumblay, S. K., & Green, C. R. (2005). Racial differences in the physical and psychosocial health among black and white women with chronic pain. *Journal of the National Medical Association, 97*, 1369–1377.

Nugraha, B., Gutenbrunner, C., Barke, A., Karst, M., Schiller, J., Schafer, P., Falter, S., Korwisi, B., Rief, W., Treede, R. D., & Pain, I. T. f. t. C. o. C. (2019, January). The IASP classification of chronic pain for ICD-11: Functioning properties of chronic pain. *Pain, 160*(1), 88–94. https://doi.org/10.1097/j.pain.0000000000001433

Pak, D. J., Yong, R. J., Kaye, A. D., & Urman, R. D. (2018, February 5). Chronification of pain: Mechanisms, current understanding, and clinical implications. *Current Pain and Headache Reports, 22*(2), 9. https://doi.org/10.1007/s11916-018-0666-8

Palmer, K. T. (2003, February 1). Pain in the forearm, wrist and hand. *Regional Musculoskeletal Conditions, 17*(1), 113–135. https://doi.org/10.1016/S1521-6942(02)00100-6

Pico-Espinosa, O. J., Skillgate, E., Tettamanti, G., Lager, A., & Holm, L. W. (2017, 01 Apr. 2017). Diabetes mellitus and hyperlipidaemia as risk factors for frequent pain in the back, neck and/or shoulders/arms among adults in Stockholm 2006 to 2010 – Results from the Stockholm public health cohort. Scandinavian Journal of Pain, 15(1), 1–7. https://doi.org/10.1016/j.sjpain.2016.11.005

Qian, M., Shi, Y., & Yu, M. (2020, November 13). The association between obesity and chronic pain among community-dwelling older adults: A systematic review and meta-analysis. *Geriatric Nursing, 42*(1), 8–15. https://doi.org/10.1016/j.gerinurse.2020.10.017

Raja, S. N., Carr, D. B., Cohen, M., Finnerup, N. B., Flor, H., Gibson, S., Keefe, F. J., Mogil, J. S., Ringkamp, M., Sluka, K. A., Song, X. J., Stevens, B., Sullivan, M. D., Tutelman, P. R., Ushida, T., & Vader, K. (2020). The revised International Association for the Study of Pain definition of pain: concepts, challenges, and compromises. *Pain, 161*(9), 1976–1982. https://doi.org/10.1097/j.pain.0000000000001939

Robinson, P. J., & Reiter, J. T. (2016). *Behavioral consultation and primary care: A guide to integrating services* (2nd ed.). Springer.

Rose, G. A., Khaw, K.-T., & Marmot, M. (2008). *Rose's strategy of preventive medicine: The complete original text.* Oxford University Press.

Rosenberger, P. H., Philip, E. J., Lee, A., & Kerns, R. D. (2011). The VHA's national pain management strategy: Implementing the stepped care model. *Federal Practitioner, 28*, 39.

Ross, A. C., Simons, L. E., Feinstein, A. B., Yoon, I. A., & Bhandari, R. P. (2017). Social risk and resilience factors in adolescent chronic pain: Examining the role of parents and peers. *Journal of Pediatric Psychology, 43*(3), 303–313. https://doi.org/10.1093/jpepsy/jsx118

Rundell, S. D., Sherman, K. J., Heagerty, P. J., Mock, C. N., & Jarvik, J. G. (2015, March). The clinical course of pain and function in older adults with a new primary care visit for back pain. *Journal of the American Geriatrics Society, 63*(3), 524–530. https://doi.org/10.1111/jgs.13241

Salazar, A., de Sola, H., Failde, I., & Moral-Munoz, J. A. (2018, October 25). Measuring the quality of Mobile apps for the Management of Pain: Systematic search and evaluation using the Mobile app rating scale. *JMIR mHealth and uHealth, 6*(10), e10718. https://doi.org/10.2196/10718

Shaheed, C. A., McFarlane, B., Maher, C. G., Williams, K. A., Bergin, J., Matthews, A., & McLachlan, A. J. (2016, January). Investigating the primary care management of low back pain: A simulated patient study. *The Journal of Pain, 17*(1), 27–35. https://doi.org/10.1016/j.jpain.2015.09.010

Shahidi, B., Curran-Everett, D., & Maluf, K. S. (2015, December 1). Psychosocial, physical, and neurophysiological risk factors for chronic neck pain: A prospective inception cohort study. *The Journal of Pain, 16*(12), 1288–1299. https://doi.org/10.1016/j.jpain.2015.09.002

Sowah, D., Boyko, R., Antle, D., Miller, L., Zakhary, M., & Straube, S. (2018, September). Occupational interventions for the prevention of back pain: Overview of systematic reviews. *Journal of Safety Research, 66*, 39–59. https://doi.org/10.1016/j.jsr.2018.05.007

Staton, L. J., Panda, M., Chen, I., Genao, I., Kurz, J., Pasanen, M., Mechaber, A. J., Menon, M., O'Rorke, J., & Wood, J. (2007). When race matters: Disagreement in pain perception between patients and their physicians in primary care. *Journal of the National Medical Association, 99*(5), 532.

Storm, L., Rousing, R., Andersen, M. O., & Carreon, L. Y. (2018). Usefulness of the STarT back screening tool to predict pain problems after lumbar spine surgery. *Danish Medical Journal, 65*, A5517.

Straube, S., Harden, M., Schroder, H., Arendacka, B., Fan, X., Moore, R. A., & Friede, T. (2016, October). Back schools for the treatment of chronic low back pain: Possibility of benefit but no convincing evidence after 47 years of research-systematic review and meta-analysis. *Pain, 157*(10), 2160–2172. https://doi.org/10.1097/j.pain.0000000000000640

Tait, R. C., & Chibnall, J. T. (2014, February–March). Racial/ethnic disparities in the assessment and treatment of pain: Psychosocial perspectives. *The American Psychologist, 69*(2), 131–141. https://doi.org/10.1037/a0035204

Thompson, T., Oram, C., Correll, C. U., Tsermentseli, S., & Stubbs, B. (2017, May 1). Analgesic effects of alcohol: A systematic review and meta-analysis of controlled experimental studies in healthy participants. *The Journal of Pain, 18*(5), 499–510. https://doi.org/10.1016/j.jpain.2016.11.009

Treede, R. D., Rief, W., Barke, A., Aziz, Q., Bennett, M. I., Benoliel, R., Cohen, M., Evers, S., Finnerup, N. B., First, M. B., Giamberardino, M. A., Kaasa, S., Kosek, E., Lavand'homme, P., Nicholas, M., Perrot, S., Scholz, J., Schug, S., Smith, B. H., … Wang, S. J. (2015, June). A classification of chronic pain for ICD-11. *Pain, 156*(6), 1003–1007. https://doi.org/10.1097/j.pain.0000000000000160.

U. S. Department of Health and Human Services. (2019). *Pain management best practices interagency task force report: updates, gaps, inconsistencies, and recommendations*. https://www.hhs.gov/ash/advisory-committees/pain/reports/index.html

Viana, M. C., Lim, C. C. W., Garcia Pereira, F., Aguilar-Gaxiola, S., Alonso, J., Bruffaerts, R., de Jonge, P., Caldas-de-Almeida, J. M., O'Neill, S., Stein, D. J., Al-Hamzawi, A., Benjet, C., Cardoso, G., Florescu, S., de Girolamo, G., Haro, J. M., Hu, C., Kovess-Masfety, V., Levinson, D., Piazza, M., Posada-Villa, J., Rabczenko, D., Kessler, R. C., & Scott, K. M. (2018, January 1). Previous mental disorders and subsequent onset of chronic back or neck pain: Findings from 19 countries. *The Journal of Pain, 19*(1), 99–110. https://doi.org/10.1016/j.jpain.2017.08.011

Von Korff, M., Scher, A. I., Helmick, C., Carter-Pokras, O., Dodick, D. W., Goulet, J., Hamill-Ruth, R., LeResche, L., Porter, L., Tait, R., Terman, G., Veasley, C., & Mackey, S. (2016, October). United States National Pain Strategy for population research: Concepts, definitions, and pilot data. *The Journal of Pain, 17*(10), 1068–1080. https://doi.org/10.1016/j.jpain.2016.06.009

Webb, R., Brammah, T., Lunt, M., Urwin, M., Allison, T., & Symmons, D. (2003). Prevalence and predictors of intense, chronic, and disabling neck and Back Pain in the UK general population. *Spine, 28*(11), 1195–1202. https://doi.org/10.1097/01.Brs.0000067430.49169.01

Weingarten, T. N., Moeschler, S. M., Ptaszynski, A. E., Hooten, W. M., Beebe, T. J., & Warner, D. O. (2008). An assessment of the association between smoking status, pain intensity, and functional interference in patients with chronic pain. *Pain Physician, 11*, 643–653.

Wijnhoven, H. A. H., de Vet, H. C. W., & Picavet, S. J. H. (2006). Explaining sex differences in chronic musculoskeletal pain in a general population. *Pain, 124*(1), 158–166. https://doi.org/10.1016/j.pain.2006.04.012

You, D. S., Albu, S., Lisenbardt, H., & Meagher, M. W. (2018). Cumulative childhood adversity as a risk factor for common chronic Pain conditions in young adults. *Pain Medicine, 20*(3), 486–494. https://doi.org/10.1093/pm/pny106

Chapter 16
Eating Disorders

C. Barr Taylor, Ellen E. Fitzsimmons-Craft, Arielle C. Smith, and Andrea K. Graham

16.1 Definition/Diagnostic Criteria

Eating disorders (EDs) are common and serious behavioral health disorders associated with high morbidity and mortality, marked impairment, and poor quality of life (American Psychiatric Association, 2013; van Hoeken & Hoek, 2020). EDs include a number of diagnostic categories as described below, with the three main clinical diagnoses being anorexia nervosa (AN), bulimia nervosa (BN), and binge eating disorder (BED). In a meta-analysis of 36 quantitative studies, Arcelus et al. (2011) reported that the weighted mortality rates (i.e., deaths per 1000 person-years) were 5.1 for AN, 1.7 for BN, and 3.3 for ED not otherwise specified (EDNOS), a categorization updated in the DSM-5 to Other Specified Feeding and Eating Disorder (OSFED), that included disorders of clinical severity other than AN, BN, and BED. The standardized mortality ratios (i.e., ratios of observed to expected deaths) were 5.86 for AN, 1.93 for BN, and 1.92 for EDNOS. They noted that one in five individuals with AN had died by suicide (Arcelus et al., 2011). Mortality associated with AN is considered to be one of the highest mortality rates of any behavioral

C. B. Taylor (✉)
Department of Psychiatry and Behavioral Sciences, Stanford University and Center for m2 Health, Palo Alto University, Palo Alto, CA, USA
e-mail: btaylor@stanford.edu

E. E. Fitzsimmons-Craft · A. C. Smith
Department of Psychiatry, Washington University School of Medicine, St. Louis, MO, USA
e-mail: fitzsimmonse@wustl.edu; arielle.smith@wustl.edu

A. K. Graham
Department of Preventive Medicine, Northwestern University, Evanston, IL, USA
e-mail: andrea.graham@northwestern.edu

W. O'Donohue, M. Zimmermann (eds.), *Handbook of Evidence-Based Prevention of Behavioral Disorders in Integrated Care*,
https://doi.org/10.1007/978-3-030-83469-2_16

health disorder (Arcelus et al., 2011). Other work has found a standardized mortality ratio of 1.50 specifically for BED (Fichter & Quadflieg, 2016).

ED diagnoses are based, for the most part, on self-reported symptoms. The Diagnostic and Statistical Manual (DSM) of the American Psychiatric Association is the standard source for definitions (American Psychiatric Association, 2013). The definitions for the most common disorders, based on the current version of the DSM (DSM-5), in adults are as follows:

16.1.1 Anorexia Nervosa (AN)

There are three key diagnostic criteria for AN: (1) restriction of energy intake relative to requirements, leading to a significantly low body weight (of note, individuals with body mass indices (BMIs) below 17 kg/m^2 are considered to have moderate to severe AN); (2) intense fear of gaining weight or of becoming fat; and (3) a disturbance in the way body weight/shape is experienced with an overevaluation of weight and shape. AN is further characterized as the restricting type if individuals have not recently engaged in bingeing or purging or as the binge eating/purging type if they have.

Historically, AN has been diagnosed in individuals with very low body weights relative to that expected for their sex/age. However, some researchers have identified individuals with "normal or high weights" who have undergone significant weight loss and who exhibit the other characteristics of AN, as well as unstable vital signs such as very low heart rates and arrhythmias indicating medical instability (Whitelaw et al., 2018). These individuals are labeled as having atypical AN (AAN), which is included under the OSFED diagnosis in DSM-5. Practitioners should thus be aware that recent, significant weight loss may be indicative of AAN in normal or overweight individuals if they have all the other features of AN.

16.1.2 Bulimia Nervosa (BN)

BN is characterized by both the presence of bingeing and "compensatory" behaviors meant to prevent weight gain, such as vomiting, misuse of laxatives, diuretics, or diet pills, fasting, and/or excessive exercise. Binge eating is defined as eating more food in a short period of time than most individuals would eat in a similar period of time under similar circumstances, and a feeling of loss of control over the eating episode (e.g., a feeling that one cannot stop eating). The binge eating and inappropriate compensatory behaviors both occur, on average, at least once a week for 3 months. Individuals with BN also unduly base their self-esteem on body shape and weight.

16.1.3 Binge Eating Disorder (BED)

BED, the third major eating disorder, is characterized by binge eating, on average, at least once a week for 3 months but without regular engagement in associated compensatory behaviors. The binge eating episodes are associated with three or more of the following: eating more rapidly than normal, eating until feeling uncomfortably full, eating large amounts of food when not hungry, eating alone out of embarrassment for what or how much one is eating, or negative emotions (e.g., disgust, guilt, depression) after overeating.

16.1.4 Purging Disorder (PD)

PD is not formally recognized in DSM-5 (it is noted as an example of OSFED), but since health-care professionals may encounter this condition in practice and see patients suffering the consequences of excessive purging, it is worth a description. (Also, some ED screening measures identify possible cases, e.g., the Stanford-Washington University Eating Disorder Screen [SWED] (Graham et al., 2019)). PD is characterized by high rates of vomiting and/or the use of diuretics or laxatives to control weight and shape in the absence of bingeing episodes.

16.1.5 Other Specified Feeding or Eating Disorder (OSFED)

In addition to AAN and PD, OSFED includes individuals with symptoms and behaviors like those of AN, BN, and BED but who do not meet the full diagnostic criteria. Much less is known about the risk factors for these disorders or how to intervene, and they will not be discussed further in this chapter.

16.2 Prevalence and Age of Onset

EDs are very common. In a recent study, the highest estimated mean annual prevalence of EDs occurred at approximately 21 years for both males (7.4%; 95% UI, 3.5%–11.5%) and females (10.3%; 95% UI, 7.0%–14.2%), with lifetime mean prevalence estimates increasing to 14.3% (95% UI, 9.7%–19.0%) for males and 19.7% (95% UI, 15.8%–23.9%) for females by 40 years. Ninety-five percent of first-time cases occurred by 25 years (Ward et al., 2019). Striegel-Moore et al. (2003) found that for White women, AN begins as early as age nine and continues to occur throughout adolescence; BN and BED typically begin somewhat later (Striegel-Moore et al., 2003). Consistent with Ward et al. (2019), they found that relatively few cases occurred after age 24. In one large US national sample, the adjusted odds ratios (AORs) for lifetime, but not 12-month, BED diagnosis was significantly lower for non-Hispanic Black respondents relative to that of non-Hispanic White respondents; AORs of BED for Hispanic and non-Hispanic White respondents did not differ significantly (Udo & Grilo, 2018). Much less is known about rates of EDs among Asians (Ning et al., 2021).

Once EDs become established, they are more difficult to treat, at least in the case of AN (Guarda, 2008), and the longer the disorder lasts, the more likely it is to have adverse effects. Proponents of prevention argue, then, that it is important both to reduce the prevalence of risk factors and to keep EDs from emerging and that, given the prevalence of disordered eating attitudes and behaviors in young women, this is of major public health importance.

16.3 Risk Factors

In recent years, a number of prospective studies have been conducted to help identify risk factors for EDs. These prospective studies, along with an even larger literature on retrospective, cross-sectional, and clinical studies, have identified a number of risk factors (Jacobi et al., 2004; Stice & Shaw, 2004; Taylor, 2017). In the ED prevention literature, the risk factors of interest have been shown to be "causative" of the disorder in that they can be reduced, with reduction associated with lower rates of onset. Across many studies, elevated perceived pressure to be thin from family, peers, and the media, internalization of the thin ideal espoused for women by Western culture, BMI, and body dissatisfaction have predicted future eating pathology (Taylor, 2017; Taylor et al., 2017). The role of dieting as a risk factor is less clear, and the results have been inconsistent, perhaps because of problems associated with measurement and/or because it so common as to be nonspecific.

In addition to the specific risk factors mentioned above, there are additional nonspecific risk factors to consider. For example, a history of adverse childhood experiences (including sexual abuse) appears to be a risk factor for the development of a number of mental health problems, including EDs (Jacobi et al., 2004; Pike et al., 2008; Sanci et al., 2008; Speranza et al., 2003). As such, prevention of adverse childhood experiences would likely reduce the onset of EDs (and other mental health problems) but is a goal beyond ED prevention. EDs are much more common in women, and, as noted previously, often begin early. These data suggest that preventive programs should begin by at least age 12, if not earlier, and that preventive programs are relevant at least into the mid-20s.

There has been some interest as to whether or not acculturation to Western society may trigger EDs. However, both greater and lesser acculturation have been identified as risk factors for the development of an ED, and this varies depending on the group studied as well as how acculturation and culture change are conceptualized and measured (Doris et al., 2015). Studies have yet to show how a change in culture may affect ED onset rates, except as applied to very contained environments.

Genetic and biological studies may eventually identify populations at particular risk and in need of targeted prevention efforts (Bulik et al., 2016;). Finally, there are a number of high-risk settings and activities that are associated with increased risk for EDs, including gymnastics and some other sports (Flatt & Taylor, 2018), classical ballet (Ringham et al., 2006), and modeling, to name a few.

While the general importance of weight and shape concerns as risk factors is well-known, it is not known if just having high weight and shape concerns is sufficient to cause an ED or if the presence of other factors is necessary for an ED to develop (Jacobi et al., 2004). Further, in a secondary analysis of a study which selected participants based on high weight concerns (Jacobi et al., 2011; Taylor et al., 2006), the most potent risk factors were comments by a coach or teacher about the participant's eating and a history of depression (Jacobi et al., 2011). This has implications for medical professionals as comments about weight, shape, and eating might have adverse consequences.

Most of the studies on weight and shape concerns have focused on young women, and much less is known about how weight/shape concerns affect young men. A study by Calzo et al. (2012) suggests that there may be important gender differences, e.g., thin young men may want to gain rather than lose weight to improve appearance. There is also less information available on weight and shape concerns as risk factors for EDs for many minority populations, e.g., the LGBTQ community. A recent systematic review found higher rates of bingeing and purging and lower body dissatisfaction, but also lower drive for thinness, in sexual minority women compared with heterosexual peers (Meneguzzo et al., 2018). Another recent study involving a very large national sample of college students found that students who identified as bisexual or other sexual orientation reported significantly greater odds of a probable ED diagnosis and greater elevations in weight and shape concerns compared to heterosexual students. Cisgender female students and gender minority students reported significantly greater odds of a probable ED diagnosis and greater elevations in weight and shape concerns compared to cisgender male students (Calzo et al., 2017).

A major, important controversy in the ED prevention field is the impact of health-care provider recommendations to lose weight for those with overweight or obesity. ED prevention experts have argued that public health attempts to encourage young men and women with "overweight" to lose weight may increase weight and shape concerns and foster unhealthy weight regulation practices, although this has not been definitively demonstrated (National Task Force on the Prevention and Treatment of Obesity, 2000). Later, we discuss how health-care professionals might discuss risk and intervention and treatment options with patients at risk for, or with early EDs, as well as overweight or obesity.

It should be noted, while many have been posited, no risk factors have been identified for AN in prospective studies, in part because of the relatively low rate of onset for AN. However, as part of a prevention study, Jacobi et al. (2018) used three characteristics to identify young girls at putative risk for AN: (1) high drive for thinness, (2) low weight or significant weight loss, and (3) high levels of perfectionism, amenorrhea, excessive exercise, or a family history of an ED. In a large sample of

German girls, ages 11 to 17, 12.1% (447/3941) were identified as at risk for AN on the basis of these risk factors (Jacobi et al., 2018).

16.4 Effective Screening

Screens can be used to identify those at possible risk for and/or with clinical disorders. (The limitations of screens are discussed elsewhere in this volume). In terms of assessing for ED risk, the Weight Concerns Scale (WCS) is one of the most widely used and studied measures (Taylor, 2017). The WCS was derived from a principal component analysis of an extensive list of self-reported ED attitudes and behaviors (Killen et al., 1993). The goal was to create a relatively brief, but psychometrically sound, instrument that did not overlap with other dimensions of EDs like purging, restraint, physical activity, and bulimia. The scale was found to have excellent stability ($r = 0.71$ for a 7-month interval (Killen et al., 1994) and $r = 0.74$ for a 12-month interval (Killen et al., 1996)) and to be sensitive to treatment differences (Taylor et al., 2006). Because the items were derived from different scales, with the items scored differently, each of the five items is adjusted to equal a maximum score of 20 (see Table 16.1), for a maximum total scale score of 100. Because the score adjustments make the WCS difficult to quickly score in clinical practice, in a sample of 4882 young women, we used a receiver operating characteristic (ROC) analysis to determine the score on items that might capture the same risk as the entire WCS. We found that a response >2 on the question, "How afraid are you of gaining 3 pounds?" (see item two in Table 16.1) had a sensitivity of 85.7% and a specificity of 78.8% for identifying individuals at high risk for an ED, based on the full WCS scale (score of 47 or greater). This one question could be added with a short screen that identifies possible EDs (e.g., the SCOFF, see Table 16.2, below) to identify individuals at risk for or with EDs.

For identifying possible EDs in clinical practice, the SCOFF is the most widely used scale (see Table 16.1). The name is a mnemonic of its five items. The SCOFF, which was developed by British researchers (hence the "one stone" criterion—a stone equals 14 pounds) consists of five items scored as yes or no (Morgan et al., 1999). A score of yes on two or more items indicates a likely case of AN or BN. In an analysis of 25 studies, the SCOFF had a pooled sensitivity of 0.86 (95% CI, 0.78–0.91) and specificity of 0.83 (95% CI, 0.77–0.88) for identifying AN and/or BN compared to a clinical interview (Kutz et al., 2020). Important to note though, the SCOFF does not identify risk, distinguish between full clinical and subclinical disorders, and may not identify BED.

If a practitioner wants to use the SCOFF to quickly and easily assess for EDs and wants to measure risk, as mentioned, the WCS may not be a viable alternative as the scoring is complicated. However, the WCS item two noted above could be added to the SCOFF, and the combined questions could identify those at risk for or with a possible ED. However, practitioners should keep in mind that item two from the

Table 16.1 Weight concerns scale

For all questions below, circle only one number				
1. How much more or less do you feel you worry about your weight and body shape than other women your age?				
1. I worry a lot less than other women				
2. I worry a little less than other women				
3. I worry about the same as other women				
4. I worry a little more than other women				
5. I worry a lot more than other women				
2. How afraid are you of gaining 3 pounds?				
(1) Not afraid	(2) Slightly afraid	(3) Moderately afraid	(4) Very afraid	(5) Terrified
3. When was the last time you went on a diet?				
1. I've never been on a diet				
2. I was on a diet about one year ago				
3. I was on a diet about 6 months ago				
4. I was on a diet about 3 months ago				
5. I was on a diet about 1 month ago				
6. I was on a diet less than 1 month ago				
7. I'm now on a diet				
4. Compared to other things in your life, how important is your weight to you?				
1. My weight is not important compared to other things in my life				
2. My weight is a little more important than some other things				
3. My weight is more important than most, but not all, things in my life				
4. My weight is the most important thing in my life				
5. Do you feel fat?				
(1) Never	(2) Rarely	(3) Sometimes	(4) Often	(5) Always

Scoring:
[100×(Q1 response-1)/4 + 100×(Q1 response-1)/4 + 100×(Q1 response-1)/6 + 100×(Q1 response-1)/3 +100×(Q1 response-1)/4]/5

WCS has not undergone the same level of extensive testing as an independent screener than has been done with the full WCS.

Several years ago, as part of a long-term ED prevention research study, we developed a short instrument that can measure both risk for and possible presence of an ED (Graham et al., 2019). The instrument includes both the WCS and items assessing clinical features of EDs based on DSM-5 criteria. Compared to a diagnostic interview, screen sensitivity ranged from 0.90 (for AN) to 0.55 (for PD) and specificity ranged from 0.99 (for AN) to 0.78 (for subthreshold BED). The final screen was programmed to be interactive so that it takes only 5–7 min to complete. The screen has since been slightly expanded to include assessment of a broader range of EDs and deployed by the National Eating Disorders Association (NEDA), the largest non-profit dedicated to EDs in the USA, as way to provide feedback to interested individuals on possible ED risk or clinical status (Fitzsimmons-Craft et al., 2019).

Table 16.2 SCOFF questions

1. Do you make yourself **S**ick because you feel uncomfortably full?
2. Do you worry that you have lost **C**ontrol over how much you eat?
3. Have you recently lost more than **O**ne stone (14 lb) in a 3-month period?
4. Do you believe yourself to be **F**at when others say you are too thin?
5. Would you say that **F**ood dominates your life?

One point for every "yes"; a score of ≥2 indicates a likely case of anorexia nervosa or bulimia

The screen is now being completed by more than 200,000 respondents per year. However, a limitation is that the algorithm is complex, and the measure cannot be easily scored by hand.

A few instruments have been developed to identify individuals with BED or subclinical BED, including those developed by pharmaceutical companies hoping to identify individuals who might then be prescribed pharmacological intervention. For example, the 7-item Binge-Eating Disorder Screener (BEDS-7) has been shown to have 100% sensitivity and 38.7% specificity for identifying cases of BED (Herman et al., 2016). Stice et al. (2004) have also developed an ED diagnostic scale based on DSM-IV.

16.5 Review of Evidence

16.5.1 Universal Prevention: Application to Health-Care Settings

Given the ubiquity of poor body image and internalization of the thin body ideal, coupled with the fact that ED risk factors begin early and that the peak onset of EDs is during adolescence, universal prevention programs would seem to be ideal to introduce in school settings. Further, if demonstrated effective, the materials might be used as psychoeducational tools in health-care settings. Early review of classroom-based interventions designed to improve body image and reduce ED attitudes and behaviors found little benefit (Pratt & Woolfenden, 2002). A more recent review suggested that more current programs could be of benefit, at least to young women, but the quality of evidence was rated as low (Chua et al., 2020), and there was little evidence that these programs resulted in meaningful reduction in ED onset. As a resource, we made one of these programs, StayingFit (Jones et al., 2014), freely available via a massive open online course (MOOC) so that it could be available for free for anyone who is interested (available at www.edx.org/course/staying-fit). The course provides basic information about body image and healthy weight regulation skills. There is some evidence that the program may support healthy weight regulation, improve weight/shape concerns among participants with EDs risk, and increase physical activity, at least in high school students (Jones et al., 2014).

Perhaps the most important role health-care providers and other authority figures (e.g., teachers) can play is to avoid messages that may stigmatize EDs, eating behaviors, overweight, or obesity, since they may inadvertently increase ED behaviors. In one of our studies, we have shown that a comment from a coach or teacher about eating was associated with increased ED risk (Jacobi et al., 2011).

16.5.2 Targeted or Selective Prevention Interventions

Preventive approaches often distinguish between universal, targeted/selective (i.e., intended for individuals at high risk for the disorder), and indicated prevention, with the latter appropriate for individuals at very high risk and exhibiting low levels of ED behaviors, including bingeing and/or compensatory behaviors. In the ED field, the distinctions between targeted/selective and indicated interventions are often arbitrary as there is a continuum of ED attitudes and behaviors. The same interventions used for targeted/selective are appropriate for those where indicated intervention is appropriate (Taylor et al., 2006). However, individuals with very high weight and shape concerns and some bingeing and/or compensatory behaviors would also be appropriate for clinical interventions. For a stepped-care approach, we recommend simply following individuals in the targeted/selective/indicated group and then moving to next-level interventions if symptoms begin or worsen.

Extensive work in the past decade has resulted in three effective targeted/selective preventive approaches at least for older adolescents and college-age women, with several programs evidencing a significant reduction in ED onset among high-risk women (Harrer et al., 2020; Martinsen et al., 2014; Stice et al., 2006, 2008; Taylor et al., 2006, 2017; Wade & Wilksch, 2018). These three programs are based on social learning theory/cognitive behavior therapy (CBT), cognitive dissonance, and media literacy/advocacy, respectively, as discussed below. Of note, psychoeducation approaches alone, particularly those with limited interactions with participants (e.g., didactic programs) and delivered to individuals at low-risk for ED onset, have limited effectiveness (Stice et al., 2007). Harrer et al. (2020) recently reported on the results of a meta-analysis of 27 studies, mostly using either social learning theory/CBT or cognitive dissonance. The relative risk of developing a subthreshold or full-threshold ED in intervention versus control was incidence rate ratio = 0.62 (95% CI [0.44, 0.87]), indicating a 38% decrease in incidence in the intervention group compared to control. Small to moderate between-group effects at posttest were found on ED symptoms ($g = 0.35$, 95% CI [0.24, 0.46], NNT = 5.10, $n_c = 26$), dieting ($g = 0.43$, 95% CI [0.29, 0.57], NNT = 4.17, $n_c = 21$), body dissatisfaction ($g = 0.40$, 95% CI [0.27, 0.53], NNT = 4.48, $n_c = 25$), drive for thinness ($g = 0.43$, 95% CI [0.27, 0.59], NNT = 4.23, $n_c = 12$), weight concerns ($g = 0.33$, 95% CI [0.10, 0.57], NNT = 5.35, $n_c = 13$), and affective symptoms ($g = 0.27$, 95% CI [0.15, 0.38], NNT = 6.70, $n_c = 18$). The effects on BN symptoms were not significant. Heterogeneity was moderate across comparisons. In the following, we briefly discuss the theoretical models on which the effective targeted/selective preventive ED interventions are based.

16.5.3 Social Learning Theory/Cognitive Behavioral Therapy (CBT)

Social learning theory assumes that behavior is affected by both external and internal processes (Bandura & National Institute of Mental Health, 1986), and following from this, disordered eating is thought to result from several processes (e.g., pressure to be thin from family members and peers, exposure to maternal and peer weight and shape concerns, the individual's internalization of the thin ideal, history of disordered eating attitudes and behaviors, history of depression and anxiety). Thus, from a social learning theory perspective, four factors are particularly important in influencing attitudes and behaviors and need to be addressed in preventive interventions: (1) modeling, (2) information, (3) instructions/persuasion from authorities, and (4) previous experience. Effective interventions incorporate each of these components. Beintner et al. (2012) reviewed ten trials of the Student Bodies intervention, based on this theoretical approach, from the USA and Germany. They reported average effect sizes on weight and shape concerns for the intervention compared to waitlist controls of 0.77 in the USA and 0.33 in Germany. Selective intervention effect sizes were 0.67 compared to 0.28 for universal, and there were no differences in effects between the two countries.

16.5.4 Dissonance Theory

Stice and colleagues (2000, 2008, 2009, 2011) have developed interventions (i.e., the Body Project) rooted in the theory that individuals become motivated to change their attitudes and behaviors, such as unhealthy expectations about weight and appearance and disordered eating behaviors, when faced with messages that contradict these very attitudes and behaviors. Thus, dissonance-based programs focus on providing participants with skills to counteract the abundant weight- and appearance-related messages prevalent in adolescents' daily lives. Programs typically involve at least two 1-h sessions and more often three or four sessions, using trained program leaders. For instance, in one session, participants are asked to write a letter to a teenage girl to encourage them not to get invested in the current, Western appearance ideal (i.e., thin ideal). Participants are then encouraged to read the letter out loud. Having written this letter, the participant experiences "cognitive dissonance" if they then follow the thin body ideal themselves. A number of studies have shown the intervention to be effective in reducing risk factors and even in reducing onset of EDs (e.g., see Harrer et al., 2020).

16.5.5 Media Literacy and Advocacy

Media literacy and advocacy interventions are based on the theory that the mass media plays a major role in perpetuating ED risk and that gaining both an understanding of this risk and developing strategies to resist media messages will reduce risk factors. The focus of these programs is to develop or enhance skills to resist social persuasion (i.e., messages about thinness), with the goal of reducing internalization of media messages about thinness and appearance. As noted above, media literacy has been shown to be an effective preventive strategy although it has not, unlike the other two effective programs discussed above, been shown to reduce case onset. For example, Wilksch and Wade (2009) studied the effects of their media literacy program on reducing ED attitudes and behaviors on high-risk female adolescents (>15 years of age). The long-term (30-month) controlled effect sizes for the media literacy program were weight concerns, ES = 0.29; dieting, ES = 0.26; and body dissatisfaction, ES = 0.20. Of note, both the social learning theory/CBT and cognitive dissonance programs include components of media literacy and advocacy.

16.5.6 Preventing AN

Given its early onset and seriousness, a number of interventions have been developed to try to prevent AN. The universal/targeted/indicated interventions described above have provided evidence mostly for reduction in non-AN EDs onset (i.e., binge/purge-type EDs). There have been some attempts to provide indicated prevention for AN. As mentioned above, in Germany, Jacobi et al. (2018) screened 3941 students, 447 of whom were considered at risk for AN, and evaluated a parent-based, online guided self-help intervention. Of these, only 256 families could be contacted and only 66 agreed to be randomized to the study. At 12-month follow-up, girls' expected body weight (EBW) percentage was significantly greater for intervention participants compared with control participants, but drop-out rates were high (66% in the treatment condition). However, no other significant effects were found on risk factors and attitudes of disturbed eating. The authors' sobering conclusion was that, given the small effects on only one outcome and the few parents who were willing to enroll and engage in the study, it might be necessary for the children's symptoms to worsen before parents are willing to engage. Given the seriousness of AN and this finding, which has been found in other studies, it may be best for individuals with AN or possible AN to receive a face-to-face intervention that involves the whole family (e.g., evidence-based family-based treatment (Lock & Le Grange, 2019)).

16.5.7 *Is Prevention Harmful?*

There has also been some concern that asking young adolescents about "ED behaviors" might be harmful in that it would expose adolescents to attitudes or behaviors they had previously not considered or would heighten their focus on weight and shape issues. In response to this concern, Celio et al. (2003) compared results from 115 sixth-grade girls who responded to questions on risky weight control behaviors and attitudes at baseline and at 12-month follow-up with the responses of 107 girls who had not been part of the baseline assessment. There were no differences in scores between the two groups on the follow-up assessment, and rates of unhealthy weight regulation behaviors decreased over time in the group assessed on two occasions. Further, and of critical importance to countering these concerns, the many large prevention trials conducted using older adolescents and college students have largely reduced EDs risk factors rather than increased them.

16.6 Stepped-Care Prevention/Intervention Model: Role of Primary Care Providers (PCPs) and Behavioral Health-Care Providers (BHCPs)

In the following, we discuss various options for stepped-care prevention/intervention for EDs, managed by PCPs and BHCPs.

The prevention/intervention process begins with the use of an evidence-based screen. As discussed above, the only evidence-based screen that categorizes individuals by risk and possible clinical status is the SWED. The SWED is designed to be interactive (using skip-out questions), but we have created a self-report pencil version for clinical practice available at www.m2health.paloaltou.edu/resources, or it can be programmed into an online survey hosting site like Qualtrics or SurveyMonkey. The alternative is to use the SCOFF and WCS item two, as discussed above. Either option will allow practitioners to sort patients into risk/diagnostic categories and associated prevention/intervention approaches as seen in Fig. 16.1. An alternative that practitioners might consider is to refer individuals who screen positive on the SCOFF and WCS item two to NEDA to complete the SWED, available at www.nationaleatingdisorders.org/screening-tool. Once they have completed the screen at NEDA, respondents will be given a number of referral options (many of them included below), including recommendation for therapy or medical assessment. However, practitioners would need to follow-up to assess patients' actual engagement in services.

It is important to note that screens provide "possible" rather than definitive diagnoses, and individuals with concerning symptoms could be missed. Further, practitioners who identify individuals as having frequent bingeing and/or purging or low weight should evaluate these patients for medical stability and the need for immediate therapy.

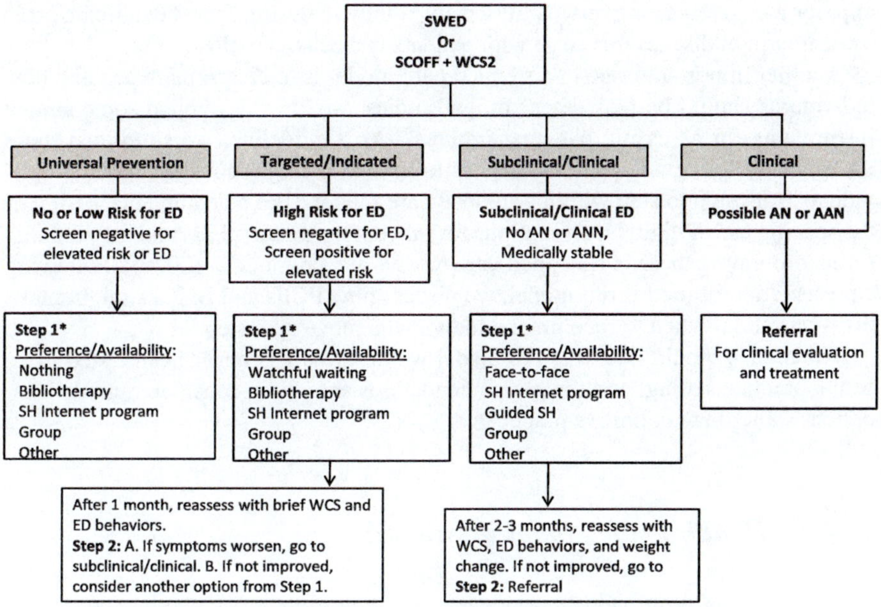

Fig. 16.1 A model of stepped-care for preventing/treating EDs in clinical practices

Although the SWED assesses BMI, the SCOFF does not. EDs, particularly BN and BED, are highly comorbid with overweight/obesity, and individuals may be interested in working on both of these issues. Interventions that combine approaches for addressing both EDs and weight loss are being evaluated, but there are none that we can currently recommend until more evidence on their efficacy, risks, and benefits is available. We note that behavioral weight loss, delivered face-to-face, has resulted in modest improvements in weight and binge eating (Grilo, 2017); however, this intervention has not been evaluated for ED prevention nor is easily scalable to large numbers of individuals. The issue of addressing weight loss in ED interventions is also complicated since food restriction/avoidance and over-exercise are significant problems in EDs, but many weight loss interventions, including widely available apps, may promote food restriction and an increased focus on exercise. If prescribed for weight loss, the clinician needs to carefully monitor their clients' use of apps for potential negative effects and in general consider how they are helping/hindering ED treatment. For example, Honary et al. (2019) interviewed people, age 18–25 and mostly males with body image concerns, to determine the potential impact of weight loss/fitness apps on maladaptive behaviors and attitudes. The most common problems reported by the sample were becoming obsessed about counting behaviors, experiencing guilt about food restriction, reducing time available for social activities, and failing to meet goals. Several respondents perceived that the app use was making their ED worse. In closing, given the large number of individuals with EDs who also want to lose weight (and for whom this may be appropriate, given their overweight/obesity, if they so desire), how health-care practitioners might discuss this issue with patients is discussed below.

Another important issue in a stepped-care model is to determine when and how individuals should be reassessed. In our studies, we have developed some simple instruments for assessing patients' progress. As a guideline, we simplified these measures to help guide professionals as to how they might consider moving individuals from step to step within a stepped-care model. (For a detailed discussion of the specific use of digital interventions for preventing/treating EDs and the potential for incorporating these in a stepped-care model, see Taylor et al. (2020)). Following a presentation of the overall model, we discuss how PCPs and BHCPs might make decisions about when to recommend individuals move up a step.

The reader should note that the model we describe has never been tested in an actual practice setting, and the recommendations should be considered guidelines/options rather than definitive practice.

16.6.1 Health Professional Messages

How health-care professionals provide feedback to individuals with potential EDs to help them decide what course of action to take before or after screening may be one of the most important factors in what paths their patients follow. We also note that people with EDs may be more likely to contact health professionals for weight reduction assistance than they are to seek treatment for their ED symptoms, which is important for practitioners to keep in mind. Several general principles include avoiding stigmatizing patients about weight or EDs, noting that restriction/dieting rarely works in the long run and may have many negative consequences, noting that healthy weight regulation strategies can be effective both for losing weight and maintaining weight loss, and explaining that many of the strategies used to address ED symptoms are consistent with healthful approaches to weight maintenance/loss (e.g., regular eating) (Kass et al., 2015). It is also likely that patients being assessed for EDs are likely to already be using one of the widely available and popular apps and programs promoted for weight loss/calorie counting (e.g., My Fitness Pal). The health-care professional should address the costs/benefits of use of such programs. The Australian National Eating Disorders Collaboration (NEDC) has developed some excellent recommendations around discussing weight-related issues with patients. For example, messages should focus on health, not weight, and have a holistic perspective which includes social, emotional, and physical aspects of health. Practitioners are also encouraged to use a collaborative approach that addresses weight stigma and promotes healthy eating practices without encouraging dieting or weight preoccupation. For more information, see www.nedc.com.au/assets/NEDC-Resources/NEDC-Resource-GPs.pdf (National Eating Disorders Collaboration, 2015). Other excellent resources for discussing these issues include: https://pediatrics.aappublications.org/content/pediatrics/111/1/204.full.pdf (American Academy of Pediatrics Committee on Adolescence, 2003) and www.nationaleatingdisorders.

org/sites/default/files/ResourceHandouts/PhysiciansRoleinEatingDisorders Prevention.pdf (National Eating Disorders Association, 2012).

The stepped-care model we provide focuses on older adolescents (where they can seek care independent of their parents) and adults, and we do not recommend this approach for children or young adolescents where a different model of care is indicated. The NEDC resource cited above discusses issues of EDs with children and adolescents.

16.6.2 *Universal Prevention*

As seen in Fig. 16.1, universal prevention would be appropriate for individuals at low or no risk for an ED. Many individuals who fall into this category are appropriate for basic psychoeducation, bibliotherapy, and for self-help programs, though we noted the limitations of those approaches earlier. We developed a program called StayingFit focused on exercise and healthy weight regulation. As mentioned, in a small randomized trial, the intervention was shown to reduce weight/shape concerns and increase physical activity in high school students (Jones et al., 2014). The program is available for free at www.edx.org/course/staying-fit.

16.6.3 *Targeted/Selective/Indicated Prevention*

Many of the prevention studies reviewed above have included individuals with low levels of ED symptoms who could be considered appropriate for indicated interventions. Here, we will review options for this group.

16.6.3.1 Watchful Waiting

Watchful waiting is an option for this group. The most important issue to monitor is an increase in bingeing and/or purging and excessive weight loss. However, what constitutes excessive in the ED field is controversial. Many argue that any sustained weight loss among individuals with BMIs in the non-overweight or obese range is excessive. Whitelaw et al. (2018) have found that in adolescents with >90% median BMI (roughly equivalent to the normal weight range or above in adults) and who had lost at least 10% of their body weight in the past 6 months or so experienced high rates of potentially serious medical problems. Of course, the reasons for the weight loss need to be determined and perhaps, systems employing a stepped-care model would consider significant weight loss as indicating medical evaluation and then consider next steps. If either bingeing or purging increase, the individual should be advised to move to the next step. Except for BMI (relevant to AN), decisions need to be based on self-report measures. Presenting the need for follow-up assessment in a non-judgmental, caring way is likely to help improve the accuracy of self-report measures.

16.6.3.2 Psychoeducation

Psychoeducation by itself has not been shown to be of much benefit for this group and is not recommended (Stice & Shaw, 2004). However, there are some resources listed in Table 16.3, which we have found helpful in incorporating/referring to, as part of other approaches.

16.6.3.3 Biblio-Prevention

A number of self-help books are available to improve body image and reduce symptoms. *Overcoming Binge Eating* (Fairburn, 2013) is a widely used self-help book for overcoming problems with binge eating and/or purging. It can also be used effectively as part of a guided self-help approach (Traviss-Turner et al., 2017). *The Body Image Workbook* (Cash, 2008) has also been widely used.

16.6.3.4 Unguided e-Health Prevention Tools

Recovery Record (www.recoveryrecord.com) is an app designed with input from ED experts to support treatment of EDs. The Recovery Record app allows self-monitoring of meals, thoughts, and feelings and provides customized meal plans

Table 16.3 Examples of resources for targeted/selective/indicated prevention

Approach	Targeted/selective/indicated
Psychoeducation	National Eating Disorders Association website (www.nationaleatingdisorders.org) NIMH Brochure (National Institute of Health, 2018) (www.nimh.nih.gov/health/publications/eating-disorders/eatingdisorders_148810.pdf)
Biblio-prevention	*Overcoming Binge Eating* (Fairburn, 2013) *The Body Image Workbook* (Cash, 2008)
Unguided e-Self-Help	Media Smart (https://mediasmart.flinders.edu.au/) (research study) Recovery Record (www.recoveryrecord.com) Jourvie (www.jourvie.com) Rise Up + Recover (www.recoverywarriers.com/app/) Student Bodies (www.m2health.paloaltou.edu)
Guided Self-Help	Recovery Record (www.recoveryrecord.com) if associated with a therapist
Individual Therapy or Group Therapy	Contact the National Eating Disorders Association helpline for help locating a provider (https://www.nationaleatingdisorders.org/help-support/contact-helpline)

and coping tactics. The program can also be linked with a treatment provider, so that a client's therapist can have access to their data. The program has been widely downloaded (Tregarthen et al., 2015) and has demonstrated high acceptability (Kim et al., 2018). A controlled trial has been conducted but not yet published. In 2019, Recovery Record has a credibility rating of 2.86/5 on PsyberGuide, a freely available online resource that evaluates available mobile mental health apps (see more information later in this chapter), a user experience rating of 2.90/5, and transparency rated as unacceptable. We are aware of two other publicly available apps that can be used as self-help for EDs, Jourvie (www.jourvie.com) and Rise Up + Recover (www.recoverywarriors.com/app/). We could find no empirical studies on their use and have not used them ourselves.

16.6.3.5 Guided Self-Help

Guided self-help has been shown to be effective in preventing EDs (Harrer et al., 2020; Taylor et al., 2017, 2020). Guided self-help should be the first choice for individuals who exhibit any bingeing or purging, which is in line with the National Institute for Health and Care Excellence guidelines from the UK www.nice.org.uk/guidance/ng69 (National Institute for Health and Care Excellence, 2017); however, the availability of such programs is limited. Options include training mental health experts or others in guiding a program like Recovery Record or the patient's use of a self-help book, such as *Overcoming Binge Eating* (Fairburn, 2013). Indeed, non-specialists can make excellent guides for these programs, and one study found that nurses were very helpful in providing guided self-help to patients with BN (Walsh et al., 2004). Graham et al. (2020) found that a program that used bachelor's-level lay therapists, trained to help patients select and use apps from a mental health app platform, was effective in reducing anxiety and depression, suggesting that a broad range of individuals may be effective in coaching/moderating evidence-based programs. A CBT-guided self-help program for EDs our team developed and tested (Fitzsimmons-Craft et al., 2020) has been made available on the SilverCloud Health platform, which is widely used by many health-care systems (e.g., Kaiser in the USA, National Health Service in the UK).

16.6.3.6 Groups

Groups (face-to-face, Internet, asynchronous, synchronous) are widely available. As mentioned, the Body Project, which is group-based, has been shown to be very effective in reducing eating disorder risk and even onset. Some evidence suggests that online communities or connections with individuals with EDs can be detrimental (Saffran et al., 2016). In the USA, a wide range of groups are offered through NEDA, the National Association of Anorexia Nervosa and Associated Disorders (ANAD), and many other resources. Practitioners wanting to recommend groups are encouraged to carefully check them out for potential harm/benefit (Taylor et al., 2020). Of note, cognitive dissonance-based prevention programs, offered as a group-based intervention, are able to be accessed through NEDA (www.nationaleatingdisorders.org/get-involved/the-body-project).

16.6.3.7 Individual Therapy

Individual therapy can be useful in helping individuals with body image problems and at risk for EDs.

16.6.4 Subclinical/Clinical BN/BED-Type EDs

The most important issues to monitor are bingeing, purging, and weight. If bingeing or purging increase, the individual should be advised to move to the next step. Some experts have also suggested that individuals who have >90% median BMI, lost at least 10% of body weight, and are exhibiting features of AN should be evaluated for possible atypical AN, which may require medical management (Whitelaw et al., 2018).

In our online guided self-help studies for individuals with EDs except AN (e.g., Fitzsimmons-Craft et al. (2020)), we have also included the expectation that individuals demonstrate a large reduction (e.g., 50%) in symptoms by about mid-point in treatment and if not, they are recommended to move on to the next step (while continuing use of the online program), which for us, has been referral to face-to-face therapy.

16.6.4.1 Watchful Waiting

Watchful waiting is probably not an option for this group. However, if an individual does not want to engage in therapy, then the practitioner should consider asking permission to recontact them in the near future to reassess their symptoms and interest in treatment.

16.6.4.2 Psychoeducation

As with those in the previous category, we do not recommend psychoeducation alone. However, if the practitioner feels the patient would benefit from knowing more about EDs, a referral to NEDA's content or other psychoeducational resources would be appropriate.

16.6.4.3 Biblio-Prevention

As mentioned, a number of self-help books are available to improve body image and reduce symptoms, for example, Fairburn (2013) and Cash (2008). However, used by themselves they are unlikely to have a significant impact. See targeted/selective for recommendations.

16.6.4.4 Unguided e-Health Prevention Tools

The same options listed for targeted/selective/indicated could be used for individuals with indicated/clinical programs. However, there are few data on their effectiveness.

16.6.4.5 Guided Self-Help

Guided self-help should be considered the first choice for individuals with clinical disorders who do not want groups or face-to-face therapy or have barriers to care for such options (e.g., limited availability in their area, concerns about cost or stigma). Guided self-help has been shown to be effective in treating EDs (Taylor et al., 2020) and can be delivered effectively by a wide variety of providers. We recently completed a large-scale randomized controlled trial (RCT) evaluating the efficacy of our team's digital CBT-guided self-help program for EDs. In this study, 690 college women with EDs from 27 universities were randomized to the intervention or a control group (i.e., referral to usual care at the college counseling/health center). For the primary outcome of ED psychopathology (measured by the Eating Disorder Examination-Questionnaire (EDE-Q) Global Score), there was a significantly greater reduction in the intervention compared to control at post-intervention and follow-up (Fitzsimmons-Craft et al., 2020). The intervention was also associated with significantly greater reductions than control in binge eating, compensatory behaviors, depression, and clinical impairment at post-intervention, with these gains sustained through follow-up for all outcomes except binge eating. (How to make this program available is discussed under targeted/indicated, above).

16.6.4.6 Groups

Group therapy is effective for a number of problems and is often used to provide evidence-based treatments such as CBT, so it is likely to be useful for treating eating disorders as well. In a meta-analysis, Grenon et al. (2017) identified 27 RCTs that provide direct comparisons with a total of 1853 participants included. Group psychotherapy was significantly more effective than waitlist controls at achieving reductions in and abstinence rates of binge eating and/or purging compared to the control groups. The authors note that the studies mostly involved small samples.

16.6.4.7 Individual Therapy

Individual therapy can be useful in helping individuals with body image problems and EDs. Many studies have shown that CBT, interpersonal psychotherapy (IPT), and other modalities are very effective for treating EDs (Kass et al., 2013).

16.6.5 Selecting the First Step

There are no guidelines in the ED field suggesting how individuals and health-care systems might order steps for universal or targeted/selective/indicated prevention. Presumably, such decisions are made in health-care practices based on considerations such as available resources, costs, evidence-base, and consumer preference. For universal prevention, watchful waiting or psychoeducation would seem to be reasonable first choices. For the targeted/selective group, any of the activities listed as a first step would seem appropriate, but those who fall into the indicated group on the basis of some bingeing/purging should be carefully monitored for increases in symptoms (e.g., every other month or so). For subclinical/clinical, self-help should be considered only if guided self-help, group, or face-to-face are not available. The most important issue for health-care providers to consider, as mentioned, is available resources and how monitoring/follow-up can occur.

16.6.6 When to Move to the Next Step

There is no empirical evidence as to when individuals should move to the next step in a universal/targeted-selective-indicated prevention/clinical intervention model for EDs. In general, we favor reassessment, though practically, it may not be realistic (or even necessary) to reassess those in the universal prevention group. In our studies of guided self-help, we routinely follow a two-step model, based on regular assessment, in which referral to face-to-face is recommended for those who are not responding (Fitzsimmons-Craft et al., 2020). The assessment consists of these items: (1) In the past week, how many times have you binged? (2) In the last week, how many times have you purged (including self-induced vomiting or use of laxatives, diuretics, or diet pills)? (3) How much did concerns about your weight/shape interfere with your life and/or cause you distress (never, rarely, sometimes, often)? Our trials usually involve asking these questions on a weekly basis. In clinical practice, it would be appropriate to change the time frame to "in the past month" and to add a question about any change in weight over that same period.

For universal, anyone who exhibits the onset of ED symptoms or excessive weight loss should be moved to self-help, guided self-help, group, or face-to-face. For targeted/selective, anyone who exhibits onset of ED symptoms or excessive weight loss should move to at least guided self-help, face-to-face, or group. As we mentioned, in our clinical trials using guided or moderated self-help for indicated, subclinical, or clinical eating disorders, we refer people to face-to-face therapy if they have not shown a 50% improvement in presenting symptoms after about 6–8 weeks (Fitzsimmons-Craft et al., 2020). We imagine that the final algorithm will need to be developed depending on the resources, standards, and interests of the providing health-care system.

16.7 Lessons Learned and Implementation

There has been considerable progress in the development of evidence-based screens and interventions to prevent and treat eating disorders. Many of the preventive and clinical interventions can be delivered by PCPs and BHCPs. While there are many barriers and issues related to introducing a stepped-care model into health-care practice and providing screening, assessment, and preventive and clinical intervention, doing so would positively improve the physical and behavioral health of many.

Acknowledgments This research was supported by R01 MH100455, K01 DK116925, and K08 MH120341 from the National Institutes of Health and NHMRC Centre of Research Excellence APP1170937 from Australia's National Health and Medical Research Council.

References

American Academy of Pediatrics Committee on Adolescence. (2003). Identifying and treating eating disorders. *Pediatrics, 111*(1) https://pediatrics.aappublications.org/content/pediatrics/111/1/204.full.pdf

American Psychiatric Association. (2013). *Diagnostic and statistical manual of mental disorders* (5th ed.). American Psychiatric Association.

Arcelus, J., Mitchell, A. J., Wales, J., & Nielsen, S. (2011). Mortality rates in patients with anorexia nervosa and other eating disorders: A meta-analysis of 36 studies. *Archives of General Psychiatry*. https://doi.org/10.1001/archgenpsychiatry.2011.74

Bandura, A., & National Institute of Mental Health. (1986). *Social foundations of thought and action: A social cognitive theory* (Prentice-Hall series in social learning theory). Prentice-Hall.

Beintner, I., Jacobi, C., & Taylor, C. B. (2012). Effects of an internet-based prevention programme for eating disorders in the USA and Germany – A meta-analytic review. *European Eating Disorders Review*. https://doi.org/10.1002/erv.1130

Bulik, C. M., Kleiman, S. C., & Yilmaz, Z. (2016). Genetic epidemiology of eating disorders. *Current Opinion in Psychiatry, 29*(6), 383–388. https://doi.org/10.1097/YCO.0000000000000275

Calzo, J. P., Blashill, A. J., Brown, T. A., & Argenal, R. L. (2017). Eating disorders and disordered weight and shape control behaviors in sexual minority populations. *Current Psychiatry Reports*. https://doi.org/10.1007/s11920-017-0801-y

Calzo, J. P., Sonneville, K. R., Haines, J., Blood, E. A., Field, A. E., & Austin, S. B. (2012). The development of associations among body mass index, body dissatisfaction, and weight and shape concern in adolescent boys and girls. *Journal of Adolescent Health*. https://doi.org/10.1016/j.jadohealth.2012.02.021

Cash, T. F. (2008). *The body image workbook: An eight-step program for learning to like your looks* (2nd ed.). New Harbinger Publications.

Celio, A. A., Bryson, S., Killen, J. D., & Taylor, C. B. (2003). Are adolescents harmed when asked risky weight control behavior and attitude questions? Implications for consent procedures. *International Journal of Eating Disorders*. https://doi.org/10.1002/eat.10188

Chua, J. Y. X., Tam, W., & Shorey, S. (2020). Research review: Effectiveness of universal eating disorder prevention interventions in improving body image among children: A systematic review and meta-analysis. *Journal of Child Psychology and Psychiatry and Allied Disciplines*. https://doi.org/10.1111/jcpp.13164

Doris, E., Shekriladze, I., Javakhishvili, N., Jones, R., Treasure, J., & Tchanturia, K. (2015). Is cultural change associated with eating disorders? A systematic review of the literature. *Eating and Weight Disorders*. https://doi.org/10.1007/s40519-015-0189-9

Fairburn, C. G. (2013). *Overcoming binge eating* (2nd ed.). Guilford Press.

Fichter, M. M., & Quadflieg, N. (2016). Mortality in eating disorders – Results of a large prospective clinical longitudinal study. *International Journal of Eating Disorders*. https://doi.org/10.1002/eat.22501

Fitzsimmons-Craft, E. E., Balantekin, K. N., Graham, A. K., Smolar, L., Park, D., Mysko, C., Funk, B., Taylor, C. B., & Wilfley, D. E. (2019). Results of disseminating an online screen for eating disorders across the U.S.: Reach, respondent characteristics, and unmet treatment need. *International Journal of Eating Disorders, 52*(6), 721–729. https://doi.org/10.1002/eat.23043

Fitzsimmons-Craft, E. E., Taylor, C. B., Graham, A. K., Sadeh-Sharvit, S., Balantekin, K. N., Eichen, D. M., Monterubio, G. E., Goel, N. J., Flatt, R. E., Karam, A. M., Firebaugh, M. L., Jacobi, C., Jo, B., Trockel, M. T., & Wilfley, D. E. (2020). Effectiveness of a digital cognitive behavior therapy-guided self-help intervention for eating disorders in college women: A cluster randomized clinical trial. *JAMA Network Open*. https://doi.org/10.1001/jamanetworkopen.2020.15633

Flatt, R. E., & Taylor, C. B. (2018). Adapting a technology-based eating disorder model for athletes. *Journal of Clinical Sport Psychology, 12*(4), 699–717. https://doi.org/10.1123/jcsp.2018-0015

Graham, A. K., Greene, C. J., Kwasny, M. J., Kaiser, S. M., Lieponis, P., Powell, T., & Mohr, D. C. (2020). Coached mobile app platform for the treatment of depression and anxiety among primary care patients: A randomized clinical trial. *JAMA Psychiatry*. https://doi.org/10.1001/jamapsychiatry.2020.1011

Graham, A. K., Trockel, M., Weisman, H., Fitzsimmons-Craft, E. E., Balantekin, K. N., Wilfley, D. E., & Taylor, C. B. (2019). A screening tool for detecting eating disorder risk and diagnostic symptoms among college-age women. *Journal of American College Health, 67*(4), 357–366. https://doi.org/10.1080/07448481.2018.1483936

Grenon, R., Schwartze, D., Hammond, N., Ivanova, I., Mcquaid, N., Proulx, G., & Tasca, G. A. (2017). Group psychotherapy for eating disorders: A meta-analysis. *International Journal of Eating Disorders*. https://doi.org/10.1002/eat.22744

Grilo, C. M. (2017). Psychological and behavioral treatments for binge-eating disorder. *Journal of Clinical Psychiatry*. https://doi.org/10.4088/JCP.sh16003su1c.04

Guarda, A. S. (2008). Treatment of anorexia nervosa: Insights and obstacles. *Physiology and Behavior*. https://doi.org/10.1016/j.physbeh.2007.11.020

Harrer, M., Adam, S. H., Messner, E. M., Baumeister, H., Cuijpers, P., Bruffaerts, R., Auerbach, R. P., Kessler, R. C., Jacobi, C., Taylor, C. B., & Ebert, D. D. (2020). Prevention of eating disorders at universities: A systematic review and meta-analysis. *International Journal of Eating Disorders*. https://doi.org/10.1002/eat.23224

Herman, B. K., Deal, L. S., Dibenedetti, D. B., Nelson, L., Fehnel, S. E., & Brown, TM. (2016). Development of the 7-item binge-eating disorder screener (BEDS-7). *Primary Care Companion to the Journal of Clinical Psychiatry*. https://doi.org/10.4088/PCC.15m01896

Honary, M., Bell, B. T., Clinch, S., Wild, S. E., & McNaney, R. (2019). Understanding the role of healthy eating and fitness mobile apps in the formation of maladaptive eating and exercise behaviors in young people. *Journal of Medical Internet Research*. https://doi.org/10.2196/14239

Jacobi, C., Fittig, E., Bryson, S. W., Wilfley, D., Kraemer, H. C., & Taylor, C. B. (2011). Who is really at risk? Identifying risk factors for subthreshold and full syndrome eating disorders in a high-risk sample. *Psychological Medicine*. https://doi.org/10.1017/S0033291710002631

Jacobi, C., Hayward, C., De Zwaan, M., Kraemer, H. C., & Agras, W. S. (2004). Coming to terms with risk factors for eating disorders: Application of risk terminology and suggestions for a general taxonomy. *Psychological Bulletin, 130*(1), 19–65. https://doi.org/10.1037/0033-2909.130.1.19

Jacobi, C., Hütter, K., Völker, U., Möbius, K., Richter, R., Trockel, M., Bell, M. J., Lock, J., & Taylor, C. B. (2018). Efficacy of a parent-based, indicated prevention for anorexia nervosa: Randomized controlled trial. *Journal of Medical Internet Research*. https://doi.org/10.2196/jmir.9464

Jones, M., Lynch, K. T., Kass, A. E., Burrows, A., Williams, J., Wilfley, D. E., & Taylor, C. B. (2014). Healthy weight regulation and eating disorder prevention in high school students: A universal and targeted web-based intervention. *Journal of Medical Internet Research*. https://doi.org/10.2196/jmir.2995

Kass, A. E., Kolko, R. P., & Wilfley, D. E. (2013). Psychological treatments for eating disorders. *Current Opinion in Psychiatry*. https://doi.org/10.1097/YCO.0b013e328365a30e

Kass, A. E., Wang, A. Z., Kolko, R. P., Holland, J. C., Altman, M., Trockel, M., Taylor, C. B., & Wilfley, D. E. (2015). Identification as overweight by medical professionals: Relation to eating disorder diagnosis and risk. *Eating Behaviors*. https://doi.org/10.1016/j.eatbeh.2014.12.013

Killen, J. D., Hayward, C., Wilson, D. M., Taylor, C. B., Hammer, L. D., Litt, I., Simmonds, B., & Haydel, F. (1994). Factors associated with eating disorder symptoms in a community sample of 6th and 7th grade girls. *International Journal of Eating Disorders*. https://doi.org/10.1002/eat.2260150406

Killen, J. D., Taylor, C. B., Hammer, L. D., Litt, I., Wilson, D. M., Rich, T., Hayward, C., Simmonds, B., Kraemer, H., & Varady, A. (1993). An attempt to modify unhealthful eating attitudes and weight regulation practices of young adolescent girls. *International Journal of Eating Disorders*. https://doi.org/10.1002/1098-108X(199305)13:4<369::AID-EAT2260130405>3.0.CO;2-0

Killen, J. D., Taylor, C. B., Hayward, C., Parish Haydel, K., Wilson, D. M., Hammer, L., Kraemer, H., Blair-Greiner, A., & Strachowski, D. (1996). Weight concerns influence the development of eating disorders: A 4-year prospective study. *Journal of Consulting and Clinical Psychology*. https://doi.org/10.1037/0022-006X.64.5.936

Kim, J. P., Sadeh-Sharvit, S., Darcy, A. M., Neri, E., Vierhile, M., Robinson, A., Tregarthen, J., & Lock, J. D. (2018). The utility and acceptability of a self-help smartphone application for eating disorder behaviors. *Journal of Technology in Behavioral Science*. https://doi.org/10.1007/s41347-018-0048-4

Kutz, A. M., Marsh, A. G., Gunderson, C. G., Maguen, S., & Masheb, R. M. (2020). Eating disorder screening: A systematic review and meta-analysis of diagnostic test characteristics of the SCOFF. *Journal of General Internal Medicine*. https://doi.org/10.1007/s11606-019-05478-6

Lock, J., & Le Grange, D. (2019). Family-based treatment: Where are we and where should we be going to improve recovery in child and adolescent eating disorders. *International Journal of Eating Disorders*. https://doi.org/10.1002/eat.22980

Martinsen, M., Bahr, R., Børresen, R., Holme, I., Pensgaard, A. M., & Sundgot-Borgen, J. (2014). Preventing eating disorders among young elite athletes: A randomized controlled trial. *Medicine and Science in Sports and Exercise*. https://doi.org/10.1249/MSS.0b013e3182a702fc

Meneguzzo, P., Collantoni, E., Gallicchio, D., Busetto, P., Solmi, M., Santonastaso, P., & Favaro, A. (2018). Eating disorders symptoms in sexual minority women: A systematic review. *European Eating Disorders Review*. https://doi.org/10.1002/erv.2601

Morgan, J. F., Reid, F., & Lacey, J. H. (1999). The SCOFF questionnaire: Assessment of a new screening tool for eating disorders. *British Medical Journal*. https://doi.org/10.1136/bmj.319.7223.1467

National Eating Disorders Association. (2012). *The physician's role in eating disorders prevention*. https://www.nationaleatingdisorders.org/sites/default/files/ResourceHandouts/PhysiciansRoleinEatingDisordersPrevention.pdf

National Eating Disorders Collaboration. (2015). *Eating disorders: A professional resource for general practitioners* (2nd ed.). https://nedc.com.au/assets/NEDC-Resources/NEDC-Resource-GPs.pdf

National Institute for Health and Care Excellence. (2017). *Eating disorders: Recognition and treatment*. https://www.nice.org.uk/guidance/ng69

National Institute of Mental Health. (2018). *Eating disorders: About more than food*. https://www.nimh.nih.gov/health/publications/eating-disorders/eatingdisorders_148810.pdf

National Task Force on the Prevention and Treatment of Obesity. (2000). Overweight, obesity, and health risk. *Archives of Internal Medicine*. https://doi.org/10.1001/archinte.160.7.898

Ning, S. K., Fitzsimmons-Craft, E. E., Austin, B. S., Wilfley, D. E., & Taylor, C. B. (2021). Estimated prevalence of eating disorders in Singapore. *International Journal of Eating Disorders, 54*(1), 7–18. https://doi.org/10.1002/eat.23440.

Pike, K. M., Hilbert, A., Wilfley, D. E., Fairburn, C. G., Dohm, F. A., Walsh, B. T., & Striegel-Moore, R. (2008). Toward an understanding of risk factors for anorexia nervosa: A case-control study. *Psychological Medicine*. https://doi.org/10.1017/S0033291707002310

Pratt, B. M., & Woolfenden, S. (2002). Interventions for preventing eating disorders in children and adolescents. *Cochrane Database of Systematic Reviews*. https://doi.org/10.1002/14651858.cd002891

Ringham, R., Klump, K., Kaye, W., Stone, D., Libman, S., Stowe, S., & Marcus, M. (2006). Eating disorder symptomatology among ballet dancers. *International Journal of Eating Disorders*. https://doi.org/10.1002/eat.20299

Saffran, K., Fitzsimmons-Craft, E. E., Kass, A. E., Wilfley, D. E., Taylor, C. B., & Trockel, M. (2016). Facebook usage among those who have received treatment for an eating disorder in a group setting. *International Journal of Eating Disorders*. https://doi.org/10.1002/eat.22567

Sanci, L., Coffey, C., Olsson, C., Reid, S., Carlin, J. B., & Patton, G. (2008). Childhood sexual abuse and eating disorders in females: Findings from the Victorian Adolescent Health Cohort Study. *Archives of Pediatrics and Adolescent Medicine*. https://doi.org/10.1001/archpediatrics.2007.58

Speranza, M., Atger, F., Corcos, M., Loas, G., Guilbaud, O., Stéphan, P., Perez-Diaz, F., Halfon, O., Venisse, J. L., Bizouard, P., Lang, F., Flament, M., & Jeammet, P. (2003). Depressive psychopathology and adverse childhood experiences in eating disorders. *European Psychiatry*. https://doi.org/10.1016/j.eurpsy.2003.04.001

Stice, E., Fisher, M., & Martinez, E. (2004). Eating disorder diagnostic scale: Additional evidence of reliability and validity. *Psychological Assessment*. https://doi.org/10.1037/1040-3590.16.1.60

Stice, E., Marti, C. N., Spoor, S., Presnell, K., & Shaw, H. (2008). Dissonance and healthy weight eating disorder prevention programs: Long-term effects from a randomized efficacy trial. *Journal of Consulting and Clinical Psychology*. https://doi.org/10.1037/0022-006X.76.2.329

Stice, E., Mazotti, L., Weibel, D., & Agras, W. S. (2000). Dissonance prevention program decreases thin-ideal internalization, body dissatisfaction, dieting, negative affect, and bulimic symptoms: A preliminary experiment. *International Journal of Eating Disorders*. https://doi.org/10.1002/(SICI)1098-108X(200003)27:2<206::AID-EAT9>3.0.CO;2-D

Stice, E., Presnell, K., Gau, J., & Shaw, H. (2007). Testing mediators of intervention effects in randomized controlled trials: An evaluation of two eating disorder prevention programs. *Journal of Consulting and Clinical Psychology*. https://doi.org/10.1037/0022-006X.75.1.20

Stice, E., Rohde, P., Gau, J., & Shaw, H. (2009). An effectiveness trial of a dissonance-based eating disorder prevention program for high-risk adolescent girls. *Journal of Consulting and Clinical Psychology*. https://doi.org/10.1037/a0016132

Stice, E., Rohde, P., Shaw, H., & Gau, J. (2011). An effectiveness trial of a selected dissonance-based eating disorder prevention program for female high school students: Long-term effects. *Journal of Consulting and Clinical Psychology*. https://doi.org/10.1037/a0024351

Stice, E., & Shaw, H. (2004). Eating disorder prevention programs: A meta-analytic review. *Psychological Bulletin*. https://doi.org/10.1037/0033-2909.130.2.206

Stice, E., Shaw, H., Burton, E., & Wade, E. (2006). Dissonance and healthy weight eating disorder prevention programs: A randomized efficacy trial. *Journal of Consulting and Clinical Psychology*. https://doi.org/10.1037/0022-006X.74.2.263
Striegel-Moore, R. H., Dohm, F. A., Kraemer, H. C., Taylor, C. B., Daniels, S., Crawford, P. B., & Schreiber, G. B. (2003). Eating disorders in white and black women. *American Journal of Psychiatry*. https://doi.org/10.1176/appi.ajp.160.7.1326
Taylor, C. B. (2017). Weight and shape concern and body image as risk factors for eating disorders. In T. Wade (Ed.), *Encyclopedia of feeding and eating disorders* (pp. 889–893). Springer.
Taylor, C. B., Bryson, S., Luce, K. H., Cunning, D., Doyle, A. C., Abascal, L. B., Rockwell, R., Dev, P., Winzelberg, A. J., & Wilfley, D. E. (2006). Prevention of eating disorders in at-risk college-age women. *Archives of General Psychiatry*. https://doi.org/10.1001/archpsyc.63.8.881
Taylor, C. B., Fitzsimmons-Craft, E. E., & Goel, N. J. (2017). Prevention: Current status and underlying theory. In W. S. Agras & A. Robinson (Eds.), *Oxford handbook of eating disorders* (pp. 247–270). Oxford University Press.
Taylor, C. B., Sadeh-Sharvit, S., Fitzsimmons-Craft, E. E., Topooco, N., Rojas-Ashe, E., & Wilfley, D. E. (2020). Utilization of technologies to support patients with eating disorders. In G. M. Reger (Ed.), *Technology and mental health: A Clinician's guide to improving outcomes* (pp. 149–170). Routledge.
Traviss-Turner, G. D., West, R. M., & Hill, A. J. (2017). Guided self-help for eating disorders: A systematic review and metaregression. *European Eating Disorders Review*. https://doi.org/10.1002/erv.2507
Tregarthen, J. P., Lock, J., & Darcy, A. M. (2015). Development of a smartphone application for eating disorder self-monitoring. *International Journal of Eating Disorders*. https://doi.org/10.1002/eat.22386
Udo, T., & Grilo, C. M. (2018). Prevalence and correlates of DSM-5–defined eating disorders in a nationally representative sample of U.S. adults. *Biological Psychiatry*. https://doi.org/10.1016/j.biopsych.2018.03.014
van Hoeken, D., & Hoek, H. W. (2020). Review of the burden of eating disorders: Mortality, disability, costs, quality of life, and family burden. *Current Opinion in Psychiatry*. https://doi.org/10.1097/YCO.0000000000000641
Wade, T. D., & Wilksch, S. M. (2018). Internet eating disorder prevention. *Current Opinion in Psychiatry*. https://doi.org/10.1097/YCO.0000000000000450
Walsh, B. T., Fairburn, C. G., Mickley, D., Sysko, R., & Parides, M. K. (2004). Treatment of bulimia nervosa in a primary care setting. *American Journal of Psychiatry*. https://doi.org/10.1176/appi.ajp.161.3.556
Ward, Z. J., Rodriguez, P., Wright, D. R., Austin, S. B., & Long, M. W. (2019). Estimation of eating disorders prevalence by age and associations with mortality in a simulated nationally representative US cohort. *JAMA Network Open*. https://doi.org/10.1001/jamanetworkopen.2019.12925
Whitelaw, M., Lee, K. J., Gilbertson, H., & Sawyer, S. M. (2018). Predictors of complications in anorexia nervosa and atypical anorexia nervosa: Degree of underweight or extent and recency of weight loss? *Journal of Adolescent Health*. https://doi.org/10.1016/j.jadohealth.2018.08.019
Wilksch, S. M., & Wade, T. D. (2009). Reduction of shape and weight concern in young adolescents: A 30-month controlled evaluation of a media literacy program. *Journal of the American Academy of Child and Adolescent Psychiatry*. https://doi.org/10.1097/CHI.0b013e3181a1f559

Chapter 17
Evidence-Based Detection, Prevention, and Behavioral Intervention for Sleep Disorders in Integrated Care

Maureen E. McQuillan, Yelena Chernyak, and Sarah M. Honaker

Sleep disorders are highly prevalent and consequential for both mental health and physical health across the lifespan. However, numerous studies suggest that sleep disorders are insufficiently identified and managed in primary care (e.g., Grandner & Chakravorty, 2017; Honaker & Meltzer, 2016). Behavioral health providers can play a key role in the prevention, detection, and treatment of sleep disorders, especially since primary care providers (PCPs) often receive limited sleep training (Mindell et al., 2013) and need to monitor and address a multitude of other concerns. Additionally, there are several sleep disorders for which behavioral health providers can play a primary role, such as insomnia, circadian rhythm sleep disorders, and nightmare disorder, as these sleep disorders respond well to brief behavioral intervention and tend to have higher prevalence than those managed primarily by physicians (e.g., obstructive sleep apnea; OSA). For both pediatric and adult patients, behavioral interventions are considered first-line treatment for insomnia, circadian rhythm sleep disorders, and nightmare disorder, but due to limited time, resources, and training, PCPs often resort to prescribing medications to address these sleep disorders (Grandner & Chakravorty, 2017; Schnoes et al., 2006). Instead, behavioral health providers are well-equipped to facilitate improved prevention, identification, and management of sleep disorders in integrated care.

There are a variety of sleep disorders, including insomnia, circadian rhythm sleep disorders, parasomnia (i.e., sleep terrors, sleep walking, and sleep talking), nightmares, hypersomnia, narcolepsy, OSA, and restless legs syndrome (RLS), each of which can present variably in adult and pediatric populations. Given the

M. E. McQuillan (✉) · S. M. Honaker
Department of Pediatrics, Indiana University School of Medicine, Indianapolis, IN, USA
e-mail: memcquil@indiana.edu

Y. Chernyak
Department of Psychiatry, Indiana University School of Medicine, Indianapolis, IN, USA

W. O'Donohue, M. Zimmermann (eds.), *Handbook of Evidence-Based Prevention of Behavioral Disorders in Integrated Care*,
https://doi.org/10.1007/978-3-030-83469-2_17

focus of this handbook, we will focus on the sleep disorders that have strong psychological contributors, namely, insomnia, circadian rhythm disorders, and nightmare disorder. Behavioral health providers can also play an important role in facilitating adherence and desensitization to treatments for OSA, including positive airway pressure (PAP) and INSPIRE devices as they become more common, but prevention and management of the other sleep disorders is emphasized here.

17.1 Definition and Diagnostic Criteria for Sleep Disorders

17.1.1 Insomnia

The DSM-5 defines insomnia as dissatisfaction with sleep quantity or quality due to one or more of the following: difficulty initiating sleep, difficulty maintaining sleep with frequent awakenings or trouble returning to sleep after awakenings, or early morning awakening with inability to return to sleep. If this sleep difficulty is present for at least 3 months and for at least three nights per week, it would be categorized as persistent insomnia (American Psychiatric Association, 2013). If symptoms are only present for 1–3 months, it would be categorized as episodic insomnia. The same diagnostic criteria are used for pediatric patients, but the sleep difficulties can present differently, particularly in young children (American Psychiatric Association, 2013). Common presenting symptoms in this age group include bedtime resistance and sleep associations. Bedtime resistance could result in difficulty initiating sleep, and a sleep association, such as needing parental presence to fall asleep and return to sleep, could affect either sleep initiation or maintenance (American Psychiatric Association, 2013).

17.1.2 Circadian Rhythm Disorders

Circadian rhythm sleep disorders, including the Delayed Sleep Phase type, the Advanced Sleep Phase type, and the Shift Work type, involve disruption in the timing of sleep, often with misalignment between the sleep schedule and societal norms.

Most commonly seen in adolescents and young adults, the Delayed Sleep Phase type presents as a delay in sleep onset with an inability to fall asleep or wake at the desired time (American Psychiatric Association, 2013). Seminal work from Carskadon and her colleagues (1998) showed that most adolescents experience a normative developmental delay in their circadian rhythm, resulting in a tendency to stay up later and wake later than preteens. These differences can be due to both psychosocial factors (e.g., social activities, academic responsibilities, extracurricular activities, and employment opportunities) as well as biological factors (e.g., slow accumulation of sleep pressure and delayed circadian phase). Moreover, school start times commonly run in opposition to this phase delay tendency (Carskadon et al., 1998), curtailing the amount of sleep adolescents are able to get on school nights. While some degree of circadian delay is developmentally normative for adolescents, a diagnosis requires a persistent inability to fall asleep or wake at the desired time, causing significant functional impairment (American Psychiatric Association, 2013).

The Advanced Sleep Phase type is more common in the elderly, who similarly tend to experience a developmentally normative shift with earlier sleep schedules as they age (Ancoli-Israel, 2005). However, a diagnosis requires not only advanced sleep onset and awakening times but also a persistent inability to stay awake or remain asleep until the desired time. Lastly, the Shift Work type can occur in patients who have variable work shifts and/or work overnight and subsequently experience insomnia or unintentionally fall asleep at undesired times.

17.1.3 Nightmare Disorder

The DSM-5 defines nightmares as recurrent episodes of extended, extremely dysphoric, and well-remembered dreams that usually involve efforts to avoid threats to survival, security, or physical integrity (American Psychiatric Association, 2013). The nightmares generally occur in the second half of a major sleep episode, and upon waking from the nightmare, the individual rapidly becomes oriented and alert. To reach diagnostic threshold, the nightmares should cause significant distress or impairment in social, occupational, or other areas of functioning, and the symptoms cannot be explained by the effects of drug or medication use, another mental disorder (e.g., posttraumatic stress disorder or delirium), or another medical condition.

17.2 Prevalence of Sleep Disorders Across the Lifespan

For each of these sleep disorders, it is imperative to acknowledge that prevalence rates may vary depending on whether the prevalence of diagnoses, problem perception, or symptom endorsement are considered. Here, we will primarily focus on diagnostic prevalence rates. Across the sleep disorders outlined below, few patients who report problematic sleep symptoms actually receive a diagnosis and subsequent treatment for their sleep disorder, suggesting that these diagnostic prevalence rates may be underestimated and highlighting the need for improved preventive guidance, identification, and management of sleep problems in integrated care.

17.2.1 *Insomnia*

The prevalence rate for insomnia diagnosis is 11% for pediatrics (Owens, 2008) and 6–15% for adults (Ohayon, 2011). As alluded to above, the prevalence of insomnia *symptoms* is much higher – up to 40% for pediatrics and up to 56% for adults (Fernandez-Mendoza et al., 2020; Léger et al., 2008; Owens, 2008).

17.2.2 *Circadian Rhythm Disorders*

The prevalence rate for DSPD among adolescents is 7–16% (Lovato et al., 2013), and this rate is much lower among adults (about 1%, Nesbitt, 2018). Advanced sleep phase disorder remains a rare diagnosis with an estimated prevalence rate of 0.04% in the general population (Curtis et al., 2019) and up to 7.13% among older adults in particular (Paine et al., 2014). Among the 16% of wage and salary workers who are shift workers, 10% are estimated to meet criteria for the shift work-type disorder due to their experiences of insomnia and/or sleepiness (Drake et al., 2004).

17.2.3 *Nightmare Disorder*

The overall prevalence rate for nightmare disorder is estimated to be 5%, but this rate is even higher (30%) among patients who have known mental health disorders (Swart et al., 2013).

17.3 Risk Factors for Sleep Disorders Across the Lifespan

A recent systematic review examined a variety of risk and protective factors associated with sleep in preschool- and school-aged children (Newton et al., 2020), spanning across biological, psychological, and environmental factors at the individual, family, and community levels. Overall, older child age, difficult temperament, previous sleep problems, externalizing psychopathology, internalizing psychopathology, electronics use at bedtime, needing a parent at bedtime, and certain parenting styles (e.g., lax or permissive parenting) were identified as risk factors for sleep problems, whereas having a consistent bedtime routine was consistently shown to be a protective factor for child sleep (Newton et al., 2020). For adults, primary risk factors include neurological or medical conditions, poor sleep hygiene or environmental factors (e.g., electronics use in the night or noisy, chaotic environments), substance use, and, most salient of all, mental health disorders (Ohayon, 2011).

17.3.1 Socioeconomic Status and Race/Ethnicity

Across the lifespan, low socioeconomic status (SES) is a risk factor for sleep problems (El-Sheikh et al., 2015; Gellis, 2011; Newton et al., 2020), potentially because individuals with fewer socioeconomic resources are more likely to experience poorer sleep environments (Hoyniak et al., 2020; Jones & Ball, 2014). Individuals with racial/ethnic minority backgrounds also tend to be at risk for experiencing sleep problems (Fernandez-Mendoza et al., 2020). For example, even among infants and toddlers, Nevarez et al. (2010) found that Black non-Hispanic infants and toddlers slept 30–60 minutes less per day than White non-Hispanic infants and toddlers. Pena and colleagues (Peña et al., 2016) found that these sleep differences by racial/ethnic background are partially, but not entirely, explained by SES. Taken together, the findings suggest that socioeconomic, racial, and ethnic disparities in sleep health exist and should be considered when working in integrated care.

17.3.2 Anxiety and Depression

Internalizing psychopathology (e.g., anxious and depressive symptoms) is associated with sleep problems across the lifespan. For pediatric patients, prevalence rates for sleep difficulties are especially high when the patient also has either depression (70–89%) or anxiety (85%; Alfano et al., 2007). Blake et al. (2018) recently reviewed various mechanisms that may explain the link between pediatric sleep problems and internalizing problems at biological (e.g., polymorphisms and dysregulation in serotonin, dopamine, and circadian clock genes and cortisol reactivity to stress), psychological (e.g., worry, rumination, dysfunctional beliefs, and attitudes), and social levels (e.g., unhelpful parenting behaviors and family stress). Other recent reviews have also shown that wakefulness in bed (e.g., due to prolonged sleep onset latency or poor sleep efficiency) tends to temporally precede the development of anxiety and depression in adolescence more so than the reverse (e.g., McMakin & Alfano, 2015), suggesting that detecting and managing sleep difficulties early in development may have downstream positive effects on mental health.

Among adults, recent research has similarly shown that about 90% of patients with depression and 70–90% of patients with anxiety report insomnia symptoms (Oh et al., 2019). In a large study of national health registry data, individuals with insomnia had a higher risk of developing anxiety and/or depression compared to individuals without insomnia, and this risk was especially high for individuals who had experienced relapse episodes of insomnia (Chen et al., 2017), highlighting the chronic nature of insomnia and the pervasive dangers associated with persistent, untreated insomnia.

17.3.3 *Attention Deficit Hyperactivity Disorder (ADHD)*

ADHD is another relevant risk factor for sleep difficulties, both for children and adults. Among children with ADHD, an estimated 25–70% experience sleep problems (Corkum et al., 1998; Tsai et al., 2016). For adults with ADHD, a recent review reported that the estimated prevalence of insomnia symptoms is 43–80% (Wynchank et al., 2017). The link between sleep difficulties and ADHD may be due to the shared neurobiological pathways involving areas of the cortex, which are responsible for regulation and arousal. Sleep difficulties may also be caused by the deleterious effects of stimulant medications on sleep onset. Currently, the recommended guideline is to assess for sleep concerns prior to initiating pharmacotherapy for ADHD to avoid worsening sleep difficulties or misdiagnosing sleep problems as ADHD.

17.3.4 *Autism Spectrum Disorder (ASD)*

Sleep problems are one of the major health concerns in individuals with ASD, with prevalence rates of about 50–80%. To date, the majority of autism research on sleep has focused on children prior to puberty, but a recent study conducted by Goldman et al., (2012) showed that sleep problems persist through adolescence for individuals with ASD. However, the nature of sleep problems tends to change across time, often switching from nocturnal fears and insomnia in childhood to DSPD in adolescence (Goldman et al., 2012).

17.4 Effective Screening of Sleep Disorders in Integrated Care

Aside from attending to these risk factors for sleep difficulties, integrated care teams can also use well-established and efficient screening tools to detect clinical and preclinical sleep problems in patients presenting to primary care. To be useful to PCPs and feasibly implemented in busy primary care settings, screening tools need to be: (1) valid indicators of increased risk, (2) easy to administer and score, (3) brief to minimize patient burden and maximize efficiency, (4) feasible for individuals with varying levels of education to complete, and (5) cost-efficient (Sheldrick & Perrin, 2009). Additionally, screening tools that assess multiple sleep domains simultaneously may be preferred as they maximize efficiency and reduce the likelihood of misdiagnosis. For example, a pediatric patient may present with prolonged sleep onset latency, which could lead to an insomnia diagnosis. However, if the child's sleep onset difficulties are determined to be caused primarily by leg discomfort, RLS may be a more accurate diagnosis and target for treatment. For a comprehensive review of pediatric screening tools, readers are encouraged to refer to a recent chapter by Hoffses et al., (2018). Here, we highlight several tools that can be used for pediatric and adult patients.

17.4.1 *Infant Sleep Questionnaire (ISQ; Morrell, 1999)*

The ISQ is a validated clinical and research tool to assess infant sleep difficulties (for ages 12–18 months). Respondents are asked to report on their child's sleep over the past month. Items assess parental perception of a sleep problem and three common areas of infant sleep disruption, specifically difficulty settling to sleep, night wakings, and taking a child to the parental bed in response to settling difficulty and/or night wakings. The ISQ consists of ten items, six of which contribute to a total score that can range from 0–38. A score of 12 or higher is designated as the cut-off for a sleep problem. The ISQ has moderate test-retest reliability (kappa = 0.76), high sensitivity (89.5%), and high specificity (93.4%).

17.4.2 *PROMIS (Forrest et al., 2018)*

The Patient-Reported Outcomes Measurement Information System (PROMIS) Pediatric Sleep Disturbance and Sleep-Related Impairment item bank has child- and parent-report items to assess sleep disturbance (15 items) and daytime sleep-related impairment (13 items) in children aged 5–17. Of the 28 items, 16 are included in the parallel PROMIS adult sleep health measures (Buysse et al., 2010). The items are reliable (Cronbach's $\alpha > 0.90$) and valid with significant associations with other measures of sleep health and impairment, including the Children's Sleep Habits Questionnaire (Markovich et al., 2015).

17.4.3 *Insomnia Severity Index (ISI)*

The ISI (Morin et al., 2011) and the Pediatric-ISI (PISI; Byars et al., 2017) have been used extensively to identify individuals experiencing difficulties with sleep onset and/or maintenance. For adults, a cutoff score of 10 has been determined to have 86.1% sensitivity and 87.7% specificity for detecting insomnia cases in the community (Morin et al., 2011). For pediatric patients, the ISI is comprised of four domains: sleep onset problems, sleep maintenance problems, daytime sleepiness, and nocturnal sleep duration. Scores range from 0 to 30 with higher scores indicative of more severe insomnia. Most importantly, this brief questionnaire takes less than five minutes to complete and score (Byars et al., 2017). The parent-report pediatric version was validated with a sample of children aged 4–10, but a subsequent version with child-report for ages 11–18 has also been developed.

17.4.4 Epworth Sleepiness Scale

The Epworth Sleepiness Scale (ESS) is an eight-item, self-administered questionnaire that contains situations commonly encountered in daily life. This measure can be completed by adolescents and adults who are instructed to rate the likelihood that he or she would fall asleep in eight situations. The total score of the ESS ranges from 0 to 24. In clinical practice, a score of ten is a frequently used cut-off to denote excessive daytime sleepiness. The ESS was initially designed for adults and then was modified for use with adolescents. For instance, the item regarding "driving in traffic" was replaced with "doing homework or taking a test" (Moore et al., 2009). Notably, recent research has shown low test-retest reliability with the ESS, potentially due to various factors that should be considered that could affect one's perceived sleepiness, such as carbohydrate intake, emotional state, physical activity, and traveling habits (Grewe et al., 2020).

17.4.5 Sleep Disorders Symptom Checklist (Klingman et al., 2017)

The Sleep Disorders Symptom Checklist (SDS-CL)-17 is a single-page instrument that was developed to screen for six sleep disorders (insomnia, obstructive sleep apnea, restless legs syndrome/periodic limb movement disorder, circadian rhythm sleep-wake disorders, narcolepsy, and parasomnias) in adults. Sensitivities and specificities for the diagnosed sleep disorders ranged from 0.64 to 0.88.

17.4.6 Pittsburgh Sleep Quality Index (PSQI; Buysse et al., 1989)

The PSQI can be used to assess patient perception of sleep patterns and problems, and use of sleep aids, over the past month. The global sum is comprised of 19 items assessing low subjective sleep quality, long sleep latency, short sleep duration, low sleep efficiency, high sleep disturbance, use of sleeping medication, and high daytime dysfunction, and a recommended cut-off score of 5 can be used to classify poor sleepers with a diagnostic sensitivity of 89.6% and specificity of 86.5%. The length of this tool may make it ill-suited for routine screening in primary care practice, but it is considered a gold-standard for use in adult sleep medicine practice and research.

17.5 Evidence-Based Prevention for Sleep Problems

In addition to the need for universal screening of sleep disorders, there are also two prime examples of evidence-based universal prevention efforts to promote sleep health prior to the onset of a sleep problem. The first, for pediatric patients, involves providing parental education at appointments during the third trimester and postpartum and through the first 6 months of an infant's life (Mindell et al., 2006). This preventative parental education usually includes recommendations for bedtime routines, consistent sleep schedules, parental handling during sleep initiation, and parental response to night wakings. Almost all programs have incorporated the recommendation that babies should be put to bed "drowsy but awake" to help them develop independent sleep initiation skills at bedtime, and enabling them to return to sleep without intervention following naturally occurring night wakings. Brief sleep guidance for all at the 4-month visit has been shown to result in fewer problematic night wakings at subsequent visits (Adachi et al., 2009; Adair et al., 1992).

The second universal prevention approach, for both pediatric and adult patients, involves promoting sleep health to not only prevent sleep disorders but also to optimize healthy sleep. Beyond the prevalence rates of diagnosed sleep disorders outlined above, experiences of insufficient sleep are also common, with prevalence rates of 20% to 41.7% in the general population (Ohayon, 2011). Among adolescents in particular, 53% obtain less than the age-appropriate recommendation of 8 hours of sleep on school nights (Gradisar et al., 2011). This pervasive problem has even been regarded as an epidemic of sleep deprivation among adolescents and a key public health concern (American Medical Association, 2010; Office of Disease Prevention and Health Promotion, 2021). Behavioral health providers can offer universal preventive guidance to prevent the development of sleep disorders as well as the downstream consequences associated with insufficient sleep for mental and physical health.

Preventive guidance could involve offering each patient in an integrated care setting sleep education (e.g., about sleep processes and developmental sleep needs) and recommendations to promote sleep hygiene (e.g., with consistent sleep scheduling and avoiding screen use and caffeine use before bed). The American Academy of Sleep Medicine (AASM), for example, provides patient-friendly handouts that integrated care teams can share with patients universally on insomnia, aging and sleep, and sleep hygiene recommendations.

For children, the ABCs of SLEEPING tool has been developed to promote universal sleep screening and promotion of healthy sleep habits (Allen et al., 2016). This is a mnemonic that was developed to serve as an organizing framework for common pediatric sleep recommendations. The mnemonic stands for (1) **a**ge-appropriate **b**edtimes and wake-times with **c**onsistency, (2) **s**chedules and routines, (3) **l**ocation, (4) **e**xercise and diet, (5) no **e**lectronics in the bedroom or before bed, (6) **p**ositivity, (7) **i**ndependence when falling asleep, (8) **n**eeds of child met during the day, and (9) equal **gr**eat sleep. To build this framework, 77 articles were systematically reviewed that provided evidence to support the promotion of these healthy sleep practices. This tool is comparable to another mnemonic, "BEARS," that was developed to help providers identify and address sleep problems by inquiring about Bedtimes, Excessive daytime sleepiness, night Awakenings, Regularity and duration of sleep, and Snoring (Owens & Dalzell, 2005).

17.6 Universal, Indicated, and Selective Prevention of Sleep Disorders

The universal screening and prevention approaches described above are low intensity but high impact, meaning that they require little cost in terms of time and effort for implementation, but they have meaningfully positive effects on sleep health. Additional universal guidance is likely not feasible as it would require more time and may not be necessary for all patients. Instead, indicated and selective guidance for those with positive screens may be both more feasible and more appropriate.

For infant sleep difficulties, selective guidance to address problematic infant night wakings (e.g., those requiring parental intervention in the night) could be offered (Honaker et al., 2020). Behavioral interventions that could be selectively offered if indicated include either modified extinction, in which a parent places an infant awake in bed and checks on her periodically until she is asleep, or parental fading, in which a parent places a child awake in bed and gradually fades the degree of parental presence over time. These behavioral strategies are highly efficacious, with more than 20 randomized control trials showing significant reductions in infant night wakings and improvements in multiple aspects of child and family functioning (Mindell et al., 2006).

Despite the well-established efficacy of behavioral intervention for infant night wakings, one factor that may determine whether universal or selective guidance for infant sleep is provided is available resources. We have determined, based on a study of a diverse sample of parents of infants presenting to PCP visits, that if resources are less available, screening for parent-perceived problems can be a selective screening approach and might identify those families who are most in need of behavioral intervention and most motivated to implement it (Honaker et al., 2021). However, if more resources are available, asking directly about night wakings, rather than parental perception of a sleep problem, could be beneficial, particularly because some parents may not see night wakings as problematic and may not be aware of interventions that can effectively reduce night wakings in infants (Honaker et al., 2021). In another study, we found that 39% of mothers were not familiar with behavioral sleep interventions for infants (Honaker et al., 2020). Thus, broad-screening for parent-reported night wakings offers an opportunity for PCPs to evaluate infants and, when needed and desired, offer intervention recommendations that could mitigate later sleep disruption and the affiliated cascade of negative health, educational, and familial correlates (Honaker et al., 2021).

The aforementioned ABCs of SLEEPING tool is another key example of screening for pediatric sleep problems and providing selective guidance as needed in response to this screen (Howlett et al., 2020). The tool includes an online questionnaire for parents, followed by electronic feedback which offers handouts summarizing evidence-based recommendations to address highlighted problem areas. In Howlett and colleagues' 2020 preliminary study of this program, 22 families and 8 healthcare workers used the tool and provided feedback. The tool was well-received, and future iterations of the tool will likely include a prioritization scheme as both families and providers indicated that it could be challenging for them to know where to start when numerous recommendations were provided. One future approach may be to use an algorithm that considers the level of empirical support for each practice area in regard to its impact on sleep as well as the severity of each problem to determine which recommendation to implement first (Howlett et al., 2020).

Another example of universal screening and selective guidance for pediatric patients is the Sleep Checkup (Honaker & Saunders, 2018), which was designed to (1) screen for pediatric sleep disorders and facilitate appropriate referrals, (2) provide basic guidance for sleep disorders with a strong behavioral or psychological component, and (3) deliver anticipatory guidance to improve sleep health and prevent sleep disorders. The Sleep Checkup was delivered by behavioral health providers in two busy urban primary care clinics. No families refused the intervention, and PCPs perceived the service to be minimally disruptive to patient flow in the clinics. The most frequently endorsed barrier to care was that parents may not express a concern about their child's sleep, limiting the number of identified cases who could benefit from selective guidance (Faruqui et al., 2011), which reiterates the importance of healthcare providers conducting universal screenings in order to detect problematic sleep, even if parents do not perceive their child's sleep habits as problematic.

For adults, the Brief Behavioral Treatment for Insomnia (BBTI; Buysse et al., 2011) could be offered by nurses in integrated care teams as selective guidance when indicated. BBTI consists of individualized behavioral instructions delivered in two intervention sessions and two telephone calls. When compared to just printed educational material (e.g., the AASM handouts discussed above), the BBTI produced significantly better self-reported sleep and health outcomes, as well as actigraphic measures of sleep, and these treatment gains were maintained at 6-month follow-up (Buysse et al., 2011).

17.7 Stepped Care

Intervention for behavioral sleep concerns should be approached in a stepwise fashion, building in intensity on a case-by-case basis based on need if lower-level strategies are deemed ineffective (Rigney et al., 2018). Lower-level strategies include universal sleep health promotion with the use of psychoeducation and biblioprevention via handouts, books, and Internet articles promoting behavioral sleep strategies, which have become readily available for patients (Ramos et al., 2006). Another form of lower-level intervention could be "watchful waiting" for concerns like snoring, nocturnal fears, and nightmares in pediatric patients, as these concerns may remit with development. However, if these lower-level strategies are deemed insufficient, providers can then increase intervention intensity.

Two key interventions to consider if additional intervention is deemed warranted are cognitive behavioral therapy for insomnia (CBT-I) and imagery rehearsal therapy for nightmares (IRT). CBT-I involves five components: sleep education and sleep hygiene, stimulus control guidelines, sleep restriction, relaxation training, and cognitive restructuring to address maladaptive thoughts and worries about sleep. The American Academy of Sleep Medicine prepared a practice parameter in 2006 summarizing the well-established efficacy of CBT-I and recommending it as the first-line treatment for insomnia (Morgenthaler et al., 2006). Imagery rehearsal therapy has similarly been shown to be highly efficacious and is the first-line treatment for treating nightmare disorder (Aurora et al., 2010). It involves rescripting and rehearsing distressing dream imagery. Both of these interventions are appropriate and effective for adolescents and adults. For younger patients, behavioral sleep interventions, such as those outlined in the selective guidance section above, are appropriate and highly effective (for a review, see Meltzer & Crabtree, 2015).

If a patient endorses symptoms of insomnia necessitating further intervention, the integrated care team can start by referring the patient to self-administered tools, including phone apps like the CBT-I coach app, SHUT-I, or SLEEPIO (Cowie et al., 2018; Ritterband et al., 2017). For pediatric insomnia, patients may benefit from the Better Nights Better Days online program, which applies the ABCs of SLEEPING framework (Allen et al., 2016). For nightmares, individuals can be referred to Internet-based self- help programs with imagery rehearsal therapy (Schredl et al., 2016). These resources are easily accessible, low-cost, and effective (van Straten & Cuijpers, 2009).

If additional assistance is deemed necessary, patients could then be referred to group-based care administered by a behavioral healthcare provider, which is cost-effective, as it maximizes the number of patients who can receive care while minimizing the amount of time and personnel required. This stepped care approach to providing CBT-I for adults with insomnia has been well-documented by Espie and colleagues (2009). Patients were first encouraged to engage in self-administered CBT-I and then invited to participate in manualized, small group CBT-I delivered by nurses if needed (Espie, 2009). For pediatric patients, 85% of pediatric insomnia treatment studies have been conducted with traditional in-person, one-to-one service provision, but 42.6% have included Internet/phone-based treatment, and 70% of adolescent studies have involved group-based care (Meltzer et al., in press), suggesting that such delivery modes are on the rise.

If these steps of care are still deemed insusfficient, then the PCP may consider referring the individual to a behavioral sleep medicine specialist. Behavioral sleep medicine providers with credentialing can be identified on the Society of Behavioral Sleep Medicine website (www.behavioralsleep.org). Referral to specialists may be particularly useful for complex cases and/or non-responders. Wickwire et al. (2020)

found that patients who were referred to a board-certified sleep medicine provider were more likely to have two or more diagnosed sleep disorders and/or medical comorbidities (e.g., asthma or heart failure) compared to patients who were not referred. However, the likelihood of no-show to specialty care is notable, with an estimated no show rate of 21.2% (Cheung et al., 2020). Factors associated with no-show include younger age, appointment type (new vs established), and insurance status (no insurance vs public insurance) (Cheung et al., 2020). These no-show rates to specialty care highlight the importance of assisting patients in primary care as much as possible given the barriers to reaching specialty clinics. Additionally, there is a notable lack of trained sleep providers, particularly outside of large, urban areas. Since 2007, the American Board of Pediatrics and the American Board of Family Medicine have certified only 251 and 138 sleep sub-specialists, respectively, compared to a population of more than 100,000 general pediatricians and more than 75,000 general family practitioners in the United States (based on American Board of Pediatrics & Board of Family Medicine in 2015).

Finally, as a last step if other exhaustive efforts have been trialed, PCPs may choose to trial medication to address sleep concerns. However, as noted above, the first-line treatment for behavioral sleep disorders are behavioral interventions. Among pediatric patients, 39.6% of PCPs have been shown to use medication alone to address sleep concerns, rather than the behavioral stepped-care approach outlined above, and 42% recommended melatonin (Schnoes et al., 2006). Additionally, many of the medications used to address sleep in pediatrics also have other indications (e.g., antihistamines, antipsychotic agents), so the number of medications that may be prescribed specifically for sleep is unclear.

17.8 Lessons Learned for Future Implementation

In summary, there is great need and opportunity for behavioral health providers to improve the prevention, identification, and treatment of sleep problems for both children and adults in integrated care. PCPs receive little sleep training (Mindell et al., 2011, 2013) and have limited time and resources to thoroughly assess sleep and implement effective interventions when indicated (Boerner et al., 2015). Behavioral health providers are well-equipped; however, to setup universal screening systems, deliver universal prevention materials through educational materials, and implement stepped care through the provision of self-help resources, small group interventions, and referral to specialty care as deemed necessary. Because psychologists require a minimum number of minutes spent with a patient and a behavioral health diagnosis in order to bill, these approaches may be best-suited for systems with trainees who cannot otherwise bill for their time, or with staff providers who have available time to provide non-billable services. The e-health prevention tools described above may also be useful in place of billable service provision.

References

Adachi, Y., Sato, C., Nishino, N., Ohryoji, F., Hayama, J., & Yamagami, T. (2009). A brief parental education for shaping sleep habits in 4-month-old infants. *Clinical Medicine & Research, 7*(3), 85–92.

Adair, R., Zuckerman, B., Bauchner, H., Philipp, B., & Levenson, S. (1992). Reducing night waking in infancy: A primary care intervention. *Pediatrics, 89*(4), 585–588.

Alfano, C. A., Ginsburg, G. S., & Kingery, J. N. (2007). Sleep-related problems among children and adolescents with anxiety disorders. *Journal of the American Academy of Child & Adolescent Psychiatry, 46*(2), 224–232.

Allen, S. L., Howlett, M. D., Coulombe, J. A., & Corkum, P. V. (2016). ABCs of SLEEPING: A review of the evidence behind pediatric sleep practice recommendations. *Sleep Medicine Reviews, 29*, 1–14. https://doi.org/10.1016/j.smrv.2015.08.006

American Psychiatric Association. (2013). *Diagnostic and statistical manual of mental disorders* (5th ed.). https://doi.org/10.1176/appi.books.9780890425596

Ancoli-Israel, S. (2005). Sleep and aging: Prevalence of disturbed sleep and treatment considerations in older adults. *The Journal of Clinical Psychiatry, 66*, 24–30.

Aurora, R. N., Zak, R. S., Auerbach, S. H., Casey, K. R., Chowdhuri, S., ... Morgenthaler, T. I. (2010). Best practice guide for the treatment of nightmare disorder in adults. *Journal of Clinical Sleep Medicine, 6*(4), 389–401.

Blake, M. J., Trinder, J. A., & Allen, N. B. (2018). Mechanisms underlying the association between insomnia, anxiety, and depression in adolescence: Implications for behavioral sleep interventions. *Clinical Psychology Review, 63*, 25–40.

Boerner, K. E., Coulombe, J. A., & Corkum, P. (2015). Barriers and facilitators of evidence-based practice in pediatric behavioral sleep care: Qualitative analysis of the perspectives of health professionals. *Behavioral Sleep Medicine, 13*, 36–51. https://doi.org/10.1080/15402002.2013.838766

Buysse, D. J., Germain, A., Moul, D. E., Franzen, P. L., Brar, L. K., Fletcher, M. E., ... Monk, T. H. (2011). Efficacy of brief behavioral treatment for chronic insomnia in older adults. *Archives of Internal Medicine, 171*(10), 887–895. https://doi.org/10.1001/archinternmed.2010.535

Buysse, D. J., Reynolds, C. F., Monk, T. H., Berman, S., & Kupfer, D. J. (1989). The Pittsburgh sleep quality index: A new instrument for psychiatric practice and research. *Psychiatry Research, 28*(2), 193–213. https://doi.org/10.1016/0165-1781(89)90047-4

Buysse, D. J., Yu, L., Moul, D. E., Germain, A., Stover, A., Dodds, N. E., ... Pilkonis, P. A. (2010). Development and validation of patient-reported outcome measures for sleep disturbance and sleep-related impairments. *Sleep, 33*(6), 781–792.

Byars, K. C., Simon, S. L., Peugh, J., & Beebe, D. W. (2017). Validation of a brief insomnia severity measure in youth clinically referred for sleep evaluation. *Journal of Pediatric Psychology, 42*(4), 466–475.

Carskadon, M. A., Wolfson, A. R., Acebo, C., Tzischinsky, O., & Seifer, R. (1998). Adolescent sleep patterns, circadian timing, and sleepiness at a transition to early school days. *Sleep, 21*(8), 871–881.

Chen, P. J., Huang, C. L. C., Weng, S. F., Wu, M. P., Ho, C. H., Wang, J. J., ... Hsu, Y. W. (2017). Relapse insomnia increases greater risk of anxiety and depression: Evidence from a population-based 4-year cohort study. *Sleep Medicine, 38*, 122–129.

Cheung, D., Sahrmann, J., Nzewuihe, A., & Espiritu, J. (2020). No-show rates to a sleep clinic: Drivers and determinants. *Journal of Clinical Sleep Medicine*, JCSM-8578.

Corkum, P., Tannock, R., & Moldofsky, H. (1998). Sleep disturbances in children with attention-deficit/hyperactivity disorder. *Journal of the American Academy of Child & Adolescent Psychiatry, 37*(6), 637–646.

Cowie, J., Bower, J. L., Gonzalez, R., & Alfano, C. A. (2018). Multimedia field test: Digitalizing better sleep using the Sleepio Program. *Cognitive and Behavioral Practice, 25*(3), 442–448.

Curtis, B. J., Ashbrook, L. H., Young, T., Finn, L. A., Fu, Y. H., Ptáček, L. J., & Jones, C. R. (2019). Extreme morning chronotypes are often familial and not exceedingly rare: The estimated prevalence of advanced sleep phase, familial advanced sleep phase, and advanced sleep–wake phase disorder in a sleep clinic population. *Sleep, 42*(10), zsz148.

Drake, C. L., Roehrs, T., Richardson, G., Walsh, J. K., & Roth, T. (2004). Shift work sleep disorder: Prevalence and consequences beyond that of symptomatic day workers. *Sleep, 27*(8), 1453–1462.

El-Sheikh, M., Keiley, M., Bagley, E. J., & Chen, E. (2015). Socioeconomic adversity and women's sleep: Stress and chaos as mediators. *Behavioral Sleep Medicine, 13*(6), 506–523. https://doi.org/10.1080/15402002.2014.940110

Espie, C. A. (2009). "Stepped care": A health technology solution for delivering cognitive behavioral therapy as a first line insomnia treatment. *Sleep, 32*(12), 1549–1558.

Faruqui, F., Khubchandani, J., Price, J. H., Bolyard, D., & Reddy, R. (2011). Sleep disorders in children: A national assessment of primary care pediatrician practices and perceptions. *Pediatrics, 128*(3), 539–546.

Fernandez-Mendoza, J., Bourchtein, E., Calhoun, S., Puzino, K., Snyder, C. K., He, F., ... Bixler, E. (2020). Natural history of insomnia symptoms in the transition from childhood to adolescence: Population rates, health disparities and risk factors. *Sleep*.

Forrest, C. B., Meltzer, L. J., Marcus, C. L., de la Motte, A., Kratchman, A., Buysse, D. J., ... Bevans, K. B. (2018). Development and validation of the PROMIS pediatric sleep disturbance and sleep-related impairment item banks. *Sleep, 41*(6), zsy054.

Gellis, L. A. (2011). Children's sleep in the context of socioeconomic status, race, and ethnicity. In M. El-Sheikh (Ed.), *Sleep and development: Familial and socio-cultural considerations* (pp. 219–244). Oxford University Press.

Goldman, S. E., Richdale, A. L., Clemons, T., & Malow, B. A. (2012). Parental sleep concerns in Autism Spectrum Disorders: Variations from childhood to adolescence. *Journal of Autism and Developmental Disorders, 42*(4), 531–538.

Gradisar, M., Gardner, G., & Dohnt, H. (2011). Recent worldwide sleep patterns and problems during adolescence: A review and meta-analysis of age, region, and sleep. *Sleep Medicine, 12*(2), 110–118.

Grandner, M. A., & Chakravorty, S. (2017). Insomnia in primary care: Misreported, mishandled, and just plain missed. *Journal of Clinical Sleep Medicine, 13*(8), 937–939.

Grewe, F. A., Roeder, M., Bradicich, M., Schwarz, E. I., Held, U., Thiel, S., ... Kohler, M. (2020). Low repeatability of Epworth Sleepiness Scale after short intervals in a sleep clinic population. *Journal of Clinical Sleep Medicine, 16*(5), 757–764.

Hoffses, K. W., Honaker, S. M., Riley, A. R., & Meadows, T. J. (2018). Screening and assessment of sleep disturbance. In *Handbook of pediatric psychological screening and assessment in primary care* (pp. 358–380). Routledge.

Honaker, S. M., McQuillan, M. E., Mindell, J. M., Downs, S., Slaven, J., & Schwichtenberg, A. J. (2021). Screening for problematic sleep in a diverse sample of infants. *Journal of Pediatric Psychology*. https://doi.org/10.1093/jpepsy/jsab050

Honaker, S. M., & Meltzer, L. J. (2016). Sleep in pediatric primary care: A review of the literature. *Sleep Medicine Reviews, 25*, 31–39. https://doi.org/10.1016/j.smrv.2015.01.004

Honaker, S. M., Mindell, J. A., Slaven, J. E., & Schwichtenberg, A. J. (2020). Implementation of infant behavioral sleep intervention in a diverse sample of mothers. *Behavioral Sleep Medicine*, 1–15.

Honaker, S. M., & Saunders, T. (2018). The sleep checkup: Sleep screening, guidance, and management in pediatric primary care. *Clinical Practice in Pediatric Psychology, 6*(3), 201–210.

Howlett, M., Jemcov, A., Adams, A., & Corkum, P. (2020). ABCs of SLEEPING tool: Improving access to care for pediatric insomnia. *Clinical Practice in Pediatric Psychology, 8*(1), 1–12.

Hoyniak, C. P., Bates, J. E., McQuillan, M. E., Albert, L. E., Staples, A. D., Molfese, V. J., Rudasill, K. M., & Deater-Deckard, K. (2020). The family context of toddler sleep: Routines, sleep environment, and emotional security induction in the hour before bedtime. *Behavioral Sleep Medicine*. https://doi.org/10.1080/15402002.2020.1865356

Jones, C. H., & Ball, H. (2014). Exploring socioeconomic differences in bedtime behaviours and sleep duration in English preschool children. *Infant and Child Development, 23*(5), 518–543. https://doi.org/10.1002/icd.1848

Klingman, K. J., Jungquist, C. R., & Perlis, M. L. (2017). Introducing the sleep disorders symptom checklist-25: A primary care friendly and comprehensive screener for sleep disorders. *Sleep Medicine Research, 8*(1), 17–25.

Léger, D., Poursain, B., Neubauer, D., & Uchiyama, M. (2008). An international survey of sleeping problems in the general population. *Current Medical Research and Opinion, 24*(1), 307–317.

Lovato, N., Gradisar, M., Short, M., Dohnt, H., & Micic, G. (2013). Delayed sleep phase disorder in an Australian school-based sample of adolescents. *Journal of Clinical Sleep Medicine, 9*(9), 939–944.

Markovich, A. N., Gendron, M. A., & Corkum, P. V. (2015). Validating the Children's Sleep Habits Questionnaire against polysomnography and actigraphy in school-aged children. *Frontiers in Psychiatry, 5*, 188.

McMakin, D. L., & Alfano, C. A. (2015). Sleep and anxiety in late childhood and early adolescence. *Current Opinion in Psychiatry, 28*(6), 483.

Meltzer, L. J., & Crabtree, V. (2015). *Pediatric sleep problems: A clinician's guide to behavioral interventions*. American Psychological Association.

Meltzer, L. J., Wainer, A., Engstrom, E., Pepa, L., & Mindell, J. A. (in press). Seeing the whole elephant: A scoping review of behavioral treatments for pediatric insomnia. *Sleep Medicine Reviews*.

Mindell, J. A., Bartle, A., Abd Wahab, N., Ahn, Y., Ramamurthy, M. B., Huong, H. T. D., … Goh, D. Y. (2011). Sleep education in medical school curriculum: A glimpse across countries. *Sleep Medicine, 12*(9), 928–931.

Mindell, J. A., Bartle, A., Ahn, Y., Ramamurthy, M. B., Huong, H. T. D., Kohyama, J., … Goh, D. Y. (2013). Sleep education in pediatric residency programs: A cross-cultural look. *BMC Research Notes, 6*(1), 130.

Mindell, J. A., Kuhn, B., Lewin, D. S., Meltzer, L. J., & Sadeh, A. (2006). Behavioral treatment of bedtime problems and night wakings in infants and young children. *Sleep, 29*(10), 1263–1276.

Moore, M., Kirchner, H. L., Drotar, D., Johnson, N., Rosen, C., Ancoli-Israel, S., & Redline, S. (2009). Relationships among sleepiness, sleep time, and psychological functioning in adolescents. *Journal of Pediatric Psychology, 34*(10), 1175–1183.

Morgenthaler, T., Kramer, M., Alessi, C., Friedman, L., Boehlecke, B., Brown, T., et al. (2006). Practice parameters for the psychological and behavioral treatment of insomnia: An update. An American Academy of Sleep Medicine Report. *Sleep, 29*, 1415–1419.

Morin, C. M., Belleville, G., Bélanger, L., & Ivers, H. (2011). The Insomnia Severity Index: Psychometric indicators to detect insomnia cases and evaluate treatment response. *Sleep, 34*(5), 601–608.

Morrell, J. M. (1999). The infant sleep questionnaire: A new tool to assess infant sleep problems for clinical and research purposes. *Child Psychology and Psychiatry Review, 4*(1), 20–26.

Nesbitt, A. D. (2018). Delayed sleep-wake phase disorder. *Journal of Thoracic Disease, 10*(Suppl 1), S103.

Nevarez, M. D., Rifas-Shiman, S. L., Kleinman, K. P., Gillman, M. W., & Taveras, E. M. (2010). Associations of early life risk factors with infant sleep duration. *Academic Pediatrics, 10*(3), 187–193.

Newton, A. T., Honaker, S. M., & Reid, G. J. (2020). Risk and protective factors and processes for behavioral sleep problems among preschool and early school-aged children: A systematic review. *Sleep Medicine Reviews, 52*, 101303. https://doi.org/10.1016/j.smrv.2020.101303

Oh, C. M., Kim, H. Y., Na, H. K., Cho, K. H., & Chu, M. K. (2019). The effect of anxiety and depression on sleep quality of individuals with high risk for insomnia: A population-based study. *Frontiers in Neurology, 10*, 849.

Ohayon, M. M. (2011). Epidemiological overview of sleep disorders in the general population. *Sleep Medicine Research, 2*(1), 1–9.

Owens, J. (2008). Classification and epidemiology of childhood sleep disorders. *Primary Care: Clinics in Office Practice, 35*(3), 533–546.

Owens, J. A., & Dalzell, V. (2005). Use of the "BEARS" sleep screening tool in a pediatric residents' continuity clinic: A pilot study. *Sleep Medicine, 6*, 63e9.

Paine, S. J., Fink, J., Gander, P. H., & Warman, G. R. (2014). Identifying advanced and delayed sleep phase disorders in the general population: A national survey of New Zealand adults. *Chronobiology International, 31*(5), 627–636.

Peña, M. M., Rifas-Shiman, S. L., Gillman, M. W., Redline, S., & Taveras, E. M. (2016). Racial/ethnic and socio-contextual correlates of chronic sleep curtailment in childhood. *Sleep, 39*(9), 1653–1661.

Ramos, K. D., Youngclarke, D. M., Child, H., Small, L. L., Reichert, B., & Holland, K. (2006). Parenting advice books about child sleep: Cosleeping and crying it out. *Sleep, 29*(12), 1616–1623.

Rigney, G., Isaacs, J., Shea, S., & Corkum, P. V. (2018). Sleep wake disorders in children. In T. Ollendick, S. White, & B. White (Eds.), *The Oxford handbook of clinical child and adolescent psychology* (pp. 382–397). Oxford University Press.

Ritterband, L. M., Thorndike, F. P., Ingersoll, K. S., Lord, H. R., Gonder-Frederick, L., Frederick, C., … Morin, C. M. (2017). Effect of a web-based cognitive behavior therapy for insomnia intervention with 1-year follow-up: A randomized clinical trial. *JAMA Psychiatry, 74*(1), 68–75.

Schnoes, C. J., Kuhn, B. R., Workman, E. F., & Ellis, C. R. (2006). Pediatric prescribing practices for clonidine and other pharmacologic agents for children with sleep disturbance. *Clinical Pediatrics, 45*(3), 229e38.

Schredl, M., Dehmlow, L., & Schmitt, J. (2016). Interest in information about nightmares in patients with sleep disorders. *Journal of Clinical Sleep Medicine, 12*(7), 973–977.

Sheldrick, R. C., & Perrin, E. C. (2009). Surveillance of children's behavior and development: Practical solutions for primary care. *Journal of Developmental & Behavioral Pediatrics, 30*(2), 151–153.

Swart, M. L., van Schagen, A. M., Lancee, J., & van den Bout, J. (2013). Prevalence of nightmare disorder in psychiatric outpatients. *Psychotherapy and Psychosomatics, 82*, 267–268.

Tsai, M. H., Hsu, J. F., & Huang, Y. S. (2016). Sleep problems in children with attention deficit/hyperactivity disorder: Current status of knowledge and appropriate management. *Current Psychiatry Reports, 18*(8), 76.

U.S. Department of Health and Human Services. Office of Disease Prevention and Health Promotion. Healthy People 2030. Increase the proportion of children who get sufficient sleep — EMC-03. https://health.gov/healthypeople/objectives-and-data/browse-objectives/children/increase-proportion-children-whoget-sufficient-sleep-emc-03. Accessed May 25, 2021.

van Straten, A., & Cuijpers, P. (2009). Self-help therapy for insomnia: A meta-analysis. *Sleep Medicine Reviews, 13*, 61–71.

Wickwire, E. M., Jobe, S. L., Parthasarathy, S., Collen, J., Capaldi, V. F., Johnson, A., … Albrecht, J. S. (2020). Which older adults receive sleep medicine specialty care? Predictors of being seen by a board-certified sleep medicine provider. *Journal of Clinical Sleep Medicine*, JCSM-8722.

Wynchank, D., Bijlenga, D., Beekman, A. T., Kooij, J. S., & Penninx, B. W. (2017). Adult attention-deficit/hyperactivity disorder (ADHD) and insomnia: An update of the literature. *Current Psychiatry Reports, 19*(12), 98.

Chapter 18
Preventing What's Preventable in Dementia

Paula E. Hartman-Stein, Daniel R. George, and Brigid K. McVaugh

18.1 Introduction

The high frequency of television and online ads for supplements, brain fitness gadgets, and other products that purportedly preserve cognitive functioning suggests that older adults are increasingly concerned about declines in memory as they age. However, given cultural stigma around memory loss, relatively few individuals discuss these worries with their primary care physicians (PCPs) or behavioral care providers (BCPs). A study conducted by the Center for Disease Control (CDC) of almost 96,000 individuals aged 45 years or older revealed that approximately 13% indicated they experienced confusion or memory loss in the previous year, but only 23% of those with such concerns raised the issues with a medical professional (National Center for Chronic Disease Prevention and Health Promotion, 2012).

Despite having limited information to guide their choices of strategies with the greatest benefits to promote cognitive wellness, many older Americans have embarked on their own experimentation by engaging in exercise, diet, meditation, participating in lifelong-learning programs, playing brain performance computer games, or taking over-the-counter supplements, with the hope that such behaviors can, in sum, prevent dementia (Hartman-Stein & LaRue, 2011). Others have a fatalistic view that nothing can be done to prevent Alzheimer's or have no interest in the

P. E. Hartman-Stein (✉)
Consultant in independent practice, Brevard, NC, USA
e-mail: paula@centerforhealthyaging.com

D. R. George
Department of Humanities, Penn State College of Medicine, Hershey, PA, USA
e-mail: dgeorge1@pennstatehealth.psu.edu

B. K. McVaugh
Consultant in Culinary Nutrition, Houston, TX, USA

W. O'Donohue, M. Zimmermann (eds.), *Handbook of Evidence-Based Prevention of Behavioral Disorders in Integrated Care*,
https://doi.org/10.1007/978-3-030-83469-2_18

topic, so they eat highly processed fast food more than vegetables and fruits, limit their reading to online posts, and/or engage in minimal exercise.

It is not merely members of the lay public who question whether lifestyle makes a difference—health providers are often dubious as well. We believe PCPs and BCPs can help patients protect and maintain their brain health, regardless of their level of belief, by advising, supporting, and teaching based on the current state of knowledge.

In 2019 the Alzheimer's Association surveyed about 1000 primary care physicians, finding that:

- Over 80% acknowledge they are on the front lines of diagnosing and providing care for Alzheimer's disease (AD) and other dementias.
- Over half of PCPs receive questions related to dementia from their patients age 65 and older or their family members every few days or more.
- More than one-quarter (27%) report being only sometimes or never comfortable answering patient questions about dementia (Alzheimer's Association, 2020a, b).

18.2 Incidence, Prevalence, and Etiologies of Dementia

The word dementia is an umbrella term referring to a wide range of medical conditions caused by brain changes. AD is a progressive neurodegenerative disorder characterized by early symptoms of difficulty recalling recent conversations, names, or events, being repetitive, having trouble following a complex train of thought, having difficulty following conversations, or withdrawing from work and social activities. Later symptoms include impairment in communicating, disorientation, confusion, poor judgment, declines in problem-solving and the ability to perform activities of daily life (Alzheimer's Association, 2020a, b; Gerontological Society of America, 2020). AD accounts for approximately 60–80% of all cases of dementia, affecting approximately 20% of individuals 80 years of age and older (Alzheimer's Association, 2020a, b; McKhann et al., 2011).

The leading hypothesis as to its etiology is that the intercellular accumulation of the protein fragment, beta-amyloid, triggers a cascade of extracellular amyloid accumulation that then cause tau proteins—structures providing stability within neurons—to twist into intracellular tangles, leading to widespread neuronal death (Selkoe & Hardy, 2016). In individuals with rare genetic mutations, levels of beta-amyloid may begin upwards of 20 years before symptoms occur (Quiroz et al., 2018). Other brain changes in AD include chronic inflammation and atrophy due to cell loss that may begin over a decade before becoming symptomatic. Microglia clear proteins and debris from dying cells, and inflammation may set in when microglia are unable to clear the debris adequately (Alzheimer's Association, 2020a, b).

However, mixed dementias—i.e., cases that encompass not only the classic hallmarks of plaques and tangles but also overlapping pathologies like vascular lesions, alpha-synuclein (the protein making up Lewy bodies), and TDP-43, a nuclear protein in common subtypes of frontotemporal dementia (FTD) and amyotrophic lateral sclerosis (ALS), appear to be more common than recognized as more than 50% of people with dementia have pathologic changes indicating more than one cause of dementia. The likelihood of having mixed dementia increases with age (Alzheimer's Disease Facts and Figures, 2020a; Winblad et al., 2016; Yu et al., 2020). Recent studies of TDP-43 suggest that more complex brain pathology leading to cognitive decline in late-life may be independent of beta-amyloid accumulation (Kawas et al., 2015; Wilson et al., 2013). Such findings indicate that treating only pathways that converge on beta-amyloid, as is the focus of current drug development, may leave untreated a significant proportion of the associated conditions in the AD phenotype that are not related to plaque and tangle pathology (e.g., vascular damage).

In a book that sparked controversy at the time, *The Myth of Alzheimer's: What you aren't being told about today's most dreaded diagnosis,* the authors dismissed the promise of a pharmaceutical panacea for AD as a cultural myth promoted by powerful drug companies (Whitehouse & George, 2008). In 2016 the pharmaceutical company, Merck, announced it was halting the late-stage trial of verubecestat, a BACE inhibitor that controlled an enzyme involved in the forming of amyloid plaques, abnormal protein clusters in the brain that have been suspected as a main cause of Alzheimer's disease. The drug did not reduce cognitive or functional decline in patients with mild-to-moderate AD and was associated with treatment-related side effects such as rash, falls and injuries, sleep disturbance, suicidal ideation, and weight loss (Egan et al., 2018).

In late 2016 the drug company, Eli Lilly, ended its clinical trial of the drug, solanezumab, after research subjects demonstrated no improvement compared to placebo. The failure of drugs in the family of BACE inhibitors developed to reduce amyloid added to doubts to the viability of the amyloid theory of AD (Hartman-Stein, 2017). Moreover, as of winter 2020, the FDA had declined to approve Biogen's drug aducanumab—a monoclonal antibody acting on different molecules than solanezumab. Researchers have made the case that given the ongoing failures of drug development, the best investment of research dollars is for prevention and improved interventions (George & Whitehouse, 2021; Whitehouse & George, 2008).

A recent major study in *JAMA Internal Medicine* published findings showing the incidence rate of dementia for people over age 65 has been dropping in the United States, from 11.6% in 2000 to 8.8% in 2012 (Langa et al., 2017). While *overall* numbers of people affected by dementia continue to rise—as one would expect, given the growing population of aging individuals who are living longer—there has been a general *decline* in both dementia incidence (the number of people diagnosed per year) and prevalence (the number of people diagnosed relative to the total number of people in the population) over the past four decades (Gao et al., 2019; Wu et al., 2017). Indeed, emerging research published in *Neurology* suggests that due to decreasing risk, older Americans' chances of developing dementia in 2021 is 13% lower than it was in 2011 (George & Whitehouse, 2021; Wolters et al., 2020). It is likely that improved vascular health at the population level, along with significantly reduced smoking rates, increased access to primary, secondary, and tertiary education, and the removal of toxins like lead from gasoline in the late twentieth century have combined to provide a more favorable milieu for the brain health of current cohorts of elders (George & Whitehouse, 2021; Livingston et al., 2020).

Despite the fact that dementia risk is dropping, the following current figures from the Alzheimer's Association (2020a, b) are sobering:

- 5.4 million Americans and 50 million people worldwide live with dementia.
- AD is the sixth leading cause of death in the United States and fifth leading cause for those age 65 and older.
- People with AD live an average of 8–10 years and as many as 20 years from onset.

18.2.1 Sequelae of Covid-19

What is not yet known is the impact of Covid-19 on the incidence of dementia and AD. In early 2021 with guidance from the World Health Organization (WHO), the Alzheimer's Association, in conjunction with 30 countries, has formed a consortium to study more than 22 million Covid-19 cases to evaluate the impact of the virus on the risk of later life cognitive decline and AD (de Erausquin et al., 2021).

18.3 Common Categories of Dementia/Diagnostic Criteria

According to the Gerontological Society of America (GSA) (2020), the most commonly used categories of dementia coded in PC settings include: dementia from AD with early onset (<age 65); dementia from AD with late onset (age 65 or older); dementia from AD, unspecified; vascular dementia with or without behavioral disturbance; dementia in other diseases classified elsewhere with or without behavioral disturbance; unspecified dementia with or without behavioral disturbance; Pick's disease (described below); other frontotemporal dementia; dementia with Lewy bodies; mild cognitive impairment; and corticobasal degeneration.

Symptoms that may indicate dementia and trigger more in-depth evaluation are deficits from baseline skills in learning and retaining new information, problem-solving, reasoning, spatial ability, orientation, word finding, following conversations, and behavioral changes such as passivity, irritability, suspicion, and misinterpreting visual or auditory stimuli (GSA, 2020).

According to the American Heart Association (AHA)/American Stroke Association (ASA), probable vascular dementia is indicated when there is cognitive impairment and imaging evidence of cerebrovascular disease, a clear temporal relationship between a vascular event (e.g., clinical stroke) and onset of cognitive deficits, and a clear relationship in the severity and pattern of cognitive impairment with the presence of diffuse, subcortical cerebrovascular pathology (Gorelick et al., 2011).

Pick's disease is a rare type of age-related dementia that affects the frontal lobes of the brain and causes speech problems like aphasia, behavior difficulties, and eventually death. It had been used interchangeably with frontotemporal dementia (FTD) but is now considered to be one of three very specific causes of FTD. Pick's disease is not usually associated with memory loss in its early stages (https://www.alzheimers.net).

FTD may occur in those 65 and older but most people with the disorder develop it a younger age (Alzheimer's Association, 2020a, b). The three subtypes are behavioral variant (bvFTD), semantic variant of primary progressive aphasia (svPPA), and non-fluent variant of primary progressive aphasia (nfvPPA). Neuropsychiatric symptoms are prominent in bvFTD.

Lewy body dementias include two related disorders, dementia with Lewy bodies (DLB) and dementia secondary to Parkinson's disease. Essential for the diagnosis is fluctuating cognition with variations in alertness, recurrent visual hallucinations, rapid eye movement sleep behavior disorder before signs of cognitive decline, and one or more features of Parkinsonism. In the early stages, there may be no memory impairment but deficits in attention, executive functioning, and visual-spatial ability may be present (Gerontological Society of America, 2020; Yamada et al., 2020).

The criteria for mild cognitive impairment (MCI) due to AD include concern regarding cognition that reflects a change reported by the patient, informant, or clinician indicating observed evidence of decline over time. In addition, there must be evidence of impairment in one or more cognitive domains, including memory while independence in functioning capacity is preserved (Albert et al., 2011). Traditionally, the MCI label has been given to patients who present with a memory complaint and some changes in intellectual function as determined by neuropsychological testing but who have relatively little impairment in activities of daily living.

A range of sub-classifications, however, has recently emerged that implies different stages of MCI: pre-MCI, early MCI, and late MCI. However, conversion rates of MCI to dementia vary significantly, and some studies observe that well over a quarter of people labeled with MCI do not progress to AD (Pandya et al., 2017) and between 14% and 41% of individuals with MCI have reverted back to "normal" cognitive functioning (Ganguli et al., 2004). Naturally, this has raised questions about the accuracy, usefulness, and ethical soundness of a label that is supposed to represent a clinical precursor to AD.

18.4 When Screening Is Warranted

The idea of widespread dementia screening in PC is debatable. Galvin et al. (2020) argue screening increases self-efficacy and improves patient-centered outcomes for lifestyle changes. However, both the Lancet Commission and the US Preventive

Services Task Force (USPSTF) conclude the evidence is lacking to support widespread pre-symptomatic screening in everyday practice (Livingston et al., 2020; US Preventive Services Task Force, 2020).

There are substantial ethical concerns about the push for early diagnosis through memory screenings. As mentioned earlier, the greatest controversy surrounds the heterogeneity observed in "pre-disease" categories such as MCI, the vagueness of its diagnostic criteria, and a lack of specific ability to predict the "disease" trajectory. If an aging person has some memory loss, but their activities of daily living are not affected, what is the value in screening them and clinically labeling them with MCI? When does the forgetfulness we may all be touched by as our brains age cross the line to "disease"? Should a clinical diagnosis be freely given by the physician or should it also require a subjective complaint from the patient or family members? This concern speaks to a broader societal question about how much power physicians (and the pharmaceutical industry) should have in defining and dictating the terms of how individuals experience disease, which can have such devastating effects in the lives of their loved ones. Indeed, it is important to remember that while markets and shareholder profits may be enlarged by diagnostic schemes that extend labels like MCI to more people, ultimately human beings with fragile, finite lives and bonds must bear the biopsychosocial consequences of disease labels (George & Whitehouse, 2021).

Screening and an accurate diagnosis are important for patients with notable impairment and/or personal or family members' concerns about their loved one's functioning. An excellent free resource for PC that can be downloaded online is *The GSA KAER Toolkit for Primary Care Teams: Supporting conversations about brain health, timely detection of cognitive impairment, and accurate diagnosis of dementia* (www.geron.org/programs-services/brain-health-cognitive-impairment-and-dementia).

The toolkit suggests that the PCP or BCP bring up the topic of brain health for educational purposes at any PC visit or as part of an annual wellness visit for every person age 65 or older. Examples of questions about concerns or change in functioning include: "Are you worried about your memory? Have you noticed any changes that concern you?" If the patient or family member raise concerns regarding memory loss or other signs of cognitive decline, then more formal screening administered by the BCP or a medical assistant who has had adequate training can administer a brief formal assessment. Front desk staff may observe behaviors such as confusion about appointments, repetition of stories or questions, or deferring to family members for basic information. In a PC setting with a large patient volume, creating an atmosphere that encourages all staff to give input will enhance patient care.

Even if no concerns arise, the BCP can use a brain health conversation to provide information about the connections between brain and heart health, medications that may affect memory, dietary patterns, and lifestyle habits that impact the brain. *Communicating with older adults: An evidence-based review of what really works* is a free resource developed by the Gerontological Society of America (GSA) containing tips for optimizing interactions between healthcare providers and older adults (Gerontological Society of America, 2012).

If screening is warranted, using a validated, brief cognitive test is advisable. The KAER toolkit recommends the Mini-Cog©, Clock Drawing test, Montreal Cognitive Assessment (MoCA), or the Saint Louis University Mental Status (SLUMS) exam. All take 10 min or less to administer. Another short test of mental status used extensively in clinical and research settings is the Mini-Mental State Exam (MMSE) developed at Johns Hopkins Medical Center (Folstein et al., 1975).

Informant questionnaires to obtain collateral information are also part of a valid screening process. The KAER toolkit lists the Ascertain Dementia eight-item Questionnaire, the Informant-based Behavioral Pathology in Alzheimer's Disease rating scale, and the Short Form of the Informant Questionnaire on Cognitive Decline in the Elderly (GSA, 2020).

Screening is not typically adequate to make a diagnosis. In most cases, we recommend when screening shows impairment, PCPs and BCPs partner with specialists such as geriatricians, geropsychologists, neurologists, neuropsychologists, or nurse practitioners with geropsychiatric expertise.

When there are symptoms of cognitive impairment, the reversible physiological causes of cognitive decline should be ruled out first through appropriate laboratory tests (e.g., thyroid or vitamin B12 deficiency). The GSA toolkit contains e-resources for PCPs and BCPs with suggestions of how to talk to patients and families about a diagnosis of dementia.

18.5 Risk Factors and Recommendations

Evidence is growing that dementia can be prevented or delayed and that healthy lifestyle changes may be beneficial for older at-risk individuals even in the presence of APOE-related genetic susceptibility to dementia (Solomon et al., 2018). Two separate international groups of scientists published their meta-analyses of research reports of both observational prospective studies (OPSs) and randomized control trials (RCTs) (Livingston et al., 2017, 2020; Yu et al., 2020). The team led by Yu et al. (2020) identified 19 modifiable factors and the Lancet Commission on dementia (Livingston et al., 2020), described 12 modifiable risk factors, accounting for 40% of dementia worldwide. To offer guidance for dementia prevention across the life span, we have summarized these evidence-based suggestions PCPs and BCPs can provide to patients from these studies.

- **Receive as much education as possible in early life and engage in cognitive activities throughout life**. As noted earlier, dementia rates are falling over the last decade in part due to increased access to education in the mid-twentieth century. Examples of life-long cognitive activities include reading, playing chess, solving problems, learning a second language, playing music, traveling to novel areas, writing narratives, and doing art work.

Additional corroborating evidence comes from a population-based longitudinal observational study in the oldest-old begun in 2003 of 587 people age 90 or older who had no signs of dementia when the study began. Participation in activities with a strong mental component, i.e., reading and church/synagogue attendance, was correlated with reduced risk of dementia as the participants aged beyond 90 (Paganini-Hill et al., 2016).

No single specific activity such as solving crossword puzzles or playing computerized games appears to protect against cognitive decline, although domain-specific training of focal skills may improve. For example, doing crossword puzzles on a regular basis improves crossword puzzle skills (Livingston et al., 2020).

The *Lancet* Commission (Livingston et al., 2020) noted that older retirement age is correlated with lower dementia risk for more cognitively demanding jobs. The take-home message is if a person's work is meaningful and mentally challenging, it may be advisable not to retire early.

Cognitive reserve theory, a concept that began in the late 1980s, may explain these findings. Cognitive reserve refers to the brain's structural and functional ability to build resilience against neurological damage, tolerate more brain pathology before signs of dementia occur, or draw upon multiple pathways in undertaking cognitive tasks. In a post-mortem analysis of 137 patients, some subjects who showed no signs of AD upon autopsy had high degrees of pathology but higher brain weights and a greater concentration of neurons compared to age-matched controls. The theory is that these individuals had cognitive reserve that served as a protective factor against cellular deterioration (Katzman et al., 1988; Whitehouse & George, 2008). Other OPS of religious orders show similar findings (Snowdon, 2003).

- **Encourage use of hearing aids for hearing deficits and protect ears from excessive noise exposure.** Cognitive reserve theory may explain that those who cannot hear properly may over time experience exponentially less cognitive stimulation.
- **Manage weight and BMI**. Given links between weight, vascular health, and brain health, it is beneficial to encourage BMI for individuals <65 to be between 18.5 and 24.9. Moreover, BMI ought to be maintained <30 in mid-life and beyond, but adults over 65 should not be overly thin and, if losing weight, they should be monitored.
- **Control vascular factors**. Ideally, systolic blood pressure should be kept to 130 mm Hg or less from age 40 on. Patients should be encouraged to maintain good condition of cerebral vessels via lifestyle or medications to avoid any cardiovascular disease. Individuals with history of stroke or cerebral micro-bleeding should be monitored for cognitive changes. Instances of atrial fibrillation should be managed and patients should be encouraged not to smoke and to avoid second hand smoke. Diet/exercise should be used to avoid diabetes while monitoring blood sugar levels for those with diabetes. Homocysteine levels should be monitored as high levels can contribute to arterial damage and result in blood clots. Vitamin B and/or folic acid can treat this condition.

- **Limit alcohol use with no more than 21 units weekly, i.e., no more than three drinks of any kind per day**. The 2020–2025 Dietary Guidelines for Americans differ somewhat in their recommendations, suggesting that for those who choose to drink, intake should be limited to one drink or less per day for women and two drinks or less in a day for men (US Department of Health and Human Services and US Department of Agriculture, 2020). While the deleterious effects of excess alcohol consumption are well-established, some mild-to-moderate alcohol consumption may be protective in reducing inflammation (Barve et al. 2017).
- **Engage in physical exercise**. Individuals 65 and older should be encouraged to engage in regular physical exercise and an active lifestyle by movement in daily activities such as taking stairs and engaging in hobbies such as yoga, dancing, and gardening. Both the Lancet Commission (Livingston et al., 2020) and Yu et al. (2020) suggest older adults maintain good cardiovascular condition, but there is no strong evidence as to what types of exercise, duration, frequency, or intensity are needed to achieve optimal cognitive functioning. Public health recommendations indicate older adults should be encouraged to engage in an active lifestyle that incorporates movement in everyday activities, and if possible, purposeful exercise with moderate to vigorous exertion including strength and aerobic training (Global Council on Brain Health, 2016).
- **Limit or avoid head trauma**. Traumatic brain injuries (TBI)—bumps, blows, or jolts to the head or neck area—can cause acute damage to the brain, and even multiple mild injuries can contribute to greater cumulative risk throughout life. Wearing helmets for contact sports and bike riding and wearing safety belts at all times should be encouraged for all ages, and caution should be taken to avoid falls (the leading cause of TBI), especially in later life stages when balance may be compromised.
- **Ensure consistent patterns of sleep**. Sleep increasingly appears to help the brain's glymphatic system remove metabolic waste that has accrued through the day. Sleep deprivation can downregulate the glymphatic system, leading to the buildup of toxic cellular waste products that can damage and impair the brain over time (Fultz et al., 2019). Several lines of evidence suggest that sleep disorders may contribute to cognitive decline and may be a promising target for prevention (Xu et al., 2020). According to the *Lancet* Commission, there is no evidence that medication for sleep is effective, but rather considerable evidence suggests its harm (Livingston et al., 2020). Thus, behavioral strategies to improve sleep are of great importance.

  BCPs can counsel patient individually or in groups on sleep hygiene including relaxing strategies before bedtime and following middle-of-the-night awakenings. Yu et al. (2020) recommended individuals get sufficient and good quality sleep but do not give specific suggestions for optimal amounts. Current health guidelines recommend at least 7 h of sleep per night, but a longitudinal observational study of 613 individuals found no differences in cognitive measures or structural measures of the brain between groups that reported 5.4, 6.2, 7, and 7.9 h of sleep over 5 points in time over 28 years. This study calls for replication, and if results are the same, it will challenge current sleep guidelines (Zitser et al., 2020).

- **Limit stress and treat depression**. Stress and depression are well-established lifespan risk factors for dementia (Livingston et al., 2017). Thus, patients should be guided toward individually tailored stress reduction strategies, e.g., practicing mindfulness-based stress reduction (Kaszniak, 2011), increasing frequency of pleasant and meaningful activities (Richards et al., 2016), and/or dealing with root causes of stress or depression. In the only RCT comparing behavioral activation to supportive therapy for preventing dementia in patients with amnestic MCI, those in the behavioral activation group had a decreased 2-year incidence of risk of memory decline (Rovner et al., 2018).

  Maintaining frequent social contacts improves mood. Research has shown that maintaining social networks is protective, and, conversely, that the effects of loneliness, isolation, and disconnection are risks comparable to smoking up to 15 cigarettes a day, obesity, physical inactivity, and air pollution (Holt-Lunstad, 2017). Social service agencies can provide regular phone or computer-based contact with isolated, vulnerable older adults. Referral to local area agencies on aging or community mental health centers is strongly recommended in such cases.
- **Medications.** Two interventions not recommended are estrogen replacement therapy and acetylcholinesterase inhibitors (Yu et al., 2020). De-prescribing anticholinergic medications is advisable. In an observational cohort study with 350 adults with follow-up of 3.2 years, anticholinergic medications were found to increase the transition from normal cognition to MCI in community-dwelling older adults without dementia (Campbell et al., 2018). Anti-hypertensive medication is the only known preventive medicine against cognitive decline (Livingston et al., 2020).

Dietary Supplements

Many dietary supplements have been promoted for maintaining or improving cognitive function. Apoaequorin, a calcium-binding protein originally derived from jelly fish, is contained in the widely advertised supplement, Prevagen. Although several animal studies on its safety have been published, human data on its efficacy are limited to published abstracts or studies posted on the company's website (Hume, 2015).

Despite the widespread advertisements for supplements, the Lancet Commission (Livingston et al., 2020) does not recommend additional vitamins, oils, or mixed dietary supplements as a means of preventing dementia because testing in trials lacked beneficial effects. However, in the 90+ study, a population-based longitudinal study, supplemental vitamin C intake around age 90 reduced risk of dementia in the oldest-old (Paganini-Hill et al., 2016).

18.6 Nutrition in the Prevention of Cognitive Decline

Because several risk factors are related to what we eat, we have included detailed information regarding research on nutrition. RCTs are somewhat limited in regard to neuroprotection. For many years, chronic disease prevention consisted of reducing intake of certain dietary components, such as saturated fat and sodium. The current major focus is on overall eating patterns and intake of bioactive compounds. Increasingly, research is demonstrating that the microbiome—the massive ecosystem of bacteria, viruses, and fungi that live in our intestinal tract and can be weakened or strengthened by the quality of our diets (and other lifestyle factors)—may have a role to play in modulating neural, immune/inflammatory, endocrine, and metabolic pathways that affect our aging brains across the lifespan. Plant-based, Mediterranean-like diets have been shown to be most beneficial to the health of our microbiota (Izaskun et al., 2018).

Some evidence suggests that individual food bioactive components protect cognitive health, including vitamins B and D, anti-oxidant vitamins, medium chain triglycerides, and long chain omega-3 fatty acids sourced from oily fish (Jennings et al., 2020). However, risks for stroke and cardiovascular disease have been the primary targets for preventing cognitive impairment (Gorelick et al., 2017), and cardioprotective diets have been extensively investigated (Appel et al., 1997; Harsha et al., 1999; Ornish, 1998; Saneei et al., 2014; Shah et al., 2017; Wright et al., 2017).

Hypertension is recognized as a modifiable risk factor for dementia (Livingston et al., 2020; Yu et al., 2020). The Dietary Approaches to Stop Hypertension (DASH) diet, formulated in the 1990s, remain a cornerstone of treatment for high blood pressure and has resulted in beneficial effects in many RCTs (Appel et al., 1997; Harsha et al., 1999).

Plant foods (e.g., vegetables, fruits, whole grains, legumes) form the foundation of all the heart healthy plans as well as fresh, whole, unprocessed foods, i.e., foods in a form as close to the original as possible.

In our experience, the general public has limited understanding as to what processed food entails, so we suggest explaining it to patients. Physical processing can be simply washing, peeling, heating, or chilling or more complex, such as milling or fermentation of grains. Some definitions refer to the number of additives that can maintain or improve food safety, freshness, taste, texture or appearance. Ultra-processed food (UPF) tends to be high in calories but generally contributes little fiber and few nutrients. While minimally processed foods are easily recognized, three classification systems rate the degree of processing in foods (Bleiweiss-Sande et al., 2019). Examples from the University of North Carolina (UNC) system give the following examples of highly processed, multi-ingredient, industrially formed mixtures that are no longer recognizable in their plant/animal source: soda, fruit drinks, lunch meat, breads made with refined flour, pastries, ice cream, processed cheese, and candy. Consuming less of these is recommended in all of the brain-heart healthy diets described below.

The role of animal products and added fats is what varies most in the recommendations of the plans. Herbs and spices are encouraged in many of these diets for flavor and for the bioactive compounds they contain. Turmeric, or Indian saffron, found in Asian curries, some pickles and yellow mustard, is promising in dementia prevention (Desai et al., 2011), but without evidence in RCTs. Curcumin, the active ingredient in turmeric, has anti-inflammatory properties (Aggarwal & Sung, 2009).

The Mediterranean diet, recommended by the World Health Organization to reduce risk of cognitive decline and described in *The Blue Zones* (Buettner, 2015), is not truly a single diet but a plant-based eating pattern, incorporating vegetables, fruits, whole grains, nuts, and oils, especially olive oil. Lifestyle habits other than diet, such as social networks, daily rituals, sense of purpose, are discussed in *The Blue* Zones and also in the low-fat Ornish plan (1998), Ornish & Ornish (2019).

The programs devised by Ornish (1998) and Esselstyn (2007) differ notably from Mediterranean-type diets in that fat, even from plant sources, is severely restricted. While RCTs are more limited, retrospective and OPS have consistently shown plant-based diets to be associated with lower risk of cognitive decline, dementia, the pathology of Alzheimer's syndrome, as well as cardiovascular disease and diabetes.

The Dash Diet, studied in RCTs to lower blood pressure, includes lean meats, poultry, fish, and eggs and allows olive and other vegetable oils (Saneei et al., 2014). The MIND Diet which combines aspects of the DASH and Mediterranean diet specifies minimum servings of green leafy vegetables (6 plus/week), berries (twice/week), nuts (5times/week), whole grains (3/day), fish (once/week), beans (4 times/week), and poultry (at least twice/week). Butter and margarine, cheese, red meat, fried foods, and sweets are limited. In a prospective study of over 900 participants over 4.5 years, moderate adherence to the MIND diet decreased AD risk (Morris et al., 2015).

In a small RCT over a six-month period, the Nordic diet improved lipid profiles and had a beneficial effect on low-grade inflammation (Uusitupa et al., 2013). This diet features beans, peas, roots, and tubers (carrots, parsnips, beets, potatoes). Fish and seafood are eaten often while red meats and animal fats are limited. Followers are encouraged to eat higher-quality meat but less of it. The Finnish Geriatric Intervention Study to Prevent Cognitive Impairment and Disability (FINGER), a 2-year long, multi-domain RCT, used "the healthy Nordic diet" similar to the Mediterranean diet (Ngandu et al., 2015).

Very low-fat plans that discourage consuming any oil, Ornish (1990, 1998) and Esselstyn (2007), emphasize eating green leafy vegetables and encourage generous amounts of all vegetables. Esselstyn's plan is vegan, while Ornish allows egg whites and nonfat dairy products. Both include whole grains and protein sources such as tofu, tempeh, beans, and legumes and limited use of nuts and seeds.

In the BROAD study, a small RCT that used a whole food plant-based (WFPB) diet, participants had improved BMI and cholesterol and reduced other risk factors, which were largely maintained at 12 months (Wright et al., 2017). The EVADE CAD trial (Shah et al., 2017), also a WFPB vegan diet, assessed multiple cardiovascular risk factors in patients with coronary artery disease treated with guideline-directed medical therapy. The vegan diet reduced systemic inflammation (measured by high sensitivity C-reactive protein).

An eight-year longitudinal study of over 22,000 people in southern Italy, age 43–67, indicated that those who ate the most UPF had the highest risk for cardiovascular disease, even among those who adhered to the Mediterranean diet, linking the consumption of junk foods to poor health outcomes (Bonaccio et al., 2020).

The table below lists diets recommended for heart and potentially brain health, the unique features of each diet, including what to avoid.

Major features of diets for heart/brain health

	Meat, fish, and poultry	Dairy	Eggs	Fat	Alcohol	Herbs and spices	Other
Vegetables, fruits, and whole grains are the foundation of all diets listed							
Mediterranean—type: 25–35% of calories from fat							
Mediterranean				Olive oil	Red wine		
DASH	Lean meats, poultry, and fish; includes eggs	Low fat and nonfat	Allowed	Limit sat fat and tropical oils	Limit	Encouraged	Nut, seeds, legumes 4–5 x/week Limit sugars
MIND	Fish emphasis	Low-fat and nonfat	Allowed	Olive oil	Limit to 1 glass/day	Include liberally	Emphasis on berries and leafy greens
Nordic	Fish emphasis	Low-fat and nonfat	Free range	Rapeseed oil	Limited	Encouraged	Fish readily available in region
Very low fat: supplementation might be required							
Ornish	None	Nonfat milk, yogurt, cheese	Whites	4 g/day; 1 low fat serving of nuts/seeds encouraged	No more than 1 glass of wine, 1 beer or 1 shot of whiskey/day	Low salt; herbs and spices for flavor	Eliminate all added oils and avocados; reduce white flour, white rice. Limit sugar
Esselstyn	None	None	None	No animal fat; no oils	Any kind in moderation	Include liberally	Avocados OK if low lipids

The US Department of Health and Human Services (HHS) and the US Department of Agriculture publish evidence-based food and beverage recommendations to promote health, prevent disease, and help people reach and maintain healthy weight. The *2020–2025 Dietary Guidelines for Americans* that provides advice for people from birth to older adulthood are a valuable resource for primary care (US Dept. of HHS & US Department of Agriculture, 2020).

Primary care providers have opportunities to directly educate patients. A first step is to have early conversations about nutrition to educate about risk factors, including targeted questions such as: How many meals/week (breakfast, lunch, and dinner) do you obtain from restaurants? When you eat at home, do you cook "from scratch" or use prepared meals or packaged products? Are there days when you do not eat any vegetables or fruits?

What are you able and willing to do to begin to eat a healthier diet?

Step 2: Provide a list of hand-outs and electronic resources that include information about healthy eating and foods to avoid, including examples of UPF. If feasible, offer individual or group programs, possibly through tele-health, to support positive, individualized, tailored changes in dietary habits (Rosenberg, Mangialasche, Ngandu, Solomon, & Kivipelto, 2020).

Step 3: Refer patients to a Registered Dietitian/Nutritionist who wants to pursue Medical Nutrition Therapy (MNT) in greater depth for optimal health and especially patients with comorbidities, such as diabetes, obesity, or those with food intolerances or allergies.

18.7 Multi-Modal Interventions

Because of the complex and multi-factorial nature of AD and other dementias, interventions that target multiple risk factors are being studied across the world. The FINGER study is the first large (1200 older adults at-risk for dementia), long-term (2 year) RCT to demonstrate positive results for improved cognition in the group that received multi-domain interventions that included exercise, diet, cognitive training, and management of metabolic and vascular risk factors (www.alzheimersprevention.org; Ngandu et al., 2015).

The FINGER lifestyle intervention is being tested in 25 other countries, including the United States, known as the World Wide FINGERS (WW-FINGERS) initiative launched in 2017 to reduce risk in different geographical, cultural, and economic settings (Kivipelto et al., 2020.) The next generation of multi-domain prevention trials have begun with a trial of 2724 computer-literate, cognitively intact participants over age 65 from Finland, France, and the Netherlands. The intervention group received support to manage cardiovascular risk factors over the Internet from a remote lifestyle coach. Data analyses have not yet been released, but if results are positive, self-management strategies may be feasible to reach a large worldwide population (Rosenberg et al., 2020).

Payment for Prevention and Management of Chronic Conditions
Educating and counseling patients about their diet, stress level, and exercise take time, and administrators of healthcare systems using fee-for-service payment may scoff at the lack of practicality of PCPs or BCPs engaging in these practices unless they can be reimbursed for such services. Once, yearly wellness visits under Medicare plans are hardly adequate from a patient care perspective, but things are changing. In 2011 a paradigm-shift in reimbursement occurred in which Medicare began to pay for 72 h of the Ornish Lifestyle Medicine under Intensive Cardiac Rehabilitation. This program includes supervised exercise by an exercise physiologist, stress management led by a certified yoga/meditation teacher, support groups run by a psychologist or social worker, and 1 h of a group meal and lecture by a dietitian (Ornish & Ornish, 2019).

In 2017 Medicare began payment in PC for chronic care management for patients with two or more chronic conditions, such as diabetes, hypertension, cardiovascular disease, depression, and risk factors for dementia. The coding for these services is beyond the scope of this chapter, but we recommend billing personnel in PC to determine the feasibility of using the chronic care management codes. BCPs can be reimbursed under the health and behavior assessment and intervention codes that are intended to improve the management of patients with medical conditions who do not have psychiatric disorders.

These changes in Medicare payment are a start; however, these sets of billing codes systems under Medicare are largely for managing chronic conditions rather than prevention. Only when prevention services are widely reimbursed or population-based approaches to integrated healthcare become common-place will prevention services become the norm in PC.

18.8 Cutting Edge of Dementia Prevention

Since the early 1970s, the neuroscientific evidence for the cognitive, emotional, and health-related benefits of meditative practices has increased exponentially from a handful of studies to over 6800 in the last few years (Goleman & Davidson, 2017). Kaszniak (2011) described a promising study of mindfulness-based stress reduction (MBSR) to improve well-being and attention task performance among caregivers of persons with dementia.

Small scale studies sponsored through the Alzheimer's Research and Prevention Foundation (ARPF) suggests that a yoga meditative practice known as Kirtan Kriya (KK) done 12 min a day is an important component of a lifestyle program for stress reduction to prevent AD along with following a plant-based diet and engaging in regular physical and mental exercise (Khalsa, 2014; Wirth et al., 2014). However, no large-scale RCTs were found to date using this meditative practice comparing it to other stress reduction techniques. In 2020 Ornish and his colleagues at the Preventive Medicine Research Institute began the first RCT to determine if the progression of early-stage AD may be slowed, stopped, or reversed. The components are a plant-based diet, moderate exercise, psychosocial support, and meditation.

The fourth pillar promoted by the ARPF, largely absent from RCTs, promotes personal growth, improvement of relationships, and finding purpose in life, similar elements included in Dean Ornish's plan for managing chronic illness (Ornish & Ornish, 2019).

18.9 Lessons Learned/Implementation

With patients who have concerns about their memory, we hope the days are over of doing nothing more than watchful waiting or reflexively prescribing drugs like donepezil, without suggesting sustainable lifestyle changes. We suggest that patients' fears about age-related memory loss are acknowledged with reassurance that there are steps that can, in many circumstances, delay or prevent further decline, even in individuals at high risk due to their genetics.

- Given a patient's age and individual risk factors, a one-size-fits-all preventive approach is not reasonable nor likely to be effective. We recommend designing a plan, with the patient's input, that reduces the individual's risk profile, beginning with two or three lifestyle changes the patient is open to trying.
- There is also no one-size-fits-all recommendation for exercising cognitive skills. A challenge that is new and stretches one's skills is good, but if the activity is too hard, people may become discouraged and stop. Engaging in fun and meaningful activities is sustainable.
- Aerobic exercise, stretching, and strength training are associated not only with cardiac and cognitive fitness but also improvement in mood (Schuch et al. 2016; Sharma et al., 2006). We recommend starting with easy, realistic goals, that take into account the patient's overall conditioning, the environment where the person lives, and readiness to change habits. A first step for sedentary patients is to increase movement in daily life, such as walking out of doors for 10–15 min a day preferably with a friend, human, or canine; using the stairs, if feasible; or using in-home exercise equipment or doing chair exercises in front of a window with a nature view for its innately calming effects (Jo et al., 2019).
- To begin improvement in nutrition, encourage eating more whole foods, less sugary and ultra-processed foods, more whole grain cereal, bread, and pasta, and reducing or eliminating red meat. Suggest incorporating fruits and vegetables at every meal (even at breakfast), such as mushrooms and spinach in an omelet of egg whites, sprinkling berries, nuts/seeds in cereal, salads, side dishes, and even desserts plus having extra vegetables as a main course. Give e-resources to the patient about healthy recipes that fit the culture and region.
- Lifestyle changes are challenging; we recommend offering group sessions, conducted virtually or in-person to reinforce and support dementia prevention strategies.

Closing Remarks

This chapter focused on the growing evidence that dementia can be delayed through modification in lifestyle, but there are limits to what following the recommendations can do. Just as the body of the most fit athlete eventually wears down with age, so does the brain. Unfortunately, dementia is often viewed as a defeat. Alzheimer's disease is feared in American society for many reasons including the stigmatizing stereotypes of loss of personhood, being shunned by others, the misconception that new learning of any kind is impossible, and the notion that the person living with dementia lacks total usefulness to his/her family and society.

A contrasting perspective is to view living with memory loss as a life stage characterized by staying in the moment, appreciating small joys, and having unexpected opportunities for increased closeness with family members. Just as in palliative care, the goal of treatment for the person with memory loss is to enhance quality and meaning to life.

The use of Montessori methods of learning and techniques such as spaced retrieval with people living with memory loss has shown that learning is possible and procedural memory skills such as piano playing, singing, reading and dancing remain intact in moderate to late stages of dementia (Camp et al., 2011; www.youtube.com/watch?v=wlAXKJfesBM). We challenge the notion that loss of personhood is inevitable with dementia. When caring for people living with dementia, a full emotional life can exist even if language is lost. Individuals with dementia may hold emotional memories of past relationships without the ability to identify them (Duffy, 1999).

Most, if not all of the strategies to promote brain health, can also be used by those living with dementia as well as with their caregivers to maximize their physical and emotional wellbeing. The goals of medical treatment are usually in the province of medication or surgery to cure or reduce symptoms. When dementia is diagnosed with no medications or surgical procedures for cure, "care" is what is left, as though the patient is actively dying rather than living on average eight to 20 more years. PCPs and BCPs can do a service to families and their patients with memory loss by emphasizing that behavioral interventions that improve quality of life are modalities of treatment, as potent as any drug, if not more so.

18.9.1 Examples of Biblio-Prevention

Anderson, N.D., Murphy, K. J., & Troyer, A.K. (2012). *Living with mild cognitive impairment*. New York: Oxford University Press.

Buettner, D. (2015). *The Blue Zones Solution: Eating and living like the world's healthiest people.* Washington DC: The National Geographic Society.

Fogler, J. & Stern, L. (2005). *Improving your memory: How to remember what you're starting to forget.* Baltimore: Johns Hopkins University Press.

Moon, Maggie. (2016). *The Mind Diet: A Scientific Approach to Enhancing Brain Function and Helping Prevent Alzheimer's and Dementia.* Berkeley: Ulysses Press.

Mosconi, L. (2020). *The XX Brain: The groundbreaking science empowering women to maximize cognitive health and prevent Alzheimer's disease.* New York: Penguin Random House.

National Institutes of Health & National Institute on Aging (2017). *Preventing. Alzheimer's disease: What do we know?* Damascus, Maryland: Penny Hill Press.

Nussbaum, P. (2010). *Save your brain: The 5 things you must do to keep your mind young and sharp.* New York: McGraw Hill.

Ornish, D. & Ornish, A. (2019). *UnDo It! How simple lifestyle changes can reverse most chronic diseases.* New York: Penguin Random House.

18.9.2 Examples of Biblio-Therapy for Caregivers

Camp, Cameron J. (2012). *Hiding the stranger in the mirror.* Solon, Ohio: Center for Applied Research in Dementia.

Joltin, A., Camp, C. J., Noble, B. H., Antenucci, V. M. (2012). *A different visit: Activities for caregivers and their loved ones with memory impairments.* Solon, Ohio: Center for Applied Research in dementia.

Mace, N. & Rabins, P. *The 36-Hour day, sixth edition: A Family Guide to caring for people who have Alzheimer Disease, other dementias, and Memory Loss.* Baltimore: Johns Hopkins Press Health Book.

Silverstone, B. & Hyman, H.K. (2008). *You & your aging parent.* New York: Oxford University Press.

Zeisel, J. (2009). *I'm still here: A breakthrough approach to understanding someone living with Alzheimer's.* New York: Penguin Group.

18.9.3 E-Health Prevention Tools

Mobile Apps

Alzheimer's Association-Alzheimer's Disease Pocketcard web version and Clinician Pocketcard app. A quick reference guide for clinicians.

Brain Performance Challenge, free mobile app developed by the Brain Performance Institute, University of Texas. Provides cognitive challenging exercises & tracking of progress.

Ted talk: Genova, L (TED talk, April 28, 2017). *What you can do to prevent Alzheimer's?*

Websites

http://alzheimersprevention.org provides info on "Four pillars" of dementia prevention including information on Kirtan Kriya meditation for cognitive health.

https://www.alz.org/help-support/brain_health/10_ways_to_love_your_brain developed by Alzheimer's Association.

http://brainwellness.com provides recipes and information on brain healthy nutrition by Nancy B. Emerson Lombardo, Ph.D.

http://www.cdc.gov/aging/publications/features/dementia-not-normal-aging.html info on the difference between normal, healthy aging and dementia.

https://www.cen4ard.com caregiver activities & training for health professionals by applied gerontologist, Cameron J. Camp, Ph.D.

https://www.centerforhealthyaging.com mental health and aging tips & resources for health professionals and older adults by geropsychologist, Paula Hartman-Stein, Ph.D.

http://www.dietaryguidelines.gov. Dietary Guidelines for Americans_2020–2025.

https://www.drreginakoepp.com/podcast on mental health and aging info by geropsychologist, Regina Koepp, PhD.

https://www.geron.org/programs-services/brain-health-cognitive-impairment-and-dementia developed by Gerontological Society of America (Fall 2020)

https://healthybrains.org/pillars info on foundations of brain health from the Cleveland Clinic.

www.Livingto100.Club weekly radio interviews, blogs and information on aging, including dementia prevention with geropsychologist, Joe Casciani, Ph.D.

www.ornish.com strategies on nutrition, stress management, physical fitness, and ways to feel emotionally supported by cardiologist and lifestyle medicine physician, Dean Ornish, M.D.

https://www.rebeccakatz.com recipes, blogs, videos on healthy nutrition from author of *The Longevity Kitchen.*

https://teepasnow.com caregiver information and programs by Alzheimer educator and occupational therapist, Teepa Snow.

https://www.youtube.com/channel/UCVgK5-w1dilMx7bPVB5yNug weekly dementia tips, strategies, and support by geropsychologist, Natali Edmonds, PhD.

Conflicts of Interest The authors declare they have no conflicts of interest.

References

Aggarwal, B. B., & Sung, B. (2009). Pharmacological basis for the role of curcumin in chronic diseases: An age-old spice with modern targets. *Trends in Pharmacological Science, 30*, 85–94.

Albert, M. S., DeKosky, S. T., Dickson, D., Dubois, B., Feldman, H. H., Fox, N. C., Gamst, A., Holtzman, D. M., Jagust, W. J., Petersen, R. C., Snyder, P. J., Carrillo, M. C., Thies, B., & Phelps, D. H. (2011). The diagnosis of mild cognitive impairment due to Alzheimer's disease:

Recommendations from the National Institute on Aging-Alzheimer's Association workgroups on diagnostic guidelines for Alzheimer's disease. *Alzheimer's Dementia, 7*(3), 270–279.

Alzheimer's Association. (2020a). Alzheimer's disease facts and figures. *Alzheimers Dementia, 16*(3), 391–460.

Alzheimer's Association. (2020b March). On the front lines: Primary care physicians and Alzheimer's care in America. *Alzheimer's & Dementia: The Journal of the Alzheimer's Association, 16*, 64–71.

Alzheimers.net. https://www.alzheimers.net

Alzheimersprevention.org. *A multidomain two-year randomized controlled trial to prevent cognitive impairment-the FINGER study*. Special Report of the Alzheimer's Research and Prevention Foundation.

Appel, L., Moore, T. J., Obarzanek, E., Vollmer, W., Svetkey, L. P., Sacks, F., et al. (1997). A clinical trial of the effects of dietary patterns on blood pressure. *New England Journal of Medicine, 336*, 1117–1124. https://doi.org/10.1056/NEJM199704173361601

Barve, S., Chen, S. Y., Kirpich, I., Watson, W. H., & Mcclain, C. (2017). Development, prevention, and treatment of alcohol-induced organ injury: The role of nutrition. *Alcohol Research: Current Reviews, 38*(2), 289–302.

Bleiweiss-Sande, R., Chui, K., Evans, E. W., Goldberg, J., Amin, S., & Sacheck, J. (2019). Robustness of food processing classification systems. *Nutrients, 11*(6), 1344. https://doi.org/10.3390/nu11061344

Bonaccio, M., Di Castelnuovo, A., Costanzo, S., De Curtis, A., Persichillo, M., Sofi, F., Cerletti, C., Donati, M. B., de Gaetano, G., & Iacoviello, L. (2020). Ultra-processed food consumption is associated with increased risk of all-cause and cardiovascular mortality in the Moli-sani Study. *The American Journal of Clinical Nutrition, 113*(2), nqaa299. https://doi.org/10.1093/ajcn/nqaa299

Buettner, D. (2015). *The blue zones solution: Eating and living like the world's healthiest people*. The National Geographic Society.

Camp, C., Zeisel, J., & Antenucci, V. (2011). Implementing the "I'm Still Here" ™ approach: Montessori-based methods for engaging persons with dementia. In P. E. Hartman-Stein & A. LaRue (Eds.), *Enhancing cognitive fitness in adults*. Springer.

Campbell, N. L., Lane, K. A., Gao, S., Boustani, M. A., & Unverzagt, F. (2018, May). Anticholinergics influence transition from normal cognition to mild cognitive impairment in older adults in primary care. *Pharmacotherapy, 38*(5), 511–519. https://doi.org/10.1002/phar.2106

De Erausquin, G. A., Snyder, H., Carrillo, M., Hosseini, A. A., Traolach, T. S., Seshadri, S., & CNS Sars-CoV-2 Consortium. (2021). The chronic neuropsychiatric sequelae of COVID-19: The need for a prospective study of viral impact on brain functioning. *Alzheimer's & Dementia*. https://doi.org/10.1002/alz.12255

Desai, A. K., Rush, J., Naveem, L., & Thaipisuttikul, P. (2011). Nutrition and nutritional supplements to promote brain health. In P. E. Hartman-Stein & A. LaRue (Eds.), *Enhancing cognitive fitness in adults*. Springer.

Duffy, M. (1999). Reaching the person behind the dementia. In M. Duffy (Ed.), *Handbook of counseling and psychotherapy with older adults*. Wiley.

Egan, M. F., Kost, J., Tariot, P. N., Aisen, P. S., Cummings, J. L., Vellas, B., et al. (2018). Randomized trial of verubecestat for mild-to-moderate Alzheimer's disease. *The New England Journal of Medicine, 378*, 1691–1703. https://doi.org/10.1056/NEJMoa1706441

Esselstyn, C. B. (2007). *Prevent and reverse heart disease*. Penguin Group.

Folstein, M. F., Folstein, S. E., & McHugh, P. R. (1975). Mini mental state: A practical method for grading the cognitive state of patients for the clinician. *Journal of Psychiatric Research, 12*(3), 189–198.

Fultz, N. E., Bonmassar, G., Setsompop, K., Stickgold, R. A., Rosen, B. R., Polimeni, J. R., & Lewis, L. D. (2019). Coupled electrophysiological, hemodynamic, and cerebrospinal fluid oscillations in human sleep. *Science, 366*(6465), 628–631. https://doi.org/10.1126/science.aax5440

Galvin, J. E., Tolea, M. I., & Chrisphonte, S. (2020). What older adults do with the results of dementia screening programs. *PLoS One, 15*(7), e0235534. https://doi.org/10.1371/journal.pone.0235534

Ganguli, M., Dodge, H. H., Shen, C., & DeKosky, S. T. (2004, July 13). Mild cognitive impairment, amnestic type: An epidemiologic study. *Neurology, 63*(1), 115–121. https://doi.org/10.1212/01.wnl.0000132523.27540.81. PMID: 15249620.

Gao, S., Burney, H. N., Callahan, C. M., Purnell, C. E., & Hendrie, H. C. (2019). Incidence of dementia and Alzheimer disease over time: A meta-analysis. *Journal of the American Geriatrics Society, 67*(7), 1361–1369.

George, D. R., & Whitehouse, P. J. (2021). *American dementia: Brain health in an unhealthy society*. Johns Hopkins Press.

Gerontological Society of America. (2012). *Communicating with older adults: An evidence-based review of what really works.* https://secure.geron.org/cvweb/cgi-bin/msascartdll.dll/ProductInfo?productcd=1947_Comm-Adults

Gerontological Society of America. (2020, Fall). *The GSA KAER toolkit for primary care teams: Supporting conversations about brain health, timely detection of cognitive impairment, and accurate diagnosis of dementia.* https://www.geron.org/programs-services/brain-health-cognitive-impairment-and-dementia

Global Council on Brain Health. (2016). *The brain-body connection: GCBH recommendations on physical activity and brain health.* A collaborative from AARP.

Goleman, D., & Davidson, R. J. (2017). *Altered traits: Science reveals how meditation changes your mind, brain and body*. Penguin Random House.

Gorelick, P. B., Furie, K. L., Iadecola, C., Smith, E. E., Waddy, S. P., Lloyd-Jones, D. M., et al. (2017). Defining optimal brain health in adults: A presidential advisory from the American Heart Association/American Stroke Association. *Stroke, 48*, e284–e303. https://doi.org/10.1161/STR.0000000000000148

Gorelick, P. B., Scuteri, A., Black, S. E., DeCarli, D., Greenberg, S. M., Iadecola, C., et al. (2011). Vascular contributions to cognitive impairment and dementia. *Stroke, 42*, 2672–2713. https://doi.org/10.1161/STR.0b013e3182299496

Harsha, D. W., Lin, P. H., Obarzanek, E., Karanja, N., Moore, T. J., & Caballero, B. (1999). Dietary approaches to stop hypertension: Summary of study results. *Journal of the American Dietetic Association, 99*(8, Supp), 35–39.

Hartman-Stein, P. (2017, March 22). Drug tests add doubt to amyloid theory on Alzheimer's disease. *The National Psychologist*. https://nationalpsychologist.com/2017/03/drug-tests-add-doubt-to-amyloid-theory-on-alzheimers-disease/103655.html

Hartman-Stein, P., & LaRue, A. (Eds.). (2011). *Enhancing cognitive fitness in adults: A guide to the use and development of community-based programs*. Springer.

Holt-Lunstad, J. (2017). The potential public health relevance of social isolation and loneliness: Prevalence, epidemiology, and risk factors. *Public Policy and Aging Report, 27*(4), 127–130. https://doi.org/10.1093/ppar/prx030

Hume, A. L. (2015, September 1). Apoaequorin for memory enhancement? *Integrative Medicine, 21*(9), 38.

Izaskun, G.-M., Selma-Royo, M., Alcantara, C., & Collado, M. C. (2018). Shifts on gut microbiota associated to Mediterranean diet adherence and specific dietary intakes on general adult population. *Frontiers in Microbiology, 9*, 890.

Jennings, A., Cunnane, S. C., & Minihane, A. M. (2020). Can nutrition support healthy cognitive ageing and reduce dementia risk? *BMJ, 369*, m2269. https://doi.org/10.1136/bmj.m2269

Jo, H., Song, C., & Miyazaki, Y. (2019). Physiological benefits of viewing nature: A systematic review of indoor experiments. *International Journal of Environmental Research and Public Health, 16*(23), 4739. https://doi.org/10.3390/ijerph16234739

Kaszniak, A. W. (2011). Meditation, mindfulness, cognition, and emotion: Implications for community-based older adult programs. In P. E. Hartman-Stein & A. LaRue (Eds.), *Enhancing cognitive fitness in adults*. Springer.

Katzman, R., Terry, R., DeTeresa, R., et al. (1988). Clinical, pathological, and neurochemical changes in dementia: A subgroup with preserved mental status and numerous neocortical plaques. *Annals of Neurology, 23*, 138–144.

Kawas, C. H., Kim, R. C., Sonnen, J. A., Bullain, S. S., Trieu, T., & Corrado, M. M. (2015). Multiple pathologies are common and related to dementia in the oldest-old. *Neurology, 85*(6), 535–542.

Khalsa, D. S. (2014-2015). A white paper: Yoga and medical meditation™ as Alzheimer's prevention medicine. In *Work of the Alzheimer's Research and Prevention Foundation*. Alzheimer's Research and Prevention Foundation.

Kivipelto, M., Mangialasche, F., Snyder, H. M., Allegri, R., Andrieu, S., Arai, H., et al. (2020). World-Wide FINGERS Network: A global approach to risk reduction and prevention of dementia. *Alzheimer's & Dementia, 16*, 1078–1094. https://doi.org/10.1002/alz.12123

Langa, K. M., Larson, E. B., & Crimmins, E. (2017). A comparison of the prevalence of dementia in the United States in 2000 and 2012. *JAMA Internal Medicine, 177*(2017), 51–58.

Livingston, G., Huntley, J., Sommerlad, A., Ames, D., Ballard, C., Banerjee, S., Brayne, C., Burns, A., Cohen-Mansfield, J., Cooper, C., Costafreda, S. G., Dias, A., Fox, N., Gitlin, L. N., Howard, R., Kales, H. C., Kivimäki, M., Larson, E. B., Ogunniyi, A., … Mukadam, N. (2020). Dementia prevention, intervention, and care: 2020 report of the lancet commission. *Lancet, 396*(10248), 413–446. https://doi.org/10.1016/50140-6736(20)30367-6

Livingston, G., Sommerlad, A., Orgeta, V., Costafreda, S. G., Huntley, J., Ames, D., Ballard, C., Banerjee, S., Burns, A., Cohen-Mansfield, J., Cooper, C., Fox, N., Gitlin, L. N., Howard, R., Kales, H. C., Larson, E. B., Ritchie, K., Rockwood, K., Sampson, E. L., et al. (2017). Dementia prevention, intervention, and care. *Lancet, 390*(10113), 2673–2734. https://doi.org/10.1016/S0140-6736(17)31363-6

McKhann, G. M., Knopman, D. S., Chertkow, H., Hyman, B. T., Jack, C. R., Jr., Kawas, C. H., Klunk, W. E., Koroshetz, W. J., Manly, J. J., Mayeux, R., Mohs, R. C., Morris, J. C., Rossor, M. N., Scheltens, P., Carrillo, M. C., Thies, B., Weintraub, S., & Phelps, C. H. (2011). The diagnosis of dementia due to Alzheimer's disease: Recommendations from the National Institute on Aging-Alzheimer's Association workgroups on diagnostic guidelines for Alzheimer's disease. *Alzheimer's & Dementia: The Journal of the Alzheimer's Association, 7*(3), 263–269. https://doi.org/10.1016/j.jalz.2011.03.005

Morris, M., Tangney, C. C., Wang, V., Sacks, F., Bennett, D., & Aggarwal, N. T. (2015). MIND diet slows cognitive decline of aging. *Alzheimer's & Dementia, 11*(9), 1015–1022. https://doi.org/10.1016/j.jalz.2014.11.009

National Center for Chronic Disease Prevention and Health Promotion. (2012). *Self-reported increased confusion or memory loss (ICML) and discussions with health care providers among adults aged 45 years or older*. cdc.gov/aging/pdf/2012-brfss-state-summary

Ngandu, T., Lehtisalo, J., Solomon, A., Levalahti, E., Ahtiluoto, S., Antikainem, R., et al. (2015). A 2-year multi-domain intervention of diet, exercise, cognitive training, and vascular risk monitoring versus control to prevent cognitive decline in at-risk elderly people (FINGER): A randomized controlled trial. *The Lancet, 385*(9984), 2255–2263. https://doi.org/10.1016/S0140-6736(15)60461-5

Ornish, D. (1990). *Dean Ornish's program for reversing heart disease*. Ballantine Books.

Ornish, D. (1998). Avoiding revascularization with lifestyle changes: The Multicenter lifestyle demonstration project. *American Journal of Cardiology, 82*, 72t–76t.

Ornish, D., & Ornish, A. (2019). *UnDo it! How simple lifestyle changes can reverse most chronic diseases*. Penguin Random House.

Paganini-Hill, A., Kawas, C. H., & Corrada, M. M. (2016). Lifestyle factors and dementia in the oldest-old: The 90+ study. *Alzheimer Disease & Associated Disorders, 30*(1), 21–26.

Pandya, S. Y., Lacritz, L. H., Weiner, M. F., Deschner, M., & Woon, F. L. (2017). Predictors of reversion from mild cognitive impairment to normal cognition. *Dementia and Geriatric Cognitive Disorders, 43*(3–4), 204–214. https://doi.org/10.1159/000456070. Epub 2017 Mar 17. PMID: 28301848; PMCID: PMC5495561.

Quiroz, Y. T., Sperling, R. A., Norton, D. J., Baena, A., Arboleda-Velasquez, J. F., Cosio, D., Schultz, A., Lapoint, M., Guzman-Velez, E., Miller, J. B., Kim, L. A., Chen, K., Tariot, P. N., Lopera, F., Reiman, E. M., & Kim, L. A. (2018). Association between amyloid and tau accumulation in young adults with autosomal dominant Alzheimer disease. *JAMA Neurology, 75*(5), 548–556.

Richards, D. A., Ekers, D., McMillan, D., Taylor, R. S., Byford, S., Warren, F. C., Barrett, B., Farrand, P. A., Gilbody, S., Kuyken, W., O'Mahen, H., Watkins, E. R., Wright, K. A., Hollon, S. D., Reed, N., Rhodes, S., Fletcher, E., & Finning, K. (2016). Cost and outcome of behavioural activation versus cognitive behavioural therapy for depression (COBRA): A randomised, controlled, non-inferiority trial. *Lancet, 388*(10047), 871–880. https://doi.org/10.1016/S0140-6736(16)31140-0

Rosenberg, A., Mangialasche, F., Ngandu, T., Solomon, A., & Kivipelto, M. (2020). Multidomain interventions to prevent cognitive impairment, Alzheimer's disease, and dementia: From FINGER to World-Wide FINGERS. *The Journal of Prevention of Alzheimer's Disease, 1*(7), 29–36. Published online October 10, 2019. https://doi.org/10.14283/jpad.2019.4

Rovner, B. W., Casten, R. J., Hegel, M. T., & Leiby, B. (2018). Preventing cognitive decline in Black individuals with mild cognitive impairment: A randomized clinical trial. *JAMA Neurology, 75*(12), 1487–1493. https://doi.org/10.1001/jamaneurol.2018.2513

Saneei, P., Salehi-Abargouei, A., Esmaillzadeh, A., & Azadbakht, L. (2014). Influence of dietary approaches to stop hypertension (DASH) diet on blood pressure: A systematic review and meta-analysis on randomized controlled trials. *Nutrition, Metabolism, and Cardiovascular Diseases, 24*(12), 1253–1261.

Schuch, F. B., Vancampfort, D., Richards, J., Rosenbaum, S., Ward, P. B., & Stubbs, B. (2016). Exercise as a treatment for depression: A meta-analysis adjusting for publication bias. *Journal of Psychiatric Research, 77*, 42–51. https://doi.org/10.1016/j.jpsychires.2016.02.023. Epub 2016 Mar 4. PMID: 26978184.

Selkoe, D. J., & Hardy, J. (2016, June 1). The amyloid hypothesis of Alzheimer's disease at 25 years. *EMBO Molecular Medition, 8*(6), 595–608. https://doi.org/10.15252/emmm.201606210. PMID: 27025652; PMCID: PMC4888851.

Shah, B., Newman, J., Woolf, K., Ganguzza, L., Guo, Y., Fisher, E., et al. (2017). Anti-inflammatory effect of whole-food plant-based vegan diet vs the American Heart Association – Recommended diet in patients with coronary artery disease: The randomized EVADE CAD Trial. *Circulation, 136*(Suppl_1), e011367.

Sharma, A., Madaan, V., & Petty, F. D. (2006). Exercise for mental health. *Primary Care Companion to the Journal of Clinical Psychiatry, 8*(2), 106. https://doi.org/10.4088/pcc.v08n0208a

Snowdon, D. (2003). Healthy aging and dementia: Findings from the Nun Study. *Annals of Internal Medicine, 139*(5 Pt 2), 450–454. https://doi.org/10.7326/0003-4819-139-5_part_2-200309021-00014

Solomon, A., Turunen, H., Ngandu, T., et al. (2018). Effect of the apolipoprotein E genotype on cognitive change during a multidomain lifestyle intervention: A subgroup analysis of a randomized clinical trial. *JAMA Neurology, 75*(4), 462–470.

US Department of Agriculture and US Department of Health and Human Services. (2020, December). *Dietary Guidelines for Americans, 2020–2025* (9th ed.). Wolters Kluwer.

US Preventive Services Task Force. (2020). Screening for cognitive impairment in older adults: US Preventive Services Task Force recommendation statement. *Journal of the American Medical Association, 323*(8), 757–763. https://doi.org/10.1001/jama.2020.0435

Uusitupa, M., Hermansen, K., Savolainen, M. J., Schwab, U., Brader, L., Mortensen, L. S., et al. (2013). Effects of an isocaloric healthy Nordi diet on insulin sensitivity, lipid profile and inflammation markers in metabolic syndrome-a randomized study (SYSDIET). *Journal of Internal Medicine, 274*(1), 52–66. https://doi.org/10.1111/joim.12044

Whitehouse, P., & George, D. (2008). *The myth of Alzheimer's: What you aren't being told about today's most dreaded diagnosis*. St. Martin's Press.

Wilson, S., Yu, L., Trojanowski, J. Q., et al. (2013 November 1). TDP-43 Pathology, cognitive decline, and dementia in old age. *JAMA Neurology, 70*(11), 1418–1424. https://doi.org/10.1001/jamaneurol.2013.3961doi:10.1001/jamaneurol.2013.3961

Winblad, B., Amouyel, P., Andrieu, S., Ballard, C., Brayne, C., Brodaty, H., et al. (2016). Defeating Alzheimer's disease and other dementias: A priority for European science and society. *Lancet Neurology, 15*, 455–532.

Wirth, M., Haase, C. M., Villeneuve, S., Vogel, J., & Jagust, W. J. (2014, August). Neuroprotective pathways: Lifestyle activity, brain pathology, and cognition in cognitively normal older adults. *Neurobiol Aging, 35*(8), 1873–1882. https://doi.org/10.1016/j.neurobiolaging.2014.02.015. Epub 2014 Feb 20. PMID: 24656834; PMCID: PMC4019766..

Wolters, F. J., Chibnik, L. B., Waziry, R., Anderson, R., Berr, C., Beiser, A., Bis, J. C., et al. (2020). Twenty-seven-year time trends in dementia incidence in Europe and the United States: The Alzheimer Cohorts Consortium. *Neurology, 95*(5), e519–e531.

Wright, N., Wilson, L., Smith, M., Duncan, B., & McHugh, P. (2017, March). The BROAD study: A randomised controlled trial using a whole food plant-based diet in the community for obesity, ischaemic heart disease or diabetes. *Nutrition & Diabetes, 7*(3), e256. https://doi.org/10.1038/nutd.2017.3

Wu, Y.-T., Beiser, A. S., Breteler, M. B., Fratiglioni, L., Helmer, C., Hendrie, H. C., et al. (2017). The changing prevalence and incidence of dementia over time—Current evidence. *Nature Reviews Neurology, 13*(6), 327.

Xu, W., Tan, C.-C., Zou, J.-J., Cao, X.-P., & Tan, L. (2020). Sleep problems and risk of all-cause cognitive decline or dementia: An updated systematic review and meta-analysis. *Journal of Neurology, Neurosurgery, and Psychiatry, 91*, 236–244.

Yamada, M., Komatsu, J., Nakamura, K., Sakai, K., Samuraki-Yokohama, M., Nakajima, K., & Yoshita, M. (2020, January). Diagnostic criteria for dementia with Lewy bodies: Updates and future directions. *Journal of Movement Disorders., 13*(1), 1–10. https://doi.org/10.14802/jmd.19052. Epub 2019 Nov 8. PMID: 31694357; PMCID: PMC6987529..

Yu, J., Xu, W., Tan, C., Andrieu, S., Suckling, J., Evangelou, E., & Vellas, B. (2020). Evidence-based prevention of Alzheimer's disease: Systematic review and meta-analysis of 243 observational prospective studies and 153 randomised controlled trials. *Journal of Neurology, Neurosurgery & Psychiatry, 9*, 1–9. https://doi.org/10.1136/jnnp-2019-321913

Zitser, J., Anaturk, M., Zsoldos, E., Mahmood, A., Filippini, N., Suri, S., Leng, Y., Yaffe, K., Singh-Manoux, A., Kivimaki, M., Ebmeier, K., & Sexton, C. (2020). Sleep duration over 28 years, cognition, gray matter volume, and white matter microstructure: A prospective cohort study. *Sleep*. https://doi.org/10.1093/sleep/zsz290

Chapter 19
Health Literacy

Catalina Vechiu and Andrea I. Mosqueda

19.1 Definition

Health literacy is a crucial component for population-based health promotion and disease prevention initiatives. Although it is widely acknowledged that health literacy skills are necessary for individuals to navigate health contexts, there is little consensus about the definition of health literacy. Some definitions emphasize individual capacity to acquire and use new information that is impacted by both innate potential and an individual's sociocultural context, while others emphasize healthcare knowledge and the dynamic nature of the healthcare context as impacting an individual's health literacy skills (Baker, 2006). Health literacy then has historically been defined as, "the degree to which individuals have the capacity to obtain, process, and understand basic health information and services needed to make appropriate decisions" (Ratzan & Parker, 2000, p. ix). This definition emphasizes:

1. *Individual capacity*: includes reading fluency, vocabulary, and listening and speaking skills. Reading fluency refers to an individual's ability to read, write, and understand written information, ability to locate and use information in documents, and numeracy (e.g., ability to understand probabilities and percentages and apply arithmetic operations) (Baker, 2006). Vocabulary includes characteristics of individuals (familiarity with the health concepts presented) and the larger healthcare system (complexity of the language or jargon utilized to communicate health concepts). Listening and effective communication skills are neces-

C. Vechiu (✉)
Edward Hines Jr. VA Hospital, Hines, IL, USA
e-mail: catalina.vechiu@va.gov

A. I. Mosqueda
Jesse Brown VA Medical Centre, Chicago, IL, USA

W. O'Donohue, M. Zimmermann (eds.), *Handbook of Evidence-Based Prevention of Behavioral Disorders in Integrated Care*,
https://doi.org/10.1007/978-3-030-83469-2_19

sary components of an individual's capacity to convey symptoms accurately, ask appropriate questions, understand medical advice or directions, and engage in shared decision-making.
2. *Healthcare knowledge*: includes an individual's prior knowledge of maintaining good health, risk factors, health beliefs, the organization and functioning of healthcare systems, and knowledge and understanding of billing and insurance processes.

Although this definition is widely utilized in public health initiatives and clinical and research settings, it maintains a focus on the characteristics and prior abilities of individuals while largely neglecting the role of health systems. To more comprehensively capture the complexity of health literacy, *Healthy People 2030* has redefined the concept to incorporate the complex role of health systems and organizations in increasing health literacy and emphasize individual ability to *apply* health information to make well-informed decisions instead of simply understanding it to make appropriate decisions (ODPHP, 2020). To this end, health literacy is comprised of *personal health literacy*, which refers to an individual's ability to find, understand, and use information to make healthcare decisions, and *organizational health literacy*, which refers to the degree to which organizations facilitate individuals to find, understand, and use information to make healthcare decisions.

Thus, shared decision-making is an essential component of behavioral health literacy.

Willis and O'Donohue (2018) have created an integrated model of behavioral health literacy that incorporates shared decision-making and patient-centered care as interconnected concepts. They define behavioral health literacy as the ability to:

1. Obtain behavioral health information that is valid and relevant in consultation with healthcare professionals
2. Evaluate and integrate behavioral health information
3. Make informed behavioral healthcare decisions utilizing this information for both treatment of disease and wellness
4. Understand factors that contribute to prevention of disease and the promotion of overall wellness

Behavioral health literacy is essential for shared decision-making and patient-centered care. Shared decision-making can be defined as an ongoing process of collaboration and discussion between the patient and provider wherein the provider actively creates and maintains rapport, evaluates a patient's preference for information and role in decision-making, and incorporates the patient's ideas, concerns, and expectations into decision-making, discussion of available option, and mutual selection of treatment course (Willis & O'Donohue, 2018). Patient-centered care can be defined as a spectrum of care that increases access to and knowledge and utilization of behavioral healthcare by incorporating the use of staff effective interpersonal skills, materials and handouts, and quality improvement (Willis & O'Donohue, 2018).

The authors propose that shared decision-making impacts behavioral health literacy and patient-centered care, in that providers ought to supply patients with accurate and complete information regarding evidence-based treatment options for their individual difficulties for patients to be active participants in their care (Willis & O'Donohue, 2018). This is particularly important as it has the potential to address the inherent dynamic and malleable nature of health literacy as a concept. The substantiative knowledge of a patient with cardiovascular disease may be vastly different than someone coping with a cancer diagnosis. Although there may be a general knowledge of health literacy domain (e.g., healthy diet and exercise), providing patients with disease-specific information and treatment options can impact their level of engagement in decision-making. This creates a need for healthcare providers to be knowledgeable about a range of behavioral health conditions, insurance policies, and evidence-based treatments. In turn, patients may feel empowered to make informed decisions, which further impacts shared decision-making and patient-centered care. Thus, health literacy is determined by individual and healthcare variables. It is a dynamic and malleable concept that represents a constellation of skills across various domains.

19.2 Prevalence

In a National Adult Literacy Study, 90 million American adults fell in the lower two levels of a five-level scale assessing the degree of proficiency needed to function in American society, and more than 40 million were categorized as functionally illiterate (Kirsch et al., 1993). Individuals with low literacy encounter challenges in reading, understanding, and integrating written information with accuracy (Nielsen-Bohlman et al., 2004). The inability to interpret written information accurately and consistently complicates skills needed to function in American society, including the demands of the healthcare system such as understanding consent forms and prescription medication information inserts.

In a review of 85 studies, the weighted prevalence of low health literacy was 26%, and that of marginal health literacy was 20% (Paasche-Orlow et al., 2005). When assessing the 85 studies individually, the reported prevalence of low health literacy ranged from 0% to 68%. The prevalence of low health literacy was significantly associated with level of education, age, and ethnicity (Paasche-Orlow et al., 2005). Specifically, the rate of high school completion was significantly associated with literacy levels. American adults with higher levels of education have higher average proficiencies (Kirsch et al., 2002). There is a positive relationship between literacy and years of education. Age also appears to have a significant association with health literacy. Paasche-Orlow et al. (2005) noted that the studies with the lowest average age had the lowest prevalence of low literacy at 15.9%, and studies in which the average age was over 50 years old had a prevalence of low literacy of 37.9%.

In addition to education and age, ethnicity and race disproportionately impact literacy. White and Asian/Pacific Islander adults have higher average health literacy than adults identifying with other ethnic and racial minorities, such as Black,

Hispanic, American Indian/Alaskan Native, and Multiracial (Kutner et al., 2006). Fourteen percent of adults that participated in the 2003 National Assessment of Adult Literacy fell in the *Below Basic* health literacy level. Twenty-four percent of Black adults and 41% of Hispanic adults were in the *Below Basic* health literacy category, compared to 9% of White and 13% of Asian/Pacific Islander adults. Hispanic adults had a higher prevalence of low health literacy than adults in any other racial and ethnic group. Furthermore, studies with higher numbers of Black participants had the highest levels of low literacy (Kutner et al., 2006; Paasche-Orlow et al., 2005).

Despite the growing number of Americans that speak a language other than English at home, research studies often exclude participants who are not Native English speakers (Paasche-Orlow et al., 2005). By excluding the non-Native English-speaking portion of the population, studies may be underestimating the prevalence of low health literacy in the United States. Paasche-Orlow et al. (2005) assessed non-Native English speakers separately. Results indicated that participants tested in Spanish had significantly higher rates of low literacy (44%) compared to participants tested in English (26%), which could be an indication that language is an important factor to consider in health literacy.

19.3 Risk Factors

Low health literacy is associated with a number of outcomes at the individual and societal levels. The estimated yearly cost of low literacy in the United States ranges from $106 to $238 billion (Liechty, 2011). Lower health literacy is associated with increased risk of hospitalization (Baker et al., 2002), higher rates of hospitalizations (Nielsen-Bohlman et al., 2004; Paasche-Orlow et al., 2005), longer hospital stays (Findley, 2015), greater emergency department visits (Mitty & Flores, 2008), and higher rates of ambulance transport (Findley, 2015). Individuals with low literacy levels tend to have higher healthcare utilization leading to increased costs.

In addition to societal costs, there are a number of costs at the individual level associated with low health literacy. Low literacy is linked to poor socioeconomic conditions (Nutbeam, 2008). Poor socioeconomic conditions are in turn linked to negative health effects. Kim (2009) indicated that individuals with low health literacy have a lower subjective sense of health and happiness and significantly higher rates of pain, arthritis, hypertension, and limitations in activity. Adults with low health literacy are also at greater risk for additional potential adverse health outcomes including high systolic blood pressure (Findley, 2015), higher mortality rates (Baker et al., 2007), and poorer health status upon presentation to treatment (Findley, 2015). Thus, health literacy poses a risk for an individual's mental and physical health.

With higher rates of chronic diseases and hospitalizations, individuals with low literacy have to navigate the healthcare system. It is well documented that the majority of healthcare materials exceed the comprehension abilities of most of the

American population (Rudd et al., 1999). American adults with low literacy encounter many challenges with navigating the healthcare system, which range from difficulty filling out forms in a medical office to comprehending and adhering to treatment plans. The absence of guidelines in plain language is associated with multiple healthcare disparities, chronic illness management, and failure to engage in healthy lifestyles (Mitty & Flores, 2008). If people do not understand guidelines and directions, then they will not be able to adequately manage their own health. Individuals with limited health literacy have less knowledge of disease management, lower rates of health promotion behaviors (Nielsen-Bohlman et al., 2004), decreased use of preventative services (DeWalt et al., 2004; Findley, 2015; Nielsen-Bohlman et al., 2004). Consequently, poorer self-management leads to worsening medical health and an increase in hospitalizations and emergency care utilization.

Providing health-related education for individuals with inadequate health literacy can be challenging. Williams et al. (1998) noted a significant relationship of functional health literacy to patients' knowledge of their chronic diseases and improper use of medical devices. This relationship has been supported by an additional study associating better reading ability to increased knowledge of health services (DeWalt et al., 2004). Providers who serve populations with low health literacy described their education and treatment efforts as challenging and exasperating (Liechty, 2011). The perceived resistance or difficulty has the potential to damage patient-provider rapport, which in turn may increase the discomfort felt by patients with low literacy and maintenance of the existing health disparity.

19.4 Effective Screening

It is imperative for health organizations to efficiently identify patients at risk for negative health outcomes through screening for low health literacy as this can facilitate prevention, early intervention, and treatment. Leading healthcare organizations have provided guidelines, recommendations, and toolkits to raise awareness of health literacy and improve patient-provider communication. For instance, the 2004 Institute of Medicine (IOM) report on health literacy indicated that "health literacy assessment should be a part of healthcare information systems and quality data collection" (IOM, 2004, p. 16). A 2013 workshop convened by IOM's Roundtable on Health Literacy further noted, "what gets measured gets managed" (IOM, 2014, p. 93), suggesting that the development of metrics to measure health literacy as part of existing programs and services may encourage health organizations to screen for health literacy status. The Joint Commission requires that hospitals attend to health literacy issues, such as providing written information in plain language and in a manner that patients can understand, encouraging patients to use information to make healthcare decisions, and engaging patients in shared decision-making (JCO, 2012). Despite public health efforts, there is no consensus about the most cost-effective, practical, and best approach to routine screening.

Screening for low health literacy has generally taken one of two approaches: a universal precautions or a hybrid approach that integrates universal precautions with targeted assistance. From a health literacy universal precautions paradigm, healthcare providers assume that all patients may experience difficulties with accessing health services and comprehending health information (Brega et al., 2015). The overarching goals of health literacy universal precautions are to make healthcare systems easier to navigate, simplify communication, and support patients in their efforts for health improvement (Brega et al., 2015). The Agency for Healthcare Research and Quality (AHRQ) developed the *Health Literacy Universal Precautions Toolkit 2.0* to assist healthcare organizations in implementing systems-level changes to address low health literacy. The toolkit offers guidance for conducting organizational assessments, developing plans to address health literacy and strategies to increase health literacy (e.g., Teach-Back method), medication management, and designing written materials and tools to help coordinate care between disciplines and improve the likelihood that patients will follow through with referrals.

The feasibility of scaling universal precautions across healthcare systems has not yet been demonstrated. In a study of 12 primary care practices that implemented specific tools from the toolkit over a period of 6 months, participating practices reported implementation barriers in the form of limited support from leadership, bureaucratic and technological challenges, competing demands and staff capacity, and limited quality improvement experiences (Mabachi et al., 2016). In an examination of whether health literacy universal precautions recommendations are being followed, only 17% of the population was offered help with forms, 29% reported their providers used the Teach-Back method to assess comprehension, and 70% always received easy-to-understand instructions from their providers (Liang & Brach, 2017). In order to achieve health literacy universal precautions, healthcare systems need to redesign workflows to integrate health literacy practices into existing services, which is an ambitious and resource-intensive undertaking.

An alternative to health literacy universal precautions is a hybrid approach that operates from a universal precautions lens and identifies patients with risk factors for low health literacy to maximize resource allocation (Hadden & Kripalani, 2019). Within this model, systems-wide screening and documentation in electronic health records (EHR) are implemented to identify patients for whom evidence-based prevention or intervention strategies can likely improve specific health outcomes. A hybrid approach incorporates some elements from the universal precautions model, namely, some resource allocation in the form of staff training in the use of the Teach-Back method, plain language with all patients, and time for data collection in addition to screening (Hadden & Kripalani, 2019). Health literacy data can present a number of opportunities for prevention and intervention strategies. These data can be accessed in real time in the patient's EHR, and providers can tailor their approach, instructions, and education to improve patients' experience. Health literacy data can also be utilized in quality improvement efforts and population based-health strategies to allocate resources for patients who are most likely to benefit from health literacy prevention and intervention strategies. This approach may be particularly beneficial given the high degree of shame associated with low health literacy or illiteracy (Parikh et al., 1996; Wolf et al., 2007).

Incorporating routine screening as part of a comprehensive health history in combination with the Teach-Back method can alleviate potential discomfort and normalize discussions of health literacy. In fact, patients are generally supportive of measures that assess and inform their medical providers of their healthy literacy level (Farrell et al., 2008; Seligman et al., 2005). There are promising findings from the last decade that have demonstrated the acceptability and feasibility of brief health literacy screening (Cawthon et al., 2014; Kindig et al., 2004). For instance, in a dissemination and implementation study of a three-item health literacy assessment tool in a hospital setting, Cawthon et al. (2014) found that the completion rate was 91.8% for inpatient admissions and 66.6% for outpatient visits. The authors identified leadership support and integration into existing workflows and infrastructure as key facilitators of rapid adoption of the screening tool.

Despite the lack of consensus regarding the most effective approach to the implementation of health literacy screening, there is overwhelming support from medical providers and patients for providers to know if patients experience difficulties with health literacy (Farrell et al., 2008; Seligman et al., 2005). There are several self-report questionnaires that have been validated and well established for use in integrated care settings that are easy to administer and provide useful information. The most common measures include (see Table 19.1).

- *Rapid Estimate of Adult Literacy in Medicine, Revised* (REALM-R; Bass et al., 2003): The REALM-R is an 11-item word recognition test utilized to identify patients at risk of low health literacy. Eleven common medical words are printed

Table 19.1 Health literacy screening tools

Name	Number of items	Time to administer	Cutoff	Language
REALM-R	11	< 2 minutes	≤ 6 = at risk of low health literacy	English
BHLS	3	1 minute	Total scores: 3–9 = lower health literacy; 10–15 = higher health literacy	English
BRIEF	4	< 2 minutes	Total scores: 4–12 = inadequate; 13–16 = marginal; 17–20 = adequate health literacy	English
S-TOFHLA	36	7 minutes	Total scores: 0–16 = inadequate; 17–22 = marginal; 23–36 = adequate literacy	English
SAHLSA	50	4–5 minutes	Total scores: 0–37 = inadequate health literacy	Spanish
NVS	6	3 minutes	Total scores: 0–1 = high likelihood of limited literacy; 2–3 = possibility of limited literacy; 4–6 = adequate literacy	English
SILS	1	<1 minute	≥ 2	English

in 18-point font, and patients are asked to read each word aloud with a time limit of 5 s per word. The first three words, "fat," "flu," and "pill" are not scored and are only administered to increase confidence and decrease anxiety. The REALM-R does not assess comprehension.

- *Brief Health Literacy Screen* (BHLS; Chew et al., 2004): The BHLS is a three-item self-report questionnaire that has been validated in outpatient, inpatient, and emergency department settings and administered by nurses during routine clinical care. Each question on the BHLS is scored on a 5-point scale that is summed, and total scores can range from 3 to15, with higher scores indicating higher health literacy levels. The three questions are: (1) "How often do you have someone help you read hospital materials?" (2) "How confident are you filling out medical forms by yourself?" and (3) How often do you have problems learning about your medical condition because of difficulty understanding written information?"
- *Brief Health Literacy Screening Tool* (BRIEF; Haun et al., 2009): The BRIEF is a four-item self-report questionnaire that incorporates the three questions from the BHLS in addition to a fourth question, "How often do you have a problem understanding what is told to you about your medical condition?" to assess difficulties with auditory health information. Scores on all four questions are summed and can range from 4 to 20.
- *Short Test of Functional Health Literacy in Adults* (S-TOFHLA; Baker et al., 1999): The S-TOFHLA is a shortened version of the TOFHLA, which is a written prose test comprised of 67 items that takes approximately 20–25 minutes to administer. The S-TOFHLA is a 36-item questionnaire from the reading comprehension subsection of the full TOFHLA that is scored on a scale of 0–36 and only takes 7 min to administer. It is as valid and reliable as the full version but much less burdensome.
- *Short Assessment of Health Literacy for Spanish Adults* (SAHLSA; Lee et al., 2006): The SAHLSA is a health literacy assessment based on the REALM test that is comprised of 50 items designed to assess a Spanish-speaking patient's ability to read and understand common medical terms.
- *Newest Vital Sign* (NVS; Powers et al., 2010): The NVS is a brief screening tool that utilizes a nutrition label from an ice cream container. Patients are provided with the label and asked six questions about the label. Patients should refer to the label while answering the questions.
- *Single-Item Literacy Screener* (SILS; Morris et al., 2006): The SILS is a single-item question designed to identify adults who experience difficulties with understanding printed health materials. The SILS asks, "How often do you need to have someone help you read instructions, pamphlets, or other written material from your doctor or pharmacy?" The SILS utilizes a Likert scale from 1 *Never* to 5 *Always*. Scores greater than 2 indicate some difficulty with reading health-related print material.

In addition to these instruments, there are many other full-length assessments, such as the REALM and TOFHLA, that are considered to be "gold standards" for measuring health literacy but are likely not feasible for implementation in integrated care settings due to their length and time needed for administration. This likely is largely dependent on the clinical setting and population of interest. The measures listed above and many others can be accessed via several repositories, including AHRQ's *Toolkit 2.0* (https://www.ahrq.gov/health-literacy/research/tools/index.html) or the *Health Literacy Tool Shed* (https://healthliteracy.bu.edu), which is the culmination of a collaboration between Boston University, RTI, and CommunicateHealth, Inc. The choice of instrument is largely dependent on clinical need, patient population, provider preference, time availability, and patient acceptability.

19.5 Evidence-Based Prevention

Promoting health literacy is a global public health goal. The relationship between low health literacy and poorer health outcomes, including higher rates of mortality and hospitalization (Baker et al., 2004; Baker et al., 2007), lower use of preventive services (White et al., 2008), poorer medication adherence (Kripalani et al., 2010), and higher use of emergency services (Baker et al., 2004), is well established. Improving the health literacy of individuals then can improve understanding of preventive care information, access to preventive care services, and improve health outcomes. Health literacy then can serve as preventive action against the onset or exacerbation of disease. Prevention efforts can be primary, secondary, or tertiary:

- *Primary prevention*: The aim of primary prevention is to prevent disease before it occurs by modifying unhealthy behaviors, increasing resistance to disease, or preventing exposure to disease. Immunizations and community-based screening initiatives are examples of primary prevention.
- *Secondary prevention*: The focus of secondary prevention is early disease detection via screening efforts. Examples include screening for high blood pressure, breast self-examinations, or Pap smears.
- *Tertiary prevention*: The aim of tertiary prevention is to mitigate the impact of an already-existing disease or prevent the onset of other severe diseases by helping patients manage complex health problems and alleviate suffering. Examples include interventions to reduce dropout rates in cardiac rehabilitation to prevent further coronary events and provision of prostheses and medical devices to improve quality of life.

There is a plethora of health literacy initiatives to create information, recommendations, and guidelines, but fewer evidence-based prevention efforts, particularly primary prevention. Emerging and evidence-based health literacy primary prevention efforts include the Black Barbershop Health Outreach Program (BBHOP), which is a partnership between medical professionals, community health volunteers, and African American-owned barbershops (Releford et al., 2013). The aim of BBHOP is to educate, screen, identify, and refer African American men at risk for diabetes and hypertension for early intervention. BBHOP developed culturally sensitive educational materials and incorporates self-administered surveys to understand the factors that prevent African American men from engaging in health-promoting behaviors. BBHOP has screened over 7000 African American men in 300 barbershops in over 20 cities across 6 states (Releford et al., 2013). Additional successful primary prevention programs include the Health Literacy Screening (HEALS) study outlined by Cawthon et al. (2014) that incorporated a brief health literacy screen into the electronic medical record in the emergency department, three primary care clinics, and all adult outpatient clinics at a large academic medical center. A systematic review of community-based programs yielded seven other studies that examined the effects of health literacy interventions that served a primary prevention function (e.g., understand food labels; Nutbeam et al., 2018).

More common than primary prevention strategies are health literacy secondary and tertiary health prevention programs. The extent to which greater health literacy can prevent the onset of disease is highly debated. Emerging evidence suggests that improving health literacy can improve comorbidities rather than preventing the first chronic disease (Liu et al., 2020). This suggests that health literacy can be a protective factor in the development of chronic diseases. A suggested theoretical pathway is that health literacy impacts health outcomes by affecting health behaviors, knowledge about health concepts, self-efficacy, and health-related perceptions (Baker, 2006; Speros, 2005; von Wagner et al., 2009). Empirical studies have yielded promising results for this proposed framework.

For instance, Fernandez et al. (2016) examined the relationship between health literacy and health perceptions and behaviors in a subsample of the Health and Retirement Study (HRS). The authors found that participants with adequate health literacy were more likely to report engaging in moderate physical activity two or more times weekly, more likely to report having a mammogram within the last 2 years, more likely to provide a correct response to a question regarding whether colon cancer screening reduces the risk of dying from colon cancer, and less likely to report current tobacco use. Interestingly, in women, 49.4% with adequate objective health literacy reported conducting monthly breast self-examinations (BSE) in comparison with 72% of those with inadequate objective health literacy (Fernandez et al., 2016). This finding is surprising and possibly related to patients' knowledge of evidence-based preventative measures. The World Health Organization does not recommend BSE (WHO, 2016) as a breast cancer screening method, and it is possible that women with higher levels of health literacy may have greater knowledge about the breast cancer guidelines and recommendations, whereas women with lower levels of health literacy may utilize BSE as a replacement to mammography for a variety of reasons (Fernandez et al., 2016; Nielsen-Bohlman et al., 2004). Similar results have been found for health literacy when assessed for specific diseases such as diabetes and HIV. Mancuso (2010) examined health literacy as a predictor of glycemic control in a sample of patients with diabetes recruited from two primary care clinics and found a strong correlation between health literacy and diabetes knowledge, such that an inadequate understanding of diabetes explained the differences found in HbA1c levels. Mancuso (2010) also found that trust in the provider was the most significant factor that impacted HbA1c levels, suggesting that the interaction with healthcare providers can influence patients' health outcomes. Although further research is necessary to elucidate the underlying mechanisms, extant evidence suggests that health literacy can be a key factor across the spectrum from prevention to treatment.

It is also possible for healthcare systems to develop programs across the spectrum of prevention. For instance, an example of a comprehensive health literacy prevention initiative can be found in the Southeastern Pennsylvania Regional Enhancements Addressing Disconnects (SEPA-READS) collaborative (Simmons et al., 2017). Nine hospitals in Southeastern Pennsylvania collaborated with several institutes and foundations to develop easy-to-read educational material on a broad range of cancer topics, plain language text messages to reduce no-show rates on the mobile mammography unit, a text messaging intervention for low-income pregnant women smokers, a comic-book-style photonovel on breast cancer from an intergenerational perspective for Chinese-Americans, and healthcare provider trainings on strategies for enhancing health literacy during patient-provider encounters (Simmons et al., 2017). Given the complexity of health literacy and the variety of extant prevention strategies, what ought prevention initiatives include? Common to many of the prevention efforts outlined here and elsewhere are the following components:

- Easy-to-understand printed and electronic materials that are newly developed or have been redesigned with a specific focus on plain language
- The use of plain language during patient encounters
- Incorporation of the Teach-Back method
- Staff training
- Support from organizational leadership and champions
- Continuous program evaluation and development

It is evident that primary, secondary, and tertiary prevention programs can positively impact the rates of identifying patients at risk of developing specific diseases (e.g., hypertension, diabetes), improve health behaviors and health knowledge, and affect the healthcare provider-patient relationship.

19.6 Intervention

In 2010, the US Department of Health and Human Services published the *National Action Plan to Improve Health Literacy*. They proposed developing a society-wide health response to health literacy targeting multiple areas, including communication skills of health professionals, clarity and accuracy of health information, cultural and linguistic adaptation of health information, and systemic changes to healthcare. Nonetheless, research on health literacy interventions has been relatively scarce (Kelly et al., 2007), and most of the existing models have focused on identifying associations between health literacy and its outcomes (Geboers et al., 2018) as opposed to identifying interventions to improve health literacy. Interventions are key, as improvements in health literacy can lead to prevention of the outcomes often associated with health literacy. Improvements in health literacy are associated with better health outcomes, such as reduced reported disease severity, greater awareness of risks for chronic diseases, and a decrease in unplanned emergency department visits and hospitalizations (Nutbeam et al., 2018). Hence, health literacy interventions can be viewed as preventative.

Healthcare providers and healthcare systems contribute to the maintenance of poor health literacy in a variety of ways, including insufficient patient education, language barriers, differing expectations between providers and patients, overuse of medical terminology, and overly technical forms/instructions (US Department of Health and Human Services, 2010). This problem begins during health professionals' training. Only a small portion of US medical schools and internal-medicine residency programs are teaching about health literacy, yet 48% of healthcare providers (physicians and nonphysicians) overestimate their understanding of health literacy issues (Coleman & Fromer, 2015). Given that health literacy is a critical factor in communication between healthcare providers and patients in their care, interventions targeting provider health literacy competency should be considered. Coleman and Fromer (2015) provided a 70-minute didactic overview of health literacy for physicians and nonphysicians. The didactic covered information on the definition of health literacy, health literacy-related outcomes, best practices for communication with patients, self-management and empowerment, and effective use of patients' social support systems. Study participants reported improved self-perceived knowledge, skills, and planned behaviors about health literacy following the didactic. The newly acquired knowledge can help providers approach patients with low health literacy in a more understanding way, provide simpler explanations of health conditions, and create a shame-free environment, in turn improving the patient-provider relationship. Despite the evidence that literacy training for healthcare providers is an important factor of health literacy intervention, more research is needed on identification and development of instructional strategies.

There are also concerns with the use of existing healthcare models, like the Stepped Care Prevention Approach, to improve health literacy. In a traditional stepped care model, healthcare professionals provide evidence-based psychological treatments in different steps (Franx et al., 2012; Ho et al., 2016). A stepped care approach typically begins with less intensive treatments, which can then be graduated to more intensive treatments if patients do not respond to prior steps. Less intensive treatments include watchful waiting, psychoeducation, and bibliotherapy. Care can then progress to individual or group therapy, as well as pharmacological treatment. Each step relies on individuals' ability to process information provided by healthcare professionals, read healthcare or self-help materials, and possess awareness of medical or mental health disorders. When more than 40 million Americans are categorized as functionality illiterate (Kirsch et al., 1993) and the reading age of some of the most popularly used self-help materials is 12.6–15.4 (Martinez et al., 2008), this is going to be a challenge. Therefore, intervention is an important area of focus within health literacy.

Researchers have approached interventions of health literacy in a variety of ways. Some researchers have attempted to identify broad categories for intervention, while others have focused on the identification of specific strategies. Nutbeam et al. (2018) postulated that health literacy can be improved through dissemination of information, effective communication, and structured education. Four broad methods of targeting mental health literacy in youth are through disseminating information in whole-of-community campaigns and community campaigns, education-based interventions, and training programs for intervention during mental health crises (Kelly et al., 2007). Examples of interventions within these four target areas are:

- *Whole-of-community intervention*: Pamphlet and poster distribution, psychoeducational website, television advertising, and educational videos
- *Community campaigns targeting youth*: Cinema, printed materials, and radio
- *Education-based interventions*: Curriculum support materials, visits to schools by health professionals, mental health information sessions, and resilience enhancement programs
- *Training programs for interventions during mental health crisis*: Course teaching recognition of risk factors for mental health disorders, applied-intervention skills training, presentations by school counseling services, and written material.

In efforts to identify more specific target areas, Brainard et al. (2016) reviewed various studies that had implemented health literacy interventions, the majority of which were delivered via interactions with healthcare professionals, with adult participants. The interventions in these studies focused on psychoeducation, skill building, behavioral change, strengthening contextual support, individual involvement at the systems live, individualization of health literacy interventions, and changes in social or cultural environments for enhancement of health literacy interventions. Health literacy interventions have been associated with increased post-intervention knowledge (Kelly et al., 2007) and significant improvements in certain health literacy aspects, including skills, self-efficiency, health knowledge, quality of life, and communication with healthcare providers (Brainard et al., 2016). Hence, it is imperative to develop specific interventions to improve health literacy.

Awareness of target areas has contributed to a shift in health literacy research with a greater focus in the development of interventions. Geboers et al. (2018) proposed a comprehensive health literacy intervention model in which outcomes are determined by the collaboration between individuals and health providers, as well as their broader social contexts. On the individual level, it is important to consider patients' interpersonal relationships, and for healthcare providers the model should also consider the entirety of the healthcare system. It is imperative to also consider the broader systemic contexts, as these include factors that can perpetuate poor health literacy. According to the proposed model, interventions targeting a combination of its five factors can improve health literacy. The five factors identified by the Geboers et al. (2018) as potential targets are:

- Context of individual

- Individuals with low health literacy
- Individual characteristics and healthcare system interactions
- Healthcare professionals
- Communication and accessibility of healthcare systems

Geboers et al. (2018) identified specific interventions such as strengthening social support systems, empowering individuals with low health literacy, improving communication between individuals and healthcare providers, skill-building (communication, awareness or health conditions), and policy change. The specific interventions are designed to target a combination of the five factors in the comprehensive health literacy intervention model.

Improvement in health literacy does not solely rest on individuals but on the collaboration of healthcare professionals, healthcare systems, and community support/engagement. A comprehensive health literacy intervention model provides multiple target areas while incorporating individuals' larger contexts. It makes both individuals and healthcare providers key players in the improvement of health literacy, contributing to the establishment of more collaborative relationships.

19.7 Role of Primary Care Providers and Behavioral Care Providers

The primary care team is uniquely situated to screen, assess, and implement strategies to enhance patients' health literacy. Typically, a patient's first point of contact with a healthcare practitioner is during the annual primary care visit. Healthcare teams can triage patients based on need by first incorporating a single item screener such as "How often do you need to have someone help you read instructions, pamphlets, or other written material from your doctor or pharmacy?" during the initial visit with a medical assistant or nursing provider. If the screen is positive, the PCP and BCP can then intervene in a number of ways:

- *Use plain language*: Using plain language means conveying information in a simple and clear way using common terms that are free of medical jargon both in written and oral communication (e.g., using "cut" instead of "abrasion," "breast health test" instead of "mammogram," etc.). Elements of plain language include using active voice instead of passive voice, breaking complex information into small chunks, organizing information so that the most important points come first, and asking open-ended questions. Plain language resources can be found at: https://www.cdc.gov/healthliteracy/developmaterials/plainlanguage.html.
- *Use the Teach-Back method*: The Teach-Back method is a simple approach for confirming that patients understand what has been communicated during a medical visit and provides an opportunity to answer questions and provide corrective information. Primary care providers can begin by asking, "We covered a lot today and I want to make sure that I explained things clearly. Let's review what

we discussed. Please describe the three things you agreed to do to help you prevent and reduce the risk of cancer" (Simmons et al., 2017).

- *Use visual aids*: The use of graphic displays of health information can help patients gain a better understanding of their medical conditions. This can be a powerful tool that can augment the oral information provided. Visual aids can also facilitate shared decision-making. Visual aid tools can be found at: http://www.vizhealth.org and https://visualsonline.cancer.gov.
- *Use and recommend technological health aids*: Actively encourage patients to use patient portals to access their health information and communicate with their providers, recommend the use of mobile applications, and telehealth options. Mobile apps provide an opportunity for self-management and tracking symptoms and can provide health information.
- *Practice culturally competent care*: Avoid making assumptions about patients' educational attainment, socioeconomic status, or the beliefs they hold about health. Promote a welcoming environment that invites patients to involve any family members or friends who are important members of their social network and can aid in decision-making.
- *Develop printed materials that promote health literacy*: Ensure that the information included in written materials is at a fifth or sixth grade level; include generous white space; integrate graphics, photographs, and conversation bubbles; and approach health literacy from a culturally sensitive lens (Simmons et al., 2017).

Attend to disease-specific and general health literacy: Ensure that handouts, brochures, or other written/digital materials include information regarding ways to maintain good health and minimize risk factors while also including separate materials that target individual diagnoses or disease processes (e.g., lifestyle modifications for diabetes management). Although time is limited during medical visits, PCPs can start this process by ensuring the use of plain language and the Teach-Back method with all patients. Providers can then engage in a "warm hand off" with a behavioral care provider who can provide targeted and brief interventions and incorporate some of the same strategies as PCPs. This can increase collaboration between various members of the integrated care team and normalize discussions of health literacy.

19.8 Lessons Learned/Implementation

A successful response to limited health literacy requires multidisciplinary collaboration and communication, coordination, and quality improvement. A systematic approach is necessary to improve the health literacy environment of a healthcare system and increase individual health literacy. To address health literacy in a coordinated and comprehensive way, several "lessons" can be considered:

- *Embed health literacy into existing systems*. Sustainable health literacy initiatives require development and implementation of health literacy procedures at an organizational level. This might require allocation of monetary funds for a designated health literacy coordinator or administrator, implementing policies that prioritize health literacy efforts, or identifying funding mechanisms that can finance staff training, development of materials, or quality improvement (ACSQHC, 2014; Simmons et al., 2017).

- *Actively and consistently update materials*. An inherent challenge is the dynamic and malleable nature of health literacy as a construct. Individuals may have a high health literacy in the general healthcare knowledge domain, in that they have a good understanding of how to maintain good health (e.g., regular physical exercise, reduce sedentary behaviors, healthy diet, minimize substance use, etc.) but may have a low health literacy regarding diabetes management, such as knowledge of medications, glucose monitoring, or lifestyle modifications that are needed to self-manage. Ensure that materials include information regarding general health literacy and disease-specific health literacy.
- *Identify leaders and champions*. Identify and support providers, administrators, or staff who can facilitate and nurture interagency relationships, advocate for health literacy policies at an organizational level, and lead development and implementation efforts.
- *Develop effective partnerships*. Action to improve health literacy can begin in one department and can flourish in collaboration with community partners and collaborators at the local, state, regional, and national levels.
- *Engage in on-going quality improvement*. Given the complexity of healthcare systems and extant gaps in research evidence for the most effective prevention and intervention programs, providers and organizations can incorporate evaluations of cost, efficiency, satisfaction, and other domains as needed into existing systems. QI efforts are likely to vary based on an organization's goals and priorities, resources, and clinical setting.

These are long-term considerations and strategies that can provide an initial framework to implement change at the organizational level. There are a number of tools that have been identified here that can provide extra assistance in the development of health literacy initiatives, including sample forms, worksheets, PowerPoint presentations, and quality improvement planning tools. Increasing the health literacy of individuals, families, and communities can have a long-standing effect throughout the medical community. Health literacy is critical for health promotion and disease prevention.

References

Australian Commission on Safety and Quality in Health Care. (2014). Health literacy: Taking action to improve safety and quality.

Baker, D. W., Williams, M. V., Parker, R. M., Gazmararian, J. A., & Nurss, S. (1999). Development of a brief test to measure functional health literacy. *Patient Education and Counseling, 38*(1), 33–42. https://doi.org/10.1016/s0738-3991(98)00116-5

Baker, D. W. (2006). The meaning and the measure of health literacy. *Journal of General Internal Medicine, 21*(8), 878–883. https://doi.org/10.1111/j.1525-1497.2006.00540.x

Baker, D. W., Gazmararian, J. A., Williams, M. V., Scott, T., Parker, R. M., Green, D., Ren, J., & Peel, J. (2002). Functional health literacy and the risk of hospital admission among Medicare managed care enrollees. *American Journal of Public Health, 92*(8), 1278–1283. https://doi.org/10.2105/ajph.92.8.1278

Baker, D. W., Gazmararian, J. A., Williams, M. V., Scott, T., Parker, R. M., Green, D., Ren, J., & Peel, J. (2004). Health literacy and use of outpatient physician services by Medicare managed care enrollees. *Journal of General Internal Medicine, 19*(3), 215–220.

Baker, D. W., Wolf, M. S., Feinglass, J., Thompson, J. A., Gazmararian, J. A., & Huang, J. (2007). Health literacy and mortality among elderly persons. *Archives of Internal Medicine, 167*(14), 1503–1509. https://doi.org/10.1001/archinte.167.14.1503

Bass, P. F., Wilson, J. F., & Griffith, C. H. (2003). A shortened instrument for literacy screening. *Journal of General Internal Medicine, 18*(12), 1036–1038. https://doi.org/10.1111/j.1525-1497.2003.10651.x

Brainard, J., Loke, Y., Salter, C., Koós, T., Csizmadia, P., Makai, A., Gács, B., & Szepes, M. (2016). Healthy ageing in Europe: Prioritizing interventions to improve health literacy. *BMC Research Notes, 9*(270). https://doi.org/10.1186/s13104-016-2056-9

Brega, A. G., Barnard, J., Mabachi, N. M., Weiss, B. D., DeWalt, D. A., Brach, C., Cifuentes, M., Albright, K., & West, D. R. (2015). *AHRQ health literacy universal precautions toolkit*. Agency for Healthcare Research and Quality.

Cawthon, C., Mion, L. C., Willens, D. E., Roumie, C. L., & Kripalani, S. (2014). Implementing routine health literacy assessment in hospital and primary care patients. *The Joint Commission Journal on Quality and Patient Safety, 40*(2), 68–76. https://doi.org/10.1016/S1553-7250(14)40008-4

Chew, L. D., Bradley, K. A., & Boyko, E. J. (2004). Brief questions to identify patients with inadequate health literacy. *Family Medicine, 36*, 588–594.

Coleman, C. A., & Fromer, A. (2015). A health literacy training intervention for physicians and other health professionals. *Family Medicine, 47*(5).

Dewalt, D. A., Berkman, N. D., Sheridan, S., Lohr, K. N., & Pignone, M. P. (2004). Literacy and health outcomes: A systematic review of the literature. *Journal of General Internal Medicine, 19*(12), 1228–1239. https://doi.org/10.1111/j.1525-1497.2004.40153.x

Farrell, T. W., Chandran, R., & Gramling, R. (2008). Understanding the role of shame in the clinical assessment of health literacy. *Family Medicine, 40*(4), 235–236.

Fernandez, D. M., Larson, J. L., & Zikmund-Fisher, B. J. (2016). Associations between health literacy and preventive health behaviors among older adults: Findings from the health and retirement study. *BMC Public Health, 16*(596). https://doi.org/10.1186/s12889-016-3267-7

Findley, A. (2015). Low health literacy and older adults: Meanings, problems, and recommendations for social work. *Social Work in Health Care, 54*, 65–81. https://doi.org/10.1080/00981389.2014.966882

Franx, G., Oud, M., de Lange, J., Wensing, M., & Grol, R. (2012). Implementing a stepped-care approach in primary care: Results of a qualitative study. *Implementation Science, 7*(1). https://doi.org/10.1186/1748-5908-7-8

Geboers, B., Reijneveld, S. A., Koot, J. A. R., & de Winter, A. F. (2018). Moving towards a comprehensive approach for health literacy interventions: The development of a health literacy intervention model. *International Journal of Environmental Research and Public Health, 15*(6). https://doi.org/10.3390/ijerph15061268

Hadden, K. B., & Kripalani, S. (2019). Health literacy 2.0: Integrating patient health literacy screening with universal precautions. *Health Literacy Research and Practice, 3*(4), e280–e285. https://doi.org/10.3928/24748307-20191028-02

Haun, J., Nolan-Dodd, V., Varnes, J., Graham-Pole, J., Rienzo, B., & Donaldson, P. (2009). Testing the BRIEF health literacy screening tool. *Federal Practitioner*, 24–30.

Ho, F. Y. Y., Yeung, W. F., Ng, T. H. Y., & Chan, C. S. (2016). The efficacy and cost-effectiveness of stepped care prevention and treatment for depressive and/or anxiety disorders: A systematic review and meta-analysis. *Scientific Reports, 6*. https://doi.org/10.1038/srep29281

IOM. (2004). *Health literacy: A prescription to end confusion.* https://doi.org/10.17226/10883.
IOM. (2014). Implications of health literacy for public health. *Implications of Health Literacy for Public Health.* https://doi.org/10.17226/18756
JCO. (2012). Provision of care, treatment, and services. *Hospital Standards, PC-02.01*, 21.
Kelly, C. M., Jorm, A. F., & Wright, A. (2007). Improving mental health literacy as a strategy to facilitate early intervention for mental disorders. *The Medical Journal of Australia, 187*(7). https://doi.org/10.5694/j.1326-5377.2007.tb01332.x
Kim, S. H. (2009). Health literacy and functional health status in Korean older adults. *Journal of Clinical Nursing, 18*(16), 2337–2343. https://doi.org/10.1111/j.1365-2702.2008.02739.x
Kindig, D. A., Panzer, A. M., & Nielsen-Bohlman, L. (Eds.). (2004). *Health literacy: A prescription to end confusion*. Retrieved from National Academies Press website: https://www.nap.edu/catalog/10883/health-literacy-a-prescription-to-end-confusion
Kirsch, I. S., Jungeblut, A., Jenkins, L., & Kolstad, K. (1993). *Adult literacy in America: A first look at the findings of the national adult literacy survey (NCES 1993–275)*. U.S. Department of Education, National Center for Education Statistics. https://nces.ed.gov/pubs93/93275.pdf
Kirsch, I. S., Jungeblut, A., Jenkins, L., & Kolstad, K. (2002). *Adult literacy in America: A first look at the findings of the national adult literacy survey (NCES 1993–275)*. U.S. Department of Education, National Center for Education Statistics. https://nces.ed.gov/pubs93/93275.pdf
Kripalani, S., Gatti, M. E., & Jacobson, T. A. (2010). Association of age, health literacy, and medication management strategies with cardiovascular medication adherence. *Patient Education and Counseling, 81*(2), 177–181. https://doi.org/10.1016/j.pec.2010.04.030
Kutner, M. E., Greenberg, E., Jin, Y., & Paulsen, C. (2006). *The health literacy of America's adults: Results from the 2003 national assessment of adult literacy (NCES 2006–483)*. U.S. Department of Education, National Center for Education Statistics. https://nces.ed.gov/pubs2006/2006483.pdf
Lee, S. Y., Bender, D. E., Ruiz, R. E., & Cho, Y. I. (2006). Development of an easy-to-use Spanish health literacy test. *Health Services Research, 41*(4 Pt 1), 1392–1412.
Liang, L., & Brach, C. (2017). Health literacy universal precautions are still a distant dream: Analysis of U.S. data on health literate practices. *HLRP: Health Literacy Research and Practice, 1*(4), e216–e230. https://doi.org/10.3928/24748307-20170929-01
Liechty, J. M. (2011). Health literacy: Critical opportunities for social work leadership in health care and research. *Health & Social Work, 36*(2), 99–107. https://doi.org/10.1093/hsw/36.2.99
Liu, L., Qian, X., Chen, Z., & He, T. (2020). Health literacy and its effect on chronic disease prevention: Evidence from China's data. *BMC Public Health, 20*(1), 1–14. https://doi.org/10.1186/s12889-020-08804-4
Mabachi, N. M., Cifuentes, M., Barnard, J., Brega, A. G., Albright, K., Weiss, B. D., Brach, C., & West, D. R. (2016). Demonstration of the health literacy universal precautions toolkit: Lessons for quality improvement. *Journal of Ambulatory Care Management, 39*(3), 199–208. https://doi.org/10.1097/JAC.0000000000000102
Mancuso, J. (2010). Impact of health literacy and patient trust on glycemic control in an urban USA population. *Nursing & Health Sciences, 12*(1), 94–104.
Martinez, R., Whitfield, G., Dafters, R., & Williams, C. (2008). Can people read self-help manuals for depression? A challenge for the stepped care model and book prescription schemes. *Behavioural and Cognitive Psychotherapy, 36*(1). https://doi.org/10.1017/S1352465807004067
Mitty, E., & Flores, S. (2008). Assisted living nursing practice: Health literacy and chronic illness management. *Geriatric Nursing, 29*(4), 230–235. https://doi.org/10.1016/j.gerinurse.2008.06.007
Morris, N. S., MacLean, C. D., Chew, L. D., & Littenberg, B. (2006). The single item literacy screener: Evaluation of a brief instrument to identify limited reading ability. *BMC Family Practice, 7*(21). https://doi.org/10.1186/1471-2296-7-21
Nielsen-Bohlman, L., Panzer, A. M., & Kindig, D. A. (Eds.). (2004). *Health literacy: A prescription to end confusion*. National Academies Press. https://doi.org/10.17226/10883

Nutbeam, D. (2008). The evolving concept of health literacy. *Social Science & Medicine, 67*(12), 2072–2078. https://doi.org/10.1016/j.socscimed.2008.09.050

Nutbeam, D., McGill, B., & Premkumar, P. (2018). Improving health literacy in community populations: A review of progress. *Health Promotion International, 33*(5). https://doi.org/10.1093/heapro/dax015

ODPHP. (2020). *Health literacy in healthy people*. Retrieved from https://health.gov/our-work/healthy-people-2030/about-healthy-people-2030/health-literacy-healthy-people.

Paasche-Orlow, M. K., Parker, R. M., Gazmararian, J. A., Nielsen-Bohlman, L. T., & Rudd, R. R. (2005). The prevalence of limited health literacy. *Journal of General Internal Medicine, 20*(2), 175–184. https://doi.org/10.1111/j.1525-1497.2005.40245.x

Parikh, N. S., Parker, R. M., Nurss, J. R., Baker, D. W., & Williams, M. V. (1996). Shame and health literacy: The unspoken connection. *Patient Education and Counseling, 27*, 33–39. https://doi.org/10.1016/0738-3991(95)00787-3

Powers, B. J., Trinh, J. V., & Bosworth, H. B. (2010). Can this patient read and understand written health information? *JAMA, 304*(1), 76–84. https://doi.org/10.1001/jama.2010.896

Ratzan, S. C., & Parker, R. M. (2000). Introduction. In C. R. Selden, M. Zorn, S. C. Ratzan, & R. M. Parker (Eds.), *National Library of medicine current bibliographies in medicine: Health literacy* (*NLM pub. No. CBM 2000–1*). National Institutes of Health, U.S. Department of Health and Human Services.

Releford, B. J., Frencher, S. K., Yancey, A. K., & Norris, K. (2013). Cardiovascular disease control through barbershops: Design of a nationwide outreach program. *Journal of the National Medical Association, 102*(4), 336–345. https://doi.org/10.1016/s0027-9684(15)30606-4

Rudd, R. E., Moeykens, B. A., & Colton, T. C. (1999). Health and literacy: A review of medical and public health literacy. *Office of Educational Research and Improvement*. https://files.eric.ed.gov/fulltext/ED508707.pdf.

Seligman, H. K., Wang, F. F., Palacios, J. L., Wilson, C. C., Daher, C., Piette, J. D., & Schillinger, D. (2005). Physician notification of their diabetes patients' limited health literacy: A randomized, controlled trial. *Journal of General Internal Medicine, 20*, 1001–1007. https://doi.org/10.1111/j.1525-1497.2005.00189.x

Simmons, R. A., Cosgrove, S. C., Romney, M. C., Plumb, J. D., Brawer, R. O., Gonzalez, E. T., Fleisher, L. G., & Moore, B. S. (2017). Health literacy: Cancer prevention strategies for early adults. *American Journal of Preventive Medicine, 53*(3), S73–S77. https://doi.org/10.1016/j.amepre.2017.03.016

Speros, C. (2005). Health literacy: Concept analysis. *Journal of Advanced Nursing, 50*(6), 633–640. https://doi.org/10.1111/j.1365-2648.2005.03448.x

U. S. Department of Health and Human Services, Office of Disease Prevention and Health Promotion. (2010). National action plan to improve health literacy. : https://health.gov/sites/default/files/2019-09/Health_Literacy_Action_Plan.pdf.

von Wagner, C., Steptoe, A., Wolf, M. S., & Wardle, J. (2009). Health literacy and health actions: A review and a framework from health psychology. *Health Education & Behavior, 36*(5), 860–877. https://doi.org/10.1177/1090198108322819

White, S., Chen, J., & Atchison, R. (2008). Relationship of preventive health practices and health literacy: A national study. *American Journal of Health Behavior, 32*(3), 227–242. https://doi.org/10.5555/ajhb.2008.32.3.227

Williams, M. V., Baker, D. W., Parker, R. M., & Nurss, J. R. (1998). Relationship of functional health literacy to patients' knowledge of their chronic disease. A study of patients with hypertension and diabetes. Archives of Internal Medicine, 158(2), 166–172. DOI: doi.org/https://doi.org/10.1001/archinte.158.2.166.

Willis, B., & O'Donohue, W. T. (2018). The neglected constructs of health literacy, shared decision-making, and patient-centered care in behavioral health: An integrated model. In. M. Duckworth & W. O'Donohue (Eds.), *Behavioral Medicine and Integrated Care* (pp. 147–174). Springer. https://doi.org/10.1007/978-3-319-93003-9_8

Wolf, M. S., Williams, M. V., Parker, R. M., Parikh, N. S., Nowlan, A. W., & Baker, D. W. (2007). Patients' shame and attitudes toward discussing the results of literacy screening. *Journal of Health Communication, 12*, 721–732. https://doi.org/10.1080/10810730701672173

World Health Organization. (2016). *Breast cancer: Prevention and control.* Retrieved from: https://www.who.int/cancer/detection/breastcancer/en/.

Index

W. O'Donohue, M. Zimmermann (eds.), *Handbook of Evidence-Based Prevention of Behavioral Disorders in Integrated Care*,
https://doi.org/10.1007/978-3-030-83469-2

V

W